Snapshots of Research

Snapshots of Research

READINGS IN CRIMINOLOGY AND CRIMINAL JUSTICE

Richard D. Hartley

University of Texas at San Antonio

Los Angeles | London | New Delhi
Singapore | Washington DC

For information:

 SAGE Publications, Inc.
2455 Teller Road
Thousand Oaks, California 91320
E-mail: order@sagepub.com

SAGE Publications Ltd.
1 Oliver's Yard
55 City Road
London EC1Y 1SP
United Kingdom

SAGE Publications India Pvt. Ltd.
B 1/I 1 Mohan Cooperative Industrial Area
Mathura Road, New Delhi 110 044
India

SAGE Publications Asia-Pacific Pte Ltd
33 Pekin Street #02-01
Far East Square
Singapore 048763

Printed in the United States of America

Library of Congress Cataloging-in-Publication Data

Snapshots of research : readings in criminology and criminal justice / editor, Richard D. Hartley.
    p. cm.
Includes bibliographical references.
ISBN 978-1-4129-8919-0 (pbk.)

  1. Criminology—Research. 2. Criminology—Research—Methodology. 3. Criminal justice, Administration of—Research. 4. Criminal justice, Administration of—Research—Methodology. I. Hartley, Richard D.

HV6024.5.S63 2011
364—dc22   2010029628

This book is printed on acid-free paper.

10   11   12   13   14   10   9   8   7   6   5   4   3   2   1

Acquisitions Editor:	Jerry Westby
Editorial Assistant:	Nichole O'Grady
Production Editor:	Catherine M. Chilton
Copy Editor:	Heidi Crossman
Typesetter:	C&M Digitals (P) Ltd.
Proofreader:	Eleni Georgiou
Cover Designer:	Bryan Fishman
Marketing Manager:	Erica DeLuca
Permissions:	Karen Ehrmann

BRIEF CONTENTS

DETAILED CONTENTS

PREFACE

This reader is intended to serve as a supplemental reader to a core research methods course in criminology or criminal justice at either the graduate or undergraduate level. The chapters include a brief introductory discussion of the basic procedures of common research methods utilized in criminology and criminal justice research along with a combination of published academic research articles. The purpose of these brief introductions is not to provide an in-depth discussion of the various research methodologies utilized by researchers in the field but rather to act as a synopsis of the material in order to provide structure and context for the selected examples of research articles that follow.

Each research example also includes an introductory paragraph that sets the stage for students regarding the topic of the research as well as the main methodology employed by the researchers. Discussion questions are also included at the end of each article. These questions serve to help students think critically about the research they have read and obtain a better appreciation for important aspects of the research process as well as enable them to connect the results and conclusions of the research back to the authors' hypotheses and theoretical underpinnings. These questions also highlight key findings or strengths and limitations of the research example.

The first chapter of the reader serves as an introduction to the research process. This chapter outlines the organization and content of the reader, summarizes the scientific method, and describes essential concepts underlying research methods in criminology and criminal justice. The emphasis is that students can better learn about research methods by reading research that has been published by scholars in the field.

The example research articles in this reader include some of the most recent criminological and criminal justice research studies that have been published in academic journals. A few articles from the late 1980s and 1990s are also included because they are exemplary of sound and principled methods of certain topics. The example articles in this reader were also chosen to represent a broad view of research involving the three major branches of the criminal justice system—policing, the courts/law, and corrections. In this way, the research examples included here are illustrative of a particular method but are also valuable and relevant to career paths that criminology and criminal justice students might be interested in pursuing. In essence, students will be learning about research methods in criminology and criminal justice while, at the same time, learning about how the system components work and how researchers go about studying them.

Some of the articles represent research that examines criminality and crime etiology (causes) or research that is relevant to important policy issues. This reader, therefore, will also expose students to how criminologists study the causes of crime and how some research aims to inform policy decisions or adoption of new criminal justice system strategies and crime prevention programs. Finally, the articles were chosen because of their appeal to students who are majoring in criminology or criminal justice. Ultimately, the idea of reading research is more attractive and enjoyable to students when the topics and subject matter are interesting to them.

This reader was constructed to follow a topical order that is logical and that parallels the chapters of some of the most widely used textbooks on research methods for criminology and criminal justice. The reader is divided into 11 chapters, each dealing with issues in social science research or with a particular research methodology used by those who study crime and justice. This variety of research topics and methods, along with the accompanying scholarly readings, will assist students in grasping the fundamentals of scientific research as well as give them a more in-depth understanding of how each of the specific methods is used through real examples of research. Some portions of these research articles have been excluded to make reading easier and to emphasize only the sections of the study that highlight the topic of that chapter. For example, certain tables and figures that are cumbersome to interpret or that are appendices in the original article as well as lengthy literature reviews may have been excluded. The research articles have been reduced in this manner to make them more consumable for a student audience.

Some of the chapters include more examples of research articles than others. This is not in order to favor one specific method over others but to exemplify the various methodological concepts that are introduced in each chapter. Instructors, therefore, may find it unnecessary to require students to read all of the articles in each chapter. Where possible, I have tried to include an example research article for each of the differing types of methodologies. However, due to the complexities of certain topics and the relative simplicity of others, the number of articles for each topic varies. For example, there is not an article for each of the various types of probability and nonprobability sampling techniques, but there are several articles included on survey research and theory and ethics.

Due to differences in pedagogy or individual preference, an instructor may want to pick and choose which of the articles in each chapter to assign to students. In smaller graduate courses, instructors could assign one of the readings in each chapter to two or three students who would be responsible for discussion, and the rest of the class would be responsible for explanation of the methods, findings, and limitations; in this way, all of the students in the class will be exposed to all of the various examples of research provided in the book but will not be burdened by an overwhelming amount of reading in each chapter. I believe that the example articles chosen provide more than enough material for students to grasp fundamental research concepts and to get a better understanding of how scholars in our field conduct their research. It is also my belief that it is better to provide instructors ample material and have them choose which articles they want to cover than to have the opposite, which is not having enough material to adequately illustrate important research concepts.

The overarching goal of this reader is to get students better acquainted with the scientific research process and with criminology and criminal justice research methods by having them read actual examples of research. This reader has been constructed on the assumption that students will be less intimidated and will more easily grasp difficult research concepts by getting their feet wet. In other words, I hypothesize that by becoming familiar with research and getting used to the format of conventional research publications, students can better understand and learn important methodological concepts.

This hypothesis, however, can only be tested with the help of students and instructors like you. If you have any suggestions for material that is not included in the book but that you believe is important to making the research process more easily understandable, or if you have specific experiences from the classroom that you would like to share, please contact me via e-mail: Richard.Hartley@utsa.edu.

ACKNOWLEDGMENTS

There are numerous persons I must thank who helped to bring this project to fruition. First and foremost, I want to thank Jerry Westby for believing in this project and for spending time traveling to several universities building support for it. I would also like to thank Nichole O'Grady, Catherine Chilton, and Heidi Crossman, who graciously guided the book from inception to publication. Special thanks are owed to the reviewers of the book's prospectus: George Burruss, Southern Illinois University at Carbondale; Mel de Guzman, The College at Brockport; Linda Keena, Southeast Missouri State University; Amy Craddock of Fayetteville State University; and Christine Tartaro, The Richard Stockton College of New Jersey. Their careful insight and suggestions have made this work both more scholarly and more student-friendly at the same time.

Finally, this book is dedicated to the "giants" of social science research whose shoulders all of us have stood on in attempt to advance our understanding of crime and justice. It is truly because of those who have come before us that we have seen farther.

Richard D. Hartley
San Antonio, TX

1

THE SCIENTIFIC METHOD AND THE RESEARCH PROCESS IN CRIMINOLOGY AND CRIMINAL JUSTICE

Education is a progressive discovery of our own ignorance.

—Will Durant

PUBLIC KNOWLEDGE OF CRIME AND CRIMINALS

Each day, persons all over the world are bombarded by information and statistics about crime and justice. Unfortunately, this information is all too often inaccurate. Many times, it is reported to the general public before the appropriate legal authorities have had the opportunity to conduct their investigations. Television reporters and news anchors as well as journalists and newspaper columnists often report stories about crime that offer up the motives for certain criminal acts or knee-jerk responses regarding what should be done with an accused offender without taking the time to conduct in-depth examinations of all of the relevant factors that may have contributed to the crime or what the most effective crime prevention measures might be for guarding against victimization.

They often also conduct interviews with, or surveys of, a few persons in a neighborhood regarding their opinions of certain types of criminal activity or personal fears about crime without really ensuring that these opinions and attitudes are reflective of everyone in the neighborhood. This daily reporting of inaccurate information and failure to obtain a true understanding of criminal events or motivations for criminal behavior gives the public a distorted view of crime and criminals. This misinformation may make us unnecessarily fearful or, worse, dangerously unaware of whom or what will actually harm or injure us. In essence, these reports of crime and criminals give us a skewed sense of the effectiveness of our criminal justice system and of our relative risk of criminal victimization.

Criminologists and other social scientists, on the other hand, have conducted a great deal of research over time regarding the causes of criminal behavior. They have undertaken studies exploring which factors are often associated with criminal behavior and have administered surveys examining public fear of crime, all in attempts to better understand criminal behavior as well as come up with best practices for crime prevention. The findings from these scientific research studies often reach conclusions that are different from media reporting of crime. So, why is it that most of the general public does not bother to read the results of research studies conducted by criminologists? Further, why is it that a majority of the public does not question the accuracy or reliability of crime information gleaned from the news?

There are probably multiple reasons, but most often the answer has to do with ease of access and comprehension. To find media-reported crime information, all people have to do is pick up a newspaper or magazine or turn on a television and they will receive short, easy to understand sound bites about crime and justice. To find scientific crime information, people have to have access to the journals that publish this research and have the skills to understand and interpret the findings, which are often written in scientific research-oriented jargon. It is not very difficult, therefore, to see why most of the public choose the former source for information on crime and criminals over the latter.

The material contained in this book is thus an effort to help students become more comfortable with reading and understanding scientific research and, ultimately, making them better consumers of information on crime and justice. Great effort is often necessary in order to encourage the students as consumers of media information to be skeptical and critical of crime statistics and crime reporting that they hear or read in the news. It is an attempt to get students to question the sources of these crime statistics as well as to think more broadly about whether this information reflects the true reality of crime and criminal behavior. For example, according to the National Crime Victimization Survey (NCVS), an annual survey of victimization (Rand, 2008), 64% of all reported rape and sexual assault victimizations against females in 2007 were committed by relatives, friends, or other acquaintances of the victim. Regardless of whether these incidents were reported to the police, local news outlets do not often disseminate this information. Rather, news reports of rape and sexual assault often report that the incidents were predatory, stranger-committed acts, the predator most often being someone who previously received prison time for similar offenses. Do these news reports of rape and sexual assault make females unnecessarily fearful of strangers yet dangerously trustworthy of those whom they know? According to the NCVS, yes!

The goal of this reader is to get you to think more critically about sources of crime information. You will be better able to do this if you are familiar with how social science researchers examine crime and justice issues. Examining scientific research will reveal how and why these research efforts are valuable as well as why you as a consumer of crime and justice information should pay more attention to research. It aims to accomplish this by discussing the fundamental ways in which social scientists, specifically criminologists and criminal justice researchers, obtain knowledge about crime and criminal justice behavior and how they go about seeking answers to important questions on these topics.

This reader has also been constructed with the belief that these goals can best be accomplished by exposing students to examples of real research. In other words, students can best learn research methods in criminology and criminal justice by reading research that has been published by scholars in the field. The compilation of research examples that are included in the following chapters provides recent and excellent examples of research that has been published in academic journals. These articles are illustrative of research that uses sound and principled research methodologies and that has explored the causes of criminal offending or examined justice issues involving the three major branches of the criminal justice system. Hopefully, as you become immersed in these examples of research, you will discover that reading and understanding scientific research in criminology and criminal justice is not as difficult as it may initially seem and that for those who will become future researchers or employees of the criminal justice system, it is indeed a very worthwhile task.

WHY CRIMINOLOGISTS CONDUCT RESEARCH USING THE SCIENTIFIC METHOD

There are other important reasons beyond information gathering that lead those who take a scientific approach to studying crime to expend a great deal of time, resources, and effort in doing so. Most of these important reasons have to do with acquiring accurate knowledge and strict adherence to the scientific method. The following pages have been written to provide a fundamental basis for understanding the procedures involved in conducting research of a scientific nature. This reader also provides discussions of some of the major limitations of the research methods used to study crime and justice.

Each year, thousands of researchers seek answers to thousands of questions about crime and justice. For example, is the death penalty an effective deterrent to homicide? Does the gender or race of defendants have an effect on the length of sentence a judge will impose on

them? Is there a relationship between age and crime? Are newspaper reports of homicide victims different dependent on the gender of the victim? Is fear of crime affected by the amount of education or annual income one has? Do delinquent friends cause an individual to be more delinquent? These questions are just a few of the thousands of questions that researchers might be interested in finding answers to in order to gain increased knowledge about crime and criminal behavior and its broader relationship to society.

What counts as research? You may have asked yourself this question if a professor assigned you a term paper and stated that you may only use empirical research as sources. You may have overheard people state that they are going to do some research on which neighborhoods are the safest in a particular city or the doctors with the best reputation in an area. Your parents may have even done some research on which colleges provide the best education at the most reasonable tuition costs. Is this research? The quick answer would be yes—anyone who investigates or employs some type of effort to seek answers to their questions or to increase their knowledge of something is doing research. But is this research scientific? Can these people be certain that their research has provided them with accurate answers? The quick answer to that question is no.

So, what is the difference? Well, primarily, the research in the above examples is probably conducted via the Internet or by asking someone who has lived in the city for a while. This research could probably also be accomplished in a few hours. The difference, therefore, is that those who conduct scientific research employ much more rigorous methods to gather the information they are seeking. Criminologists and other social scientists use systematic, well-established research practices to seek answers to their questions. This is what makes their research empirical. Scientific researchers also restrict their questions and explanations in more tangible ways than the everyday researcher (Ellis, Hartley, & Walsh, 2010). Social scientists follow what is referred to as the scientific method in order to get objective answers to their questions and to ensure that the answers they get are valid and reliable.

The problem with the answers that everyday citizens obtain or that are provided by local television reporters on the street is that there is a high likelihood that they may not reflect the true nature of reality. In other words, the answers are most likely erroneous. This is why researchers in criminology and criminal justice also utilize theory (both probability and criminological) and statistics (both mathematical and inferential) in their research endeavors. Theory and statistics help scientific researchers limit the amount of error associated with research results. After reading the rest of this chapter, you will be more familiar with the reasoning behind the use of the scientific method for research in criminology and criminal justice.

THE SCIENTIFIC METHOD

The scientific method is a tool that helps criminology and criminal justice researchers systematically study crime and justice using methods that are logical (that make sense), that reduce the likelihood of error (that ensure answers are accurate and reliable), and that make results open to scrutiny by other researchers (that enables others in the field to examine and question the findings). Bachman and Schutt (2008) point out some of the ways in which the scientific method is superior to methods that the average person might use to seek answers to their questions: (1) The scientific method uses procedures for selecting persons or groups for study that are representative of the population the researcher wants to study, (2) the scientific method relies on systematic measurement to reduce inaccuracies in observation, (3) the scientific method makes

use of certain criteria to establish cause, and (4) the scientific method resists change and ensures objectivity by allowing others to examine and be critical of findings and results.

Figure 1.1 represents an illustration of the scientific research process. As shown in this figure, there are several important steps involved in the scientific method that must be followed to be sure that all the characteristics listed above are true for a particular research study. The steps involved in the scientific method are also referred to as the wheel of science (Wallace, 1971) and include theory, hypotheses, data collection, and empirical generalization. Although research can begin at different stages in the process (deductive versus inductive approaches), there is some debate about the appropriate starting point and the proper way to conduct research. Pure researchers (those concerned with advancing knowledge) believe that all research should begin with theory. Researchers who take a more applied approach, on the other hand, may start by collecting and analyzing data and then looking for theoretically appropriate explanations for what they have observed. Chapter 2 will provide a further discussion of deductive and inductive research, but for now, the importance of theory in the research process cannot be understated.

Theory is important in crime research because there are many competing ideas (theories) about why persons engage in criminal behavior. For instance, some might believe that young adults are more likely to engage in criminal activity if they hang out with others (friends) who are criminal. Maybe you personally know someone who has engaged in unlawful behaviors and have observed that person hanging out with others who are also delinquents or criminals. But does having criminal friends make someone more prone to commit illegal acts? Further, how can we be sure that the delinquent friends are to blame for an individual's criminal behavior? The answer is that we cannot be sure, and we cannot say that criminal friends

Figure 1.1   The Research Circle

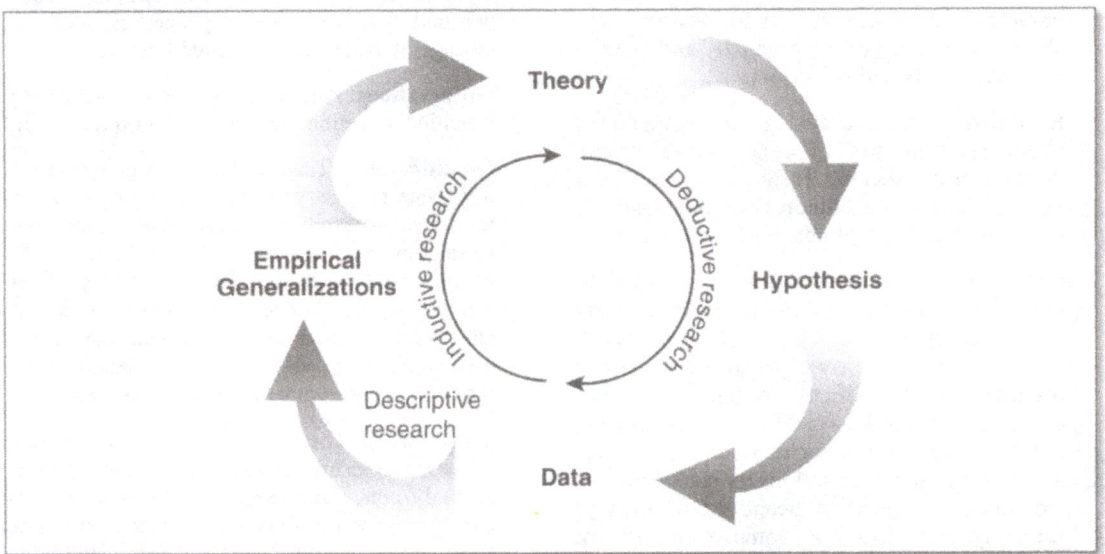

cause persons to commit crime based on one or a few individuals who we know. But we could conduct scientific research to find out if this theory of criminal friends influencing criminal behavior is a plausible explanation. This theory could be tested by following the steps outlined in the scientific method. The scientific method enables researchers to test theories through hypotheses, observations, and empirical generalization.

In order to test the theory that criminal activity is more likely for an individual who has friends who are criminal, several procedures must be followed. To test theories, researchers need to formulate hypotheses, make decisions about measuring or quantifying variables, make decisions about how to collect the data and from whom, undertake procedures to collect the data (observations must be made), and finally, analyze the data. Before beginning a discussion of the steps involved in the scientific method, it is necessary to define a few terms that will make the research process seem a little less complicated.

More than a few university professors have observed that students put off taking a course in research methods until they absolutely have to (their last semester before graduation). One of the main reasons that most students avoid research methods classes is the language that researchers use to describe the research process. This "research shock," as Hagan (2010, p. 15) describes it, can be intimidating but, once learned, can greatly assist students in understanding the process of research. It is, therefore, actually important to take a research methods class as early as possible because it will ultimately help you understand materials and research presented in other required courses. Some straightforward definitions of widely used language in research methods follow:

Units of Analysis: The people, places, and things that researchers study; the objects of their research. Common units of analysis in criminology and criminal justice research include individuals, groups, and institutions.

Theory: A plausible explanation of reality. Criminological theories, for example, provide possible reasons why crime occurs or why individuals commit crime. Crime theories also allow us to understand, organize, and predict criminal events and behaviors.

Hypothesis: An educated guess or statement about relationships between variables and derived from theory. Hypotheses spell out expectations about theoretical relationships between variables and observed phenomena.

Concepts: Abstract ideas that are created to explain our reality. For example, weight is a fairly simple concept constructed to explain how heavy something is. Some concepts in social science research can be difficult to understand. For example, everyone knows the concept of religion, but have they ever thought about what makes some people religious and others not? How can we measure religion in people or in society? Similarly, crime is a fairly complex concept that different persons, at different places, and in different times, have defined differently. Depending on what behaviors are included in conceptualizing crime, it may or may not be difficult to study.

Operationalization: This is another word for measurement; a description of how the concepts in our research are going to be measured. Crime for instance may be measured as counts (number of homicides, robberies, or burglaries), or it may be measured as a rate (count per certain number of population). Religion, for example, could be operationalized by frequency of church attendance, amount of belief in a higher power, or level of dedication to prayer practices. Operationalization allows researchers to make abstract concepts more concrete, which makes them more amenable to scientific study.

Variables: Concepts that have been operationalized, or traits that can have different values. For example, different neighborhoods could have different numbers of burglaries in a specified time period. Burglary, therefore, is a trait (variable) of neighborhoods that can take on different values. Dependent variables are the traits we are attempting to predict: the caused variable. Independent variables are those we assume are influencing the traits we are studying. Independent variables that might influence the number of burglaries in a neighborhood could include: number of street lights, number of entrances (exits) to the neighborhood, average value of properties, and percentage of owned versus rented houses.

Observations: Any data gathered or collected by watching, counting, interviewing, or questioning.

Quantification: The practice of assigning numerical value to observations. Quantifying observations helps researchers categorize and understand them. For instance, if I tell you I weigh 200 pounds, you will have a fairly good idea of my weight. Pounds are a way to quantify an individual's weight. Crime rates, for instance, are a way to quantify crime per a unit of population so that researchers can compare crime across cities.

Empiricism: The practice of using methods based on experiments and observation. In order to study concepts, researchers need to empirically measure variables. This means they need to make observations or gather data using well-established scientific methods.

Generalizability: The ability of a researcher to infer the results of a research study based on a sample back to the larger population from which the sample was drawn.

THE RESEARCH PROCESS

Theory

The scientific method involves tests of theory. Many criminological theories exist as attempts to explain the reality of crime and criminal behavior. Some of these theories are categorized as macrolevel (societal causes), and others, microlevel (individual causes). The previously mentioned idea that persons may learn criminal behavior through interactions with criminal friends has been proposed as a criminological theory called differential association theory (Sutherland, 1939; 1947). Sutherland proposed this complex theory of learning in which he set forth nine postulations regarding how criminal behavior might be learned.

One of these nine postulations included concepts that related the idea of differential association to human interactions. Sutherland stated that "a person becomes delinquent because of an excess of definitions favorable to violation of the law over definitions unfavorable to violation of the law" (Akers, 2000, p. 72). In other words, those who have contact with persons who have values favoring law violation will also learn to favor law violation. Another of Sutherland's postulates stated that these differential associations may vary in frequency, duration, priority, and intensity. From the postulations of differential association theory, and through use of the scientific method, researchers can formulate hypotheses that could test Sutherland's theory. These hypotheses may look similar to the ones in the following section. (Obviously these hypotheses are simple examples. A true test of the differential association theory would require more elaborate and well thought out hypotheses based on the various components of differential association theory.)

Hypotheses

Hypothesis 1: Those who have more criminal friends will be more likely to engage in criminal behavior.

Hypothesis 2: The greater the amount of time spent with criminal friends (frequency, duration), the more likely it is that the individual will engage in criminal behavior.

Hypothesis 3: The more meaningful these associations with criminal friends are (priority, intensity), the more likely it is that the individual will engage in criminal behavior.

In order for researchers to test hypotheses, they must make decisions about how to operationalize (measure) important concepts from the theory. Researchers also need to specify the measurement of concepts so that they can collect data on them. These concepts may have already been very well defined and measured

by other researchers; therefore, researchers sometimes use previously constructed measures. Conceptualization and operationalization of concepts, therefore, are primary steps in research testing theory. For tests of criminological theory, one of the first concepts that researchers need to operationalize is crime or criminality. Making a decision about how to operationalize crime or criminality can sometimes prove difficult. For example, should all offenses, petty crimes, and misdemeanors, as well as felonies, be included in this definition of crime? Does crime include only offenses for which a person has been caught and arrested by the police? What about those who have committed crimes but were not caught, or situations where crimes occurred but no one notified authorities? Some researchers believe a better method of operationalizing crime or criminality is to ask persons about crimes they have committed, which would allow inclusion of those crimes that did not come to the attention of police.

Whichever operational definition a researcher chooses, a primary step is to establish what it means to be criminal so that researchers can distinguish between criminals and noncriminals as well as evaluate levels of criminality in individuals. After a decision has been made about the most appropriate way to measure crime, researchers also need to operationalize other key concepts related to the theoretical explanations for criminal behavior. The next step in the scientific method is deciding on a research design.

Research Design

Choosing a research design includes deciding the methods to be used to conduct the research or to test the theory. Researchers might already have a specific research design in mind prior to deciding the operationalization of key concepts; however, the ways in which researchers decide to measure variables may influence the type of methodological design they can use. For example, if crime is defined by police arrests, researchers must choose a design that enables them to study police records. If, on the other hand, researchers want to include criminal behaviors both known and unknown to the police, they might choose a design that allows them to study a broader population than arrestees. This step is also where researchers need to specify the unit of analysis to be studied.

Units of analysis in criminology research, especially in tests of microlevel theories, are often individuals. As stated above, perhaps a researcher decides to ask individuals to report their level of criminal behavior, whether or not they have criminal friends, and how much contact they have with these friends. Many researchers have used this method of data collection to obtain information about individuals' criminal behavior. This method of collecting data (observations) is referred to as self-report survey research because it entails asking individuals to answer questions about their behavior via a survey.

Much more will be said about survey research in Chapter 7; however, for now, keep in mind that a lot of what we know about criminal and other behaviors has been collected by simply asking individuals to self-report on their attitudes, opinions, and behaviors. Researchers usually also collect demographic information along with behavioral information from these individuals such as sex, age, and race or ethnicity in order to assess differences in behaviors between groups.

Included in the research design stage is a decision about whom this info is going to be solicited from. In other words, who are the research subjects (those who the survey will be administered to)? Obviously being able to administer the survey to all persons in a particular city, state, or even country would be the best way to test hypotheses about a theory. However, due to limited time and resources, most researchers are only able to study a small group of persons from the population. This group is referred to as a sample. The way in which this sample is chosen is very important to scientific-based research because in order for researchers to conclude anything about the reality of observed relationships, such as the correlation between having criminal friends and engaging in criminal behavior, they need to be able to study a group of subjects (sample) that is representative of the population they wish to study.

A sampling procedure called random sampling is the best way to obtain a group for study to ensure that the findings are true for the larger population as well. Random sampling is a technique that allows researchers to select subjects in such a way that every member of the population has an equal probability to be in the sample. This is important because it means that the sample the researchers study will resemble the larger population—it will be what scientists refer to as a representative sample. If researchers are able to obtain a representative sample, it means that they can be more certain that the results of the research based on the sample hold true for the population from which the sample was drawn.

This is referred to as generalizability, or the extent to which researchers can state that what is true about their sample is also true for the larger population. Sometimes, however, it is difficult to get a random sample, especially when studying specific types of crime or rare and obscure criminal behaviors. If researchers cannot obtain a random sample, they have to be more cautious about stating that the results and findings of the research are true, or generalizable, to the entire population of offenders. Much more will be said in Chapter 6 about the different types of sampling techniques used by social science researchers, which are generally categorized into two types: probability and nonprobability.

Observations (Data Collection)

Once a sample has been selected for study, researchers can collect data. As stated earlier, a great deal of research on criminal behavior has been collected via self-report survey. Survey research is not as easy to do as it may first seem. Numerous issues arise regarding the types of questions to ask, the way to ask these questions, and the best method to use to fill out the questionnaire (whether the subjects should fill it out or if the researcher should ask the subjects questions and fill out the survey for them). Data can be collected from a sample at one point in time (cross-sectional data) or can be collected from the same sample over time (longitudinal data). More will be said about survey research in Chapter 7, but past research has shown that results can vary depending on how questions are asked.

Once data has been collected or observations have been made, researchers analyze the data utilizing some type of statistical techniques. Statistics can refer to the characteristics of the individuals in the sample as well as the mathematical tests and procedures used to analyze data collected from these individuals (Champion & Hartley, 2010). Researchers today have access to very powerful statistical programs that can help them conclude all sorts of things about the data collected. Not to complicate things, but there are certain stringent assumptions regarding the data collected that must be met in order to employ many of these statistical tests.

At the simplest level, this stage also consists of describing the data you have collected. For instance, what percentage of your sample reported engaging in criminal behaviors? Further, what percentage reported having contacts with criminal friends? What was the average number of criminal friends that those who engaged in crime had? Researchers usually also report whether any of these results differ by gender, age, race, ethnicity, or educational level of the individuals studied. Theories of crime may hold true for some groups and not for others (for example, a particular crime theory may hold true for males but not females), and distinguishing these differences might be

important to advancing theoretical knowledge. Finally, did any of the persons who reported that they had engaged in crime report no associations with criminal friends, or did anyone report having criminal friends but did not engage in crime? If this is the case, there might be something else, another variable, or a combination of variables other than associations with criminal friends that is responsible for the criminal behavior of the group studied.

Most criminologists understand that crime is a very complex phenomenon, and that one variable alone cannot explain all criminal behaviors. Researchers often test a number of hypotheses, which examine many factors that may be influential of crime. This involves measuring more concepts and collecting more data in order to tap into other dimensions of criminal offending. It also involves utilizing more advanced statistical techniques, namely multivariate statistics. Multivariate statistics examine the relationships between two or more variables. Because crime is a complex phenomenon, most researchers who study it employ some type of multivariate statistical analysis in their research. Statistical analysis is important to the research process. Wallace (1971) asserts that "statistical tests provide the most 'objective,' most rigorous, and most sensitive rules available for measuring the fit between hypothesis and finding" (p. 81). A discussion of multivariate statistical tests is beyond the scope of this reader; however, if students are seriously considering conducting research in the future, it would be wise to enroll in a social science statistics class to get a better understanding of these techniques.

Researchers make use of both quantitative and qualitative research methods in tests of criminological theory. Quantitative research involves the collection of numerical data or the application of statistical techniques to the collected data. Most research published in academic journals includes some type of quantitative analysis, although the number of outlets publishing qualitative research is increasing.

Qualitative research involves data collection of a more personal nature: data that is more related to the senses and cannot necessarily be described with numbers.

Qualitative researchers often conduct research in the field and collect more than just demographic information or attitudes and opinions; rather, they make more in-depth observations. Most researchers who conduct qualitative research get more involved in their data collection techniques and may even interact with, or participate in, the customs or behaviors (participant observations) of those they are studying. Qualitative researchers do not necessarily know the nature of the data they are going to collect in advance. They conceptualize and categorize the data collected and construct themes, inferences, and theoretical explanations after data collection.

Both quantitative and qualitative research will be discussed further in Chapters 8 and 9. More recently, researchers have begun to utilize both quantitative and qualitative research methodologies in a single study. These studies are referred to as mixed methods research designs, and both the advantages and disadvantages of combining quantitative and qualitative methods will be discussed in Chapter 10. For now, keep in mind that a considerable amount of both types of research, as well as mixed methods research, have been employed in the study of crime and criminal behavior and in examinations of the administration of justice.

Empirical Generalizations

The last step in the scientific research process comes after the data has been gathered and the appropriate analyses have been performed. Researchers at this stage assess whether their results support their hypotheses. In other words, this step involves inferring the findings back to theory to determine whether the results support or refute the theory. For example, if the results from the surveys reveal

that those who report being criminal also report having a greater number of criminal friends, the findings have provided some support for the theory of criminal friends being correlated with criminal behavior (differential association theory). Researchers, however, realize that one study does not make or break a theory. It may be that with another group of subjects, the findings would be different. It also may be that even though the study sample was randomly selected, some subjects refused to respond to the questionnaire. Participation in research, especially involving human subjects must be voluntary; subjects must be able to choose whether to provide information.

If too many of the subjects that have been randomly selected for study do not agree to fill out the questionnaire, the responses may not represent the larger population from which the sample was selected. In other words, the sample would no longer be random or representative. For example, perhaps in the survey research above, the most criminal individuals were also the most likely to decline to provide information, or perhaps some subjects lied about their criminal behavior on the survey. More will be said about the truthfulness of self-report data in Chapter 7. For now, keep in mind that a great feature of science is that it is cumulative and self-correcting (Ellis et al., 2010). In other words, the results of numerous studies must be considered together in an assessment of a particular theory, and if error is present in sample selection procedures or in the way in which important concepts were operationalized, future research studies by others will uncover these errors and correct them with new research findings.

This is also the reason why criminologists and other researchers never make statements such as "this study *proves*" or "our findings show that criminal friends *cause* crime." Human behavior is very complex, and researchers can never state that their results will hold true for everyone. What criminologists can say is that their findings show a correlation between two variables (for example, the number of criminal friends one has and the presence of criminal behavior). What this means is that scientists can use the findings of their research to make predictions—they may say, for example, that those who have more criminal friends are more likely to engage in criminal activity, but they do not consider these findings to be deterministic or that every person who has criminal friends will be criminal.

One of the criteria for assessing the merit of a theory is whether it is testable. Theories have to be tested in order to advance scientific knowledge. Akers (2000), for instance, states that "if a theory cannot be tested against empirical findings, it has no scientific value" (p. 7). Numerous research studies have tested a number of criminological theories; some of these tests provide support for these theories while others do not. What students of scientific research also need to bear in mind is that theories cannot really be proven to be true. If they could, they would no longer be theories (plausible explanations); they would be considered scientific facts. Another desirable attribute of a theory is that it is subject to being falsified (Ellis et al., 2010). This may seem a bit counterintuitive; why do researchers put forth time and effort to test something that cannot be proven true? In science, if a theory cannot be falsified, it is not considered to be a good theory. Good theories, therefore, are both testable and falsifiable.

In science, just testing theory is neither good enough nor is it the end of the research process. Researchers also need to verify and validate the results of theory tests. Verification simply refers to "confirmation of the accuracy of findings" (Hagan, 2010, p. 6), or being more sure of the results by conducting more research. Results can also be validated by replicating the same research with different samples or populations. Researchers often replicate research that others before them have conducted to verify the results of previous research. This verification and validation

process illustrates the cumulative nature of science and epitomizes a now-famous phrase credited to Isaac Newton in the late 1600s. Newton declared in a letter to colleague Robert Hooke that "if I have seen farther than others, it is because I have stood on the shoulders of giants." What this means is that all scientific research relies on previous scientific research in order to advance knowledge.

Research, therefore, is a neverending process; once researchers have conducted a theory test, depending on the results, they will conduct additional studies to further verify and validate their findings or they will modify their tests by choosing new research methods or selecting different samples. In either case, researchers revert back to the scientific method and begin the research process all over again. Researchers have recently begun to integrate theories in their tests of crime etiology. Many researchers have attempted to test competing theories in a single study. This makes sense, as crime is a very complex phenomenon. By including concepts that measure different theories in a single study, researchers are controlling for each of these theories in attempts to determine which have the strongest effects on criminal behavior. In other words, they are attempting to assess causal relationships by controlling for other possible causal factors (measures of other theories).

POSITIVISM AND THE RESEARCH PROCESS

Auguste Compte, a French sociologist (and the so-called father of sociology), is said to be the first to emphasize the need for scientific rigor in the study of human behavior. Compte proposed using quantitative methods and mathematics as a basis for social science research. Although some critics claim that others before Compte had already proposed these ideas (see, for instance, Heilbron, 1990), Compte's six-volume *Courses in Positive Philosophy*, which was published from 1830 to 1842, were the impetus for the use of empirical measurement in the social sciences. Positivism is a philosophy that states that researchers cannot seek to understand reality unless they can measure it (Hagan, 2005). Positivism entails strict adherence to the scientific method and positivists believe that the only way to acquire knowledge is through use of the scientific method. In other words, researchers cannot understand the truth unless they can somehow measure it.

A related philosophy, referred to as postpositivism, argues that it is not possible for scientists to objectively measure reality. From this perspective, it is argued that the observations researchers make are skewed by their prejudices and biases. The only way to observe an objective view of reality is through agreement among the scientific community about the true nature of reality (Wallace, 1983). Both perspectives believe, however, in adherence to the scientific method. They also believe that through research and measurement we can discover the true reality of social phenomena.

Official statistics can be misleading, depending on how they are measured. Let's say, for instance, that a student wishes to attend the University of Texas. This student's parents, however, would rather that he attend the University of Nebraska in Lincoln because it is their alma mater, and Lincoln is much safer than Austin. The student's father has looked up the latest homicide data from the Uniform Crime Reports (UCR) available from the FBI's website. He tells the student that the Austin, Texas metro area observed 33 homicides in 2008, and that Lincoln, Nebraska observed only 6 homicides for the same year. The student might conclude that his father is correct and that he would be safer, as well as make his parents feel better, if he attended the University of Nebraska.

After sleeping on it, however, the student decides that he would really rather be a Longhorn than a Husker but also knows he needs to convince his parents that he will be safe. How could a student find the truth (reality) about how dangerous the two different cities are? How could he find an objective way to measure the relative occurrence of crime from city to city? One way is to look at crime rates; crime rates (the number of crimes per unit of population) are a method of measuring the amount of crime in a city so that it can be compared with crime in other cities. The student decides to collect more data on homicide in the two cities. In examining the data, the student notices that the UCR also reports that there are over 1.6 million persons living in the Austin metropolitan areas versus only about 300,000 persons living in Lincoln (USDOJ, 2009a).

The student decides that to get a true idea of the reality of safety in the two cities, a better way to measure homicide is as a rate, which controls for the population of the cities. If homicide is measured as a rate rather than as the absolute number of homicides, the student observes that both cities have homicide rates of 2.0 per 100,000 persons. Using the rate to measure the number of homicides is a better way to assess the relative risk of homicide in these two cities. In other words, the student now has a better picture of the true reality of homicide across the two cities, and he can now reassure his parents that he will be just as safe in Austin.

Obviously, this is a simple measurement example, and looking only at homicide gives no knowledge of the risk of victimization for other crimes such as robbery, assault, or burglary. Previous research has also shown that victimization rates vary by age, gender, race, and lifestyle (see, for examples, Rand, 2009); as such, there are multiple factors related to the risk of victimization of an individual. With this simple example, however, it is easy to see that researchers cannot uncover the true nature of phenomena unless they can find objective ways to measure them; researchers also need accurate measures of what they are studying.

THE PROBABILISTIC NATURE OF SCIENCE

In the earlier discussion of the scientific method and the research process, it was stated that researchers assume that the phenomena they study are probabilistic. What this means is that researchers assume that "effects will most often occur when certain causes are present" (Hagan, 2010, p. 6). This assumption allows researchers to predict patterns and trends in crime or to explain relationships among groups. Because social scientists believe that the things they study are probabilistic, they can make predictions about relationships between variables based on observations they have made. This does not mean, however, that these predictions will be true all of the time or that these patterns will hold for every individual subject.

For example, if a researcher conducts a study that shows a strong negative relationship between level of education and delinquency (higher education associated with lower delinquency), this researcher is not predicting that everyone who does not receive a high school diploma will become delinquent. Neither does it mean that if a majority of those who do not finish high school do not commit delinquent acts that this researcher was wrong. What it means is that there is a strong relationship between high school graduation and delinquency, and researchers can therefore predict that changing graduation rates will affect delinquency rates. Further, it suggests that those who do not graduate are probably most at risk for becoming delinquent. In the next chapter, a more in-depth discussion will be presented about the ways that researchers estimate relationships between variables (correlations) as well as how they estimate the probability that the results of their research are accurate (statistical significance). Now that you know more about the scientific method and the research process, the next step is to learn how to read research that has been published in academic journals.

HOW TO READ PUBLISHED RESEARCH

Most published research follows a basic format. This format provides a structure for researchers to follow when writing up a description and summary of their research. Although, this structure varies by discipline and the particular journal that the research is published in, most scientific research reports that are published follow a conventional format. This format includes an abstract, an introduction, a review of previous literature, a methods section, a findings or results section, a discussion or conclusion section, and references.

Reading research that is published in academic journals can sometimes be intimidating. However, knowing the general information that is included in each of these sections can make reading published research less daunting. It would also be wise for those who are going to be reading published research to familiarize themselves with how to read tables. In most research articles, data and findings are presented in tabular format. Examining the tables included in a published article can often be a quick and simple way to understand the characteristics of the data collected for a study as well as the findings and results of the study.

Published research can also sometimes be quite lengthy. As such, the examples included in this book have been modified somewhat for ease of reading. This means that you will not see all of the sections listed above in all of the examples of research in this reader. Some sections, such as the literature review or discussion, may have been shortened or removed to make the articles easier to read or in an effort to highlight the particular method that the researchers used. A brief summary of the material that is commonly included in each of these sections follows:

Abstract. The abstract is usually around 150–200 words, depending on the journal, and gives a synopsis of what the research is about. The abstract provides a quick way for the reader to get an overview of the research study. It can assist other researchers in decisions about whether the research study could be used to frame their own research studies without having to read the entire article.

Introduction. The introduction section is an opportunity for the researcher to establish the importance of the research topic. It is also where the authors make the argument that the topic is in need of research. For example, perhaps the number of juveniles being tried as adults is increasing, and the authors argue that it is necessary to examine how juveniles are treated in adult court. Or perhaps a particular topic or phenomenon has not received a lot of attention by researchers in the past; often, the lack of research on a particular subject is the impetus for the research.

Review of Literature (Literature Review; Review of Previous Research). The literature review section provides a framework for the research that the authors are conducting. Literature simply refers to the previous research that has already been conducted on a topic. The review of literature, therefore, provides a clear picture of what is currently known about the topic of study, what limitations are inherent in the existing research, and where existing research is lacking. In a sense, similar to the introduction, the literature review can emphasize the importance of the research topic but in this case, in a more academic sense.

The review of literature also includes a description of the theoretical framework that was used for study. Good research will have a well-formulated, theoretical framework as its foundation. This theoretical discussion helps readers understand the authors' hypotheses, what they were based on, and how they were formulated. In some publications, the hypotheses will be placed at the end of the literature review; in others, they will be found in the methods section. This may depend on the discipline or the preferences of the authors or journal.

Methods. The methods section is the meat of the research article and entails a description of the research design that was utilized for the study. It should outline the methods used by the researchers to gather data. It should also discuss the sampling technique employed to obtain the subjects for the study and the way the variables were measured. Outlining these procedures is important because the research design and sampling technique will allow the reader to be able to interpret the results of the study. The methods section of a published research article should also include any limitations inherent in the research design or in the sampling procedures. For example, researchers should disclose how many of the originally obtained subjects dropped out of the study or did not consent to participate. In mail surveys, for instance, authors would want to differentiate between the number of surveys mailed out and the number of surveys completed and returned. The difference between these two is referred to as sample attrition and is very important to the generalizability of the findings and the study's overall influence in increasing knowledge or testing theory.

A final component of the methods section includes a discussion of the sample. This section is usually found under the headings of descriptive statistics or univariate statistics and is important so that the reader can get an idea of the characteristics of the sample subjects. The methods section is also where the authors should discuss the statistical analysis to be performed with the data. Although the statistical analysis section can be somewhat complex, it is important for the authors to present this information so that the reader can understand the techniques used in analyzing the data.

Results (Findings). The results section describes the findings of the research. In this section, the authors need to inform the reader about whether the hypotheses of the study were supported. Dependent on whether the hypotheses were correct or not, the authors will also want to discuss what this means from a theoretical perspective. In other words, did the results provide support for, or refute, the theory that was tested.

Authors will also want to note whether there were any unexpected or even contradictory findings. Many times, researchers will get results that are opposite of what they expected, or even that defy interpretation, according to previous research and theory.

The information and statistical output in the results section is usually presented in tabular format as well as described within the text. Again, it would be beneficial to be adept at reading various types of tables. Researchers create tables to display results because in this format the results make sense to other social science researchers. These tables also help the reader follow the in-text description of the study's results. A helpful resource for students just learning about statistical output and reading published research is a book entitled *From Numbers to Words: Reporting Statistical Results in the Social Sciences*. This book by Morgan, Reichert, and Harrison (2002) provides more detailed information regarding the structure, format, and interpretation of research publications. If you are considering conducting your own research, or you are a master's student with an upcoming thesis requirement, you would be wise to pick up a copy of this book.

Conclusion (Discussion). In the conclusion section of publications, authors give the reader a broader picture of the research study. Some of the findings may be reiterated to emphasize their significance to the discipline or for theory. Here the authors should also bring the study full circle and relate the results back to the hypotheses and literature review or introduction sections of the study. Authors will highlight the key findings and discuss what has been gained scientifically from this research study as well as what future researchers might consider when conducting research on the same topic or using the same methodology. Depending on the journal, some publications may also include a paragraph or two regarding policy implications that the research might have in the discussion section.

References. The references section of a research article gives the reader complete information about the previous research that was used in the current study. Remember Newton's phrase about standing on the shoulders of giants? Authors need to cite and provide full information for all of the sources that were used in the current publication to frame and build the sections of their research described above. The reader can then use these sources of information to get access to additional research that has been conducted on the topic or that discuss the specific methodological or statistical techniques employed in the current research study.

2

CRIMINOLOGICAL THEORY AND THE SCIENTIFIC METHOD

To say that theory is the cornerstone of research is an understatement. Theoretical knowledge of crime and justice enables researchers to do many valuable things. Theoretical knowledge allows researchers to explain current events and to predict future ones. For example, theory allows researchers to explain why some persons commit crime in their early adolescent years and then desist offending as they age or why other offenders persist as criminals into adulthood and become what are known as life course persistent (Moffitt, 1993). Criminological theories also allow researchers to assess the effect of other noncriminal events on criminal offending (Ellis, Hartley, & Walsh, 2010). For example, if the country experiences an economic downturn, will property crime increase? If a higher percentage of newborn infants are male as opposed to female this year, does that mean that crime will spike in 15 to 20 years? Many researchers have sought to explain the questions like those posed above through the use of criminological theories.

Theories also enable researchers to organize and classify scientific observations. For example, researchers have used the chivalry or paternalism theory to explain why judges hand out more lenient sentences to females than to males who have committed similar offenses. These theories contend that judges try to protect female defendants from the harshness of prison, or that judges view female offenders as less blameworthy and culpable than male offenders (Steffensmeier, 1980; Steffensmeier, Kramer, & Ulmer, 1998). Others have argued that this leniency toward female defendants can be explained through a more nuanced version of the theory of paternalism called familial paternalism—the idea that because females are the primary caregivers for dependent children, judges are more lenient on them in order to keep the family intact (Daly, 1989; 1994). Others still have contended that there may be some practical or organizational theories that guide judges' decisions; there are not as many prison beds for females offenders, so they are sent to prison less often (Dixon, 1995; Johnson, Ulmer, & Kramer, 2008; Steffensmeier, Kramer, & Streifel, 1993; Ulmer & Kramer, 1996).

Finally, theories are the driving force behind scientific research studies; theories assist in guiding and shaping research questions, methodologies, and hypotheses. Bachman and Schutt (2008) note that researchers "who connect their work to theories…develop conclusions with more implications for other research" (p. 31). Recall that in Figure 1.1 in Chapter 1, theory was atop the wheel of science; most researchers in criminology and criminal justice utilize theory as a foundation for their scientific research studies. Theories help researchers understand and explain criminal events. Explanation and prediction are important for criminology and criminal justice; as such, evaluating and advancing criminological theory is a central component of research. Research that evaluates policies and programs toward crime prevention or rehabilitation (evaluation research) is also an important endeavor for the discipline and larger society. Evaluation research will be discussed further in Chapter 11.

useful predictions for every social situation or research problem that we seek to investigate. Moreover, we may find unexpected patterns in the data we collect. . . . In either situation, we should reason inductively, making whatever theoretical sense we can of our unanticipated findings. (p. 34)

Clearly, this emphasizes the idea that the research process does not have a definite starting or stopping point. Research is a continual process of deductively testing hypotheses drawn from theory and inductively making sense of observations from which new hypotheses can be drawn. This circular process is precisely how researchers advance knowledge in the social and behavioral sciences.

DEDUCTION VERSUS INDUCTION

Theory and research are connected through two main processes: deductive reasoning and inductive reasoning. Deductive reasoning starts at the top of the wheel of science with theory. The researcher draws hypotheses from theory and tests them through observations or data collection (Babbie, 2010). Inductive reasoning, on the other hand, is a bottom-up approach; the researcher starts with observations or data and then seeks to find patterns in the data that may be explained through theory (Bachman & Schutt, 2008). These two approaches are important in scientific research, and criminology is replete with examples of both. These seemingly opposing methods, however, are not mutually exclusive, and numerous research studies have used both to advance knowledge. Bachman and Schutt explain the importance of both deduction and induction in the research process:

We cannot test an idea fairly unless we use deductive reasoning, stating our expectations in advance and setting up a test in which our idea could be shown to be wrong (falsified). . . . Yet theories, no matter how cherished, cannot make

CORRELATION VERSUS CAUSATION

Causation is the key to research in the social sciences. The goal of research is to identify causal relationships between variables. When criminologists test theories about the causes of crime or undertake research exploring other important questions in the field, they usually only examine factors they believe are related or correlated with crime. Vold, Bernard, and Snipes (2002) state that the research process involves procedures where "assertions of theory are tested against the observed world of the facts" (p. 5). In other words, criminologists study the relationship between crime and other social variables by testing theory against real-world observations. Researchers use statistical tests in attempts to assess the direction and strength of relationships between variables.

However, just because researchers find relationships between variables does not mean that one is causing the other. A very important rule of research is that correlation does not equal causation. Researchers can assess the relationship between two variables by making observations or by gathering data. A simple example is the relationship between a person's height and weight. Researchers might believe that height will predict weight. Data can be collected on students' heights and weights to assess the relationship between these two variables. Generally, the hypothesis would be that taller people are heavier than shorter people; increases in height will be associated with increases in weight. This, however, will not be the case for all people, we may have very tall persons who are skinny and weigh less than very short persons who are muscular.

Once this data is collected and displayed (usually in graphical format, also known as a scatterplot or scattergram), the true relationship between the variables of height and weight can be examined. Statistical techniques exist to assist in assessing the strength of relationships between two variables; one of these is credited to Karl Pearson and is referred to as Pearson's r statistic. The Pearson's r is correlation coefficient; a number that denotes how strong and in what direction the relationship is between two variables. If the data reveals that increases in height are associated with increases in weight, there is a positive relationship between the two variables. If the opposite is observed—decreases in weight for increases in height—there is a negative relationship between these variables.

Correlation coefficients range from −1 to +1, and a coefficient of 0 would mean no relationship between the variables. The closer the coefficient is to either +1 or −1, the stronger the relationship is. In social science research, 0 (or no) relationships rarely occur (researchers usually find some relationship between the variables they study). Similarly, two variables are seldom perfectly correlated (where one variable is the only cause of the other). Pearson's r is an invaluable tool to assess the relationship between two variables. Again, however, even if a strong relationship is observed between two variables, researchers have to be careful in concluding causality; in the social and behavioral world, many variables are often related to one another, but not one variable alone is completely associated with or causing another.

Remember that correlation does not equal causation, and researchers "should not be fooled into thinking that a cause-effect relationship has been found simply because two variables are correlated" (Ellis et al., 2010, p. 87). Criminologists, for example, have discovered many factors that have relationships to crime. If criminologists could prove that only one variable causes crime, it would be easy for them to predict the circumstances in which crime would occur and, therefore, institute mechanisms to prevent it altogether.

Criminologists also have to control for other possible causing variables, which are sometimes called rival causal factors. If these so-called rival causal factors are not controlled for, criminologists may mistakenly conclude that one or more of the independent variables they are examining are causes of crime; this is what researchers refer to as a spurious relationship. Bachman and Schutt (2008) state that "a causal effect is said to occur if variation in the independent variable is followed by variation in the dependent variable, when all other things are equal" (p. 114). This inclusion of all else being equal is a very important step in assessing causation, as researchers must control for other factors that may be causing a change in the dependent variable.

NULL VERSUS RESEARCH HYPOTHESES

In Chapter 1, hypotheses were defined as statements about the relationship between variables. Hypotheses are important in research because they describe expectations about theoretical relationships between variables. Hypotheses are the machinery that drives tests of theory. There are two types of hypotheses: research hypotheses and null hypotheses. Research hypotheses are statements outlining the predicted relationship between the variables of interest. Research hypotheses are derived from theory. Null hypotheses, on the other hand, are simply statements showing no observed relationship between variables. In some studies, researchers will specifically list their research hypotheses and test them through observations and statistical analysis. In other studies, researchers will simply state the null hypothesis (that no relationship exists between the variables studied) and then make observations, conduct analyses, and determine whether the opposite is true—that there is a relationship between the variables of interest.

Often the null hypothesis is implied rather than explicitly stated; however, all scientific research indirectly tests null hypotheses by testing research hypotheses (Ellis et al., 2010). Both cannot be true. Either there is a relationship between variables, or there is not. By testing the null hypotheses, researchers can make decisions about the truthfulness of research hypotheses.

Champion and Hartley (2010) describe some of the reasons why researchers test null hypotheses:

1. Testing null hypotheses makes tests of theory seem more objective; even though a theory may make specific statements about the relationship between variables, researchers test the theory with different samples of individuals or through observations at different points in time. In order to be objective, researchers often assume there is no observed relationship until they demonstrate otherwise. If researchers observe that a relationship exists, it lends greater support for theory.

2. In criminology and criminal justice research, null hypotheses are conventional. It is wise to follow established practices of the discipline. Researchers in criminology and criminal justice commonly test null hypotheses in their research.

3. Null hypotheses lend themselves well to probability theory. All hypothesis testing makes use of probability theory to evaluate and assess relationships. Researchers employ statistical techniques to assess whether the relationship between variables is statistically significant (in other words, that the relationship could not have occurred by chance). In essence, researchers are testing

the relationships between variables (research hypotheses) based on probability theory, using statistical techniques.

TYPE I AND TYPE II ERRORS

Based on probability theory, tests of null hypotheses are associated with two types of error: Type I and Type II. When researchers test hypotheses based on real-world observations, they are examining whether relationships exist between variables. If they find that a relationship exists, they reject the null hypothesis, which assumes no relationship. There is, however, some chance that researchers could be wrong in stating that a relationship exists when it actually does not or in stating that no relationship exists when in actuality one does. Simply put, a Type I error occurs if a researcher rejects the null hypothesis when it is actually true, and a Type II error occurs if a researcher accepts the null hypothesis when it is, in fact, false (Ellis et al., 2010).

When researchers test hypotheses, there is always a chance of error associated with the tests; researchers utilize probability theory to minimize the risk of making either of these errors. If researchers could test hypotheses by studying the entire population, they would not have to rely on probability theory. However, since researchers usually only study samples (a small group of persons, places, or things) from the population, they must rely on probability theory and statistics to ensure they are not making erroneous generalizations about the nature of reality based on their obtained sample.

PROBABILITY THEORY AND STATISTICAL SIGNIFICANCE

Using probability theory in research allows for prediction of the risk of making errors. Employing statistical techniques in research allows for application of mathematical procedures to research results and hypothesis tests. Conventionally, researchers will accept a 5% chance of making errors in the decision about rejecting or failing to reject the null hypotheses. Statistical tests provide researchers with a probability level associated with their results. If this probability level is 0.05 or below, a researcher can safely reject the null hypothesis and conclude that a statistically significant relationship does, in fact, exist between the variables under study. What this means is that there is less than a 5% chance that the researcher is wrong in rejecting the null hypothesis and supporting the research hypothesis. By utilizing the 0.05 probability level, researchers can state that only five times in 100 tests of the hypotheses using these data would they be wrong in rejecting the null hypothesis.

Probability levels are ordinarily denoted by the letter P and are usually given for each variable in the study. Most research articles will present the results of these tests in tabular format and denote significant variables with an asterisk. Researchers then provide a key at the bottom of the table, noting that an asterisk (*) indicates a probability level less than or equal to 0.05 ($* p \leq 0.05$); in other words, a statistically significant relationship has been observed. Probability levels and statistical significance are very important concepts to understand as you read the research articles included in this book. Mastering these concepts will enable students to quickly assess which of the independent variables in a study are significantly related to (have statistically significant relationships with) the dependent variable. Probability and statistical significance will be a recurrent theme throughout the following chapters and in the examples of research provided here.

RESEARCH READING

This research article tests two competing theories of the causes of delinquent behavior: self-control theory and social learning theory. Meldrum, Young, and Weerman argue that although strong support has been found for both of these theories in existing research studies, there has been a disagreement about how best to operationalize the key concepts from these theories. Thus, the current study attempts to provide a more inclusive test of self-control and social learning theories by examining the key concepts of both theories within the same study. Pay specific attention to the authors' discussion of how the concepts from the two theories have been operationalized in past research, as well as what they aim to accomplish by testing these two theories on a sample of students in the Netherlands. Findings reveal that perhaps these theories are more complementary in explanations of delinquency than previously thought.

Source: Meldrum, R. C., Young, J. T. N., & Weerman, F. M. (2009). Reconsidering the effect of self-control and delinquent peers: Implications of measurement for theoretical significance. *Journal of Research in Crime and Delinquency, 46*(3), 353–376.

Authors' Note: This research is supported by funding from the Netherlands Organization for Scientific Research. We would like to thank Carter May, Travis Pratt, Jerald Herting, Tim Wadsworth, and the anonymous reviewers for their useful comments and suggestions.

RECONSIDERING THE EFFECT OF SELF-CONTROL AND DELINQUENT PEERS

Implications of Measurement for Theoretical Significance

Ryan C. Meldrum, Jacob T. N. Young, and Frank M. Weerman

Abstract: Prior research examining the effect of self-control and delinquent peers on crime suggests that both variables are strong correlates and that controlling for one fails to eliminate the effects of the other. Yet prior research was based on indirect and possibly biased indicators of peer delinquency. Recent research using direct measures of delinquent peers, as reported by respondents' peers themselves, indicates that the relationship between peer delinquency and self-reported delinquency is smaller than when respondents report on their peers' behavior. The present study extends this line of work by examining the effect of self-control on delinquency when controlling for these two measures of delinquent peers. The results indicate that the effect of self-control is greater in magnitude in models using the direct measure of peer delinquency relative to models that rely on the traditional measure of delinquent peers. An interaction between self-control and the direct measure of peer delinquency was also found. Implications for future theory testing are discussed.

INTRODUCTION

Gottfredson and Hirschi's (1990) self-control theory and Akers's (1977) social learning theory have been two of the most widely tested, debated, and empirically supported criminological theories to date. Research indicates that key concepts from both theories are "strong predictors of crime, and that controlling for one see of variables is unlikely to eliminate the effects of the other" (Pratt and Cullen 2000:948). Moreover, this research has also found that the effect sizes of variables representing the two theories are similar (although see Perrone et al. 2004). Thus, current evidence suggests that the two theories make comparable contributions to our understanding of delinquent and criminal behavior.

Although there is strong empirical support for social learning theory and self-control theory, significant controversy has surrounded the measurement of key concepts from the two theories. For example, Akers (1991) contended that self-control theory is tautological if measures of deviant behavior are being used to predict criminal behavior. In an effort to address such criticisms, researchers have since developed attitudinal indicators of self-control (e.g., Grasmick et al. 1993). Research has subsequently indicated that regardless of whether self-control is measured behaviorally or attitudinally, it is a strong predictor of crime (Evans et al. 1997; Pratt and Cullen 2000; Tittle, Ward, and Grasmick 2003).

With respect to social learning theory, there is good reason to believe that much of the observed effect of delinquent peers found in tests of the theory may be due to measurement error, not normative influence. Specifically, Gottfredson and Hirschi (1987, 1990), along with many other researchers (Davies and Kandel 1981; Jussim and Osgood 1989; Wilcox and Udry 1986) have argued that because the traditional measurement of peer behavior has relied on respondents' perceptions of peer behavior, individuals may be imputing their own behavior onto peers. Many researchers (e.g., Coleman 1961; Kandel 1978; Reiss and Rhodes 1964) have made use of alternative measures of peer behavior that are not subject to the issues created by projection, principally by having respondents identify who their peers are and directly obtaining measures of behavior from these peers. This technique has come to be known as the "social network method" or the "direct method" (Aseltine 1995; Baerveldt et al. 2004; Haynie 2001, 2002; Haynie and Osgood 2005; Weerman and Smeenk 2005). Recent research investigating the effect of direct measures of peer delinquency indicates that the effect size is one half to one third in comparison with the effect size of the traditional measure of delinquent peers (Weerman and Smeenk 2005).

If, as the research suggests, the effect of delinquent peers is much smaller than what has been previously found, there may be important implications for research examining the relative strength of self-control and delinquent peers as predictors of crime. Haynie and Osgood (2005) brought this point to light:

> Overestimating the effects of peer delinquency in past research has also resulted in underestimating the influence of other factors. . . . Furthermore, it is likely that these same methodological weaknesses have distorted the findings of many studies that have pitted normative influence against other causal processes. (p. 1124)

Following this argument, it is reasonable to suggest that studies that have rejected Gottfredson and Hirschi's (1990) contention that self-control is the most important variable for explaining delinquency and crime may have been premature because of problems associated with the use of indirect measures of peer delinquency.

It is important to emphasize that findings from past research investigating the relative strength of self-control and delinquent peers have been based on a body of literature that relied entirely on indirect measures of peer delinquency (Baron 2004; Burton et al. 1994, 1998; Evans et al. 1997; Perrone et al. 2004). And although previous research has focused on the change in the strength of the effect of delinquent peers when moving from an indirect measure to a direct measure, research has yet to examine the effect of competing theoretical variables, such as self-control, when placed into models using a direct measure of peer delinquency. Such a test would seem critical for establishing a more precise understanding of the importance of these variables as explanations of delinquency and, in a broader sense,

help better delineate one of the ongoing debates concerning the relevance of control theories and learning theories in general.

The present study is the first to investigate these relationships cross-sectionally and longitudinally, using both a direct measure of delinquent peers as well as the traditional measure of delinquent peers. The data used are uniquely suited to investigating these relationships in that they contain both a validated measure of self-control as well as a research design that allows for the validation of friendship networks needed to establish the direct measure of delinquent peers in addition to the indirect measure of delinquent peers. To provide readers with a more thorough understanding of the current state of evidence regarding the strength of self-control and delinquent peer effects we provide an overview of the prior literature on the topic. Attention is then given to the issues surrounding the measurement of delinquent peer associations. After describing the current study, we present an analysis that examined the effect of self-control on delinquency when controlling for the two different measures of delinquent peers. Consideration is then given to the possible interactive relationship between self-control and delinquent peers. Concluding remarks address the findings, limitations of the current study, and implications for future research.

PRIOR RESEARCH ON SELF-CONTROL AND DELINQUENT PEERS

Considerable attention has been devoted to testing the major components of self-control theory. Most important, a variety of studies have found self-control to predict various delinquent and criminal behaviors (for example Baron 2004; Burton et al. 1998; Evans et al. 1997; Grasmick et al. 1993; Hay 2001; Pratt and Cullen 2000). Yet at the same time, Gottfredson and Hirschi's (1990) contention that self-control should be the single cause of crime has not been supported. Of particular interest, several studies have found that the introduction of self-control into models examining the effect of delinquent peers fails to eliminate the delinquent peer effect (Baron 2004; Burton et al. 1994, 1998; Evans et al. 1997; Perrone et al. 2004).

In addition to the inability of self-control to eliminate the effect of delinquent peers, a meta-analysis conducted by Pratt and Cullen (2000) indicated that the effect of social learning variables, such as delinquent peer associations, are as strong as the effect of various measures of self-control. Moreover, recent research indicates that the effect of peer delinquency may be stronger than the effect of self-control. Specifically, using the Add Health data, Perrone et al. (2004) found that the effect of an indirect measure of peer delinquency was twice as strong as the effect of a five-item measure of self-control tapping risk-seeking behaviors. Thus, the current literature suggests not only that self-control fails to eliminate the effect of competing theoretical variables such as delinquent peers but that the significance of self-control theory as an explanation for delinquency and crime may not be as important as the contribution made by variables derived from rival learning theories.

MEASURING DELINQUENT PEER ASSOCIATIONS

Although evidence suggests that self-control may not be as consequential as having delinquent friends, there is reason to question the reliance on indirect measures of peer delinquency that have formed the basis for all comparisons of self-control and delinquent peer effects. Specifically, many researchers (e.g., Jussim and Osgood 1989; Wilcox and Udry 1986) contend that respondents may impute their qualities onto their friends when they report on friends' behavior, what has been referred to as "assumed similarity" or "projection" (Byrne and Blaylock 1963; Newcomb 1961). In support of this, recent research by Matsueda and Anderson (1998) and Zhang

and Messner (2000) found that adolescent-reported peer delinquency, to a certain extent, reflects self-reported delinquency.

In an effort to avoid the problem of having respondents report on their friends' behavior, researchers have made use of alternate methods for measuring peer delinquency using social-networking data (i.e., Add Health, Netherlands Institute for the Study of Crime and Law Enforcement [NSCR] School Project) that allow for the direct measurement of peer delinquency. Recent research indicates that the use of direct measures of peer delinquency results in a correlation with self-reported delinquency that is one half to one third in size compared with the use of indirect measures of delinquent peers (Iannotti and Bush 1992; Kandel 1996; Weerman and Smeenk 2005), providing support for the argument that the effect of peer delinquency has been overestimated in research that has relied on respondents' reports of peer delinquency.

THE PRESENT STUDY

Although past research has compared the effect sizes of direct and indirect measures of delinquent peers, no research has examined how differences in the measurement of delinquent peers might have influenced research testing the relative strength of self-control and delinquent peers when examined together. Research assessing the relative strength of self-control and the improved measure of delinquent peers can potentially lead to a more precise understanding of the significance of self-control theory and social learning theory as explanations of delinquent and criminal behavior. Moreover, such research would also contribute to the larger debate regarding latent-trait versus social environment perspectives of criminal offending.

In an effort to fill this gap in the literature, the aim of the present study was to examine for the first time the effect sizes of self-control and the two measures of delinquent peers cross-sectionally and longitudinally. Consistent with Gottfredson and Hirschi's (1990) claim that self-control should be the most important predictor of crime, the main hypothesis tested in this study was that the effect size of self-control should be substantially larger than the effect sizes of the direct measure of delinquent peers. Results consistent with this hypothesis would garner greater support for self-control theory and call into question the significance of the delinquent peer effect proffered by proponents of social learning theory. On the other hand, if the effect of the direct measure of delinquent peers is comparable in magnitude with the effect of self-control, the implication would then be that key predictors from self-control theory and social learning theory both substantially contribute to our understanding of involvement in delinquent and criminal behavior, and the claim made by Gottfredson and Hirschi (1990) that self-control is the single explanation of crime would appear to be an overstatement.

Given that past research has found that the effect of delinquent peers on self-reported delinquency varies across levels of key theoretical variables (Wright et al. 2001), we also investigated a secondary hypothesis. Specifically, the hypothesis tested was that the effect of self-control should vary according to different levels of direct peer delinquency. As Evans et al. (1997) suggested, perhaps self-control theory and social learning theory should not be viewed as opposing theoretical frameworks, but rather, the two, in conjunction, can provide a better overall explanation of patterns of criminal offending. Results indicative of an interaction between self-control and peer delinquency would support this argument, as well as provide partial support to the life-course interdependence model as described and tested by Wright et al. (2001).

METHODS

Sample Description

The data used in this study came from the NSCR School Project, a Netherlands-based study that focuses on peer network formation,

personal development, and school interventions in the development of problem behavior and delinquency. The data analyzed here were from the first two waves of the longitudinal study, which began in 2002. The sampling procedure was guided by two aims: first, to obtain a relatively "high risk" sample with a substantial proportion of delinquent respondents and, second, to achieve enough variation in school contexts and student populations to be able to better generalize results. To achieve this, schools and students in the lower educational strata of a major Dutch city with inner-city problems were oversampled, and additional students were recruited from schools in smaller cities and towns in the vicinity.

The full sample consisted of 1,978 students from the first and third grades of 12 schools with a total population of 2,370 first and third graders. Ages ranged from 11 to 18 years, but because of the cohort design of the study, respondents aged 13 and 15 years dominated (32% and 25%, respectively). The majority of respondents (58%) lived in the city area, a substantial number (34%) lived in one of two medium-sized cities (about 120,000 inhabitants) nearby, and some respondents (8%) were recruited at a school in a smaller town (about 15,000 inhabitants). As a consequence of selecting a large city, more than one third of the sample consisted of respondents with foreign backgrounds, but respondents with Dutch parents were still the majority (63%).

Measures

Respondents' delinquency. Respondents' delinquency was measured using self-reports regarding a variety of offenses. Respondents were asked if they had ever committed an offense and, if so, how often during the reference period, which covered the interval between the last summer holiday prior to the beginning of the school year and the time when the survey was administered (April and May). The measure used in this study came from the following questions: "In the last year, how many times did you" "steal

Table 2.1 Descriptive Statistics (*n* = 1,929)

Variable	M	SD	Minimum	Maximum
Controls				
Age (years)	14.03	1.31	11.00	18.00
Male	.54	.49	.00	1.00
Friends outside of school	2.02	.75	1.00	3.00
Unstandardized process scales				
Attachment to parents	3.64	.53	1.00	6.12
Attachment/commitment to school	4.57	.77	1.00	5.84
Attachment to peers	4.37	.65	1.25	5.94
Time spent with peers	2.15	.51	.76	3.06
Self-control	2.72	.72	.45	4.91
Indirect peer delinquency	1.19	.28	1.00	3.00
Direct peer delinquency	.30	.37	.00	4.00
Self-reported delinquency (counts), wave I (*n* = 1,929)	.29	.66	.00	5.00
Self-reported delinquency (counts), wave 2 (*n* = 1,364)	.21	.57	.00	5.00

small things from shops worth less than 5 euros," "steal things worth more than 5 euros," "break or enter to steal something" "rob someone," and "hit somebody so hard he or she gets wounded/hurt?" (α = .613). Because the response categories were ordinal and top coded, the responses were recoded into a binary measure that reflected whether a respondent reported engaging in each behavior. These were then summed to create a count of how many different offenses were committed by the respondent. To examine the robustness of the effect of the variables of interest on respondent delinquency longitudinally, a measure of the same delinquency items reported one year later was also created for respondents who were in the second wave of the sample.

Peer delinquency: indirect and direct measures. The construction of the indirect measure of peer delinquency followed the conventional method in criminology (e.g., the National Youth Survey; see Elliot, Huizinga, and Ageton, 1985). The index of indirect peer delinquency was created from items for which respondents were asked how many of their friends had committed each of the five acts for which the respondent also self-reported (α = .714). The response categories for each of the variables were *no one, some, most* or *all.* The direct measure of peer delinquency was constructed using social network questions (comparable with the Add Health method; see Haynie 2001). Respondents were provided with a numbered list of all students in their schools who were of the same grade level. The number of students on this list varied between schools (roughly between 50 and 150) but usually spanned more than one classroom. Respondents were asked to fill in the numbers of those students with whom they usually associated (a maximum of 10). The direct peer delinquency measure was constructed by linking the nominations of school friends with those persons' answers to the five delinquency questions above. The number of different offenses committed by each nominated school friend were summed and then scaled by the number of nominated school friends to control for different sizes of the respondents' personal networks. The direct measure of peer delinquency was therefore the average number of various delinquent acts reported by the respondents' peer groups.

Direct measurement of peer delinquency was not available for all respondents. Only school friends who answered the self-report questions about delinquent behavior themselves were used in the computation of the direct peer delinquency scores. Forty-nine respondents chose no friends at all and were excluded from the analysis. To examine possible differences between the two groups of missing cases and the full sample, mean delinquency levels and percentages involved in delinquency were examined. These analyses indicated, however, that the missing cases did not differ significantly with regard to delinquency from those included in the sample.

Self-control. The measure of self-control consists of three subscales (i.e., impulsivity, risk-seeking, anger) adapted from Grasmick et al. (1993) totaling 12 items: "I often do things without thinking first"; "I make fun if I can, even if it leads to trouble"; "I say what I think immediately"; "I often do what I feel like immediately"; "I like to do exciting and adventurous things"; "I like to try out scary things"; "I love doing dangerous things"; "I think it's stupid to do things for fun where you might get hurt" (reverse coded); "People better stay away from me when I am angry"; "I would rather hit someone than talk when I am angry at them"; "I can talk out arguments calmly" (reverse

coded); and "I get angry easily" ($\alpha = .783$). Response categories were on a five-point, Likert-type scale ranging from *completely agree* to *completely disagree,* with higher values indicating greater self-control. Preliminary analyses using confirmatory factor analysis suggested that; the subscales represent three dimensions of a single common factor.

Analytic Plan

As a first step, a cross-sectional analysis of the conventional comparison of the effect of self-control and the indirect measure of delinquent peers on self-reported delinquency is presented. This is included to compare the present results with those of past studies that used indirect measures of peer delinquency. This is followed by a model examining the effect of self-control and the direct measure of delinquent peers, providing the test of the main hypothesis of interest. To check the robustness of the results, a longitudinal analysis of the effect of the same variables of interest on self-reported delinquency one year later is considered. The analysis concludes by considering the interactive effect of self-control and direct peer delinquency, providing the test of the secondary hypothesis.

Given that the measure of self-reported delinquency was a variety index of delinquent behavior, Poisson regression would normally be used. It is viewed as the appropriate model for the regression of count data, and linear regression can produce biased, inefficient, and inconsistent estimates of parameters with count data (Long 1997). However, because the measure of self-reported delinquency in this study was overdispersed, a negative binominal regression model was used to describe the relationship between self-control, peer delinquency, and respondent delinquency. The negative binomial model is similar to a Poisson model in that it considers the expected count of events as a function of the rate at which a behavior occurs but takes into account overdispersion. Extensive discussion of the negative binomial can be found in Long (1997) and

Hilbe (2007), and a thorough treatment using Stata appears in Long and Freese (2005).

RESULTS

Interaction Analysis

Table 2.2 shows the results for the models reported in Table 2 [not shown] when multiplicative interaction terms between self-control and the direct measure of peer delinquency are added. Model 1 investigates the possible interaction cross-sectionally, while model 2 considers the same relationship longitudinally. Although model 1 suggests that the interaction between the direct measure of delinquent peers and self-control is not significantly different from zero, model 2 indicates a significant interactive effect between self-control and the direct measure of peer delinquency longitudinally, providing partial support for the secondary hypothesis. The coefficient for the interaction term can be interpreted in multiple ways. First, the interaction analysis indicates that the estimate for the effect of self-control becomes less negative as the value of peer delinquency increases, suggesting that the strength of self-control as a deterrent of delinquency decreases as peer delinquency increases. Second, the estimate for the effect of peer delinquency becomes more positive as the value of self-control increases, meaning that the strength of peer delinquency as a facilitator of delinquency by the respondent becomes stronger as self-control increases.

Figure 2.1 illustrates the interactive relationship between self-control and the direct

Table 2.2   Negative Binomial Regression of Self-Reported Delinquency on the Direct Measure of Peer Delinquency and Self-Control, With Interactions

	Cross-Sectional (n=1949)	Longitudinal (n = 1,364)
Variable	*Model 1*	*Model 2*
Peer delinquency (direct measure)	.198**(.068)	.243** (.075)
Self-control	−.473** (.077)	−.343** (.105)
Self-control × peer delinquency (direct measure)	.032 (.050)	.125* (.055)
Constant	−2.125 (.485)	−.711 (.747)
Log a	−.467 (.239)	.188 (.311)
Log pseudo-likelihood	−1,18.381	−706.755
AIC	2,382	1,433
BIC	2,443	1,485

Note: AIC = Akaike information criterion; BIC = Bayesian information criterion. Unstandardized coefficients with robust standard errors corrected for clustering in parentheses are shown. All equations include additional controls for sex, age, age squared, friends outside of school, attachment to parents, attachment to peers, attachment or commitment to school, and time spent with peers. The estimates do not change substantially when the interaction terms are added, so these variables are not shown in the table. The complete table is available on request.

*$p < .05$. **$p < .01$.

Figure 2.1 Effect of Self-Control on Self-Reported Delinquency Across Different Levels of Peer Delinquency

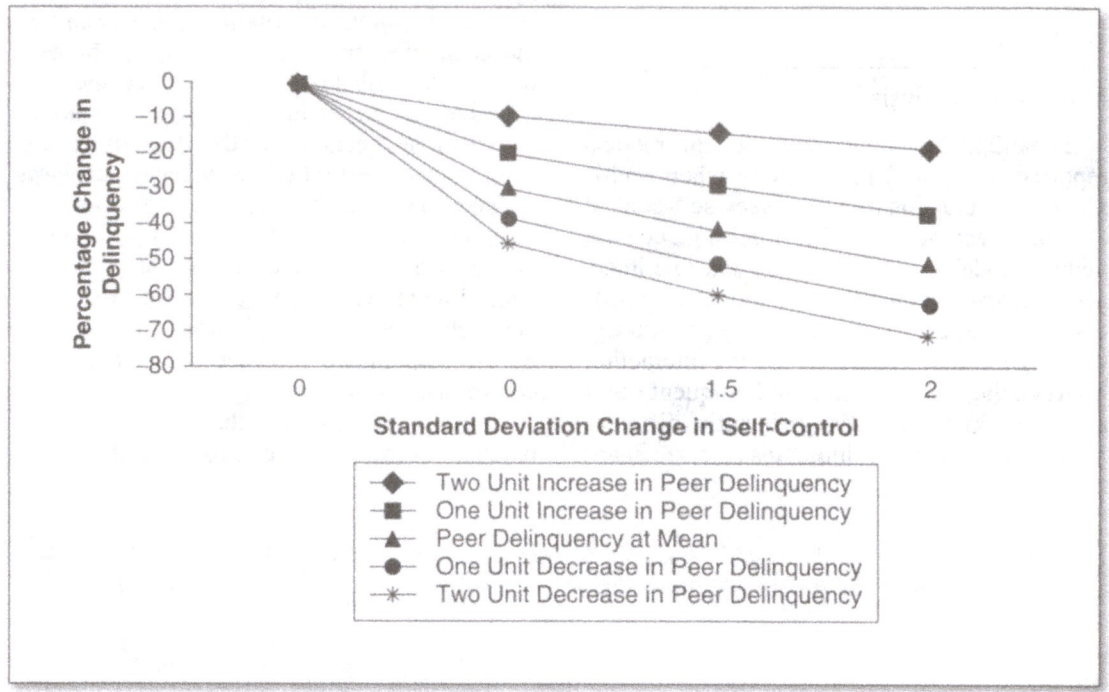

measure of peer delinquency from model 2 of Table 2.2. Figure 2.1 shows that the effect of self-control on self-reported delinquency varies across different levels of the direct measure of peer delinquency. When peer delinquency is at its mean, there is a 29% decrease in self-reported delinquency for an increase of one standard deviation in self-control. However, when peer delinquency is two standard deviations higher than the mean, there is a 9% decrease in self-reported delinquency for an increase of one standard deviation in self-control. The results indicate that as one's peer

DISCUSSION AND CONCLUSION

In this study, the relative effects of self-control and delinquent peers on self-reported

delinquency were investigated cross-sectionally and longitudinally using both direct and indirect measures of peer delinquency. The main hypothesis tested was that the effect of self-control should be greater than the effect of peer delinquency when a more refined, direct measure of peer delinquency was considered. Support for this hypothesis was found using a cross-sectional and longitudinal measure of delinquent behavior. Still, however, a moderate effect of peer delinquency (and time spent with peers) remained, indicating that Gottfredson and Hirschi's (1990) claim that self-control is the single explanation of crime is an overstatement.

Partial support for the secondary hypothesis of an interaction between self-control and peer delinquency was also found. Specifically, the longitudinal interaction analysis indicated that the deterrent effect of self-control weakens as peer delinquency increases, and the facilitating effect of peer delinquency strengthens as self-control increases. The finding of a positive rather than negative coefficient for the interaction term may seem counterintuitive, but it may be consistent with self-control theory. For example, consider two individuals who have the same level of self-control, but one has more delinquent peers. The interaction results suggest that the effect of self-control will be weaker for the individual with more delinquent peers. Thus, in the context of high peer delinquency, self-control plays a less prominent role. Consider an alternative example of the same two individuals in which one has a higher level of self-control than the other, but both have the same number of delinquent peers. The interaction suggests that the effect of having delinquent peers will be stronger for the individual with higher self-control, because the individual with lower self-control requires less facilitation to engage in delinquency. Thus, in the context of higher self-control, peers play a stronger role in promoting delinquent behavior. It should be emphasized, however, that the finding of an interaction between self-control and peer delinquency should be taken with caution and further explored in future research given the small t value (2.27) found in the longitudinal analysis.

These findings have important implications that require discussion. First, and contrary to previous research (Perrone et al. 2004; Pratt and Cullen 2000), we found that when a more refined measure of delinquent peers is considered in models examining the relative effect sizes of self-control and delinquent peers, the effect of self-control is stronger. Moreover, the estimate for self-control substantially increased when the indirect measure of peer delinquency was replaced with the direct measure. This provides strong support for the suggestion made by Haynie and Osgood (2005) that variables representing theories in opposition to social learning theory may have been underestimated in past research as a result of reliance on perceptual measures of peer delinquency.

Second, the finding that self-control and the direct measure of peer delinquency interact suggests that the theoretical integration of self-control theory and social learning theory may lead to a more precise understanding of the contours of criminal offending and that the two theories should perhaps be viewed not as competing but rather complementary to each other (see also Evans et al. 1997). This finding is also consistent with the life-course interdependence model tested by Wright et al. (2001). Early socialization processes (e.g., the development of self-control) that occur prior to the age at which children begin to spend a significant amount of time with peers may explain initial offending trajectories, but when children enter school and begin spending more time with peers, these trajectories may shift for some individuals because of group process factors that arise during early adolescence. Warr (2002) described a number of these factors, including fear of ridicule, status striving, and the diffusion of responsibility within a group.

In sum, we found that self-control has a larger effect on self-reported delinquency than delinquent peers when a more precise measure of delinquent peers is considered, garnering more support for self-control theory than social learning theory. At the same time, however, the results also suggest that an integrated model including concepts from the two theories might prove to be fruitful. Continued investigation of these relationships with additional efforts devoted to the improvement of measuring important theoretical concepts will help provide a more complete and nuanced understanding of human behavior as it relates to issues of delinquency and crime.

REFERENCES

Agnew, Robert 1991. "The Interactive Effects of Peer Variables on Delinquency." *Criminology* 29:47-72.

Akers, Ronald L. 1977. *Deviant Behavior: A Social Learning Approach*. 2d ed. Belmont, CA: Wadsworth.

Akers, Ronald L. 1991. "Self-Control as a General Theory of Crime." *Journal of Quantitative Criminology* 7:201-11.

Aseltine, Robert H. 1995. "A Reconsideration of Parental and Peer Influences on Adolescent Deviance." *Journal of Health and Social Behavior* 36:103-21.

Baron, Stephen W. 2004. "Self-Control, Social Consequences, and Criminal Behavior: Street Youth and the General Theory of Crime." *Journal of Research in Crime and Delinquency* 40:403-25.

Baerveldt, Chris, Marijtje Van Duijn, Lotte Vermeij, and Diann Van Hemert. 2004. "Ethnic Boundaries and Personal Choice: Assessing the Influence of Individual Inclinations to Choose Intra-Ethnic Relationships on Pupils' Networks." *Social Networks* 26:55-74.

Brownfield, David, and Ann Marie Sorenson. 1993. "Self-Control and Juvenile Delinquency: Theoretical Issues and an Empirical Assessment of Selected Elements of a General Theory of Crime." *Deviant Behavior* 14:243-64.

Burton, Velmer S., Francis T. Cullen, T. David Evans, Leanne Fiftal Alarid, and R. Gregory Dunaway. 1998. "Gender, Self-Control, and Crime." *Journal of Research in Crime and Delinquency* 35:123-47.

Burton, Velmer S., Francis T. Cullen, David Evans, and Gregory Dunaway. 1994. "Reconsidering Strain Theory: Operationalization, Rival Theories, and Adult Criminality." *Journal of Quantitative Criminology* 10:213-40.

Byrne, Don and Barbara Blaylock. 1963. "Similarity and Assumed Similarity Between Husbands and Wives," *Journal of Abnormal Psychology* 67:636-40.

Coleman, James S. 1961. *The Adolescent Society*. Glencoe, IL: Free Press.

Costeilo, Barbrara J. and Paul R. Vowell. 1999. "Testing Control Theory and Differential Association: A Reanalysis of the Richmond Youth Project Data." *Criminology* 37:815-42.

Davies, Mark and Denise R, Kandel, 1981. "Parental and Peer Influences on Adolescents' Educational Plans." *American Journal of Sociology* 87:363-87.

Elliot, Delbert S., David Huizinga, and Suzanne S. Ageton, 1985. *Explaining Delinquency and Drug Use*. Beverly Hills, CA: Sage.

Evans, David T., Francis T. Cullen, Velmer S. Burton, R. Gregory Dunaway, and Michael L.

Benson. 1997. "The Social Consequences of Self-Control: Testing the General Theory of Crime." *Criminology* 35: 475-504.

Gottfredson, Michael R. and Travis Hirschi. 1987. "The Methodological Adequacy of Longitudinal Research on Crime." *Criminology* 25:581-614.

Gottfredson, Michael R., and Travis Hirschi. 1990. *A General Theory of Crime*. Palo Alto, CA: Stanford University Press.

Grasmick, Harold G., Charles R. Tittle, Robert J. Bursik, and Bruce Arnekley. 1993. "Testing the Core Empirical Implications of Gottfredson and Hirschi's General Theory of Crime." *Journal of Research in Crime and Delinquency* 30:5-29.

Hagan, John and Bill McCarthy. 1998. *Mean Streets: Youth Crime and Homelessness*. Cambridge, UK: Cambridge University Press.

Hay, Carter. 2001. "Parenting, Low Self-Control, and Delinquency: A Test of Self-Control Theory." *Criminology* 39:707-36.

Haynie, Dana L. 2001. "Delinquent Peers Revisited: Does Network Structure Matter?" *American Journal of Sociology* 106:1013-57.

Haynie, Dana L. 2002. Friendship Networks and Delinquency: The Relative Nature of Peer Delinquency." *Journal of Quantitative Criminology* 18:99-134.

Haynie, Dana L. and Wayne D. Osgood. 2005, "Reconsidering Peers and Delinquency: How Do Peers Matter?" *Social Forces* 84:1109-30.

Hawdon, James E. 1999. "Daily Routines and Crime: Using Routine Activities as Measures of Hirschi's Involvement." *Youth & Society* 30:395-415.

Hilbe, Joseph M. 2007. *Negative Binomial Regression*. Cambridge, UK: Cambridge University Press.

Hirschi, Travis. 1969. *Causes of Delinquency*. Berkeley: University of California Press.

Iannotti, Ronald J. and Patricia J. Bush. 1992. "Perceived vs. Actual Friends' Use of Alcohol, Cigarettes, Marijuana, and Cocaine: Which Has the Most Influence?" *Journal of Youth and Adolescence* 21:375-89.

Jussim, Lee and Wayne D. Osgood. 1989. "Influence and Similarity Among Friends: An Integrative Model Applied to Incarcerated Adolescents." *Social Psychology Quarterly* 52:98-112.

Kandel, Denise B. 1978. "Homophily, Selection and Socialization in Adolescent Friendships." *American Journal of Sociology* 84:427-36.

Kandel, Denise B. 1996. "The Parental and Peer Contexts of Adolescent Deviance: An Algebra of Interpersonal Influences." *Journal of Drug Issues* 26:289-315.

Kempf, Kimberly L. 1993. "The Empirical Status of Hirschi's Control Theory." Pp. 143-85 in *New Directions in Criminological Theory* Vol. 4, edited by Freda Adler and William S. Laufer. New Brunswick, NJ: Transaction.

Lauritzen, Steffen L. and Thomas S. Richardson 2002. "Chain Graph Models and Their Causal Interpretation." *Journal of the Royal Statistical Society, Series B* 64:321-61.

Loeber, Rolf, David P. Farrington, Magda Stouthamer-Loeber, Terrie E. Moffitt, Avshalom Caspi, Helene Raskin White, Evelyn H. Wei, and Jennifer B. Myers. 2003. "The Development of Male Offending: Key Findings from Fourteen Years of the Pittsburgh Youth Study." Pp. 93-136 in *Taking Stock of Delinquency: An Overview of Findings from Contemporary Longitudinal Studies,* edited by Terence P. Thornberry and Marvin D. Krohn. New York: Plenum.

Long, Scott. 1997. *Regression Models for Categorical and Limited Dependent Variables.* Thousand Oaks, CA: Sage.

Long, Scott and Jeremy Freese. 2001. *Regression Models for Categorical Dependent Variables Using Stata.* College Station, TX: Stata Press.

Matsueda, Ross L. 1982. "Testing Control Theory and Differential Association: A Causal Modeling Approach." *American Sociological Review* 47:489-504.

Matsueda, Ross L. and Kathleen Anderson. 1998. "The Dynamics of Delinquent Peers and Delinquent Behavior." *Criminology* 36:269-308.

Newcomb, Theodore M. 1961. *The Acquaintance Process.* New York: Holt, Rinehart & Winston.

Osgood, Wayne D., Janet K. Wilson. Patrick M. O'Malley, Jerald G. Bachmnn, and Lloyd Johnston. 1996. "Routine Activities And Individual Deviant Behavior," *American Sociological Review* 61:635-55.

Pearl, Judea. 2000. *Causality: Models, Reasoning, and Inference.* New York: Cambridge University Press.

Perrone, Dina, Christopher J. Sullivan, Travis C. Pratt, and Satenik Margaryan. 2004."Parental Efficacy, Self-Control, and Delinquency: A Test of a General Theory of Crime on a Nationally Representative Sample of Youth." *International Journal of Offender Therapy and Comparative Criminology* 48:298-312.

Pratt, Travis C. and Francis T, Cullen. 2000. 'The Empirical Status of Gottfredson and Hirschi's General Theory of Crime: A Meta-Analysis.' *Criminology* 38:931-64.

Reiss, Albert J. and A. Lewis Rhodes. 1964. 'An Empirical Test of Differential Association Theory.' *Journal of Research in Crime and Delinquency* 1:5-18.

Sutherland, Edwin H. 1947. *Principles of Criminology.* 4th ed. Philadelphia: Lippincott.

Thornberry, Terence P. and Marvin D. Krohn. 1997. "Peers, Drug Use, and Delinquency." Pp. 218-33 in *Handbook of Antisocial Behavior,* edited by David M. Stoff, James Breiling, and Jack D. Maser. New York: John Wiley.

Tittle, Charles R., David A. Ward, and Harold G. Grasmick. 2003. "Self-Control and Crime/ Deviance: Cognitive vs. Behavior Measures." *Journal of Quantitative Criminology* 19:333-65.

Warr, Mark. 1993. "Age, Peers, and Delinquency." *Criminology* 31:17-40.

Warr, Mark. 2002. *Companions in Crime: The Social Aspects of Criminal Conduct.* Cambridge, UK: Cambridge University Press.

Warr, Mark and Mark Stafford. 1991. "The Influence of Delinquent Peers: What They Think or What They Do?" *Criminology* 29:851-6.

Weerman, Frank M. and Wilma H. Smeenk. 2005. "Peer Similarity in Delinquency for Different Types of Friends: A Comparison Using Two Different Measurement Methods." *Criminology* 43:499-523.

Wilcox, Steven and J. Richard Udry. 1986. "Autism and Accuracy in Adolescent Perceptions of Friends' Sexual Attitudes and Behaviors." *Journal of Applied Social Psychology* 16:3 61-74.

Wright, Bradley R., Avshalom Caspi, Terrie E. Moffitt, and Phil A. Silva. 2001. "The Effects of Social Ties on Crime Vary by Criminal Propensity: A Life-Course Model of Interdependence." *Criminology* 39:321-51.

Zhang, Lening and Steven F. Messner. 2000. "The Effects of Alternative Measures of Delinquent Peers on Self-Reported Delinquency." *Journal of Research in Crime and Delinquency* 37:323-37.

DISCUSSION QUESTIONS

1. What are some of the controversies surrounding measurement of concepts testing self-control theory and social learning theory?

2. What is the social network method as a means to operationalize peer delinquency under social learning theory?

3. What is the main hypothesis these authors are testing? What is their secondary hypothesis?

4. How did these researchers ensure that their sample would include delinquent students?

5. In Table 2.1, what is the average age of the subjects? How many friends outside of school did these subjects have on average?

6. According to Figure 2.1, by what percent does self-reported delinquency change for a student with a two unit decrease in peer delinquency with a self-control score that is two standard deviations above the mean compared with a student with the mean amount of peer delinquency and a self-control score one standard deviation above the mean?

7. Did these researchers find support for their main hypothesis? What do they conclude about these two theories? Are they competing theories?

8. How do the two theories being researched interact? In other words, how does the effect of self-control change as peer delinquency increases, and how does the effect of having delinquent friends on facilitation of delinquency change as self-control increases?

RESEARCH READING

In this research, Chamlin and Cochran examine institutional anomie theory (IAT). IAT is a macrolevel theory that seeks to explain crime rates in nations as a product of the competition between social institutions. Specifically, the theory's founders contend that where cultural goals of material wealth are strong and there is an imbalance of power between the economy and other social institutions, strain (anomie) exists that causes high rates of serious crime. Chamlin and Cochran explore IAT and its testability using macrolevel data from several nations around the world. Specifically, these authors explore measurement issues as they relate to some of the underlying assumptions of the theory. They argue that although IAT seems logical, its assumptions are not easily testable or falsifiable. Recall that testability and falsifiability are desirable attributes of theoretical perspectives.

Along with these conceptual measurement issues, the authors point out that there have been no direct tests of institutional anomie theory. Specifically, Chamlin and Cochran examine two primary assumptions of IAT on both homicide and robbery rates for 73 nations. Their

Source: Chamlin, M. B., & Cochran, J. K. (2007). An evaluation of the assumptions that underlie institutional anomie theory. *Theoretical Criminology*, *11*(1), 39–61. Copyright © 2007 Sage Publications.

results lead them to argue that IAT may only be useful in explaining societal level causes of violent crime in Western, developed nations.

AN EVALUATION OF THE ASSUMPTIONS THAT UNDERLIE INSTITUTIONAL ANOMIE THEORY

Mitchell B. Chamlin and John K. Cochran

Abstract: Messner and Rosenfeld's institutional anomie theory [IAT] postulates that a pervasive cultural mandate to obtain material wealth, coupled with an anomie normative environment that arises from a pronounced imbalance of power in favor of the economy over all other societal institutions, is responsible for the high rates of serious crime found in the United States. Though intuitively appealing, this perspective is not readily amenable to falsification. Consequently, most empirical evaluations of institutional anomie theory have examined the additive and multiplicative effects of the structural antecedents of the institutional imbalance of power and anomie on violent and property crime rates. Our research takes a different tack. We examine the theory's underlying assumptions and suggest that the applicability of IAT may be limited to advanced, western nation-states.

INTRODUCTION

Approximately a decade ago, Messner and Rosenfeld (1994) identified two characteristics of the United States that ostensibly differentiate it from all other nation-states. First, compared to the inhabitants of other countries, residents place a disproportionate emphasis on the accumulation of property. According to this view, the preoccupation with material success goals is so pronounced that other definitions of achievement, such as becoming a good parent or donating time and money to the less fortunate, have become superfluous. Second, compared to the inhabitants of other countries, residents of the United States are plagued with 'exceptionally' high levels of serious crime, especially homicide.

In *Crime and the American Dream,* Messner and Rosenfeld (1994) devote considerable time and energy exploring the association between these two distinctive features of the United States. Indeed, their primary contribution to the ongoing elaboration of anomie theory may rest with their explication of how an almost compulsive conformity to the conventional norms and values concerning material success goals can promote dysfunctional changes in noneconomic institutions and, as a consequence, higher levels of crime.

Of course, Messner and Rosenfeld (1994) were not the first to contend that conforming to the dominant value system can be criminogenic. Indeed, the recognition that the fundamental contradictions that permeate the cultural and social structures of the American social system are inherently anomie represents the creative insight that undergirded Robert Merton's version of anomie theory. In brief, Merton (1938, 1968) recognized that the social structure cannot effectively deliver what the dominant value system promises: universal access to legitimate means to secure material success goals. According to Merton, American culture places a preeminent emphasis on monetary rewards (i.e., the 'American Dream'). Although socially accepted methods for acquiring property are also instilled in the populace, a preoccupation with the 'ends' often relegates the norms associated with the 'means' to a position of less importance. When the social structure fails to provide sufficient means to achieve success goals in the prescribed fashion, an increase in the rate of crime is the anticipated result. In the context of blocked opportunities, the contradictions between the values concerning the means and ends produce a state of anomie, which, in turn, motivates some segments of society to engage in criminal activities to procure monetary goals.

Messner and Rosenfeld (1994,1997a, 2001, 2005), like Merton, contend that American culture places a disproportionate emphasis on material success goals. Also consistent with Merton, they maintain that the contradictions implicit in the dominant value system produce strong pressures to employ the most efficacious means to obtain monetary rewards (1994: 84-5). However, their conceptualization of the impact of the social structure on the emergence of anomie within macrosocial units and, in turn, on levels of instrumental crime, departs dramatically from that of Merton's.

In brief, Messner and Rosenfeld question Merton's decision to restrict his analysis of the relationship between social structure and anomie to only one facet of this dimension of the social system, the legitimate opportunity structure (1994: 15). In further contrast to Merton, they argue that an expansion of economic opportunities, rather than lessening the level of anomie in society, may actually intensify culturally induced pressures to use extralegal means to acquire monetary rewards. In so far as economic vitality reinforces a societal preoccupation with the goal of material success, it is likely to heighten the level of anomie with a collectivity (1994: 62, 88-101). Hence, they conclude that the elimination of structural impediments to conventional opportunities cannot, in and of themselves, do much to reduce crime rates (1994: 108).

Rather than focusing solely on the limitations of the economy as the primary source of structural pressure to innovate, Messner and Rosenfeld's analysis explores the criminogenic influence of a variety of social institutions in American society. Drawing heavily on Marxist theory, they argue that the cultural penchant for pecuniary rewards is so all-encompassing that the major social, institutions (i.e., the polity, religion, education and the family) lose their ability to regulate passions and behavior. Instead of promoting other social goals, these institutions primarily support the quest for material success (i.e., the 'American Dream'). For example, Messner and Rosenfeld contend that 'education is regarded largely as a means to occupational attainment, which in turn is valued primarily insofar as it promises economic rewards' (1994: 78). To the extent that social institutions are subservient to the economic structure, they fail to provide alternative definitions of self-worth and achievement that could serve as countervailing forces against the anomie pressures of the American Dream.

To summarize, Messner and Rosenfeld's institutional anomie theory holds that a pervasive cultural mandate to obtain material wealth, coupled with an anomie normative environment that arises from a pronounced imbalance of power in favor of the economy over all other societal institutions, is responsible for the high rates of serious crime found in the USA.

There can be little doubt that Messner and Rosenfeld's (1994, 2001) theoretical contribution to the anomie tradition evidences both originality and sophistication. Unfortunately, not unlike Durkheim's and Merton's versions of anomie theory, their formulation is not readily amenable to direct falsification. For example, using macrolevel data, how does one measure the 'dominance of the economy in the institutional balance of power', 'the effectiveness of noneconomic institutional controls' or 'anomie? As a consequence, no direct tests of institutional anomie have appeared in the research literature. Rather, beginning with Chamlin and Cochran's (1995) analysis of state-level data, scholars have attempted to indirectly assess institutional anomie theory by examining the additive and multiplicative effects of various economic variables on violent and profit-motivated crime rates (Messner and Rosenfeld, 1997b; Piquero and Piquero, 1998; Savolainen, 2000; Maume and Lee, 2003).

One should not underestimate the value of indirect tests of macrosocial theory. Nonetheless, in the absence of direct indicators of the intervening processes that distinguish institutional anomie theory from other macrosocial perspectives that also make claims about economic conditions affecting crime rates, it may prove useful to employ an alternative strategy to evaluate Messner and Rosenfeld's theoretical ideas. Therefore, in lieu of offering yet another iteration of the structural multivariate models that have been used to indirectly assess institutional anomie theory, the present investigation examines the veracity of two of the key assumptions underlying this theoretical schema.

SERIOUS CRIME AMONG NATION-STATES

In the preface to the first edition of *Crime and the American Dream*, Messner and Rosenfeld assert that the first purpose of their book is to 'present a reasonably cogent explanation of the exceptionally high levels of serious crime in the United States' (1994; iii). This statement presupposes that offense rates for 'serious crime' within the United States are substantially higher than those of other nation-states. Should this observation be erroneous, then there would be no need to devise a theory to explain how and why the American social system is uniquely organized to promote criminality.

Therefore, before explicating their contribution to the evolution of anomie theory, Messner and Rosenfeld (1994: 22) seek to establish that the United States does indeed have inordinately high rates of 'serious crime'. Toward this end, they compare rates of robbery and homicide per 100,000 population across 16 advanced, industrialized countries, including the United States. As expected, they report that the robbery rate (1988) was more than two times higher for the United States than that reported for any other nation-state; and that the disparity between the US homicide rate and that for the remainder of the sample was even more pronounced. Thus, they conclude that '[w]hen it comes to lethal violence, America remains the undisputed leader of the modern world' (1994: 22).

In the most recent edition of *Crime and the American Dream* (2001), Messner and Rosenfeld reexamined robbery (1997) and homicide (1993-5) rates for the same sample of 16 industrialized countries. Once again,

they report that the United States suffers from substantially higher rates of robbery and homicide than the other 15 nation-states. While now recognizing that some countries (e.g., the Russian Federation) experience higher rates of homicide than the United States, Messner and Rosenfeld still affirm that '[t]he more serious the offense, the greater the actual or potential harm to the victim, and the more unrestrained its character, the more the United States diverges from other advanced industrial societies' (2001: 21).

We are somewhat surprised by Messner and Rosenfeld's decision to restrict the reference group for their cross-national comparison of serious crime rates to a small number of 'advanced industrial nations' (1994: 22). From a practical standpoint there is no reason to limit the analyses to these countries. The data used by Messner and Rosenfeld (International Police Organization reported crime statistics, World Health Organization vital statistics), as well as other sources (the United Nations surveys on crime trends) contain information for an appreciably larger number of both advanced, and developing, nation-states.

Further, we see no substantive or theoretical justification for excluding less 'advanced' countries from any cross-national comparisons. Messner and Rosenfeld (1994, 2001) offer no explanation (that we can discern) for changing the focus of their book from explaining why the United States has exceptionally high crime rates (1994: iii) to explaining why the United States has higher crime rates than other 'developed' countries (1994: 21). There is nothing inherent in Durkheimian anomie theory or, for that matter, the American revisions of Durkheim's work, that would require them to do so.

According to our understanding of Durkheimian theory, the relationship between modernization and anomie depends on the degree to which a society is able to adapt to the new cultural and structural arrangements. For example, during periods of rapid social change there is not enough time for the social system to adjust to new macrostructural conditions. Commenting on the transition from agrarian to industrial economies (the 'rapid social change' that captures his attention in *The Division of Labor in Society)*, Durkheim laments that '[t]hese new conditions of industrial life naturally demand a new organization, but as these changes have been accomplished with extreme rapidity, the interests in conflict have not yet had time to be equilibrated' (1933: 370). Norms and values that clearly define social roles and expectations within agricultural communities quickly become obsolete. As a result, they lose much of their power to hold in check the rising aspirations and expectations of societal members facing fundamental changes in the social and economic order. Until new norms and values can emerge to replace the old, a state of anomie emerges, extricating individuals from the external constraints of society. Thus, they become free to pursue their singular wants and desires, including acts of crime and deviance (Durkheim, 1933: 353-73, 1951: 246-57).

In short, societal evolution is criminogenic because it initially disrupts the bonds of solidarity that had generated macrosocial integration in more homogeneous, simple societies (the social deregulation hypothesis). Thus, from a Durkheimian perspective, modernization, not unlike the religious composition of nation-states, is just another social fact that one should take into account when attempting to understand the interrelationships cross-nationally among social structure, anomie and crime (Webb, 1972; Krohn, 1978; Messner, 1982). Consequently, it appears self-evident (at least to us) that one should sample countries that vary with respect to their level of modernization (development) when making cross-national comparisons of crime rates.

Similarly, we find nothing in the writings of either Merton (1938, 1968) or Messner and Rosenfeld (1994) that would recommend excluding lesser developed nations from a cross-national comparison of crime rates. On the contrary, they seem to suggest that there is no country more anomie than the United States and, as a consequence, the USA could be expected to generate more profit-motivated crime than any other nation, regardless of its

level of industrial development. Indeed, Merton viewed the USA as 'the *polar type* in which great emphasis upon certain success goals occurs without equivalent emphasis upon institutional means' (1968: 136, emphasis added). Similarly, Messner and Rosenfeld (2001: 61) contend that the American Dream, with its emphasis on individualism and materialism, encourages people to 'adopt an "anything goes" mentality in the pursuit of personal goals', as well as an 'anomie cultural environment' that is ultimately responsible for the USA's high levels of crime.

Thus, from a Mertonian as well as an institutional anomie perspective, we can find no justification for excluding less developed nations from cross-cultural comparisons of crime rates. On the contrary, these approaches suggest to us that the United States, because of its unique cultural evolution, should be expected to suffer from higher rates of serious crime than other countries regardless of their level of development.

Hence, in order to reevaluate the claim that the USA is plagued by disproportionately high levels of serious crime, we compared official crime data from a larger, and more developmentally diverse, sample of nation-states. Specifically, we employed data from the *Seventh United Nations Survey on Crime Trends and the Operations of Criminal Justice Systems, 1998-2000* (United Nations Office on Drugs and Crime, 2002). Following Messner and Rosenfeld (1994, 2001) we compared homicide and robbery rates per 100,000 population for the USA with the other countries in the sample. We defined homicide as completed homicides (death deliberately inflicted on another person, including infanticide) reported to the police; while we defined robbery as thefts of property from a person, overcoming resistance by force or threat of force (United Nations Office on Drugs and Crime, 2002). To minimize yearly fluctuations in reporting crime, figures were averaged, when possible, for the three years of the survey (1998-2000).

Table 2.3 presents the ascending rank order of nations with respect to the mean

Table 2.3   Ascending Rank Order of Nations With Respect to Mean Homicide and Robbery Rates, 1998–2000

Rank	Mean Homicide Rate per 100,000 Population		Mean Robbery Rate per 100,000 Population	
	Nation	Homicide Rate	Nation	Robbery Rate
1	Pakistan	0.06	Pakistan	0.53
2	Qatar	0.36	Yemen	1.00
3	Japan	0.53	Qatar	1.13
4	Saudi Arabia	0.61	Thailand	1.50
5	Hong Kong	0.79	Azerbaijan	1.78
6	Norway	0.93	Turkey	2.33
7	Singapore	0.96	Saudi Arabia	2.77
8	Indonesia	0.97	India	3.04
9	Denmark	0.99	Japan	3.38
10	Ireland	1.02	Armenia	3.63
11	Tunisia	1.04	Paraguay	5.03
12	Switzerland	1.09	Georgia	6.00
13	New Zealand	1.14	Philippines	7.70
14	Germany	1.19	Tunisia	9.71
15	Spain	1.20	S. Korea	10.48
16	Iceland	1.25	Iceland	11.15
17	Slovenia	1.26	Macedonia	12.12
18	Netherland	1.27	Greece	16.28
19	Greece	1.31	Singapore	17.04
20	Italy	1.40	Romania	17.47
21	England & Wales	1.50	China	18.20
22	Chile	1.56	Slovenia	22.09
23	Canada	1.62	Slovakia	24.29
24	Australia	1.63	Sri Lanka	25.14
25	Czech Republic	1.68	Kyrgyzstan	28.96

(Continued)

Table 2.3 (Continued)

Rank	Mean Homicide Rate per 100,000 Population		Mean Robbery Rate per 100,000 Population	
	Nation	Homicide Rate	Nation	Robbery Rate
26	France	1.69	Indonesia	31.40
27	S. Korea	2.08	Hungary	32.19
28	Macedonia	2.19	Zambia	34.18
29	Mauritius	2.27	Switzerland	34.50
30	Romania	2.35	Norway	36.09
31	Hungary	2.47	France	37.64
32	Slovakia	2.54	Czech Republic	42.79
33	Malaysia	2.59	Ukraine	43.55
34	Finland	2.61	Finland	44.97
35	Dominica	2.74	New Zealand	46.88
36	Portugal	2.95	Hong Kong	51.06
37	Azerbaijan	3.13	Bulgaria	51.98
38	Armenia	3.75	Belarus	53.41
39	India	3.83	Denmark	53.50
40	Costa Rica	4.07	Malaysia	58.79
41	Uruguay	4.14	Papua New Guinea	59.54
42	Bulgaria	4.22	Moldova	59.96
43	Yemen	4.57	Colombia	63.32
44	Georgia	4.70	Italy	66.46
45	United States	4.87	Germany	75.21
46	Poland	5.05	Seychelles	78.08
47	Seychelles	6.67	Dominica	78.08
48	Zimbabwe	6.89	Zimbabwe	79.40
49	Argentina	7.23	Guatemala	80.87
50	Moldova	7.75	Ireland	83.58
51	Philippines	7.80	Latvia	88.92
52	Barbados	7.89	Russia	89.70
53	Ukraine	8.60	Canada	92.61

Rank	Mean Homicide Rate per 100,000 Population		Mean Robbery Rate per 100,000 Population	
	Nation	*Homicide Rate*	*Nation*	*Robbery Rate*
54	Kyrgyzstan	8.72	Mauritius	93.43
55	Thailand	8.81	Jamaica	98.92
56	Lithuania	8.92	Lithuania	102.70
57	Zambia	9.25	Netherlands	106.57
58	Papua New Guinea	9.44	Poland	114.16
59	Latvia	9.91	Australia	122.34
60	Belarus	10.04	Venezuela	140.79
61	Paraguay	13.43	Barbados	142.36
62	Mexico	14.72	Portugal	152.40
63	Russia	19.03	*United States*	154.98
64	Estonia	21.90	England & Wales	155.72
65	Venezuela	25.99	Swaziland	251.22
66	Guatemala	26.68	Mexico	270.27
67	Jamaica	33.34	Estonia	328.28
68	S. Africa	56.02	S. Africa	408.37
69	Colombia	59.34	Costa Rica	484.32
70	Swaziland	89.29	Uruguay	604.35
71	–	–	Chile	681.53
72	–	–	Argentina	959.72
73	–	–	Spain	1310.40

Source: The Seventh United Nations Survey on Crime Trends and the Operations of Criminal Justice Systems, 1998-2000 (United Nations Office on Drugs and Crime, 2002).

homicide and robbery rates (1998-2000), respectively. Consistent with Messner and Rosenfeld's (1994, 2001) previous analyses, we find that the USA continues to endure relatively high rates of homicide (4.87 per 100,000) and robbery (1.54.98 per 100,000).

None the less, further inspection of Table 2.3 reveals that the United States may not be quite as 'criminogenic' as prior comparisons would have us believe.

Consider the distribution of homicides. The USA ranks 45th out of the 70 nations that completed the United Nations survey instrument. Put alternatively, slightly more than a third of the sample reported that their mean homicide rate was greater than that of the USA. However, if we exclude the so-called developing and Third World nation-states from our comparisons, we find that the US homicide rate is appreciably higher than the advanced countries in the sample (with a rate 65 percent greater than its nearest rival, Portugal).

The pattern of robbery rates, though more in line with the observations of Messner and Rosenfeld, also raises doubts as to whether or not the United States is truly an 'outlier' with respect to the incidence of serious crime. The mean robbery rate of 155 per 100,000 population places the United States at the 86th percentile (63 out of 73 nations). Note however, that 2 advanced, industrial countries (Spain, England, and Wales), as well as 8 other, less developed, nations report higher robbery rates than the United States.

Taken together, our analyses indicate that while the official homicide and robbery rates for the USA are substantial, they are not exceptional. Only when we focus on a very restricted sub-sample of primarily Western European nation-states does the US' 'serious' crime rate appear to be particularly egregious.

MATERIAL SUCCESS GOALS AMONG NATION-STATES

According to institutional anomie theory, what distinguishes the American value system from those in other advanced capitalist nations is the almost coercive demand placed upon its citizenry to accumulate income, wealth and status. Indeed, as Messner has recently reaffirmed, '[t]he special feature of the American Culture, however, is the extent to which money *signifies* success; it is the *metric* of success' (2003: 98-9). Thus, from this perspective, the preoccupation with material success is the distal, catalytic agent that is responsible for the generation of the more proximate causes of the unusually high levels of serious crime found within the USA (i.e., the dominance of the economy in the institutional balance of power, anomie and weak institutional controls [Messner and Rosenfeld, 1994: 83-4]).

As we lamented earlier, these more immediate causal processes are not readily amenable to operationalizing (for a similar view see Chamlin and Cochran, 1995; Messner, 2003). None the less, we have been able to locate a data source, the World Values Survey (WVS), that contains cross-national measures of the cultural acceptance of pecuniary success goals. Thus, while we are unable to directly examine the extent to which the USA experiences the *consequences* of the adherence to the American Dream, we can, at a minimum, determine whether or not the USA disproportionately embraces material success goals (the second assumption of institutional anomie theory).

Admittedly, we are not the first to endeavor to use the WVS to evaluate institutional anomie theory. Recently, Jensen employed cross-national attitudinal measures from the 1993-4 World Values Survey, in order to determine the extent to which the USA is 'institutionally unbalanced with primacy accorded to economic roles over familial, civic or religious roles' (2002: 58).

The WVS, which grew out of a study conducted by the 1981 European Values Survey group, is designed to provide cross-national data amenable to the examination of the influence of cultural dimensions of social life on political and social systems. Specifically, the WVS utilizes stratified, multi-stage, probability sampling techniques to measure cross-cultural attitudes, values and beliefs of citizens, 18 and older. The 3rd wave (1995-7), which contains the items used to determine the extent to which nations differ with respect to their acceptance of monetary success goals, was administered to over 60 macrosocial units (both nation-states and sub-national regions), representing a majority of the world's population, various levels of economic prosperity (with per capita incomes as low as $300 a year, to societies with per capita incomes as high as $30,000 per year) and various forms of political representation (from long-established democracies to authoritarian regimes).

Our examination of the survey instrument revealed two questions that appear, on their face, to be valid indicators of the differing emphases social systems place on the acquisition of material rewards. Each captures an important aspect of Messner and Rosenfeld's (2001: 61-4) conceptualization of the 'American Dream'.

The first question focuses on respondents' goals when seeking employment. Individuals were asked to pick one of four options (good income, job security, friendly colleagues or feelings of accomplishment) as the most important factor in selecting a job. To capture the extent to which respondents place monetary rewards above all others, we report the percentage of people stating that a good income is the most important attribute of gainful employment.

The second question more directly taps respondents' views concerning how much weight should be placed on material success goals. Specifically, sample members were asked whether or not less emphasis on money and material possessions would be a good thing, a bad thing or does not matter. To facilitate comparisons to Jensen's (2002) study, we decided to estimate the degree to which citizens accept material success goals as the percentage of respondents stating that less emphasis on money and material possessions is a good thing.

Table 2.4 presents the rank order of nations with respect to the acceptance of material success goals. The third column reports the percentage of respondents stating that financial rewards are the most important feature of work while column five reports the percentage of respondents stating that less

emphasis on money and material possessions is a good idea.

Inspection of column 3 reveals that approximately 32 percent of the respondents residing within the USA feel that money is the most important reason to go to work. However, almost 60 percent of the sample (26 nations) report even higher levels of agreement with this position. Seven of the eight countries with the most citizens agreeing with the cultural exhortation that monetary compensation is the most important reason for securing employment are former Soviet republics. None of these nation-states, however, are among those included in Messner and Rosenfeld's (1994, 1997a, 2001) cross-national comparisons of reported levels of serious crime.

The distribution of nation-states with respect to the second indicator of the acceptance of material success goals is even more striking. Comparable to what Jensen (2002) reports upon the analysis of a previous wave of the WVS, we find that approximately 69 percent of Americans agreed with the assertion that less emphasis on money and material possessions is a good thing. Put in a larger perspective, this result indicates that among the nations in the sample, only *three* countries (although two of three are advanced, western nations) have *less* of a problem with de-emphasizing material success goals than does the USA. Interestingly, and consistent with what we found with respect to attitudes toward employment goals, four of the ten nations that have the lowest percentage of their populace reporting that the de-emphasis of material success goals is a good thing are former Soviet or Warsaw Pact nations.

The results are clear. When compared to a larger and more heterogeneous (with respect to economic development) sample of countries, we find no evidence in support of Messner and Rosenfeld's (1994, 2001; Messner, 2003) core assumption that American culture places an unparalleled emphasis on the acquisition of goods and services. Rather, it appears that the

Table 2.4 Rank Order of Nations With Respect to Measures of Material Success Goals, 1995-7

Rank	Income Is the Most Important Feature of Work		Less Emphasis on Money and Material Possessions Is Good	
	Nation	Percent in Agreement	Nation	Percent in Agreement
1	Norway	9.0	S. Africa	29.4
2	Sweden	10.3	Bangladesh	30.2
3	Japan	11.0	India	33.2
4	Finland	12.5	Moldova	33.5
5	Taiwan	17.3	Lithuania	37.1
6	Puerto Rico	17.8	Philippines	38.5
7	Turkey	17.9	Peru	43.3
8	S. Korea	18.1	Bulgaria	43.4
9	Slovakia	19.4	Croatia	43.8
10	Ghana	21.1	Ghana	43.8
11	Switzerland	21.4	Belarus	45.0
12	Australia	22.3	Estonia	45.6
13	Philippines	23.2	S. Korea	45.6
14	Brazil	23.8	China	46.2
15	Argentina	25.3	Bosnia	46.9
16	Spain	26.3	Serbia	47.1
17	Germany	26.7	Latvia	47.8
18	Venezuela	29.7	Nigeria	47.8
19	United States	32.1	Japan	48.1
20	Croatia	32.5	Russia	48.6
21	Dominican Rep.	32.6	Ukraine	48.8
22	Mexico	32.9	Slovenia	49.1
23	Bangladesh	35.1	Puerto Rico	50.7
24	China	35.3	Montenegro	51.6
25	Macedonia	35.9	Dominican Rep.	51.7

Rank	*Income Is the Most Important Feature of Work*		*Less Emphasis on Money and Material Possessions Is Good*	
	Nation	*Percent in Agreement*	*Nation*	*Percent in Agreement*
26	Latvia	36.4	Venezuela	52.4
27	Estonia	37.5	Taiwan	53.6
28	Serbia	37.6	Finland	54.5
29	Peru	38.6	Macedonia	55.4
30	Montenegro	40.0	Mexico	57.8
31	India	40.2	Chile	58.5
32	Nigeria	41.0	Armenia	58.7
33	S. Africa	45.0	Poland	59.1
34	Chile	45.4	Colombia	59.4
35	Russia	46.8	Germany	60.8
36	Bulgaria	47.8	Norway	60.9
37	Uruguay	48.4	Azerbaijan	64.0
38	Belarus	50.1	Brazil	64.5
39	Armenia	52.3	England & Wales	65.36
40	Moldova	52.3	Georgia	66.5
41	Georgia	54.4	Turkey	67.9
42	Georgia	54.4	Australia	68.9
43	Lithuania	54.4	Argentina	68.9
44	Bosnia	56.8	United States	68.9
45	Azerbaijan	63.6	Spain	73.7
46			Sweden	74.0
47			Uruguay	75.0

Source: World Values Survey (1995-7).

fledgling, market economies that emerged from the dissolution of the Soviet Union most enthusiastically embrace the so-called 'American Dream'. However, when we restrict our analyses to only advanced, industrialized nation-states, especially those located in Western Europe, our findings fall more in line with the assumptions of institutional anomie theory.

IMPLICATIONS

In essence, the fundamental contribution of institutional anomie theory to the larger discussion about the relationships among macrosocial phenomena, anomie and variations in deviant behavior is rooted in Messner and Rosenfeld's (1994) insightful delineation of the role that balance plays in the generation of high rates of serious crime. Not only do they recognize, as Merton (1938, 1968) did before them, that the *imbalance* between culturally prescribed success goals and structured opportunities to realize these goals is inherently anomie, but they also recognize that the *imbalance* between the economy and other social institutions exacerbates this condition. To the extent that noneconomic institutions become subservient to the economic structure, they fail to provide alternative definitions of self-worth and achievement that could serve as countervailing forces against the anomie pressures of the American Dream. Thus, Messner and Rosenfeld (1994, 2001) postulate that a pervasive cultural mandate to obtain material wealth, coupled with an anomie normative environment that arises from a pronounced imbalance of power in favor of the economy over all other societal institutions, is responsible for the high rates of serious crime found in the United States.

Though intuitively appealing, institutional anomie theory is not readily amenable to falsification. Indeed, we are in total accord with Messner's observation that institutional anomie 'like the anomie tradition more generally' employs concepts that 'defy easy operationalization' (2003: 107). Consequently, most empirical evaluations of institutional anomie theory have examined the additive and multiplicative effects of the structural antecedents of the institutional imbalance of power and anomie on violent and property crime rates.

Our research takes a different tack. Rather than continuing to specify and estimate the conditional effects of economic variables on crime rates, which we believe provides ambiguous evidence concerning the efficacy of institutional anomie theory, we examine the theory's underlying assumptions about the American experience with serious crime and material success goals.

To review, Messner and Rosenfeld (1994, 1997a, 2001) assert that the United States suffers from 'exceptionally' high levels of serious crime (particularly homicide and robbery), as well as a singular preoccupation with material success goals (the American Dream). In short, their 'thesis is that the American Dream itself exerts pressures toward crime by encouraging an anomie cultural environment in which people are encouraged to adopt an "anything goes" mentality in the pursuit of personal goals' (1994: 68).

To summarize, our study fails to sustain Messner and Rosenfeld's characterizations of American society as exceptional. The cross-sectional analyses of the nations that completed the seventh United Nations survey of crimes known to the police point to the conclusion that while American homicide and robbery rates are substantial, they are not exceptional. Rather, the data indicate that an appreciable number of countries, both advanced industrial as well as developing nations, are plagued by serious crime rates that are comparable to, or surpass, those reported by the United States.

Further, we find no evidence that can sustain the contention that Americans are disproportionately obsessed with the pursuit of material success goals. The findings derived from the World Values Survey are clear and consistent. A majority of the countries included in the sample reported that more of their citizens ranked income as the most important feature of work than did their counterparts in the USA. Furthermore, only three nations in the sample had a higher percentage of respondents agreeing with the statement that less emphasis on money and material possessions is a good thing than did the USA. Indeed, as we discussed earlier, the distribution of responses with respect to these two survey items suggests to us that inhabitants of developing countries, such as the former Soviet Republics, rather than only individuals residing in the USA, are disproportionately driven by material success goals.

While it is beyond the scope of this article to attempt to revise institutional anomie theory, we offer one possible avenue of inquiry based on the recent theoretical work of Chamlin and Cochran (2005). In brief, Chamlin and Cochran (2005; 22) posit that the interrelationships among economic inequality, the legitimacy of social institutions and cross-national homicide rates may depend on the level of societal development. Drawing on the observations of an eclectic array of social theorists (Bonger, 1916; Lenin, 1939; Ford, 1953; Blau, 1964; Weber, 1968; Steinberg, 1978; Blau and Blau, 1982; Bukovansky, 2002), they conclude that an important consequence of the evolution of societies from traditional, agrarian communities to industrialized, modern social systems is the increasing rejection of custom and heredity to legitimate the extant social, economic and political order. Rather, modern societies, particularly those grounded in the European intellectual revolutions of the 18th and 19th centuries (e.g., Rationalism and Romanticism) tend to rely on rational-legal authority to legitimate the manner in which they allocate positions in the social structure (Marx, 1906, 1963; Durkheim, 1933, 1938; Lefebvre, 1967; Weber, 1968; Voltaire, 1971; Locke, 1982). Thus, they hypothesize that the effect of economic inequality on cross-national homicide rates should be mediated by the perceived legitimacy of the stratification system in modern societies, but not in traditional, less developed societies.

A similar process may be at work here. That is to say, it is possible that the same cultural context (i.e., the intellectual movements of post-Renaissance Europe) that is hypothesized to determine whether or not the perceived legitimacy mediates the effects of economic inequality on homicide, may also condition the interrelationships among economic institutions, noneconomic institutions, anomie and serious crime.

In sum, we agree with Messner's assertion that the falsification of institutional anomie theory awaits the 'formulation of more explicit definitions of key concepts and the specification of appropriate measurement strategies' (2003:107). Nonetheless, we believe that our examination of the core assumptions of institutional anomie theory is informative and may stimulate further elaboration of this perspective.

REFERENCES

Becker, Gary S. (1971) *The Economics of Discrimination*. Chicago, IL: University of Chicago Press.

Blalock, Hubert M., Jr. (1967) *Toward a Theory of Minority-Group Relations*. New York: Capricorn.

Blalock, Hubert M., Jr. (1991) 'Are There Really any Constructive Alternatives to Causal-Modeling?', *Sociological Methodology* 21: 325-35.

Blau, P.M. (1964) *Exchange and Power in Social Life*. New York: Wiley.

Blau J.R. and P.M. Blau (1982) 'The Cost of Inequality: Metropolitan Structure and Violent Crime', *American Sociological Review* 47(1): 114-29.

Bonger, W. (1916) *Criminality and Economic Conditions*. Boston, MA: Little, Brown & Company.

Bukovansky, M. (2002) *Legitimacy and Power Politics*. Princeton, NJ: Princeton University Press.

Chamlin, Mitchell B. and John K, Cochran (1995) 'Assessing Messner and Rosenfeld's Institutional Anomie Theory: A Partial Test', *Criminology* 33(3): 411-29.

Chamlin, Mitchell B. and John K. Cochran (2005) 'Ascribed Economic Inequality and Homicide among Modern Societies', *Homicide Studies* 9(1): 3-29.

Durkheim, Emile (1933) *The Division of Labor in Society*. New York: Free Press.

Durkheim, Emile (1938) *The Rules of Sociological Method*. New York: Free Press.

Durkheim, Emile (1951) *Suicide*. New York: Free Press.

Ford, F.L. (1953) *Robe and Sword*. New York: Harper & Row.

Jensen, Gary (2002) Institutional Anomie Theory and Societal Variations in Crime: A Critical Appraisal', *International Journal of Sociology and Social Policy* 22(7/8): 45-74.

Krohn, Marvin (1978) 'A Durkheimian Analysis of International Crime Rates', *Social Forces* 57(2): 654-70.

Lefebvre, G. (1967) *The Coming of the French Revolution*. Princeton, NJ: Princeton University Press.

Lenin, V.I. (1939) *Imperialism: The Highest Stage of Capitalism*. New York: International Publishers.

Lenski, Gerhard (1988) 'Rethinking Macro-sociological Theory', *American Sociological Review* 53(2): 163-71.

Liska, Allen E. (1992) *Social Threat and Social Control*. Albany, NY: State University of New York Press.

Locke, J. (1982) *Second Treatise of Government*. Arlington Heights, IL: Harlan Davidson.

Marx, K. (1906) *Capital*. New York: Random House.

Marx, K. (1963) *Poverty of Philosophy*. New York: International Publishers.

Maume, Michael O. and Matthew R. Lee (2003) 'Social Institutions and Violence: A Sub-National Test of Institutional Anomie Theory', *Criminology* 41(4): 1137-72.

Merton, Robert K. (1938) 'Social Structure and Anomie', *American Sociological Review* 3(5): 672-82.

Merton, Robert K. (1968) *Social Theory and Social Structure*. New York: Free Press.

Messner, Steven F. (1982) 'Societal Development, Social Equality, and Homicide: A Cross-National Test of a Durkheimian Model', *Social Forces* 61(1): 225-40.

Messner, Steven F. (2003) 'An Institutional-Anomie Theory of Crime: Continuities and Elaborations in the Study of Social Structure

and Anomie', *Cologne Journal of Sociology and Social Psychology* 43(1): 93-109.

Messner, Steven F. and Richard Rosenfeld (1994) *Crime and the American Dream*. Belmont, CA: Wadsworth.

Messner, Steven F. and Richard Rosenfeld (1997a) *Crime and the American Dream* (2nd edn). Belmont, CA: Wadsworth.

Messner, Steven F. and Richard Rosenfeld (1997b) 'Political Restraint of the Market and Levels of Criminal Homicide: A Cross-National Application of Institutional Anomie Theory', *Social Forces* 75(4): 1393-416.

Messner, Steven F. and Richard Rosenfeld (2001) *Crime and the American Dream* (3rd edn). Belmont, CA: Wadsworth.

Messner, Steven F. and Richard Rosenfeld (2005) The Present and Future of Institutional Anomie Theory', in Francis T. Cullen, John Paul Wright and Kristie R. Blevins (eds) *Taking Stock: The Status of Criminological Theory Advances in Criminological Theory*, pp. 127-48. New Brunswick, NJ: Transactions Publishers.

Piquero, Alex and Nicole L. Piquero (1998) 'On Testing Institutional Anomie Theory with Varying Specifications', *Studies on Crime and Crime Prevention* 7(1): 61-84.

Savolainen, Jukka (2000) 'Inequality, Welfare State, and Homicide: Further Support for the Institutional Anomie Theory', *Criminology* 38(4): 1021-42.

Steinberg, J. (1978) *Locke, Rousseau, and the Idea of Consent*. Westport, CT: Greenwood Press.

United Nations Office on Drugs and Crime (2002) *Seventh United Nations Survey on Crime Trends and the Operations of Criminal Justice Systems, 1998-2000*. http://www.unodc.org Voltaire, F.A. (1971) *Philosophical Dictionary*. Middlesex, England: Penguin Books.

Voltaire, F.A. (1971) *Philosophical Dictionary*. Middlesex, England: Penguin Books.

Webb, Steven D. (1972) 'Crime and the Division of Labor: Testing a Durkheimian Model', *American Journal of Sociology* 78(3): 643-56.

Weber, M. (1968) *Economy and Society*. Ed. Guenther Roth and Claus Wittich. Berkeley, CA: University of California Press.

World Values Survey (1995-7) *World Values Survey,* http://www.worldvaluessurvey.org

DISCUSSION QUESTIONS

1. What does IAT postulate is the cause of crime, especially violent crime?

2. Why do Messner and Rosenfeld suggest that the United States specifically has high violent crime rates?

3. Why do Chamlin and Cochran disagree that the United States leads the world in lethal violence?

4. According to Table 2.3, where does the United States rank in the world for homicide and robbery?

5. What two indicators do these authors use as a way to operationalize the concepts underlying IAT?

6. What do the authors find when they look at these indicators? Does US culture place an extraordinary emphasis on the goal of attaining wealth according to these indicators?

7. What do Chamlin and Cochran believe may be a valuable measure in mediating the relationship between institutional competition and violent crime rates?

RESEARCH READING

Armstrong and colleagues examine previous research that has used the National Youth Survey (NYS) to test a number of criminological theories. Specifically, these authors examine the scales utilized in theory tests that were developed based on NYS data. Their research reveals that researchers have used the same constructs to test different theories using the same NYS items. Based upon this, Armstrong and colleagues identify NYS items that future researchers should pay attention to in order to strengthen subsequent tests of criminological theory.

AN ASSESSMENT OF SCALES MEASURING
——— CONSTRUCTS IN TESTS OF CRIMINOLOGICAL THEORY ———
BASED ON NATIONAL YOUTH SURVEY DATA

Todd A. Armstrong, Daniel R. Lee, and Gaylene S. Armstrong

Abstract: Researchers have utilized the National Youth Survey (NYS) data to test a variety of theoretical explanations of criminal behavior. Here, the authors offer an assessment of scales used in tests of criminological theory based on NYS data. The authors conducted this assessment to provide results informing

Source: Armstrong, T. A., Lee, D. R., & Armstrong, G. S. (2009). An assessment of scales measuring constructs in tests of criminological theory based on national youth survey data. *Journal of Research in Crime and Delinquency, 46*(1), 73–105. Copyright © 2009 Sage Publications.

future tests of theory. Their analyses focus on understanding the extent to which scales representative of different theories are actually based on the same item content. They test for two distinct processes that may explain this phenomenon. In the first process, scales measuring a given construct are attributed to different theories. In the second process, scales measuring different constructs are based on the same items. Results show that both of the processes described above contribute to the use of the same NYS items in scales that are attributed to different theories. To inform future tests of theory, the authors identify the sections of the NYS where each of these processes are most prevalent, in effect identifying the areas of the NYS that future tests of theory should treat with the greatest care. Based on the implications of each process identified above, the authors also offer some suggestions to strengthen future tests of theory using NYS data.

INTRODUCTION

While the importance of criminological theory is evident in the volume of research that has accumulated, it could be argued that criminologists have made only modest progress in the development of criminological theories. In fact, Bernard and Snipes (1996) went so far as to state that "criminological research has tended toward a million modest little studies that produce a million tiny conflicting results" (p. 303). Despite this state of evidence, empirical assessments of the nature of theory tests are lacking. Instead, works devoted to the advancement of criminological theory have tended toward volumes addressing particular types of theory (Farrington 2005), works discussing particular types of theoretical development and the development of theory in general (Bernard 1990; Messner, Krohn, and Liska 1989), reviews of the literature (Leonard 1993), and recently, meta-analyses of tests of particular criminological theories (Pratt and Cullen 2000, 2005; Pratt et al. 2006). Here, we begin to address this gap in the literature by offering an empirical assessment of scales used in tests of theory based on National Youth Survey (NYS) data. Specifically, we explore both the theory to which scales measuring a given type of construct are attributed and the extent to which scales measuring different constructs are based on the same items.

CONSTRUCTS INCORPORATED IN TESTS BASED ON NYS DATA

The NYS was initiated as an epidemiological assessment of delinquent behavior among American youth. This assessment centered around a test of a new integrated theory of delinquency (Elliott Huizinga, and Ageton 1985). This integrated theory synthesized traditional strain, social control, and social learning perspectives (Elliott et al. 1985:11). The NYS also included a number of questions suitable for the operationalization of constructs important to labeling theory. Consequently, a majority of tests of criminological theory based on the NYS data have focused on these theories. Here, we briefly review key constructs within each of these theoretical traditions. In this review, we emphasize the specific iterations of theories that appear most frequently among tests of theory based on NYS data.

Among tests of criminological theory incorporating constructs from control theory, a strong majority are grounded in Hirschi's (1969) version of control theory. Hirschi's theory identified four key constructs: attachment, commitment, involvement and beliefs. Attachment is the bond one has with others and is described by Hirschi as "the essence of internalization of norms, conscience, or superego" (p. 18). Commitment can be understood as the extent to which an individual has a "stake in conformity" (Toby 1957). Individuals with higher levels of commitment are less willing to jeopardize their investment in conventionality by engaging in criminal acts. Involvement refers to the amount of time spent pursuing conventional activities such as studying or spending time with the family. Individuals with higher levels of involvement are thought to be restrained from delinquent behavior as a function of effort invested in conventionality. Beliefs refer to the extent to which an individual endorses conventional values and norms. Hirschi stated, 'The less a person believes he should obey the rules, the more likely he is to violate them" (p. 26).

Not surprisingly, tests of criminological theory incorporating constructs from social learning theory are largely based on Akers's (1998) social learning theory. Constructs central to Akers' theory include definitions, differential association, differential reinforcement, and mimicry. Of these constructs, definitions and differential association play a central role in tests of theory based on NYS data. Akers described definitions as "orientations, rationalizations, definitions of the situation and other attitudes that label the commission of an act as right or wrong, good or bad, desirable or undesirable, justified or unjustified" (p. 78). Differential association refers to the extent to which an individual differentially associates with those who commit criminal behavior or espouse delinquent definitions. Through differential association, an individual can learn delinquent definitions and thereby become more likely to engage in acts of crime and delinquency.

With regard to strain theory, tests based on NYS data typically draw on Agnew's (1992) general strain theory (for an exception, see Menard 1995). In general strain theory, strain leads to pressure for adaptation. In some cases, this adaptation is crime. Agnew (2001) stated, "Crime may be a method for reducing strain (e.g., stealing the money you desire), seeking revenge, or alleviating negative emotions (e.g., through illicit drug use)" (p. 319). There are three types of strain within general strain theory: (1) failure to achieve positively valued goals, (2) the removal or threatened removal of positively valued stimuli, and (3) the presentation or threatened presentation of negatively valued stimuli.

Key labeling theory constructs included in tests of theory based on NYS data are most often derived from contemporary versions of labeling theory (Matsuda 1992; Heimer and Matsuda 1994). These contemporary versions of labeling theory typically emphasize the influence of reflected appraisals. Reflected appraisals are the impression that an individual has of the appraisals of the self by others (Heimer and Matsueda 1994). Important types of reflected appraisals include an individual's impression of the perceptions of the self held by parents, teachers, and friends.

IMPLICATION OF THE CURRENT WORK

Through our investigation of the use of NYS data in tests of theory, we provide evidence with which to strengthen tests of criminological theory. The debate regarding the processes that shape tests of criminological theory is manifested in works devoted to theoretical advancement (see Bernard 1990; Messner et al. 1989) and in discussions included in works defining the different theories within the criminological tradition (see Akers 1998:3–20). While these processes are clearly of interest to theoreticians, by and large they have not been empirically assessed. An empirical assessment of the processes that shape the aggregate body of evidence on criminological theory will provide information that can help to advance this body beyond "a million modest little studies that produce a million tiny conflicting results" (Bernard and Snipes 1996:303).

As noted above, we are interested in the extent to which the tendency of criminological theories to claim similar constructs influence the empirical validation of theory. While the conceptual overlap between different criminological theories has been acknowledged (for examples see Agnew 1995; Tittle 1995), the areas in which this overlap tends to manifest itself in tests of theory has not been empirically assessed. Our investigation offers such an assessment and identifies the constructs that most often are offered by tests of theory as being representative of multiple theoretical traditions.

By identifying which constructs tend to be attributed to different theories in tests assessing the empirical veracity of different theoretical traditions, we in effect identify the constructs that need to be treated with additional sophistication. When tests of theory tend to attribute a specific type of construct to multiple theoretical traditions, it is particularly important to make an effort to consider the causal structure implied in these tests. This consideration should include an effort to incorporate in theory tests elements that fully quantify the causal processes that distinguish one theoretical tradition from other explanations of crime and deviance and an effort to include elements that test the competing assumptions of theories.

Careful consideration of the theoretical causal structure that is implied by a test will move us in the direction of "critical" or "crucial" tests of theory. As described by Liska, Krohn, and Messner (1989), critical tests pit the assumptions and propositions of one theory against another by quantifying the specific causal processes that distinguish one theory from another. These tests, described earlier in the work of Hempel (1966:25-28) and Stinchcombe (1968:27-28), provide results that "simultaneously lend credibility to one theory while raising doubts about another" (Liska et al. 1989:2). While we recognize not every construct attributed to multiple theories may lend itself to a critical test, we argue that when tests of theory tend to attribute the same construct to multiple theories, the incorporation of elements that will provide evidence potentially distinguishing between the different theoretical approaches is important. Absent such elements, we should anticipate that tests attributing the same construct to different theories will, all else being equal, tend to produce equivalent support for both theories. With this in mind, our analysis informs future tests of theory by identifying the theoretical constructs that existing tests tend to attribute to multiple theories. The incorporation of these constructs in theoretical tests should be accompanied by elements that will distinguish between the different theories to which the construct may be attributed.

Collectively, our result inform both the structure and measurement of tests of criminological theory and potentially improve the nature of evidence upon which we base our theoretical preferences.

DATA AND METHOD

The current work is an analysis of tests of criminological theory that utilize NYS data. The NYS, developed by Elliott et al. (1985), is based on a probability sample of U.S. households in 1976. The probability sample was derived using a multistage, cluster sampling design, through which 8,000 households were selected to participate. These households included 2,360 eligible youth, ages 11 to 17 on December 31, 1976, who were physically and mentally capable of being interviewed. Of these youth, about 73 percent or 1,725 agreed to participate in the study. Initial interviews were conducted in 1977 with an additional eight waves of interviews extending through 1993.

One of the primary purposes of the NYS data collection was to test an integrated theoretical explanation of delinquency (Elliott et al. 1985). Consequently, the NYS contains a number of sections designed to measure constructs from diverse theoretical traditions including control, differential association/social learning, labeling, and strain theory. In part because of the broad variety of theoretical constructs included, the NYS has had a tremendous impact on criminological theory. A list of studies using NYS data provided by the Interuniversity Consortium for Political and Social Research (ICPSR) includes 131 journal articles. A quick review of this list shows that many of these studies test theories or theoretical issues.

To identify tests of theory using NYS data, we used a number of search engines including Criminal Justice Abstracts, Sociological Abstracts, and PsychlNFO. This list was then cross-referenced with a list of studies using NYS data compiled by the ICPSR. Studies that met the following criteria were included in the analyses: (1) published in a peer-reviewed journal, (2) analyzed existing NYS data, and (3) included measures of theoretical constructs. Eighty-one articles met our criteria. Among the articles, we found 586 scales measuring theoretical constructs. In our analysis, we excluded scales incorporated in tests of theory as control variables (N = 152) and scales included in nontheoretical frameworks (N= 127), leaving 307 scales measuring theoretical constructs.

We included theoretical constructs that were central to the causal processes that define a particular theoretical tradition and tertiary constructs when these constructs were attributed by the authors to a specific theory. Examples of constructs central to a particular theory include the attachment, commitment, involvement, and belief constructs within Hirschi's (1969) social control theory. Tertiary constructs include those that are hypothesized by a particular theoretical tradition to mediate the effect of primary causal variables. For example, Agnew's (1992) discourse on general strain theory suggests that delinquent peers may mediate the influence of strain on delinquency. Consistent with this theoretical speculation, Mazerolle and Maahs (2000) incorporated a measure of exposure to delinquent peers, noting that "general strain theory asserts that the presence of delinquent peers may strengthen the link between strain and delinquency" (p. 761).

Construct and Theory Categories

After identifying scales measuring theoretical constructs, we then identified the theory and construct that the scale measured. In each case, scales were classified according the usage of the scale by the author(s) of the papers under consideration. Construct and theory categorization schemes were developed through a review of NYS studies. In this review, we first gathered information describing the construct quantified by each scale included in our analysis and the title of each scale employed by the author(s) of the study in

which the scale was included. Next, this information was sorted into construct categories. Once construct categories were developed, the titles and descriptions of scales were rechecked to ensure that they had been appropriately classified.

Classifications were originally completed by each author of this article. Subsequent to original classifications, discrepancies across authors were resolved through discussion amongst the authors. During this discussion, we referenced the articles in which the scales were included; when we were in agreement, the construct categorization scheme was finalized. Next, we identified the theory to which each of the scales had been attributed by the author(s) of the theory test in which the scale was included. These theories were then sorted into general categories. The resultant categorization schemes for theory and construct are presented in the appendix.

One of the principal challenges we faced when creating our theory and construct categories was to create theory and construct categorization schemes that qualified as reasonable groupings but would also lead to results that were readily interpretable. Recognizing that detailed construct and theory categories would introduce a substantial amount of complication into our results, we tended to err on the side of aggregation. This led to construct and theory categories where there is, in some instances, variation within category. This variation can be seen in our control theory category and in our attitudes construct category.

The control theory category includes Hirschi's (1969) social control theory as well as Gottfredson and Hirschi's (1990) self-control theory. While recent work has argued that social bond and self-control might not be as distinct as first conceptualized (Gottfredson 2006; Hirschi 2004), it seems reasonable to suggest that authors using NYS items to test social control theory or self control theory may use distinct items. While we recognize this possibility, we felt that acknowledging distinct versions within a given theoretical tradition would have resulted in undue complication. We are comfortable with this decision primarily because it leads to a more conservative test. By grouping theories within a single tradition together, we decrease the likelihood that measures based on the same items will be attributed to different theories.

There is also variation within our construct categories. In particular, our attitudes category includes measures of attitudes regarding antisocial behavior and attitudes regarding marriage/children and the family. While we recognize conceptual differences among these different types of attitudes, we feel our construct categorization scheme is reasonable. Grouping attitude measures together results in a conservative test, as fewer categories decrease the likelihood that particular NYS items will be found to have been incorporated in measures of distinct constructs.

In sum, we feel that our theory and construct categories allow us to offer a conservative test of both the extent to which distinct theories are represented by the same constructs and the extent to which scales measuring distinct constructs are based on the same NYS items. Furthermore, the categories used in this test also facilitate an analysis that can incorporate all tests of theory using NYS data while presenting results that are readily interpretable.

ANALYSIS

In our analysis, we first assessed the frequency with which tests of theory based on NYS data have used the same NYS items in scales quantifying constructs that are attributed to different criminological theories. If tests are structured in such a way that different theories are represented by scales composed of the same items, we would anticipate that the magnitude of the relationship between these scales and measures of crime and delinquency would also be similar or identical, contributing to a body of evidence where the different theoretical paradigms

within the criminological tradition have similar empirical support.

Subsequent to testing the extent to which individual NYS items are incorporated in scales quantifying multiple theories, we next explored two possible explanations for this tendency. The first of these two explanations is based on the recognition that there is overlap among the theoretical constructs incorporated by the different theoretical traditions within criminology. When two criminological theories claim the same construct, we would anticipate that tests of these two criminological theories would often incorporate scales measuring these constructs. Furthermore, we would anticipate that these scales would be based on the same items. To test the extent to which such conceptual overlap is manifested in tests of criminological theory, we explored the extent to which scales measuring a particular type of construct are attributed to distinct criminological theories.

Next, we test the possibility that distinct scales representing different theories are composed of the same items. That is, a given NYS item is used in scales quantifying multiple constructs that are in turn attributed to different theories. Explained in this way, the use of a single item in scales measuring different theories is attributed to the measurement of the constructs quantified by these scales.

Are NYS Items Used in Scales Offered as Measures of Distinct Criminological Theories?

In this section of our analysis, we identified the number of theories in which each NYS item has been used. To do this, we identified each of the NYS items used in the scales incorporated in the tests of theory included in our analysis. We then created an item-level database describing the use of these items. Information in this database included the total number of different theories measured by the scales that incorporated a given NYS item.

Summary values for all NYS items are presented in the first row of Table 2.5. On average,

Table 2.5   The Use of National Youth Survey (NYS) Items in Scales Representing Criminological Theories

	Theories Measured by Scales Incorporating Distinct Items: M(SD)	Diversity Index (SD)	Number of Scales: M(SD)
Overall	1.91 (1.07)	.289 (.263)	4.43 (4.56)
NYS section			
One	1.32(0.48)	.148 (.226)	2.26 (1.10)
Two	3.00 (0.50)	.482 (.049)	12.33 (2.29)
Three	4.50 (0.53)	.386 (.052)	17.70 (4.50)
Four	1.50 (0.71)	.240 (.339)	6.00 (2.83)
Five	1.25 (0.50)	.125 (.250)	2.50 (1.00)
Six	1.26 (0.44)	.095 (.166)	3.71 (2.83)
Seven	2.81 (0.83)	.528 (.086)	4.44 (1.86)
Eight	2.78 (0.67)	.468 (.260)	2.89 (0.78)
Nine	2.36 (0.50)	.539 (.199)	3.50 (1.16)
Ten	2.00 (0.00)	.420 (.000)	10.00 (0.00)
Eleven	2.33 (1.00)	.080 (.121)	4.33 (2.83)

distinct NYS items were used in scales that measured 1.91 different theories. If we restrict our analysis to items that were used more than once, this value increases to 2.18 different theories. These values show that the same NYS items are often included in many scales and also offered as representative of different theories.

The extent to which conceptual overlap potentially accounts for the use of NYS items in scales attributed to multiple theories is illustrated by results presented in Table 2.5. Results presented in Table 2.5 show that items taken from section 2 have been included in scales attributed to a variety of theories. This is not surprising, as the items in section 2 measure attitudes regarding antisocial behavior including crime, delinquency, deviance, violence, and drug and alcohol use. These items seem to be appropriate for use in scales measuring either the beliefs construct from

Hirschi's (1969) social control theory and the definitions construct from Akers's (1998) social learning theory. As such, much of the tendency of tests of theory to use items in section 2 to test multiple theories may be driven by conceptual overlap between Hirschi's social control theory and Akers's social learning theory.

Do Tests of Competing Theories Incorporate the Same Constructs?

In this section of our analysis, we assessed the influence of the tendency of theories to claim similar or identical constructs on tests of theory. To do this, we explored the distribution of scales measuring a particular construct type across the different criminological theories. Results for this section of our analysis are presented in Table 2.6. The extent to which tests

Table 2.6 Frequency Distribution of Scales Across Theory

Construct Type	Theory									
	Control	Differential Association Social Learning	Integrated	Labeling	Routine Activities	Strain	Other	More Than One	Total	Percentage Outside Modal Theoretical Category
Attachment	19	1	1	8	2		2		33	42.4
Attitudes	19	12	4	5		1	3		44	56.8
Commitment	10	1		1	1				13	23.1
Delinquent peers	3	27	5	5	2	1	2	6	51	47.1
Disapproval	2		6	6			2		16	62.5
Involvement	10	2	6	2					20	50.0
Labeling	3	3	1	30					37	23.3
Normlessness	5		7						12	41.7
Strain			3	4		27			34	25.9
Social isolation	3			3					6	50.0
Time spent	4	4	1		7		1		17	58.8

Mean = 43.8.

of theory tend to attribute similar or identical constructs to different theories is reflected by the distribution of scales measuring a particular type of construct across the different theories. For example, measures of attitudes were attributed to control theory *(N = 19)*, differential association theory *(N = 12)*, integrated theory *(N = 4)*, labeling theory *(N = 5)*, strain theory *(N = 1)* and other theories *(N = 3)*.

To quantify the distribution of constructs across theories, we calculated the percentage of scales lying outside the modal theoretical category. For example, in the studies under consideration, there were 33 scales measuring attachment. Of these scales, 19 were in the modal category of control theory. The remaining 14 scales (42.4 percent) were distributed across the theories outside of the modal theoretical category. Higher percentages of constructs outside the modal theoretical category are indicative of greater dispersion of constructs across theories.

Across the 283 scales included in Table 2.6, 124 (43.8 percent) were attributed to theories outside the modal theoretical category for those scales. The distribution of these scales across theory was widest for scales measuring parental or peer disapproval, scales measuring how time is spent, and scales measuring attitudes toward acts of crime and deviance. The results presented in Table 2.6 show that in tests of theory based on NYS data, different criminological theories are often represented by the same constructs. This demonstrates that the tendency of theory tests to use NYS items in scales attributed to different theories is at least in part attributable to the tendency of theories to incorporate similar or identical constructs.

The attribution of the same constructs to different theories indicates that future tests of theory employing these constructs need to pay careful attention to model specification and should attempt to provide evidence distinguishing between theories by quantifying the causal processes that distinguish one theoretical tradition from another. This implication of

our results is fully addressed in our Discussion and Conclusions section.

DISCUSSION AND CONCLUSIONS

Bernard and Snipes (1996) stated that "criminological research has tended toward a million modest little studies that produce a million tiny conflicting results" (p. 303). Our results suggest that these million modest little studies and million tiny conflicting results are in part attributable to the structure of tests of criminological theory. Specifically, we found that distinct criminological theories are often represented by scales containing the same items. Subsequent analyses showed that this tendency is due to two distinct processes. In the first process, tests of theory attribute the same constructs to different theories. In the second process, tests of theory quantify distinct theoretical constructs with scales incorporating the same NYS items.

We now offer a discussion of the implications of our results for future tests of criminological theory. In this discussion, we first address the implications of the tendency of tests of theory to attribute scales measuring the same theoretical constructs to different criminological theories. In short, we argue that results showing that tests of theory frequently attribute the same theoretical constructs to distinct theories, and this demonstrates that theory tests need to move beyond simple associational tests to quantify the causal processes that distinguish one theory from another.

Implication of the Attribution of Scales Measuring Similar Constructs to Multiple Theories

As part of our analysis, we offered an empirical assessment of the extent to which tests of theory tend to attribute scales measuring a given type of theoretical construct to distinct theories. While prior literature has noted the conceptual overlap among theories, the extent to which this overlap influences tests of theory has not yet been empirically assessed. Our results show that among tests of theory based on NYS data, distinct theories are often represented by measures of the same theoretical construct.

The tendency of tests of theory to attribute scales measuring the same constructs to distinct theories can be understood as a function of the conceptual overlap among theories. To illustrate, consider the similarity between the definitions construct from Akers's (1998) social learning theory and the beliefs construct from Hirschi's (1969) social control theory. As noted in our literature review, Hirschi stated that "the beliefs most obviously relevant to delinquency are those bearing on the goodness or badness of delinquent behavior" (p. 198), while Akers stated that definitions "label the commission of an act as right or wrong, good or bad, desirable or undesirable, justified or unjustified" (p. 78). The conceptual overlap between beliefs as described by Hirschi and definitions as described by Akers has led authors to use the same NYS items in scales that are attributed in their respective studies to either social learning theory or to social control theory (for example, see measures included in Agnew 1991; Hochstetler et al. 2002).

While we are convinced of the value of our focus on the NYS, we also recognize the need to extend our analysis to other data sets before conclusions regarding the measurement properties of scales measuring theoretical constructs included in the larger body of literature may be drawn. Other data sets may have unique features potentially impacting the processes found to influence empirical tests of theory utilizing NYS data. Replicating the current work with other data sets will directly inform the generalizability of our results and provide additional information describing the processes that shape the aggregate body of evidence present in tests of criminological theory.

Bernard (1990) stated that "despite 20 years of extensive research, criminology has not made scientific progress in the sense of falsifying some theories and accumulating verified knowledge in the context of other theories" (p. 325). Our analysis of scales included in tests of theory based on NYS data suggests that this state of evidence may be influenced by the quantification of theoretical constructs and by the tendency of tests of criminological theory to attribute particular types of theoretical constructs to more than one theory. Regarding the quantification of theoretical constructs, our analysis indicates that future tests of criminology should pay increased attention to the discriminant validity of scales measuring key theoretical constructs. Recognizing that the tendency of tests of theory to attribute a particular type of theoretical construct to more than one theory is a function of conceptual overlap among theories, we argue that to provide evidence to help move the field forward, tests incorporating these constructs should focus on fully quantifying the causal processes that distinguish one theoretical tradition from other explanations of crime and deviance and testing the competing assumptions of theories.

REFERENCES

Agnew, Robert. 1991. "A Longitudinal Test of Social Control Theory and Delinquency." *Journal of Research in Crime and Delinquency* 30:47-87.

Agnew, Robert. 1992. "Foundation for a General Strain Theory of Crime and Delinquency." *Criminology* 30:47-87.

Agnew, Robert. 1995. 'Testing the Leading Crime Theories: An Alternative Strategy Focusing on Motivational Processes " *Journal of Research in Crime and Delinquency* 32:363-98.

Agnew, Robert. 2001. "Building on the Foundation of General Strain Theory: Specifying the Types of Strain Most Likely to Lead to Crime and Delinquency." *Journal of Research in Crime and Delinquency* 38:319-61.

Agresti, Alan and Barbara Finlay Agresti. 1978. "Statistical Analysis of Qualitative Variation." *Sociological Methodology* 10:204-37.

Akers, Ronald L. 1998. *Social Learning and Social Structure: A General Theory of Crime and Deviance.* Boston: Northeastern University Press.

Andrews, D. A. and J. L. Bonta. 1995. *The Level of Service Inventory-Revised.* Toronto, Canada: Multi-Health Systems.

Becker, Howard S. 1963. *Outsiders: Studies in the Sociology of Deviance.* New York: Free Press.

Bernard, Thomas J. 1990. "Twenty Years of Testing Theories: What Have We Learned and Why?" *Journal of Research in Crime and Delinquency* 27:325-47.

Bernard, Thomas J. and Jeffery B. Snipes. 1996. "Theoretical Integration in Criminology." Pp. 301-48 in *Crime and Justice: A Review of Research,* vol. 20, edited by Michael Tonry. Chicago: University of Chicago Press.

Campbell, Donald T. and Donald W. Fiske. 1959. "Convergent and Discriminant Validation by the Multitrait-Multimethod Matrix." *Psychological Bulletin* 56:81-105.

Elliott, Delbert S., David Huizinga and Suzanne S. Ageton. 1985. *Explaining Delinquency and Drug Use.* Thousand Oaks, CA: Sage.

Farrington, David P. 2005. *Integrated Developmental and Life-Course Theories of Offending.* New Brunswick, NJ: Transaction Publishers.

Farrington, David P., Rolf Loeber, Magda Stouthamor-Louber, Wilmoet B. Van Kamtnen and Laura Schmidt. 1996. "Self-reported Delinquency and a Combined Delinquency Seriousness Scale Based on Boys, Mothers, and Teachers: Concurrent and Predictive Validity for African-Americans and Caucasians." *Criminology* 34:493-517.

Garofalo, James. 1987. "Reassessing the Lifestyle Model of Criminal Victimization." Pp. 23-42 in *Positive Criminology,* edited by Michael R. Gottfredson and Travis Hirschi. Newbury Park, CA: Sage.

Gottfredson, Michael R. 1986. "Substantive Contributions of Victimization Surveys." Pp. 252-87 in *Crime and Justice: An Annual Review of Research,* vol. 7, edited by Michael Tonry and Norvall Morris. Chicago: University of Chicago Press.

Gottfredson, Michael R. 2006. "The Empirical Status of Control Theory in Criminology." Pp. 77-100 in *Taking Stock: The Status of Criminological Theory,* edited by Francis T. Cullen, John Paul Wright, and Kristie R. Blevins. Piscataway, NJ: Transaction Publishers.

Gottfredson, Michael R. and Travis Hirschi. 1990. *A General Theory of Crime.* Stanford, CA: Stanford University Press.

Grasmick, Harold G., Charles R. Tittle and Robert J. Bursik. 1993. "Testing the Core Implications of Gottfredson and Hirschi's General Theory of Crime." *Journal of Research in Crime and Delinquency* 30:5-29.

Harer, Miles and Neil P. Langan. 2001. "Gender Differences in Predictors of Prison Violence: Assessing the Predictive Validity of a Risk Classification System." *Crime and Delinquency* 47:513-36.

Heimer, Karen and Ross L. Matsueda. 1994. "Role-Taking, Role Commitment, and Delinquency: A Theory of Differential Social Control." *American Sociological Review* 59:365-90.

Hempel, Carl. 1966. *Philosophy of Natural Science.* Englewood Cliffs, NJ: Prentice Hall.

Hindelang, Michael, J., Michael R. Gottfredson and James Garofalo. 1978. *Victims of Personal Crime: An Empirical Foundation for a Theory of Personal Victimization.* Cambridge, MA: Ballinger.

Hindelang, Michael, Travis Hirschi and Joseph J. Weis. 1981. *Measuring Delinquency.* Thousand Oaks, CA: Sage.

Hirschi, Travis. 1969. *Causes of Delinquency.* Berkeley: University of California Press.

Hirschi, Travis. 2004. "Self-Control and Crime." Pp. 537-52 in *Handbook of Self-Regulation: Research, Theory, and Applications,* edited by R. F. Baumeister and K. D. Vohs. New York: Guilford.

Hochstetler, Andy, Heith Copes and Matt DeLisi 2002. "Differential Association in Group and Solo Offending." *Journal of Criminal Justice* 30:559-66.

Hoffmann, John P. 1993. "Exploring the Direct and Indirect Family Effects on Adolescent Drug Use." *Journal of Drug Issues* 23: 535-57.

Hoffmann, John P. 1994. "Investigating the Age Effects of Family Structure on Adolescent

Marijuana Use." *Journal of Youth and Adolescence* 23:215-35.

Huizinga, David and Delbert S. Elliott. 1986. "Reassessing the Reliability and Validity of Self-Report Delinquency Measures." *Journal of Quantitative Criminology* 2:293-327.

Kempf, Kimberly. 1993. "The Empirical Status of Hirschi's Control Theory." Pp. 143-188 in *New Directions in Criminological Theory,* vol. 4, edited by Freda Adler and William S. Laufer. New Brunswick: Transaction Publishers.

Kroner, Daryl G. and Jeremey F. Mills. 2001. "The Accuracy of Five Risk Appraisal instruments in Predicting Institutional Misconduct and New Convictions." *Criminal Justice and Behavior* 28:471-89.

Lauritsen, Janet L. 1993. "Sibling Resemblance in Juvenile Delinquency: Findings from the National Youth Survey." *Criminology* 31:387-409.

Lemert, Edwin M. 1967. *Human Deviance, Social Problems, and Social Control.* Englewood Cliffs, NJ: Prentice Hall.

Leonard, Kimberly K. 1993. "The Empirical Status of Hirschi's Control Theory." Pp. 143-85 in *New Directions in Criminological Theory,* vol. 4, edited by F. Adler and W. Laufer. New Brunswick, NJ: Transaction Publishers.

Liska, Allen E., Marvin D. Krohn and Steven F. Messner. 1989. "Strategies and Requisites for Theoretical Integration in the Study of Crime and Deviance." Pp. 1-20 in *Theoretical Integration in the Study of Deviance and Crime: Problems and Prospects,* edited by Steven F. Messner, Marvin D. Krohn, and Allen E. Liska. New York: State University of New York Press.

Longshore, D., J. A. Stein and S. Turner. 1998. "Reliability and Validity of Self-Control Measure: A Rejoinder." *Criminology* 36:175-82.

Longshore, D., S. Turner, and J. A. Stein. 1996. "Self-Control in a Criminal Sample: An Explanation of Construct Validity." *Criminology* 34:209-28.

Matsueda, Ross L. 1992. "Reflected Appraisals, Parental Labeling, and Delinquency: Specifying a Symbolic Interactionist Theory." *American Journal of Sociology* 97:1577-611.

Matsueda, Ross L. and Karen Anderson. 1998. 'The Dynamics of Delinquent Peers and Delinquent Behavior." *Criminology* 36:269-308.

Mazerolle, Paul and Jeff Maahs. 2000. "General Strain and Delinquency: An Alternative Examination of Conditioning Influences." *Justice Quarterly* 17:753-77.

Mead, George, H. 1934. *Mind, Self and Society.* Chicago: University of Chicago Press.

Menard, Scott. 1995. "A Developmental Test of Mertonian Anomie Theory" *Journal of Research in Crime and Delinquency* 32:136-74.

Merton, Robert, K. 1938. "Social Structure and Anomie." *American Sociological Review* 3: 672-82.

Messner, Steven F., Marvin D. Krohn and Allen E. Liska. 1989. *Theoretical Integration in the Study of Deviance and Crime: Problems and Prospects.* Albany: State University of New York Press.

Mihalic, Shannon W. and Delbert Elliott. 1997. "Short- and Long-Term Consequences of Work." *Youth & Society* 28:464-98.

Moffitt, Terrie, E. 1993. "Life-Course-Persistent and Adolescence-Limited Antisocial Behavior: A Developmental Taxonomy." *Psychological Review* 100:674-701.

Paschall, Mallie J., Miriam L. Ornstein and Robert L. Flewelling. 2001. "African American Male Adolescents' Involvement in the Criminal Justice System: The Criterion Validity of Self-Report Measures in a Prospective Study." *Journal of Research in Crime and Delinquency* 38:174-87.

Paternoster, Ray and Robert Brame 1997. "Multiple Routes to Delinquency? A Test of Developmental and General Theories of Crime." *Criminology* 35:49-80.

Paternoster, Ray and Paul Mazerolle. 1994. "General Strain Theory and Delinquency: A Replication and Extension." *Journal of Research in Crime and Delinquency* 31: 235-63.

Piquero, Alex. 1999. 'The Validity of Incivility Measures in Public Housing." *Justice Quarterly* 16:793-818.

Piquero, Alex and Andre B. Rosay. 1998. "The Reliability and Validity of Grasmick et al.'s Self-Control Scale: A Comment on Longshore et al." *Criminology* 36:157-73.

Pratt, Travis C. and Francis T. Cullen. 2000. "The Empirical Status of Gottfredson and Hirschi's General Theory of Crime: A Meta Analysis." *Criminology* 38:931-64.

Pratt, Travis C. and Francis T. Cullen. 2005. "Assessing Macro-Level Predictors and Theories of Crime: A Meta-Analysis." Pp. 373-450 in *Crime and Justice: A Review of Research,* vol. 32, edited by Michael Tonry. Chicago: University of Chicago Press.

Pratt, Travis C., Francis T. Cullen, Kristie R. Blevins, Leah E. Daigle and Tamara D. Madensen. 2006. "The Empirical Status of Deterrence Theory: A Meta-Analysis." Pp. 367-95 in *Taking Stock: The Empirical Status of Criminological Theory-Advances in Criminological Theory,* vol. 15, edited by Francis T. Cullen, John Paul Wright, and Kristie R. Blevins. New Brunswick, NJ: Transaction Publishers.

Rebellon, Cesar J. 2002. "Reconsidering the Broken Homes/Delinquency Relationship and Exploring Its Mediating Mechanism(s)." *Criminology* 40:103-35.

Stinchcombe, Andrew J. 1968. *Constructing Social Theories.* New York: Harcourt, Brace and World.

Sutherland, Edwin, J. 1947. *Principles of Criminology.* 4th ed. Philadelphia: Lippincott.

Tannenbaum, Frank. 1938. *Crime and the Community.* New York: Columbia University Press.

Taylor, Ralph B. 1999. "The Incivilities Thesis: Theory, Measurement, and Policy." Pp. 65-68 in *Measuring What Matters: Proceeding from the Policing Research Institute Meetings,* edited by R. Langworthy. Washington, DC: National Institute of Justice.

Tittle, Charles. 1995. *Control Balance: Toward a General Theory of Deviance.* Boulder, CO: Westview.

Toby, Jackson. 1957. "Social Disorganization and Stake in Conformity: Complementary Factors in the Predatory Behavior of Hoodlums." *Journal of Criminal Law, Criminology and Police Science* 48:12-17.

Worral, John L. 2006. "The Discriminant Validity of Perceptual Incivility Measures." *Justice Quarterly* 23:359-83.

DISCUSSION QUESTIONS

1. Which criminological theories have been tested using data from the National Youth Survey?

2. Why do these authors report that it is important to identify the constructs that are attributed to different theories?

3. What type of sampling design did NYS researchers use to obtain their sample? In what years was the NYS data collected? What was the primary purpose of the NYS?

4. According to the results in Tables 2.5 and 2.6, did these authors find that different theories are represented by the same constructs? Did they find that scales measuring different constructs are based on the same NYS items?

5. What explanations do these authors give for their findings? What does this mean for future theory tests based on NYS data?

6. What do you think of the quote given at the beginning of the Discussion section? What does this say about advancing knowledge in criminology?

7. What do these researchers believe all researchers need to do to strengthen future tests of theory?

3

Ethics in the Research Process

There have been numerous examples of unethical research studies in the social and behavioral sciences, and ethical issues are ever-present in criminal justice and criminology research. As such, many safeguards and guidelines have been put in place to oversee ethical issues as they relate to research, especially research that involves human subjects. This chapter will discuss the role of researchers in minimizing harm to subjects of research as well as the responsibility that researchers themselves must take on as scientists.

Remember the discussion of positivism in the first chapter and the idea that we can observe an objective reality? In this spirit, researchers must be as objective as possible when conducting research. What this means is that the researcher should not have a vested interest in the results of the research. Researchers should not, in advance of the study, wish or hope that they find certain results. This is especially true for research that is evaluating the effectiveness of programs. One could imagine the pressure felt by researchers to conclude that a program aimed at reducing violence among family members or helping drug addicts not to relapse back into addiction is successful and effective. Sometimes these programs are relying on research-proven success in order to continue to receive governmental funding. Program staff will not welcome results that

reveal no effectiveness or lack of success in outcomes if it means that their jobs are on the line.

In the broader scientific sense, however, researchers who conduct research to advance knowledge in the discipline or who conduct tests of criminological theories, also have a responsibility to conduct this research in a professional and objective manner. Some may argue that pure objectivity in research is impossible as all human beings bring some preferences and biases to the table and that these will ultimately affect observations. Nonetheless, no matter the type of research being conducted, researchers in criminology and criminal justice should strive for objectivity by following the rules and guidelines put in place regarding the selection of the samples to be studied, the observations and data collection procedures, analysis of the data, and reporting and dissemination of the results and conclusions of the research.

Due to both unethical and harmful research studies that have been conducted in the past, the federal government has set up screening committees to oversee research in the United States. These committees are known as Institutional Review Boards (IRB) and are mostly set up in colleges and universities around the country to ensure that research is being conducted in accordance with federal rules. Prior to IRBs, researchers themselves would have to make decisions about the ethical appropriateness of their research (Ellis, Hartley, & Walsh, 2010). Most research today must be approved by an IRB in order to commence. Although this can sometimes mean an additional and often time-consuming extra step in the research process, it is a necessary step to ensure the emotional and physical well-being of research subjects.

Hagan (2005) lists some ethical guidelines that those conducting research in criminology and criminal justice specifically should adhere to. These include: (1) avoid research that may be potentially harmful to subjects, (2) honor all agreements made to subjects, (3) be objective and professional in conducting research and in reporting the results, and (4) maintain the confidentiality of subjects. All those who are thinking about conducting research in the future would be wise to keep these guidelines in mind to maintain professionalism in the discipline and to ensure compliance with federal regulations.

INFORMED CONSENT

Informed consent involves notifying the subjects of research about the purposes of the research study so that they may make an informed choice about whether to participate in the study or not. Often, this means getting subjects (questionnaire respondents, subjects of experiments, or face-to-face interviewees) to read and sign an informed consent form. At other times, like observations in public or research of an ethnographic nature (observations or participation in the customs and culture of groups), consent is implicit based upon IRB approval of the research study. Research involving human subjects must be voluntary, which means that subjects are to be treated as autonomous persons. In other words, persons must be able to decide for themselves whether they want to participate as a subject of the research. No one should be forced or coerced to participate as a subject of research.

Informed consent forms ensure the requirements regarding autonomy and voluntariness.

RESPECT FOR SUBJECTS OF RESEARCH

Researchers also have an ethical obligation to keep all commitments or promises made to research subjects. Often subjects who consent to participate in a study will be debriefed by researchers afterward to ensure that they understand the purposes of the research they have just participated in and to provide them an opportunity to ask any questions about the methods used to collect the data, the intended use for the collected data, the outlets for reporting research results, or the opportunity to express any other ethical concerns that they may have as a result of being a part of the research. Researchers, therefore, should not collect any information other than that which they explicitly proposed to the IRB and should not use the data or results for any purposes other than that which was stated via the informed consent form. Informing participants of the purposes of the research and keeping promises to them shows respect for them as subjects of research.

Researchers have gathered a lot of data from subjects who have readily volunteered information via participation in studies. A great deal of what we know about human behavior and the nature and causes of criminal offending has come from simply asking persons to provide information about their lives. As such, in order for the continued sharing of information by subjects, a mutual trust between researcher and subject must be maintained by all who conduct research in the social and behavioral sciences.

CONFIDENTIALITY

Ethical concerns are specifically salient to research in criminology and criminal justice.

Researchers in these fields study behaviors that are most often violations of the law. As such, they may be asking persons to respond to questions of a very personal nature, and that could subject the participants to legal sanctions if the information was made public. Researchers in this field also study the behavior of groups such as gangs or other types of offenders (prostitutes, residential burglars, drug dealers), which could subject them to scrutiny by law enforcement or even compromise their own safety. Ellis and colleagues (2010) note that those conducting research in criminology and criminal justice "must balance the need for scientific knowledge with their ethical principles and safety" (p. 372).

The best way to uphold ethical standards in criminal justice research is to ensure anonymity, or at least confidentiality, of the information collected from subjects. Anonymity refers to procedures undertaken to collect anonymous information—that which is not attached to the identity of the subjects. This may be difficult in studies using direct observation where researchers observe specific individuals engaged in specific behaviors. Confidentiality, on the other hand, is a guarantee by the researcher not to disclose the identity of the subject who provided information. This is the case where the researcher has information on the subject's identity but promises not to reveal that information as part of the reporting or dissemination of the responses or results.

If researchers cannot guarantee the confidentiality of the subjects, they should not collect this information; as part of the ethical guideline to respect subjects, promises made to subjects regarding confidentiality should be strictly adhered to. Researchers are vested with considerable protections in maintaining the confidentiality of the subjects of their research. The government would have to provide a compelling reason to a grand jury or judge in order to force researchers to reveal the identity of subjects or to turn over information they have collected as part of a research study (Pearson, 2009; Williams, Dunlap, Johnson, & Hamid, 1992). Researchers have an ethical obligation to keep subject identities private. That being said, however, researchers in the past have been incarcerated (although very few) for failing to provide authorities with the identities of research subjects or with information they have collected about criminal behaviors as part of a research study (Monaghan, 1993). Researchers can be granted what are known as certificates of confidentiality—which are issued by the National Institutes of Health, the Department of Justice, and other agencies—that provide the researchers protection from disclosure of information about subjects in criminal, civil, administrative, and even legislative proceedings (Department of Health and Human Services, 2003). These certificates can be granted regardless of whether the funding source is at the local, state, or federal level.

Unless a researcher is willing to risk prosecution (and possibly incarceration) for maintaining confidentiality of subjects, it is best not to collect any identifying information from subjects who provide information on criminal behaviors (Frankfort-Nachmias & Nachmias, 1992). Obviously, not all criminal justice research rises to this level of ethical and legal scrutiny. However, for researchers who collect personal information or data on criminal activity, or researchers who observe or even participate in criminal activities as part of their research, it would be wise to keep in mind the issues discussed here regarding the ethical propriety of research. Ethical issues regarding ethnography and participant observation will be further discussed in Chapter 8 regarding qualitative research. Where identifying information is collected as part of a research study seeking to collect data on criminal or delinquent behavior, researchers can obtain a certificate of confidentiality to provide protection against disclosure.

RESEARCH READING

This article provides a discussion of the possible conflict between research ethics, namely confidentiality of subjects, and the law. Researchers, especially criminologists, have an obligation to conduct research with ethical propriety, especially research that involves human subjects. Most notably for criminology researchers is maintaining the confidentiality of research subjects. These authors discuss the conflict between ethical obligations of researchers and the legal protections given to them in Canada and the United States. They provide examples of past research where the courts and other entities have ordered researchers to disclose the identity of their research subjects. These authors contend that better codes of ethics need to be in place regarding confidentiality and the law, and they suggest that if researchers are concerned about these issues, the best remedy may be to collect anonymous data.

THE ETHICS AND LAW OF CONFIDENTIALITY
IN CRIMINAL JUSTICE RESEARCH

A Comparison of Canada and the United States

John Lowman and Ted Palys

Abstract: The Academy of Criminal Justice Sciences Code of Ethics and the American Society of Criminology Draft Code of Ethics raise the possibility of a conflict arising between research ethics and the law relating to evidentiary and testimonial privilege. However, they say nothing about the form that legal threats to research confidentiality may take in Canada and the United States, the two countries where these codes apply, nor do they describe the strategies that researchers can employ to protect confidential research information in court. The purpose of this article is to address these matters. It begins with a brief description of the role that confidentiality plays in protecting research participants and maintaining the validity and reliability of criminal justice research. It then describes the legal context in which the researchers' ethical obligations unfold and the strategies that researchers can employ to protect confidential research information when third parties use legal force to try to obtain it. The article argues that the ethical responsibilities of researchers studying criminal justice issues are best fulfilled and their research participants best protected when researchers use their understanding of law to design research so as to anticipate the evidentiary requirements of the courts. It concludes with a discussion of the respective advantages and disadvantages of statutory as compared to common law protections for research confidentiality.

> *Confidential information provided by research-participants must be treated as such by criminologists, even when this information enjoys no legal protection or privilege and legal force is applied.*
>
> —American Society of Criminology Draft Code of Ethics, paragraph 30; Academy of Criminal Justice Science *Code of Ethics*, paragraph 19

Source: Lowman, J., & Palys, T. (2001). The ethics and law of confidentiality in criminal justice research: A comparison of Canada and the United States. *International Criminal Justice Review, 11*(1), 1–33. Published by Sage Publications on behalf of Georgia State University Research Foundation. Copyright © 2001 Sage Publications.

INTRODUCTION

With this sentence (taken from the 1989 American Sociological Association's [ASA] Code of Ethics) the American Society of Criminology (ASC) Draft Code of Ethics and Academy of Criminal Justice Sciences (ACJS) Code of Ethics raise the possibility of a conflict arising between research ethics and the law relating to evidentiary and testimonial privilege. Both affirm that the criminologist's primary obligation is to ethics. However, none of these codes say anything about the form that legal threats to research confidentiality may take. And, while all enjoin researchers in one way or another to "anticipate possible threats to confidentiality" (e.g., ACJS Code of Ethics, paragraph 18), none describe the legal protections and privileges that researchers can employ to protect confidential research information in court.

Although confidentiality is essential to many different types of research, nowhere is it more important than in research where subjects are asked to divulge information about criminal activity and criminal justice processes, especially when this concerns criminal activity or rights violations that have not been detected. The primary role of research ethics is to ensure that subjects are not harmed by their participation in research. When subjects divulge information about crime or criminal justice processes, it is our ethical responsibility to ensure that the information cannot be used against them. Without a guarantee of confidentiality and confidence in our willingness and ability to maintain it, neither offenders nor those who prosecute, process, and incarcerate them—police, prison guards, prosecutors, and judges—are likely to reveal sensitive information about the nature of their activity and the operation of the criminal justice system.

The purpose of the current article is to address these issues as they pertain to criminal justice research in Canada and the United States. The article begins with a brief description of the role that confidentiality plays in protecting research participants. It then describes the legal context in which a researcher's ethical obligations unfold and discusses how researchers most effectively can protect confidential research information when third parties use legal force to try to obtain it. Because the ASC and ACJS ethics codes apply in both Canada and the United States, we describe the history of conflicts between ethics and law in both countries. The comparison itself is instructive because of the very different experiences of researchers in the two countries.

CONFIDENTIALITY IN CRIMINAL JUSTICE RESEARCH

The need for confidentiality arises in relationships where one party is vulnerable because of the trust reposed in the other. These include relationships where one party provides information to another because of the latter's commitment to confidentiality. For this reason, a confidential relationship is a fiduciary relationship *par excellence*.

The researcher-participant relationship is unique among relationships in which confidentiality may be considered integral to the functioning of the relationship. If research participants face a risk because of their participation in our research, it is usually because we have walked into their lives and exposed them to it. Generally, research participation is voluntary, and it is conducted without undue coercion or promise of reward. Some research participants are paid for their time, such as students in psychology experiments or criminal offenders, but the payment is usually nominal. Although participants may derive satisfaction at someone lending them an ear and perhaps even hope to change the world by revealing private information to a researcher, research participants are generally motivated by their desire to help create knowledge for the greater good.

The primary purpose of research ethics is to ensure that research participants are not harmed by their involvement in research. With respect to risks produced by third party intrusion, our commitment to confidentiality and anonymity provides the key foundations for this protection. When research can be conducted in a way that maintains research participant anonymity, the threat of violating confidentiality because of some unwanted third party intrusion is minimal. Clearly, whenever data can be gathered anonymously, they should be.

However, in many types of research, anonymity is not an option. Researchers who want to link particular individuals across different databases or track certain participants over time must have a means of identifying research participants. When working with large databases, a variety of techniques can be used to sever identifying information and either destroy it or store it separately, preferably in another country.

Unless they are involved in longitudinal studies or are tracking individuals across databases, quantitative researchers generally do not experience the problem of recording incriminating information, and they rarely carry it in their heads. But the more qualitative and inductive the research becomes, the more difficult it is to use technical devices to protect research participants. Ethnographers and other researchers working with a limited number of key informants or developing case histories, where participants are chosen on the basis of their reputation or institutional affiliation and position, can delete identifying information from interview transcripts and field notes, but they cannot delete it from their memories.

Of course, confidentiality is not essential across the entire spectrum of research. With relatively innocuous topics confidentiality may be of little concern to participants. Also, some research participants prefer to be named, as is their right. However, when research participants divulge personal information that could harm their reputation, self-esteem, or well-being, and especially when secrecy is cherished in the social world under study, the researcher-participant relationship is predicated on trust. Trust cannot be built on a promise of confidentiality that, depending on whether law enforcement authorities or interested third parties want the information, may or may not be kept.

POTENTIAL CONFLICTS BETWEEN RESEARCH ETHICS AND LAW

There are at least four areas of potential conflict between the law and the ethical requirement of confidentiality:

1. When researchers learn about certain crimes and are statutorily obliged to report them (i.e., mandatory reporting laws that do not exempt researchers; these vary by jurisdiction but may include, for example, elder abuse, child abuse, and spousal assault).

2. When researchers learn about potential future crime and may be held liable for harm to third parties that they could have prevented.

3. When nongovernmental third parties subpoena researchers to testify about issues arising in high-stakes litigation.

4. When prosecutors, grand juries, congressional committees, and various public bodies subpoena researchers to testify about crimes or other offenses that research participants may have revealed to them. Coroners also can subpoena researchers if they think that they might have information relevant to an inquest.

In general, the first two areas are situations where researchers' violation of confidentiality would be a matter of their own initiative, independent of compulsion. In contrast, subpoenas create the threat of compelled revelation after the fact. Depending on the kind of research that they are conducting, criminologists could find themselves confronting dilemmas in any of these four areas. However, historically, in the U.S. at least, it is the third and fourth categories—both involving the possibility of subpoena and orders for disclosure—that have represented the greatest threat to researchers and their participants.

SUBPOENAS AND COURT ORDERS FOR DISCLOSURE: A BRIEF HISTORY

The general duty that all citizens have to testify when called upon-and the contempt of court that they can be charged with if they do not-constitutes the principal threat to research confidentiality. In the U.S. since the 1960s, dozens of researchers have received subpoenas and been asked—and occasionally ordered—to violate research confidences (Bond, 1978; Caroll & Knerr, 1975; Cecil & Wetherington, 1996), In Canada, we know of only one such instance (see below).

Challenges to Research Confidentiality in the United States

In the United States, the principal threats to research confidentiality have come from congressional committees and grand juries and from private interests using the discovery process in civil litigation. Since 1970, an extensive secondary literature has developed to describe these problems.

One of the first recorded instances of third party attempts to obtain confidential research information involved the FBI's threat to subpoena some of the sex research records of the Kinsey Institute at Indiana University. The FBI withdrew when members of the Institute made it clear that, regardless of the legal consequences, they would not release confidential research information (Caroll & Knerr, 1973).

Conflicts between research ethics and law proliferated during Richard Nixon's presidential administration when politicians, law enforcement officials, prosecutors, and grand juries began trying to co-opt research for law enforcement purposes:

1. In 1971 a local county prosecutor subpoenaed a researcher studying a federally sponsored income maintenance program in New Jersey. The prosecutor was interested in determining whether any participants had illegally collected welfare while receiving income maintenance. The researcher refused to reveal the names of his participants on the grounds that he had guaranteed them anonymity (Bond, 1978).

2. In 1972 Samuel Popkin, a Harvard political scientist, spent eight days in jail for refusing to reveal to a grand jury the identities of the persons he interviewed regarding the Pentagon Papers, a secret war study (Caroll & Knerr, 1973; O'Neil, 1996).

3. In 1973, as part of its investigation into criminal liability arising from the Attica prison riot, the New York State Attorney's Office subpoenaed the records of the State Governor's Commission on the riot. In this instance, the court ruled that, because of the threat to research that a violation of confidentiality would cause, it was in the public interest that the subpoena be quashed (Nejelski & Finsterbusch, 1973).

By the mid-1970s, Caroll and Knerr (1975) were able to identify some two dozen instances of congressional committees, law enforcement agencies, prosecutors, and grand juries harassing researchers for information to aid the investigation and prosecution of research participants. These developments had profound implications for criminology because of their potential to compromise research where anonymity was not possible.

Since that time, although the number of such cases has declined, two of the most important occurred:

1. Mario Brajuha was conducting participant observation research on "the sociology of the American restaurant" when the restaurant where he was working and observing burned down under suspicious circumstances. A grand jury subpoenaed Brajuha to testify and produce his field notes to help their investigation. Brajuha refused. In the end, Brajuha

was able to anonymize his field notes before submitting them, thereby protecting the identities of his participants (Brajuha & Hallowell, 1986; *In re Grand Jury Subpoena Dtd,* 1984).

2. University of Washington graduate student Richard Scarce was engaged in research with animal rights activists when an animal care facility at the university was vandalized. When the grand jury investigating the case subpoenaed Scarce, he refused to reveal information that would violate the confidentiality of individual participants. His claim of privilege was denied both at trial and on appeal. Scarce maintained confidentiality nevertheless, and he spent 159 days in jail until the judge deemed that his incarceration was no longer "coercive" but "punitive," at which time he was released (*In re Grand Jury Proceedings. James Richard Scarce,* 1993; Scarce, 1994, 1999).

The threat from congressional committees, grand juries, and prosecutors appears to have declined over the past 20 years. However, from the mid-1970s onwards, another broad threat posed by large corporations embroiled in high-stakes litigation came to the fore. Corporations became interested in research findings in order to either discredit them or enlist them in support of the corporation's case. The following summary of cases on compelled disclosure gives a sense of the wide range of research affected:

1. Marc Roberts, a Harvard public health professor, interviewed employees of Pacific Gas and Electric Company (PG&E) in a study of utility company decision-making regarding environmental issues. Subsequently, a company sued PG&E for breach of contract. Roberts's interview notes were subpoenaed because the plaintiff believed that they might have a bearing on the case. Roberts refused to provide them, arguing that compelled disclosure of confidential information would stifle research into public policy, the very subject in which the public interest is greatest (see *Richards of Rockford Inc.* v. *Pacific Gas and Electric,* 1976).

2. In 1982, two Dow Chemical Company herbicides were the subject of cancellation hearings before the Environmental Protection Agency. When independent research conducted at the University of Wisconsin was cited at the hearings, Dow subpoenaed the researchers, asking them to produce complete documentation of the research. The researchers refused, arguing that the subpoena was excessive and amounted to harassment (*Dow Chemical* v. *Allen,* 1982).

3. Arthur Herbst, Chair of Obstetrics and Gynecology at the University of Chicago, had compiled a registry of more than 500 women with vaginal and cervical adenocarcinoma dating back to 1940 and had published several articles based on data in the registry. In 1984, plaintiffs brought an action against several drug companies alleging that a drug that they manufactured caused cervical cancer. Dr. Herbst's research was cited in support of the claim. One of the companies subpoenaed Herbst, ordering that he produce every record in the registry. Herbst refused, stating that information in the registry was confidential and that his and similar research would be impossible to conduct in the future if that confidence were to be violated (*Deitchman* v. *E. R. Squibb & Sons, Inc.,* 1984).

4. On two occasions, American Tobacco Company subpoenaed Irving Selikoff of the Mount Sinai School of Medicine, in order to challenge his research regarding links between smoking and cancer (*In re American Tobacco Co.,* 1989a, 1989b). In another case, Dr. Paul Fischer of the University of Georgia Medical School had surveyed three- and six-year-old children to determine whether they were able to identify R. J. Reynolds Tobacco Company's "Joe Camel" character. They were.

As part of a suit against them in California, RJR subpoenaed Fischer, initially demanding all documentation in relation to his study, including the names of all the children who had taken part (Fischer, 1996; *R J. Reynolds Tobacco Co.* v. *Fischer,* 1993). Both Selikoff and Fischer resisted the subpoenas.

5. In 1992, the Exxon Shipping Co. was sued for liability arising from the *Exxon Valdez*

oil tanker disaster. Upon hearing of research being conducted by University of Alabama sociologist J, Steven Picou regarding community stress in Alaskan coastal villages following the disaster, the shipping company subpoenaed Picou's field notes. Picou challenged the subpoena (Picou, 1996).

6. Professors Michael Cusumano and David Yoffie of Harvard University and the Massachusetts Institute of Technology had interviewed 40 Netscape employees regarding their "browser war" with Microsoft. Not long after the interviews were conducted, Microsoft became embroiled in defending itself against charges of antitrust violations. With respect to the browser wars, Microsoft argued that the stunning increase in market share that it enjoyed at Netscape's expense was not because of the predatory business practices of which Microsoft stood accused but was due to poor business decisions by their rivals at Netscape. Microsoft subpoenaed the two researchers and asked for all interview tapes, transcripts, data files, correspondence, and field notes pertaining to the browser wars. The researchers refused, claiming that these materials were privileged (*In re Michael A. Cusumano and David B. Yoffie,* 1998).

We will review the outcomes of these cases as we delve more deeply into the implications of U.S. jurisprudence for protecting confidential research information. Although none of the civil cases is explicitly "criminological," one can easily imagine situations where researchers studying corporate or white-collar crime might find themselves in the cross fire between corporate litigants and government agencies. Also, U.S. criminologists must remain mindful of the threat posed by grand juries investigating specific cases.

Challenges to Research Confidentiality in Canada

In Canada, the situation is very different. There are no grand juries and, to our knowledge, prosecutors have not pressured researchers to yield the identity of research participants who have disclosed information about their own criminal activity. And we have not yet found an example of a corporation involved in high-stakes litigation dragging a Canadian researcher into court. Indeed, we can find just one instance where the threat of compelled disclosure has arisen. The case involved a coroner's court and Simon Fraser University (SFU) criminology graduate student Russel Ogden, whose MA thesis included interviews with people who had witnessed or assisted in the suicides and euthanasia of persons with AIDS.

When he submitted his ethics application to the SFU Research Ethics Review Committee, Ogden made it clear that he proposed to provide "absolute confidentiality" to his participants. How else could research with persons potentially facing first degree murder charges be conducted? The university ethics committee approved the proposal.

After a local newspaper published an article on the research, the Vancouver Coroner subpoenaed Ogden and a journalist to attend an inquest into the death of an "unknown female" who may have been one of Ogden's subjects. Ogden appeared but refused to reveal the identity of any of his participants, whereupon the Coroner threatened to take action against him for contempt of court. Ogden's lawyers argued that his research met the Wigmore criteria, a common law test that Canadian courts use to adjudicate claims of privilege, which we describe later in this article. In the end, the Coroner acknowledged the public interest privilege that made Ogden's research possible and released him "from any stain or suggestion of contempt" (*Inquest of Unknown Female,* 20 October 1994, oral reasons for judgment of the Honourable L. W. Campbell, 91-240-0838, Burnaby, B.C., p. 10).

The Simon Fraser University Research Ethics Controversy

Although Ogden won the day in Coroner's court, the experience set in motion a prolonged controversy at SFU over the university's treatment of Ogden and subsequent changes to the university's research ethics policy. It took an internal inquiry and the caustic comments of a judge to resolve the controversy over the administration's treatment of Ogden (Lowman & Palys, 2000). In 1998, the university president apologized to Ogden for the university's failure to appear on his behalf in court, paid his legal fees and lost wages, and undertook to represent other researchers should they ever find themselves in the same predicament. The controversy over changes to the ethics policy proved more difficult to resolve.

The controversy about the ethics policy revolved around a "limited confidentiality consent statement" that university administrators and the ethics committee imposed in order to ensure that there would not be a repeat of the problems that they perceived to have been caused by Ogden's guarantee of absolute confidentiality (Lowman & Palys, 1998a). A new "screening" question was added to the ethics review application form asking, "Does information to be obtained from subjects include information on activities that are or may be in violation of criminal or civil law?" Applicants who answered in the affirmative—mostly criminologists—were required to tell participants, "Any information that is obtained during this study will be kept confidential to the full extent permitted by law.... It is possible as a result of legal action the researcher may be required to divulge information obtained in the course of this research to a court or other legal body." Framed in this way, the statement had a severe impact on certain kinds of criminological research. What kind of prospective participants would talk to a researcher about their offenses if they thought that the researcher would hand the information to a court so that they could be prosecuted?

When pressed about the ethics of this approach, the vice president for research gave three justifications for use of the limited confidentiality consent statement:

1. Because researcher-participant privilege is not recognized in Canadian statutory law, there is no point in challenging a subpoena.

2. Researchers are "not above the law of the land" and the University cannot condone law breaking because it must respect the Rule of Law. Consequently, the university cannot approve an unlimited guarantee of confidentiality because it implies that a researcher would deliberately break the law by refusing to comply with a court order to disclose confidential research information.

3. Therefore, in the interest of informed consent, it is necessary to warn prospective participants of the legal limits to confidentiality. (Clayman, 1997; testimony in *Russel Ogden v. Simon Fraser University,* 1998)

We refer to this doctrine as the "law of the land" or *caveat emptor* approach to research ethics. It put criminologists and researchers from several other disciplines in a catch-22 situation, because the SFU research ethics policy also says, "There is a professional responsibility of researchers to adhere to the ethical norms and codes of conduct appropriate to their own disciplines." No North American ethics code that we know of absolutely subordinates research ethics to the law of confidentiality, including the disciplinary codes that apply to our own research fields, criminology and sociology.

Consequently, several SFU criminologists refused to use the limited confidentiality consent statement, on the following grounds:

1. It abrogates the researcher's ethical responsibility to do everything legally possible to protect research participants from harm. As we demonstrate below, academic researchers *can* use a case-by-case analysis in common law to assert privilege, as Ogden did.

2. Far from satisfying the requirements of informed consent, the limited confidentiality consent statement provides information only about the *legal* limit of confidentiality. It says nothing about the researcher's *ethical* stand, because it assumes that law establishes the ethical limit.

3. Although researchers are not above the law of the land, many social science ethics codes recognize that the researcher's primary

professional obligation in the last instant is to ethics, not law. Consequently, in those rare circumstances where law and ethics conflict, researchers must oppose compelled disclosure if it creates an ethical conflict.

As the ensuing discussion demonstrates, this "ethics-first" position is based on the disciplinary norms and standards of various disciplinary ethics codes and on the *Tri-Council Policy Statement,* the new national ethics code created by Canada's three federal research funding agencies (Canadian Institutes of Health Research, Natural Sciences and Engineering Research Council, & Social Sciences and Humanities Research Council, 1998). Although the ethics-first position holds that, in the last instance, law must be subordinated to ethics, the researcher's goal nevertheless should be to avoid ever having to violate a court order to disclose confidential information. The ethical and legal strategy that we present next is designed to do just that and, in the process, to maximize the legal protections available for research participants.

RESEARCH CONFIDENTIALITY: THE CRIMINOLOGICAL TRADITION

Reflecting on the obvious threat that U.S. courts and grand juries posed to research participants and the integrity of research, Marvin Wolfgang wrote a series of articles (1976, 1981, 1982) outlining the appropriate ethical response. Wolfgang summarized the criminologist's ethical responsibility to maintain confidentiality in this way:

> [The researcher] is a neutral, disinterested recipient of data collected only for scientific research purposes. The purpose for obtaining the information is to aid the scholarly enterprise and to provide guidance for a rational social policy. Data obtained that could have direct untoward consequences to subjects are not the possession of the state but of science. . . . The social scientist is not a representative of any branch of government with an obligation to execute certain police or judicial duties. (1981, p. 351)

In a subsequent section entitled "What should a research center do if the police, prosecutor or court requests the files?" Wolfgang states, "Our position is clear: we would not honor the request. We would make every effort, short of using aggressive force, to prevent the files from being examined or taken from the Center's premises. We would, if necessary, enter into litigation to protect the confidentiality of the records" (pp. 352-353). He adds that, even if a researcher were to be charged as an accessory or with contempt, "we would still maintain a posture of unwillingness to reveal names" (p. 353).

In fact, in the U.S. the general response of researchers to threats to confidentiality from third parties, be they agents of the state or private litigants, has been precisely the approach that Wolfgang outlined: resistance, resistance, resistance. They have been aided in this task by their respective disciplinary associations, who have contributed by filing *amicus curiae* briefs in court[4] and have developed codes of ethics that make it clear that researchers have an ethical obligation to maintain confidentiality unless the research participant wishes to waive that right. If its Draft Code is accepted, ASC will have institutionalized that approach in criminology, as ACJS already has.

The Rights and Interests of Researchers

Researchers have personal and collective interests beyond their ethical obligation to protect research participants. They have a broad interest in protecting academic freedom in order to maintain independence from both corporations and the state. Also, they have an interest in protecting unpublished data in order to maintain priority and timeliness of publication and would rather not deplete resources responding to expansive and time-consuming subpoenas.

Courts have been sensitive to these concerns— when researchers have both articulated them and presented evidence to document them— because the judiciary appears to attach a high social value to the role of research in advancing public knowledge. Several court decisions include strong statements about the social value of research and the need to protect academic freedom. For example, the court of appeals characterized Dow Chemical's subpoena *(Dow Chemical v. Allen,* 1982) as a threat of "substantial intrusion into the exercise of university research . . . capable of chilling the exercise of academic freedom," which would "inevitably tend to check the ardor and fearlessness of scholars." The court quashed the subpoena. Similarly, in its decision to quash Microsoft's subpoena of Cusumano and Yoffie, the court stated that "allowing Microsoft to obtain the notes, tapes, and transcripts it covets would hamstring not only the respondents' future research efforts but also those of other similarly situated scholars. This loss of theoretical insight into the business world is of concern in and of itself. Even more importantly, compelling the disclosure of such research materials would infrigidate the free flow of information to the public, thus denigrating a fundamental First Amendment value" *(In re Michael A. Cusumano and David B. Yoffie,* 1998, p. 9). Given that Microsoft's market capitalization dropped by tens of billions of dollars when Judge Jackson issued his initial opinion, the court's protection of Cusumano and Yoffie's research participants stands as powerful testimony to the value that it placed on research.

In other instances, it is hardly surprising that courts have ordered researchers to produce information that does not identify research participants. Researchers should be accountable for the information that they disseminate. If their findings are relevant to the adjudication of a case and are not available elsewhere, then the party disadvantaged by that information has as much right to challenge the researcher's methodology and interpretive validity as the opposing party has to introduce it.

Generally speaking, the courts have balanced these obligations of researchers with a concern for safeguarding academic freedom. In particular, courts have been especially likely to protect researchers when a subpoena appears to be part of a strategy of harassment, when the researcher is independent, when the party issuing the subpoena has not clearly demonstrated its relevance, and when other sources of information are available to speak to the issue at hand (Crabb, 1996; Wiggins & McKenna, 1996).

At the same time, the information that researchers are asked to disclose would not exist in the first place were it not for the researchers' pledge of confidentiality. Consequently, while researchers have a duty to inform courts about the knowledge that they produce, they also are obliged not to harm research participants in the process, and the courts have consistently respected that obligation.

The Rights and Interests of Research Participants

When U.S. courts have compelled researchers to disclose information, they typically have ordered *partial* disclosure, where the part being protected is research participant identity. For example, in *Deitchman v. E. R Squibb & Sons, Inc.* (1984), Dr. Herbst was ordered to testify and to produce documentation from his confidential data registry. But the court also ordered that the names of the women in the registry be redacted (Crabb, 1996, pp. 10-12). Similarly, in *In re American Tobacco Company* (1989a, 1989b), Dr. Selikoff was ordered to testify and to produce data tapes for the courts, but with participant names redacted (Wiggins & McKenna, 1996, p. 70). In the *Exxon Valdez* case, the court directed Dr. Picou to show his field notes to a sociologist hired by Exxon, but the court warned the Exxon sociologist that he would be held in contempt if he violated the confidentiality of Picon's respondents (Picou, 1996).

The biggest challenge to research confidentiality will come when a criminal defendant's right to a fair trial is pitted against researcher-participant privilege. The only case we have found that came close to doing so involved Richard Leo's observation of police interrogation practices (1995). A public defender subpoenaed Leo as a percipient witness during a felony court criminal trial, seeking his field notes and testimony regarding one of the interrogations that he observed. After attempting to get the subpoena quashed, Leo complied with the judge's order to testify. Leo has publicly stated (1995) that he will "always regret that decision" and that, for the sake of the integrity of the research enterprise, he should have refused to testify.

We suggest that Leo's concern was misplaced and emerged largely because of failure to distinguish the locus of privilege. If "researcher privilege" were at issue, then Leo's regret would be understandable to the extent that he allowed a court order to thwart what would be seen as his professional obligation. However, as is the case with attorney-client privilege, where the privilege is that of the *client* and *not* the lawyer, researcher-participant privilege should be seen to lie not primarily with the researcher but with the research *participant*. The ACJS Code of Ethics recognizes this important distinction by asserting that "subjects of research are entitled to rights of personal confidentiality unless they are waived" (p. 14). It turns out that Leo's was a false ethical dilemma. He reports that his police officer participants actually *wanted* him to testify because they believed, as did he, that his eyewitness testimony would corroborate their view of the interrogation. Understanding that the privilege was *theirs* and not his would have led Leo to ask them whether they wanted to waive privilege; presumably in this case the answer would have been "yes" and the ethical dilemma would have been resolved.

Because Leo chose to testify, the question of privilege in that case was not the subject of a legal decision, leaving open the question of what the courts would do if researcher-participant privilege conflicted with a defendant's right to a fair trial. No doubt the resolution would depend on the particular interests at stake in the case, if indeed the matter ever arose in court. If during the course of research a researcher were to discern convincing evidence that an individual was being falsely accused, the researcher would likely have to wrestle with the ethical issues involved well before any court issued a subpoena.

There are only three cases where courts have ordered researchers to divulge participant names or information that could be linked to them: two grand jury cases *(Popkin* and *Scarce)* and *Atlantic Sugar, Ltd. v. United States* (1980). One noteworthy point about each of these cases is that, for a variety of reasons, the researchers in question would have had a hard time satisfying the first Wigmore criterion. For example, neither Popkin nor Scarce was able to demonstrate that their communications with particular individuals were confidential, a problem that may well have been alleviated had their research protocols anticipated the evidentiary requirements of the Wigmore test (Palys & Lowman, in press). The *Atlantic Sugar* case raises an entirely different issue, which relates to the problems created by a priori limitations of confidentiality, which we consider next.

Should Confidentiality Ever Be Limited?

The essence of the ASA code on which the ASC and ACJS codes are based is that researchers should know the law that is relevant to their research, only make promises that they are willing to maintain, and be forthright with research participants about what they are promising. Consequently, ASA obliges researchers to discuss confidentiality as well as any factors that "may limit or alter guarantees of confidentiality" (ASA Code of Ethics 1997, section 11.02(a)) that are made to research participants. One such factor is the unanticipated discovery of serious prospective harm. A higher ethic might cause a researcher to violate a guarantee of confidentiality in order to prevent loss of life or serious bodily harm. But is this possibility a reason to limit confidentiality *a priori*? We suggest that there is a defensible ethical position that the answer is "no," although there may well be a reason to *violate* a guarantee of confidentiality, depending on the research and the pledge that is made.

Is There a General Duty to Report Crime?

One concern that deserves attention in any consideration of the law regarding confidentiality is the proposition that researchers who learn about civil or criminal offenses are *required* to disclose such information to the authorities. Historically, a citizen who failed to report a felony was responsible for "misprision of felony" in common law. Indeed, in the United States Code, misprision of felony is still an offense: "Whoever, having knowledge of the actual commission of a felony cognizable by a court of the United States, conceals and does not as soon as possible make known the same to some judge or other person in civil or military authority under the United States, shall be fined under this title or imprisoned not more than three years, or both" (Title 18, § 4).

Had the courts construed misprision of felony broadly, the chilling effect on ethnographic and other kinds of field research would have been so great that many of the sociological classics of the twentieth century could not have been written. But in U.S. jurisprudence the phrase "conceals and does . . . not make known" has been construed quite narrowly. As Teitelbaum (1983, p. 21) explains, "the essence of the crime lies in the commission of acts that impede, rather than in omission to aid, the administration of justice." In other words, silence alone does not constitute misprision of felony. Of course, as Teitelbaum warns, because some states also have misprision statutes, researchers in the U.S. should also familiarize themselves with relevant state law and jurisprudence.

Mandatory Reporting Laws

Although there is no general duty to report crime, there are some offense-specific mandatory reporting laws. They vary across state jurisdictions, sometimes including and sometimes exempting researchers, and include reporting of child and elder abuse. In some jurisdictions reporting of venereal disease also is mandatory.

Mandatory reporting laws create a difficult dilemma for researchers. On the one hand, we all have an ethical responsibility to protect each other from the harms that are the subject of mandatory reporting laws. However, persons conducting research with the intention of reporting offenses that they can anticipate hearing about would appear to be self-consciously building a law-enforcement role into their research. They might consider seeking a reporting exemption from state authorities. If they do not secure an exemption and if they can anticipate learning of activities that are the subject of mandatory reporting laws but feel that the value underlying the mandatory reporting law outweighs the value of the research, then they should not conduct the research. If they feel that the value of the research outweighs the value underlying the mandatory reporting law and the research is not protected by a research shield law, they should make an unlimited guarantee of confidentiality and stick to it. If they do not anticipate discovering activities falling under the ambit of mandatory reporting laws, they may treat such discovery as an instance of unanticipated "heinous discovery."

CONCLUSION

Most contemporary disciplinary ethics codes recognize that law may conflict with the researcher's ethical obligation to protect confidential research information, particularly the identity of research participants, and call on researchers to anticipate these problems by becoming familiar with the laws of evidentiary privilege that apply to their conduct as researchers. The purpose of the current article has been to facilitate this understanding by providing a general introduction to U.S. and Canadian law relating to researcher-participant privilege and contrasting the experience of researchers in the two countries. The article identifies the various statutes and common law tests applicable to researcher-participant privilege and considers the advantages and disadvantages of research-participant shield laws as opposed to the case-by-case analysis that occurs when researchers use common law to assert evidentiary privilege.

We suggest that in the U.S. researchers should apply for confidentiality or privacy certification whenever their research is eligible for it and should campaign for expansion of the areas of research that are eligible for such protection. In lieu of this protection, they should familiarize themselves with state laws and design their research so as to maximize their chances of satisfying the evidentiary criteria laid out in the Wigmore test.

In Canada, because there is no statutory protection for researchers other than the provisions of the *Statistics Act,* which apply only to Statistics Canada employees, researchers should encourage the legislature to introduce confidentiality certification. Until such legislation is in place, they should design their research with the Wigmore test in mind, as it is the only device that they have for protecting confidential research information in court.

REFERENCES

Alexander, L. (1983). Proposed legislation to improve statistical and research access to federal records. In R. F. Boruch & J. S. Cecil (Eds.), *Solutions to ethical and legal problems in social research* (pp. 273-292). New York: Academic Press.

Atlantic Sugar, Ltd. v. U.S., 85 Cust. Ct. 128 (1980).

Bond, K. (1978). Confidentiality and the protection of human subjects in social science research: A report on recent developments. *The American Sociologist, 13,*144-152.

Brajuha, M., & Hallowell, L. (1986). Legal intrusion and the politics of field work: The impact of the Brajuha case. *Urban Life, 14,*454-478.

Canadian Institutes of Health Research, Natural Sciences and Engineering Research Council, & Social Sciences and Humanities Research Council. (1998). *Tri-council policy statement: Ethical conduct for research involving humans.*

Ottawa, Canada: Department of Supply and Services. Available: http://www.sshrc.ca/english/programinfo/policies/index.htm.

Caroll, J., & Knerr, C. (1973). Confidentiality of social science research sources and data: The Popkin case. *Political Science Quarterly, 6,*268-280.

Caroll, J., & Knerr, C. (1975). A report of the APSA confidentiality in social science research data project. *Political Science Quarterly, 8,*258-261.

Cecil, J., & Wetherington, G. T. (Eds.). (1996). Court ordered disclosure of academic research: A clash of values of science and law [Special issue]. *Law and Contemporary Problems, 59,* 1-191.

Clayman, B. (1997, October 30). The law of the land. *Simon Fraser News,* p. 5.

Comarow, M. (1993, December 15). Are sociologists above the law? *The Chronicle of Higher Education,* A44.

Cotchett, J. W., & Elkind, A.B. (1993). *Federal courtroom evidence* (3rd ed.). New York: Butterworth.

Crabb, B. B. (1996). Judicially compelled disclosure of researchers' data: A judge's view. *Law and Contemporary Problems, 59,* 9-34.

Daisley, B. (1994, December 9). Clear evidence needed to invoke Wigmore rules. *The Lawyer's Weekly,* p. 28.

Deitchman v. E. R. Squibb & Sons, Inc., 740 F.2d 556 (7th Cir. 1984).

Dow Chemical Co. v. Allen, 672 F.2d 1262 (7th Cir. 1982).

Fanning, J. (1999). *Privacy and research: Public policy issues,* unpublished manuscript, Office of the Assistant Secretary for Planning and Evaluation, United States Department of Health and Human Services.

Fischer, P. M. (1996). Science and subpoenas: When do the courts become instruments of manipulation? *Law and Contemporary Problems, 59,* 159-168.

Friedson, E., (1976). The legal protection of social research; Criteria for definition. In P. Nejelski (Ed.), *Social research in conflict with law and ethics* (pp. 123-137). Cambridge, MA: Ballinger.

In re American Tobacco Co., 866 F.2d 552 (2nd Cir. 1989a).

In re American Tobacco Co., 880 F.2d 1520 (2nd Cir. 1989b).

In re Grand Jury Proceedings. James Richard Scarce, 5 F3d 397 (9th Cir. 1993).

In re Grand Jury Subpoena Dtd. January 4,750 F.2d 223 (2nd Cir. 1984).

In re Michael A. Cusumano and David B. Yoffie [United States of America v. Microsoft Corporation], No. 98-2133, United States Court of Appeals for the First Circuit (1998). Available: http://www.law.emory.edu/lcircuit/dec98/98-2133.01ahtml

Inquest of Unknown Female, 91-240-0838, Burnaby, B.C. (1994).

Iutcovich, J., Hoppe, S., Kennedy, J., & Levine, F. J. (1999). Confidentiality and the ASA Code of Ethics: A response from COPE. *Footnotes, 27,* 5.

Jaffee v. Redmond, 518 U.S.I (1996).

Lempert, R. O., & Saltzburg, S. A. (1982). *A modern approach to evidence: Text, problems, transcripts, and cases* (2nd ed.). St. Paul, MN: West Publishing Company.

Leo, R. (1995). Trial and tribulations: Courts, ethnography, and the need for an evidentiary privilege for academic researchers. *American Sociologist, 26,* 113-133.

Levine, F., & Kennedy, J. M. (1999). Promoting a scholar's privilege: Accelerating the pace. *Law and Social Inquiry, 24,* 967-976.

Lowman, J., & Palys, T. S. (1998a). *The history of limited confidentiality at SFU.* Submission prepared for the SFU Ethics Review Policy Revision Task Force. Available: http://www.sfu.ca/~palys/history.htm.

Lowman, J., & Palys, T.S. (1998b, June). When research ethics and law conflict. *CAUT Bulletin,* pp. 6-7.

Lowman, J., & Palys, T. S. (1999, February). Confidentiality and the 1997 ASA *Code of Ethics:* A query. *Footnotes,* p. 5.

Lowman, J., & Palys, T. S. (2000). Ethics and institutional conflict of interest: The research confidentiality controversy at Simon Fraser University. *Sociological Practice, 2,* 245-264.

Madden, T. J., & Lessin, H. S. (1983), Statutory approaches to ensuring the privacy and confidentiality of social science research information: The Law Enforcement Assistance Administration experience. In R. F. Boruch & J. S. Cecil (Eds.), *Solutions to ethical and legal problems in social research* (pp. 263-272). New York; Academic Press.

Marshall, M. (1992). *When is a secret not a secret?* Available: http://www.cookdukecox.com/newsletters/issue6-1992/secret.htm.

McLaughlin, R. H. (1999). From the field to the courthouse: Should social science research be privileged? *Law and Social Inquiry, 24,* 927-966.

Moynihan, D. (1999). Thomas Jefferson Researcher's Privilege Act of 1999. Available: http://www.senate.gov/member/ny/moynihan/general/072699b.htm.

Nejelski, P., & Finsterbusch, K. (1973). The prosecutor and the researcher: Present and prospective variations on the Supreme Court's Branzburg decision. *Social Problems, 21,* 3-21.

Nejelski, P., & Peyser, H. (1976). A proposed researcher's shield statute: Text and summary of commentary. In P. Nejelski (Ed.), *Social research in conflict with law and ethics* (pp. 163-187). Cambridge, MA: Ballinger Publishing Company.

Nelson, R. I., & Hedrick, T. E. (1983). The statutory protection of confidential research data; Synthesis and evaluation. In R. F. Boruch & J. S. Cecil (Eds.), *Solutions to ethical and legal problems in social research* (pp. 213-238). New York: Academic Press.

O'Neil, R, M. (1996). A researcher's privilege: Does any hope remain? *Law and Contemporary Problems, 15,* 35-50.

Palys, T. S., & Lowman, J. (2000). Ethical and legal strategies for protecting confidential research information. *Canadian Journal of Law and Society, 15,* 39-80.

Palys, T. S., & Lowman, J. (in press). Anticipating law: Research methods, ethics and the common law of privilege. *Sociological Methodology,*

People v. Newman, 345 N.Y.S. 2d 502 (N.Y. Ct App. 1973).

Picou, J. S. (1996). Compelled disclosure of scholarly research: Some comments on "high stakes" litigation. *Law and Contemporary Problems, 59,* 149-157.

Privacy Protection Study Commission. (1977). *Personal privacy in an information society.* Washington, DC: U.S. Government Printing Office.

R. v. Gruenke, 3 S.C.R. 263 (1991).

R. J. Reynolds Tobacco Co. v. Fischer, 427 S.E, 2d810(Ga. Ct. App. 1993).

Richards of Rockford, Inc. v. Pacific Gas and Electric Co., 71 F.R.D. 388 (N.D. Cal. 1976).

Russel Ogden v. Simon Fraser University. Burnaby Registry of the British Columbia Provincial Court: Case No. 26780(1998). Text of the decision available: http://www.sfu.ca/~palys/steinbrg.htm.

Scarce, R. (1994). (No)trial (but) tribulations: When courts and ethnography conflict. *Journal of Contemporary Ethnography, 23,* 123-149.

Scarce, R. (1999). Good faith, bad ethics: When scholars go the distance and scholarly associations do not. *Law and Social Inquiry, 24,* 977-986.

Smith v. Jones, I S.C.R. 455 (1999).

Sopinka, J., Lederman, S. N., & Bryant, A. W. (1992). *The law of evidence in Canada.* Toronto: Butterworth.

Teitelbaum, L. E. (1983). Spurious, tractable and intractable legal problems: A positivist approach to law and social science research. In R, F. Boruch & J. S. Cecil (Eds.), *Solutions to ethical and legal problems in social research* (pp. 11-48). New York: Academic Press.

Traynor, M. (1996). Countering the excessive subpoena for scholarly research. *Law and Contemporary Problems, 59,* 119-148.

U.S. Census Bureau. (1999). *Confidentiality: No sharing of census data.* Los Angeles: Regional Office. Wiggins, E. D., & McKenna, J. A. (1996). Researchers' reactions to compelled disclosure of scientific information. *Law and Contemporary Problems, 59,* 67-94.

Wigmore, J. H. (1905). *A treatise on the system of evidence in trials at common law. Including the statutes and judicial decisions of all jurisdictions of the United States, England, and Canada.* Boston: Little, Brown and Company.

Wolfgang, M. (1976). Ethical issues of research in criminology, In P. Nejelski (Ed.), *Social research in conflict with ethics and the law* (pp. 25-34). Cambridge, MA: Ballinger Publishing Company.

Wolfgang, M. (1981). Criminology: Confidentiality in criminological research and other ethical issues. *Journal of Criminal Law and Criminology, 72,* 345-361.

Wolfgang, M. (1982). Ethics and research. In F. Elliston & N. Bowie (Eds.), *Ethics, public policy, and criminal Justice research* (pp. 391-418). Cambridge, MA: Oelgeschlager, Gunn, and Hain, Publishers, Inc.

DISCUSSION QUESTIONS

1. What do Lowman and Palys argue is missing from the ASC (American Society of Criminology) and ACJS (Academy of Criminal Justice Sciences) codes of ethics?

2. What do these authors suggest in regard to the collection of data related to criminal behavior if researchers want to avoid third-party intrusion?

3. Of the potential conflicts between research ethics and the law, which do these authors say poses the greatest threat to criminologists?

4. Are law enforcement officials the only entity that has been interested in gaining access to data collected by researchers?

5. How do Canada and the United States differ on these issues?

6. Describe the rights and interests of both researchers and research participants in these issues about confidentiality. What should researchers be accountable for? What is most often protected?

7. What do these authors say about the duty to report crimes and how this duty affects a researcher's ability to conduct research?

8. Ultimately, what do researchers have to decide between when conducting research on criminal behavior?

RESEARCH READING

A topic of concern in criminological research involving human subjects is always how to design and conduct studies that can advance knowledge of phenomena while, at the same time, afford safety and protection to subjects. This article provides information regarding ethical conduct in research with vulnerable participants, namely research that includes interviewing subjects who have been victims of partner violence. Logan and colleagues discuss ethical concerns regarding the recruitment of subjects for studies of sensitive topics. More specifically, they provide information on approaches that have dual purposes of enhancing ethical protection of subjects and assisting with recruitment strategies of subjects in both rural and urban settings. Their study reveals that ethical considerations, specifically in the case of partner violence victimization, does not hinder but may, in fact, enhance recruitment of subjects for study.

COMBINING ETHICAL CONSIDERATIONS
—————— WITH RECRUITMENT AND FOLLOW-UP STRATEGIES ——————
FOR PARTNER VIOLENCE VICTIMIZATION RESEARCH

TK Logan, Robert Walker, Lisa Shannon, and Jennifer Cole

Abstract: In general, the literature on research ethics and the literature on recruitment and retention of research participants tend to be separated by different purposes and principles. This article uses multiple methods to compile information about research ethics with vulnerable participants as well as with recruitment and follow-up strategies, including (a) literature reviews, (b) key informant interviews, (c) focus group interviews, (d) a pilot study to test ideas for study implementation, and (e) documentation of recruitment and follow-up efforts for a longitudinal study of 757 women with partner violence victimization experiences. This article shows how considering research ethics may actually enhance recruitment and follow-up strategies with women experiencing partner violence victimization.

INTRODUCTION

One question that typically emerges in planning research on other sensitive topics is how to design and implement meaningful studies while considering safety and protection of human participants (Azar, 2002; Lynn & Nelson, 2005; Oakes, 2002; Sieber, 1998), especially when the design includes interviews with survivors of partner violence. Within the last 15 years there have been several papers and reports disseminated to the research community about recruitment and follow-up of women with partner violence victimization experiences (e.g., Dutton et al., 2003; Rumptz, Sullivan, Davidson, & Basta, 1991; Sullivan, Rumptz, Campbell, Eby, & Davidson, 1996). Furthermore, the general literature on recruitment and follow-up of behavioral research participants is considerable and can be also applied to partner violence studies (e.g., Brown, Long, & Milliken, 2002; Brown-Peterside et al., 2001;

Source: Logan, T. K., Walker, R., Shannon, L., & Cole, J. (2008). Combining ethical considerations with recruitment and follow-up strategies for partner violence victimization research, *Violence Against Women, 14*(11), 1226–1251. Copyright © 2008 Sage Publications.

Cotter, Burke, Loeber, Navratil, 2002; Hall et al., 2003; Hough, Tarke, Renker, Shields, & Glatstein, 1996; Ribisl et al., 1996). Although ethical issues were not addressed explicitly in many of these articles, they were implicitly addressed. However, the literature on research ethics and the literature on recruitment and retention of research participants tend to be separated by different purposes and principles. This separation makes it difficult to see how careful attention to research ethics can enhance the methodological rigor of behavioral research.

More specifically, when studying sensitive topics such as partner violence victimization, it is easy to envision potential harm related to participation. This concern, for example, may result in overly constrained outreach and follow-up procedures with victims to reduce a variety of possible risks. On the other hand, when examining the research methodology literature, there is strong encouragement to use assertive methods to recruit and follow up participants because of the threats to generalizability and the robustness of findings resulting from low recruitment and follow-up rates. Hence, there is a gap in the literature on how to bridge the ethical with methodologically effective follow-up strategies.

Using a variety of methods including process and quantitative measures on the implementation of a major longitudinal study of women with partner violence victimization experiences, this article provides information on approaches to consider that enhance ethical protections as well as the recruitment and follow-up strategies for a community-based research study. Specifically, the article describes the processes used to develop recruitment and follow-up strategies with women who had experienced partner violence in rural ($n = 378$) and urban ($n = 379$) environments as well as the outcomes of those strategies. The overall intent of this article is to increase awareness of how ethical considerations can potentially enhance recruitment and follow-up of research participants.

METHOD

Procedure

This study used several methods to compile information about ethical conduct in research with vulnerable participants as well as recruitment and follow-up strategies, including (a) literature reviews, (b) key informant interviews, (c) focus group interviews, (d) a pilot study to test implementation ideas, and (e) documentation of recruitment and follow-up efforts in a large, longitudinal study of partner violence victims. It should be noted that all of the methods (except the literature reviews) were approved by the University of Kentucky Human Subjects Internal Review Board.

Literature review. Literature on human behavioral research ethics was reviewed in addition to the literature on recruiting and maintaining contact with behavioral research study participants and specifically for recruitment and follow-up of women who had experienced violence by an intimate partner. In addition, literature on rural areas was examined to better understand contextual differences that can dramatically affect study recruitment and follow-up rates.

Key informant interviews. Victim service representatives, mental health providers, and judges in the rural and urban areas targeted for the specific study were interviewed. This step was conducted to increase protocol sensitivity to protective issues as well as cultural factors that could affect participant responses to recruitment or follow-up procedures. These interviews were done informally as the study implementation began to ensure a smooth study implementation in the targeted communities. While doing these interviews, interviewees were generous in providing advice about ensuring successful study implementation and follow-up.

Focus groups. A series of focus groups were conducted to generate a better understanding of the rural and urban areas targeted and key informant ideas about research participation, perception of risks, and steps that might be important to reduce risks (Logan, Evans, Stevenson, & Jordan, 2005; Logan, Shannon, & Walker, 2005; Logan, Stevenson, Evans, & Leukefeld, 2004).

Focus groups were conducted with 128 female volunteers, all of whom were over the age of 18 and did not have current protective orders against a male intimate partner. A total of eight community focus groups were conducted, two in an urban county *(n = 30)* and two each in three selected rural counties *(n = 98)*. Women were recruited for focus groups using advertisements in the local newspaper, radio public service announcements, and flyers placed at bus stops, laundromats, grocery stores, libraries, coffee shops, bookstores, and other key community locations. Informed consent was obtained from all participants, and women were told that they would be asked to discuss a variety of topics related to violence against women. Discussion specifically regarding research in the focus groups was guided by three major questions: (a) What would make you feel safe to talk to a researcher about your experiences? (b) What kind of ad (newspaper, radio, or television) would you be most likely to respond to by calling about the study? and (c) What would the ad need to say in order to make you feel safe to participate in a study about violence against women? In addition, 30 women were recruited for focus group participation through rape crisis centers using key contacts at each center. Three groups were conducted in one rural county *(n = 18)* and three were conducted in two urban counties *(n = 12)*. The focus groups provided an opportunity to both refine the ethical dimensions (protection from undue risk of harm and freedom of choice) of the study and develop, improve, and tailor research study recruitment and follow-up strategies.

Pilot study. A small pilot study was conducted with 8 rural women and 15 urban women to examine women's perceptions of the proposed study recruitment procedures in the selected rural and urban areas, interview content, and the time to complete interviews (Logan, Walker, Cole, Ratliff, & Leukefeld, 2003). This pilot study guided the protocol development for the larger longitudinal study and directed attention to possible differences in recruitment and/or follow-up in the two areas.

Analysis

Qualitative information from the key informant interviews, focus groups, and pilot study interviews were categorized into themes to illustrate relevant issues related to recruitment and/or follow-up. Interviewer logs of contact attempts were coded, entered into SPSS, and analyzed with descriptive and bivariate statistics for rural and urban comparisons. In addition, locating and interview completion strategies and characteristics of participants were examined for those classified into the minimal effort, moderate effort, and intensive effort groups based on the locator effort index score to complete the follow-up interview. Results from five main methods are synthesized in this article to provide qualitative and quantitative information about research ethics considerations combined with recruitment and follow-up strategies for rural and urban women in partner violence victimization research.

RESULTS

Results of Literature Review, Key Informant Interviews, Focus Groups, Pilot Interview, and Documentation of Recruitment And Follow-Up Efforts

Basic research ethics relies on the three guiding Belmont principles (Brody & Waldron, 2000; National Science Foundation [NSF], 2006). The first principle, beneficence, involves maximizing possible benefits while minimizing possible harms to participants and society. The second principle is respect for persons, which includes providing adequate and comprehensive information about the research study and any risks likely to occur in comprehensible language as well as providing participants with the opportunity to choose what will and will not happen to them. This principle implies that considering culture and norms and allowing participants the maximum degree of control over interview conditions while still maintaining research integrity is critical. And the third principle, justice, means the research is fair and does not exploit or ignore one group to benefit another. Adhering to the justice principle also includes sensitivity to cultural conditions to ensure results are interpreted within the appropriate cultural contexts.

Within this context, nine key themes emerged across the five different methods that were important to consider in research ethics as well as community-based research with partner violence victims: (a) community collaboration, (b) emphasizing study participation benefits, (c) consideration of transportation and child care, (d) consideration of partner issues, (e) increasing participant comfort, (f) ensuring participant understanding of the research process and goals, (g) considering the necessity and challenges of home visits, (h) interviewer flexibility, and (i) participant safety and data quality monitoring.

Community Collaboration. There were three main subthemes that emerged within this overall theme: (a) awareness and credibility of the study, (b) issues of trust related to the community context in the rural area, and (c) correct interpretation of results.

Women in the focus groups emphasized that the awareness, credibility, and reputation of the study would be enhanced if victim service agencies knew about the study. Building community collaboration and ensuring all the key agencies were aware of and comfortable with the study would increase the likelihood of secondary referrals to the study, it is also possible that women thinking about participating would ask others in the community (e.g., victim advocates) about the study before deciding to participate.

In addition, community-specific service referrals were a key part of the study protocol and were given to each participant at the end of the study. Community collaboration was beneficial in this aspect because study staff had personal contact with the referral resource agencies that participants might use. It became clear from the focus groups that women did not just want referrals in terms of phone numbers; they prefer more information about the agencies to which they are being referred. Thus, to verify the accuracy of the information, all research staff members were required to network with the agencies, learn about and visit those agencies, and periodically call the phone numbers of the referrals that we were giving to the women. Surprisingly, phone numbers to local services were sometimes changed or even disconnected, so calling all of the numbers at least twice a year was mandatory. In addition, it was surprising to be put on hold, for example, when calling the suicide hotline. So having more detailed information about the referrals interviewers were making was important. Providing women with accurate information on community resources is in line with the principle of beneficence by increasing the likelihood that women would obtain information that might benefit them.

A second major reason that community collaboration was critical to the success of our study had to do with issues of trust in the targeted rural area. The targeted rural area for this study was in Appalachia. The Appalachian rural areas have long distrusted outsiders because of their history of being negatively exploited by others, such as business (e.g., the coal industry), government, filmmakers, and researchers (Billings, Norman, & Ledford, 1999; Duncan, 1999). In addition, the targeted rural areas are characterized by extreme poverty (Appalachian Regional Commission, 2000; Duncan, 1999) and a high prevalence of drug use, including misuse of prescription narcotics. For example, during the time this particular study was being done the target rural areas had been under scrutiny by the national media for significant prescription drug abuse problems, including Oxycontin (Drug Enforcement Agency [DEA], 2003; "US NY: The Alchemy of Oxycontin," 2001; "US: Oxycontin Deaths Said to Be Up Sharply," 2002) and Lorcet, Lortob, Vicodin, Valium, and Xanax ("Addicted and Corrupted," 2003; "Agency OKs More Pills in Chase," 2003; "Drugs in This Story," 2003; "Drug Overdose Numbs Appalachian," 2003; "Lesser-Known Favorites Cheap, Abundant," 2003). In fact, Kentucky was ranked third in the nation at that time in terms of per capita prescriptions overall (Kaiser Family Foundation, 2001), and 10 eastern Kentucky counties were listed in the top seven areas receiving the most narcotics per capita from 1998 to 2001 (DEA, as cited in "Map of Narcotic Distribution in the U.S.," 2003). This historical context of lack of trust, focus on local drug problems by the media, and the negative media coverage often given to the Appalachian rural areas increased the need to work within the community rather than coming from the outside to do research. It also added to the need for increased sensitivity to research ethics to prevent harm or perceived harm resulting from the study procedures.

The third major reason for collaborating with each of the targeted communities was related to ensuring appropriate interpretation of study results. The community agencies were invited into the interpretive process to ensure the most accurate interpretations, as well as to provide feedback to the targeted communities. Sharing results with the community was also important in continuing to build trust and relationships within both the rural and urban communities. The victim advocacy groups were especially concerned about this because they believed that in the past researchers asked them for help and then disappeared without ever giving them anything in return. They were very interested in learning about the results of the studies that were conducted in their communities. Several strategies were used as part of the feedback process. As a strategy to maintain community collaboration throughout the duration of the study, newsletters containing some preliminary data results and other information regarding partner violence were sent to all of the key community agencies. These newsletters were sent two or three times a year throughout the duration of the study. Also, presentations were made to various key agencies throughout the duration of the project. This process contributed to the ethical principles of respect for persons and beneficence. Furthermore, presenting to specific agencies, especially in the rural areas, was appreciated because it is sometimes difficult for these agencies to get speakers who are willing to travel to their agency and to present to the small group of staff members. In addition, these presentations fulfilled an important educational requirement for staff in some of these agencies.

Study participation benefits. Women in the focus groups were clear that payment for participation was important because women were giving up their time to provide valuable information to researchers. On the other hand, focus group participants were also very clear that monetary compensation was not the only critical incentive to participation. In fact, women in the focus groups emphasized that letting participants know that the study might help other women in similar situations was critical to their motivation to participate; this more intrinsic motivation has also been noted by others (e.g., Hough et al., 1996; Ribisl et al., 1996). One focus group participant said, "The [recruitment] ad should be focused on the woman's voice being heard, making a difference, and helping other victims." Another woman said, "[It is important to tell women] how the information is being used, how it is helping others." Key informants stressed the principle of beneficence by stating that sharing the study findings may benefit society and that individual participants may take satisfaction in knowing how their information benefited others.

Transportation and child care. Any study that is to be successfully completed with women must consider transportation and child care. This became especially important in the rural areas targeted for the study. There was no public transportation system in any of the rural communities and many of the women did not have their own transportation (Logan et al., 2004; U.S. Department of Commerce, Bureau of the Census), in addition, there was either limited, unreliable, or no taxi service in the rural areas, which made travel to and from an interview location difficult for some women. Rural focus group participants suggested—which pilot interview participants confirmed—that women participating in our study would likely be driven to the interview by a relative, friend, or even a partner. Sometimes those partners would be waiting out in the parking lot for them, and sometimes women would have to leave because of the time constraints of their driver. Although this issue occasionally came up in the urban area, for the most part urban women had alternative options (e.g., bus, taxi), were more likely to have their own transportation, or were able to schedule an interview at a setting closer to their neighborhood because of the increased options in the more densely populated area (e.g., public libraries, a restaurant, a hospital).

Child care was another issue that had to be considered. In the rural areas especially, daycare centers were limited. Rural focus group participants warned us that not all men would be interested in watching the children while their partners went to an appointment. This in part is potentially related to the more rigid gender-role stereotypes perceived to be an issue in the rural areas (Fahnestock, 1992; Goeckermann et al., 1994; Logan et al., 2003). Another consideration mentioned in the research literature as a barrier to service utilization but that may also be relevant for research participation was that women may not feel comfortable leaving their children in the care of others, especially if they are concerned about their violent partner's access to and/or behavior toward the children (Logan, Cole, Shannon, & Walker, 2006). Hence, providing incentives to women who needed to make special provisions for child care became not only a practical matter but an ethical issue as well.

Partner issues. Attention to participant and interviewer safety is an important consideration

and it has been noted in the research literature (e.g., Dutton et al., 2003; Hall et al., 2003). Focus group members expressed concern about how women's participation in the study could pose a risk to their safety because it could potentially aggravate their partners' negative feelings. The focus groups advised using only female interviewers to reduce the likelihood of a male partner's jealousy. Focus group participants also suggested that male partners might interrogate participants about where they were going and what they were doing, and that this kind of negative partner reaction could be detrimental to a longitudinal study. In fact, while conducting the longitudinal study, several of the women we interviewed were being stalked and harassed while at the interviews (although overall this occurred to about 1% of participants).

With staff and participant safety in mind, several study-specific safety protocols were developed on the basis of key informant interviews and focus group suggestions. Some of the safety protocols included a neutral study title, constant communication between study staff about interview locations and status, sending two interviewers together (when possible) if the interview was to take place in the participant's home, and practicing what to do in situations that were potentially risky. In addition, interviewers were trained in how to maintain participant confidentiality while talking to various people about participants' whereabouts in preparing for follow-ups. Although these people's names were given by the participants themselves at baseline for us to contact in case the participants could not be reached at their primary address and phone number, it could still potentially be risky, which made careful planning and training critical in this process. Also, constant reinforcement of safety strategies and focus on them were important throughout the course of the study.

Participant comfort. Focus group members suggested strategies to increase participant comfort during a research interview. These suggestions included making sure the interviewer was friendly and did not act cold and/or uninterested, making sure to diminish possible stigma associated with victimization (e.g., the title of the study should be general rather than about specific problems or issues that were stigmatizing), making sure the interview area was private and comfortable, and providing participants with the choice of time and place. Choice of time and place was especially important for women's willingness to participate in the study, by increasing their comfort, and safety, as well as to effectively address child care and other scheduling considerations. This theme is especially relevant to the principle of respect for persons.

In the rural area, focus group participants emphasized the importance of confidentiality, pointing to the greater difficulty of maintaining confidentiality in smaller communities. The lack of confidentiality and privacy in the rural areas for receiving all kinds of services (e.g., mental health services, health services) was mentioned in the focus groups and it was also a concern about participation in a research study. At the same time, focus group participants believed that women would not be comfortable talking to someone who did not understand the rural area. Consequently, they suggested that interviewers be residents of the rural area, although not necessarily from the immediate area targeted for the study. This notion of matching the interviewer to participant characteristics has been noted in other publications as well (e.g., Brown et al., 2002; Hall et al., 2003).

Furthermore, several strategies were used to ensure that women understood the sensitive nature of the questions before they participated, but some women might still have had concerns about being judged or might have felt embarrassed. Interviewers were trained to be especially sensitive to this issue. For example, although most of the study focused on experiences of victimization, it also elicited information about drug use, sexual behavior, and lifetime partners. It was critical to train the research staff to convey an absence of any moral judgment about the women's behavior and to also reflect acceptance of their experiences. This

became an even bigger issue during the follow-up period, because some of the women continued their relationship with their violent partners and were therefore hesitant to participate in the study. In response to this issue, interviewers were instructed to tell all participants at the end of the baseline interview that it did not matter whether they continued a relationship or were in a new relationship, and that whatever their situation, their participation was valued.

Participant understanding. Brown et al. (2002) interviewed a variety of individuals employed as study recruiters to get their perspective on recruitment for research participation. One critical finding from that study is that many in the community do not understand research. In other words, many participants confused research with social service programs, just did not understand what the study was about or what participation involved. Therefore, distinguishing the present research study from social service provision was a major ethical concern for the investigators. For this study, a variety of techniques were used to increase understanding of the study, such as face-to-face recruitment, informational brochures (which presented the information in the consent form in a much more user-friendly and engaging presentation), careful informed consent procedures, and follow-up informational mailings. This issue related directly to the ethical principle of respect for persons and clarified how this study needed to be extremely careful in administering informed consent. Merely reading the forms was insufficient; explanation and examples needed to be offered to make sure participants understood exactly what they were agreeing to in order not to experience undue risk or become disillusioned with the study and hence discontinue participation. Again, taking care to treat participants ethically likely enhanced follow-up efforts, because if participants are treated with respect and are well informed about the research study they are more likely to continue participation.

Challenges of home visits. Much of the literature on following up research participants suggests that home visits may be necessary (e.g., Brown-Peterside et al., 2001; Hall et al., 2003; Rumptz et al., 1991). Home visits were used in the present study only when participants preferred this setting for the interview. Interviewing participants at their homes was challenging for study staff, particularly in rural areas where it was not uncommon for interviewers to travel 2 to 4 hr to a participant's residence. Many women lived in small hollows with unpaved roads and in homes with no identifiable addresses. Another unanticipated challenge in visiting homes was encountering conditions of extreme deprivation. Staff training addressed preparation for how to respond in cultural conditions that were shaped by extreme poverty beyond what interviewers had seen before. These interviews had to be conducted with the same respect for the person as were the interviews with middle-class women.

Interviewer flexibility. Attention to ethical principles and practicality called for a high degree of situational flexibility. The issue of flexibility in responding to participants was raised in the focus groups when discussing the importance of giving participants a choice of interview time and place. The importance of accommodating participants' unique circumstances was emphasized in staff trainings. Examples of interviewers demonstrating flexibility were evident in the following situations: slow and careful reading of response options to a visually impaired participant, conducting interviews in unusual places and with frequent interruptions, keeping an eye on children, and conducting follow-up interviews at the spur of the moment.

However, there were many other instances requiring flexibility that the research team did not anticipate. For example, participants scheduling appointments and then not showing up are a part of all research studies. Even so, this study found that no-shows could dampen interviewers' morale and motivation. Staff had to be reminded how chaotic participants' lives were and that successful follow-ups often meant several attempts

to reschedule. No-shows were particularly difficult in the rural area, where an interviewer might spend 2 hr to get to the location, an hour waiting for a participant, and then 2 hr driving back to the office. The ethical principles of respect for persons and beneficence were presented to the staff in training around how to keep a consistently respectful and understanding attitude toward participants.

A more challenging ethical concern arose in the context of maintaining privacy while also giving participants choice over interview time and location. Home visits may mean the presence of other family members, even multiple family members. Maintaining complete privacy in these situations proved difficult at times. Although to some extent flexibility from an interviewer was expected, it was still challenging and required creativity and reflection.

Participant safety and data quality monitoring. In addition to the standard human subjects research requirements (e.g., written consent, full disclosure of risks and benefits, informing participants of their rights as a research subject, strict adherence to confidentiality standards, Certificate of Confidentiality from the National Institute of Health), this study incorporated additional participant safety and data quality-monitoring activities that were applied to all aspects of the study. Additional activities to ensure participant safety and data quality included quarterly trainings with interviewers and other staff about human participants research for the duration of the study; random site audits to verify that all precautions were being taken to secure data; specific protocols for participant safety and comfort, adverse events, and study protocol violations were developed and disseminated in writing and verbally; intensive data monitoring and quality control of every aspect of the study; random participant verifications for 5% of participants to verify participation, understanding of the project, consent, and satisfaction, to answer any questions, and to verify locator information (this aspect of the study was written into each consent form and explained to each participant); extensive data entry audits and verifications; and weekly data reports, including recruitment and interview reports, contact tracking reports, no-show/refusal reports, and returned mail reports were conducted on a regular basis. Standardized instruments were used to record results of all aspects of data safety and quality monitoring. Interviewer documentation of all contacts with participants was also included as a part of the participant safety and data quality-monitoring procedures. This documentation of efforts to recruit and follow up women demonstrates the thoroughness, persistence, and creativity that are required to obtain high response rates with a vulnerable population, which enhances the study's methodological rigor.

DISCUSSION

This article presented information about how specific ethical considerations and recruitment and follow-up strategies were developed and implemented for a large longitudinal study of partner violence victims. Even with the initial recruitment, this study presented unique ethical and recruitment challenges. However, this article describes how close attention to research ethics does not impede but may actually enhance recruitment and follow-up strategies. Anecdotally, key informants reported that the study's reputation for strict ethical adherence made women more trusting of it, and the informal community communications about the study may have encouraged participation. Subsequent to the data collected in the study and to the results shown in this article, the major findings of the study have been shared with the participating communities in several regional conferences, both in the rural and urban areas. Furthermore, in addition to the initial key agency collaborations at the beginning of the study, maintaining that information-sharing component throughout the duration of the study was important, although

it was time consuming. Putting together and mailing newsletters and personally presenting study results to individual agencies adds a time and monetary cost component that was not initially anticipated but proved to be valuable for this study as well as for future collaborations. In part, community collaboration is built on the principle of respect for persons. Community collaboration shows respect for potential participants, but also to the communities within which victim participants live. Community collaboration was also in accord with the justice principle because inclusion of community perspectives in the interpretation of results helped to ensure appropriate understanding of the findings in the cultural context. Furthermore, by engaging the community in the design and structure of study methods and through the use of piloting study procedures and interviews, investigators can tailor projects that not only contribute to the scientific importance of their current area of study but also prepare communities to trust future research projects (Ribisl et al., 1996). Failure to adhere to research ethics could easily lead communities to the opposite perspective and could impede future studies of critical human behavior and health problems.

One of the lessons to be learned through this process was that patience may be critical to developing an ethically sound and methodologically rigorous study. Considerable time and effort went into the key informant interviews, the focus groups, and the prestudy pilot before launching the full study. Careful prestudy activity yields valuable information to shape study methods for maximal research gains and at the same time ensure attention to ethics. Furthermore, it is important to note that extensive and detailed participant safety and data quality-monitoring procedures were used to ensure adherence to study protocols, to monitor for problems and respond to those problems consistently across research sites and staff, and to ensure safety for interviewers, participants, and quality of data collection. However, this level of monitoring was also intensive and time consuming. Initially, this level of monitoring made staff uncomfortable until they fully understood the value of the procedures, which was integrated into the continual and ongoing training and quality control.

Future research is needed to address the unanswered question as to the net impact of careful attention to research ethics through institutional review board monitoring on the effectiveness of reducing risk to human participants (Mueller & Furedy, 2001). Although this study suggests that careful attention to ethics can be combined with rigorous research design and implementation, other studies may show more tension between the two driving factors guiding behavioral research in the community. Future research should examine whether specific ethical considerations may result in impediments to study implementation.

There were limitations to this study. First, the study as presented in this article actually combines a family of smaller studies that were related to a larger federally funded research project on partner violence victims with protective orders. Each of the studies is limited by the use of self-report information, and each of the smaller studies is limited by relatively small sample sizes. The described recruitment and follow-up methods may have somewhat limited generalizability because the study was done in a largely rural state, although one of the sites was urban. Also, the focus groups and key informant interviews were convenience samples limiting generalizability. Furthermore, the quantitative results from the large study cannot be generalized to women who did not obtain protective orders for partner violence. Also, the contact logs may have under-reported activity because it was very difficult for interviewers to log every contact even with all of the quality control and emphasis on this activity.

However, even with these limitations, this article suggests that combining ethical considerations with recruitment and follow-up strategies can enhance study success. Perhaps the most important conclusion from this study is that researchers must place an extraordinarily high premium on the value of the individual research participant. If any single ethical principle runs throughout this study, it is the idea of respect for persons. Respect for persons led to engagement with key informants, focus groups, and careful piloting. It also shaped the amount of care and time used in recruiting and following up with women whose victimization experiences suggested great risk of safety and for attrition from the study. Respect for persons also meant respecting the unique culture of rural Appalachians as well as urban women. Perhaps the most important point of all is that community-based research requires input from the target population, key agencies, the community as well as the research and practice literature to ensure study procedures are appropriate, successful, and ethical.

REFERENCES

Addicted and corrupted. (2003, January 19). *Lexington Herald Leader.* Retrieved February 20, 2003, from http://www.kentucky.com/mld/heraldleader/new/special_packages/5033813.htm

Agency OKs more pills in chase. (2003, January 19). *Lexington Herald Leader.* Retrieved February 20, 2003, from http://www.kentucky.com/mld/heraldleader/news/special_packages/4982321.htm

Appalachian Regional Commission. (2006). *County economic status in Appalachia, FY 2006.* Retrieved December 12, 2006, from http://www.arc.gov/index.

Azar, B. (2002). Ethics at the cost of research? *Monitor on Psychology, 33(2),* 38-40.

Billings, D., Norman, G. & Ledford, K. (1999). *Confronting Appalachian stereotypes: Back talk from an American region.* Lexington: University Press of Kentucky.

Brody, J., & Waldron, H, (2000). Ethical issues in research on the treatment of adolescent substance abuse disorders. *Addictive Behaviors, 25,* 217-228.

Brown, B., Long, H., & Milliken, N. (2002). What's to know about study recruitment? We asked recruiters. *Women's Health Issues, 12,* 116-121.

Brown-Peterside, P., Rivera, E., Lucy, D., Slaughter, I., Ren, L., Chiasson, M., et al. (2001). Retaining hard-to-reach women in HIV prevention and vaccine trials: Project ACHIEVE. *American Journal of Public Health, 91,* 1377-1379.

Cotter, R., Burke, J., Loeber, R., & Navratil, J. (2002). Innovative retention methods in longitudinal research: A case study of the departmental trends study. *Journal of Child and Family Studies, 11,* 485-498.

Drug Enforcement Agency. *DEA briefs & background, drugs and drug abuse, state factsheets, Kentucky.* Retrieved May 10,2003, from http://www.usdoj.gov/dea/pubs/states/kentuckyp .html

Drug overdose numbs Appalachia. (2003, January 19). *Lexington Herald Leader,* Retrieved February 20, 2003, from http://www.kentucky .com/mld/heraldleader/news/special,, packages/4982326.htm

Drugs in this story. (2003, January 26). *Lexington Herald Leader,* Retrieved February 20, 2003, from http://www.kentucky.com/mld/herald-leader/news/special_packages/5033812.htm

Duncan, C., (1999). *Worlds apart: Why poverty persists in rural America.* New Haven, CT: Yale University Press.

Dutton, M., Munroe, A., Jouriles, E., McDonald, R., Krishnan, S., McFarlane, J., et al. (2003). *Recruitment and retention in intimate partner violence research.* Washington, DC: National Institute of Justice, Office of Justice Programs, U.S. Department of Justice.

Fahnestock, K, (1992, Summer). Not in my county. *The Judges Journal,* pp. 1-15.

Goeckermann, C., Hamberger, K., & Barber, K, (1994). Issues of domestic violence unique to rural areas. *Wisconsin Medical Journal, 93,* 473-479.

Hall, E., Zuniga, R., Cartier, J., Anglin, M., Danila, B., Ryan, T, et al (2003). *Staying in touch: A field-work manual of tracking procedures for locating substance abusers in follow-up studies.* University of California. Retrieved January 2004 from http://www.uclaisap.org/tracking-manual/manual.html

Hough, R., Tarke, H., Renker, V., Shields, P., & Glatstein, J. (1996). Recruitment and retention of homeless mentally ill participants in research. *Journal of Consulting and Clinical Psychology, 64,* 881-891.

Kaiser Family Foundation. (2001). *State health fact sheets online: 50 state comparison, number of prescriptions per capita.* Retrieved February 13, 2003, from http://www.statehealthfacts .kff.org

Lesser-known favorites cheap, abundant. (2003, January 19). *Lexington Herald Leader.* Retrieved February 20, 2003, from http//www.kentucky.com/mld/hearldleader/news/special_packages/4982335.htm

Logan, T., Cole, J., Shannon, L., & Walker, R. (2006). *Partner stalking: How women respond, cope, and survive.* New York: Springer.

Logan, T., Evans, L., Stevenson, E., & Jordan, C. (2005). Barriers to services for rural and urban rape survivors. *Journal of Interpersonal Violence, 20,* 591-616.

Logan, T., Shannon, L., & Walker, R. (2005). Protective orders process and barriers in rural and urban areas: A multiperspective study. *Violence Against Women, 11,* 876-911.

Logan, T., Stevenson, E., Evans, L., & Leukefeld, C. (2004). Rural and urban women's perceptions of barriers to health, mental health, & criminal justice services: Implications for victim services. *Violence and Victims, 19,* 37-62.

Logan, T., Walker, R., Cole, J., Ratliff, S., & Leukefeld, C. (2003). Qualitative differences among rural and urban intimate violence victimization experiences and consequences: A pilot study. *Journal of Family Violence, 18,* 83-92.

Lynn, M, & Nelson, D. (2005). Common (mis) perceptions about IRB review of human subjects research. *Nursing Science Quarterly, 16,*264-270.

Map of narcotic distribution in the U.S. (2003, January 19). *Lexington Herald Leader.* Retrieved February 20, 2003, from http://www.kentucky.com/mld/hearaldleader/news/special_packages/4979633.htm

Mueller, J., & Furedy, J. (2001). Reviewing for risk: What's the evidence that it works? *Observer, 14(7),* 1-5.

National Science Foundation. (2006). *Frequently asked questions and vignettes.* Retrieved February 6, 2007, from www.nsf.gov/bfa/dias/policy/hsfaqs.jsp#c.

Oakes, J. (2002). Risks and wrongs in social science research. *Evaluation Review, 26,* 443-479.

Ribisl, K., Walton, M., Mowbray. C., Luke, D., Davidson, W., & Bootsmiller, B. (1996).

Minimizing participant attrition in panel studies through the use of effective retention and tracking strategies: Review and recommendations. *Evaluation and Program Planning, 19,* 1-25.

Rumptz, M., Sullivan, C., Davidson, W., & Basta, J, (1991). An ecological approach to tracking battered women over time. *Violence and Victims, 6,* 237-244.

Sieber, J. (1998). Planning ethically responsible research. In L. Bickman & D. Rob (Eds.). *Handbook of applied social research methods* (pp. 127-156). Thousand Oaks, CA: Sage.

Sullivan, C., Rumptz, M., Campbell, R., Eby, K., & Davidson, W. (1996). Retaining participants in longitudinal community research: A comprehensive protocol. *Journal of Applied Behavioral Science, 32,* 262-276.

U.S. Department of Commerce, Bureau of the Census. (2000). *Census 2000.* Available from http://www.census.gov/main/www/cen2000.html

US NY: The alchemy of Oxycontin: From pain relief to drug. Media Awareness Project. (2001, July 29). *New York Tunes.* Retrieved February 13, 2003, from http://www.mapinc.org/drugnews/v0l/n1369/a04.html

US: Oxycontin deaths said to be up sharply. Media Awareness Project. (2002, April 15). *New York Times.* Retrieved February 13, 2003, from http://www.mapinc.org/drugnews/v02/n732/a02.html

DISCUSSION QUESTIONS

1. Describe the methods used by Logan and colleagues to recruit female volunteers for their focus groups.

2. Describe the three Belmont Principles as they relate to treatment of human subjects of research.

3. From the results of this study, how does collaborating with members of the community help researchers with recruitment of subjects for this type of research? Why was community collaboration especially important in rural areas?

4. What unique considerations do these researchers say need to be made for research using females as subjects in order for it to be successful? Will appointments with research subjects always go according to plan? Why?

5. In regard to safety of both the interviewers and the subjects, what are some protocols that emerged from this study that future researchers could use to decrease potential risks when interviewing vulnerable subjects?

6. What is an interesting finding from interviews of recruiters regarding community knowledge of research?

7. Why do Logan and colleagues believe that attention to ethics in research studies of this type may actually enhance subject participation?

4

CONCEPTUALIZATION AND MEASUREMENT

In Chapter 1, it was stated that concepts are human-created ideas that represent reality. Concepts allow researchers to gain a better understanding of the social world we live in. For example, intelligence is a concept—a human-created idea to measure how smart an individual is. Researchers interested in intelligence and its relationship to other variables (crime, for example) could not study varying levels of intelligence in individuals and whether it influences behaviors without first conceptualizing what intelligence is and constructing methods for measuring it. Intelligence has been measured in the past by an intelligence quotient (IQ), in order that persons can be compared on this concept. Incidentally, IQ has been used both as a dependent variable (which individual or societal factors influence someone's IQ) and an independent variable (IQ's influence of other behaviors such as crime). Psychologists continue to debate whether current methods for measuring IQ are accurate and whether IQ should be measured uniformly across all groups and cultures in society (Weinberg, 1989). This debate notwithstanding, intelligence is a concept that has been defined and measured to make it possible for researchers to study it.

Conceptualization is a very important step in the research process. Researchers cannot study particular phenomena unless they first define what it is exactly that they are studying. Conceptualization involves identifying important attributes and describing and defining them to make them amenable for study. Blalock (1982) states that "conceptualization involves a series of processes by which theoretical constructs, ideas, and concepts are clarified, distinguished, and given definitions" (p. 11). A primary reason why researchers often come to contradictory conclusions in studies of the same topic is that individual researchers have conceptualized the same phenomenon in slightly different ways. Crime, for instance, is a very broad concept, and depending on how a researcher conceptualizes crime, different variables may be shown to be influential in the occurrence of it.

For example, if a researcher wants to study the influence of gender on crime, the types of criminal behaviors included in the study will greatly influence whether gender has an effect on crime. If the researcher only studies violent crime, he or she may find a large gender effect (males have a greater likelihood to commit violent crime); however, if the same researcher includes only property and public order crimes in his or her conceptualization of crime, a gender effect may be less pronounced. Beyond conceptualization, a researcher must also construct ways to operationalize concepts. The way in which concepts are measured may also influence the significance of the relationship between independent and dependent variables.

CONCEPTUAL VERSUS OPERATIONAL DEFINITIONS

Researchers almost always report the ways in which their independent and dependent variables were conceptualized and operationalized in their research. This helps the consumers of this research understand exactly what the researchers studied and may also help interpret some of the findings from the study. Researchers usually distinguish between conceptual and operational definitions of concepts. A conceptual definition might be found in a dictionary, whereas an operational definition is more empirical and outlines how a concept will be measured or observed for study (Ellis, Hartley, & Walsh, 2010).

For example, say a researcher believes that religiosity is related to crime; the hypothesis is that those who are more religious are less likely to be criminal. Religiosity is a common concept; less obvious is how religiosity can be measured in an individual. Perhaps church attendance would be a good measure of religiosity. The researcher may want to collect information on how many times per year or month an individual attends church services. Maybe, however, there are some persons who are very religious but do not attend church. The same researcher may also want to ask individuals about their belief in a higher power, or whether or not they pray. These preceding measures might all be ways to operationalize religiosity so that the absence or presence or variability of

religiosity can be observed for selected individuals in order to assess religiosity's relationship to criminal offending.

Issues in conceptualization and operationalization in criminology and criminal justice research are ever present as there is always debate about the most appropriate ways to measure certain phenomena and because researchers across the globe adopt different methods for measuring the same concepts of interest. From a research standpoint, conceptualization and operationalization are important steps in transforming abstract concepts about the social world into more concrete, observable ideas. There is also a great deal of debate about how accurate and exact measures of crime and justice variables should be.

VALIDITY, RELIABILITY, AND PRECISE MEASUREMENT

Although variables can be measured at different levels (Stevens, 1946; see also Bachman and Schutt, 2008 for a more in-depth discussion of levels of measurement), accuracy, consistency, and precision in measurement are also important steps in the research process. In order to advance knowledge in the discipline, researchers have to make their best attempts to ensure that their measures are accurate. In other words, are researchers observing what they intended to observe? Accurate observations are critical to getting accurate results and making conclusions that reflect the true reality of phenomena. Some concepts are easier to accurately measure than others; a respondent's age, sex, and education level can be measured more accurately than their attitudes or opinions of a particular subject. Measurement error is one of the most persistent problems threatening social and behavioral science researchers' ability to get accurate results. Accuracy in measurement is comprised of three elements: validity, reliability, and precision (Ellis et al., 2010).

Validity

Validity refers to the extent to which researchers measure what they planned to measure. In other words, are the variables used in the study good indicators of what the researchers are trying to study? There are different ways to assess the validity of measures. Some simply involve researchers asking themselves if their measures seem like logical and common sense ways to measure concepts (face validity). Others seek outside criteria to assess the validity of measures; researchers asking a respondent to self-report drug use could validate the response by also asking the participant to provide a urine sample (criterion validity). Further still, researchers may want to ensure that they are examining the full range or meaning of the concept (content validity) or that their measures fit with philosophical or theoretical ideas of the concept they are attempting to measure (construct validity).

Even though researchers may use all of the preceding ways in assessing the validity of their measures, problems with validity may still persist. Constructing valid measures are a continual problem in criminology and criminal justice because researchers in these disciplines study very complex and difficult concepts (Ellis et al., 2010). Hagan (2005) notes that "validity is never entirely demonstrated or proven; rather, invalidity is lessened, or researchers are able to express greater degrees of confidence in their data" (p. 280).

Reliability

Reliability, on the other hand, has to do with the consistency and stability of measures. Will the measures, if repeated using the same subjects, yield the same results? For example, a scale, if calibrated correctly, is a very reliable measure of weight—much more reliable than having someone guess a person's weight based on his or her height and body type. The radar gun that police officers use to measure the speed of passing cars is another example of a reliable way to measure a concept—in this case, the velocity of automobiles. Just as with validity, there are some common ways for researchers to assess the reliability of their measures. They could administer the same survey to the same respondents twice to assess consistency (test-retest methods), or have two different persons gather observations and assess the consistency between the two (inter-rater reliability). Often, researchers assess reliability of their measures using what is known as the split-half technique; the instrument or questionnaire is divided into two halves, both of which measure the same concept; however, the scores from the two halves are examined separately and compared to assess the reliability of the measures.

Although both validity and reliability are concerned with measurement accuracy, they are not the same thing. You probably know people who, to make themselves feel better, set their scale back 5 pounds. Each day they weigh themselves, provided their weight does not change much from day to day, it displays the same weight. Thus, this scale is reliably measuring their weight (consistent from day to day) but it is not valid because they set it so they weigh 5 pounds less than their true weight, and thus the scale is not accurate. Researchers would be wise to assess the validity and reliability of their measures before gathering data or making observations with the sample they intend to study. There are no remedies for invalid or unreliable measures if they are found after the data has been collected. Most researchers conduct pilot tests (tests on a small group of people) to ensure validity and reliability of their measures.

Precise Measurement

Accuracy of measurement also refers to the fact that researchers can make observations or measure variables with varying degrees of preciseness. For example, using a scale is a very precise way to measure weight; having students guess weight, however, is a very crude way to measure weight. As a general rule, precise measurements are superior to imprecise ones; however, a high degree of precision may not be necessary for every project, nor desirable for that matter. Ultimately, it will depend on the purposes of the research. For example, measuring someone's annual income to the exact dollar, or age to the exact year, is more precise than using categories of income or age (for example, <$10,000, $10,001–$29,999, $30,000–$49,999, $50,000+; <19, 20–29, 30–39, 40–49, 50+). Similarly, measuring the implementation of a new policy at its exact date is more precise than measuring it by the decade it was implemented (summer of 1996 versus 1990s). However, these more precise measures may not always be necessary.

Obviously, operationalization of concepts will depend a great deal on the amount of precision that is required in the study. If knowing that someone's income is in between $30,000–$49,000 or that someone is in their 40s satisfies the purposes of a specific research study, then the additional effort to more precisely measure concepts may not be worth it; in other words, this may be time wasted for both the researcher and the respondent. Further, some respondents may not know their exact annual income because it varies from year to year. Researchers also want to avoid asking questions that require respondents to spend a great deal of time trying to recall answers. Measures that elicit easily recalled responses are ultimately likely to be more accurate.

RESEARCH READING

Conceptualization is an important step in the research process. If researchers want to examine social phenomena, they must first define what it is exactly that they intend to study as well as what the parameters of their research subject are. In other words, researchers need to construct both conceptual and operational definitions of their topics in order to ensure that they are observing and measuring exactly what they wanted to. The article by Gibbs makes it clear that the things researchers are interested in studying are often difficult to conceptualize and measure. Although terrorism has probably been discussed and redefined numerous times since this article was first published, it is nonetheless a good example of why conceptualization is a very important step in the research process.

Gibbs here reveals that some phenomena are not always as easy to define and measure as they may seem. Issues with conceptualization and operationalization are ever present in social science research and are often the reason for conflicting findings in research of the same topic. In considering terrorism, Gibbs provides a good example of some of the implications of definitions that are too broad or too narrow. As you will see, a definition of terrorism can be quite complex, and complexity is not necessarily what researchers want when studying a topic; however, simplifying terrorism can make researching it problematic as well.

Source: Gibbs, J. P. (1989). Conceptualization of terrorism. *American Sociological Review, 54*(3), 329–340.

CONCEPTUALIZATION OF TERRORISM

Jack P. Gibbs

Abstract: Many issues and problems surround the conceptualization of terrorism. Most definitions of the term are indefensible if only because they do not speak to those issues and problems. An assessment of contending definitions can transcend purely personal opinions; and an assessment can be undertaken without a theory, even though an impressive theory is the ultimate justification of its constituent definitions. The present conceptualization goes beyond a definition of terrorism by emphasizing the definition's bearing on five major conceptual questions, each of which introduces a major issue and/or problem. Then it is argued that thinking of terrorism and other sociological phenomena in terms of control promotes recognition of logical connections and/or empirical associations, each of which could become a component of a theory.

INTRODUCTION

Definitions of terrorism are controversial for reasons other than conceptual issues and problems. Because labeling actions as "terrorism" promotes condemnation of the actors, a definition may reflect ideological or political bias (for lengthy elaboration, see Rubenstein 1987). Given such considerations, all of which discourage attempts to define terrorism, it is not surprising that Laqueur (1977, p. 5) argued that

> a comprehensive definition of terrorism does not exist, nor will it be found in the foreseeable future. To argue that terrorism cannot be studied without such a definition is manifestly absurd.

Even granting what Laqueur implies—that terrorism is somehow out there awaiting definition—it is no less "manifestly absurd" to pretend to study terrorism without at least some kind of definition of it; leaving the definition implicit is the road to obscurantism.

Even if sociologists should overcome their ostensible reluctance to study terrorism (for a rare exception, see Lee 1983), they are unlikely to contribute to its conceptualization. The situation has been described succinctly by Tallman (1984, p. 1121): "Efforts to explicate key concepts in sociology have been met with stifling indifference by members of our discipline."

There are at least two reasons why sociologists commonly appear indifferent to conceptualizations. First, Weber and Parsons gave the work a bad name in the eyes of those sociologists who insist (rightly) on a distinction between substantive theory and conceptual analysis. Second, conclusive resolutions of conceptual issues are improbable because the ultimate justification of any definition is an impressive theory that incorporates the definition. Nonetheless, it is crippling to assume that productive research and impressive theories are possible without confronting conceptual issues and problems. The argument is not just that theorizing without a definition is sterile, nor merely recognition that theory construction and conceptualization should go hand in hand. Additionally, one can assess definitions without descending to purely personal opinion, even when not guided by a theory.

Systematic tests of a theory require definitions of at least some of the theory's constituent terms; but test findings, even those based on the same units of comparison, will diverge if each definition's empirical applicability is negligible, meaning if independent observers disagree when applying the definition to identify events or things. To illustrate, contemplate a question about any definition of terrorism: How much do independent observers agree in judging whether or not President Kennedy's assassination was terrorism in light of the definition? As subsequent illustrations show, simple definitions may promote agreement in answers to the Kennedy question and yet be objectionable for theoretical reasons; but the immediate point is that an empirically applicable definition does not require a theory. By contrast, given evidence that a definition promises negligible empirical applicability, no theory can justify that definition.

Still another "atheoretical" criterion is the definition's consistency with convention. That criterion cannot be decisive, because it would preclude novel definition, but it is important when the field's professionals must rely on "outsiders" for data and, hence, presume appreciable congruence between their definitions and those of the outsiders. That consideration is particularly relevant here, because in analyzing terrorism social scientists often rely on reports of government officials, journalists, and historians.

Conceptual issues and problems haunt virtually all major terms in the social and behavioral sciences, and any definition is ambiguous if it does not answer questions bearing on those issues and problems. There are at least five such questions about terrorism. First, is terrorism necessarily illegal (a crime)? Second, is terrorism necessarily undertaken to realize some particular type of goal and, if so, what is it? Third, how does terrorism necessarily differ from conventional military operations in a war, a civil war, or so-called guerrilla warfare? Fourth, is it necessarily the case that only opponents of the government engage in terrorism? Fifth, is terrorism necessarily a distinctive strategy in the use of violence and, if so, what is that strategy?

The questions are answered in light of a subsequent definition of terrorism, but more than a definition is needed. The pursuit of a theory about terrorism will be furthered by describing and thinking about terrorism and all other sociological phenomena in terms of one particular notion, thereby promoting the recognition of logical and empirical associations. The most appropriate notion is identified subsequently as "control," but a defense of that identification requires a definition of terrorism (not of "terror").

A Definition of Terrorism

Terrorism is illegal violence or threatened violence directed against human or nonhuman objects, provided that it:

(1) was undertaken or ordered with a view to altering or maintaining at least one putative norm in at least one particular territorial unit or population;

(2) had secretive, furtive, and/or clandestine features that were expected by the participants to conceal their personal identity and/or their future location;

(3) was not undertaken or ordered to further the permanent defense of some area;

(4) was not conventional warfare and because of their concealed personal identity, concealment of their future location, their threats, and/or their spatial mobility, the participants perceived themselves as less vulnerable to conventional military action; and

(5) was perceived by the participants as contributing to the normative goal previously described (supra) by inculcating fear of violence in persons (perhaps an indefinite category of them) other than the immediate target of the actual or threatened violence and/or by publicizing some cause.

Clarification, Issues, and Problems

In keeping with a social science tradition, most definitions of terrorism are set forth in a fairly brief sentence (see, e.g., surveys by Oots 1986, pp. 5-8, and Schmid and Jongman 1986, pp. 32-38). Such definitions do not tax the reader's intellect or patience, but it is inconsistent to grant that human behavior is complex and then demand simple definitions of behavioral types.

The Illegality of Terrorism. Rubenstein's definition (1987 p. 31) is noteworthy if only because it makes no reference to crime or illegality: "I use the term 'terrorism' . . . to denote acts of small-group violence for which arguable claims of mass representation can be made." However, even granting that terrorism is an illegal action, there are two contending conceptions of crime, one emphasizing the reactions of officials as the criterion and the other emphasizing normative considerations (e.g., statutory law). Because of space limitations, it is not feasible to go much beyond recognizing the two contending conceptions. It must suffice to point out that an action may be illegal or criminal (in light of statutes and/or reactions by state officials) because of (1) where it was planned; (2) where it commenced; and/or (3) where it continued, especially in connection with crossing a political boundary. Such distinctions are relevant even when contemplating the incidence of terrorism.

One likely reaction: But why is terrorism necessarily a crime? The question suggests that classes of events or things exist independently of definitions. Thus, it may appear that "stones" and "humans" denote on to logically given classes, but in the context of gravitational theory stones and humans are not different. However, to insist that all definitions are nominal is not to imply that conventional usage should be ignored; and, again, the point takes on special significance when defining terrorism. The initial (unnumbered) part of the present definition is consistent, with most other definitions and also with this claim: most journalists, officials, and historians who label an action as "terrorism" evidently regard the action as illegal or criminal. However, it is not denied that two populations may differ sharply as to whether or not a particular action was a crime. As a necessary condition for an action to be terrorism, only the statutes and/or reactions of officials in the political unit where the action was planned or took place (in whole or in part) need identify the action as criminal or illegal.

Violence and Terrorism. Something like the phrase "Violence or threatened violence" appears in most definitions of terrorism (see Schmid and Jongman 1988, p. 5). As in those definitions, the phrase's key terms are here left as primitives; and whether they must be defined to realize sufficient empirical applicability can be determined only by actual attempts to apply the definition.

Despite consensus about violence as a necessary feature of terrorism, there is a related issue. Writers often suggest that only humans can be targets of violence, but many journalists, officials, and historians have identified instances of destruction or damage of nonhuman objects (e.g., buildings, domesticated animals, crops) as terrorism. Moreover, terrorists pursue their ultimate goal through inculcation of fear and humans do fear damage or destruction of particular nonhuman objects.

The Ultimate Goal of Terrorists. The present definition indicates that terrorists necessarily have a goal. Even though it is difficult to think of a human action that is not goal oriented, the consideration is controversial for two reasons. One reason is the allegation that terrorists are irrational or mentally ill (see, e.g., Livingston 1978, pp. 224-39; and Livingstone's commentary, 1982, p. 31 on Parry), which raises doubts as to whether terrorists have identifiable goals. The second reason why part 1 of the definition is controversial: many sociologists, especially Durkheimians, do not emphasize the purposive quality of human behavior, perhaps because they view the emphasis as reductionism. In any case, a defensible definition of virtually any term in sociology's vocabulary requires recognition of the relevance of internal behavior (e.g., perception, beliefs, purpose). Thus, without part 1 of the present definition, the distinction between terrorism and the typical robbery becomes obscure. The typical robber does not threaten violence to maintain or alter a putative norm; he or she is concerned only with behavioral control in a particular situation.

A defensible definition of a norm is not presumed (see Gibbs 1981, pp. 9-18, for a litany of difficulties). Rather, it is necessary only that at least one of the participants (those who undertake the violent action or order it) view the action as contributing to the maintenance or alteration of some law, policy, arrangement, practice, institution, or shared belief.

Part l of the definition is unconventional only in that goals of terrorists are not necessarily political. Many definitions create the impression that all terrorism is political (for a contrary view, see Wilkinson 1986, p. 51), but the very term "political terrorism" suggests at least two types. The concern of social scientists with terrorism typologies is premature (see, e.g., the commentary by Oots [1986, pp. 11, 30] on Mickolus's notions of international, transnational, domestic, and interstate terrorism). No terrorism typology amounts to a generic definition (see the survey in Schmid and Jongman 1988, pp. 39-59), and without the latter the former is bound to be unsatisfactory.

Military Operations and Terrorism. To repeat a previous question; How does terrorism necessarily differ, if at all, from conventional military operations in a war, civil war, or so-called guerrilla warfare? The question cannot be answered readily because there are no clearly accepted definitions of conventional military operation, war, civil war, and guerrilla warfare. "Guerrilla" is especially troublesome because journalists are prone to use the word without defining it but such as to suggest that it is synonymous with terrorism (a usage emphatically rejected by Laqueur 1987 and Wilkinson 1986).

Conventional military operations differ from terrorism along the lines indicated by parts 2, 3, and 4 of the definition. However, the definition does not preclude the possibility of a transition from terrorism to civil war. One tragic instance was the Easter Rising in Ireland (1916), when rather than perpetuate the terrorism tradition, a small group of Irish seized and attempted a permanent defense of government buildings in Dublin, vainly hoping that the populace would join them in open warfare.

Today, it is terrorism rather than civil war that haunts Northern Ireland, and the term, "guerrilla warfare" has no descriptive utility in that context.

Terrorism as a Special Strategy. One feature of terrorism makes it a distinctive (though not unique) strategy in violence. That feature is described in part 5 of the definition.

Part 5 is controversial primarily because it would exclude actions such as this threat: "Senator, if you vote for that bill, it will be your death warrant." Why would such a threat not be terrorism? A more theoretically significant answer is given subsequently. Here it must suffice to point out that scores of writers have emphasized "third party" or "general" intimidation as an essential feature of terrorism; and journalists, officials, or historians only rarely identify "dyadic intimidation" (X acts violently toward Y but *not* to control Z's behavior) as terrorism.

"State Terrorism" as a Special Issue. Zinam's definition (1978, pp. 244-45) illustrates one of many reasons why definitions of terrorism are so disputable: "[Terrorism is] the use or threat of violence by individuals or organized groups to evoke fear and submission to obtain some economic, political, sociopsychological, ideological, or other objective, " Because the definition would extend to the imposition of legal punishments by government officials to prevent crimes through general deterrence, in virtually all jurisdictions (see Morris 1966, p. 631), some aspects of criminal justice would qualify as terrorism; and Zinam's definition provides no basis for denying that it would be "state terrorism." Even granting that a state agent or employee acts for the state only when acting at the direction or with the consent of a superordinate, there is still no ostensible difference between the use or threat of violence in law enforcement and Zinam's terrorism.

Had Zinam defined terrorism as being necessarily illegal or criminal, then many instances of violence by a state agent or employee at the direction or with the consent of a superordinate would not be terrorism. However, think of the numerous killings in Nazi Germany (Erust Roehm, the Storm Troop head being a well-known victim) during the Night of the Long Knives (June 30, 1934). Hitler ordered the slaughter, and at the time the killings were illegal in light of German statutes; but Hitler publicly acknowledged responsibility, and the only concealment was that perceived as necessary to surprise the victims. Surely there is a significant difference between such open, blatant use of coercion by a state official (dictator or not) and the situation where regime opponents are assassinated but officials disavow responsibility and the murders are so secretive that official complicity is difficult to prove. The "rule of terror" of Shaka, the famous Zulu chief, is also relevant. Shaka frequently ordered the execution of tribal members on a seemingly whimsical basis, but the orders were glaringly public (see Walter 1969). Shaka's regime illustrates another point: in some social units there may be no obvious "law" other than the will of a despot, in which case there is no basis to describe the despot's violence as illegal. The general point: because various aspects of government may be public violence, to label all of these aspects "terrorism" is to deny that terrorism has any secretive, furtive, or clandestine features.

Given the conceptual issues and problems that haunt the notion of state terrorism, it is hardly surprising that some writers attribute great significance to the notion, while others (e.g., Laqueur 1987, pp. 145-46) seem to reject it. The notion is not rejected here, and the following definition does not make it an extremely rare phenomenon. State terrorism occurs when and only when a government official (or agent or employee) engages in terrorism, as previously defined, at the direction or with the consent of a superordinate, but one who does not publicly acknowledge such direction or consent.

The foregoing notwithstanding, for theoretical reasons it may prove desirable to limit the proposed definition of terrorism (supra) to nonstate terrorism and to seek a quite different definition of state terrorism. Even so, it will not do to presume that all violence by state agents is terrorism. The immediate reason is that the presumption blurs the distinction between terrorism and various kinds or aspects of law enforcement. Moreover, it is grossly unrealistic to assume that all instances of genocide or persecution along racial, ethnic, religious, or class lines by state agents (including the military) are terrorism regardless of the means, goals, or circumstances. Nor is it defensible to speak of particular regimes (e.g., Stalin's, Hitler's, Pol Pot's) as though all of the related violence must have been state terrorism. For that matter, granted that the regimes were monstrous bloodbaths, it does not follow that the state agents in question made no effort whatever to conceal any of their activities and/or their identity. Readers who reject the argument should confer with American journalists who attempted to cover Stalin's Soviet Union, Hitler's Germany, or Pol Pot's Cambodia. Similarly, it is pointless to deny that secretive, clandestine, or furtive actions have been characteristic of "death squads" (many allegedly "state") in numerous Latin American countries over recent decades. It is commonly very difficult to prove that such groups murder with the knowledge and/or consent of state officials; but the difficulty is one justification for identifying the murders as terrorism, even though the state-nonstate distinction may be debatable in particular instances.

Difficulties in Empirical Application

One likely objection to the present definition of terrorism is its complexity; but, again, demands for simplicity are inconsistent with human behavior's complexity. Nonetheless, application of the definition does call for kinds of information that may not be readily available. Reconsider a previous question: Was President Kennedy's assassination terrorism? The present definition does not permit an unequivocal answer, largely because there are doubts about the goals of the assassination and whether or not it was intimidation. If terrorism were defined as simply "the illegal use or threat of violence," an affirmative answer to the Kennedy question could be given; but the definition would also admit (inter alia) all robberies and many child abuses. Similarly, the phrase "for political purposes" would justify an affirmative answer to the Kennedy question; but the implication would be a tacit denial of apolitical terrorism, and divergent interpretations of "political" are legion. Finally, although a definition that specifically includes "murder of a state official" would maximize confidence in an affirmative answer to the Kennedy question, there must be doubts about the feasibility of such an "enumerative" definition of terrorism. And what would one make of the murder of a sheriff by his or her spouse?

The general point is that a simple definition of terrorism tends to delimit a class of events so broad as to defy valid generalizations about it (reconsider mixing presidential assassinations, robberies, and child abuses) or so vague that its empirical applicability is negligible. In the latter connection, the Kennedy illustration indicates the need to grant this methodological principle: the congruence dimension (but not the feasibility dimension) of a definition's empirical applicability is enhanced when independent observers agree that the definition cannot be applied in a particular instance because requisite information is not available. If that principle is not granted, sociologists will try to make do with simple definitions and whatever data are readily available.

Presumptive and Possible Terrorism. Comparative research on terrorism commonly is based on the use of the term "terrorism" by journalists or officials. Hence, insofar as the use of data on presumptive terrorism can be justified, a definition's utility is enhanced by its correspondence with the use of the term "terrorism" by journalists and officials. Although only potentially demonstrable, my claim is that the present definition corresponds more with such use of the term than does any simpler definition, such as: terrorism is illegal violence.

Even when terrorism research is based on descriptions of violent events, as in newspaper stories, there may be cases that can be designated as possible terrorism even though the information is not complete; and a definition's empirical applicability can be assessed in terms of agreement among independent observers in such designations. In that connection, the present definition points to the kind of information needed for truly defensible research on terrorism, which is not the case when investigators try to make do with a much simpler definition, or no definition at all.

Toward a Theory of Terrorism

The presort definition of terrorism does not answer any of a multitude of questions, such as: Why does the incidence of terrorism vary among political units and over time? Although it is an illusion to suppose that any definition answers empirical questions, a definition may be much more conducive than are alternatives to thinking about phenomena; if so, the definition furthers the pursuit of a theory.

Summary and Conclusion

An impressive theory of terrorism requires more than a conceptualization that confronts issues and problems. A definition of terrorism must promise empirical applicability and facilitate recognition of logical connections and possible empirical associations. Such recognition requires a notion that facilitates describing and thinking about terrorism; and the notion must be compatible with each of three possible explanatory mechanisms: strict causation, selective survival, and purposiveness.

The notion of control is the most promising candidate. Although that notion has no equal when it comes to underscoring human behavior's purposive quality, it is not alien to any particular explanatory mechanism. All of sociology's subject matter can be described and thought of in terms of control (at least as it has been conceptualized here), and the notion is particularly relevant in the study of terrorism. That phenomenon and attempts to prevent it are nothing less than one vast attempt at control.

REFERENCES

Becker, Jillian. 1988. *Terrorism in West Germany.* London: Institute for the Study of Terrorism.

Catton, William R. 1966. *From Animistic to Naturalistic Sociology.* New York: McGraw-Hill.

Clark, Robert P. 1986. "Patterns in the Lives of ETA members." Pp. 283-309 in *Political Violence and Terror,* edited by Peter H. Merkl. Berkeley: University of California Press.

Davis, Kingsley. 1959. "The Myth of Functional Analysts as a Special Method in Sociology and Anthropology." *American Sociological Review* 24:757-72.

Durkheim, Emile. 1949. *The Division of Labor in Society.* New York: Free Press.

Gibbs, Jack P. 1981. *Norms, Deviance, and Social Control.* New York: Elsevier.

Harris, Marvin. 1979. *Cultural Materialism.* New York: Random House.

Laqueur, Walter. 1977. *Terrorism.* London: Weidenfeld and Nicolson.

————. 1987. *The Age of Terrorism.* London: Weidenfeld and Nicolson.

Lee, Alfred M. 1983. *Terrorism in Northern Ireland.* Bayside, NY: General Hall.

Livingston, Maritis H., ed. 1978. *International Terrorism in the Contemporary World.* Westport, CT: Greenwood.

Livingstone, Neil C. 1982. *The War Against Terrorism.* Lexington, MA: Heath.

Morris, Norval. 1966. "Impediments of Penal Reform." *University of Chicago Law Review,* 33:627-56.

Noakes, Jeremy. 1986. "The Origins, Structure and Function of Nazi Terror." Pp. 67-87 in *Terrorism, Ideology, and Revolution,* edited by Noel O'Sullivan. Brighton, England: Harvester.

Oots, Kent I. 1986. *A Political Organization Approach to Transnational Terrorism.* Westport. CT: Greenwood.

Parsons, Talcott. 1951. *The Social System.* New York: Free Press.

Rubenstein, Richard E. 1987. *Alchemists of Revolution.* London: L.B. Tauris.

Schmid, Alex P. and Albert I. Jongman. 1988. *Political Terrorism.* Rev. ed. Amsterdam: North-Holland.

Skocpol, Theda. 1979. *States and Social Revolution.* London: Cambridge University Press.

Taillman, Irving. 1984. Book Review. *Social Forces* 62:1121-22.

Walter, Eugene V. 1969. *Terror and Resistance.* New York: Oxford University Press.

Weber, Max. 1978. *Economy and Society.* 2 vols. Berkeley: University of California Press.

Wilkinson, Paul. 1986. *Terrorism and the Liberal State.* 2nd ed. New York: New York University Press.

Zinam, Oleg. 1978. "Terrorism and Violence in Light of a Theory of Discontent and Frustration." Pp. 240-63 in *International Terrorism in the Contemporary World,* edited by Marks H. Livingston. Westport, CT: Greenwood.

DISCUSSION QUESTIONS

1. Why does Laqueur argue that a definition of terrorism does not exist? Why does Gibbs argue that social scientists are often indifferent to conceptualization?

2. One of the first issues Gibbs discusses is the illegality of terrorism. What are some of the issues that Gibbs raises regarding defining terrorism as a crime?

(Continued)

(Continued)

3. Under certain definitions of terrorism, why might the military operations of some countries be considered as terrorism, in essence making their governments terrorists?

4. According to this article, do terrorists have goals? What makes terrorists any different than other criminals (such as murderers)?

5. What are some of the difficulties with empirical application of terrorism? In other words, why is it difficult to measure?

6. What does this author conclude about whether the assassination of President Kennedy was an act of terrorism?

7. What does Gibbs conclude regarding what is necessary to the formulation of a theory of terrorism?

RESEARCH READING

This research article examines whether the ways in which questions about sexual and physical victimization are asked to inmates affects the reporting of these acts. Wolff and colleagues argue that not much is known regarding the prevalence of violence inside correctional settings because researchers have not been consistent with their definitions of victimization. Their purpose is to explore the difference between using questions that are very broad or general versus those that are related to specific acts. The results of this study reveal that depending on how questions are worded, the prevalence rates of sexual and physical violence vary. Their research demonstrates the importance of asking the right questions and in the correct manner in order that researchers obtain accurate measures. Accurate measures of the amount of victimization that occurs inside prison are important to developing programs to reduce and control it.

MEASURING VICTIMIZATION INSIDE PRISONS

Questioning the Questions

Nancy Wolff, Jing Shi, and Ronet Bachman

Abstract: Violence and victimization inside the prison setting are accepted as facts, although the facts about their prevalence remain uncertain. Variation in the methods used to estimate rates of sexual and

Authors' Note: This study was supported by the Office of Justice Programs (Grant #OJP-2004-RP-BX-0012) and the National Institute of Mental Health (Grant #P20 MH66170). The authors acknowledge with gratitude the generous and helpful comments they received from Dr. Richard Tewksbury in the development of the manuscript.

Source: Wolff, H., Jing, S., & Bachman, R. (2008). Measuring victimization inside prisons: Questioning the questions. *Journal of Interpersonal Violence, 23*(10), 1343–1362. Copyright © 2008 Sage Publications.

physical victimization contribute to the wide range in estimates appearing in the prison literature. This article focuses on the questions used in the prison victimization literature to elicit information on victimization from inmates, compared to questions used in the general victimization literature. The questions used in the National Violence Against Women and Men Surveys are used to estimate sexual and physical victimization rates for an entire prison system. Rates of victimization were found to vary significantly by specificity of the question, definition of perpetrator, and clustering of behaviors. Facts about victimization inside prison will become more certain when the methodology becomes more standardized and consistent with definitions of victimization.

INTRODUCTION

Some people housed in America's prisons are victimized both sexually and physically by other inmates and staff (Bowker, 1980; Gaes & Goldberg, 2004; Lockwood, 1980; Toch, 1985). This statement once considered a myth is now readily accepted as fact. What remains less evidence based, however, concerns how many people inside prison are victimized in particular ways and by whom. These issues have been the source of considerable investigation over the past two decades, especially with respect to sexual victimization. Representative prevalence rates remain elusive, with ranges varying from less than 1% to 40% for sexual victimization (Gaes & Goldberg, 2004) and 10% to 25% for physical victimization (Wooldredge, 1998). Extant studies are characterized by probability and convenience samples of inmates with (uncontrolled) nonresponse rates of 50% or higher drawn from a small number of prison facilities, by survey questions that require varying degrees of subjective interpretation, by varying recall or reflection periods, and by survey administration strategies that vary in their ability to minimize stigma and shame, as well as danger to the inmate.

In an effort to focus the measurement of victimization inside prisons, this study controls for certain types of methodological bias (sample size, time period, and survey administration) to investigate the framing of questions that are used to elicit information about victimization inside prison. Although framing of questions is a central focus of survey and violence research, it has not received careful investigation in the measurement of sexual or physical victimization inside prisons. The purpose of this study is to explore the use of general questions about victimization framed in terms of "assault" (a broadly and commonly used term in the victimization literature; cf. Kilpatrick, 2000) versus specific questions about particular acts or behaviors on the rate of physical and sexual victimization inside prisons during a 6-month time period.

LITERATURE REVIEW

One of the basic components of survey research is the phrasing of questions to measure what is intended (Presser et al., 2004). Questions cannot be reasonably phrased, however, until there is clarity about what is to be measured. In the prison victimization literature, what is to be measured is interpersonal violence resulting from one person (the perpetrator or aggressor) harming another person (the victim) in particular ways: physically, sexually, psychologically, or emotionally. Violence might be manifested as an actual (i.e., hitting, coercing, or forcing sexual contact), attempted (i.e., striking out but missing the person, attempting forced sexual contact), or a threatened act that is harmful. The harmful act might have occurred at any point, because the person was under the authority of the correctional entity; the act occurred at one or more prisons operated by that entity; or the act occurred once or multiple times and been perpetrated by inmates, staff, or both. Furthermore, the harmful act might have been reported to authorities and have led to further or more severe mistreatment because it was reported;

likewise, it might have resulted in medical and/or mental health treatment.

Given the multidimensionality of violence, being clear about what is to be measured means limiting the definition first in terms of (a) whether the goal is to measure harmful acts that are committed, attempted, or threatened; and (b) the types of acts that are considered harmful. Sexual violence, as defined by the National Center for Injury Prevention and Control (NCIPC), is divided into nonconsensual sexual acts, consisting of forced or threatened sex acts, including vaginal, oral, and anal sex; and abusive sexual contacts, including intentional touching of specified areas of the body (Basile & Saltzman, 2002). Nonconsensual sexual acts are defined to be consistent with notions of rape, attempted rape, or sexual assault. *Physical abuse* is typically defined as a threat or an attempt to do bodily harm and may or may not involve a weapon. As such, definitions of sexual and physical violence share three commonalities in that they do the following: (a) produce interpersonal harm (which may be manifested physically, emotionally, and/or psychologically); (b) may be completed, attempted, or threatened; and (c) include specific types of behavior. These commonalities define the domains of what is to be measured by questions in surveys about victimization inside prisons. These domains can be described in terms of place, time, and perpetrator.

Victimization questions used in the prison victimization literature have been idiosyncratic and, as such, have generated rates of victimization that cannot be meaningfully compared across studies based on correctional populations or the general population. More meaningful and useful prevalence rates would be available if prison-based studies used modified questions based on the NVAW survey. Modification is needed because the weapons (and language for these weapons) and the type of perpetrators are different in prison settings, although the harmful behaviors or acts are the same as are their types of commission (i.e.,

completed, attempted, or threatened). The study described next used both general and specific questions to measure sexual and physical victimization inside male and female prisons located in a single mid-Atlantic state. The specific questions were modified from the NVAW. The questions were framed to measure bid time and 6-month prevalence rates of both sexual and physical victimization within a state prison system.

METHOD

Sampling

A sample of 7,443 inmates was drawn from a single state $(N = 22,231)$, inclusive of 12 adult male facilities and 1 adult female facility. Inmates were excluded from the sample if they were younger than 18 or in administrative segregation custody, detention, death row, a sex offender treatment facility, or otherwise too sick to participate in the survey. Also excluded were inmates residing in halfway houses or off-site at the time of the survey. In total, 85% $(n = 18,956)$ of the inmate population was eligible. Data were collected from June through August 2005. Inmates housed in the general population $(n = 18,956)$ were invited by researchers to participate in the survey. Enough time inside the facility was requested to collect a 40% probability sample from the general population, typically requiring between 2 and 5 days. A 66% random sample of inmates was selected from a population frame in advance with the expectation of a 60% response rate among those randomly selected, yielding the expected 40% sample target within the allotted time at the facility. Target samples across facilities ranged from 26% to 53%, with a mean target sample of 40% $(SD = 0.061)$. Data collection at the facility with a target sample of 26% was prematurely terminated because of a lockdown situation (unrelated to the study) at the facility.

Procedures

The survey was administered using an audio-computer-administered survey instrument (audio-CASI) available in English and Spanish. Respondents sat at a laptop computer in a private location and were read the questions via headset and responded via mouse. Thirty computer stations were available and researchers were available for assistance. Completing the English version of the instrument by audio-CASI took approximately 60 minutes, whereas the Spanish version took approximately 90 minutes. Participants were provided the option of a Spanish version (68 respondents [0.9%] completed the Spanish version). The recruitment protocol, the consent procedures, and the consent form were approved by the appropriate university and Department of Corrections (DOC) institutional review boards. Participants were informed about the survey through inmate liaison representatives and an informational video about the survey (played on the inmate television channel). DOC staff was not involved in the recruitment or marketing of the survey. Participants were not compensated for their participation to reduce any overt coercion.

Participants

Of the 18,956 inmates from general population eligible to participate, approximately 13,000 were briefed on the survey and 7,443 (57% response rate) were recruited and completed the survey. A total of 6,879 men *(M* age = 33.9, *SD* = 6.5) and 564 women aged 18 or older participated in the study *(M* age = 35.5, SD = 6.4). Over two thirds (68.4%) of the female inmate respondents were non-White and 83.1% of the male respondents were non-White. These demographic statistics are equivalent to the general prison population (67.3% of females are non-White, with a mean age of 35.4 years; 79.8% of the males are non-White, with a mean age of 34.4). The survey sample overrepresented the Hispanic (inclusive of White and non-White; 14.5% female; 19.9% male) population within the prison (10.1% female; 15.0% male).

Instruments

The questions regarding sexual victimization were adapted from the NVAW survey (Tjaden & Thoennes, 2000). Violence was measured using four general questions for each type of perpetrator (inmate or staff member). The general questions were as follows: Have you been sexually assaulted (physically assaulted) by (inmate/staff member) within the past 6 months? Have you ever been sexually assaulted (physically assaulted) by (inmate/staff member) on this bid? In contrast to community-based studies of victimization, a 6-month reflection period, instead of a 12-month period, was selected in the phrasing of questions for three reasons. First, one of our study objectives was to measure interfacility variation in victimization rates. Given the tendency of inmates to move between and among facilities, a 6-month reflection period provided greater stability within the denominator of the prevalence rates for each facility. Second, the literature suggests that inmates are at greatest risk of sexual victimization in the first 6 months at a facility. Limiting the reflection period to 6 months allowed us to test (analysis to be conducted in the future) whether, indeed, victimization rates are highest when inmates first arrive at a facility. Third, given the frequency of violence expected inside prison, especially in terms of physical victimization, more reliable reporting is expected from shorter reflection periods. Longer reflection periods, say 12 months, are most appropriate for low probability events. Prevalence rates for 6-month periods, in combination with the bid time prevalence rates, can be linearized to approximate 12-month rates under alternative growth rate assumptions. Only findings based on the 6-month data are presented herein.

Ten additional questions about specific types of sexual victimization were used (e.g., "During the past 6 months, has (another inmate or staff member) ever . . . touched you, felt you or grabbed you in a way that you felt was sexually threatening or made you have sex by using force or threatening to harm you or someone close to you?"). The specific sexual assault questions were clustered to reflect definitions of sexual violence developed by the NCIPC.

Behavior-specific questions about physical victimization were framed in terms of whether another inmate (or staff member) has done any of the five specific behaviors "during the past 6 months." The five specific questions relating to physical victimization were collapsed into two categories differentiated by whether a weapon was involved (i.e., with or without weapon). The specific questions were collapsed into categories of physical victimization involving and not involving a weapon.

Statistical Analysis

Unweighted data are presented here because the emphasis is on question phrasing. It is noteworthy, however, that nearly identical results are generated with weighted data. Unless otherwise indicated, the significance level used to assess the validity of the null hypotheses is $p < .05$. Prevalence of sexual and physical victimization measures the number of people in the population experiencing sexual and physical victimization within a 6-month period.

RESULTS

Rates of inmate victimization varied significantly by phrasing of the victimization question. As shown in Table 4.1, specific questions, phrased in terms of specific types of behavior, produced rates of victimization that were 1.1 to 9 times larger than rates based on the general question, phrased in terms of sexual or physical assault for both inmate and staff perpetrators. Rates of inmate-on-inmate victimization reported by women based on the specific questions dramatically increased relative to the general question and relative to their male counterparts. Less dramatic yet still significant (except for female inmate rates by staff) increases occurred in the estimated rates for physical victimization within gender or across gender groups.

The rates of sexual victimization, according to Table 4.1, could be reported as low as 1.7% of male inmates to as high as 10.7%, depending on whether respondents were asked if they had been sexually assaulted in the past 6 months by another inmate or whether they had experienced various types of sexually explicit (and abusive) behavior by another inmate or a staff person during that same time period. The range of rates for female inmates was even larger, ranging from 2.5% to 26.4%. If experiences of physical and sexual victimization are combined and inclusive of both inmate and staff perpetrators, roughly 40% of female and male inmates experienced some form of victimization within a 6-month period in this state prison system.

Using questions that focus on inmate-on-inmate rape understates the rape experience of male (1.6% vs. 3.0%) and female (3.7% vs. 5.0%) inmates. Similarly, using questions phrased in terms of rape or sexual assault, as measured by nonconsensual sexual acts, understates exposure to sexual victimization within a prison setting (males: 3.0% vs. 9.4%; females: 5.0% vs. 25.0%). Likewise, important gender and perpetrator patterns are masked when physical victimization questions do not distinguish the use of weapons in the commission of physically assaultive acts.

Table 4.2 explores the response patterns to the general and specific questions. Nearly all of those who reported "no" to all the specific questions about sexual victimization also reported "no" to the general questions. Yet of those who said "yes" to at least one of the

Table 4.1 Six-Month Prevalence Rates (Per 1,000) for Victimization by Gender, Type of Perpetrator, and Phrasing of the Survey Question

Phrasing of the Survey Question	Male Inmates (N = 6,897)						Female Inmates (N = 564)					
	Inmate	95% Confidence Interval	Staff	95% Confidence Interval	Either or Both	95% Confidence Interval	Inmate	95% Confidence Interval	Staff	95% Confidence Interval	Either or Both	95% Confidence Interval
Sexual victimization by type of perpetrator												
General	17	14 to 20	27	23 to 31	37	32 to 41	25	12 to 39	27	13 to 40	45	28 to 62
Specific	39	35 to 44	73	67 to 79	99	92 to 106	226	192 to 261	84	61 to 107	264	227 to 300
Combined	44	40 to 49	79	73 to 86	107	99 to 114	230	195 to 265	86	62 to 109	264	227 to 300
Nonconsensual	16	13 to 19	21	18 to 25	30	26 to 34	37	22 to 53	20	8 to 31	50	32 to 68
Abusive, sexual	36	32 to 41	69	63 to 75	94	87 to 101	216	182 to 252	74	52 to 96	250	214 to 285
Physical victimization by type of perpetrator												
General	73	67 to 79	164	155 to 172	198	188 to 207	102	77 to 127	59	39 to 78	138	109 to 166
Specific	194	185 to 203	220	210 to 230	326	315 to 337	203	170 to 237	65	44 to 85	228	193 to 263
Combined	207	198 to 217	261	251 to 272	360	315 to 371	224	190 to 259	91	67 to 115	260	223 to 296
Without weapon	119	111 to 126	148	140 to 157	218	208 to 228	164	133 to 195	52	33 to 70	187	155 to 220
With weapon	145	136 to 153	158	149 to 167	251	241 to 261	100	75 to 125	25	12 to 38	114	88 to 140
Combined sexual and physical victimization by type of perpetrator												
General	80	74 to 87	173	164 to 182	210	200 to 220	117	914 to 144	71	50 to 92	158	128 to 188
Specific	208	198 to 217	249	239 to 259	357	345 to 368	336	297 to 375	125	98 to 152	383	342 to 423
Combined	223	213 to 233	289	278 to 299	390	378 to 401	350	310 to 389	142	113 to 171	400	359 to 440

Table 4.2 Percentage of Inmates Responding to Specific and General Phrasing of Victimization Question by Gender and Type of Perpetrator

Response to Specific Questions	Male Inmates		Female Inmates	
	General, % Yes	General, % No	General, % Yes	General, % No
	Sexual Victimization, Inmate-on-Inmate by Response to General Question			
Specific, Yes	30.0	70.0	9.7	90.3
Specific, No	0.6	99.4	0.5	99.5
	Sexual Victimization, Staff-on-Inmate by Response to General Question			
Specific, Yes	28.9	71.1	31.1	68.9
Specific, No	0.6	99.4	0.2	99.8
	Physical Victimization, Inmate-on-Inmate by Response to General Question			
Specific, Yes	30.6	69.4	39.5	60.5
Specific, No	1.7	98.3	2.7	97.3
	Physical Victimization, Staff-on-Inmate by Response to General Question			
Specific, Yes	55.2	44.8	50.0	50.0
Specific, No	5.3	94.7	2.7	97.3

specific questions, roughly 7 in 10 reported "no" to the general question, except for the inmate-on-inmate responses by the female respondents in which 9 in 10 reported "no" to the general question while responding "yes" to at least one of the specific questions.

The general physical victimization, especially for staff-on-inmate form of victimization, yields responses more consistent with the specific questions (yes-yes combinations). Yet the slightly lower proportion reporting "no" to the specific question and "yes" to the general question regarding physical victimization (ranging from 1.7% to 5.3%, compared to the 0.2% to 0.6% for the sexual victimization questions) suggests that types of physically abusive behavior for the specific behavior question are not fully representative of the behavior that respondents consider physically assaultive.

DISCUSSION

The results of this research illustrate the importance of question wording when attempting to measure sexual and physical victimization. More specific behavior questions elicit information on violent or abusive behaviors that are threatened or attempted; behaviors, like actual completed behaviors, create a sense of psychological and emotional distress and fear within the victim and the environment. In general, specific behavior questions increase the percentage of people reporting sexual and physical victimization inside prisons within a specific reference period. Questions focusing on specific types of behavior also provide more detail about actual victimization, allowing it to be delineated into types, such as nonconsensual sexual acts or abusive sexual conduct (Fisher, Cullen, & Turner, 2000). More specificity on the types of sexual victimization is critically important for prevention strategies because abusive sexual conduct is often considered a precursor to nonconsensual sexual acts (Lockwood, 1980). Defining the source of victimization to include both inmates and staff also increases the prevalence of victimization, in some cases doubling the estimated rate. The effect of including staff as perpetrators appears to depend on the type of victimization and gender.

Although it is clear that the form of the question and its scope affects estimates of victimization within a prison, it also affects the ability to compare violence in prisons to that in the general population residing in the community. Using the same questions, the NVAW survey found that 0.2% of women reported being raped (attempted or completed) during a 12-month period (Tjaden & Thoennes, 2000), compared to 4.6% of women and 2.7% of men during a 6-month period in prison. (Note: In the NVAW survey, fewer than 5 male victims in a sample of 8,000 reported being raped and, as such, no estimates were calculated.) Rates of physical assault for a 12-month period were 1.3% for females and 0.9% for males in the general population, compared to 22.8% of females and 32.6% of males in prison, again during a 6-month period.

Comparing victimization rates inside prison to those in the general population is problematic, because people inside prison are not representative of the general population. Given the strong correlation between poverty and criminalization (Jargowsky, 1997; Wilson, 1987) and between poverty and victimization (Rennison & Rand, 2003), a more appropriate comparison group may be inner-city areas— areas more representative of the places where people residing in prison once lived and where they will eventually return after completing their sentences (Travis, 2005). Teplin, McClelland, Abram, and Weiner (2005) used the NCVS to estimate 12-month prevalence rates of crime victimization for "central cities." For central cities over a 12-month period, rates of rape or sexual assault were estimated at 0.23% for women, 0.025% for men. Rates of physical assault for men and women were estimated at, respectively, 1.6% and 1.1%, in inner cities based on the NCVS questions on sexual and physical assault. Although the screening questions for the NCVS are less specific than those used in the NVAW, they still generate rates, adjusted to central city areas, which are substantially smaller than rates of victimization estimated for male and female prisons over a time period half in length.

One of the central advantages of using victimization questions that are used in national surveys is that it allows meaningful comparisons across groups in different settings and geographical areas. As such, it becomes clear that prisons are more violent places than the general population and central city environments. It remains unclear whether this is because the prison environment congregates people prone toward violence, because the secluded nature and power structure of the prison environment facilitates violence, or because the deprivation within the environment foments the stresses that cause violence. Also, it is unclear to what extent group-to-group violence motivates or directs interpersonal violence. These data simply suggest that prison environments are more violent and that the people residing there live with the consequences and fear of victimization during their incarceration, and the data also suggest areas where more research is needed.

Putting prison victimization methods on par with those in the general victimization literature is long overdue. What is being measured—victimization—is independent of setting and needs only to be translated to a prison context in terms of type of perpetrator and names of weapons (e.g., "shanks"). Standardization of methods will provide more useful information for identifying the sources and context of victimization, which can then be used to develop policies to prevent violence inside prisons and to treat and protect those who have been victimized. The Commission on Safety and Abuse in America's Prisons (2006) is calling for actions that will make correctional settings safer. Collecting reliable and valid data on victimization inside prisons is a necessary first step toward this goal in terms of identifying how much victimization is occurring and what types of violence occur and by whom, as well as providing guidance on how best to prevent violence and how much treatment is needed to respond to the trauma and other consequences associated with violence.

It is important to keep in mind that our findings are based on a single state prison system. Whether these rates generalize to other prisons systems is an empirical issue that requires future research. Yet for this single state system, our findings indicate that people inside prisons are at greater risk of sexual and physical victimization than the average citizen in the community, even central cities characterized by poverty. For this reason, prisons can be considered a natural laboratory for systematically studying violence in terms of its causes, its consequences, and ways to prevent and treat it. In particular, researchers studying violence in prison have an opportunity to develop and inform the literature on the measurement of victimization and its prevention. Interpersonal violence, whether sexual or physical, has many dimensions and manifestations, with actual, attempted, and threatened violence having consequences that affect physical health (such as HIV infection) as well as psychological and emotional well-being. The challenge is to measure the dimensionality of different forms of violence, to explore the interdependence between and among these dimensions, and to develop interventions to prevent its onset and to treat its occurrence in ways that addresses the ensuing layers of harm. Yet in advancing the literature, it is critical that prison-based research incorporates standard measures of victimization and methods of collection to ensure valid estimates and comparisons across settings.

REFERENCES

Bachman, R. (2000). A comparison of annual incidence rates and contextual characteristics of intimate-partner violence against women from the National Crime Victimization Survey (NVAWS). *Violence Against Women, 6,* 839-867.

Basile, K. D., & Saltzman, L. E. (2002). *Sexual violence surveillance: Uniform definitions and recommended data elements.* Atlanta, GA: National Center for Injury Prevention and Control, Centers for Disease Control and Prevention.

Beck, A. J., & Hughes, T. A. (2005). *Sexual violence reported by correctional authorities, 2004* (National Criminal Justice Report 210333). Washington, DC: U.S. Department of Justice.

Bowker, L. (1980). *Prison victimization.* New York: Elsevier North Holland.

Bureau of Justice Statistics. (2004). *Data collections for the Prison Rape Elimination Act of 2003.* Retrieved July 9, 2006, from http://www.ojp.usdoj.gov/bjs/pub/pdf/dcprea03.pdf

Butler, T., Donovan, B., Levy, M., & Kaldor, J. (2002). Sex behind the prison walls. *Australian and New Zealand Journal of Public Health, 26(4),* 390-391.

Commission on Safety and Abuse in America's Prisons. (2006). *Confronting confinement.* Retrieved June 19, 2006, from http://www .prisoncommission.org/report.asp

Fisher, B. S., Cullen, F. T., & Turner, M. G. (2000). *The sexual victimization of college women* (National Criminal Justice Report 182369). Washington, DC: U.S. Department of Justice.

Fuller, D. A., & Orsagh, T. (1977). Violence and victimization within a state prison system. *Criminal Justice Review, 2,* 35-55.

Gaes, G. G., & Goldberg, A. L. (2004). *Prison rape: A critical review of the literature* (Working paper). Washington, DC: National Institute of Justice.

Hensley, C, Tewksbury, R., & Castle, T. (2003). Characteristics of prison sexual assault targets in male Oklahoma correctional facilities. *Journal of Interpersonal Violence, 18(6),* 595-607.

Jargowsky, P. A. (1997). *Poverty and place: Ghettos, barrios, and the American city.* New York: Russell Sage.

Kilpatrick, D. G. (2000). *Rape and sexual assault.* Retrieved June 7, 2007, from http://www.musc .edu/vawprevention/research/sa.shtml

Lockwood, D. (1980). *Prison sexual violence.* New York: Elsevier.

Maitland, A. S., & Sluder, R. D. (1998). Victimization and youthful prison inmates: An empirical analysis. *The Prison Journal, 78,* 55-73.

Presser, S., Rothger, J. M., Couper, M. P., Lessler, J. T., Martin, E. L., Martin, J., & Singer, E. (2004). *Methods for testing and evaluating survey questionnaires.* Hoboken, NJ: John Wiley.

Rennsion, C. M., & Rand, M. R. (2003). *Criminal victimization, 2002* (National Criminal Justice Report 199994). Washington, DC: Bureau of Justice Statistics.

Straus, M. A. (1979). Measuring intrafamily conflict and violence: The conflict tactics (CT) scales. *Journal of Marriage and the Family, 41,* 75-88.

Straus, M. A., & Gelles, R. J. (1999). *Physical violence in American families.* New Brunswick, NJ: Transaction Publishing.

Struckman-Johnson, C, & Struckman-Johnson, D. (2000). Sexual coercion rates in seven midwestern prison facilities. *The Prison Journal, 80,* 379-390.

Struckman-Johnson, C, & Struckman-Johnson, D. (2002). Sexual coercion reported by women in three midwestern prisons. *Journal of Sex Research, 23,* 217-227.

Struckman-Johnson, C, & Struckman-Johnson, D. (2006). A comparison of sexual coercion experiences of men and women in prison. *Journal of Interpersonal violence, 21,* 1591-1615.

Struckman-Johnson, C, Struckman-Johnson, D., Rucker, L., Bumby, K., & Donaldson, S. (1996). Sexual coercion reported by men and women in prison. *Journal of Sex Research, 33,* 67-76.

Teplin, L. A., McClelland, G. M., Abram, K. M., & Weiner, D. A. (2005). Crime victimization in adults with severe mental illness: Comparison with the National Crime Victimization Survey. *Archives of General Psychiatry, 62,* 911-921.

Tewksbury R. (1989). Fear of sexual assault in prison inmates. *The Prison Journal, 69,* 62-71.

Tjaden, P., & Thoennes, N. (2000). *Full report of the prevalence, incidence, and consequences of violence against women: Findings from the national violence against women survey* (National Criminal Justice Report 183781). Washington, DC: National Institute of Justice and the Centers for Disease Control and Prevention.

Toch, H. (1985). Warehouses of people. *Annals of American Academy of Political and Social Science, 478,* 58-72.

Travis, J. (2005). *But they all come back: Facing the challenges of prisoner reentry.* Washington, DC: Urban Institute.

Wilson, W. J. (1987). *The truly disadvantaged: The inner-city, the underclass and public policy.* Chicago: University of Chicago Press.

Wooden, W. S., & Parker, J. (1982). *Men behind bars: Sexual exploitation in prison.* New York: Plenum.

Wooldredge, J. D. (1994). Inmate crime and victimization in a southwestern correctional facility. *Journal of Criminal Justice, 22,* 367-381.

Wooldredge, J. D. (1998). Inmate lifestyles and opportunities for victimization. *Journal of Research in Crime and Delinquency, 35,* 480-502.

DISCUSSION QUESTIONS

1. How much have prevalence rates of sexual and physical victimization varied in past research?

2. Why do Wolff and colleagues believe it is important for researchers to clarify what they want to measure, especially regarding violence?

3. How did these researchers solicit information from prison inmates? Regarding ethics of subjects, do you think respondents would have been less comfortable answering questions about victimization through face-to-face interviews with the researchers?

4. How much difference in victimization rates did these researchers find for general versus specific questioning?

5. In Table 4.2, did some inmates who answered yes to a specific question confirming they had been victimized, also report no, that they had not to a more general question about victimization? What does this reveal?

6. In what ways are specific questions about violent victimizations better for research?

7. What do these researchers say are some of the problems with comparing victimizations rates inside prison versus rates of the general population not in prison?

8. What are some of the limitations of this research study?

RESEARCH READING

Racial profiling has become a well-recognized and popular buzz word to both researchers and the general public alike. The authors of the current article, however, point out that relatively little is known about the cause of racial profiling. They contend that a lack of conceptualization of racial profiling is the reason for this void in knowledge. In this article, Batton and Kadleck attempt to conceptualize racial profiling in order to make it more amenable for future researchers to assess causality. Specifically, they outline four conceptual issues and the implications each has for data collection and analysis of racial profiling. Pay particular attention to the separate discussions of conceptualization and operationalization issues regarding racial profiling and how the two are related but different. The appendix provides information on the various different types of definitions that have been used to define racial profiling. This appendix is a great example of the difficulty in coming up with universal conceptualizations of phenomena that are of interest to social science researchers.

Source: Batton, C., & Kadleck, C. (2004). Theoretical and methodological issues in racial profiling research. *Police Quarterly*, *7*(1), 30–64. Copyright © 2004 Sage Publications.

THEORETICAL AND METHODOLOGICAL ISSUES IN RACIAL PROFILING RESEARCH

Candice Batton and Colleen Kadleck

Abstract: Racial profiling has generated a significant amount of social concern in American society. Yet little is known about the etiology of this phenomenon, in part because its defining characteristics have yet to be identified and conceptualized. In this article, the authors summarize and organize the existing racial profiling literature and establish a strong conceptual foundation for future racial profiling research. Four issues that must be explicitly addressed in the conceptualization process of research on racial profiling are identified and described; realm of activity, level of aggregation and unit of analysis, population of interest, and characteristics of the incident. These factors have methodological implications in terms of data collection control variables, and methods of analysis.

INTRODUCTION

Racial disparities in the justice system have long been of interest to researchers who have documented disproportionate numbers of racial and ethnic minorities at virtually every stage of justice processing (Walker, Spohn, & DeLone, 2000). The latest issue to garner scholarly attention with respect to race is racial profiling, a term generally used to describe situations in which race or ethnicity functions as an indicator of criminal propensity, typically by law enforcement officers in the context of a traffic stop (Harris, 1997, 1999a; Maclin, 1998; U.S. General Accounting Office, 2000). Although racial profiling is a relatively new concept that has only recently generated broad social concern, discrimination on the basis of race has long plagued the U.S. criminal justice system (Kennedy, 1999; Walker, 2001).

The broad, sweeping consequences of racial profiling for minorities, police, and society in general make it an issue worthy of scholarly attention. The necessity of research is further underscored by the flurry of legislative action and reforms to law enforcement policies that have occurred due to heightened concern over racial profiling and the potential civil liberties violation it constitutes (Commission on Accreditation for Law Enforcement Agencies, 2002; Harris, 1999b; Strom, Brien, & Smith,

2001; Walker, 2001). Although there have been recent efforts to measure the extent of racial profiling, much of the existing literature fails to adequately conceptualize the problem in that there is no consensus on the meaning of racial profiling or what it entails. We use the term *racial profiling* to refer to the use of discretionary authority by law enforcement officers in encounters with minority motorists, typically within the context of a traffic stop, that result in the disparate treatment of minorities. The defining characteristics of racial profiling incidents have yet to be identified, but in this article, we suggest several factors that should be considered.

CONCEPTUAL FRAMEWORK

Social and Cultural Foundation of Racial Profiling

With the "sociological imagination," C. Wright Mills (1961) stressed the importance of situating phenomena in their broader social and cultural context to more fully understand them. Toward that end, we begin by defining racial profiling and discussing its historical roots. The term *racial profiling* has been used to loosely refer to a variety of instances in which minorities, African Americans in particular, are treated distinctly because of their skin color by persons occupying various social roles (e.g., store owners, taxi drivers, police) (Meeks, 2000). Although a broad conception is not incorrect, we use *racial profiling* to refer to a narrower range of social behavior-specifically, the use of discretionary authority by law enforcement officers in encounters with minority motorists, typically within the context of a traffic stop.

The roots of racial profiling run deep. Throughout the course of American history, minorities, and Blacks in particular, have been subjected to differential treatment by the criminal justice system (Donziger, 1996; Kennedy, 1999; Meeks, 2000; Tonry, 1995; Williams & Murphy, 1990). In the mid-1800s, slave patrols were implemented as an arm of the law to search for disobedient and runaway slaves (Reichel, 1988; Williams & Murphy, 1990). Following the abolition of slavery, "Black codes" were enacted in many states in attempts to legally limit the rights and liberties of Blacks. Although the federal government banned "Black codes" in 1868, many Southern states still attempted to use the legal system to maintain White supremacy with Jim Crow laws, which required separate facilities for Blacks (e.g., schools, rail cars, bathrooms) (Free, 1996; Williams & Murphy, 1990). It was not until the Civil Rights Act of 1964 that it became illegal to discriminate on the basis of "race, color, . . . or national origin" (Legal Information Institute, 2002). Although discrimination is prohibited, it is well documented that racial disparities exist at virtually every stage of U.S. criminal justice system processing (Donziger, 1996; Free, 1996; Mauer, 1994; Tonry, 1995; Walker, 1999; Walker et al., 2000). It is within this social and historical context that racial profiling emerged.

Several facets of police training and experiences are conducive to racial profiling. First, profiling is generally viewed as an efficient law enforcement technique for getting contraband off the street and "netting" persons who are wanted (Cleary, 2000: Harris, 1999b, 2002; Kennedy, 1999; Milazzo & Hansen, 1999). Unless it is the sole factor prompting a stop, the use of race/ethnicity in profiling is generally not believed to constitute discrimination. In consideration of this, racial profiling may occur in conjunction with anti-crime crackdowns. For example, in an attempt to get guns off Kansas City streets, a high crime rate area was assigned extra patrols with the task of establishing "reasonable suspicion" to perform searches, many of which occurred in the context of traffic stops (Sherman, Shaw, & Rogan, 1995). Although minorities were not explicitly targeted, 92% of residents in the targeted area were non-White, Uniform Crime Report (UCR) statistics indicating disproportionate minority involvement in crime also support the use of race in profiling (Taylor & Whitney, 1999). Although they have been criticized by academics for not accurately reflecting the nature and extent of crime or the characteristics of criminals, UCR statistics constitute police reality in that they reflect arrests and offenses known to the police (Robinson, 2000). Scholars may argue that self-report and victimization surveys paint a different image of racial differences in criminal behavior, but it is unknown to what extent police are aware of this information. On a related note, officers are trained to look for persons who do not belong or appear suspicious (Johnson, 1983; Maclin, 1998). As Skolnick (1994) noted, citizen reports of "suspicious" persons more often involve minorities than Whites, which reinforces linkages between criminality and minorities.

Drug interdiction training also facilitates racial profiling as drug courier profiles are more likely to target minorities, African Americans and Hispanics in particular (Cole, 1999; Donziger, 1996; Harris, 2002; Leitzel, 2001; Maclin, 1998; Tonry, 1995; Walker et al., 2000). Harris (1999b) argued that racial profiling was institutionalized in law enforcement in the mid-1980s through Operation Pipeline, a Drug Enforcement Agency (DEA) training program on using traffic violations as pretexts for stopping persons who fit drug courier profiles, especially on roads known as drug "pipelines." Once a stop is made on the pretext of a traffic violation, the officer has a better opportunity to determine whether a search is warranted (Cole, 1999). Even with no evidence, consent for a search may be requested. Motorists can refuse, but they may believe that consent is not required or that cooperation decreases the risk of a citation (Cole, 1999; Harris, 1999a, 2002). If consent is not given, a canine unit may be summoned in an attempt to establish probable cause for a full search (Harris, 1999a, 2002; Meeks, 2000). The idea that training includes race/ethnicity as a risk factor is important because training influences officer behavior (McNamara, 1967; Niederhoffer, 1967; Walker, 1999).

All of these factors contribute to the perpetuation of stereotypes that link criminality with racial and ethnic minorities (Harris, 1999b; Kennedy, 1997). These stereotypes permeate police work and are manifested through the use of discretionary authority contributing to the belief that searches of minorities and their vehicles are likely to be "productive" in terms of netting contraband and criminals (Cole, 1999; Johnson, 1983; Milazzo & Hansen, 1999; Ramirez, McDevitt, & Farrell, 2000; Robinson, 2000). The result is a self-fulfilling prophecy as officers target vehicles operated by minorities and simultaneously pay less attention to others (Harris, 1999b; Ramirez et al., 2000). Interestingly, "hit rate" research indicates that drugs are found in a smaller percentage of vehicles operated by minorities than by Whites (Harris, 1999a; Ramirez et al., 2000). Officers vary in the extent to which they are cognizant of how race affects their use of discretion, with many denying that it has any effect at all (Johnson, 1983; Ramirez et al., 2000; Robinson, 2000).

Finally, it should be noted that U.S. Supreme Court decisions on the constitutionality of pretext stops also facilitate racial profiling. In 1996, the use of drug courier profiles and pretext stops was upheld by the Court in *Whren v. United States* as long as race is not the only motivating factor for the stop or search (Cole, 1999; Harris, 1999b; Kennedy, 1999). Whether this constitutes racial profiling is the subject of debate. Although some define racial profiling as occurring when race is the

only factor motivating a stop or search, others argue that it encompasses situations when race is used as one of a constellation of factors (Cleary, 2000; Fridell et al., 2001; Kennedy, 1999; Walker, 2001). Harris (1999b) argued that any use of race is problematic because "police are therefore free to use Blackness as a surrogate indicator or proxy for criminal propensity" (p. 291). In other words, race becomes a proxy for risk of criminal behavior (Gaynes, 1993; Hemmens & Levin, 2000; Johnson, 1983; Kennedy, 1999; Mann, 1993). The U.S. Supreme Court handed down a similar decision in 1976 supporting the actions of Border Patrol agents who used drivers' ethnic heritage as a factor in the decision to stop and search vehicles on the southern California border (Meeks, 2000).

Explicitly identify factors that should be taken into account in the conceptualization and operationalization of racial profiling.

CONCEPTUALIZATION OF RACIAL PROFILING

It is difficult to overstate the importance of clear conceptualization in the research process. A firm understanding of the meaning and parameters of key concepts is necessary for identifying valid and reliable measures and adequately operationalizing variables. A strong conceptual framework is also important for model development in terms of specifying causal mechanisms and relevant control variables. The following discussion focuses on four factors central to the conceptualization of racial profiling; realm of activity, level of aggregation, population of interest, and incident characteristics.

Realm of Activity

It has been well documented that profiling in a broad sense occurs in many realms of activity and by persons occupying a multitude of social roles. Studies indicate that race and sex are very powerful determinants of the manner in which individuals interact with others. They are particularly important in interactions between strangers who do not have any other prior knowledge of each other and therefore must rely on outward appearances to "size up" and make assessments about the other person (Anderson, 1990, 1999; Leitzel, 2001). It has been argued that African Americans are discriminated against by retailers who assume that they either do not have any money or are more likely to shoplift, by taxi cab drivers who fear criminal victimization, and by Customs agents searching for contraband on the basis of skin color (Cole, 1999; Meeks, 2000).

Although this type of "profiling" undoubtedly occurs and is likely based at least in part on race, of particular interest here is racial profiling that occurs in the context of police interactions with minority motorists. First, racial profiling by police is likely to be distinct from that done by others because of the discretionary authority of the police and the power differential that exists between police and those they stop. Second, traffic law and vehicle code enforcement is an area in which officers have broad discretion, in part because of the sheer number of vehicles operated in violation of the law (Ramirez et al., 2000; Walker, 2001). Vehicle stops, most of which involve suspected traffic or vehicle code violations, are also discretionary as they are largely proactive, or officer-initiated, as opposed to other types of encounters, which are more likely to be reactive, or driven by service calls and citizen complaints (Mastrofski et al., 1998; Walker, 2001). Vehicle stops are also distinct from many other types of police-citizen encounters in terms of their situational characteristics, the absence of a "victim" demanding that justice be served, and the potential outcomes (Smith & Visher, 1981; Worden, 1989). Therefore, a distinction should be made between racial profiling in the context of interactions between police and minority motorists and other social settings.

Unit of Analysis and Aggregation

In the process of conceptualizing racial profiling, it is important to consider the unit of analysis and the possibility of effects at different levels of aggregation. The most basic unit of analysis is the incident, or the individual vehicle stop. For this unit of analysis, data must be collected on the characteristics of all vehicle stops that occur within a specific geographical area during a set period of time, Incident data are important because officer decision making is affected by the characteristics of incidents. Officers tend to have a limited amount of time and information to use in deciding whether to stop a vehicle, thus they rely on various aspects of the situation (e.g., driver behavior, seriousness of the violation, location of the stop, other traffic conditions, and vehicle characteristics) (Worden, 1989). As Walker (2001) noted, the context in which the stop occurs should be considered.

Although data should be incident level, it is important to consider the possibility of effects across officers, districts, and/or agencies. At the officer level, the risk of racial profiling may vary because of differences in attitudes and beliefs about the relationship between race/ethnicity and criminality. Officer-level differences may also stem from differences in training and guidelines from supervisors (Verniero & Zoubek, 1999), which could be detected by controlling for shift or beat. District effects are possible as several factors related to the distribution of crime vary across police districts including the (a) demographic characteristics of residents, (b) extent of social disorganization (e.g., population density, mixed use areas, rental properties), and (c) number of officers assigned to an area (Bursik & Webb, 1982; Klinger, 1997; Reiss, 1986; Schuerman & Kobrin, 1986; Shaw & McKay, 1942). Klinger (1997) also argued that the structure of the division of police labor in conjunction with the autonomous nature of patrol work results in district variation in policing norms. Finally, agency-level effects are possible as a result of variation in goals, operating philosophies, and organizational culture (Engel, Calnon, & Bernard, 2002; Fridell et al., 2001). This is consistent with research by Mastrofski, Ritti, and Hoffmaster (1987) on drunk driving enforcement and Fyfe (1982) on police use of lethal force; both studies found that agency philosophies affect officer behavior.

Population of Interest

Identifying and defining the population at risk is central to the conceptualization of racial profiling. Are all persons "at risk" or are particular racial/ethnic groups more likely than others to be targeted? The popular phrase "driving while Black" implies that African Americans are the targets of racial profiling. Studies that focus solely on the experiences of African American motorists, such as Harris (1999a), further support this idea. However, other racial and ethnic minorities are also likely to be targeted. As Mann (1993) noted, Americans stereotype the race or ethnicity of criminals as African American, Hispanic, or Native American, depending on the type of crime and area of the country.

The extent to which various minority groups are targeted in racial profiling likely depends on the racial and ethnic composition of the population. Particular minority groups may be at greater risk in areas where their numbers are relatively large. For example, African Americans may be at greater risk than others in the South because they comprise a relatively large proportion of the minority population. According to the U.S. Census Bureau (2000, pp. 25-27), in 2000, 90% to 95% of the minority population was comprised of African Americans in states like Louisiana, Mississippi, and Alabama. The composition of the minority population differs in states such as Texas and California, where African Americans comprised 39.6% and 16.5% of the 2000 minority population, respectively. In both of these states, approximately one third of the population in 2000 was comprised of Hispanics, and in California about 10% of the total population and 27% of the minority population was comprised of Asians.

The race/ethnicity of known drug couriers and drug-related offenders should also be considered in conceptualizing the at-risk population. Officers are likely to rely on their own experiences as well as the collective experiences of the agency, which they are exposed to through radio communications, supervisor reports and messages, and informal exchanges of information. Thus, if the majority of drug trafficking arrestees in an area are young, Asian males, they may be at greater risk for racial profiling than African Americans or Hispanics, even if the latter comprise a relatively large proportion of the minority population in that jurisdiction.

Characteristics of the Incident

Anecdotal evidence suggests that the nature and quality of the encounter is a crucial aspect of racial profiling (Fridell et al., 2001). Although discussions frequently focus on the use of pretext stops, what happens during the stop is as important as the "reason" for it. Several factors are identified below as potential defining characteristics of racial profiling incidents.

Length of Delay

Anecdotal evidence suggests that minorities are more likely to be detained by law enforcement officers for traffic violations and for longer periods of time (Fridell et al, 2001; Harris, 1999a; Ramirez et al., 2000). Although a White driver may be detained relatively briefly for a traffic violation for the amount of time it takes to issue a warning or a citation, it has been argued that minorities are likely to be detained longer as more extensive questioning, background checks, and/or searches are conducted. Investigating the extent to which minorities are subjected to longer delays and the reason for them is an important aspect of racial profiling research.

Searches

Anecdotal evidence suggests that searches are an important aspect of racial profiling. Several facets of searches need to be more closely examined, including racial/ethnic differences in the likelihood of being searched, the rationales underlying searches, and nature of the search. Clearly, the most basic question is whether minority motorists and their vehicles are more likely than Whites to be searched, presumably because of a suspicion that drugs will be found. In a study of police-public contact in 1999, Langan, Greenfeld, Smith, Durose, and Levin (2001, p. 2) found that Blacks and Hispanics were twice as likely as Whites to be searched during a traffic stop. They also found that younger drivers were searched more often.

The circumstances surrounding the search are also important-specifically, the basis for initiating the search (i.e., visible contraband, odor, canine alert, inventory search prior to impoundment, consent search) (Fridell et al., 2001; Ramirez et al., 2000). If an individual refused consent to a search, was a canine unit summoned (Cole, 1999)? If so, how was the dog used (i.e., interior vehicle search, exterior vehicle search)? Were the search results positive, and if so, what was recovered (e.g., drugs, paraphernalia, weapons) (Fridell et al., 2001)? Another important aspect is whether the motorist felt pressured to consent to a search out of fear of receiving a citation or ignorance of the right to refuse consent (Cole, 1999; Harris, 1997; Meeks, 2000). However, it may not be possible to accurately measure this facet of searches.

Property Damaged

As alluded to above, allegations of property damage have frequently been made by minority motorists claiming that either their vehicle or personal belongings were damaged in the course of officers or canine units conducting a search of their vehicle (Harris, 1999a). Personal property might be damaged if belongings are carelessly rifled through, thrown on the ground, or exposed to inclement conditions (e.g., rain, snow, mud). Property may also be damaged as a result of police dogs scratching the exterior of the vehicle or entering the vehicle and damaging the upholstery. Damaged property may be indicative of being treated

with a lack of respect and therefore may tap into the qualitative nature of the encounter.

Information and Demeanor

The extent to which the officer provides or requests information may also be important in conceptualizing racial profiling. For example, there is evidence that officers frequently do not give a reason for the stop, even when asked directly by the motorist. This may indicate a lack of professionalism, but Fridell et al. (2000, p. 14) noted that minorities tend to attribute officer rudeness, discourtesy, and unwillingness to provide the reason for the stop to racial bias. It should be noted, however, that Langan et al. (2001, p. 15) found few racial differences (i.e., 1.5% of Whites, 2% of Blacks, and 2.3% of Hispanics) in drivers reporting that no reason was given for the stop. Researchers should also document whether officers ask inappropriate or irrelevant questions about where the individuals have been or where they are going. In cases involving minorities driving more expensive cars, people report being asked who the car belongs to, as if the car did not belong to them. These questions may be particularly revealing when they have little to do with the underlying traffic violation (Harris, 1999a).

The demeanor of the officer is an important aspect of the interaction. This refers to the manner in which the officer treats and interacts with the individual; is the person treated with courtesy and respect or is the officer rude and suspicious? Information on officer demeanor would likely provide important insights into the issue of racial profiling, but this facet of the interaction is virtually impossible to measure without direct observation, which may itself have an impact on officer behavior. Furthermore, officer demeanor is likely to be partially a function of motorists' demeanor. As Kennedy (1999, p. 7) noted, a "downward spiral" may occur if the motorist expresses resentment at having been stopped because of racial/ethnic heritage and the officer responds to the perceived hostility in kind. On a related note, Engel et al. (2002)

reported that non-White suspects may be more disrespectful toward police, which could be linked with higher arrest rates for minorities, especially young Black males. Although Lundman (1996) found that citizen demeanor affects the likelihood of arrest, other factors must also be considered, such as severity of the offense (Klinger, 1996; Worden, Shepard, & Mastrofski, 1996).

Restraint and Use of Force

Another aspect of the incident to consider is the use of restraints on the driver and/or passengers. Restraints might include handcuffs, leg shackles, or being placed in the patrol car. The use of restraints typically suggests that the officer had reason to believe the person was dangerous or posed a threat to his or her safety. The more frequent use of restraints with minority motorists may be an indication of racial bias in that the decision to use them may stem from preconceptions on the part of the officer about racial differences in criminality, in their study of police-public contact. Langan et al. (2001) found that Blacks (6.4%) and Hispanics (5%) were more likely to be handcuffed during a stop than Whites (2.5%). Blacks (2%) and Hispanics (2%) were also more likely than Whites (<1%) to have force or the threat of force used against them.

Disposition of Stop

Racial profiling may be linked with racial/ethnic differences in the disposition or outcome of a traffic stop (e.g., winning, citation) (Fridell et al., 2001). Differences in incident dispositions may reflect the extent to which the stop was based on an actual traffic violation as opposed to a traffic violation being the pretext for the stop. Stops initiated on the basis of a minor infraction that do not result in a citation, but do result in a search or attempted search, are consistent with DEA training on the use of pretext stops. Ramirez et al. (2000, p. 50) suggested the following disposition codes: oral warning, written warning,

arrest made, arrest by warrant, criminal citation, traffic citation-hazardous, traffic citation-nonhazardous, courtesy service/citizen arrest, and no action taken.

METHODOLOGICAL IMPLICATIONS OF CONCEPTUAL DEFINITION

The conceptualization of a problem has implications for conducting research on that phenomenon. In the following, a variety of methodological issues that follow from the conceptual framework on racial profiling established above are discussed.

Operationalization

In establishing the conceptual framework, four factors were discussed as central to racial profiling research: realm of activity, level of aggregation, population of interest, and characteristics of the incident. In the following, the operationalization of these concepts is discussed as well as the implications for data collection.

Realm of Activity

The conceptualization of racial profiling has implications both for its operationalization as a variable and for data collection. With respect to the realm of activity, we argue that the data collected should pertain to interactions between law enforcement officers and motorists that occur during officer-initiated vehicle stops. Ramirez et al. (2000) defined a stop "as any time an officer initiates contact with a vehicle resulting in the detention of an individual and/or vehicle" (p. 43). Although the majority of stops will likely involve traffic law violations, other highly discretionary vehicle stops (e.g., investigative stops) should also be included (Fridell et al, 2001). For example, in their investigation of Operation Valkyrie, the ACLU found that Illinois state troopers assigned to drug interdiction units stopped

Hispanic motorists 2 to 3 times more frequently than troopers in other units (Harris, 1999a). However, as Fridell et al. (2001, p. 123) noted, collecting data on vehicle stops as opposed to traffic stops compounds the problem of identifying an appropriate baseline for comparison.

Although data on the outcome of the stop should be recorded, it should not serve as the basis for sample selection. Instead, data should be recorded on all vehicle stops to avoid bias and accurately assess the nature and extent of racial profiling (Cleary, 2000; Fridell et al., 2001). Data should be collected on the date, time, and location of the stop to fully understand the context in which the stop occurred (Cordner, Williams, & Zuniga, 2001; Ramirez et al., 2000).

Level of Aggregation

Researchers should be cognizant of the level of aggregation that characterizes their data. Most racial profiling studies have examined department-level data (Cleary, 2000), with the exception of legal research, such as Laraberth's study of the Maryland State Police (ACLU, 1996). Agency-level data are likely to uncover important information and may be necessary to protect the anonymity and confidentiality of the officers being studied, especially in relatively small departments. As Cleary (2000, p. 28) noted, officers often perceive the collection of identification information as a serious threat, which can affect both behavior and morale.

Although these are legitimate concerns, identifying the parameters of the issue is important and agency-level data may obscure differences among officers and districts. To the extent that research findings serve as the basis for policy and program reforms, it is important to know, for example, whether racial profiling involves a large group of officers, all officers working in a particular district or shift, or only a few officers. Previous research indicates that the percentage of traffic stops involving minorities varies by officer

(ACLU, 1996) and district (Cordner et al., 2001). Therefore, whenever possible, data should be collected in a way that allows for aggregation at the officer, district, and agency level. At the same time, researchers should take precautions to protect the confidentiality and anonymity of participants and be cognizant of how the data collection process might impact the behavior of officers (Ramirez et al., 2000). Researchers should also control for factors such as beat assignments, especially with data aggregated at the officer level, that may be related to the likelihood of encountering minority motorists.

Population of Interest

Identifying the population of interest and establishing a baseline measure of this group is perhaps the most difficult aspect of operationalizing racial profiling (Ramirez et al., 2000). As Cleary (2000) noted, "there is typically no perfect baseline measure against which to gauge police stop practices" (p. 24). One common approach is to use the racial/ethnic composition of the community as a baseline against which to compare the racial distribution of traffic stops (Cleary, 2000; Engel et al., 2002). See, for example Cox, Pease, Miller, and Tyson (2001); Nixon (2001); Texas Department of Public Safety (2000), and Verniero and Zoubek (1999). However, this approach is problematic because it assumes that all members of racial/ethnic subgroups drive and thus are at risk of being stopped (Walker, 2001). Also implicit is the assumption of vehicle ownership and a valid driver's license, both of which vary by race/ethnicity (Doyle & Taylor, 2000; Polzin, Chu, & Rey, 2000).

Given these issues, some researchers have used the racial/ethnic composition of the driving population as a baseline measure (Harris, 1999a). For example, a study of North Carolina State Highway Patrol data used district residents holding a valid driver's license as a baseline for comparisons (Zingraff et al., 2000). Although an improvement, this measure is also problematic in that the racial/ethnic composition of the driving population within a particular jurisdiction varies across different stretches of roadway, times of the day, and days of the week (Cleary, 2000; Guiliano, 2000; Valenzuela, 2000). Furthermore, it assumes no racial/ethnic differences in traffic violations and equipment failure rates (Zingraff et al., 2000). As Engel et al. (2002) noted, it is possible that certain subgroups of the population (e.g., young Black males) drive more aggressively and commit more moving violations. Finally, both measures fail to account for nonresidents traveling in the area under study, which itself impacts baseline measures (Cox et al., 2001). Walker (2001) argued that such problems may well be insurmountable and suggested an "early warning system" approach as an alternative to attempts to establish a baseline.

Another challenge is the determination of race/ethnicity by law enforcement officers (Cleary, 2000). The racial/ethnic categories used in police record keeping vary across agencies (Cleary, 2000; Ramirez et al., 2000), which is logical given regional variations in the composition of the population. Research on racial profiling should employ racial/ethnic categories that are socially meaningful within the jurisdiction of the agency. However, to facilitate comparisons with previous research, the categories should be able to be collapsed to reflect those used in the UCRs. Also, the number of categories should be relatively small to enhance the reliability and validity of the measures and to minimize error in the data collection process. Although they may not match motorists' self-assessments, officer determinations of race/ethnicity are generally best because their perceptions (rather than actual race/ethnicity) are what is central to the issue of racial profiling (Cleary, 2000). However, as Walker (2001, p. 74) noted, contextual factors impede the ability of officers to determine race/ethnicity, including tinted car windows and limited vision at night.

In addition to recording the motorists' race/ethnicity, data on age and sex should also be collected to determine whether disparities exist along these dimensions as well (Fridell et al., 2001). For example, the Washington State Patrol and Criminal Justice Training Commission (2001) found that drivers younger than 30 were more likely to be cited, regardless of race. In their North Carolina study, Zingraff et al. (2000) found that age played a role in racial differences in that Black males aged 23 to 49 (23%) and 49 and older (70%) were more likely to receive a citation than their White counterparts. Finally, Cordner et al. (2001) found a greater proportion of San Diego traffic stops involved males rather than females.

Characteristics of the Incident

Research on racial profiling must determine the extent to which racial disparities exist in the characteristics of stops. In looking at the characteristics of the incident, the focus is on what happens from the time the stop is initiated to when it is completed. To the extent that the data are available in agency records and activity logs, collecting and coding data on several factors should be relatively straightforward. For example, Zingraff et al. (2000) measured length of delay in minutes and then computed mean delay times by race. It may be possible to collect data on length of delay if the times that the stop was initiated and that the officer returned to service were recorded on activity logs or could be determined by reviewing in-car camera tapes or communications with dispatch, both of which may be time-date stamped.

Data should be collected on whether a vehicle search was conducted. With Missouri data, Nixon (2001) calculated search rates (i.e., number of searches/number of stops) by race. Similarly, Verniero and Zoubek (1999) and the Texas Department of Public Safety (2000) looked at search percentages by race. Data should also be collected on the basis or reason for the search and whether it involved a canine unit. For example, Cordner et al. (2001) distinguished between nine types of searches in San Diego (i.e., inventory, incident to arrest, consent, Fourth Amendment waiver, other basis, odor of contraband, contraband visible, evidence of criminal activity, and canine alert). Finally, information on the search outcome is important. In their North Carolina study, Zingraff et al. (2000) looked at the percentage of searches resulting in citations and warnings by race.

Researchers should attempt to determine whether restraints were used and, if so, what type of restraint (handcuffs, placed in police car). Data on this facet of the incident should be available in police reports. Researchers should also attempt to determine whether force (e.g., held at gunpoint) was used by the officer.

Data on the disposition of the stop should be available in activity logs and/or warning and citation records. Information should be collected on whether the motorist was released without a ticket, given a verbal warning, issued a warning or citation for a traffic violation, or arrested as a result of a vehicle search. Although several researchers have looked at whether or not citations or warnings were issued, with the goal of discerning racial disparities (Texas Department of Public Safety, 2000), information on the nature of the warning, citation, or arrest is also desirable. See, for example, Cox et al. (2001, p. 4) and Ramirez et al. (2000, p. 19). It is also important to distinguish between warnings and citations issued in the context of traffic accidents, as did Zingraff et al. (2000) in their study of North Carolina Highway Patrol data.

Although data collection on some incident characteristics may be relatively straightforward, gathering information on other characteristics is likely to prove more challenging, if not impossible. For example, it would be difficult to identify a valid measure of property damage given that both motorists and officers may falsify information to further their own interests. Furthermore, in cases in which property damage is disputed, it would be virtually impossible to determine the truth of the situation. Although it may be possible to rely on in-car video cameras, if available, to some extent, the angle or quality of video footage is often insufficient to allow for a clear determination. When possible, data should be collected on whether damage occurred to either the vehicle or its contents during the course of a search.

It is also likely to be very difficult, if not impossible, to collect data on the nature of the officer-citizen interaction to get at requests for information and demeanor. Demeanor is highly subjective. Although it may be possible in some cases to use videos from in-car cameras to see basic aspects of officer-motorist interaction during stops, the quality of the footage is often rather poor, as noted above, and typically does not include sound. With better quality videos that include sound, it may be possible to see facial expressions and body language and to hear the nature of the exchange of information as well as the tone. Although it may be possible for a separate observer to record information about the nature of the interaction, his or her presence is likely to have its own independent effects on the outcome of the interaction.

Summary and Conclusions

In recent years, racial profiling has generated a significant amount of controversy and social concern in American society. Although stories about racial profiling abound, very little is known about the etiology of this phenomenon. In this article, we attempt to summarize and organize the existing literature on racial profiling and establish a strong conceptual foundation for future racial profiling research. We argue that the failure to adequately conceptualize racial profiling is one of the primary problems with current research. In an effort to fill this gap, we identify and describe four issues that must be explicitly addressed in the conceptualization process of research on racial profiling: realm of activity, level of aggregation, population of interest, and characteristics of the incident. These factors are central to the concept of racial profiling and have implications for the future direction of racial profiling research.

One of the primary tasks for future research is to accurately document the nature and extent of racial profiling in American society, which is no small task. Although it may be difficult (if not impossible) to accurately assess all of the factors that impact racial profiling, there is still a significant amount of work that can be done to further knowledge on the issue and enhance our understanding of the factors that influence it. Of particular importance is the development of multivariate models that attempt to control for the effects of a variety of factors with the goal of constructing more complete and accurate causal models. It is important to move beyond simple comparisons across racial/ethnic categories of the likelihood of being pulled over or of being issued a citation. We have identified several factors that should be controlled for in racial profiling research, but note that this list is not exhaustive. Instead, as more is learned about vehicle stops and the factors that affect police decision making within that context, additional potential control variables are likely to be identified. As models continue to be refined, a better sense of the relative impact of the factors discussed will emerge.

APPENDIX

The table below categorizes the different ways that the term *racial profiling* is used in the literature. In addition to variation between sources in terms of whether an explicit definition of racial profiling is provided, there are subtle and not-so-subtle variations in the implied and explicitly stated meanings of the term.

Definitions of Racial Profiling

Cleary (2000, pp. 5-6)—Conceptual

> "Under the narrow definition, racial profiling occurs when a police officer stops, questions, arrests, and/or searches someone solely on the basis of the person's race or ethnicity. . . . Under the broader definition, racial profiling occurs when a law enforcement officer uses race or ethnicity as one of several factors in deciding to stop, question, arrest, and/or search someone."

Fridell et al. (2001, p. 5)—Conceptual

> "Racially biased policing occurs when law enforcement inappropriately considers race or ethnicity in deciding how to intervene in a law enforcement capacity."

Harris (1999a)—Conceptual and Operational

> "African-Americans call it 'driving while Black'-police officers stopping, questioning, and even searching Black drivers who have committed no crime, based on the excuse of a traffic offense." (p. 265)

> "The task was the same as Lamberth's . . . use statistics to test whether Blacks in Ohio were being stopped in numbers disproportionate to their presence in the driving population." (p. 281)

Kennedy (1999, p. 11)—Conceptual

> "Properly understood, then, racial profiling occurs whenever police routinely use race as a negative signal that, along with an accumulation of other signals, causes an officer to react with suspicion."

Langan, Greenfeld, Smith, Durose, and Levin (2001, p. 20)—Operational

> "One definition of racial profiling is 'using race as a key factor in deciding whether to make a traffic stop.' Another definition is 'using race as a key factor in deciding whether, during a traffic stop, to search the vehicle or the driver.'"

Meeks (2000, pp. 4-5)—Conceptual

> Racial profiling is "the tactic of stopping someone only because of the color of his or her skin and a fleeting suspicion that the person is engaging in criminal behavior."

Minnesota Department of Public Safety (2000, p. 2)—Conceptual

> "To help determine whether motor vehicle drivers in Minnesota are being stopped by law enforcement officers because of their race."

Muharrar (1998, p. 1)—Conceptual

"Racial profiling—the discriminatory practice by police of treating Blackness (or brownness) as an indication of possible criminality."

Newport (1999) for Gallup Organization—Operational

"It has been reported that some police officers stop motorists of certain racial or ethnic groups because the officers believe that these groups are more likely than others to commit certain types of crimes. Do you believe that this practice, known as 'racial profiling,' is widespread or not?"

Nixon (2001, p. 1)—Operational

"Racial profiling . . . defined as the inappropriate use of race when making a decision to stop, search, cite, or arrest a person."

Ramirez, McDevitt, and Farrell (2000, p. 3)—Conceptual

"Racial profiling is defined as any police-initiated action that relies on the race, ethnicity, or national origin rather than the behavior of an individual or information that leads the police to a particular individual who has been identified as being, or having been, engaged in criminal activity."

Taylor and Whitney (1999, p. 507)—Conceptual

"'Racial profiling' by the police, that is, the practice of questioning Blacks in suspicious circumstances in disproportionate numbers in the expectation that they are more likely than people of other races to be criminals."

United States General Accounting Office (2000, p. 1)—Conceptual

"Racial profiling of motorists by law enforcement-that is, using race as a key factor in deciding whether to make a traffic stop."

Verniero and Zoubek (1999, p. 5)—Conceptual

"We choose to define 'racial profiling' broadly enough to encompass any action taken by a sole trooper during a traffic stop that is based upon racial or ethnic stereotypes and that has the effect of treating minority motorists differently than nonminority motorists."

Walker (2001, p. 64)—Conceptual

"Racial profiling refers to allegations that police officers stop African American drivers for alleged traffic violations on the basis of race and not because of legitimate suspicion of any law violation."

Washington State Patrol (2001, p. 1)—Conceptual and Operational

"'Racial profiling,' or the targeting of certain racial groups during the course of conducting traffic stops"

"Officer-initiated contacts of violators . . . [should be] . . . racially proportionate to two standards: driving-age populations and collisions."

Meaning of Racial Profiling Assumed or Inferred Through Examples

Cohen, Lennon, and Wasserman (2000, p. 2)—No Definition

"The well-founded belief that authorities use racial profiles to justify more intensive observation and questioning of people of color has fed escalating tensions between police and minority communities."

Cordner, Williams, and Zuniga (2001)—No Definition

Used the term *racial profiling* but did not define it. Compared the percentage of minorities and Whites in the population to the percentage of minority and White drivers stopped.

Harris (1999b)—No Definition

Used the term *racial profiling* but did not define it. Instead provided examples, talked about "driving while Black" and the use of race in pretext stops.

Leitzel (2001)—No Definition

Used term *racial profiling* but did not define it. Used term *race-based policing* more often, inferring that it is the practice of using race alone or in concert with other factors as a reason to stop or detain a person.

Texas Department of Public Safety (2000)—No Definition

Used term *racial profiling* but did not define it. Referred to instances of inappropriate use of race in decisions regarding motorists.

References

American Civil Liberties Union. (1996). *Report of John Lamberth, Ph.D.* (In the Courts). Retrieved February 12, 2002, from www.aclu.org/court/lamberth.html

Anderson, E. (1990). *Streetwise: Race, class, and change in an urban community.* Chicago: University of Chicago Press.

Anderson, E. (1999). *The code of the street: Decency, violence, and the moral life of the inner city.* New York: Norton.

Bursik, R. J., & Webb, J. (1982). Community change and patterns of delinquency. *American Journal of Sociology, 88,* 24-42.

Chambliss, W. (1994). Policing the ghetto underclass: The politics of law and law enforcement. *Social Problems, 41,* 177-194.

Cleary, J. (2000). *Racial profiling studies in law enforcement; Issues and methodology.* St. Paul; Minnesota House of Representatives, Research Department.

Cohen, J. D., Lennon, J. J., & Wasserman. R. (2000). *End racial profiling.* Blueprint, volume 8. Retrieved July 13, 2002 from http://www.ndol.org/blueprint/fall2000/cohen-lennon-wasserman.html

Cole, D. (1999). *No equal justice; Race and class in the American criminal justice system.* New York: New Press.

Commission on Accreditation of Law Enforcement Agencies. (2002, March 29). *Racial profiling update—2000 state actions.* Retrieved April 13, 2002, from www.calea.org/newweb/news/2000Stateactions.htm

Cordner, G., Williams, B., & Zuniga, M. (2001). *Vehicle stops for the year 2000: Executive summary.* San Diego, CA: San Diego Police Department.

Council on Crime and Justice. (2001). *Minneapolis Police traffic stops and driver's race; Analysis and recommendations.* Minneapolis, MN: Author.

Cox, S., Pease, S., Miller, D., & Tyson, C. B. (2001). *Interim report of traffic stops statistics for the state of Connecticut.* Rocky Hill, CT: Office of the Chief State's Attorney, State of Connecticut Retrieved June 24, 2002 from http://web.wtnh.com/Report_Narrative.pdf

Decker, S. (1981). Citizen attitudes toward the police: A review of past findings and suggestions for future policy. *Journal of Police Science and Administration. 9,* 80-87.

Donziger, S. R. (1996). *The real war on crime: The report of the National Criminal Justice Commission.* New York; HarperCollins.

Doyle, D. G., & Taylor, B. D. (2000). Variation in metropolitan travel behavior by sex and ethnicity. In Battelle (Ed.), *Travel patterns of people of color* (pp. 181-244). Washington, DC: Federal Highway Administration.

Engel, R. S., Calnon, J., & Bernard, T. J. (2002). Theory and racial profiling: Shortcomings and future directions in research. *Justice Quarterly, 19,* 249-273.

Fridell, L., Lunney, R., Diamond, D., Kubu, B., with Scott, M., & Laing, C. (2001). *Racially biased policing: A principled response.* Washington, DC: Police Executive Research Forum.

Free, M. D. (1996). *African Americans and the criminal justice system.* New York: Garland.

Fyfe, J. J. (1982). Blind justice; Police shootings in Memphis. *The Journal of Criminal Law and Criminology, 73,*707-722.

Gaynes, E. (1993). The urban criminal justice system: Where young + Black + male = probable cause. *Fordham Urban Law Journal, 20, 621.*

Guiliano, G. (2000). Residential location differences in people of color. In Battelle

(Ed.), *Travel patterns of people of color* (pp. 91-136). Washington, DC; Federal Highway Administration.

Harris, D. A. (1997). "Driving while Black" and all other traffic offenses: The Supreme Court and pretextual traffic stops. *The Journal of Criminal Law and Criminology, 87,* 544-582.

Harris, D. A. (1999a). The stories, the statistics, and the law; Why 'driving while Black' matters. *Minnesota Law Review, 84,* 265-325.

Harris, D. A. (1999b). *Driving while Black: Racial profiling on our nation's highways.* Retrieved May 23, 2001, from the American Civil Liberties Union Web site: www.aclu.org/profiling/report/index.html

Harris, D. A. (2002). *Profiles in injustice: Why racial profiling cannot work.* New York: New Press.

Hemmens, C., & Levin, D. (2000). Resistance is futile; The right to resist unlawful arrest in an era of aggressive policing. *Crime and Delinquency, 46,* 472-496.

James, J. (2000). The dysfunctional and the disappearing: Democracy, race and imprisonment. *Social Identities, 6,* 483-493.

Jensen, G. (2000). Prohibition, alcohol, and murder; Untangling countervailing mechanisms. *Homicide Studies, 4,* 18-36.

Johnson, S.L. (1983). Race and the decision to detain a suspect. *Yale Law Journal, 93,* 214-258.

Kennedy, R. (1997). *Race, crime and the law.* New York; Pantheon.

Kennedy, R. (1999, September 13). Suspect policy. *The New Republic, 13,* 30. Retrieved March 29, 2002, from http://www.tnr.com/archive/0999/091399/coverstoryO91399.html

Klinger, D, A. (1996). Bringing crime back in: Toward a better understanding of police arrest decisions. *Journal of Research in Crime and Delinquency, 33,* 333-336.

Klinger, D. A. (1997). Negotiating order in patrol work: An ecological theory of police response to deviance. *Criminology, 35,*277-306.

Kreft, I., & de Leeuw, J. (1998). *Introducing multilevel modeling.* Thousand Oaks, CA: Sage.

Langan, P. A., Greenfeld, L. A., Smith, S. K., Durose, M. R., & Levin, D. J. (2001). *Contacts between the police and the public: Findings from the 1999 National Survey* (No. NCJ 184957). Washington, DC: Bureau of Justice Statistics, U.S. Department of Justice.

Lawson, B. (1992). *The underclass question.* Philadelphia: Temple University Press.

Legal Information Institute. (2002). *Civil rights; An overview.* Ithaca, NY: Cornell Law School. Retrieved March 2, 2002 from www.law.cornell.edu/topics.civilrights.html

Leitzel, J. (2001). Race and policing. *Society, 38,* 38-43.

Lundman, R. J. (1996). Demeanor and arrest: Additional evidence from previously unpublished data. *Journal of Research in Crime and Delinquency, 33,* 306-323.

Maclin, T. (1998). Terry v. Ohio's Fourth Amendment legacy: Black men and police discretion, *St. John's Law Review, 72,* 1271-1321.

Mann, C. R. (1993). *Unequal justice: A question of color.* Bloomington: Indiana University Press.

Mastrofski, S. D., Parks, R, B., Reiss, A. J., Warden, R. E., DeJong, C., Snipes, J. B., et al. (1998). *Systematic observation of public policy: Applying field research methods to policy issues* (NIJ No. NCJ 172859). Washington, DC: Government Printing Office.

Mastrofski, S. D., Ritti, R. R., & Hoffmaster, D. (1987). Organizational determinants of police discretion: The case of drinking-driving. *Journal of Criminal Justice, 15,* 387-402.

Mauer, M. (1994). *Americans behind bars; The international use of incarceration, 1992-93,* Washington, DC: The Sentencing Project.

McNamara, J. H. (1967). Uncertainties in police work; The relevance of police, recruits' backgrounds and training. In D. J. Bordua (Ed.), *The police: Six sociological essays* (pp. 163-252). New York: John Wiley.

Meeks, K. (2000). *Driving while Black: Highways, shopping malls, taxicabs, sidewalks; how to fight back if you are a victim of racial profiling.* New York; Broadway Books.

Milazzo, C., & Hansen, R. (1999, October 30-November 3). *Race relations in police operations: A legal and ethical perspective.* Paper presented at the 106th Annual Conference of the International Association of Chiefs of Police, Charlotte, NC.

Mills, C. W. (1961). *The sociological imagination.* New York: Grove.

Minnesota Department of Public Safety. (2000, November), *Racial profiling report.* Retrieved September 13, 2001, from mnclu.org/nr_racial_profiling.html

Muharrar, M. (1998, September/October). *Media blackface; "Racialprofiling" in news reporting.* Retrieved May 23, 2001, from www.fair .org/extra/9809/media-blackface.html

Newport, F. (1999). *Racial profiling is seen as widespread, particularly among young Black men.* Princeton, NJ: The Gallup Organization. Retrieved May 23, 2001 from www.gallup .com/poll/releases/pr991209.asp

Niederhoffer, A. (1967). *Behind the shield: The police in urban society.* Garden City, NY: Doubleday.

Nixon, J. (2001). *2000 annual report of Missouri traffic stops.* Jefferson City: Missouri Attorney General's Office.

Polzin, S. R, Chu, X., & Rey, J. R, (2000). Demographics of people of color. In Battelle (Ed.), *Travel patterns of people of color* (pp. 27-44). Washington, DC: Federal Highway Administration.

Ramirez, D., McDevitt, J., & Farrell, A. (2000). A *resource guide on racial profiling data collection systems; Promising practices and lessons learned* (USDOJ No. NCJ 184768). Washington, DC: Government Printing Office.

Reichel, P. L. (1988). Southern slave patrols as a transitional police type. *American Journal of Police, 7, 51-77.*

Reiss, A. J., Jr. (1986). Why are communities important in understanding crime? In A. J. J. Reiss & M. Tonry (Eds.), *Communities and crime* (pp. 1-34). Chicago: University of Chicago Press.

Robinson, M. (2000). The construction and reinforcement of myths of race and crime. *Journal of Contemporary Criminal Justice, 16, 133-156.*

Schuerman, L., & Kobrin, S. (1986), Community careers in crime. In A. J. J. Reiss & M. Tonry (Eds.), *Communities and crime* (pp. 67-100). Chicago: University of Chicago Press.

Shaw, C, & McKay, H. (1942). *Juvenile delinquency and urban areas.* Chicago: University of Chicago Press.

Sherman, L., Shaw, J. W., & Rogan, D.P. (1995). *The Kansas City gun experiment* (NIJ No. NCJ 150855). Washington, DC: National Institute of Justice.

Skolnick, J. (1994), *Justice without trial* (3rd ed.). New York: Macmillan.

Smith, D. A., & Visher, C. A. (1981). Street-level justice: Situational determinants of police arrest decisions. *Social Problems, 29(2),* 167-177.

Strom, K., Brien, P., & Smith, S. (2001). *Traffic stop data collection policies for state police, 2001* (BJS No. NCJ 191158;. Washington, DC: U.S. Department of Justice, Bureau of Justice Statistics.

Taylor, J., & Whitney, G. (1999). Crime and racial profiling by U.S. police: Is there an empirical basis? *The Journal of Social, Political, and Economic Studies, 24,* 485-509.

Texas Department of Public Safety. (2000, October). *Traffic stop data report.* Retrieved June 20, 2002, from www.txdps.state.tx.us/director_ staff/public_information/ trafrep2q00.pdf

Toby, J. (2000). Are police the enemy? *Society, 37,* 38-43.

Tonry, M. (1995). *Malign neglect: Race, crime, and punishment in America.* New York: Oxford University Press.

Torres, D. A. (1987). *Handbook of state police, highway patrols, and investigative agencies.* New York: Greenwood.

U.S. Census Bureau. (2000). *Statistical abstract of the United States 2000.* Washington, DC: Government Printing Office.

U.S. General Accounting Office. (2000). *Racial profiling limited data available on motorist stops* (Tech. Rep. No. GAO/GGD-00-41). Washington. DC: Author.

Valenzuela, A. (2000). Race, inequality, and travel patterns among people of color. In Battelle (Ed.), *Travel patterns of people of color* (pp. 1-26). Washington, DC: Federal Highway Administration.

Verniero, P., & Zoubek, P. H. (1999). *Interim report of the state police review team regarding allegations of racial profiling.* Office of the Attorney General, New Jersey Department of Law and Public Safety. Retrieved June 19, 2002 from www.state.nj.us/lps/intm_419.pdf

Walker, S. (1999). *The police in America: An introduction* (3rd ed.). Boston; McGraw-Hill College.

Walker, S. (2001). Searching for the denominator: Problems with police traffic stop data and an early warning system solution. *Justice Research and Policy, 3,* 63-95.

Walker, S., Spohn, C., & DeLone, M. (2000). *The color of justice: Race, ethnicity, and crime in America.* Belmont, CA: Wadsworth/Thomson Learning.

Washington State Patrol & Criminal Justice Training Commission. (2001, January). *Report to the legislature on routine traffic stop data.* Retrieved June 20, 2002, from Washington State Patrol Web site: www.wa.gov/wsp/reports/demogra2.doc

Wilbanks, W. (1987). *The Myth of a racist criminal justice system.* Monterey, CA: Brooks/Cole.

Williams, H., &, Murphy. P. (1990). *The evolving strategy of police: A minority view* (N1J No. 13). Washington, DC: Government Printing Office.

Wilson, W. J (1992). *The ghetto underclass.* Newbury Park, CA: Sage.

Worden, R. E. (1989). Situational and attitudinal explanations of police behavior: A theoretical reappraisal and empirical reassessment. *Law and Society Review, 23,* 668-711.

Worden, R. E., Shepard, R. L., & Mastrofski, S. D. (1996). On the meaning and measurement of suspects' demeanor toward the police: A comment on "demeanor and arrest." *Journal of Research in Crime and Delinquency, 33,* 324-332.

Zingraff, M. T., Mason, H. M., Smith, W. R., Tomuskovic-Devey, D., Warren, P., McMurray, H. L., et al. (2000, November 1). *Evaluating North Carolina State Highway Patrol data; Citations, warnings, and searches in 1998.* Retrieved June 20, 2002, from www.nccrimecontrol.org/shp/neshpreport.htm

DISCUSSION QUESTIONS

1. According to these authors, is racial profiling a relatively new phenomenon?

2. Batton and Kadleck outline four factors they believe are central to conceptualizing racial profiling. They point out that in broader contexts, race and sex influence social interactions. Why do these authors argue that police interactions are different?

3. What is problematic about using the incident (individual traffic stop) as the unit of analysis in racial profiling research?

4. What is it about the incidents (the traffic stops) themselves that is important to analyze?

5. Why might racial profiling be greater in some areas of the country than others?

6. What, according to these authors, is the most difficult component of measuring racial profiling?

7. What are some of the ethical issues that might arise in research on racial profiling?

8. Could the persons who are stopped by law enforcement also have a role in the outcome of that stop?

5

SAMPLING PROCEDURES

Because most researchers cannot study the entire population of persons they would like to, they usually employ procedures to obtain a sample of that population. Sampling is a procedure that allows researchers to study a selected part of the population. One of the first steps in sampling is determining the population the researcher wishes to study. A population in research terms is the entire group of elements a researcher wants to study (Bachman & Schutt, 2008); the population is sometimes also referred to as the sampling frame.

For example, maybe a researcher is interested in studying the population of high school age boys in a particular city or wants to assess the riot policies of all maximum security prisons in the United States. Around election time, many agencies attempt to study the entire voting public by sampling only a few individuals to determine who is likely to be the next president. The key is that in order to obtain a sample that is similar to the population researchers want to study, they need to first specify that population. Once the population is specified, researchers can attempt to obtain a representative sample or a sample that has all the same characteristics of the population (Ellis, Hartley, & Walsh, 2010).

REPRESENTATIVE AND NONREPRESENTATIVE SAMPLES

Representative samples allow researchers to generalize the findings from their study to the larger population. The ability to generalize the findings of a study is a very desirable feature of research. For instance, if 16% of the voting population is Hispanic females, researchers will want to select a sample that contains the same percentage of Hispanic females. Often, obtaining a representative sample is a difficult endeavor; researchers may not have the time or resources to select a representative sample, or the population researchers want to study might be very difficult to define (for some criminal offenses, say prostitution or narcotics trafficking, the entire population of offenders is very difficult to identify). If the characteristics of the sample do not match the population's characteristics, the study contains what is known as sampling error. Not to be confused with measurement error, *sampling error* refers to biases in the research results based on the way in which the sample was selected, not the way in which the concepts or variables in a study were measured.

Because of the difficulty in obtaining representative samples, researchers in criminology and criminal justice often study nonrepresentative samples. Ultimately, if the goal of the research study is to assess the relationship between variables or to test theoretical arguments across different samples of the population, obtaining a representative sample may not be necessary (Ellis et al., 2010).

PROBABILITY SAMPLING DESIGNS

Probability sampling designs are those that allow researchers to obtain representative samples. Probability sampling designs allow each sampling unit an equal chance of being selected in the sample (Hagan, 2005). Most researchers use simple random sampling to obtain probability samples. This entails obtaining a list of members of the population and then randomly selecting the sample from this list. Advances in technology have greatly helped researchers be able to select random samples from large populations; computer programs can generate random samples from a list of subjects. Researchers who conduct telephone surveys often employ random digit dialing programs to obtain random samples.

Other probability sampling methods include stratified random sampling and cluster sampling. Stratified random samples rely on the distribution of the characteristics of a population in order to select a sample that is representative of these characteristics (Hagan, 2005). Researchers using this method partition (or stratify) the population according to certain characteristics (often demographic characteristics such as age, sex, race), then randomly select individuals from these groupings to obtain a sample that is representative. Cluster sampling involves similar techniques and is useful for large or widely dispersed populations.

Cluster sampling involves randomly dividing the population into clusters and then a random sample is selected from each cluster (Bachman & Schutt, 2008). Clusters could include states, counties, cities, or neighborhoods. The National Crime Victimization Survey (NCVS) is an example of research that uses a cluster sampling technique to study victimization in the United States. Even when a sample's characteristics do not resemble the population, a technique called weighting can be employed to make the obtained sample more representative of the population (Ellis et al., 2010). Due to its complexity, however, weighting can only be done through computerized statistical programs.

NONPROBABILITY SAMPLING DESIGNS

Nonprobability sampling methods are those where EPSEM (Equal Probability of Selection Method) is violated. Often, researchers cannot obtain representative samples. This may especially be the case for criminological and criminal justice research. Many times, researchers study criminals who have been arrested or convicted of crimes. These studies have been criticized because they are not representative of the true population of offenders (the true population of offenders would include both criminals who have been arrested and convicted and those who have not). Because researchers are not often able to identify those who have committed offenses but have not been caught, they are really studying, for lack of a better phrase, unsuccessful criminals. Again, however, based upon the purposes of a research study, or simply because the true population cannot be identified, researchers study those whom they can; these samples are often not representative.

The main types of nonprobability sampling designs used for criminology and criminal justice topics include: convenience sampling, purposive sampling, quota sampling, and snowball sampling (Bachman & Schutt, 2008). Convenience samples are just that: convenient. Often, researchers select a sample for study because the subjects are easy to obtain or are available for study. If you have ever participated in a research study as part of a university course, the professor was conducting research by way of a convenience sample. The only reason you were selected to be in the study was because you enrolled in the class—that made it convenient for the professor to use you as a subject of research. While not representative or generalizable, these samples are relatively cheap and easy to obtain. The local television station journalist is utilizing convenience sampling every time he or she conducts interviews with persons on the street; again, the problem with these samples is that we really cannot be sure that the responses obtained reflect those of the entire population the reporter wants to generalize to.

Purposive sampling is another nonprobability sampling design and is similar to convenience sampling; these samples are chosen based on the researcher's needs or skills. Maybe the purpose is to simply study a group of DWI defendants at one city court to gain an understanding of their attitudes toward drinking and driving. In this case, going to the courthouse to survey or interview these offenders provides a sample for the purpose of the research. Again, these samples are not representative, and the responses and results of these studies cannot be generalized to the larger population of DWI offenders.

Quota samples attempt to overcome the limitations of convenience or purposive samples by selecting a sample that resembles the population's characteristics, however, not through use of random sampling. Quota sampling is the nonprobability analog of stratified probability sampling (Hagan, 2005). Even though researchers using quota sampling have selected a sample that resembles the population on some characteristics, they do not know whether the sample is truly representative regarding all characteristics (Bachman & Schutt, 2008). Therein lies the problem with these samples: we have no way of knowing how generalizable the results from them are. Ellis and colleagues (2010) state that quota samples are nothing more than convenience samples chosen based on some population characteristic.

The last type of nonprobability sampling design is called snowball sampling and is utilized where subjects may be difficult to obtain or where behaviors are rare. Snowball sampling "entails obtaining a first subject and, on the basis of this subject, obtaining an entrée and introduction to a second subject, then a third, and so forth" (Hagan, 2005, p. 143). Subjects such as prostitutes or drug dealers may be difficult to identify, yet if a researcher is able to obtain one or two subjects, these subjects can probably introduce or refer him or her to other subjects. If a researcher wants to study drug dealers or gang members, for instance, obtaining one or two subjects can "snowball" into a large sample because these initial subjects interact with, or know, other subjects engaging in similar behaviors (Bachman & Schutt, 2008). Again, however, because researchers will likely not obtain the entire population of offenders, this sampling technique does not allow them to generalize their results. Nonetheless, some offenders and some behaviors are rare and difficult to study; thus, a snowball design may be the only opportunity a researcher has to study a specific population.

GENERALIZABILITY AND STATISTICAL INFERENCE

Because the goal of social scientific research is to advance knowledge, research using representative samples is better able to generalize its findings to the larger population. Generalizability, therefore, is a desirable attribute of research. To the extent researchers can generalize their results, they can have greater certainty that their findings are accurate and represent reality. The extent to which criminologists specifically can do this enables them to advance knowledge about crime etiology or the nature of criminal events. How a researcher selects a sample obviously plays an important role in the ability to generalize the findings.

Sample generalizability also depends on the amount of sampling error present in research. Luckily, researchers can determine the amount of sampling error that exists with mathematical tools called inferential statistics. Inferential statistics allow researchers to estimate "how likely it is that a statistical result based on data from a random sample is representative of the population from which the sample was selected" (Bachman & Schutt, 2008, p. 103).

Similar to the discussion in Chapter 2 about hypothesis testing, generalizations about populations based on findings from samples are always associated with a probability level (Champion & Hartley, 2010). If researchers randomly select their samples, they can generalize their results based upon the calculated P value associated with them. The 5% rule applies here as well; if the probability level (P) associated with the results is less than 0.05, this means that there is less than a 5% chance that the results are erroneous, and these findings can be inferred to the larger population from which the sample was drawn.

In the research studies that you will read in this book, you will notice that researchers only interpret the results that reach this 0.05 threshold. The results that have p values greater than 0.05 are not interpreted or inferred as true for the larger population because there is a greater than 5% chance that they are due to error. If researchers could study an entire population, they would have no need for inferential statistics, as research results would simply be descriptions of the characteristics of the population. Some critics have argued against the use of inferential statistics in criminology and criminal justice research where the researcher has not obtained a representative sample (see, for instance, Berk, 2004); nonetheless, by convention, most studies make use of probability levels and inferential statistics.

RESEARCH READING

Corporate crime has recently garnered more spotlight as national scandals of corporate malfeasance have been made public. Public concern and law enforcement efforts have historically always been more focused toward street-level offenders. The downfall of Enron, WorldCom, and Bernard Madoff, and with them the retirement and savings plans of employees and shareholders, have renewed public interest in the consequences that these types of white-collar offenses can have. Unnever and colleagues study a national probability sample to examine public support for tougher regulations and sanctions for corporate executives. The results not surprisingly show public support for getting tough on corporate crime. What is interesting, however, is that their results reveal differing attitudes across racial groups regarding punishment for corporate crime.

PUBLIC SUPPORT FOR GETTING TOUGH ON CORPORATE CRIME

Racial and Political Divides

James D. Unnever, Michael L. Benson, and Francis T. Cullen

Abstract: The recent wave of corporate wrongdoing has raised the issue of whether the public is concerned about the control of lawlessness in the business world. Using a national probability sample, we

Source: Unnever, J. D., Benson, M. L., & Cullen, F. T. (2008). Public support for getting tough on corporate crime: Racial and political divides. *Journal of Research in Crime and Delinquency, 45*(2), 163–190. Copyright © 2008 Sage Publications.

explore whether Americans want to enact stricter regulations of the stock market and advocate more punitive criminal sanctions for corporate executives who conceal their company's true financial condition. The findings reveal that Americans generally favor getting tough on corporate illegality. The analysis also indicates, however, that group differences exist in public support for punitive corporate crime control policies. Although liberals and conservatives equally support punishing corporate criminals more harshly, African Americans are more likely than Whites to endorse more restrictive and more punitive policies toward corporate criminals. We conclude that punitive attitudes are socially constructed beliefs that reflect the dynamics of conflicted class and racial relations.

INTRODUCTION

Since the inception of crime-related opinion polls, an important issue has been to understand why some Americans hold more punitive attitudes regarding crime control than others (Beckett and Sasson 2000; Cullen, Fisher, and Applegate 2000; Roberts and Hough 2005; Roberts and Stalans 2000). In recent years, this line of research has taken on particular urgency as the United States has adopted ever more punitive crime control policies. Indeed, since the 1980s, the United States has waged a "war on crime"—a development variously held to manifest a "penal harm movement" (Clear 1994), a "prison experiment" (Currie 1998), a "culture of control" (Garland 2001), "penal populism" (Roberts et al. 2003), and "harsh justice" (Whitman 2003).

The war on crime that was launched in the 1980s, however, was not directed with equal vigor at corporate crime. As Simon (2006) notes, during the Reagan administration, funding designated for prosecuting corporate crime by the U.S. Department of Justice was reduced. This lack of attention on corporate crime was not new. As Sutherland (1949) noted, a distinguishing feature of corporate crime is the differential implementation of the criminal law. Whereas so-called ordinary street crimes are handled almost exclusively within the criminal justice system, it is no secret that violations of law by corporations have traditionally been dealt with via civil or regulatory proceedings. The reasons for this differential enforcement are historically complex. In part, however, they reflect the belief among some policymakers and economic theorists that free markets are self-correcting. Using the criminal law to control harmful corporate behavior is inefficient and would only get in the way of this built-in self-regulating mechanism (Pontell 2005). Opposing this point of view are those who believe that government controls, either in the form of regulations or criminal laws, are necessary and appropriate (Snider 1990).

Throughout the history of the United States the popularity of these differing viewpoints—free markets, government regulations, or criminal laws—as means of controlling harmful corporate behavior has fluctuated. The 1980s inaugurated a period of deregulation, but the deregulation of the 1980s and 1990s had been preceded by expansions of regulations in the 1960s and 1970s. In addition, since the 1970s a social movement against white-collar crime has been evident, which has resulted in increased use of the criminal law against corporations (for a recent review, see Cullen et al. 2006).

The growth of regulation and criminal laws directed at business often follows a three-step pattern of scandal, outcry, and response. First, a scandal of some sort is discovered. This provokes the second step—public outcry demanding governmental action—that is followed by the third step—some sort of governmental action, either a showcase prosecution or more importantly new laws and regulations. We believe that the United States is undergoing such a scenario now. The first phase of the process—the discovery of a scandal—has been well-documented and extensively publicized.

Since the turn of the twenty-first century, the United States has been in the midst of what the U.S. General Accounting Office (U.S.

GAO) has labeled a "wave" of corporate scandals. These scandals involve massive corporate financial fraud, which the U.S. GAO (2005:1) defines as "criminal activity involving various types of unlawful, nonviolent conduct committed by corporations, individuals, or both, including theft or fraud and other violations of trust, for example, securities fraud and financial institution fraud." Among the more prominent offenders are such large corporations as Halliburton, Lucent, Xerox, Rite Aid, Cendant, Sunbeam, Waste Management, Enron Corporation, Global Crossing, K-Mart. WorldCom, Adelphia, Xerox, and Tyco (Simon 2006). The financial costs of these frauds have been enormous. The collapse of Enron alone resulted in approximately US$70 billion in lost market capitalization and devastated thousands of investors, pensioners, and employees. Similarly, the WorldCom collapse is the largest corporate bankruptcy in U.S. history.

Furthermore, a U.S. GAO (2002) report commissioned to investigate restatements of corporate financial statements found that about 10 percent of all listed companies announced at least one restatement because of accounting irregularities and that the number of restatements increased approximately 145 percent between January 1997 and June 2002. The alleged financial frauds committed by Enron, WorldCom, Qwest, Tyco, and Global Crossing, by themselves, are estimated to total about US$460 billion (Rezaee 2005). As a point of comparison, the annual loss for larceny-theft was estimated by the Federal Bureau of Investigation (2005:52) to be US$5.1 billion. Needless to say, the media attention on these corporate crime cases and their aftermaths has been enormous.

In light of this recent wave of corporate crime, it is important to assess the current state of American public opinion about the control of corporate wrong-doings. Public sentiments are potentially important in shaping crime control policy (Roberts et al. 2003). Indeed, scholars have argued that the legitimacy of the criminal justice system can be undermined if the government fails to respond to well-publicized corporate crimes that result in multitudes of harmed victims (Moore and Mills 1990). This can be particularly true if these crimes occur when the public is expressing sentiments that something should be done to stop an emerging crime wave of corporate offending.

Policymakers have argued that the public holds relatively benign opinions toward white-collar crime, including behaviors that occurred in "corporate suites." For example, the President's Commission on Law Enforcement and the Administration of Justice (1968; 158) concluded that: "the public tends to be indifferent to business crime or even to sympathize with the offenders who have been caught." Researchers, however, questioned the accuracy of this depiction and took on the task of assessing public sentiments toward corporate crime (Braithwaite 1982; Cullen et al 1983; Cullen, Link, and Polanzi 1982; Frank et al. 1989; Hans and Ermann 1989; for a summary, see Evans, Cullen, and Dubeck 1993). Different methods were used to probe citizens' attitudes, including rankings of crime seriousness, preferred sentencing recommendations, and assessments of vignettes. Regardless of the research design, the public displayed a surprising willingness to sanction corporate crime, especially when the harm was perceived as high. What remains unclear, however, is the extent to which this consensus has remained intact after the turn of the twenty-first century. There is an emerging understanding that the public continues to view white-collar offenses as relatively serious and worthy of punishment (Kane and Wall 2006; Piquero, Carmichael, and Piquero forthcoming; Schoepfer, Carmichael, and Piquero 2007). Still, the extant research remains slim and in need of further investigation.

To help fill this void, we use a national, probability sample conducted in 2002 to examine two policies related to corporate crime control. First, we investigate the degree to which Americans support greater regulation of the stock market, which has served as a conduit for many financial frauds. Second, we investigate the degree to which Americans want stricter penalties, including longer prison terms, for corporate executives who conceal their company's true financial condition. These analyses thus reveal the degree to which Americans support social reforms that address the root causes of corporate crime (e.g., further regulating the stock market) and whether they endorse punishing corporate criminals more severely.

Most importantly, we attempt to advance the extant research by examining not only general attitudes toward corporate crime control policy, but also how these opinions are affected by political orientation and race. These factors are two of the most salient predictors of public policy attitudes. They often create a wide policy gap in how members of these groups "see the world," especially in regards to crime control (Unnever forthcoming). Given the dearth of previous research, however, it is not clear how political orientation—liberals versus conservatives—and race are related to corporate crime control.

There are fundamental differences between how liberals and conservatives want to solve entrenched social problems such as crime. In general, conservatives favor punitive policies, including mass incarceration, that target "irresponsible" criminals, whereas liberals want to attack the root causes of crime (Beckett and Sasson 2000; Jacobs and Carmichael 2002). We assess whether this "political divide" is reproduced in attitudes toward the control of corporate criminals. As we argue below, there are reasons to believe that it is not and that the roles will actually be reversed. Accordingly, we provide an empirical test of the "switch hypothesis" put forward by Zimring and Hawkins (1978).

Similarly, we explore whether the "racial divide" in support for punitive crime control policies—that is particularly evident in public support for the death penalty—is also reproduced in American attitudes toward the punishment of corporate criminals (Cochran and Chamlin 2006). African Americans generally endorse less punitive responses to street crime than Whites, but is this divide replicated with respect to corporate crime? We use comparative conflict theory to inform this analysis (see Hagan, Shedd, and Payne 2005).

METHODS

Data

The current project analyzes data that were generated from a poll, conducted July 11-15, 2002, by ABC News and *The Washington Post*. This poll is part of a continuing series of monthly surveys conducted by these agencies with the purpose of soliciting public opinion on a range of political and social issues. The universe included people aged 18 and over living in households with telephones in the nation's contiguous 48 states. The sample included households in the continental United States that were selected via random digit dialing procedures to insure that all possible listed and unlisted phone numbers were included with equal probability of selection. Within households, the respondent selected was the adult living in the household who last had a birthday and who was home at the time of the interview. The sample included 1,512 respondents. The final data were weighted using demographic information from the Census to adjust for sampling and non-sampling deviations from population values. The respondents were classified into one of 48 cells based on age, race, sex, and education. Weights were assigned so that the proportion in each of these 48 cells matched the actual population proportions according to the Census Bureau's most recent Current Population Survey (ABC News/The *Washington Post* 2002). We use the weighted sample in the analysis.

Dependent Variables

We analyze two dependent variables. These measures examine different forms of corporate crime control policies. Table 5.1 shows the variables in our analyses, including variable names, coding categories, and descriptive statistics.

Regulating the stock market. Our first dependent variable assesses the degree to which Americans support efforts to control corporate wrongdoing via policies that would affect the functioning of the economy. It is based on the following question: "Do you

Table 5.1 Coding of Variables

Variable	Coding and/or Range	Mean	Standard Deviation
Dependent variables			
Regulating stock market	Scores range from 1 to 3 with higher values indicating greater support for new regulations	1.78	.94
Stiffer penalties	Scores range from 1 to 4 with larger values indicating more support for stiffer penalties	3.69	.64
Independent variables			
Conservative	Scores range from 1 to 3 with higher values indicating a more conservative political orientation	2.13	.74
African American	1 = *African American*, 0 = *other*	0.7	.26
Covariates			
Income	Score range from 1 = under $8,000 to 10 = *$100,000 or more*	6.65	2.32
Employed	1 = employed full time, 0 = other	.56	.49
Financially hurt	1 = financially hurt, 0 = other	.40	.49
Age	In years	45.59	15.55
Male	1 = male, 0 = female	.47	.49
Education	Scores range from 1 to 6 with larger values indicating more education	4.10	1.13
Urban	Scores range from 1 (*rural area*) to 4 (*large city*)	2.52	1.02
Southerner	1 = lives in South, 0 = other regions	.35	.47
Catholic	1 = Catholic, 0 = other	.22	.41
Conservative protestant	1 = born-again or evangelical Christian, 0 = other	.43	.49
Government trust	A scale that ranges from 0 to 2, with higher values indicating less trust	1.36	.76

think there should be more government regulation of the stock market, less regulation, or should government regulation of the stock market stay as it is?" Responses were receded so that higher values indicate greater support for regulating the stock market. There were three response categories: (1) *less,* (2) *stay the same,* and (3) *more.*

Stiffer penalties. Our second dependent variable measures the degree to which Americans believe that corporate criminals need to be punished more severely. It is based on the following question: "Do you support or oppose stricter penalties, including longer prison terms and higher fines, for corporate executives who conceal their company's true financial condition?" The response categories were recoded so that higher values indicate greater support for more severe penalties (1 = *oppose strongly,* 2 = *oppose somewhat,* 3 = *support somewhat,* and 4 = *support strongly).*

Corporate crime encompasses many different types of offenses, ranging from those with only financial effects to those with more serious physical and environmental consequences. Here, we focus on only one type: financial fraud. This is a limitation of our analysis. It is possible that the results could differ by other types of corporate illegality, including crimes involving violence (e.g., injuries from unlawful workplace hazards). Accordingly, further elaborations and tests of the current study may want to examine other types of corporate crime.

Independent Variables

Race. A focus of this project is whether there is a racial divide in support for a more punitive approach to controlling corporate crime. As noted, the prior literature on punitiveness indicates that African Americans are less punitive than Whites (Cochran and Chamlin 2006; Unnever and Cullen 2007a). We constructed a binary variable (African American) to measure the respondent's race with African Americans coded 1 and Whites coded 0.

Political orientation. As noted earlier, researchers have found that political orientation is one of the most robust and consistent predictors of punitiveness toward criminal offenders (Beckett and Sasson 2000). Our measure of political ideology is similar to the one used in prior research (Applegate et al. 2000; Borg 1997; Stack 2000, 2003; Unnever and Cullen 2005; Unnever, Cullen, and Applegate 2005; Young 1992). The variable conservative is based on the following question: "Would you say your views on most political matters are liberal, moderate, or conservative?" Responses were recoded so that larger values indicated a more conservative political orientation (1 = *liberal,* 2 = *moderate,* and 3 = *conservative*). Those who answered "don't think in those terms" or "no opinion" were deleted from the analysis.

Analytical Strategy

A cumulative logit model was used to analyze our two dependent variables because each had ordinal categories. We replicated the results presented in Table 5.3 using ordinal regression and ordinary least squares. The results were substantively the same. Standardized logistic regression coefficients are presented in Table 5.3. List-wise deletion of missing cases was used. There was no indication of multicollinearity. An ordinary least squares analysis of the data showed that no variance inflation factor exceeded 1.36. The sample size for each regression equation is reported in Table 5.3.

RESULTS

We first examine the degree to which Americans support a more restrictive and punitive approach to controlling corporate crime (see Table 5.2). Two relevant findings

Table 5.2 Public Support for Controlling Corporate Crime

Public Support	Percentage
Regulating the stock market	
Less	58.7
About the same	6.5
More	34.8
Support for tougher penalties for corporate executives	
Oppose strongly	1.9
Oppose somewhat	3.9
Support somewhat	16.3
Support strongly	77.7

emerge. First, the frequencies reveal a lack of support for further regulating the stock market; only 34.8 percent reported that they supported more regulation. Indeed, the majority of Americans, 58.7 percent, reported that they thought there should be less regulation of the stock market. However, the data replicate the findings of prior research in regards to punishing corporate criminals more severely. A sizeable majority of Americans, 77.7 percent, strongly support stricter penalties, including longer prison terms and higher fines for corporate executives who conceal their company's true financial condition. Only 6.5 percent of Americans either "oppose strongly" or "oppose somewhat" punishing corporate criminals more severely.

Model 1 of Table 5.3 assesses whether African Americans and Whites have significantly different "cognitive landscapes" when considering whether there should be further government regulation of the stock market and the degree to which corporate criminals should be punished more severely. The results reveal that African Americans and Whites differ significantly in their opinions. Notably, African Americans are significantly more likely than Whites to want stricter government regulation of the stock market and longer prison sentences and higher fines for corporate criminals while controlling for the other covariates. These findings are quite pronounced as the standardized regression coefficients indicate that race is the most substantive predictor of support for these policies.

The analysis in model 1 omitted political orientation. It could be argued that any race effect is really a political orientation effect (i.e., because African Americans are more liberal). In model 2 of Table 5.3, we include political orientation in the regression equations. The results reveal that conservatives are significantly less likely to endorse more government regulation of the stock market. However, the data also show that there is no "political divide" when conservatives and liberals consider whether corporate criminals should be punished more severely. Liberals are as equally likely to support "getting tough" on corporate crime as conservatives.

Comparing the results across models 1 and 2, the data indicate that political orientation does partially mediate the "gap" between African Americans and Whites in their opinions about stricter regulation of the stock market. Political orientation mediated nearly 14 percent of the racial divide in whether the government should further regulate the stock market. However, the results also show that including political orientation in the regression equation exacerbates the gap between African Americans and Whites regarding whether corporate criminals should be punished more severely. Political orientation increased the likelihood that African Americans would be more punitive than Whites.

DISCUSSION

America declared a war on crime in the 1980s—that is, a war on street crimes. To some segments of the American population,

Table 5.3 Analysis of Support for "Getting Tough" on Corporate Crime (standardized logistic regression coefficients)

Variable	Model 1		Model 2	
	More Stock Regulations	*Stiffer Penalties*	*More Stock Regulations*	*Stiffer Penalties*
African American	.129***	.149**	.113**	.155**
Conservative	—	—	−.092**	.29
Income	.023	.133**	.023	.136**
Employed	−.015	.132**	−.019	.131**
Financially hurt	.089*	.074	.086*	.076
Age	.050	.197***	.052	.196***
Male	.045	.128**	.044	.125**
Education	−.099*	.053	−.102*	.055
Urban	.074	−.055	.072	−.053
Southerner	.063	−.034	.070	−.32
Catholic	.063	−.014	.066	−.013
Conservative protestant	−.030	−.091	−.011	−.098
Government trust	−.075*	.047	−.76	.045
Max-rescaled *R*-square	.059*** ($n = 890$)	.013*** ($n = 900$)	.082*** ($n = 886$)	.104*** ($n = 896$)

*** $p < .001$; ** $p < .01$; * $p < .05$ (two-tailed tests of significance).

the "excesses" of liberal courts in the 1960s had created an atmosphere where street crime—gang violence, juvenile murders—flourished and had to be curtailed (Beckett and Sasson 2000; Coulter 2006). However, the United States did not embark on a parallel, equally vigorous war on corporate crime. Some have argued that this failure to advance a second front on crime reflected the priorities of the American public. Policymakers have

argued that Americans do not want to get tough on corporate crime because they do not consider it serious. Or, there is no need to get tough on corporate crime because free markets are self-correcting and new criminal laws would impede this built-in self-regulating mechanism (Pontell 2005). Others, however, have questioned these assumptions. Indeed, research conducted in the 1980s found that Americans by and large agree that corporate crime is serious and that it warrants the attention of the criminal justice system.

Past research shows that Americans support harshly punishing corporate criminals, but it does not address whether their support for corporate crime control extended to tighter regulation of the stock market. Previous studies have also failed to fully investigate whether Americans who support getting tough on street crime, such as political conservatives, also express the same level of support for getting tough on corporate crime. The current project addressed these issues.

REFERENCES

ABC News/The *Washington Post*. 2002. *ABC News/The Washington Post Poll* July 2002. ICPSR version. Horsham, PA: Taylor Nelson Sofres Intersearch. Ann Arbor, Ml: Interuniversity Consortium for Political and Social Research.

Applegate, Brandon K., Francis T. Cullen, Bonnie S. Fisher, and Thomas Vander Ven. 2000. "Forgiveness and Fundamentalism: Reconsidering the Relationship between Correctional Attitudes and Religion." *Criminology* 38:719-54.

Baker, David N., Eric G. Lambert, and Morris Jenkins. 2005. "Racial Differences in Death Penalty Support and Opposition: A Preliminary Study of White and Black College Students." *Journal of Black Studies* 35:201-24.

Barkan, Steven E. and Steven F. Cohn. 1994. "Racial Prejudice and Support for the Death Penalty by Whites." *Journal of Research in Crime and Delinquency* 31:202-9.

Beckett, Katharine and Theodore Sasson. 2000. *The Politics of Injustice: Crime and Punishment in America*. Thousand Oaks, CA: Pine Forge Press.

Benson, Michael L, 2002. "Prosecuting Corporate Crime: Problems and Constraints," Pp. 381-91 in *Crimes of Privilege: Readings in White-Collar Crime,* edited by Neal Shover and John P. Wright. New York: Oxford University Press.

Benson, Michael L. and Francis T. Cullen. 1998. *Combating Corporate Crime: Local Prosecutors at Work*. Boston: Northeastern University Press.

Benson, Michael L. and Kent R. Kerley. 2001. "Life Course Theory and White-Collar Crime." Pp. 121-36 in *Contemporary Issues in Crime and Criminal Justice: Essays in Honor of Gilbert Geis,* edited by Henry N. Pontell and David Shichor. Upper Saddle River, NJ: Prentice Hall.

Benson, Michael L., William J. Maakestad, Francis T. Cullen, and Gilbert Geis. 1998. "District Attorneys and Corporate Crime: Surveying the Prosecutorial Gatekeepers." *Criminology* 26:505-18.

Bobo, Lawrence and Devon Johnson, 2004. "A Taste for Punishment; Black and White Americans' Views on the Death Penalty and the War on Drugs." *Du Bois Review* 1:151-80.

Borg, Marian J. 1997. "The Southern Subculture of Punitiveness? Regional Variation in Support for Capital Punishment" *Journal of Research in Crime and Delinquency* 34:25-46.

Braithwaite, John. 1982. "Challenging Just Deserts: Punishing White-Collar Criminals." *Journal of Criminal Law and Criminology* 73:723-63.

Buckler, Kevin, James D. Unnever, and Francis T. Cullen. Forthcoming. "Perceptions of Injustice Revisited: A Test of Hagan el al.'s Comparative Conflict Theory." *Journal of Crime and Justice*.

Chiricos, Ted, Kelly Welch, and Mark Gertz. 2004. "Racial Typification of Crime and Support for Punitive Measures." *Criminology* 24:359-89.

Clarke, James W. 1998. "Without Fear or Shame: Lynching, Capital Punishment, and the Subculture of Violence in the American South." *British Journal of Political Science* 28:269-89.

Clear, Todd R. 1994. *Harm in American Penology: Offenders, Victims, and Their Communities*. Albany: State University of New York Press.

Cochran, John K. and Mitchell B. Chamlin. 2006 'The Enduring Racial Divide in Death Penalty Support." *Journal of Criminal Justice* 34:85-99.

Coulter, Ann. 2006. *Godless: The Church of Liberalism*. New York: Random House.

Cullen, Francis T., Gray Cavender, William J. Maakestad, and Michael L. Benson. 2006. *Corporate Crime under Attack: The Fight to Criminalize Business Violence*. Cincinnati, OH: LexisNexis/Anderson.

Cullen. Francis T., Bonnie S. Fisher, and Brandon K. Applegate. 2000. 'Public Opinion about Punishment and Corrections." Pp. 1-79 in *Crime and Justice: A Review of Research,* vol.27, edited by Michael Tonry. Chicago: University of Chicago Press.

Cullen, Francis T., Bruce G. Link, and Craig W. Polanzi. 1982. "The Seriousness of Crime Revisited: Have Attitudes Toward While-Collar Crime Changed?" *Criminology* 20:8:5-102.

Cullen. Francis T, Richard A. Mathers, Gregory A. Clark, and John B. Cullen, 1983. "Public Support for Punishing White-Collar Crime: Blaming the Victim Revisited?" *Journal of Criminal Justice* 11:481-93.

Currie, Elliott. 1998. *Crime and Punishment in America.* New York: Metropolitan Books.

Dilulio, J. J., Jr. 1995. "The Coming of the Super-Predators." *The Weekly Standard,* November 27, pp. 23-8.

Evans, T. David, Francis T. Cullen, and Paula J. Dubeck. 1993. "Public Perceptions of Corporate Crime." Pp. 85-114 in *Understanding Corporate Illegal Behavior,* edited by Michael B. Blankenship. New York: Garland.

Federal Bureau of Investigation [FBI]. 2005. *Crime in the United States 2004: Uniform Crime Reports.* Washington, DC: U.S. Government Printing Office.

Fleury-Steiner, Benjamin. 2002. "Narratives of the Death Sentence: Toward a Theory of Legal Narrativity." *Law and Society Review* 36:549-77.

Frank, James, Francis T. Cullen, Lawrence F. Travis III, and John Bointrager. 1989. "Sanctioning Corporate Crime: How Do Business Executives and the Public Compare?" *American Journal of Criminal Justice* 13:136-69.

Garland, David. 2001. *The Culture of Control: Crime and Social Order in Contemporary Society.* Chicago: University of Chicago Press.

Geis, Gilbert. 1978. "Deterring Corporate Crime" Pp. 278-96 in *Corporate and Governmental Deviance: Problems of Organizational Behavior in Contemporary Society* edited by M. David Ermann and Richard J. Lundman. New York: Oxford University Press.

Grasmick, Harold G. and Anne L. McGill. 1994. "Religion, Attributional Style, and Punitiveness Toward Juvenile Offenders." *Criminology* 32:23-46.

Hagan, John and Celesta Albonetti. 1982. "Race, Class and the Perception of Criminal Injustice in America." *American Journal of Sociology* 88:329-55.

Hagan, John, Carla Shedd, and Monique R. Payne. 2005. "Race, Ethnicity, and Youth Perceptions of Criminal Injustice." *American Sociological Review* 70:381-407.

Hans, Valerie P. and David Ermann. 1989. "Responses to Corporate Versus Individual Wrongdoing." *Law and Human Behavior* 13:151-66.

Henderson, Martha, Francis T. Cullen, Liqun Cao, Sandra L. Browning, and Renee Kopache. 1997. "The Impact of Race on Perceptions of Criminal Injustice," *Journal of Criminal Justice* 26:1-16.

Hogan, Michael J., Ted Chiricos, and Marc Gertz. 2005. "Economic Insecurity, Blame, and Punitive Attitudes," *Justice Quarterly* 22:392-412.

Jacobs, David and Jason T. Carmichael. 2002. The Political Sociology of the Death Penalty: A Pooled Time-Series Analysis." *American Sociological Review* 67:109-31.

Jacobs, David, Jason T. Carmichael, and Stephanie L. Kent. 2005. "Vigilantism, Current Racial Threats, and Death Sentences." *American Sociological Review* 70:656-77.

Jacobs, David, Zhenchao Qian, Jason T. Carmichael, and Stephanie L. Kent. 2007. "Who Survives on Death Row? An Individual and Contextual Analysis." *American Sociological Review* 72:610-33.

Kane, John and April D. Wall. 2006. *The 2005 National Public Survey on White Collar Crime.* Fairmont, WV: National White Collar Crime Center.

Miller, Joanne I., Peter H. Rossi, and Jon E. Simpson. 1991. "Felony Punishments: A Factorial Survey of Perceived Justice in Criminal Sentencing." *Journal of Criminal Law and Criminology* 82:396-422.

Moon, Melissa M., John P. Wright, Francis T. Cullen. and Jennifer A. Pealer. 2000. "Putting Kids to Death: Specifying Public Support for Juvenile Capital Punishment." *Justice Quarterly* 17:663-84.

Moore, Elizabeth and Michael Mills. 1990. "The Neglected Victims and Unexamined Costs of White-Collar Crime;" *Crime & Delinquency* 36:408-18.

Ogletree, Charles J., Jr. 2002. "Black Man's Burden: Race and the Death Penalty in America" *Oregon Law Review* 81:15-38.

Oshinsky, David M. 1996. *"Worse Than Slavery": Parchman Farm and the Ordeal of Jim Crow Justice*. New York: Simon and Schuster.

Paternoster, Raymond and Sally Simpson. 2002. "A Rational Choice Theory of Corporate Crime." Pp. 194-210 in *Crimes of Privilege: Readings in White-Collar Crime*, edited by Neal Shover and John Paul Wright. New York: Oxford University Press.

Peffley, Mark and Jon Hurwitz. 1998. "Whites' Stereotypes of Blacks: Sources and Consequences." Pp. 58-99 in *Perception and Prejudice: Race and Politics in the United States*, edited by Jon Hurwitz and Mark Peffley. New Haven. CT: Yale University Press.

Piquero, Nicole L., Stephanie Carmichael, and Alex R. Piquero. Forthcoming. "Assessing the Perceived Seriousness of White-Collar and Street Crimes." *Crime & Delinquency*.

Pontell, Henry N. 2005. "White-Collar Crime or Just Risky Business? The Role of Fraud in Major Financial Debacles." *Crime, Law and Social Change* 42:309-24.

President's Commission on Law Enforcement and Administration of Justice. 1968. *Challenge of Crime in a Free Society*, Washington. DC: U.S. Government Printing Office.

Rezaee, Zabihollah. 2005. "Causes, Consequences, and Deterrence of Financial Statement Fraud." *Critical Perspectives on Accounting* 16:277-98.

Roberts, Julian V. and Mike Hough. 2005. *Understanding Public Attitudes to Criminal Justice*. Maidenhead, UK; New York: Open University Press.

Roberts, Julian V. and Loretta J. Stalans. 2000. *Public Opinion, Crime, and Criminal Justice*. Boulder, CO: Westview.

Roberts, Julian V., Loretta J. Stalans, David Inder-maur, and Mike Hough. 2003. *Penal Populism and Public Opinion: Lessons from Five Countries*. New York: Oxford University Press.

Sampson, Robert J. and William Julius Wilson. 1995. "Toward a Theory of Race, Crime, and Urban Inequality." Pp. 37-54 in *Crime and Inequality*, edited by John Hagan and Ruth D.

Petersen. Stanford, CA: Stanford University Press.

Savelsberg. Joachim J. 2002. "Religion, Historical Contingencies, and Institutional Conditions of Criminal Punishment: The German Case and Beyond." *Law and Social Inquiry* 29:375-402.

Schoepfer, Andrea, Stephanie Carmichael, and Nicole L. Piquero. 2007. "Do Perceptions of Punishment Vary Between White-Collar and Street Crimes?" *Journal of Criminal Justice* 35:151-63.

Shover, Neal and Andy Hochstetler. 2005. *Choosing White Collar Crime: Doing Deals and Making Mistakes*. New York: Cambridge University Press.

Simon, David R. 2006. *Elite Deviance*. Boston: Pearson Education.

Simpson, Sally S. 2002. *Corporate Crime, Law, and Social Control*. Cambridge, UK: Cambridge University Press.

Snider, Laureen. 1990. "Cooperative Models and Corporate Crime: Panacea or Cop-Out" *Crime A Delinquency* 36:373-90.

Soss, Joe, Laura Langbein, and Alan R. Metelko. 2003. "Why Do White Americans Support the Death Penalty?" *Journal of Politics* 65:397-421.

Stack. Steven. 2000. "Support for the Death Penalty: A Gender-Specific Model." *Sex Roles* 3: 163-79.

_____. 2003. "Authoritarianism and Support for the Death Penalty: A Multivariate Analysis." *Sociological Focus* 36:333-52.

Sutherland, Edwin H. 1949. *White Collar Crime*. New York: Holt. Rinehart and Winston.

Thornton, Bill and Diana Knox. 2002. "'Not in My Back Yard': The Situational and Personality Determinants of Oppositional Behavior." *Journal of Applied Social Psychology* 32:2554-74.

Tolnay, Stewart E., E. M. Beck, and James L. Massey. 1992. "Black Competition and White Vengeance: Legal Execution of Blacks as Social Control in the Cotton South. 1890 to 1929." *Social Science Quarterly* 73:621-44.

Tolnay, Stewart E., Glenn Deane, and E. M. Beck. 1996. "Vicarious Violence: Spatial Effects on Southern Lynchings, 1890-1910." *American Journal of Sociology* 102:788-815.

Tonry, Michael. 1999. "Why Are U.S. Incarcertion Rates So High?" *Crime & Delinquency*, 45:419-37.

_____. 2004. *Thinking about Crime: Sense and Sensibility in American Penal Culture,* New York: Oxford University Press.

U.S. General Accounting Office [GAO]. 2005. *Criminal Debt Court-Ordered Restitution Amounts Far Exceed Likely Collections for the Crime Victims in Selected Financial Fraud Cases.* Washington. DC: Author.

_____. 2002. *Financial Restatements, Trends, Market Impacts, Regulatory Responses, and Remaining Challenges.* Washington. DC: Author.

Unnever, James D. Forthcoming. "Two Worlds Far Apart: Black-White Differences in Beliefs About Why African American Men Are Disproportionately Imprisoned." *Criminology.*

Unnever, James D. and Francis T. Cullen. 2005. "Executing the Innocent and Support for Capital Punishment: Implications for Public Policy." *Criminology and Public Policy* 4:3-37.

_____. 2006. "Are Christian Fundamentalists Radical Supporters of Capital Punishment?" *Journal of Research in Crime and Delinquency* 43:169-17.

_____. 2007a. "Reassessing the Racial Divide in Support for the Capital Punishment: The Continuing Significance of Race." *Journal of Research in Crime and Delinquency* 44:124-58.

_____. 2007b. "The Racial Divide in Support for the Death Penalty: Does White Racism Matter?" *Social Forces* 85:1281-1301.

Unnever, James D., Francis T. Cullen, and Brandon Applegate. 2005. "Turning the Other Cheek: Moving Beyond Fundamentalism in Explaining Punitive Ideology" *Justice Quarterly* 22:304-39.

Unnever, James D., Francis T. Cullen, and Bonnie S. Fisher. 2005. "Empathy and Support for Capital Punishment." *Journal of Crime and Justice* 24:1-34.

_____. 2007. "'A Liberal Is Someone Who Has Not Been Mugged': Criminal Victimization and Political Beliefs." *Justice Quarterly* 24:309-334.

Unnever, James D., Francis T. Cullen, and Cheryl Lero Jonson. Forthcoming. "Race, Racism, and Support for Capital Punishment." In *Crime and Justice: A Review of Research,* edited by Michael Tonry. Chicago: University of Chicago Press.

Unnever, James D., Francis T. Cullen, and James D, Jones. 2008. "Public Support for Attacking the 'Root Causes' of Crime: The Impact of Egalitarian and Racial Beliefs." *Sociological Focus* 41:1-33.

Unnever, James D. and Paulette Higgins. 1995. "The Legislative History of the Surface Mining Control and Reclamation Act of 1977." *Capitalism Nature Socialism* 6:77-90.

Vogel, Brenda L. and Ronald E. Vogel. 2003. "The Age of Death: Appraising Public Opinion of Juvenile Capital Punishment." *Journal of Criminal Justice* 31:169-83.

Weisburd, David, Stanton Wheeler, Elin Waring, and Nancy Bode 1991. *Crimes of the Middle Classes: White-Collar Offenders in the Federal Courts.* New Haven, CT: Yale University Press.

Whitman. James Q. 2003. *Harsh Justice: Criminal Punishment and the Widening Divide Between America and Europe.* New York: Oxford University Press.

Wortley, Scott, John Hagan. and Ross Macmillan. 1997. "Just Des(s)erts? The Racial Polarization of Perceptions of Criminal Injustice." *Law and Society Review* 31:637-76.

Young, Robert L. 1992. "Religious Orientation, Race and Support for the Death Penalty." *Journal for the Scientific Study of Religion* 31:76-87.

Young, T. R. 1986. "A Marxian Theory of Crime" Retrieved from http://www.etext.org/Politics/Progressive.Sociologists/authors/Young.TR/marxian-theory-of-crime. Accessed February 23,2008.

Yu, Olivia and Lening Zhang. 2006. "Does Acceptance of Corporate Wrongdoing Begin on the 'Training Ground' of Professional Managers?" *Journal of Criminal Justice* 34:185-94.

Zimring, Franklin E. 2003. *The Contradictions of American Capital Punishment.* New York: Oxford University Press.

Zimring, Franklin E. and Gordon Hawkins. 1978. "Ideology and Euphoria in Crime Control." *University of Toledo Law Review* 10:370-88.

Zimring, Franklin E. and David T. Johnson. 2006. "Public Opinion and the Governance of Punishment in Democratic Political Systems." *Annals of the American Academy of Political and Social Science* 605:265-80.

DISCUSSION QUESTIONS

1. Comparatively, what are the losses associated with corporate versus street crime? What has traditionally been the attitude of the public toward white-collar crime?

2. What two areas are these authors exploring with regard to public opinions? What factors about the subjects are they controlling for?

3. How was the sample that these researchers studied obtained? Who did they study? Do you think this is a representative sample? What did the researchers do to make it more representative?

4. According to Table 5.1, what other variables were part of the study? Why do you think the authors included these factors?

5. What do the results from Table 5.2 regarding attitudes toward regulating the stock market and supporting tougher penalties for corporate executives reveal?

6. According to Table 5.3, which independent variables were significantly related to the dependent variables at the 0.05 level?

7. Were the expected political and racial divides in public opinion regarding corporate crime observed in this sample?

8. Did subjects who had been financially hurt in the past support more regulation and tougher sanctions?

9. Do you think these researchers would get similar results if they obtained another sample? Why or why not?

RESEARCH READING

Wilcox and colleagues study an interesting aspect of criminal behavior: opportunity. Several previous studies have shown that opportunity has a strong relationship to crime. The authors of the current study examine school victimization as it relates to gender differences in opportunity. They study victimization through a longitudinal self-report survey of students in the seventh grade. They looked at both school-based theft and physical assault using data from over 10,000 students nested within 111 schools in Kentucky. To obtain their sample, they employed a multistage, stratified sampling procedure of 120 counties in Kentucky. Pay special attention to how these authors selected their sample by clustering subjects first within counties then within schools in those counties.

Source: Wilcox, P., Skubak Tillyer, M., & Fisher, B. (2009). Gendered opportunity? School-based adolescent victimization. *Journal of Research in Crime and Delinquency, 46*, 245–269. Copyright © 2009 Sage Publications.

——— GENDERED OPPORTUNITY? ———

School-Based Adolescent Victimization

Pamela Wilcox, Marie Skubak Tillyer, and Bonnie S. Fisher

Abstract: Researchers have shown that criminal opportunity significantly predicts school-based adolescent victimization. However, little is known about the extent to which opportunity for school-based victimization might be gendered. In this study, the authors drew from criminal opportunity and feminist research and extended the principle of homogamy to explore how gender interacts with opportunity and school-based victimization. Data collected from 2001 to 2004 from 10,522 students in 111 middle and high schools throughout Kentucky were used to examine whether indicators of criminal opportunity placed students, particularly girls, at heightened risk for school-based theft and physical assault victimization. The results of gender-specific hierarchical logistic regression models indicated that measures of criminal opportunity were significantly related to theft and assault for both sexes. Equality-of-coefficient tests supported gendered effects for some opportunity indicators, with differences indicating that the effects of risk and protective factors for victimization were heightened for girls.

INTRODUCTION

Despite the downward trend in school victimization when looking at 10-year aggregate trajectories and the rarity of extreme or lethal school violence, "less serious" incidents are still abundant and considered "everyday" occurrences in our nation's schools (De Voe et al. 2005). Several studies have suggested that *criminal opportunity,* the extent to which offenders and victims or targets come into contact with each other in the absence of capable guardianship, is key in understanding the etiology of school victimization, but much remains unknown (see Campbell Augustine et al. 2002; Garofalo, Siegel and Laub 1987; Schreck, Miller, and Gibson 2003). In particular, research to date has neither explicated nor tested how opportunity may operate differently across gender. The implicit assumption of previous studies, therefore, has been that "opportunity" is a "one size fits all students" concept. We think this assumption deserves empirical study to determine if gendered opportunities for school-based victimization exist.

With the present study, we built on recent etiological work on school victimization in the tradition of criminal opportunity theory but also extended this body of research with an important examination of the possible conditioning effects of gender. More specifically, we explored a "gendered opportunity" approach to school-based victimization by estimating gender-specific hierarchical logistic regression models of school-based theft and physical assault victimization using data from 10,522 students in 7th to 10th grade nested within 111 Kentucky schools.

THE PRESENT STUDY

Although the previously reviewed research has shown support for a perspective on school-based victimization that emphasizes opportunity-based risk factors at both individual and school levels, we believe that this line of inquiry can be refined further by examination of cross-gender differences in factors heretofore presumed to represent opportunity equally for all. More specifically, we question the assumption of the generalizability of individual opportunity-related risk and protective factors across gender through an exploratory gender-specific analysis of school-based victimization.

Data

The data for our exploration of possible gender differences in opportunity-related correlates of school victimization come from the Rural Substance abuse and Violence Project (RSVP), a prospective longitudinal study conducted between spring 2001 and spring 2004 throughout Kentucky. We used all four waves of the student component of RSVP, collected through annual self-report surveys of a panel of students who were enrolled in seventh grade during the 2000-2001 academic year. Participants were selected through a multistage procedure involving, first, a stratified sampling of 30 of Kentucky's 120 counties.[2] Within the 30 selected counties, the principals of all public schools containing seventh graders were asked to participate, with 65 of the 74 principals agreeing. Finally, all seventh graders within the 65 participating schools, a total of 9,488 students, were targeted for inclusion in the sample. A parental consent procedure was used, and active consent was granted by the parents of 43 percent of the targeted population, leaving 4,102 sample participants.[3] Of those participants, we received completed surveys from 3,692 students in wave 1, 3,638 students in wave 2, 3,050 students in wave 3, and 3,040 students in wave 4.[4]

The response rate was generally consistent with other studies of students that used active parental consent, yielding rates ranging from 35 percent to 60 percent (Esbensen et al. 1996). Comparing demographic characteristics from our sample with Kentucky Department of Education (KDE) enrollment data for the 65 original schools in our sample, we found that the racial composition of our sample was fairly close to the KDE population data. Specifically, in wave 1, our sample percentage non-White was 9.55 percent, while the corresponding figure from the KDE data

(which includes all students in the selected schools, not just seventh graders) was 10.18 percent. In contrast, our sample did appear to underrepresent boys, with about 45.5 percent of the wave 1 respondents being male compared with 51.9 percent for the KDE data.

Finally, sample attrition that occurred across waves did not appear to be systematically related to race or gender. The sample was 90.5 percent White and 45.4 percent male at wave 1, and it was 90.9 percent White and 45.9 percent male at wave 4. Considering race and gender combined, the sample at wave 1 was as follows: 4.8 percent non-White male, 5.0 percent non-White female, 42.7 percent White male, and 47.5 percent White female. By wave 4, the race and gender composition of the sample was 4.3 percent non-White male, 4.3 percent non-White female, 42.2 percent White male, and 49.2 percent White female. Despite little evidence of race and gender patterns in attrition, previous victims were slightly more likely to drop out of the sample. At each wave, the mean rate of victimization was lower among the participants who remained in the sample compared with those who had dropped out by wave 4. For instance, the mean rate of victimization was 1.0 among wave 1 participants who remained in the sample by wave 4, while the mean rate of victimization was 1.4 among wave 1 participants who had dropped out by wave 4. The wave 2 mean rate of victimization was 1.06 for those remaining in the sample throughout the study period; this wave 2 victimization rate was 1.5 for those who had dropped out by wave 4. Finally, wave 3 victimization was also lower among those staying in the sample compared with those dropping out by wave 4 (.95 vs. 1.3).

Across all four waves, one or more observations were recorded from 3,977 of the 4,102 respondents whose parents granted consent. To examine the effects of interest across as many school- and grade-level contexts as possible, we pooled the individual data across years, leaving a sample of 13,420 data points (person-years) within 111 school contexts. Listwise deletion of cases with missing data on variables within the sample left 10,522 data points nested within 111 schools for analysis.

Measures of Variables

Theft and assault victimization during the current school year were the dependent variables. Theft victimization was a dichotomous variable that measures whether students had money or property stolen (without force) on school grounds or at school-related activities. Assault victimization was a dichotomous variable measuring whether students were physically attacked on school grounds or at school-related activities. Although opportunity structures are often crime specific, findings from previous studies (reviewed above) suggested that the opportunity-related variables used in this study would correlate similarly with both types of victimization.

RESULTS

Theft Victimization

The results of the final hierarchical logistic model of theft victimization for boys are presented in Table 5.4. Consistent with theory and previous victimization research, involvement in school sports, impulsive personality, self-reported criminal behavior, and delinquent peers significantly increased the likelihood of school-based theft victimization for boys. Examination of odds ratios for those effects indicated that a one-unit increase in each of these variables was associated with an increase in the odds of theft victimization of 8 percent, 34 percent, 80 percent, and 177 percent, respectively. Socioeconomic status was also significantly related to male theft victimization.

The results of our final hierarchical logistic model of theft victimization risk at school for girls (Table 5.4) indicated that higher student GPA, involvement in school sports, involvement in school activities, impulsive personality, delinquent peers, and self-reported criminal behavior were associated with increased risk for female theft victimization. Of particular note, the odds ratios for delinquent peers and self-reported criminal behavior were quite large, suggesting that the odds of female theft victimization increased 2.78 and 3.09 times, respectively, with each one-unit increase in delinquent associations and own delinquency. Conversely, attachment to parents and attachment to peers significantly reduced the risk for theft victimization at school for female students. In terms of control variables, higher levels of socioeconomic status increased the likelihood of theft victimization at school for girls, as was the case for boys.

To more fully explore the possible gendered effects of situational opportunity on theft victimization risk at school, the last column in Table 5.4 provides the z scores from the test for the equality of regression coefficients ($\alpha < .05$). The results show that the regression coefficients for attachment to parents, student GPA, attachment to peers, and self-reported criminal behavior were significantly different for boys and girls.

Assault Victimization

As with the models of theft victimization, we produced gender-specific unconditional (intercept-only) models of assault victimization risk to determine if significant variation existed across schools.

The findings reported in Table 5.5 indicate that involvement in school activities, impulsive personality, delinquent peers, and self-reported criminal behavior increased the risk for assault victimization at school for boys. In addition, assault risk was higher for White male students and those boys reporting higher levels of socioeconomic status. Conversely, student GPA, attachment to peers, and involvement in school sports significantly

Table 5.4   Hierarchical Logistic Models of School-Based Theft Victimization Risk by Gender

Variable	Model A: Boys			Model B: Girls			Test of Equality of Regression Coefficient
	Coefficient	SE	Odds Ratio	Coefficient	SE	Odds Ratio	z Score
Individual (level 1) fixed effects							
Attachment to parents	.02	.05	1.02	−.22*	.04	.81	3.75*
Attachment to school	.02	.07	1.02	−.09	.07	.92	1.11
Student grade point average	−.03	.04	.97	.12*	.04	1.12	−2.65
Attachment to peers	−.04	.05	.96	−.20*	.06	.82	2.05*
Involvement in school sports	.08*	.02	1.08	.09*	.02	1.10	−.35
Involvement in school activities	.04	.02	1.04	.05*	.02	1.05	−.35
Impulsive personality	.29*	.05	1.34	.37*	.06	1.44	−1.02
Delinquent peers	1.02*	.15	2.77	1.02*	.15	2.78	.00
Self-reported criminal behavior	.59*	.13	1.80	1.13*	.22	3.09	−2.11*
Race	.13	.13	1.14	−.12	.11	.89	1.47
Socioeconomic status	.05*	.02	1.06	.05*	.02	1.05	.00
Wave 2	−.07	.09	.93	−.13	.07	.88	.53
Wave 3	−.21*	.10	.81	−.27*	.10	.76	.42
Wave 4	−.41*	.11	.66	−.54*	.11	.58	.84
School (level 2) fixed effects							
Intercept	−.19*	.05	.82	.00	.04	.99	

Variable	Model A: Boys			Model B: Girls			Test of Equality of Regression Coefficient
	Coefficient	SE	Odds Ratio	Coefficient	SE	Odds Ratio	z Score
Random Effects	Model A: Boys			Model B: Girls			
	SD	Variance Component		SD	Variance Component		
Mean victimization risk	.35	.13*		.32	.10*		
Attachment to parents slope				.18	.03*		
Attachment to school slope	.33	.11*		.31	.09*		
Student grade point average slope	.19	.04*					
Involvement in school sports slope	.11	.01*					
Self-reported criminal behavior slope	.59	.35*		.69	.47*		
Race slope	.52	.27*					
Level 1 extra binomial error	.98	.96		.99	.98		

Note: Level 1: $n = 4,840$ boys, $n = 5,682$ girls; level 2: $n = 111$ schools.

* $\alpha < .05$.

reduced the likelihood of assault victimization at school for boys.

The results presented in Table 5.5 indicate that involvement in school sports, involvement in school activities, impulsive personality, delinquent peers, and self-reported criminal behavior increased the risk for assault victimization at school for girls. The effect of self-reported criminal behavior is particularly noteworthy, with the odds of assault victimization increasing some 25 times per unit increase in delinquency. In addition, assault risk was significantly higher for White female students. In contrast, attachment to parents and attachment to peers significantly reduced the risk for assault victimization at school for female students.

Table 5.5 also provides the z scores from the test of differences in coefficients across male and female assault victimization models. As Table 5.5 indicates, regression coefficients for involvement in school sports and self-reported criminal behavior were significantly different across male and female students in estimating assault victimization. Both of these variables enhanced the likelihood of assault victimization for girls much more so than boys. In contrast, reporting assault victimization during wave 2 and wave 3 (in comparison with wave 1) was reduced significantly more so for boys as opposed to girls.

Table 5.5 Hierarchical Logistic Models of School-Based Assault Victimization Risk by Gender

Variable	Model A: Boys			Model B: Girls			Test of Equality of Regression Coefficient
	Coefficient	SE	Odds Ratio	Coefficient	SE	Odds Ratio	z Score
Individual (level 1) fixed effects							
Attachment to parents	−.11	.06	.90	−.17	.05	.84	.77
Attachment to school	−.04	.08	.96	.06	.05	.95	−.94
Student grade point average	−.11*	.04	.90	−.05	.05	.95	−.94
Attachment to peers	−.22*	.05	.80	−.36*	.07	.70	1.63
Involvement in school sports	−.06*	.02	.94	.08*	.02	1.08	−4.95
Involvement in school activities	.11*	.02	1.11	.09*	.03	1.10	.55
Impulsive personality	.39*	.06	1.48	.54*	.05	1.72	−1.92
Delinquent peers	.77*	.13	2.17	.80*	.18	2.22	−.14
Self-reported criminal behavior	.89*	.17	2.44	3.23*	.38	25.39	−5.68*
Race	.28*	.13	1.33	.28*	.13	1.32	.00
Socioeconomic status	.08*	.02	1.08	.01	.03	1.01	1.94
Wave 2	−.40*	.08	.67	−.17*	.06	.84	−2.30*
Wave 3	−.96*	.10	.38	−.66*	.09	.52	−2.23*
Wave 4	−1.25*	.10	.29	−1.16*	.11	.31	−.61
School (level 2) fixed effects							
Intercept	−.05	.05	.95	−1.04*	.04	.35	

| Variable | Model A: Boys | | | Model B: Girls | | | Test of Equality of Regression Coefficient |
	Coefficient	SE	Odds Ratio	Coefficient	SE	Odds Ratio	z Score
Random Effects				SD	Variance Component	SD	Variance Component
Mean victimization risk				0.35	.12*	0.24	.06*
Attachment to parents slope				0.31	.09*		
Involvement in school sports slope				0.12	.02*		
Self-reported criminal behavior slope				88	.78*	2.27	5.18*
Level 1 extra binomial error				0.98	0.96	0.99	0.97

Note: Level 1: $n = 4,840$ boys, $n = 5,682$ girls; level 2: $n = 111$ schools.

* $\alpha < .05$.

DISCUSSION

Recently, studies on school victimization have begun to move from descriptive to causal, with theory and empirical research implicating criminal opportunity as a key component to understanding school victimization. In the present study, we sought to examine an implicit assumption within this area of research, that is, that presumed indicators of opportunity for school victimization operate similarly across student subpopulations, namely, girls and boys. Although we had no ability to test actual perceptions of offenders in this study, we grounded our exploratory examination of the conditional role of gender in previous work suggesting that gender may be used by offenders to assess target vulnerability and gratifiability. As such, we wondered whether risk and protective factors would exhibit stronger effects for girls as opposed to boys. Several statistically significant differences in effects were found,

providing modest support for the idea that gender helps shape perceived opportunity.

This possible interpretation for gender-specific effects is consistent with previous work pointing to the perceived vulnerability of female targets on the part of offenders (Finkelhor and Asdigian 1996; Miller 1998; Mustaine and Tewksbury 2002; Schwartz and Pitts 1995), but it nonetheless remains speculative. There are undoubtedly other possible reasons why gender differences in indicators of opportunity emerge, but we are unaware of strong theory or prior research that would elucidate such possibilities. As such, we provide one possible theoretical interpretation of such differences: that gender exacerbates indicators of opportunity because it also provides cues (perhaps misguided) to offenders about opportunity.

The specific ways in which gender-conditioned opportunity indicators varied across type of victimization remain in question. On one hand, this is not altogether surprising, given that opportunity structures that facilitate one type of victimization are not necessarily conducive to all types of victimization. Nonetheless, the measures of opportunity-related risk and protective factors were not obviously crime specific, and as such, we expected them to exhibit similar main effects and conditional effects (conditional on gender) across theft and assault models.

The one risk factor that was moderated by gender regardless of crime type was self-reported criminal involvement. It was the strongest predictor of both theft and violent victimization for female students, and its effect was much larger than for male students. Although previous research has addressed the intertwined nature of offending and victimization (Lauritsen et al. 1991, 1992; Sampson and Lauritsen 1990), our findings suggest that this close coupling is especially discernable for female adolescents. Jensen and Brownfield (1986) originally suggested that the effects of gender on victimization might be mediated by exposure in the form of delinquent involvement. Our study reframes this debate as one of moderation rather than mediation. Future work should aim to understand more fully the dynamics behind this robust conditional effect, but preliminary interpretation is that female delinquents represent particularly opportunistic targets of victimization from an offender vantage point.

Although interesting gender-specific findings did emerge from this exploration, we should not lose sight of the fact that many predictors were consistent, regardless of gender. For instance, theft victimization was similarly positively related to involvement in sports, impulsivity, and delinquent peers for both male and female students. Theft victimization was equally negatively related to grade level (as measured by the wave variable) for both male and female students. Assault victimization was equally negatively related to attachment to peers and grade level for both genders, and it was positively related to involvement in nonsports activities, impulsive personality, and delinquent peers

similarly across male and female models. Overall, the fact that more of the individual-level effects examined here were similar as opposed to different across gender suggests that general opportunity reduction strategies in school should, in many instances, yield similar benefits to both male and female students. Despite that general tendency, those interested in school crime prevention should also be attuned to the possibility that gender may, in some situations, help define opportunity.

In conclusion, our study is important in its delineation of both gender specific and gender-neutral opportunity-related risk factors regarding school victimization. However, it is limited in several important ways, necessarily qualifying our findings. For instance, the Kentucky-based sample, combined with a limited response rate, raises suspicion about the generalizability of our findings to middle and high school students across the United States. Furthermore, as noted in the description of the sample above, attrition occurred across the four waves of data collection, with patterns of attrition at least loosely related to victimization. Given such limitations, although we think that our findings provide a new direction for better understanding of school-based victimization, replication with other samples is clearly needed. Nonetheless, it is noteworthy that the RSVP longitudinal sample has produced findings consistent with long-standing criminological theory and other data sources, so we have no reason to believe that it is unusual (see, e.g., Ousey and Wilcox 2007; Wilcox et al. 2006).

Another possible limitation of our study relates to temporal order. To use students from as many school contexts and grade levels as possible, we treated each student-year within the panel as a unique case. Hence, we were not able to carefully control the temporal ordering of independent and dependent variables. Although this is considered a limitation by many, we justify our decision with our belief that victimization opportunity is highly situational, with *situational* referring to the immediate context at hand. Therefore, the idea that one-year lagged independent variables predict current-year victimization seems somewhat far fetched; instead, we simply assume the effects to be contemporaneous. However, modeling contemporaneous rather than lagged effects opens the possibility that our specification of causal order between opportunity-related risk factors and student victimization is incorrect. This approach, furthermore, does make it difficult to discern whether opportunity contexts are at least partially developmentally defined, an idea hinted at by the significant effects of several of the wave dummy variables for assault victimization. In particular, risk for assault declined over the waves of the study more so for boys as opposed to girls. Although not the focus of this study, the potentially dynamic nature of gendered opportunity structures is clearly an issue deserving attention in future research.[9]

Finally, our analysis did not allow us to fully unpack the reasoning behind the gendered effects we found. We interpreted these conditional effects using offender decision-making and opportunity frameworks, but that interpretation is admittedly speculative. Future work is suggested for gaining clarity regarding the ways in which gender transforms risk and protective factors for adolescents while at school. This work could perhaps incorporate information from offenders about how gender affects perceived target suitability or tap, from victim surveys, more explicit measures of the dimensions of opportunity highlighted here as possibly key in understanding gender-specific effects. Thus, despite its limitations, our study provides an agenda for continued exploration of the notion of gendered opportunity.

REFERENCES

Andaman, Eric A. and David M. S. Kimweli. 1997. "Victimization and Safety in Schools Serving Adolescents." *Journal of Early Adolescence* 17:408-38.

Astor, Ron Avi, Heather Ann Meyer, and William J. Behre. 1999. "Unowned Places and Times: Maps and Interviews about Violence in High Schools." *American Educational Research Journal* 36:3-42.

Bastian, Lisa D. and Bruce M. Taylor. 1991. *School Crime: A National Crime Victimization Survey Report.* Washington, DC: U.S. Government Printing Office.

Blackwell, Brenda Sims, Christine S. Sellers, and Sheila M. Schlaupitz. 2002. "A Power-Control Theory of Vulnerability to Crime and Adolescent Role Exits Revisited." *Canadian Review of Sociology and Anthropology* 39:199-218.

Campbell Augustine, Michelle, Pamela Wilcox, Graham C. Ousey, and Richard R. Clayton. 2002. "Opportunity Theory and Adolescent School-Based Victimization." *Violence and Victims* 17:233-53.

Cohen, Lawrence E., James R. Kluegel, and Kenneth C. Land. 1981. "Social Inequality and Predatory Criminal Victimization: An Exposition and Test of a Formal Theory." *American Sociological Review* 46:505-24.

Crowe, Timothy D. 1990. "Designing Safer Schools." *School Safety* Fall:9-13.

DeVoe, Jill E, Katherin Peter, Margaret Noonan, Thomas D. Snyder, and Katrina Baum. 2005. *Indicators of School Crime and Safety: 2005.* NCES 2006-001/NCJ 210697. Washington, DC: U.S. Government Printing Office.

Dillman, Don A. 1978. *Mail and Telephone Surveys: The Total Design Method.* New York: John Wiley.

Esbensen, Finn-Aage, Elizabeth Piper Deschenes, Ronald E. Vogel, Jennifer West, Karen Arboit, and Lesley Harris. 1996. "Active Parental Consent in School-Based Research: An Examination of Ethical and Methodological Considerations." *Evaluation Review* 20:737-53.

Felson, Marcus. 1986. "Linking Criminal Choices, Routine Activities, Informal Control and Criminal Outcomes." Pp. 119-28 in *The Reasoning Criminal,* edited by Derek B. Cornish and Ronald V. Clarke. New York: Springer-Verlag.

Finkelhor, David and Nancy L. Asdigian. 1996. "Risk Factors for Youth Victimization: Beyond a Lifestyles Theoretical Approach." *Violence and Victims* 11:3-20.

Garofalo, James, Leslie Siegel, and John Laub. 1987. "School-Related Victimizations among Adolescents: An Analysis of National Crime Survey (NCS) Narratives." *Journal of Quantitative Criminology* 3:321-38.

George, Rani and George Thomas. 2000. "Victimization among Middle and High School Students: A Multilevel Analysis." *High School Journal* 84:48-57.

Hindelang, Michael J., Michael R. Gottfredson, and James Garofalo. 1978. *Victims of Personal Crime: An Empirical Foundation for a Theory of Personal Victimization.* Cambridge, MA: Ballinger.

Jensen, Gary F. and David Brownfield. 1986. "Gender, Lifestyles, and Victimization: Beyond Routine Activity." *Violence and Victims* 1:85-99.

Laidler, Karen Jo and Geoffrey Hunt. 2001. "Accomplishing Femininity among Girls in the Gang." *British Journal of Criminology* 41:656-78.

Lauritsen, Janet L., John H. Laub, and Robert J. Sampson. 1992. "Conventional and Delinquent Activities: Implications for the Prevention of Violent Victimization among Adolescents." *Violence & Victims* 7:91-108.

Lauritsen, Janet L., Robert J. Sampson, and John H. Laub. 1991. "The Link between Offending and Victimization among Adolescents." *Criminology* 29:265-92.

Maher, Lisa. 1997. *Sexed Work: Gender, Race and Resistance in a Brooklyn Drug Market.* Oxford, UK: Clarendon.

Messerschmidt, James W. 1993. *Masculinities and Crime.* Lanham, MD: Rowman & Littlefield.

Miller, Jody. 1998. "Up It Up: Gender and the Accomplishment of Street Robbery" *Criminology* 36:37-66.

Mullins, Christopher W. and Richard Wright. 2003. "Gender, Social Networks and Residential Burglary." *Criminology* 41:813-39.

Mustaine, Elizabeth Erhardt and Richard Tewksbury. 2002. "Sexual Assault of College Women: A Feminist Interpretation of a Routine Activities Analysis." *Criminal Justice Review* 27:89-123.

Osgood, D. Wayne, Amy L. Anderson, and Jennifer N. Shaffer. 2005. "Unstructured Leisure in the After-School Hours." Pp. 45-64 in *Organized Activities as Contexts of Development: Extracurricular Activities, After-School and Community Programs,* edited by Joseph L. Mahoney, Reed W. Larson, and Jacquelynne S. Eccles. Mahwah, NJ: Lawrence Erlbaum.

Ousey, Graham and Pamela Wilcox. 2007. "The Interaction of Antisocial Propensity and Life-Course Predictors of Delinquent Behavior Differences by Method of Estimation and Implications for Theory." *Criminology* 45:401-41.

Paternoster, Raymond, Robert Brame, Paul Mazerolle, and Alex Piquero. 1998. "Using the Correct Statistical Test for the Equality of Regression Coefficients" *Criminology* 36:859-66.

Raudenbush, Stephen W., Anthony S. Bryk, and Richard T. Congdon. 2000. *HLM 6 Hierarchical Linear and Nonlinear Modeling.* Chicago: Scientific Software International.

Sampson, Robert J. and Janet L. Lauritsen. 1990. "Deviant Lifestyles, Proximity to Crime and the Offender-Victim Link in Personal Violence" *Journal of Research in Crime & Delinquency* 27:110-39.

Schreck, Christopher J. 1999. "Criminal Victimization and Low Self-Control: An Extension and Test of a General Theory of Crime" *Justice Quarterly* 16:633-54.

Schreck, Christopher J. and Bonnie S. Fisher. 2004. "Specifying the Influence of Family and Peers on Violent Victimization: Extending Routine Activities and Lifestyle Theories." *Journal of Interpersonal Violence* 19:1021-41.

Schreck, Christopher J., Bonnie S. Fisher, and J. Mitchell Miller. 2004. 'The Social Context of Violent Victimization: A Study of the Delinquent Peer Effect" *Justice Quarterly* 21:23-47.

Schreck, Christopher J., J. Mitchell Miller, and Chris L. Gibson. 2003. 'Trouble in the School Yard: A Study of the Risk Factors of Victimization at School." *Crime & Delinquency* 49:460-84.

Schreck, Christopher J., Eric A. Stewart, and Bonnie S. Fisher. 2006. "Self-Control, Victimization, and Their Influence on Risky Lifestyles: A Longitudinal Analysis Using Panel Data." *Journal of Quantitative Criminology* 22:319-40.

Schreck, Christopher, J. Richard A. Wright, and J. Mitchell Miller. 2002. "A Study of Individual and Situational Antecedents of Violent Victimization" *Justice Quarterly* 19:159-80.

Schwartz, Martin D. and Victoria L. Pitts. 1995. "Exploring a Feminist Routine Activities Approach to Explaining Sexual Assault." *Justice Quarterly* 12:9-31.

Steffensmeier, Darrel. 1983. "Organization Properties and Sex Segregation in the

Underworld: Building a Sociological Theory of Sex Differences in Crime." *Social Forces* 61:1010-32.

Stewart, Eric A., Kirk W. Elifson, and Claire E. Sterk. 2004. "Integrating the General Theory of Crime into an Explanation of Violent Victimization among Female Offenders." *Justice Quarterly* 21:159-81.

Stimson, James A. 1985. "Regression in Space and Time: A Statistical Essay." *American Journal of Political Science* 29:914-47.

Wilcox, Pamela, Michelle Campbell Augustine, Jon Paul Bryan, and Staci D. Roberts. 2005.

"The 'Reality' of Middle School Crime: Objective vs. Subjective Experiences among a Sample of Kentucky Youth." *Journal of School Violence* 4:3-28.

Wilcox, Pamela, Kenneth C. Land, and Scott A, Hunt. 2003. *Criminal Circumstance: A Dynamic, Multicontextual Criminal Opportunity Theory.* Hawthorne, NY: Aldine de Gruyter.

Wilcox, Pamela, David C. May, and Staci D. Roberts. 2006. "Student Weapon Possession and the 'Fear and Victimization Hypothesis': Unraveling the Temporal Order." *Justice Quarterly* 23:502-29.

DISCUSSION QUESTIONS

1. Describe the authors' multistage sampling procedure.
2. What was their response rate? Attrition rate? Were any groups under-represented because of these?
3. What were the main dependent variables examined in this study?
4. In Table 5.4, which variables predict both boys' and girls' theft victimization? Are any of the variables significant for boys and not girls, or vice versa?
5. In Table 5.5, are there variables that predict physical assault for boys and not girls, or vice versa?
6. What theoretical explanation do these authors provide for gender differences in victimization?
7. What do these authors say about their ability to generalize the results of their study based on their response rates?

RESEARCH READING

Anderson and Sample examine the degree to which citizens access sex offender registry information as well as those citizens' attitudes and feelings about the registry and whether or not they respond to this information with preventative measures. They explore this topic using a representative sample of Nebraska residents through a telephone survey utilizing random digit dialing. The survey asked those 19 years old and older about awareness of, and access to, Nebraska's sex offender registry. The results reveal that a majority of persons knew about the registry but very few had accessed it. Of those that did get information about sex offenders from the registry, very few took any preventative measures.

Source: Anderson, A. L., & Sample, L. L. (2008). Public awareness and action resulting from sex offender community notification laws. *Criminal Justice Policy Review, 19*(4), 371–396. Copyright © 2008 Sage Publications.

PUBLIC AWARENESS AND ACTION RESULTING FROM SEX OFFENDER COMMUNITY NOTIFICATION LAWS

Amy L. Anderson and Lisa L. Sample

Abstract: Few studies have examined the degree to which citizens access registry information or take preventive action in response. Survey responses from a representative sample of Nebraska residents were used to examine the degree to which people access registration information, the feelings this information invokes, and if preventive measures are subsequently taken by citizens. The results suggest that the majority of citizens had not accessed registry information, although the majority of people knew the registry existed, and few respondents took any preventive measures as a result of learning sex offender information. The implications of the results on notification laws are discussed.

INTRODUCTION

At a time when most measures of sex offending were depicting declines in sex crimes, sex offenders were receiving an extraordinary amount of legislative attention. For instance, from 1996 to 2005, the Federal Bureau of Investigation reported a 2.4% decline in reporting forcible rape to police (Federal Bureau of Investigation, 2005), and a review of the National Crime Victimization Survey for this same period reveals a 35% decline in victimization for rape and sexual assault (Sample, 2001). Yet despite these reported declines in offending, many sex offender laws proliferated across the country during this same period including civil commitment, chemical castration, residency restrictions, prohibitions of sex offenders from some public places, and electronic monitoring of convicted offenders (Levenson, 2007; Sample, 2001). Few of these laws have been as far-reaching in terms of their application, however, than the community notification laws passed during the mid-1990s.

Megan's Law was passed in 1996 as an amendment to the Wetterling Act (Tide XVII of the Violent Crime Control and Law Enforcement Act of 1994,42 U.S.C.A. §14071), making it mandatory for all states to disclose information about registered sex offenders to the public. The notification of sex offender information was further facilitated with the passage of the Prosecutorial Remedies and Other Tools to End the Exploitation of Children Today ("PROTECT") Act of 2003 (PL- 08-21, section 604), requiring all states to provide Internet websites of registration information.

Many scholars have suggested that the passage of these community notification laws was the result of a "moral panic" about sex offending, particularly the victimization of children (Gavin, 2005; Hinds & Daly, 2000; Jenkins, 1998; Quinn, Forsyth, & Mullen-Quinn, 2004; Sample, 2001; Steinbeck, 1995; Zgoba, 2004). In other words, these laws are often seen as the products of exaggerated concern stimulated by extensive media coverage of a few isolated incidents of sexually related homicides against children (Sample, 2006). Legislation is often the natural outgrowth of a moral panic, as the very nature of moral panics implies that some action must be taken to address a problem (Ben-Yehuda, 1990; S. Cohen, 1972; Sutherland, 1950). In the case of sex offending, however, the passage of community notification laws was only one measure taken to address the behavior. Unlike other legislation often resulting from moral panics, these laws required that private citizens take some action as well.

Community notification laws are premised on the notion that citizens should be informed of sex offenders' information and whereabouts, so they may take some preventive action to protect themselves and their children (Caputo & Brodsky, 2003; M. Cohen & Jeglic, 2007; Levenson, 2007; Pawson, 2007; Tewksbury, 2002, 2005; Zevitz, 2006). Consistent with such theories as the routine activities perspective (L. E. Cohen & Felson, 1979), preventive measures may take many forms but often include "target hardening" techniques such as increased surveillance of people and places, additional security measures for homes, and improved self-defense procedures. These citizens' actions are expected to augment the public safety afforded by other sex offender legislation and law enforcement activities. To this end, private citizens have become somewhat responsible for community safety, as they are responsible for proactively accessing sex offender information and subsequently formulating some preventive action plan.

Although scholars have investigated the degree to which notification laws have the ability to achieve their informative goals (Levenson, Brannon, Fortney, & Baker, 2007; Phillips, 1998), little research examines the degree to which citizens actually access registry information or take action in response (Lovell, 2007). This study examines the degree to which community notification laws inform the public of sex offender information and preventive action from citizens. Specifically, a random sample of Nebraska residents was surveyed to discern the degree to which people access registration information, the feelings invoked by this information, and the types of actions taken by citizens as a result of this information. Our examination is not intended to diminish the sex offender problem, demean legislators' attempts at addressing the behavior, or make light, of the harm that victims endure. Rather, our findings are meant to shed further light on the effectiveness of community notification laws at enhancing public safety. Our results, however, also have implications for the study of moral panic legislation, as they highlight the

actions taken by the public as a result of moral panics beyond the subsequent enactment of legislation.

Our study begins with an examination of the impetus of community notification laws and a review of the effectiveness of this sex offender reform. We proceed with a discussion of our data collection and analytic techniques followed by a discussion of our results and the implications for the future of sex offender policies and reforms.

BACKGROUND

In the late 1980s and early 1990s, three specific incidents of sexual homicides against children were catalysts for contemporary registration and community notification laws. In October 1989, an armed, masked stranger abducted Jacob Wetterling, 11, near his home in Minnesota (National Criminal Justice Association, 1997) and he was never found. His case resembled that of a boy in a neighboring town who was abducted and sexually attacked earlier that year. The police believed that the same man was involved in both of the incidents, which led them to believe that they were searching for a repeat sex offender. Although the Wetterling abduction drew attention to the repetitiveness of sex offenders' behaviors, it was the homicide of Polly Klaas and Megan Kanka that brought this issue to the forefront of the policy agenda (Jenkins, 1998).

In 1993, the media widely disseminated the story of Polly Klaas, a 12-year-old girl who was abducted from her bedroom, sexually assaulted, and subsequently killed. Only one year later, the media reported that 7-year-old Megan Kanka was missing from her New Jersey home; she was later found sexually assaulted and murdered (Jenkins, 1998). Previously convicted sex offenders who were released from prison had murdered both Polly Klaas and Megan Kanka. The parents of these murdered children actively lobbied state and federal legislators for remedies to address the repeat behavior of sex offenders.

In 1994, the Jacob Wetterling Crimes Against Children and Sexually Violent Offender Registration Act mandated that 10% of a state's funding under the Edward Bryne Memorial State and Local Law Enforcement Assistance grant program be used to establish a statewide system for registering and tracking convicted sex offenders (M. Cohen & Jeglic, 2007; Hinds & Daly, 2000; Levenson et al., 2007). Law enforcement personnel were responsible for creating sex offender registries, obtaining addresses, phone listings, driver's license numbers, photographs, and other information from sex offenders upon their conviction, in addition to verifying addresses, updating registry information, and apprehending persons for failure to comply. To date, all states have complied with the requirements of the Wetterling Act (Sample, 2001).

The Wetterling Act was soon amended by the passage of "Megan's Law" in 1996, which requires states to make sex offender registry information available to the public. This burden again fell on law enforcement personnel and could be accomplished in several ways, such as door-to-door solicitation, answering requests for information over the phone, or providing registry listings in media outlets and on the Internet. The implementation of Megan's Law, however, has been affected by the passage of the federal PROTECT Act of 2003 (PL-108-21, section 604), which requires all states to create Internet websites that contain various information about registered sex offenders.

Most scholars acknowledge that these laws were passed on misinformation and faulty assumptions about sex offenders and their behaviors, with no research-based evidence of effectiveness, and with little thought to the long-term consequences for offenders (M. Cohen & Jeglic, 2007; Levenson et al., 2007; Sample, 2006; Sample & Bray, 2003, 2006; Sample & Kadleck, 2008; Tewksbury, 2002,

2005; Zevitz, 2003; Zevitz & Farkas, 2000b). Nevertheless, researchers have recently started investigating the effectiveness of community notification laws at informing the public and the degree to which they may affect sex offenders' behavior.

The utility of community notification laws is premised on the accuracy of sex offender information, yet empirical and journalistic investigations consistently reveal a significant amount of error in descriptions of sex offenders and their addresses (Lees & Tewksbury, 2006; Tewksbury, 2002). Not only is incorrect descriptive information about offenders often included on registry websites, sex offenders also provide false addresses for their residences, which should not be surprising given the magnitude of their past crimes. To this end, on their very surface, these laws may be ineffective at informing the public, increasing the surveillance of offenders, and preventing future assaults simply because of the inaccuracy of information included in registry listings.

Even when information on sex offender registries is assumed to be correct, and notification procedures occur as intended, there are scholars who are still skeptical of these laws' ability to reduce offending (Adkins, Huff, & Stageberg, 2000; Avrahamian, 1998; Petrosino & Petrosino, 1999; Schram & Milloy, 1995; Tewksbury, 2002; Walker, Madden, Vasquez, VanHouten, & Ervin-McLarty, 2005; Zevitz, 2006; Zevitz & Farkas, 2000b).

Research soliciting the public's perceptions of sex offenders and sex offender legislation suggests much knowledge and support of notification laws, yet none of these studies asked respondents about the degree to which they regularly access registration information, or how citizens use this information to protect themselves and their families. These questions appear particularly salient in light of the passage of the PROTECT Act and the requirement of Internet websites to inform the public as to the whereabouts of offenders. Given the access the public has to computers either at home, school, or public libraries, the PROTECT Act should provide information to virtually any citizen wishing to protect themselves and their children from convicted sex offenders, thereby enhancing public safety beyond what was witnessed under previous door-to-door, flyer, or news media notification procedures. These enhancements to community safety, however, can only be achieved to the degree that citizens access this information and act on it.

This study seeks to fill the gaps in our knowledge about the effectiveness of notification laws by investigating the degree to which people access information concerning sex offenders and subsequently take action based on this information. We also add to the body of literature on notification laws by investigating people's fear associated with sex offender information. To this end, our study is, in part, a replication of previous studies examining public perceptions of notification laws. Rather than concentrating on citizens' perceptions of the law and offenders, however, we focus on citizen access and actions associated with notification information.

DATA AND METHODS

This study employs a sample of residents from Nebraska to explore three specific research questions: To what degree do citizens access the sex offender registry information? Do citizens feel safer armed with this information? and Are actions taken as a result of learning sex offender information? All of these questions are consistent with the goals of notification legislation.

At least one of the goals of Nebraska's community notification law is clearly stated within the statute:

> The legislature determined that state police should assist efforts of local law enforcement agencies to protect their communities by requiring sex offenders to register with local law

enforcement agencies as provided by the Sex Offender Registration Act. This information is to be used to provide public notice and information about a registrant so a community can develop constructive plans to prepare themselves and their family. (NE 29-4002)

Although some may maintain that notification laws may have been passed simply to demonstrate legislators' abilities to respond to public fear and concern, the Nebraska statute makes specific inference to the public's need to take some proactive preventive measures, or at the very least, construct a community protection plan. With this in mind, Nebraska legislators constructed a three-tiered notification system to inform citizens of sex offender information, based on a risk assessment of offenders' propensity to reoffend.

The Nebraska State Patrol (NSP) compiles information about convicted sex offenders. For sex offenders assessed as low/Level 1 risk for reoffending, NSP notifies only law enforcement agencies likely to encounter the sex offender. If the risk level for reoffending is moderate/Level 2, schools, daycare centers, and religious and youth organizations that are in the registrant's county of residence are notified, in addition to local law enforcement agencies. For offenders assessed as most at risk for reoffending, high/Level 3, the general public is notified through news media releases in the registrant's area and through the state's Internet, registration website, which can be accessed by citizens 24 hours a day. Level 3 notifications via the Internet began in Nebraska in January 2000. Local law enforcement agents may utilize additional news releases, community meetings, or direct contact with neighbors to provide further notice of sex offenders' presence in the community.

We believe the fact that Nebraska only informs citizens of the Level 3 offenders, or those offenders believed to pose the most danger to society, makes it well suited for our research purposes. The offenders listed on the sex offender registry are consistent with public perceptions of the type of sex offenders from which people would want to protect themselves and their families. It is possible, then, that Nebraska could represent the "best case" in terms of citizens proactively checking sex offender registries and taking action.

Sampling Design

The interviewers for the Nebraska Annual Social Indicators Survey (NASIS) used Random Digit Dialing (RDD) to select survey respondents. This was facilitated by the Genesys sample generation program, which generates telephone numbers based on known area codes, prefixes within each area code, and working phone number ranges within each prefix. Because several people aged 19 years or older often reside in telephoned homes, a probability process was necessary to select persons to be surveyed in each residence. In this process, the interviewers asked whoever answers the telephone the number of adults living in the home, and based on a random selection by computer, the interviewer requests to speak with the adult who is the oldest, youngest, middle, and so forth. If the designated respondent was not present in the home at the time of the call, the interviewer probed for a time when the respondent was likely to be home in order to make a return call to the designated person. The Nebraskans that were not contacted to participate in the survey included those who were younger than 19 years of age, in institutional custody, living in group quarters or military installations, transient, or without a telephone or a landline.

A total of 9,674 telephone numbers were sampled, of which 5,558 were households. Only 20% of the phone numbers for homes resulted in a ring but no answer after 15 attempts and were subsequently excluded from the sample. In total, of the 5,558 contacts made, approximately 33% completed the survey resulting in a sample of 1,821 adult Nebraska residents aged 19 years or older. The demographic traits of the sample are presented in Table 5.6. One limitation of telephone survey research, which can be seen in the age distribution of the respondents, is that those aged 19 to 24 are underrepresented compared with population estimates due to factors such as transience and cell phones. Additionally, females were slightly overrepresented. Appropriately, weights were computed and used in all of our analyses that adjusted for these age and gender differences from population figures. Thus, the NASIS is a representative sample of individuals aged 19 and older living in the state of Nebraska.

As seen in Table 5.6, the weighted sample was split almost evenly between men and women, and the majority were presently married and living with their partners. Approximately 45% of respondents had children in the home, with about 20% of them having children aged 5 years or younger. This sample characteristic works well for our purposes, as one could logically argue that people with children in the home, particularly young children, should be most vested in accessing sex offender information and taking action as a result.

Survey Instrument and Variables

Data for this study were collected as part of a larger survey conducted in Nebraska that elicits responses on a number of social well-being questions. Generally included in this survey are questions to determine citizens' financial well-being, their health and health care status, their access to state parks and other social services in the state, and their overall mental health status. In total, the survey instrument is 68 pages long and takes almost an hour to administer. We were allowed 1 minute of questions, which amounted to six questions on this survey. The interviewers collected the data from respondents from November 2006 to March 2007 using a standardized coding instrument. All questions included in the survey were closed-ended.

Our independent variables were created from basic demographic information collected

Table 5.6 Demographic Characteristics of Sample ($N = 1,821$)

Independent Variable	Category	Frequency
Gender	Male	901 (49.5%)
	Female	919 (50.5%)
	Missing	1 (0.0%)
Age range	19 to 24	217 (11.9%)
	25 to 44	667 (36.6%)
	45 to 64	616 (33.8%)
	65 and older	312 (17.1%)
	Missing	9 (0.5%)
Marital status	Married	1246 (68.4%)
	Single/never married	313 (17.2%)
	Divorced, separated, living apart	157 (8.6%)
	Widowed	101 (5.6%)
	Missing	4 (0.2%)
Education	Less than high school	82 (4.5%)
	High school/General Equivalency Diploma (GED)	474 (26%)
	Some college or college graduate	963 (52.9%)
	Some graduate school or graduate degree	299 (16.4%)
	Missing	3 (0.2%)
Children in the home	No children in the home	998 (54.8%)
	Children in the home	823 (45.2%)
Family income	Less than $20,000	182 (10%)
	$20,000 or more	1,539 (84.5%)
	Missing	101 (5.5%)
Race	Caucasian only	1,628 (89.4%)
	Other/multiple racial/ethnic groups(s)	191 (10.5%)
	Missing	3 (.2%)
Urban/rural	City or town	1,445 (79.3%)
	Farm or open country	375 (20.6%)
	Missing	1 (0.1%)

from respondents and included: gender, age, marital status, children, education, income, race, and whether the respondent lived in a rural or urban area. Gender was a dichotomous variable where male = 0 and female = 1. Age, in years, was a categorical variable and was coded 19 to 24 years = 1.25 to 44 years = 2.45 to 64 years = 3, and 65 and older = 4. Additionally, marital status was also a categorical variable and was coded so that those who were never married = 0; currently married and living together = 1; divorced, separated, or married but living separately = 2; and widowed = 3. The presence of children in the home was a dichotomous variable and was coded 0 if there were no children in the home and 1 if there was at least one child in the home. The education measure was coded as a categorical variable where those with less than a high school degree = 0, a high school degree only = 1, some college or college degree = 2, and 1 to 6 years of graduate school = 3. Finally, the respondents that reported living on a farm or in the open country were coded 0 and respondents were coded as a 1 if they reported living in a city or town. The income measure was a dichotomous variable coded 0 if the family income of the respondent was less than $20,000 and was coded 1 for those that made more than $20,000 a year.

A dichotomous variable was created for race (Caucasian = 1). The respondents were asked, What race or races do you consider yourself to be? The response categories were the same as found in the U.S. Census and respondents could choose multiple categories. The responses were recoded such that each respondent fell into one of the following mutually exclusive categories: (a) Caucasian; (b) African American; (c) Hispanic/Latino; (d) Asian, Pacific Islander, or Hawaiian; (e) Native American; and (f) respondents who responded as Other or those who self-identified with more than one racial or ethnic category. Those that responded being Caucasian and no other racial or ethnic group made up more than 91% of the sample, with the next largest racial/ethnic group being those in the Other/multiple race group (3.5% of the sample). Each other group was about 2% of the sample or less. This limited distribution of non-White respondents led to our decision to create a White/non-White dichotomous variable.

People's awareness and access of sex offender registry information first was assessed by asking respondents if they were aware of the sex offender registry in Nebraska (no = 0, unsure = 1, and yes = 2). Those who answered *yes* were asked if they had ever accessed Nebraska's sex offender registry (no = 0, yes = 1). If they had, then respondents were asked how many times they had accessed this information and the responses were coded as once = 1; 2 to 5 times = 2; and 5 times or more = 3. To determine people's opinions of registry information, respondents were asked if they felt safer knowing registry information, and if they thought this information would help keep their families safer (no = 0, yes = 1). Finally, respondents were specifically asked if they had taken any preventive measures as a result of registry information (no = 0, yes = 1).

In addition to the information gathered through the above closed-ended questions, qualitative data were also collected. Specifically, interviewers recorded any comments citizens gave while responding to the questions. For instance, when asked if they had ever accessed registry information, respondents often volunteered more information beyond *yes* or *no*. Some stated they read information in the paper, some specifically stated they had never been on the Internet registration website, and still others suggested that other members of the family had accessed information but the specific respondent had not. The interviewers collected these unsolicited comments as direct quotes. Although some of the questions received more qualitative responses than other questions, none had more than 22 recorded responses. This low qualitative response rate could be a function of the length of the survey or people's unwillingness to articulate further thoughts and opinions. Regardless of the reason, this response rate should be kept in mind when interpreting our results.

RESULT

We disaggregate the results into three sections. First, we examined respondents' knowledge of and access to the Nebraska sex offender registry. Second, we examined respondents' perceptions of safety, both personal and familial, resulting from accessing the registry. Finally, we examined whether respondents took any preventive measures after they accessed the registry.

We begin each section by presenting the overall results for our main research questions (see Table 5.7), which is merely presenting the frequencies for each category for each question. We then present any significant findings from chi-squared tests, which determined whether there was an association between the demographic characteristics of the survey

respondents and their answers to questions about the sex offender registry. We do not report these results in a single table, however. Rather, we discuss the demographic data frequency distributions for each question followed by individualized discussions of statistically significant (i.e., $p < .05$) chi-squared tests where appropriate.

Awareness and Access of Registry Information

The overwhelming majority of Nebraska respondents were aware that a sex offender registry existed in their state (89.8%). Results of the chi-squared tests showed an association between being aware of the registry and gender ($\chi^2 = 9.494$, $df = 2$, $p = .009$), age ($\chi^2 = 70.377$, $df = 6$, $p = .000$), marital status ($\chi^2 = 52.241$, $df = 6$, $p = .000$), education ($\chi^2 = 89.487$, $df = 6$, $p = .000$), children ($\chi^2 = 13.802$, $df = 2$, $p = .001$), income ($\chi^2 = 39.675$, $df = 2$, $p = .000$), and race ($\chi^2 = 105.23$, $df = 2$, $p = .000$).

Specifically, men were more likely to be unsure if there was a registry (10.8%) compared to women (7.6%) or to say there was no

Table 5.7   Awareness, Feeling, and Action Resulting From Notification

Dependent Variable	Yes	No	Unsure	Valid N
Aware of registry	1,609 (89.8%)	18 (1.0%)	164 (9.2%)	1,791
Accessed registry	558 (34.8%)	1,046 (65.2%)		1,605
Feel family is safer	478 (87.6%)	68 (12.4%)		546
Personally feel safer	484 (88.0%)	66 (12.0%)		551
Taken preventive action	209 (37.6%)	346 (62.4%)		555
	1	*2 to 5*	*5 or More*	
Times accessed the registry	119 (21.3%)	278 (49.8%)	161 (28.9%)	558

sex offender registry in Nebraska (1.5% to .6%). The respondents with children were more likely to say yes (92.6%) compared to those with no children in the home (87.6%), although those with no children were more likely to say they were unsure (11.5% to 6.4%). Respondents whose race was Caucasian only were less likely to answer that there was not a registry (.4%) or to be unsure (7.8%) than respondents who were not Caucasian only (6.6% and 21.9%, respectively). Almost 92% of White respondents were aware that there was a sex offender registry in Nebraska, compared with 71.6% in the Other racial/ethnic category.

There was a sizable difference with respect to income and knowledge of the registry, as almost 93% of those making $20,000 or more reported being aware of the registry, compared to only about 79% of those making less than $20,000.

Additionally, more than 20% of those making less than $20,000 reported being unsure whether there was a sex offender registry, whereas less than 7% of those making $20,000 or more reported being unsure.

An examination of the association between age and registry awareness showed considerable variation between the age categories. For example, just about 79% of respondents between the ages of 19 and 24 reported knowing the registry existed, whereas another 19% were unsure and 2.4% said no. This compares with more than 93% of respondents between both the ages of 25 and 44 and the ages of 45 to 64 who knew of the registry. Similarly, of those aged 65 and older, about 82% knew of the registry but almost 17% of this age group reported being unsure (compared to 5.3% of 25 to 44-year-olds and 6.4% of 45- to 64-year-olds who reported being unsure).

The association between marital status and awareness of the registry also varied by the marital category examined. About 92% of respondents who were either currently married or had been married in the past but were separated or divorced said they were aware there was a registry in Nebraska. These percentages compare with about 80% of widowed respondents and 82% of never-married respondents who reported being aware of the registry. Similarly, 15% of the never-married respondents and more than 16% of widowed respondents reported being unsure as to whether there was a registry, although only about 7% of married respondents and 8% of divorced or separated respondents said they were unsure. Finally, the never-married and widowed were more likely to say that the registry did not exist compared with the married and divorced or separated groups (3.3% and 3.1% compared to .4% and 0%, respectively).

With regard to education, results indicated that as education increased, awareness of the registry increased and uncertainty of the registry decreased. For example, 6.3% of respondents with less than a high school degree said there was no registry, just more than 25% said they were unsure, and 68.4% said there was a sex offender registry in Nebraska. These numbers compare to 1.1%, 15.5%, and 83.5% for those with a high school degree only; .7%, 5.9%, and 93.4% for those with some college or a college degree; and .7% who said no, 5.1% who were unsure, and 94.2% who said yes that had 1 to 6 years of graduate education. It is clear that having at least some college is associated with having knowledge of the sex offender registry.

Despite the widespread awareness of the registry, only a little more than one third (34.8%) of respondents had accessed this information. The majority of the respondents accessing sex offender information were women ($\chi^2 = 35.431$, $df = 1$, $p = .000$), had children in the home ($\chi^2 = 81.815$, $df = 1$, $p = .000$), had a family income of $20,000 or more ($\chi^2 = 7.220$, $df = 1$, $p = .007$), and lived in a city or town ($\chi^2 = 19.962$, $df = 1$, $p = .000$). Additionally, an association was found between accessing the registry and age ($\chi^2 = 136.251$, $df = 3$, $p = .000$), marital status (χ^2 = 13.745, df = 3, p = .003), and education (χ^2 = 30.049, df = 3, p = .000).

Specifically, almost 42% of females reported accessing the State of Nebraska sex offender registry, whereas only about 27% of males reported actually accessing the registry. Similarly, about 46% of respondents with children in the home said they had accessed the registry, whereas only about 25% of those without children said they had accessed the registry. Those with a higher income were also more likely to check the registry (36.1%) than those who made less than $20,000 a year (24.6%), and respondents who lived in a city or town were more likely to have checked the registry than respondents who lived on a farm or in the open country (37.6% to 24.6%).

In terms of the association between age and checking the registry, the highest percentage was for the age group of 25 to 44, with 50.3% of this age category saying they had checked the registry. This compares with about 32% of 19- to 24-year-olds who checked the registry, 29.1% of 45- to 64-year-olds, and only 10.9% of those aged 65 and older. In terms of marital status, the results showed that comparable percentages of those never-married, married, or divorced and separated respondents had checked the registry (34.7%, 36%, and 35.9%, respectively), whereas considerably fewer widowed respondents reported accessing the sex offender registry (15.4%).

Finally, the association between checking the registry and education was similar to the findings for awareness of the registry. In particular, only 17% of those with a high school degree reported checking the registry and about 25% of respondents with only a high school degree said they had checked. These percentages compare to about 39% of respondents with some college or a college degree and 38.8% of those with 1 to 6 years of graduate education that reported checking the registry.

Most of these people (78.7%) who had accessed registry information had done so more than once, with about half of the respondents

who did access the registry reporting doing so between two and five times (49.8%) and another 28.9% checking it five or more times. The only demographic variable significantly associated with the number of times a respondent reported checking the registry was the respondent's marital status (χ^2 = 13.396, df = 6, p = .037). Married respondents were more likely to have checked the registry across all response categories (about 20% checked it once, about 51% checked it two to five times, and 29% checked it five or more times), whereas those respondents who reported being separated, divorced, or married living separately were disproportionately likely to have reported checking the registry five or more times (44%, with 32% checking between two to five times and 24% checking once). About 25% of respondents that had never been married said they checked it once, more than 55% said they checked it two to five times, with not quite 20% saying they checked it five or more times. For widowed respondents, 30% reported checking the registry once, 60% had checked it two to five times, and only 10% of this group reported checking the sex offender registry five or more times.

When respondents noted reasons for being aware of or accessing the registry, the majority noted they had read this information in the newspaper (15 of 22 people). Some specifically stated that they had not accessed this information online. To this end, it appears that the media may provide a more effective venue for community notification than the computer.

Approximately 65% of respondents stated that they had not accessed the sex offender registry. Few respondents offered reasons for why they had not personally accessed the information. When respondents did comment on reasons for not checking the registry, people suggested that it was friends', neighbors', family members', or schools' responsibility to inform them of sex offender information. Respondent 18 noted, "[Notification is] done through school" Others explained, "sister-in-law accesses the information" (Respondent 10), "my wife has" (Respondent 7), or "[my neighbor], she's a teacher and she gets the neighborhood registry" (Respondent 22). Still others noted that "friends have" (Respondent 2), and "my daughter has because she has a son" (Respondent 16). These findings suggest that notification of sex offender information is a rather passive endeavor, with people learning of information in a secondhand manner. They also suggest that citizens may not take the responsibility for learning about sex offender information personally, and see this as a duty better left to others.

Even when respondents do access registry information, it seems that this access is more related to employment needs or requirements than personal interest and safety. Respondent 15 noted, "[Work] in a licensed day care, automatically on an alert list." Respondent 12 explained, "[Access] due to her job, I work with mentally handicapped, so it helps to make them aware to protect themselves." Respondent 7 explains that he or she had not accessed the registry at home, "but at business and school." Landlords, such as Respondent 13, also noted they "look at it because they have tenants." In sum, it appears that accessing registry information has become more of a professional responsibility than a personal one.

Perceptions of Safety Resulting From Registry Information

Only a total of 551 people of 1,821 (30.2%) responded to questions regarding their perceptions of personal safety as a result of sex offender information due to the fact that only 34% had accessed registry information and the skip pattern of the survey. Of these respondents, approximately 88% reported feeling safer after learning the whereabouts of convicted sex offenders.

The only demographic variables related to whether the respondent felt personally safer knowing the information were children in the home ($\chi^2 = 7.965$, $df = 1$, $p = .005$) and age ($\chi^2 = 20.874$, $df = 3$, $p = .000$). Ninety-one percent of respondents with children in the home reported feeling personally safer with the information provided by the sex offender registry compared to about 83% of respondents with no children who reported feeling safer.

The association between age and feeling personally safer after retrieving the sex offender information was somewhat interesting. In particular, 100% of respondents between the ages of 19 and 24 reported feeling safer after checking the registry. This compares with about 89% of those aged 25 to 44, 85% of those 45 to 64, and about 67% of those aged 65 and older that reported feeling personally safer. Those older than the age of 65 appear to be the most skeptical group in terms of translating the sex offender information into a feeling of personal safety, whereas those aged 19 to 24 could be considered the least skeptical, as they feel considerably safer as an age group when accessing the sex offender information. Both of these findings are interesting in light of the evidence presented earlier that these are the very groups least likely to have known about or checked the registry in the first place. It seems that when they do check it, the young people feel safer while the older respondents have more mixed views.

The findings that respondents generally felt personally safer may be overstated, however. When further comments were offered by respondents, most qualified their response by stating that registry information made them feel only *somewhat* or *a little* safer. Furthermore, some citizens "question the accuracy" (Respondent 4) and quantity of information about sex offenders. Respondent 8 noted, "Would like it [information] to be more specific as to what kind of sex offender they are, whether adult or child." Respondent 17 explained, "You can only see Level 3 offenders in Nebraska and would like to see all levels." Despite concerns regarding the quality and quantity of information, some respondents

Q:SOR3

How many times have you accessed the State of Nebraska's sex offender registry? Would you say . . .

1 Never

2 Once

3 Two to five times

4 Five or more times

If (SOR3 = 1) skip to END; if (SOR3 > 4) skip to END

Q:SOR4

Have you taken any preventive measures as a result of the information?

1 Yes

5 No

Q:SOR5

Do you think this information will help keep you and your family safe?

1 Yes

5 No

Q:SOR6

Do you feel safer knowing this information?

1 Yes

5 No

REFERENCES

Adkins, G., Huff, D., & Stageberg, P. (2000). *The Iowa sex offender registry*. Des Moines: Iowa Department of Human Rights.

Avrahamian, K. A. (1998). A critical perspective: Do "Megan's Laws" really shield children from sex-predators? *Journal of Juvenile Law, 19,* 301-317.

Becker, H. S. (1963). *Outsiders; Studies in the sociology of deviance.* New York: The Free Press.

Ben-Yehuda, N. (1990). *The politics and morality of deviance.* New York: State University of New York Press.

Caputo, A. A., & Brodsky, S. L. (2003). Citizens coping with community notification of released sex offenders. *Behavioral Sciences & the Law,* 22(2), 239-252.

Cohen, L. E., & Felson, M. (1979). Social change and crime rate trends: A routine activities approach. *American Sociological Review,* 44(4), 588-608.

Cohen, M., & Jeglic, E. L. (2007). Sex offender legislation in the United States: What do we know? *International Journal of Offender Therapy and Comparative Criminology,* 57(4), 369-383.

Cohen, S. (1972). *Folk devils and moral panics: The creation of the Mods and Rockers.* London: MacGibbon and Kee.

Conrad, P., & Schneider, J. W. (1980). *Deviance and medicalization, from badness to sickness.* St. Louis: Mosby.

Elbogen, E. B., Patry, M., & Scalora, M. (2003). The impact of community notification laws on sex offender treatment attitudes. *International Journal of Law and Psychiatry, 26.*

Evans, M K. (2007). *Citizens' perceptions of sex offender community notification in Nebraska.* Unpublished thesis, University of Nebraska at Omaha.

Federal Bureau of Investigation. (2005), *Crime in the United States.* Washington, DC: Department of Justice.

Francis, B., & Soothill, K. (2000). Does sex offending lead to homicide? *The Journal of Forensic Psychiatry, 11* (1), 49-61.

Gaines, L. K., & Kraska, P. B. (2003). *Drugs, crime, and justice: Contemporary perspectives.* Prospect Heights, IL: Waveland Press.

Gavin, H. (2005). The social construction of the child sex offender explored by narrative. *The Qualitative Report, 10*(3), 395-415.

Hinds, L., & Daly, K. (2000). The war on sex offenders: Community notification in perspective. *Australian and New Zealand Journal of Criminology, 13*(3), 284-306.

Jenkins, P. (1998). *Moral panic: Changing concepts of the child molester in modern America.* New Haven, CT: Yale University Press.

Lees, M., & Tewksbury, R. (2006). Understanding policy and programmatic issues regarding sex offender registries. *Corrections Today. 68(1),* 54-57.

explained that the information "will make you more aware, which makes you safer" (Respondent 20). To this end, some citizens appear to have derived a casual model for public safety with regard to sex offenders in which registry information makes them more aware, and awareness translates to some enhanced level of perceived public safety.

In addition to feeling personally safer after learning sex offender information, the majority of respondents (87.6%) also felt that the registry would help keep their families safe as well. There were no significant differences across the demographic variables in terms of whether the respondent believed the information would help keep them and their family safe. Respondents' comments suggest that this information may only "somewhat" (Respondent 8) or "to a certain extent" (Respondent 21) make their families safer, or the information "could increase safety" (Respondent 13). One respondent concludes, "[The information does] not necessarily make your family safer, it will just make them more aware." Moreover, the accuracy of information was again in question. As one respondent stated, "It should [make families safer], if they register and are where they are suppose to be." On the other hand, another respondent noted that "only when they're behind bars" will families be safer.

Preventive Measures-Resulting From Registry Information

A little more than one third of respondents answered *yes* when asked if they had taken any preventive measures as a result of sex offender registry information. The chi-squared tests revealed a significant association between taking preventive action and both gender ($\chi^2 = 4.007$, $df = 1$, $p = .045$) and having children ($\chi^2 = 6.337$, $df = 1$, $p = .012$). Approximately 41% of females said they had taken preventive measures, whereas only about 32% of males reported taking preventive action. Similarly, about 42% of those with children reported taking preventive

action, whereas 31% of those with no children in the home reporting taking action.

Respondents' comments suggest that the most common action taken by citizens if they obtain sex offender information may be to "spread the word" (Respondent 12). Respondent 3 stated, "I talked to my kids," and Respondent 15 mentioned, "I told my daughters." Beyond sharing the information with children, Respondent 20 explained, "I forwarded the information [to friends]." Respondent 21 stated, "I used to look it up for children and send it to their parents." Additionally, two respondents explained that they inform tenants and/or renters about the presence of a sex offender on their properties.

Although sharing sex offender information was a common response to receiving it, the respondents took other actions as well. Respondent 14 reported "locking the door when I'm home alone." Respondent 12 explained, "I'm a little more cautious." Still another respondent, Respondent 4, stated that upon learning the whereabouts of sex offenders, "I had to evict one from my apartments. They're there and children are there."

Surprisingly, 62% of the respondents who answered this question reported that they had not taken any preventive measures. It is difficult to shed further light on why people do not take action because respondents offered no qualitative comments in this regard. Perhaps the enhanced feelings of safety reported by the majority of respondents precluded any further action.

CONCLUSION

Despite federal legislation mandating public access to sex offender registries, it seems that the majority of people in Nebraska do not proactively seek sex offender information using the Internet-based sex offender registry. A lack of awareness of the registry cannot explain this finding, as most people reported being aware of the availability of sex offender information.

When the public accesses this information, however, it appears to make people feel safer themselves and for their families, yet most do not take any preventive measures to ensure these perceptions of safety. Respondents' comments did not suggest any situational crime prevention techniques taken on behalf of themselves or their families, such as installing home security systems, enhancing locking devises, installing security cameras, or more actively monitoring public spaces where children dwell. This is surprising given the concern and attention that sex crimes against children invoke; however, it is likely that people do not live in a constant state of moral panic. These findings suggest several implications for not only community notification procedures but also for the resulting legislation of moral panics more generally.

Implications for Notification Laws

To the degree that community notification laws were intended to make people feel safer, the provision of reporting sex offender information to the public may have achieved this goal. If the laws were intended to have appreciable effects on actual public safety, however, it seems likely that these laws will fall short of that goal. It will be difficult for notification to inform the public of sex offenders' whereabouts and thereby increase the informal surveillance of offenders if only about one third of the population accesses this information. Moreover, only about one third of people armed with sex offender information take any preventive measures, so it is likely that even if more people access this information, few will act on it. Although the optimum percentage of the public that should access registry information or take protective measures as a result remains unknown, it seems likely that legislators intended community notification to be a broad-based policy intended to aid as many citizens possible. To this end, it is likely that more than one third of the population was the

target of this legislation. If greater enhancements to public safety, particularly for children, are going to be observed, it seems some adjustments are needed to community notification procedures.

Although the public appears aware of the sex offender registry, few reported accessing this information using the Internet. Because people are deriving information about sex offenders through the media, states would be wise to advertise registry websites in media outlets to increase the access to this information. Public service announcements may go a far way to publicizing the ease with which citizens can access sex offender information online. Simply providing sex offender information to the public may not be enough, however.

Few people took any preventive action based on the sex offender information they had learned. It is possible that people believe that simply accessing sex offender information is a protective action in and of itself. It may be more likely, however, that citizens do not take preventive measures after learning of sex offenders' whereabouts simply because they do not know what actions to take. Campaigns could be conducted by law enforcement agencies to inform the public what preventive measures may be taken as a result of sex offender information. It would be prudent to include prevention information on sex offender registry websites, in news releases of registry information, and at community meetings about sex offenders' presence (Evans, 2007). To the degree to which notification laws were intended to enhance public safety through private actions, media campaigns and more prevention information appears imperative to accomplish this goal. This is not to say, however, that this information will automatically spur the public into preventive action. Given the results of this research, it is possible that these efforts will have little effect on community action plans or parents' protective measures toward their children.

In order for people to devise prevention strategies, they need accurate information about

offenders and trends in offending. Citizens need to be reassured that the information in sex offender registry is accurate and up-to-date. Law enforcement agencies should inform the public as to their verification procedures. If citizens were aware of the ways in which law enforcement agents monitor the movements of sex offenders, they may have more confidence in the information included in registration listings. More important, prevention strategies should be founded on empirical information about sex offenders' patterns of behavior.

Media accounts of children sexually assaulted and killed by strangers who were repeat sex offenders leave the public with the impression that they have more to fear from strangers than from people known to them (Sample, 2006; Sample & Kadleck, 2008). Empirical evidence, however, suggests that, most sexual assaults are committed by persons known to their victims (Sample, 2001; Snyder, 2000), that few sex offenders kill their victims (Francis & Soothill, 2000; Sample, 2006), and that the vast majority of sexual assaults reported to police occurred in a residence and not in a public park or school zone (Snyder, 2000). To that end, campaigns to inform the public about prevention strategies should include discussions about techniques by which to recognize signs of victimization in the home.

Limitations

As with all survey research, participation in this study was voluntary. To this end, despite our efforts at randomization and the weighting of data, participants' views may vary significantly from those who chose not to participate. The extent to which this selection bias affects our results remains unknown and this should be kept in mind when reviewing our research findings.

Another caveat concerns the degree to which our results can be generalized beyond Nebraska to residents in other states. Although the

PROTECT Act of 2003 mandates all states to create Internet websites, there is variability across the states concerning the types of offenders included in sex offender registries and the type of information included about offenders (Sample & Bray, 2003). Nebraska includes only sex offenders assessed as high risk for reoffending on their website, whereas other states (e.g., Illinois) include all convicted offenders in their notification procedures, regardless of assessed risk. Some states include photographs of offenders and the exact crime for which offenders were convicted, and others do not. To the degree that registries and notification procedures vary across states, it is unlikely that the findings from Nebraska citizens can be generalized to all citizens at large. This study is exploratory in nature, however, and therefore was not intended to be representative of residents in other states. Our purpose was simply to explore the degree to which the public accesses registry information and the results thereof, thereby providing a baseline for other researchers.

APPENDIX: STATE OF NEBRASKA SEX OFFENDER REGISTRY SURVEY QUESTIONS

Q:SOR1

Is there a sex offender registry in the State of Nebraska? Would you say . . .

1 Yes

5 No

7 Or you are unsure

If (SOR1 > 1) END

Q:SOR2

Have you ever accessed Nebraska's sex offender regi

1 Yes

5 No

if (SOR2 > 1) END

Levenson, J. S. (2007). The new scarlet letter: Sex offender policies in the 21st century. In D. Prescott (Ed.), *Applying knowledge to practice: Challenges in the treatment and supervisions of sexual abusers*. Oklahoma City, OK: Wood 'N' Barnes Publishing & Distribution.

Levenson, J, S., Brannon, Y. N., Fortney, T., & Baker, J. (2007). Public perceptions and community protection policies. *Analyses of Social Issues and Public Policy, 7*(1), 137-161.

Levenson, J. S., & Cotter, L. P. (2005). The effect of Megan's Law on sex offender reintegration. *Journal of Contemporary Criminal Justice, 21*(1), 49-66.

Loseke, D. R. (1989). Violence is violence . . . or is it? The social construction of "wife abuse" and public policy. In J. Best (Ed.), *Images of issues: Typifying contemporary social problems*. New York: Aldine de Gruyter.

Lovell, E. (2007). *Megan's Law: Does it protect children?* London: Policy and Public Affairs, NSPCC.

Malesky, A., & Keim, J. (2001). Mental health professionals' perspectives on sex offender registry web sites. *Sexual Abuse: A Journal of Research and Treatment, 13*(1), 53-63.

Martin, M., & Marinucci, C. (2006, July 18). Support behind tough sex offender initiative. *San Francisco Chronicle*.

Mustaine, E. E., Tewksbury, R., & Stengel, K. M. (2006). Social disorganization and residential locations of registered sex offenders: Is this a collateral consequence? *Deviant Behavior, 27*(3), 329-350.

National Criminal Justice Association. (1997). *Sex offender community notification*. Washington, DC: Author.

Pawson, R. (2007). *Does Megan's Law work? A theory-driven systematic review*. London: University of London.

Petrosino, A. J., & Petrosino, C. (1999). The public safety potential of Megan's Law in Massachusetts; An assessment from a sample of criminal sexual psychopaths. *Crime and Delinquency, 45*(1), 140-158.

Phillips, D. M. (1998). *Community notification as viewed by Washington's citizens*. Olympia: Washington State Institute for Public Policy.

Quinn, J. F, Forsyth, C, J., & Mullen-Quinn, C. (2004), Societal reaction to sex offenders: A review of the origins and results of the myths surrounding their crimes and treatment amenability. *Deviant Behavior, 25*(3), 215-232.

Redlich, A. D. (2001). Community notification: Perceptions of its effectiveness in preventing child sexual abuse. *Journal of Child Sexual Abuse, 70*(3), 91-116.

Sample, L. L. (2001). *The social construction of the sex offender*. Unpublished dissertation, University of Missouri–St. Louis.

Sample, L. L. (2006). An examination of the degree to which sex offenders kill. *Criminal Justice Review, 37*(3), 230-250.

Sample, L. L., & Bray, T. M. (2003). Are sex offenders dangerous? *Criminology & Public Policy, 3*(1), 59-82.

Sample, L. L., & Bray, T. M. (2006). Are sex offenders different? An examination of re-arrest patterns. *Criminal Justice Policy Review, 77*(1), 83-102.

Sample, L. L., & Kadleck, C. (2008). Sex offender laws: Legislators' accounts of the need for policy. *Criminal Justice Policy Review, 19*(1), 40-62.

Schram, D. D., & Milloy, C. D. (1995). *Community notification: A study of offender characteristics and recidivism*. Olympia: Washington State Institute for Public Policy.

Snyder, H. N. (2000). *Sexual assault of young children as reported to law enforcement: Victim, incident, and offender characteristics*. Washington, DC: U.S. Department of Justice. Bureau of Justice Statistics.

Steinbock, B. (1995). A policy perspective. *Criminal Justice Ethics, 14*(1), 212-234.

Strauss, A. L., & Corbin, J. M. (1998). *Basics of qualitative research: Techniques and procedures for developing grounded theory* (2nd ed.). Thousand Oaks, CA; Sage.

Sutherland, E. H. (1950). The diffusion of sexual psychopath laws. *The American Journal of Sociology, 56*(2), 142-148.

Telpner, B. J. (1997). Constructing safe communities: Megan's Law and the purposes of punishment. *Georgetown Law Journal, 85*(6), 2039-2068.

Tewksbury, R. (2002). Validity and utility of the Kentucky sex offender registry. *Federal Probation, 66*(1), 21-26.

Tewksbury, R. (2005). Collateral consequences of sex offender registration. *Journal of Contemporary Criminal Justice, 21*(1), 67-81.

Tewksbury, R., & Lees, M. (2006). Perceptions of sex offender registration: Collateral consequences and community experiences. *Sociological Spectrum, 26*(3), 309-334.

Walker, J. T, Madden, S., Vasquez, B. E., VanHouten, A, C, & Ervin-McLarty, G. (2005). *The influence of sex offender registration and notification laws in the United States:* Retrieved December 15, 2005, from www.acjc.org

Zevitz, R. G. (2003). Sex offender community notification and its impact on neighborhood life. *Crime Prevention and Community Safety: An International Journal, 20*(1), 41-61.

Zevitz, R. G. (2004). Sex offender placement and neighborhood social integration: The making of a scarlet letter community. *Criminal Justice Studies, 17*(2), 203-223.

Zevitz, R. G. (2006). Sex offender community notification: Its role in recidivism and offender reintegration. *Criminal Justice Studies, 19*(2), 193-208.

Zevitz, R. G., & Farkas, M. A. (2000a). The impact of sex-offender community notification on probation/parole in Wisconsin. *International Journal of Offender Therapy and Comparative Criminology, 44*(1), 8-21.

Zevitz, R. G., & Farkas, M. A. (2000b). Sex offender community notification: Examining the importance of neighborhood meetings. *Behavioral Sciences and the Law, 18*(2/3), 393-408.

Zgoba, K. M. (2004). Spin doctors and moral crusaders: The moral panic behind child safety legislation. *Criminal Justice Studies, 17*(4), 385-404.

DISCUSSION QUESTIONS

1. Why did laws regarding sex offending proliferate across the country at a time when official statistics revealed that sex crimes were declining?

2. What premise were community notification laws based on?

3. How do these authors' research questions line up with sex offender notification laws?

4. After using random digit dialing to call a household, how did the interviewers decide who in the house to survey? Who was not included in the study?

5. What was the response rate in this study? Were any groups in the sample over-represented compared to population statistics? Under-represented? How did the authors remedy this?

6. Why do these authors say that they were able to collect both quantitative and qualitative data?

7. According to Table 5.7, although a majority of people were aware of the registry, very few had actually accessed it. Despite very few persons accessing the registry, what do the results show about attitudes toward safety because of it?

8. What were some of the preventative measures taken by those who gave qualitative information?

9. What do the results of this research say about the goals for implementing sex offender registries? Or preventive measures taken by parents because of them?

RESEARCH READING

In this research by Wright and colleagues, they conduct interviews with 105 active residential burglars in St. Louis, Missouri. The purpose of their research was to study those who were not incarcerated. In other words, they wanted to study successful, rather than unsuccessful, criminals. This article outlines how these authors were able to obtain a sample of active criminals. Specifically, it describes their snowball sampling technique as well as the difficulties they encountered in conducting field research. Their results reveal that, by studying those who have been incarcerated for burglary, we get a distorted view of the characteristics of residential burglars. Their sample differed in a number of important ways from traditional samples of burglars collected through the criminal justice system.

——— A SNOWBALL'S CHANCE IN HELL ———

Doing Fieldwork With Active Residential Burglars

Richard Wright, Scott H. Decker, Allison K. S. Redfern, and Dietrich L. Smith

Abstract: Criminologists long have recognized the importance of field studies of active offenders. Nevertheless, the vast majority of them have shied away from researching criminals "in the wild" in the belief that doing so is impractical. This article, based on the authors' fieldwork with 105 currently active residential burglars, challenges that assumption. Specifically, it describes how the authors went about finding these offenders and obtaining their cooperation. Further, it considers the difficulties involved in maintaining an on-going field relationship with those who lead chaotic lives. And lastly, the article outlines the characteristics of the sample, noting important ways in which it differs from one collected through criminal justice channels.

INTRODUCTION

Criminologists long have recognized the importance of field studies of active offenders. More than 2 decades ago, for example, Polsky (1969, p. 116) observed that "we can no longer afford the convenient fiction that in studying criminals in their natural habitat, we would discover nothing really important that could not be discovered from criminals behind bars." Similarly, Sutherland and Cressey (1970) noted that:

Those who have had intimate contacts with criminals "in the open" know that criminals are not "natural" in police stations, courts, and prisons,

and that they must be studied in their everyday life outside of institutions if they are to be understood. By this is meant that the investigator must associate with them as one of them, seeing their lives and conditions as the criminals themselves see them. In this way, he can make observations which can hardly be made in any other way. Also, his observations are of unapprehended criminals, not the criminals selected by the processes of arrest and imprisonment. (p. 68)

And McCall (1978, p. 27) also cautioned that studies of incarcerated offenders are vulnerable to the charge that they are based on "unsuccessful criminals, on the supposition that successful criminals are not apprehended

Source: Wright, R., Decker, S., Redfern, A. K., & Smith, D. L. (1992). A snowball's chance in hell: Doing fieldwork with active residential burglars. *Journal of Research in Crime & Delinquency, 29*(2), 148–161. Copyright © 1992 Sage Publications.

or at least are able to avoid incarceration." This charge, he asserts, is "the most central bogeyman in the criminologist's demonology" (also see Cromwell, Olson, and Avery 1991; Hagedorn 1990; Watters and Biernacki 1989).

Although generally granting the validity of such critiques, most criminologists have shied away from studying criminals, so to speak, in the wild. Although their reluctance to do so undoubtedly is attributable to a variety of factors (e.g., Wright and Bennett 1990), probably the most important of these is a belief that this type of research is impractical. In particular, how is one to locate active criminals and obtain their cooperation?

The entrenched notion that field-based studies of active offenders are unworkable has been challenged by Chambliss (1975) who asserts that:

> The data on organized crime and professional theft as well as other presumably difficult-to-study events are much more available than we usually think. All we really have to do is to get out of our offices and onto the street. The data are there; the problem is that too often [researchers] are not. (p. 39)

Those who have carried out field research with active criminals would no doubt regard this assertion as overly simplistic, but they probably would concur with Chambliss that it is easier to find and gain the confidence of such offenders than commonly is imagined. As Hagedorn (1990, p. 251) has stated: "Any good field researcher . . . willing to spend the long hours necessary to develop good informants can solve the problem of access."

We recently completed the fieldwork for a study of residential burglars, exploring, specifically, the factors they take into account when contemplating the commission of an offense. The study is being done on the streets of St. Louis, Missouri, a declining "rust belt" city. As part of this study, we located and interviewed 105 active offenders. We also took 70 of these offenders to the site of a recent burglary

and asked them to reconstruct the crime in considerable detail. In the following pages, we will discuss how we found these offenders and obtained their cooperation. Further, we will consider the difficulties involved in maintaining an on-going field relationship with these offenders, many of whom lead chaotic lives. Lastly, we will outline the characteristics of our sample, suggesting ways in which it differs from one collected through criminal justice channels.

LOCATING THE SUBJECTS

In order to locate the active offenders for our study, we employed a "snowball" or "chain referral" sampling strategy. As described in the literature (e.g., Sudman 1976; Watters and Biernacki 1989), such a strategy begins with the recruitment of an initial subject who then is asked to recommend further participants. This process continues until a suitable sample has been "built."

The most difficult aspect of using a snowball sampling technique is locating an initial contact or two. Various ways of doing so have been suggested. McCall (1978), for instance, recommends using a "chain of referrals":

> If a researcher wants to make contact with, say, a bootlegger, he thinks of the person he knows who is closest in the social structure to bootlegging. Perhaps this person will be a police officer, a judge, a liquor store owner, a crime reporter, or a recently arrived Southern migrant. If he doesn't personally know a judge or a crime reporter, he surely knows someone (his own lawyer or a circulation clerk) who does and who would be willing to introduce him. By means of a very short chain of such referrals, the researcher can obtain an introduction to virtually any type of criminal. (p. 31)

This strategy can be effective and efficient, but can also have pitfalls. In attempting to find active offenders for our study, we avoided seeking referrals from criminal justice officials for both practical and methodological reasons. From a practical standpoint, we elected not to use contacts provided by police or probation officers, fearing that this would arouse the suspicions of offenders that the research was the cover for a "sting" operation. One of the offenders we interviewed, for example, explained that he had not agreed to participate earlier because he was worried about being set up for an arrest: "I thought about it at first because I've seen on T.V. telling how [the police] have sent letters out to people telling 'em they've won new sneakers and then arrested 'em." We also did not use referrals from law enforcement or corrections personnel to locate our subjects owing to a methodological concern that a sample obtained in this way may be highly unrepresentative of the total population of active offenders. It is likely, for instance, that such a sample would include a disproportionate number of unsuccessful criminals, that is, those who have been caught in the past (e.g., Hagedorn 1990). Further, this sample might exclude a number of successful offenders who avoid associating with colleagues known to the police. Rengert and Wasilchick (1989, p. 6) used a probationer to contact active burglars, observing that the offenders so located "were often very much like the individual who led us to them."

A commonly suggested means of making initial contact with active offenders other than through criminal justice sources involves frequenting locales favored by criminals (see Chambliss 1975; Polsky 1969; West 1980). This strategy, however, requires an extraordinary investment of time as the researcher establishes a street reputation as an "all right square" (Irwin 1972, p. 123) who can be trusted. Fortunately, we were able to short-cut that process by hiring an ex-offender (who, despite committing hundreds of serious crimes, had few arrests and no felony convictions) with high status among several groups of Black street criminals in St. Louis. This person retired from crime after being shot and paralyzed in a gangland-style execution attempt. He then attended a university and earned a bachelor's degree, but continued to live in his old neighborhood, remaining friendly, albeit superficially, with local criminals. We initially met him when he attended a colloquium in our department and disputed the speaker's characterization of street criminals.

Working through an ex-offender with continuing ties to the underworld as a means of locating active criminals has been used successfully by other criminologists (see, e.g., Taylor 1985). This approach offers the advantage that such a person already has contacts and trust in the criminal subculture and can vouch for the legitimacy of the research. In order to exploit this advantage fully, however, the ex-offender selected must be someone with a solid street reputation for integrity and must have a strong commitment to accomplishing the goals of the study.

The ex-offender hired to locate subjects for our project began by approaching former criminal associates. Some of these contacts were still "hustling," that is, actively involved in various types of crimes, whereas others either had retired or remained involved only peripherally through, for example, occasional buying and selling of stolen goods. Shortly thereafter, the ex-offender contacted several street-wise law-abiding friends, including a youth worker. He explained the research to the contacts, stressing that it was confidential and that the police were not involved. He also informed them that those who took part would be paid a small sum (typically $25.00). He then asked the contacts to put him in touch with active residential burglars.

Figure 5.1 outlines the chain of referrals through which the offenders were located. Perhaps the best way to clarify this process involves selecting a subject, say 064, and identifying the referrals that led us to this person. In this case, the ex-offender working on our project contacted a street-wise, noncriminal

Figure 5.1 "Snowball" Referral Chart

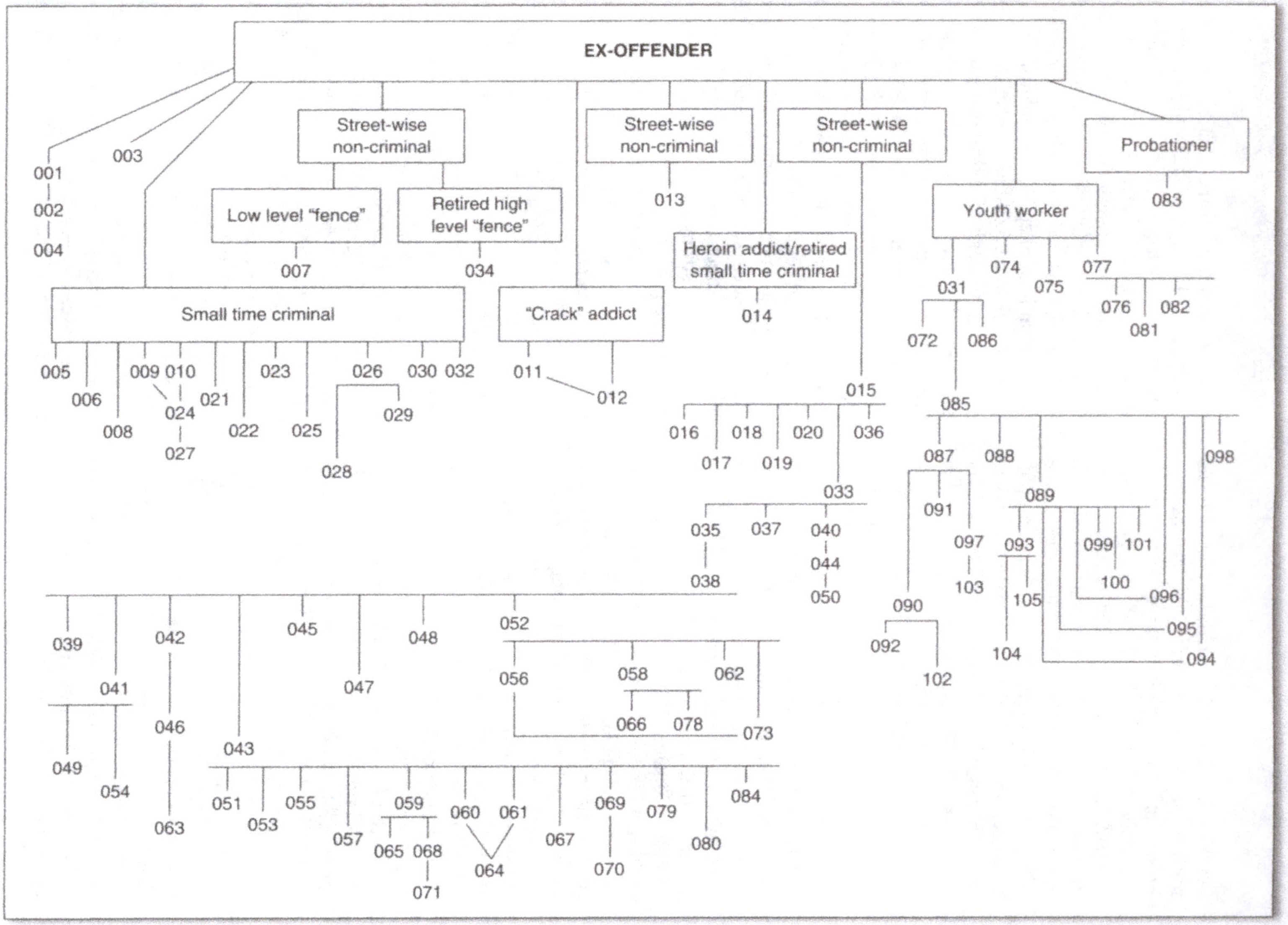

acquaintance who put him in touch with the first active burglar in the chain, offender 015. Offender 015 referred 7 colleagues, one of whom—033—put us in touch with 3 more subjects, including 035, who in turn introduced us to 038, who referred 8 more participants. Among these participants was offender 043, a well-connected burglar who provided 12 further contacts, 2 of whom—060 and 061—convinced 064 to participate in the research. This procedure is similar to that described by Watters and Biernacki (1989, p. 426) in that "the majority of respondents were not referred directly by research staff." As a consequence, our sample was strengthened considerably. After all, we almost certainly would not have been able to find many of these individuals on our own, let alone convince them to cooperate.

Throughout the process of locating subjects, we encountered numerous difficulties and challenges. Contacts that initially appeared to be promising, for example, sometimes proved to be unproductive and had to be dropped. And, of course, even productive contact chains had a tendency to "dry up" eventually. One of the most challenging tasks we confronted involved what Biernacki and Waldorf (1981, p. 150) have termed the "verification of eligibility," that is, determining whether potential subjects actually met the criteria for inclusion in our research. In order to take part, offenders had to be both "residential burglars" and "currently active." In practice, this meant that they had to have committed a residential burglary within the past 2 weeks. This seems straightforward, but it often was difficult to apply the criteria in the field because offenders were evasive about their activities. In such cases, we frequently had to rely on other members of the sample to verify the eligibility of potential subjects.

We did not pay the contacts for helping us to find subjects and, initially, motivating them to do so proved difficult. Small favors, things like giving them a ride or buying them a pack of cigarettes, produced some cooperation, but yielded only a few introductions. Moreover, the active burglars that we did manage to find often were lackadaisical about referring associates because no financial incentive was offered. Eventually, one of the informants hit on the idea of "pimping" colleagues, that is, arranging an introduction on their behalf in exchange for a cut of the participation fee (also see Cromwell et al. 1991). This idea was adopted rapidly by other informants and the number of referrals rose accordingly. In effect, these informants became "locators" (Biernacki and Waldorf 1981), helping us to expand referral chains as well as vouching for the legitimacy of the research, and validating potential participants as active residential burglars.

The practice of pimping is consistent with the low level, underworld economy of street culture, where people are always looking for a way to get in on someone else's deal. One of our contacts put it this way: "If there's money to make out of something, I gotta figure out a way to get me some of it." Over the course of the research, numerous disputes arose between offenders and informants over the payment of referral fees. We resisted becoming involved in these disputes, reckoning that such involvement could only result in the alienation of one or both parties (e.g., Miller 1952). Instead, we made it clear that our funds were intended as interview payments and thus would be given only to interviewees.

FIELD RELATIONS

The success of our research, of course, hinged on an ability to convince potential subjects to participate. Given that many of the active burglars, especially those located early in the project, were deeply suspicious of our motives, it is reasonable to ask why the offenders were willing to take part in the research. Certainly the fact that we paid them a small sum for their time was an enticement for many, but this is not an adequate explanation. After all, criminal opportunities abound and even the inept "nickel and dime" offenders in the sample could have earned more had they spent the time engaged in illegal activity. Moreover, some of the subjects clearly were not short of cash when they agreed to participate; at the close of one interview, an offender pulled out his wallet to show us that it was stuffed with thousand dollar bills, saying:

> I just wanted to prove that I didn't do this for the money. I don't need the money. I did it to help out [the ex-offender employed on our project]. We know some of the same people and he said you were cool.

Without doubt, many in our sample agreed to participate only because the ex-offender assured them that we were trustworthy. But other factors were at work as well. Letkemann (1973, p. 44), among others, has observed that the secrecy inherent in criminal work means that offenders have few opportunities to discuss their activities with anyone besides associates-which many of them find frustrating. As one of his informants put it: "What's the point of scoring if nobody knows about it?" Under the right conditions, therefore, some offenders may enjoy talking about their work with researchers.

We adopted several additional strategies to maximize the cooperation of the offenders. First, following the recommendations of experienced field researchers (e.g., Irwin 1972; McCall 1978; Walker and Lidz 1977; Wright and Bennett 1990), we made an effort to "fit in" by learning the distinctive terminology and phrasing used by the offenders. Here again, the assistance of the ex-offender proved invaluable. Prior to entering the field, he suggested ways in which questions might be asked so that the subjects would better understand them, and provided us with a working knowledge of popular street terms (e.g., "boy" for heroin, "girl" for cocaine) and pronunciations (e.g., "hair ron" for heroin). What is more, he sat in on the early interviews and critiqued them afterwards, noting areas of difficulty or contention and offering possible solutions.

A second strategy to gain the cooperation of the offenders required us to give as well as take. We expected the subjects to answer our questions frankly and, therefore, often had to reciprocate. Almost all of them had questions about how the information would be used, who would have access to it, and so on. We answered these questions honestly, lest the offenders conclude that we were being evasive. Further, we honored requests from a number of subjects for various forms of assistance. Provided that the help requested was legal and fell within the general set "of norms governing the exchange of money and other kinds of favors" (Berk and Adams 1970, p. 112) on the street, we offered it. For example, we took subjects to job interviews or work, helped some to enroll in school, and gave others advice on legal matters. We even assisted a juvenile offender who was injured while running away from the police, to arrange for emergency surgery when his parents, fearing that they would be charged for the operation, refused to give their consent.

One other way we sought to obtain and keep the offenders' confidence involved demonstrating our trustworthiness by "remaining close-mouthed in regard to potentially harmful information" (Irwin 1972, p. 125). A number of the offenders tested us by asking what a criminal associate said about a particular matter. We declined to discuss such issues, explaining that the promise of confidentiality extended to all those participating in our research.

Much has been written about the necessity for researchers to be able to withstand official coercion (see Irwin 1972; McCall 1978; Polsky 1969) and we recognized from the start the threat that intrusions from criminal justice officials could pose to our research. The threat of being confronted by police patrols seemed especially great given that we planned to visit the sites of recent successful burglaries with offenders. Therefore, prior to beginning our fieldwork, we negotiated an agreement with police authorities not to interfere in the conduct of the research, and we were not subjected to official coercion.

Although the strategies described above helped to mitigate the dangers inherent in working with active criminals (see, e.g., Dunlap et al. 1990), we encountered many potentially dangerous situations over the course of the research. For example, offenders turned up for interviews carrying firearms including, on one occasion, a machine gun; we were challenged on the street by subjects who feared that they were being set up for arrest; we were caught in the middle of a fight over the payment of a $1 debt. Probably the most dangerous situation, however, arose while driving with an offender to the site of his most recent burglary. As we passed a pedestrian, the offender became agitated and demanded that we stop the car: "You want to see me kill someone? Stop the car! I'm gonna kill that motherfucker. Stop the fuckin' car!" We refused to stop and actually sped up to prevent him jumping out of the vehicle; this clearly displeased him, although he eventually calmed down. The development of such situations was largely unpredictable and thus avoiding them was difficult. Often we deferred to the ex-offender's judgment about the safety of a given set of circumstances. The most notable precaution that we took involved money; we made sure that the offenders knew that we carried little more than was necessary to pay them.

CHARACTERISTICS OF THE SAMPLE

Unless a sample of active offenders differs significantly from one obtained through criminal justice channels, the difficulties and risks associated with the street-based recruitment of research subjects could not easily be justified. Accordingly, it seems important that we establish whether such a difference exists. In doing so, we will begin by outlining the demographic characteristics of our sample. In terms of race, it nearly parallels the distribution of burglary arrests for the City of St. Louis in 1988, the most recent year for which data are available. The St. Louis Metropolitan Police Department's Annual Report (1989) reveals that 64% of burglary arrestees in that year were Black, and 36% were White. Our sample was 69% Black and 31% White. There is divergence for the gender variable, however; only 7% of all arrestees in the city were female, while 17% of our sample fell into this category. This is not surprising. The characteristics of a sample of active criminals, after all, would not be expected to mirror those of one obtained in a criminal justice setting.

Given that our research involved only currently active offenders, it is interesting to note that 21 of the subjects were on probation, parole, or serving a suspended sentence, and that a substantial number of juveniles—27, or 26% of the total—were located for the study. The inclusion of such offenders strengthens the research considerably because approximately one third of arrested burglars are under 18 years of age (Sessions 1989). Juveniles, therefore, need to be taken into account in any comprehensive study of burglars. These offenders, however, seldom are included in studies of burglars located through criminal justice channels because access to them is legally restricted and they often are processed differently than adult criminals and detained in separate facilities.

Prior contact with the criminal justice system is a crucial variable for this research. Table 5.8 sets out whether, and to what degree, those in our sample have come into official contact with that system. Of primary interest in this table is the extent to which our snowball sampling technique uncovered a sample of residential burglars unlikely to be encountered in a criminal justice setting, the site of most research on offenders.

More than one-quarter of the offenders (28%) claimed never to have been arrested. (We excluded arrests for traffic offenses, "failure to

Table 5.8 Contact With Criminal Justice System

	Frequency	Percentage
Subject ever arrested (for any offense)?		
No	28	28
Yes	72	72
Total	100	
Subject ever arrested, convicted, incarcerated (for burglary)?		
No arrests	44	42
Arrest, no conviction	35	33
Arrest, conviction, no jail/prison	4	4
Arrest, conviction, jail/prison	22	21
Total	105	

appear" and similar minor transgressions, because such offenses do not adequately distinguish serious criminals from others.) Obviously, these offenders would have been excluded had we based our study on a jail or prison population. Perhaps a more relevant measure in the context of our study, however, is the experience of the offenders with the criminal justice system for the offense of burglary, because most previous studies of burglars not only have been based on incarcerated offenders, but also have used the charge of burglary as a screen to select subjects (e.g., Bennett and Wright 1984; Rengert and Wasilchick 1985). Of the 105 individuals in our sample, 44 (42%) had no arrests for burglary, and another 35 (33%) had one or more arrests, but no convictions for the offense. Thus 75% of our sample would not be included in a study of incarcerated burglars.

We turn now to an examination of the patterns of offending among our sample. In order to determine how many lifetime burglaries the offenders had committed, we asked them to estimate the number of completed burglaries in which they had taken part We "bounded" this response by asking them (a) how old they were when they did their first burglary, (b) about significant gaps in offending (e.g., periods of incarceration), and (c) about fluctuations in offending levels. The subjects typically estimated how many lifetime burglaries they had committed in terms of a range (e.g., 50-60), then were prompted with questions about the variation in their rate of offending over the course of their burglary career. We recorded what offenders agreed was a conservative estimate of the number of lifetime burglaries. More than half of the sample (52%) admitted to 50 or more lifetime burglaries. Included in this group are 41 offenders (40% of the total) who have committed at least 100 such crimes.

The measure of lifetime burglaries, of course, does not provide an estimate of the rate of offending. For that, we calculated "lambda" (Blumstein and Cohen 1979)—that is, the annual number of lifetime burglaries—for each subject by using our interview data. We arrived at this figure by subtracting age at first burglary from age at time of initial interview; from this, we subtracted the number of years each offender spent "off the street" in a secure residential facility (prison, jail, secure detention, or treatment center). This gave us the denominator for the lambda measure, the number of years at risk. The number of lifetime burglaries was divided by years at risk to get lambda. Approximately two thirds of the sample (68%) averaged 10 or fewer burglaries a year over the course of their offending careers-a finding not out of line with lambda estimates for burglary derived from arrest data (Blumstein and Cohen 1979). It should be noted, however, that there was great variability in the rate of offending among our sample; 34% committed, on average, less than five burglaries a year while, at the other extreme, 7% committed more than 50 such crimes yearly. This subgroup of exceptionally high rate offenders accounted for 4,204 of the 13,179 residential burglaries (32%) reported by our subjects. This result compliments previous research based on self-reports by prison inmates that has shown great variability in individual crime rates, with a small group of very active criminals being responsible for a disproportionate number of offenses (e.g., Greenwood 1982; Petersilia, Greenwood, and Lavin 1977).

The final portion of the analysis compares offenders who have and have not ever been arrested for anything in terms of (a) their total lifetime burglaries, and (b) their lambda (see Table 5.9).

The differences for these measures are pronounced. The mean lifetime burglaries for those who have never been arrested for anything is nearly double that for those who have been arrested. The variability in the group that has not been arrested is evident in the standard deviation (s = 324). A small subsample of this group has committed very few lifetime burglaries. Those in this subsample are mostly juvenile females who have offended infrequently over a very short period of time. But

Table 5.9 Comparisons of Sample Members by Any Previous Arrest Status

	Number	Mean	s	t*
Total lifetime burglaries by any previous arrest				
Yes	67	120	166	
				.04
No	20	232	324	
N	87			
Lifetime burglary lambdas				
Yes	67	13	21	
				.03
No	20	28	38	
N	87			

* Because sample selection was not random, the t-test results must be interpreted cautiously.

for this, there would be even larger differences between the groups. The mean lambda for those who have not been arrested is twice that for their arrested counterparts. This measure also displays considerable variation, as evidenced by the high standard deviation. Nevertheless, among those who have not been arrested, there are a number of offenders whose existence often has been doubted, namely high-rate criminals who successfully have avoided apprehension altogether.

CONCLUSION

By its nature, research involving active criminals is always demanding, often difficult, and occasionally dangerous. However, it is possible and, as the quantitative information reported above suggests, some of the offenders included in such research may differ substantially from those found through criminal justice channels. It is interesting, for example, that those in our sample who had never been arrested for anything, on average, offended more frequently and had committed more lifetime burglaries than their arrested counterparts. These "successful" offenders, obviously, would not have shown up in a study of arrestees, prisoners, or probationers—a fact that calls into question the extent to which a sample obtained through official sources is representative of the total population of criminals.

Beyond this, researching active offenders is important because it provides an opportunity to observe and talk with them outside the institutional context. As Cromwell et al. (1991) have noted, it is difficult to assess the validity of accounts offered by institutionalized criminals. Simply put, a full understanding of criminal behavior requires that criminologists incorporate field studies of active offenders into their research agendas. Without such studies, both the representativeness and the validity of research based on offenders located through criminal justice channels will remain problematic.

REFERENCES

Dennett, Trevor and Richard Wright. 1984. *Burglars on Burglary: Prevention and the Offender*. Aldershot, England: Gower.

Berk, Richard and Joseph Adams. 1970. "Establishing Rapport with Deviant Groups." *Social Problems* 18:102-17.

Biernacki, Patrick and Dan Waldorf. 1981. "Snowball Sampling: Problems and Techniques of Chain Referral Sampling." *Sociological Methods & Research* 10:141-63.

Blumstein, Alfred and Jacqueline Cohen. 1979. "Estimation of Individual Crime Rates from Arrest Records." *Journal of Criminal Law and Criminology* 70:561-85.

Chambliss, William. 1975. "On the Paucity of Research on Organized Crime: A Reply to Galliher and Cain." *American Sociologist* 10:36-39.

Cromwell, Paul, James Olson, and D'Aunn Avery. 1991. *Breaking and Entering: An Ethnographic Analysis of Burglary*. Newbury Park, CA: Sage.

Dunlap, Eloise, Bruce Johnson, Harry Sanabria, Elbert Holliday, Vicki Lipsey, Maurice Barnett, William Hopkins, Ira Sobel, Doris Randolph, and Ko-Lin Chin. 1990. "Studying Crack Users and Their Criminal Careers: The Scientific and Artistic Aspects of Locating Hard-to-Reach Subjects and Interviewing Them about Sensitive Topics." *Contemporary Drug Problems* 17:121-44.

Greenwood, Peter. 1982. *Selective Incapacitation*. Santa Monica, CA: RAND.

Hagedorn, John. 1990. "Back in the Field Again: Gang Research in the Nineties." Pp. 240-59 in *Gangs in America*, edited by C. Ronald Huff. Newbury Park, CA: Sage.

Irwin, John. 1972. "Participant Observation of Criminals." Pp. 117-37 in *Research on Deviance*, edited by Jack Douglas. New York: Random House.

Letkemann, Peter. 1973. *Crime as Work*. Englewood Cliffs, NJ; Prentice-Hall.

McCall, George. 1978. *Observing the Law*. New York: Free Press.

Miller, S. M. 1952. "The Participant Observer and Over-Rapport." *American Sociological Review* 17:97-99.

Petersilia, Joan, Peter Greenwood, and Marvin Lavin. 1977. *Criminal Careers of Habitual Felons*. Santa Monica, CA: RAND.

Polsky, Ned. 1969. *Hustlers, Beats, and Others*. Garden City, NJ: Anchor.

Rengert, George and John Wasilchick. 1985. *Suburban Burglary: A Time and a Place for Everything*. Springfield, IL: Thomas.

———. 1989. Space, Time and Crime: Ethnographic Insights into Residential Burglary, Final report submitted to the National Institute of Justice, Office of Justice Programs, U.S. Department of Justice.

Sessions, William. 1989. *Crime in the United States—1988*. Washington, DC: U.S. Government Printing Office.

St Louis Metropolitan Police Department. 1989. *Annual Report—1988/89*. St. Louis, MO: St. Louis Metropolitan Police Department.

Sudman, Seymour. 1976. *Applied Sampling*. New York: Academic Press.

Sutherland, Edwin and Donald Cressey. 1970. *Criminology*—8th Edition, Philadelphia, PA: Lippincott.

Taylor, Laurie. 1985. *In the Underworld*. London: Unwin.

Walker, Andrew and Charles Lidz. 1977. "Methodological Notes on the Employment of Indigenous Observers." Pp. 103-23 in *Street Ethnography*, edited by Robert Weppner. Beverly Hills, CA: Sage.

Watters, John and Patrick Biernacki. 1989. "Targeted Sampling: Options for the Study of Hidden Populations," *Social Problems* 36:416-30.

West, W. Gordon. 1980. "Access to Adolescent Deviants and Deviance." Pp. 31-44 in *Fieldwork Experience: Qualitative Approaches to Social Research*, edited by William Shaffir, Robert Stebbins, and Allan Turowitz. New York: St. Martin's.

Wright, Richard and Trevor Bennett, 1990. "Exploring the Offender's Perspective: Observing and Interviewing Criminals." Pp. 138-51 in *Measurement Issues in Criminology*, edited by Kimberly Kempf. New York: Springer-Verlag.

DISCUSSION QUESTIONS

1. Why do these authors believe that field research is important? Why have criminologists shied away from participant observation?

2. How did the authors get their first few subjects? In other words, how did they gain entry into the world of burglary? Why was this person beneficial?

3. In looking at Figure 5.1, what were some of the problems encountered with their snowball sampling method? What did they have to do for some subjects?

4. These authors say the success of this kind of research depends on subjects' participation. What three things specifically did they do to ensure success?

5. What were some of the dangers they encountered in conducting this research?

6. How were the characteristics of their sample different from traditional criminal justice samples?

7. What do they conclude about field research and samples from official sources?

6

EXPERIMENTAL AND QUASI-EXPERIMENTAL RESEARCH DESIGNS

Recall the discussion in Chapter 2 regarding causation. Determining causation is the goal of most research in criminology and criminal justice. However, also recall that researchers in the social sciences are very tentative when it comes to establishing cause—that Variable A caused a change in Variable B. Researchers proceed with caution when making statements about causality because one study alone does not prove a causal relationship. Numerous research studies over time concluding that relationships between variables exist is the only way to build up support for the idea that one variable is the cause of another. Another reason those who conduct social and behavioral science research rarely make causal statements is that they are cognizant of the fact that in the real world multiple factors are influencing variables such as crime. Disentangling the multiple influences of certain dependent variables is a complex task. Nonetheless, there is a specific type of research design that is better at establishing cause: experimental designs.

Experimental research designs entail the researcher directly manipulating the variables being studied (Ellis, Hartley, & Walsh, 2010). Experiments are unique because most other research methods involve the researcher recording observations, collecting data, or analyzing data that has been previously gathered. Experiments are said to be the best type of research design because they enable the researcher more certainty in establishing cause. In order to establish cause, a researcher must satisfy three conditions: an association between variables, an observed time order, and nonspuriousness (Bachman & Schutt, 2008).

SOLVING THE CAUSALITY PROBLEM

Two variables could be causally related if there is a correlation between them, if the cause occurs before the effect, and if no other variable could have caused the relationship. If these three criteria are established, variables are said to be causally related. To show a correlation between variables, a researcher must establish a relationship between them. "If two things do not vary together in some systematic way…then the one cannot cause the other" (Vold, Bernard, & Snipes, 2002, p. 6). Crime researchers sometimes have problems with this criterion; even though a lot of the variables they study are related, in the real world, there are not many perfect correlations. The second criterion requires that the cause occurs before the effect. Logically, it does not make sense to say one variable is the cause of another if it did not occur first. Similarly, in criminological research, time order is not always clear. Often, the relationships between the variables resemble the chicken/egg scenario: which came first? For example, does drug use cause crime, or are criminals more likely to also use drugs?

The final criterion, nonspuriousness, entails establishing that nothing else could have caused the relationship. This requires researchers to rule out rival causal factors as influences of change in the dependent variable. Again, this can be a difficult task as so many of the variables studied in the social sciences are interrelated. Experimental research designs specifically seek to disentangle the relationships that exist in the social world.

True Experimental Designs Versus Quasi-Experimental Designs

True experiments are the best at being able to satisfy all three criteria related to causal inference. Three characteristics of true experiments specifically assist researchers in satisfying the causal criteria. True experiments have an experimental (treatment) group and a control group, random assignment of subjects to these groups, and a pre-observation and postobservation period. Because there is random assignment to treatment and control groups, the groups are assumed to be equal. Also, in true experiments, one group (the experimental group) gets the treatment (independent variable), and the other does not. Finally, because observations of the groups are made both before and after the treatment, researchers can establish whether the treatment (independent variable) has an effect on the outcome (dependent variable).

There are many variations of true experimental designs, but their hallmark is random assignment to treatment and control groups. Because researchers can assume equivalence of these two groups, they can assess whether exposing one to some treatment causes a change from observation Time 1 to Time 2. In other words, any difference observed between the experimental and control group from Time 1 to Time 2 must be due to the treatment (independent) variable. Using experiments, researchers can isolate whether the treatment has an influence.

It is not easy to conduct true experiments in criminology; crime does not happen in a laboratory. Thus, it is difficult for researchers studying crime and justice issues to randomly assign subjects to experimental and control groups. In fact, it may not be ethical to do so (should some drug offenders not be given treatment while other are treated to ascertain whether this drug treatment works?). Researchers may also have trouble manipulating the independent variable and controlling rival causal factors (can researchers be sure that a probation officer has randomly assigned probationers to intensive supervision probation (treatment) and regular probation (control) and not assigned these based on the defendants' demeanors or his or her dealings with them in the past?). Thus, quasi-experimental designs are a more practical way for criminologists to conduct experiments.

Quasi-experiments differ from true experiments in that they are lacking one or more of the three features of a true experimental design. Subjects may not be randomly assigned (for instance, drug offenders who receive drug court versus jail will be assigned by the judge), there may not be a control group (researchers might observe the impact of a new drinking and driving law on the incidence of arrests for DWI), or there may not be a pretest (researchers observe recidivism rates of two groups of offenders who are released from prison, one group who went through a reentry program prior to release and another group who did not).

Quasi-experiments lend themselves better to crime and justice research because the features of true experiments are often difficult to realize in the real world. Obviously, because they lack one or more of the features of true experiments, quasi-experiments are not as good at establishing cause. However, because they do not require the stringency of random assignment or the degree of control or two observation points, quasi-experiments are more amenable to research in natural settings. Researchers who utilize quasi-experimental designs try to emulate true experiments by employing methods to rule out rival causal factors, such as matching experimental and control groups on some characteristics. Again, however, the problem is that the researcher cannot be sure that the groups are truly equivalent because they were not randomly assigned.

RESEARCH READING

Experiments are the best research designs in assessing causality; yet, they are often difficult to conduct in criminal justice research because crime does not happen in a lab. In other words, it is difficult to control variables in the real world. In the article, Weisburd outlines some of the difficulties in conducting experiments in criminal justice research, which include ethical, political, and practical barriers.

——— RANDOMIZED EXPERIMENTS IN CRIMINAL JUSTICE POLICY ———

Prospects and Problems

David Weisburd

Abstract: In theory, experimental designs provide the most reliable method to establish a relationship between interventions and outcomes. However, in practice, randomized experiments have remained a much less common choice for criminal justice evaluators than have nonexperimental methods. This article focuses on factors that have traditionally inhibited the use of randomized experiments as a tool for developing criminal justice policy. In this context, the main ethical, political, and practical barriers that face experimenters are described. General principles for identifying circumstances less or more amenable for developing randomized experiments are also defined. In concluding, it is argued that experiments are possible in many circumstances and can provide a powerful tool for developing criminal justice policy.

INTRODUCTION

Randomized experiments are often advocated as an ideal tool for evaluating public policy (e.g., see Farrington, Ohlin, & Wilson, 1986). However, in practice, randomized experiments have remained a much less common choice for criminal justice evaluators than have nonexperimental methods. Although recent reviews suggest that the use of experimental methods is more common than had once been assumed (see Dennis, 1988; Petrosino, 1997; Weisburd,

Source: Weisburd, D. (2000). Randomized experiments in criminal justice policy: Prospects and problems. *Crime & Delinquency, 46*(2), 181–193. Copyright © 2000 Sage Publications.

Sherman, & Petrosino, 1990), randomized experiments are noted more for their rarity than for their substantive importance in research and practice in criminology.

In this article, I focus on factors that have traditionally inhibited the use of randomized experiments as a tool for developing criminal justice policy. In this context, I describe the main ethical, political, and practical barriers that often face experimenters. I also define general principles for identifying circumstances less or more amenable for developing randomized experiments, with the goal of staking out guidelines for defining when implementation of experimental designs is most likely to be successful in practice. Before turning to the substance of the article, I begin with a description of the major advantage of experimental over nonexperimental research.

RANDOMIZATION AS A METHOD OF RULING OUT COMPETING CAUSES

Our primary task in evaluation research is to identify whether a particular intervention has an impact on specific outcomes. In policy-related research, this often translates to a concern with whether a treatment or sanction reduces crime or recidivism. Our methodological problem is that we want to isolate the effects of interventions from other confounding causes. For example, it would not be a very fair comparison to look simply at recidivism rates for those sentenced and not sentenced to prison to assess whether there is a deterrent effect of imprisonment. We know at the outset that more serious offenders are more likely to be sentenced to prison, and such people are also more likely to be recidivists.

Using nonexperimental designs, we commonly take two approaches to such evaluation questions. In the first, we try to fairly identify the effect of the intervention through a controlled statistical design. If, for example, we wanted to know whether a new probation intervention worked, we would compare those who received treatment and those who did not, taking into account confounding control variables. The reason for the statistical control is that there are other factors that affect whether a probationer reoffends, and these are not likely to be evenly distributed between those who have and have not received treatment. It might be, for example, that the probationers in the program are younger than those who are not in the program. Given the fact that younger offenders would be more likely to commit new crimes, if this issue is not taken into account, it might look as if the intervention failed merely because the people subject to it were more likely to reoffend in the first place.

Whereas a statistical design can account for such confounding factors, in practice there will always be some doubt as to whether all such influences can be identified by the researcher. This is the case, in part, because criminality is a difficult problem to explain, and thus, many relevant confounding influences will be unknown at the outset. But it also is due to the fact that it is often not feasible in a study to collect information on all the factors a researcher may think are important.

A second alternative to a true experimental design is what is usually called a quasi-experiment (Campbell & Stanley, 1966). In a quasi-experiment, confounding factors are not taken into account through statistical controls but through some direct method of comparison, such as matching places or people or looking at the effects of an intervention over time. Returning to our probation example, we might try to identify a group of offenders that were very similar to the ones who received the new intervention in terms of social and criminal backgrounds but who were not involved in the program. We would then look at whether the probationers who participated in the program were less likely to reoffend than those who did not. We could also look at their prior behavior and compare it with their experiences after joining the program. Again, however, as with statistical designs, investigators can seldom rule out all alternative explanations for their findings. It is always possible and even likely that the matched comparison group will differ in important ways from the treatment group. Although the researcher can sometimes use statistical controls to account for such confounding (see Berk, 1987), data for such statistical controls must be available in the first place. In turn, as with statistical control designs more generally, it is difficult for the researcher to completely rule out the possibility that an unmeasured cause is responsible for the outcomes observed.

In a true randomized experimental design, an investigator can make a direct link between interventions and their impacts without concern about the confounding impacts of other variables. This is made possible through the technique of random assignment. The investigator takes a sample of potential subjects, either people or places, and then randomly allocates some to a treatment and some to a control condition. The treatment group will receive the proposed program or treatment. The control group is either ignored or given some traditional criminal justice intervention. Through this simple act of randomization, the investigator is now able to state that there is no systematic difference between the treatment and control groups beyond the fact that one group will receive the experimental intervention and the other will not. Although the groups are not necessarily the same on every characteristic— indeed, there are likely to be differences—such differences can now be assumed to be distributed randomly and are part and parcel of the stochastic processes taken into account in statistical tests. If when the experiment ends, the investigator finds a statistically significant improvement in the treatment group, he or she can directly attribute the cause to treatment itself. Other causes have been ruled out through random allocation of treatment.

As our discussion illustrates, experimental designs provide in theory the most reliable method to establish a relationship between interventions and outcomes. Given this fact, it

is natural to ask why researchers and practitioners are often resistant to experimental research. The answer lies in ethical, practical, and political problems often encountered in experimental studies.

ETHICAL PROBLEMS IN EXPERIMENTAL RESEARCH DESIGNS: WEIGHING COSTS AND BENEFITS

One major stumbling block in the development of randomized experiments has been the moral concerns that confront both experimenters and criminal justice practitioners who attempt to carry out such projects. The problem may be phrased simply: Is it ethical to allocate criminal justice sanctions or treatments on the basis of research rather than legal criteria?

In making such decisions, it is important to differentiate at the outset the nature of the criminal justice intervention that is evaluated, and this leads to my first principle.

Principle 1: In the case of experiments that add additional resources to particular criminal justice agencies or communities or provide treatments for subjects, there are generally fewer ethical barriers to experimental research.

When researchers seek to provide a new resource to offenders or communities, it is unlikely for ethical problems to be raised. Adding police to a neighborhood (e.g., see Sherman & Weisburd, 1995) or providing rehabilitation services to offenders (e.g., see Weisburd & Taxman, 2000) does not provide any special moral concerns for experimenters or practitioners beyond those that would exist in nonexperimental research programs.

However, this assumes that the control group will continue to gain traditional levels of criminal justice intervention. Accordingly, these types of experiments become tests of whether a new intervention is better than an existing one. Where treatment is withdrawn from control subjects, serious ethical questions are likely to emerge. This is why criminal justice experiments can often be defined as including treatment and *comparison* groups rather than treatment and *control* groups.

The area where experimental study has produced the most serious ethical problems has been in what might be termed "sanctioning experiments." In this case, decisions about the processing of individual offenders are made through random allocation rather than the traditional discretionary decision-making powers of criminal justice agents. Although such experiments have been rarer, when they are carried out, as was the case in the Minneapolis Domestic Violence Experiment (Sherman & Berk, 1984), they usually have a good deal of impact on public policy. The problem here, of course, is whether it is legitimate to base the decision to arrest, sentence, or imprison on the basis of random allocation.

Traditionally, experimenters have argued that there should be a balance between the criminal justice system's need to find answers to difficult questions and its commitment to equity in the allocation of sanctions. It must be remembered that sanctioning experiments allocate sanctions that are legally legitimate to impose on offenders. The ethical concerns raised by an experimental design are not connected to the sanction itself but rather to how it is applied to a sample of individuals for whom such a sanction could be brought. The question usually asked is whether the potential benefit to be gained from learning how sanctions affect offenders should outweigh the temporary suspension of what we generally think of as equity in criminal justice processing.

But ethical concerns in sanctioning experiments depend on how we define the questions our research seeks to answer. For example, I know of no major objections that were raised to the California Reduced Prison Experiment (Berecochea & Jaman, 1981), even though thousands of offenders were in practice left in prison for longer periods of time based on a random allocation scheme. The reason for this

appears to be that the study was an assessment of whether reducing the sentences of offenders had an impact on recidivism. That is, the program released some offenders earlier than would have been their natural release date from prison. Thus, the experiment becomes a test of whether one can be lenient in the allocation of sanctions. On one level, there is very little real difference between experiments that seek to assess less punitive criminal justice interventions and those such as the Minneapolis Domestic Violence Experiment that examine the influence of more punitive sanctions. In both types of studies, one group receives a more punitive sanction than the other. However, a second principle regarding ethical barriers to experimentation can be drawn from this observation:

Principle 2: Experiments that test sanctions that are more lenient than existing penalties are likely to face fewer barriers than those that test sanctions more severe than existing penalties.

POLITICAL BARRIERS TO EXPERIMENTATION

This second principle leads me to another potential problem in developing experimental research. For criminal justice practitioners, there may be political costs to experimentation. Whereas reducing penalties for some offenders may not raise traditional ethical questions, it may raise important political concerns. I suspect, for example, that many policy makers and practitioners in the United States today would be hesitant to develop a high-visibility experiment that tests the potential for leniency in criminal justice policy. The political climate now is much less sympathetic to experiments such as the reduced prison experiment, in good part because public policy in the United States has taken a much more punitive turn in the past decade.

An equally difficult political situation is likely to develop when additional criminal justice resources are distributed through random allocation. For example, in the Jersey City Drug Market Analysis Experiment (Weisburd & Green, 1995), citizens in nonexperimental areas wanted to know why their neighborhoods were not receiving the increased police attention that was given to experimental sites. If citizens become concerned enough about the inequality of interventions that are produced in an experiment, they may exert political pressures that lead to the cessation of experimental conditions. In some sense, this problem is similar to that encountered in recent medical research, where interest groups fight to have experiments abandoned in midstream to provide medication to all who might benefit from it.

These observations lead to two additional principles. The first concerns the extent to which an experiment receives public attention.

Principle 3: Experiments that have lower public visibility will generally be easier to implement.

Political difficulties are less likely to emerge when experiments are less visible to the public. Researchers in this context must resist the temptation to tell too much about experimental studies before they are complete.

The second principle relates to the circumstances in which it will be easiest for researchers to defend random allocation in the context of the politics of the allocation of treatments.

Principle 4: In cases where treatment resources are limited, there is generally less political resistance to random allocation.

As long as communities or individuals believe that they have not been systematically excluded, experiments do not provide a significantly more difficult political problem than do nonexperimental program evaluations (see Campbell & Stanley, 1966). In this regard, it is seldom the case that a new program or treatment can be brought to more than just a few areas or a limited number of subjects. For example, in the HIDTA drug treatment experiment (Weisburd & Taxman,

2000), practitioners were much less resistant to an experimental design because they could not provide treatment to all eligible subjects. In this case, random allocation can provide a type of pressure valve for allocating scarce criminal justice resources. In such cases, it can be politically safer to apply treatment on the basis of random allocation than on other criteria.

One additional principle develops from the potential consequences of experimentation for communities:

Principle 5: Randomized experiments are likely to be easier to develop if the subjects of intervention represent less serious threats to community safety.

It is much easier for policy makers and practitioners to defend the use of randomization when the potential risks to the community are minimized. This is one reason why few experiments have been carried out with high-risk violent crime offenders (for exceptions, see Love, Allgood, & Samples, 1986; Shaw, 1974).

PRACTICAL PROBLEMS FOR STUDIES: OVERCOMING DESIGN LIMITATIONS

Practical barriers to experimentation have perhaps been even more significant in explaining resistance to experimental studies in criminal justice than have ethical or political concerns. Although I cannot review the full range of methodological issues facing experimenters in this article, we can focus on some of the more central concerns and conditions under which they become more or less problematic for experimental researchers.

Right at the outset, there is the very considerable difficulty of getting practitioners to agree to random allocation in the justice system. This problem relates both to the ethical and political difficulties I raised earlier as well as the very real concern that allowing random allocation interferes with the everyday workings of the institutions that are affected. To some extent, public acceptance of the experimental model in clinical trials in medicine has helped to overcome such barriers in the United States—where experimentation in policing and corrections, for example, has become more common. It is also true that experiments are attractive to practitioners and policy makers because they are easier to understand in terms of design than are more common correlational methods. Accordingly, experimenters often find it much easier to get practitioners to try out experiments than they expect at the outset.

At the same time, there are certain conditions under which experiments will be much more difficult to develop, and this leads to my sixth principle.

> *Principle 6:* Experiments will be most difficult to implement when the researcher attempts to limit the discretion of criminal justice agents who generally operate with a great degree of autonomy and authority.

Judges, in this regard, are generally more resistant to random allocation than are other criminal justice agents. And even when they do agree to experiments, they often subvert them through misassignment of subjects. A good example of this is the Denver Drunk Driving Experiment (Ross & Blumenthal, 1974) conducted in the mid-1970s. Judges were expected to randomly allocate fines and two types of probation to convicted drunk drivers. In practice, however, the judges circumvented the randomization process in more than half of the cases, mostly in response to defense attorney pleas to have their clients receive fines rather than probation.

But even in the case of judges, the likelihood of success of randomization is linked to the nature of the decisions they are being asked to make. And this leads to a subprinciple:

> *Subprinciple:* Where treatment conditions are perceived as similar in leniency to control conditions,

it will be easier to carry out a randomized study involving high-authority and high-autonomy criminal justice agents.

For example, in Project Muster (Weisburd, 1991), a probation experiment in New Jersey, judges correctly randomized subjects in all but one or two cases. Here, judges were being asked to sentence selected offenders violated for failure to pay fines to a program that involved intensive probation and job counseling. There was no restraint put on their sentencing decisions for other violated probationers beyond the fact that they could not be sentenced to Project Muster. Given the fact that relatively few offenders if any would have been sentenced to jail in such cases, the judges did not feel compromised in choosing Muster versus traditional probation.

The relatively large number of police experiments carried out in recent years in the United Sates suggests another principle.

> *Principle 7:* Systems in which there is a strong degree of hierarchical control will be conducive to experimentation even when individual actors are asked to constrain temporarily areas where they have a considerable degree of autonomy.

In military-style criminal justice agencies such as the police and certain corrections agencies, it is often easier to develop experimental research because criminal justice actors act within a rigid hierarchical structure. This is particularly the case where the discretion that is reduced is in choice of target rather than in choice of action or decision. For example, in experiments in Minneapolis (Sherman & Weisburd, 1995) and Jersey City (Weisburd & Green, 1995), police officers were sent to experimental crime hot spots and restricted from operating in control areas with a good deal of success.

Hierarchical control also explains, in part, why in policing it has been possible to conduct experiments even when the differences between control and treatment conditions have been significant and the criminal justice agent has traditionally exercised considerable autonomy. The best known examples of such experiments are the six domestic violence studies supported by the National Institute of Justice (see Sherman, 1995), in which spouse abusers were randomly allocated to either arrest or nonarrest conditions. These studies did not evidence the kind of subversion I alluded to earlier in the Denver Drunk Driving Experiment. However, they do illustrate the importance of providing options for overriding random allocation when the criminal justice agent believes that random allocation would place the public in serious danger. In the Minneapolis Domestic Violence Experiment (Sherman & Berk, 1984), some 18% of the cases were overidden in this way. Overrides present a less serious problem for experimental designs when they are made before offenders are allocated to a control or treatment condition. If such decisions are made after random allocation, the advantages of a randomized design are seriously challenged.

As is apparent, randomization provides an initial stumbling block for researchers. The problem of maintaining the integrity of experimental treatments is the most difficult task for researchers once randomization has been successfully implemented (see Boruch, 1997; Dennis, 1990; Petersilia, 1989; Weisburd, 1993). Although treatment integrity is an issue in any research design, it is particularly important in randomized studies because there is little option for taking into account treatment failures once the experiment has begun. Experiments in this sense are fairly inflexible as contrasted with nonexperimental designs (see Clarke & Cornish, 1972). In nonexperimental studies, variablity in the implementation of a particular treatment can be taken into account in the context of a multivariate statistical model. In and experiment, one is constrained by randomization.

This is illustrated, for example, in the California Special Intensive Parole Experiment (Reimer & Warren, 1957), in which parole officers in the control group ended up increasing their contacts with offenders to almost the same degree as those in the experimental group. The not surprising result was a showing that the treatment was not effective, although, of course, this derived from a failure to implement the proposed treatment. Similarly, in the California Parole Research Project (Johnson, 1962), control subjects often had more contact with their parole officers than the treatment group. In a statistical control design, these problems might be overcome by including a variable that accounted for number of contacts and relating that factor to outcomes. There is no similar way to account for implementation failures in an experimental design. Indeed, attempts at non-experimental analysis of an experimental design are usually suspect.

What this means is that experiments cannot be seen as merely a before-and-after effort by researchers. The "black box" representing what is actually happening in the control and treatment groups is extremely important to open and analyze. Given the relative inflexibility of experimental designs, developing methods of keeping track of and ensuring treatment integrity is crucial. For example, in the Minneapolis Hot Spots Experiment (Sherman & Weisburd, 1995), which sought to test the effectiveness of increased police patrol in crime hot spots, Lawrence Sherman and I conducted thousands of hours of observations to monitor actual police presence. These observations allowed us to ensure the integrity of the treatments administered. However, that study illustrates that keeping track of experiments can be a very time-consuming and costly enterprise.

Of course, not all experiments present the same degree of difficulty. Where the experimental treatment involves a routine action on the part of criminal justice agents, experiments will generally be no more expensive in monitoring than are nonexperimental designs. This is the case, for example, in studies that involve one-shot interventions. The investigator in this case need only ensure that offenders were placed in a particular condition, such as violation, arrest, or prison. However, this leads to my final principle:

Principle 8: Where treatments are relatively complex, involving multiple actions on the part of criminal justice agents or actions that they would not traditionally take, experiments can become prohibitively cumbersome and expensive.

At this point, I think it important to at least note briefly the relationship between the question of cost per site or subject and the problem of statistical power. Simply stated, the statistical power of an experiment is the probability that a specific outcome will lead to a significant result (see Lipsey, 1990; Weisburd, 1998). Given the importance attached to statistical significance in research findings, statistical power becomes a very crucial concern in the design of a research effort. One does not want to design a study in such a way that even if the treatment has the effect desired, the study is not powerful enough to show a significant impact. This is precisely what occurs in many criminal justice studies (see Brown, 1989)—which are underpowered and may be seen as doomed to failure from the outset (Sherman & Weisburd, 1995).

Experimental studies have, all else being equal, a power advantage over designs that use statistical controls. This derives from the fact that one does not need to take into account multiple control variables in statistical tests of study outcomes. Nonetheless, because experimental studies are often more expensive to run per subject than are nonexperimental designs, all else is usually not equal. The number of cases in a study has a direct impact on the likelihood of rejection of the null hypotheses. Larger studies are, all else being equal, more powerful than smaller ones. In this context, the expense of some types of experimental studies is sometimes raised as a barrier to experimental research.

Whereas this issue is an important one, it is worthwhile reflecting for a moment on the number of cases needed to reach an acceptable level of power in most experimental designs. If one expects at the outset a moderate difference

of, for example, 20% between experimental and control conditions, a sample of more than 100 per group is usually enough to achieve a relatively high level of statistical power. Accordingly, experimental studies can provide statistically powerful research findings with a relatively small number of cases.

CONCLUSION

Experimental designs are not appropriate for every evaluation study in criminal justice. Nonetheless, experiments are possible in many circumstances and can provide a powerful tool for developing criminal justice policy. There is no reason to exclude experimental designs at the outset either for ethical, political, or practical reasons, though this is often the case in criminal justice study. The task is to identify under what conditions experiments can be successfully implemented.

I have defined eight principles that may help researchers and practitioners to assess when experimentation will be most feasible. Briefly noted, they are as follow:

1. There are generally fewer ethical barriers to experimentation when interventions involve the addition of resources.

2. There are generally fewer objections to experiments that test sanctions that are more lenient than existing criminal justice penalties.

3. Experiments with lower public visibility will generally be easier to implement.

4. In cases where treatment cannot be given to all eligible subjects, there is likely to be less resistance to random allocation.

5. Randomized experiments are likely to be easier to develop if the subjects of intervention represent less serious threats to community safety.

6. Experimentation will be more difficult to implement when experimenters try to limit the discretion of criminal justice agents who traditionally act with significant autonomy and authority.

7. It will be easier to develop randomized experiments in systems in which there is a high degree of hierarchical control.

8. When treatments are relatively complex, involving multiple actions on the part of criminal justice agents, experiments can become prohibitively cumbersome and expensive and accordingly less feasible to develop.

REFERENCES

Berecochea, J. E., & Jaman, D. R. (1981). *Time served in prison and parole outcome: An experimental study* (Report No. 2). Sacramento: California Department of Corrections Research Division.

Berk, R. A. (1987). Causal inference as a prediction problem. In D. Gottfredson & M. Tonry (Eds.), *Prediction and classification*. Chicago: University of Chicago Press.

Boruch, R. (1997). *Randomized experiments for planning and evaluation*. Thousand Oaks, CA: Sage.

Brown, S. E. (1989). Statistical power and criminal justice research. *Journal of Criminal Justice, 17*,115-122.

Campbell, D., & Stanley, J. (1966). *Experimental and quasi-experimental designs for research*. Chicago: Rand McNally.

Clarke, R.V.G., & Cornish, D. B. (1972). *The controlled trial in institutional research-paradigm or pitfall for penal evaluators?* London: H. M. Stationery Office.

Dennis, M. L. (1988). *Implementing randomized field experiments: An analysis of criminal and civil justice research*. Unpublished doctoral dissertation, Northwestern University, Evanston, IL.

Dennis, M. L. (1990). Assessing the validity of randomized field experiments: An example from drug abuse treatment research. *Evaluation Review, 14(A)*, 347-373.

Farrington, D. P., Ohlin, L. E., & Wilson, J. Q. (1986). *Understanding and controlling crime*. New York: Springer Verlag.

Johnson, B. M. (1962). *Parole performance of the first year's releases: Parole research project, evaluation of reduced caseloads* (Research Report No. 27). Sacramento: California Youth Authority.

Lipsey, M. W. (1990). *Design sensitivity: Statistical power for experimental research*. Thousand Oaks, CA: Sage.

Love, C.T., Allgood, J. G., & Samples, F.P.S. (1986). The Butner research projects. *Federal Probation, 50,* 32-39.

Petersilia, J. (1989). Implementing randomized experiments: Lessons from BJA's intensive supervision project. *Evaluation Review, 13,* 435-458.

Petrosino, A. J. (1997). *"What works?" Revisited again: A meta-analysis of randomized experiments in individual-level interventions*. Unpublished dissertation, Rutgers University, School of Criminal Justice, New Brunswick, NJ.

Reimer, E., & Warren, M. (1957). Special intensive parole unit: Relationship between violation rate and initially small caseload. *National Probation and Parole Association Journal, 3,* 222-229.

Ross, H. L., & Blumenthal, M. (1974). Sanctions for the drinking driver: An experimental study. *Journal of Legal Studies, 3,* 53-61.

Shaw, M. (1974). *Social work in prison*. London: H. M. Stationery Office.

Sherman, L. W. (1995). *Policing domestic violence: Experiments and dilemmas*. New York: Free Press.

Sherman, L. W., & Berk, R. (1984). *The Minneapolis Domestic Violence Experiment* (Police Foundation Report No. 1). Washington, DC: The Police Foundation.

Sherman, L. W., & Weisburd, D. (1995). General deterrent effects of police patrol in crime "hot spots": A randomized controlled trial. *Justice Quarterly, 12(4),* 625-648.

Weisburd, D. (1991). *Project muster: The external evaluator's report*. Trenton: New Jersey Administrative Office of the Courts.

Weisburd, D. (1993). Design sensitivity in criminal justice experiments. *Crime and Justice, 17,* 337-339.

Weisburd, D. (1998). *Statistics in criminal justice*. Belmont, CA: Wadsworth.

Weisburd, D., & Green, L. (1995). Policing drug hot spots: The Jersey City Drug Market Analysis Experiment. *Justice Quarterly, 12,* 711-735.

Weisburd, D., Sherman, L. W., & Petrosino, A. (1990). *Registry of randomized experiments in criminal sanctions, 1950-1983*. Los Altos, CA: Sociometics Corporation, Data Holdings of the National Institute of Justice.

Weisburd, D., & Taxman, F. (2000). Developing a multi-center randomized trial in criminology: *The case of HIDTA. Journal of Quantitative Criminology, 16*(3).

DISCUSSION QUESTIONS

1. What is a quasi-experiment, and how does it control for confounding factors?

2. What does the technique of random assignment allow researchers to assume about the study groups? Why?

3. What are some of the ethical problems that Weisburd discusses regarding randomized experiments in criminal justice research?

4. What are some of the political barriers in conducting experiments for criminal justice topics?

5. Practically, what are some of the issues with experimental studies in criminal justice research?

6. What does Weisburd say about statistical significance and statistical power as they relate to experiments in past criminal justice research?

RESEARCH READING

Lowenkamp and colleagues examine an application of a cognitive behavioral therapy program using a quasi-experimental design. These authors state that much research has been conducted regarding the best methods of reducing recidivism and that cognitive behavioral therapy has been shown to be effective. Thinking for a Change (TFAC) is a cognitive behavioral curriculum designed to help offenders gain prosocial skills and attitudes. The curriculum assists offenders in using newly obtained skills to restructure their thought patterns of criminal offending and feelings of others. These researchers believe that their test of TFAC is a true test (real world) because it was implemented by those in the community corrections setting. Their purpose is to provide a more practical and methodologically sound test of a cognitive behavioral therapy program.

A QUASI-EXPERIMENTAL EVALUATION OF THINKING FOR A CHANGE

A "Real-World" Application

Christopher T. Lowenkamp, Dana Hubbard, Matthew D. Makarios, and Edward J. Latessa

Abstract: Due to the popularity of cognitive behavioral interventions, programs that follow this model are often assumed to be effective. Yet evaluations of specific programs have been slow in coming. The

Source: Lowenkamp, C. T., Hubbard, D., Makarios, M. D., & Latessa, E. J. (2009). A quasi-experimental evaluation of thinking for a change: A "real-world" application. *Criminal Justice and Behavior, 36,* 137–146. Copyright © 2009 Sage Publications. Published by Sage Publications on behalf of the Association for Correctional and Forensic Psychologists.

current investigation seeks to bridge this gap by evaluating the effectiveness of Thinking for a Change (TFAC), a widely used cognitive behavioral curriculum for offenders. Furthermore, this evaluation provides a "real-world" test of TFAC, because it was implemented by line staff in a community corrections agency as opposed to being a pilot project implemented by program developers. The results of the analyses indicate that offenders participating in the TFAC program had a significantly lower recidivism rate than similar alleluia's that were not exposed to the program.

INTRODUCTION

Over the past three decades, much has been learned in regards to "what works" in reducing recidivism (Andrews, Bonta, & Hoge, 1990; Gendreau, 1996; Gendreau, French, & Taylor, 2002; Palmer, 1995). One finding that has consistently appeared is the effectiveness of cognitive behavioral therapy (CBT) in reducing recidivism (Landenberger & Lipsey, 2005). As a result, a variety of cognitive behavioral curricula that target criminal populations have surfaced. One such curriculum, Thinking for a Change (TFAC), has been developed by Bush, Glick, and Taymans (1997) with the support of the National Institute of Corrections. TFAC is becoming increasingly popular with implementation at some level in more than 45 states (personal communication with Steve Swisher, National Institute of Corrections, July 15, 2006). To date, however, very few evaluations of the TFAC program have been conducted (Reeves, 2006). In addition, although each study adds to the knowledge base on the effectiveness of TFAC, each study has limitations that are inherent in applied research.

Consequently, the purpose of the current study is to overcome some of the practical and methodological limitations of previous research using a quasi-experimental evaluation of the TFAC program. Practically, the program under evaluation was implemented and delivered by practitioners in the correctional system without the assistance and monitoring of an evaluator. Thus, this application of TFAC is a "real-world" application rather than a demonstration project. This has particular relevance because some research (see, for example, Lipsey, 1995) indicates that demonstration projects, managed

by an involved evaluator or program designer, produce larger treatment effects than the same programs implemented in a "real-world" setting. Furthermore, because the program was delivered by correctional practitioners that were a part of the justice system, this study will provide correctional agencies with a more realistic picture of the effectiveness of a readily available cognitive behavioral curriculum.

THE INCREASING DEMAND FOR COMMUNITY SUPERVISION

Over the past 10 years, prison populations increased by nearly 30%, from 1,078,000 inmates in 1995 to more than 1.4 million by the end of 2005 (Harrison & Beck, 2006). Given the large increase, many states have relied more heavily on community supervision agencies to reduce prison populations by both diverting offenders from prison and by providing early release to community control (Latessa & Smith, 2007). Consequently, the corresponding 31% increase of offenders under probation or parole supervision between 1995 and 2005 (from 3,757,000 to 4,947,000) is not surprising (Glaze & Bonczar, 2006).

The building and operation of prisons come at great cost to many other social services and needs of the community (Weisfeld, 2007). Although there is certainly a population of offenders that need to be incarcerated out of concern for public safety, policy makers have realized that much can be done to reduce state prison populations (Public Safety Performance Project, 2007). Thus, given the costs of prisons and the cuts these cause in other areas of state budgets, many state policies have begun to focus on stopping the growth of prison populations (Public Safety Performance Project, 2007).

Although community supervision provides a fiscally prudent alternative to prison, it is not without its own unique costs. As Petersilia (2000) notes, there are political, economic, and social consequences associated with offenders returning to the community while on supervision. A major source of problems for community supervision agencies is that they are expected to serve more offenders with fewer resources. For example, correctional populations tripled from 1982 to 1999 while at the same time there was little more than a doubling of staff (Gifford, 2002). Resources clearly have not kept pace with increasing numbers.

Perhaps the most important issue facing community supervision is that of public safety, which is usually measured through rates of recidivism. Although the recidivism rates of offenders supervised in the community range from 16% to 65% (Latessa & Smith, 2007), a significant percentage of recidivists are returned to prison for revocations due to technical violations. Furthermore, revocations are becoming an increasingly larger proportion of the prison population (Cohen, 1995). Given the widespread use of community supervision and the high costs associated with recidivism (both in terms of public safety and reincarceration), the need to maximize the effectiveness of community supervision is pressing.

Reducing Recidivism in Community Supervision

One promising approach to reducing the recidivism of offenders on probation is to provide treatment services to offenders (for a review, see Cullen & Gendreau, 2000). Although probation alone is generally ineffective at reducing recidivism (Gendreau & Goggin, 1996), research indicates that if probation supervision is treatment focused, it can effectively reduce

criminal behavior (Aos, Miller, & Drake, 2006; Hanley, 2002; Lowenkamp & Latessa, 2005; Petersilia & Turner, 1993; Taxman, Yancey, & Bilanin, 2006). However, it is important to note that not all treatment efforts are equally effective. Programs that adhere to specific principles of effective intervention have been shown to have the greatest impact on recidivism (Andrews, Zinger, et al., 1990) and should therefore serve as the basis of community supervision-based treatment services.

The three major principles of effective intervention—risk, need, and responsivity (Andrews, Zinger, et al., 1990; Andrews, Bonta, & Hoge, 1990; Andrews, Bonta, & Wormith, 2006; Lowenkamp & Latessa, 2005; Lowenkamp, Latessa, & Smith, 2006; Lowenkamp, Pealer, Latessa, & Smith, 2006)—are designed to provide a blueprint of effective intervention for correctional agencies to follow. Translated into practice, the principles of effective intervention suggest delivering behaviorally based programs (e.g., cognitive behavioral treatment), to higher risk offenders (those with the higher likelihood of recidivism), while focusing on relevant criminogenic needs (e.g., antisocial attitudes, values, and beliefs). Recent research suggests that probation agencies that follow these aspects have lower rates of recidivism than those which do not (Lowenkamp, Latessa, & Smith, 2006; Taxman et al., 2006).

At the core of providing effective correctional interventions in the community is delivering behaviorally based programming. Behavioral programming is based on the presumption that behavior is learned. Furthermore, once a particular behavior has been initiated, it is maintained or discouraged by the consequences of the behavior on one's attitudes, values, and beliefs (for a theoretical discussion, see Bandura, 1986; for an application to offending behavior, see Andrews & Bonta, 2006). For offenders to be retrained to exhibit prosocial behaviors, they must be given the opportunity to learn prosocial skills and attitudes. Meta-analytic reviews have consistently identified behavioral programs to be one of the most effective forms of correctional interventions aimed at reducing recidivism (e.g., Dowden & Andrews, 2000; Garrett, 1985; Lipsey, Chapman, & Landenberger, 2001; Wilson, Bouffard, & MacKenzie, 2005; Wilson, Gallagher, & MacKenzie, 2000).

COGNITIVE BEHAVIORAL THERAPY AND CORRECTIONAL INTERVENTIONS

There are a number of justifications for using CBT with correctional populations (Andrews & Bonta, 2006). First, unlike many correctional programs that are based on so-called "common sense" approaches (Latessa, Cullen, & Gendreau, 2002), CBT is based on scientifically derived theories (cognitive and behavioral). Second, CBT is based on active learning, not talk therapy and consequently focuses on the *present* (how offenders currently think and behave), not past events that cannot be changed (Andrews & Bonta, 2006). Third, it targets major criminogenic needs in a structured group setting (Andrews & Bonta, 2006). Finally, cognitive behavioral programming has consistently been shown to reduce the recidivism of program participants (for a review, see Landenberger & Lipsey, 2005).

TFAC is a cognitive behavioral therapy developed to integrate cognitive skills and cognitive restructuring modalities of offender treatment. At its core, TFAC uses problem solving to teach offenders prosocial skills and attitudes. Consisting of 22 lessons, each lesson teaches participants important social skills, such as active listening and asking appropriate questions to more complex restructuring techniques, such as recognizing the types of thinking that leads them into trouble and understanding the feelings of others. As such, TFAC both stresses interpersonal communication skills development and confronts thought patterns that lead to problematic behaviors.

Landenberger and Lipsey's (2005) meta-analyses of cognitive behavioral programs provides some insight into the effectiveness of TFAC. They reviewed 58 studies of cognitive behavioral programs and found that, on average, these programs reduced recidivism by 25%. Furthermore, they examined several different cognitive behavioral curricula, including five evaluations of TFAC. Landenberger and Lipsey (2005) found that TFAC was effective in reducing recidivism, as the results indicated that the effects of the five studies were not different than that average reduction in recidivism of 25%. However, none of the studies included in the analysis had been published in peer reviewed journals, and they had other methodological limitations (such as short follow-up periods, lack of statistical controls, and small sample sizes). Furthermore, Landenberger and Lipsey (2005) encourage continued studies of CBT, as very few of the studies they were able to locate (6 out of 58) were randomized studies in "real-world" settings.

Recently, Golden, Gatchel, and Cahill (2006) provided the first published outcome evaluation of TFAC. They examined the effects of TFAC on a sample of probationers and found that, compared to those who did not attend the program, participants who completed the program experienced reductions in problem-solving skills and in proportion of the group who committed a new offense. Although informative, this research had a follow-up time limited to 1 year and used a three group analysis which excluded treatment dropouts from the experimental group.

A three-group analysis compares differences in the recidivism between participants who (a) completed treatment, (b) dropped out of treatment, and (c) received no treatment. The experimental group is separated into treatment completions and dropouts because it is assumed that individuals who did not get the full dose of treatment will "water down" the true treatment effect. Unfortunately, comparing treatment completions to a control group creates a selection bias, because offenders who are likely to drop out of treatment (because they are unmotivated to change or are higher risk) exist in both groups but are only eliminated from the treatment group. Furthermore, as the selection bias is created by eliminating unmotivated and/or higher risk individuals from the treatment group, this process will tend to inflate the treatment effect. To address this issue, the present research includes all individuals who attended at least one session of TFAC in the treatment group regardless of whether they successfully completed the treatment.

This research also offers two other methodological advances over prior evaluations of TFAC. To measure recidivism, this research uses the outcome of arrest which is superior to some of the previous evaluations of TFAC that used intermediate outcomes such as pre/post measures of attitudes (Reeves, 2006). Furthermore, the follow-up time for the outcome is longer than previous studies, and while variable, averages just more than 2 years. In sum, this research provides an evaluation of TFAC in a real-world setting, while addressing the methodological limitations of prior research by using (a) a two group analysis, (b) arrest as a measure of recidivism, and (c) an extended follow-up.

METHOD

Research Location and Procedures

The Tippecanoe County probation department is located in central Indiana and provides services to adult offenders brought into the correctional system for a felony or misdemeanor offense. In addition to the probation department, Tippecanoe County also has a community corrections division that complements services provided by probation. Staff from both community corrections and probation provide TFAC services to offenders. The National Institute of Corrections provided the initial training for the Tippecanoe County employees, after which the agency developed their own training program and provided subsequent training for new facilitators as the program grew and new staff were added.

Offenders were referred to the TFAC program directly from court (as a condition of their probation sentence) or from their probation officer as a sanction for violation behavior. Probationers enrolled in the TFAC program were expected to complete all 22 sessions. The number of sessions attended ranged from 2 to 22 with an average of 20. The high average was likely due to almost 75% of the treatment group completing all 22 sessions. The program was delivered over 11 weeks (2 sessions each week for a total of 22 sessions) with an average of 12 participants in each class (class size ranged from 5 to 20). The TFAC program was typically administered by two facilitators; however, with larger classes, as many as four facilitators were used.

Participants

The participants in this study ($n = 217$) were individuals in Tippecanoe County that were placed on probation for a felony offense. Of the total, there were 121 treatment cases. Inclusion into the treatment group required that the individual on probation was referred to and attended at least one session of TFAC. Comparison cases ($n = 96$) consist of offenders that were placed on probation during the same time period as the treatment cases but were not referred to TFAC. Cases were also required to have at least a 6-month follow-up period to be included in the study. For the treatment group, the follow-up requirement began 6 months from the time that they left the TFAC program, whereas the control group follow-up was based on the time they began probation. The demographic statistics of the two groups are contained in Table 6.1. The two groups were very similar in terms of age, race, and gender, with no statistically significant differences detected. Overall, the sample was predominantly White (84%), male (71%), and on average 33.5 years old.

Measures

Since all offenders did not have a standardized risk/need assessment completed in their files, a risk measure was created that was based on factors used in prior analyses (Lowenkamp, Pealer, Latessa, & Smith, 2006; Lowenkamp & Latessa, 2005). Each offender was coded on seven factors based on file information. These factors included prior arrests (0 = *none*, 1 = *one or more*), prior prison commitments (0 = *none*, 1 = *one or more*), prior community supervision violation (0 = *none*, 1 = *one or more*), prior drug problem (0 = *no indication of a drug problem*, 1 = *some indication of a drug problem*), prior alcohol problem (0 = *no indication of an alcohol problem*, 1 = *some indication of an alcohol problem*), employed at arrest (0 = *unemployed at arrest*, 1 = *employed at arrest*), and education (0 = *completed less than Grade 12*, 1 = *high school graduate or above*). These factors were summed together to give a risk score that ranged in value from

0 to 7. Three categories (low, moderate, and high risk) were created based on the composite score.

The correlation between risk and any new arrest is 0.19 ($p = .006$). The recidivism rates by risk level were 20% for low-risk, 31% for moderate-risk, and 50% for high-risk ($\chi^2 = 7.938$, $p = .019$). The two groups did differ significantly on this measure (see Table 6.1), with the treatment group scoring slightly higher than the comparison group (4.0 versus 3.5; $t = 2.46$; $p = .015$). Differences in risk between treatment and control groups may confound the final results, although the higher risk of the treatment groups suggests that the results would favor a null treatment effect. Still, to ensure the accuracy of the treatment effect, the final results control for differences in risk between the two groups.

Also, since offenders were followed for unequal periods of time, it was necessary to adjust for time at risk to recidivate. To do so, a variable was created that measured the number of months of follow-up time that recidivism was tracked. For the comparison group, the follow-up period began when the offender was placed on probation. For the treatment group, the follow-up period began when the offender entered the TFAC

Table 6.1 Descriptive Statistics for Independent Variables

Variable	Treatment (N = 121)	Comparison (N = 96)
Race (% White)	88	80
Gender (% male)	72	71
Age (average in years)	33.6	33.5
Time-at-risk (average in months)*	21.4	32.4
Risk score (average)*	4.0	3.5
Recidivism (% rearrested)*	23	6

*$p \leq .05$.

program. As indicated in Table 6.1, on average the comparison group has a considerably longer follow-up period than the treatment group *(t = 5.10; p = .000)*. Since differences in time at risk can also confound the final results, this measure was included in all multivariate models.

To operationalize recidivism, a dichotomous variable indicating whether the offender received an arrest for a new criminal charge (misdemeanor or felony offense) was created. These data were retrieved from county and local databases; worth noting is that the measure is limited to offenses that were reported only in Tippecanoe County.

RESULTS

Results from the bivariate analysis of the impact of participation in the TFAC program are presented in Table 6.1. These indicate that there is a statistically significant difference in the proportion of individuals who recidivated between the treatment and control groups. Specifically, 23% of the treatment group

recidivated (i.e., were rearrested for new criminal behavior) whereas 36% of the comparison group recidivated ($\chi^2 = 3.93; p = .047$). Thus, the difference in the odds of recidivating between the control and treatment groups indicates that the control group was 1.57 (or 57%) more likely to be arrested during the follow-up.

Since the groups differed significantly on several key variables, multivariate logistic regression was used to predict recidivism while controlling for time at risk, race, gender, age, and risk level. The results of this model are presented in Table 6.2. According to the results, the significant predictors of recidivism were age, risk category, and group membership. More specifically, younger offenders, higher-risk offenders, and offenders in the comparison group were more likely to be arrested for new criminal behavior during their follow-up.

Exponent B (Exp [B]) presents the change in the odds ratio for the dependent variable, which results from a one unit change in the independent variable of interest. As such, it is centered on 1.00, with values above 1 indicating increases in the odds of recidivism and

Table 6.2 Multivariate Logistic Regression Model Using All Treatment Cases

Variable	B	SE	Sig	Exp(B)
Group*	0.67	0.35	0.05	1.95
Risk category	0.82	0.26	0.00	2.26
Gender	0.01	036	0.99	1.01
Race	−0.75	0.55	0.17	0.47
Age*	−0.04	0.02	0.03	0.96
Time at risk	0.20	0.13	0.12	1.22
Constant	−1.68	0.79	0.03	0.19

*$p \le .05$.

values below 1 indicating decreases in the odds of recidivism. The coefficient for group membership indicates that when controlling for confounding factors, the odds of the comparison group being arrested during the follow-up were almost double (Exp [B] = 1.95) that of the treatment group. Comparing the differences in odds of being arrested in the bivariate analysis (1.57) to those of the multivariate analysis (1.95) indicates that controlling for confounding factors produces increases in the treatment effect.

Figure 6.1 presents the adjusted recidivism rates for the treatment and comparison groups, holding all other independent variables constant. At 28%, the adjusted rate of recidivism for the treatment group is modestly lower than that of the comparison group's rate of 43%. This indicates that adjusting for the net effects of risk, age, race, gender, and follow-up time produces a recidivism rate of the treatment groups which is 15 percentage points lower than that of the comparison group.

DISCUSSION

The results of the current study indicate that participation in the TFAC program, as delivered by the Tippecanoe County probation department, is associated with an appreciable reduction in recidivism. This shows that a specific cognitive behavioral curriculum that is readily available to correctional agencies can work to reduce recidivism. Furthermore, the program was delivered by community corrections staff that did not necessarily possess any exceptional qualifications or credentials aside from training on the facilitation of the TFAC program. Also, unlike many evaluations of cognitive programs, neither was this study a demonstration project nor was it

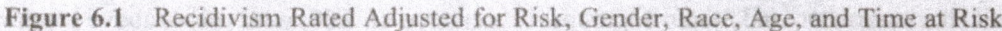

Figure 6.1 Recidivism Rated Adjusted for Risk, Gender, Race, Age, and Time at Risk

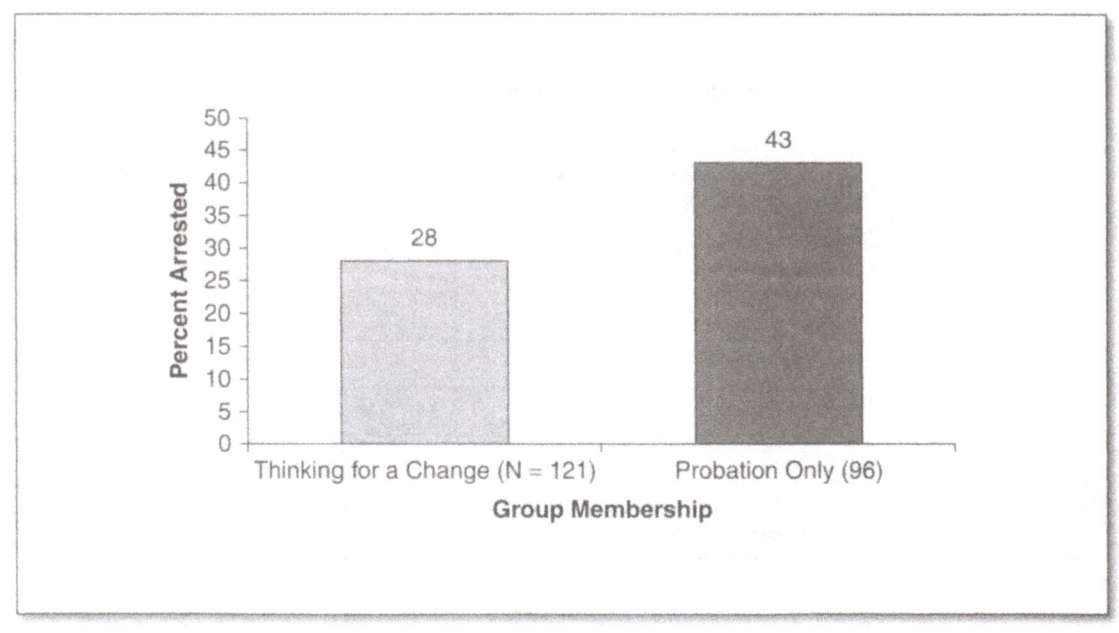

delivered in an "optimal" or "artificial" environment. In sum, the current research indicates that a program that was delivered in a real-world setting was effective in reducing the recidivism of its participants.

While the results of this evaluation are encouraging, there are a number of limitations that should be noted. First and foremost, the participants in this study were not randomly assigned to the differing treatment conditions. Although the comparison and treatment groups were similar on most factors, there is still a possibility that there was some selection bias in assigning offenders to the TFAC groups. Again, some of this concern is tempered by the fact that the two groups of offenders were similar on demographic characteristics except for risk—a difference which favored the comparison group. The other identified difference between the two groups, length of follow-up time, is another limitation. We would have preferred a standardized time frame and lengthier follow-up period; unfortunately, certain contextual factors and data limitations prohibited this from occurring.

While an experimental design with standardized follow-up would be preferred, this limitation is not fatal, as statistical controls were implemented to adjust for potentially confounding factors. Furthermore, the potential for bias due to risk favors the control group (who were of lower risk), suggesting that, if anything, differences in risk would produce conservative estimates. While the same cannot be said for time at risk (the control group spent more time at risk, which potentially could lead to artificial increases in the recidivism of the control group), our analyses that control for this factor show that time at risk failed to be a significant predictor of recidivism, indicating that this factor is not confounding the present results.

The current investigation indicates that probation and similar community supervision agencies may be able to use their staff to provide meaningful rehabilitative services that lead to reductions in recidivism. Furthermore, this research is consistent with recent research that suggests that TFAC in particular (Golden et al., 2006) and cognitive behavioral programs in general (Landenberger & Lipsey, 2005) can produce meaningful reductions in recidivism. This is important, because it suggests that community corrections agencies can work toward the goal of enhancing public safety through the implementation of programming which has been shown to be effective in a "real-world" setting.

No single study in social sciences is definitive, and the current investigation is no exception. Further research should seek to conduct randomized trials to investigate the impacts of the TFAC program. Furthermore, while effective on this sample of probationers in Tippecanoe County, Indiana, practitioners and scholars should not jump to conclusions about the generalizability of this research. Future evaluations, if conducted across multiple jurisdictions and with varied samples of offenders, would help to speak to the generalizability of TFAC in reducing recidivism. Also, continued testing of the efficacy of TFAC and other cognitive behavioral curricula will aid in the development of a base of knowledge to inform correctional agencies in making decisions regarding adoption and implementation of correctional programming.

REFERENCES

Andrews, D. A., & Bonta, J. (2006). *The psychology of criminal conduct* (4th ed). Cincinnati, OH: Anderson.

Andrews, D. A., Bonta, J., & Hoge, R. (1990). Classification for effective rehabilitation: Rediscovering psychology. *Criminal Justice & Behavior, 17,*19-52.

Andrews, D. A., Bonta, J., & Wormith, S. J. (2006). The recent past and near future of risk and/or need assessment. *Crime & Delinquency, 52,*7-27.

Andrew, D. A., Zinger, I., Hoge, R. D., Bonta, J., Gendreau, P., & Cullen, F. T. (1990). Does correctional treatment work? A clinically relevant and psychologically informed meta-analysis. *Criminology, 8,*369-404.

Aos, S., Miller, M., & Drake, E. (2006). *Evidence-based public policy options to reduce future prison construction, criminal justice costs, and crime rates.* Olympia: Washington State Institute for Public Policy.

Bandura, A. (1986). *Social foundations of thought and action: A social cognitive theory,* Englewood Cliffs, NJ: Prentice-Hall.

Bush, J., Glick, B., & Taymans, I. (1997). *Thinking for a change: Integrated cognitive behavior change program.* National Institute of Corrections. Washington, DC: U.S. Department of Justice.

Cohen, R. L. (1995). *Probation and parole violators in state prison, 1991.* Washington, DC: Bureau of Justice Statistics.

Cullen, F. T., & Gendreau, P. (2000). Assessing correctional rehabilitation; Policy, practice, and prospects. In J. Horney (Ed.), *Criminal justice 2000, volume 3: Policies, processes, and decisions of the criminal justice system* (pp. 109-175). Washington, DC: National Institute of Justice.

Dowden, C., & Andrews, D. A. (2000). Effective correctional treatment and violent reoffending: A meta-analysis. *Canadian Journal of Criminology, 42,*449-467.

Garrett, C. J. (1985). Effects of residential treatment on adjudicated delinquents: A meta-analysis. *Journal of Research in Crime & Delinquency, 22,*287-308.

Gendreau, P. (1996). The principles of effective interventions with offenders. In A. T. Harland (Ed.), *Choosing correctional options that work: Defining the demand and evaluating the supply* (pp. 117-130). Thousand Oaks, CA: Sage.

Gendreau, P., & Goggin, C. (1996). Principles of effective correctional programming. *Forum on Corrections, 8,*38-41.

Gendreau, P., French, S., & Taylor, A. (2002). *What works (what doesn't work)-revised 2002: The principles of effective correctional treatment.* Unpublished Manuscript, University of New Brunswick at Saint John.

Gifford, S. (2002). *Justice expenditures and employment in the United States, 1999.* Washington, DC: Bureau of Justice Statistics.

Glaze, L. E., & Bonczar, T. P. (2006). *Probation and parole in the United States, 2005.* Washington, DC: U.S. Department of Justice.

Golden, L. S., Gatchel, R. J., & Cahill, M. A. (2006). Evaluating the effectiveness of the National Institute of Corrections' "Thinking for a Change" program among probationers. *Journal of Offender Rehabilitation, 42,* 55-73.

Hanley, D. (2002). *Risk differentiation and intensive supervision: A meaningful union?* Doctoral Dissertation, Division of Criminal Justice: University of Cincinnati. (UMI No. 3062606)

Harrison, P. M., & Beck, A. J. (2006). *Prisoners in 2005.* Washington, DC: United States Department of Justice.

Landenberger, N., & Lipsey, M. (2005). The positive effects of cognitive behavioral programs for offenders: A meta analysis of factors associated with effective treatment. *Journal of Experimental Criminology, 1,* 451-476.

Latessa, E. J., & Smith, P. (2007). *Corrections in the community.* Cincinnati, OH: Anderson.

Latessa, E. J., Cullen, F., & Gendreau, P. (2002). Beyond correctional quackery-Professionalism and the possibility of effective treatment. *Federal Probation, 66,*43-49.

Lipsey, M. W. (1995). What have we learned from 400 research studies on the effectiveness of treatment with juvenile delinquents? In J. McGuire (Ed.), *What works? Reducing reoffending* (pp. 63-78). New York: John Wiley.

Lipsey, M. W., Chapman, G. L., & Landenberger, N. A. (2001). Cognitive behavioral programs for offenders. *Annuls of the American Academy of Political and Social Science, 578,* 144-157.

Lowenkamp, C. T., & Latessa, E. J. (2005). *Evaluation of Ohio's CCA funded programs.* Unpublished Report, University of Cincinnati, Division of Criminal Justice.

Lowenkamp, C. T, Latessa, E. J., & Smith, P. (2006). Does correctional program quality really matter? The impact of adhering to the principles of effective interventions. *Criminology & Public Policy, 5,* 575-594.

Lowenkamp, C. T., Pealer, J., Latessa, E. J., & Smith, P. (2006), Adhering to the risk principle: Does it matter for supervision-based programs? *Federal Probation, 4,* 3-8.

Palmer, T. (1995). Programmatic and nonprogrammatic aspects of successful intervention: New directions for research. *Crime & Delinquency, 41,* 100-131.

Petersilia, J. (2000). *When prisoners return to the community: Political, economic, and social consequences.* Washington, DC: National Institute of Justice.

Petersilia, J., & Turner, S. (1993). Intensive probation and parole. In M. Tonry (Ed.), *Crime & Justice: A Review of Research* (pp. 281-335). Chicago: University of Chicago Press.

Public Safety Performance Project. (2007). *Public safety, public spending: Forecasting America's prison population, 2007-2011.* Washington, DC: The Pew Charitable Trusts.

Reeves, D. W. (2006). *Investigation of the impact of a cognitive skills educational program upon adult criminal offenders placed on supervised probation.* Doctoral Dissertation, Northern Arizona University. (UMI No. 3213110)

Taxman, F. S., Yancey, C, & Bilanin, J. (2006). *Proactive community supervision in Maryland: Changing offender outcome.* Baltimore: Maryland Division of Parole and Probation.

Weisfeld, N. E. (2007). *Realigning state-local relationships to save correctional dollars.* Washington, DC: The Pew Charitable Trusts.

Wilson, D. B., Bouffard, L. A., & MacKenzie, D. L. (2005). A quantitative review of structured, group-oriented, cognitive-behavioral programs for offenders. *Criminal Justice & Behavior, 32,* 172-204.

Wilson, D. B., Gallagher, C. A., & MacKenzie, D. L. (2000). A meta-analysis of corrections-based education, vocation, and work programs for adult offenders. *Journal on Research in Crime & Delinquency, 37,* 347-368.

DISCUSSION QUESTIONS

1. Why do these researchers believe their study is a more practical test of TFAC? What has been a problem of the past research on these programs?

2. What has occurred that has caused an increasing demand for community-based supervision programs?

3. What are some of the reasons for using cognitive behavioral programs with offenders in jail or prison?

4. How did these offenders get into the TFAC program? In other words, how were the treatment and control groups selected for this study? In Table 6.1, what are the similarities and differences between the two groups?

5. What do these authors list as some of the variables that may confound the results? What did they do to attempt to control these rival causal factors?

6. How do these researchers operationalize success? What is a limitation of this operational definition?

7. According to the results of this study, was TFAC an effective program at reducing recidivism? What were the differences in recidivism rates? Which other variables were significant predictors of recidivism?

8. What are some of the limitations of this experimental research? What do these authors mean when they state that "no single study in the social sciences is definitive"?

RESEARCH READING

Evidence-based research is becoming more popular as the powers that be are looking for programs that are more effective than traditional criminal justice outcomes. Researchers are, therefore, looking to evaluate programs in order to find out what works in reducing recidivism rates. Perez specifically used a quasi-experimental research design to examine the effectiveness of a residential substance abuse treatment program. She matched offenders in this program with regular probationers who did not receive treatment. Her findings revealed that the substance abuse program did not have a statistically significant effect on her measures of recidivism but that those who participated in the treatment program were less likely to be arrested for a new offense. Those in the treatment group, on the other hand, were more likely to violate their probation. This study is an excellent example of how findings can change dependent on how program success is defined.

APPLYING EVIDENCE-BASED PRACTICES TO COMMUNITY CORRECTIONS SUPERVISION

An Evaluation of Residential Substance Abuse Treatment for High-Risk Probationers

Deanna M. Pérez

Abstract: This study sought to evaluate the effectiveness of residential substance abuse treatment in reducing recidivism among high-risk offenders. The study employed a quasi-experimental research design to match 82 probationers who participated in residential drug treatment programs to 82 probationers with similar demographics and criminal history who did not attend treatment. The findings revealed that residential substance abuse treatment had no statistically significant effect on several dichotomous measures of recidivism but that treatment participation substantially reduced the amount of criminal activity in which offenders engaged in during the 18-month follow-up period. Furthermore, among those arrested, the treatment group was more likely to be charged with a probation violation, whereas controls were substantially more likely to be arrested for a new criminal offense. The results serve as the foundation for future examinations into the efficacy of residential drug treatment for high-risk offenders under community supervision.

INTRODUCTION

Over the past decade, research has advanced the application of evidence-based practices (EBP) or what has come to be widely referred to as "what works" in the field of correctional rehabilitation (Cullen & Gendreau, 2000; Latessa, 2004; MacKenzie, 2000, 2001; Sherman, Gottfredson, MacKenzie, Eck, Reuter, & Bushway, 1997). EBP draws on science to inform the operational practice of services and programs for offenders. The aim is to employ

Source: Pérez, D. M. (2009). Applying evidence-based practices to community corrections supervision: An evaluation of residential substance abuse treatment for high-risk probationers. *Journal of Contemporary Criminal Justice, 25*(4), 442–458.

empirically tested practices that produce reductions in recidivism among offenders (MacKenzie, 2005). A large and growing body of empirical research has identified those aspects of correctional programming that are common to the most effective treatment interventions.

According to Cullen and Gendreau (2000), successful interventions are based soundly in theory and research and designed to target dynamic predictors of recidivism. Dynamic factors are those characteristics of offenders that are mutable, such as drug use, antisocial attitudes, and employment skills. Furthermore, the most successful programs apply cognitive-behavioral treatment (CBT) techniques to help offenders modify their thoughts regarding criminal and risky behaviors. CBT with correctional populations have been conceptualized as cognitive restructuring, cognitive or coping-skills development, and life skills training (Carey, 1997, Wilson, Bouffard, & MacKenzie, 2005). The focus of treatment is on restructuring the cognitive distortions and dysfunctional thought processes of the offender that lend to inappropriate, deviant, and illegal behavior.

Correctional research on EBP consistently finds that the principles of risk and needs are a necessary component of effective correctional interventions (Andrews, 2000; Andrews & Bonta, 1998; Gendreau & Goggin, 2000; Latessa, Cullen, & Gendreau, 2002). The risk principle states that supervision and treatment programming should be commensurate with the risk level, or probability of recidivism, of the offender (Andrews, 2002; Lowenkamp & Latessa, 2005). Specifically, intensive services should be directed at moderate to high-risk offenders rather than provided indiscriminately. Empirical research and meta-analyses have shown that correctional programs that follow the risk principle yield the largest reductions in recidivism (Dowden, Antonowicz, & Andrews, 2003; Lovins, Lowenkamp, Latessa, & Smith, 2007; Lowenkamp & Latessa, 2004).

The needs principle recommends that interventions for offenders target known predictors

of crime and recidivism. In particular, correctional treatment should focus on dynamic risk factors, commonly referred to as "criminogenic needs" (Andrews et al., 1990; Cullen & Gendreau, 2000). Dynamic risk factors, such as low self-control, dysfunctional family tics, and antisocial values, are characteristics of an individual that are mutable. Whereas we know that certain static factors (e.g., offense history) highly predictive of recidivism cannot be modified, dynamic predictors can potentially be changed. Substance abuse is viewed as one of the most critical criminogenic needs among the offender population (Hiller, Knight, & Simpson, 2006; Karberg & James, 2005).

Although most research into the effectiveness of correctional rehabilitation programs has focused on interventions within correctional facilities, less research has examined community corrections programming (Hiller et al., 2006). A limited number of outcome evaluations of community residential drug treatment have found mixed results for such programs (but see Krebs, Strom, Koetse, & Lattimore, 2009 who found that nonresidential treatment was more effective than residential treatment in delaying time to recidivism). For example, an evaluation of the Brooklyn Drug Treatment Alternative-to-Incarceration Program (DTAP), a program that diverts to residential drug treatment prison-bound offenders, found that 4% of DTAP participants were rearrested compared to 13% of similar nonparticipants (Sung, 2003). More recently, in their evaluation of a probation-based residential drug treatment facility, Hiller et al. (2006) found that treatment completers were significantly less likely to recidivate in the second year after treatment than noncompleters and controls, whereas all groups recidivated at the same rate in the first year. Given these mixed results, the evidence to date on the efficacy of residential drug treatment programs remains equivocal (Chanhatasilpa, MacKenzie, & Hickman, 2000; MacKenzie, 1997). To address this deficiency, the current study employs a quasi-experimental design to evaluate the effectiveness of residential substance abuse programs to reduce recidivism among offenders under community corrections supervision.

METHOD

This research used a quasi-experimental design to examine the hypothesis that high-risk offenders under community corrections supervision who participated in residential drug treatment would have lower rates of recidivism than a matched group of offenders who did not receive treatment. While randomization to the treatment or control condition is the "gold" standard (Maxfield & Babbie, 1995), this study was a retrospective evaluation of offenders who had previously participated in treatment; thus, it was not possible to conduct a randomized experiment. An alternative option was to match offenders on factors related to the dependent variable, recidivism (Cook & Campbell, 1979).

During the period December 2001 to June 2002, 82 probationers/parolees were funded to participate in residential drug treatment—these participants comprised the treatment group. The control group was constructed by matching the treatment participants to 82 offenders with similar demographics and criminal history who did not attend substance abuse treatment. The treatment participants were matched to controls based on sex, race, age, probation district, primary offense, and supervision level (a proxy for criminal history). It is possible that relevant variables were not included in the matching process; however, the literature has consistently found that the factors on which the offenders were matched are strongly related to recidivism (Chung, Hill, Hawkins, Gilchrist, & Nagin, 2002; Farrington, 1995; Hepburn & Albonetti, 1994). The follow-up period for the study was 18 months.

Program Description

The participants of this study were sampled from one of seven treatment facilities located in a southeastern state that provided residential drug treatment to offenders who were under the community supervision of the state department of corrections (DOC). The programs were designated approved providers and were similar in the services they provide their clients, each offering residential treatment that included individual and group therapy, family counseling, psycho-education, relapse prevention, and aftercare. All of the facilities also addressed similar issues in counseling, such as motivational issues to resist drug use, identifying triggers for drug use, reinforcing and creating new coping skills that do not involve drug use, replacing drug-using activities with non-drug-using activities, and the legal consequences of continued drug use. In addition, all of the facilities offered services to address domestic violence and physical abuse, HIV/AIDS testing and education, and postdischarge follow-up.

The treatment centers were also similar in the types of clients they treated. The average age of the clients they served was mid-30s and most frequently presented with cocaine or opiate abuse. Clients were primarily daily users, and most had been using drugs and/or alcohol since they were adolescents. All the facilities employed the services of recovering addicts and reported high completion rates for criminal justice clients.

There were two primary differences between the treatment centers. Length of stay in treatment varied by program; however, all of the programs required a minimum of 1 month stay. In addition, the facilities differed in the proportion of the population represented by criminal justice clients (i.e., clients currently in the system whose stay at the treatment center was funded by DOC). The two largest facilities reported that criminal justice clients were approximately 50% of their population, and the remaining five facilities estimated that criminal justice clients comprised 10% to 25% of the population. All of the treatment programs advised that the criminal justice and noncriminal justice populations interacted, both in programming and socially.

Data Collection

Official criminal records and probation officer and treatment provider reports were the sources for pretreatment data as well as post-treatment data for a period of 18 months following the completion date of treatment for the experimental group and the start date of supervision for the control group. For the experimental participants who did not complete treatment, the follow-up period began on the date of discharge from treatment to the community. A questionnaire was mailed to the probation officer of each study participant requesting information on demographic characteristics (i.e., sex, race, age, marital status, and education level); primary offense; criminal history; histories of substance abuse and mental health treatment; and number of technical violations, new criminal arrests, and revocations. Criminal history and recidivism data were also obtained from the state police criminal information database. This included historical and follow-up data on number and type of arrests and convictions. The state institution and local jail information systems were searched to locate historical and recommitment data.

Measures

Independent variables. The primary variable of interest was treatment participation. The study examined whether attending residential drug treatment reduced recidivism among high-risk offenders under community corrections. Those receiving treatment services were compared to a matched control group of offenders who did not receive treatment services.

The matching variables included sex and race of the offender, with males and African Americans coded I. In addition, offenders were matched on date of birth, which was used to compute their age. The district in which offenders were supervised was used as a matching factor to account for potential regional effects. Offenders were matched by specific district; however, the variable was aggregated into central, eastern, or western regions. The western region saved as the reference category.

Offenders were also linked according to the crime codes for their primary offense. In instances where an exact match could not be made, a code within the same category was selected that had similar sentencing guidelines (e.g., if the treatment participant had a primary offense of Schedule I or II Drugs, Distribution, but an exact match was not available in the database, the offender was matched according to the most analogous offense, in this case. Schedule I or II Drugs. Possession, with intent to sell, distribute, etc.). After offense-specific matching was completed, offenses were aggregated into one of four categories: drug, property, violent, or other. The other group represented the variable of reference with three dummy variables included for the remaining offense categories. The final matching variable was supervision level, coded as intensive, regular, or relaxed, where relaxed served as the reference category and intensive and regular supervision were dummy variables.

Given the nonrandom design of this study, a number of risk factors identified as best predictors of recidivism were measured (Farrington, 1995). These factors fall into the domains of social bonds, substance abuse, and criminal history. Two measures of social bonds were created: marital status and level of education. Marital status was comprised of three categories, single (the referent group), married/cohabitating, or divorced/separated, based on the hypothesis that the latter two variables represent stronger social bonds than being single. Education was a dummy variable coded 0 for high school dropout and I for high school graduate/more, where the latter indicated a stronger bond to society.

To capture substance abuse, two dichotomous measures were created. The first was a variable that measured history of alcohol/drug treatment based on the probation officer's report. The second was a dichotomous measure for prior drug arrest. Although these two variables are not the optimal measure of substance abuse, they are frequently used in substance abuse research (Belenko, 1998) and were the best measures available.

Several measures of criminal history were created; all of the measures were based on official adult records. Arrest measures included an official record of at least one prior adult arrest, whether prior arrest included any violent offense, and mean number of prior arrests. Two variables representing conviction history were recorded: any official prior conviction and mean number of prior convictions. Last, a history of at least one prior incarceration was used to measure criminal history.

Dependent variables. Multiple measures of recidivism were created from official criminal records for an 18-month time follow-up period. Official data were used to create the following variables: number of new arrests, number of new incarcerations, proportion of new arrests, type of offense, proportion of new convictions, and proportion of new incarcerations occurring during the 18-month follow-up period.

Data Analysis

Chi-square tests were conducted to examine differences between the prevalence of arrests, convictions, and incarcerations for the treatment and control groups. It is important to note that, due to the small sample sizes, the analyses may have lacked the statistical power necessary to detect significant differences; thus sole reliance on statistical significance at the disregard of substantive significance is inadvisable (Cohen, 1988; Dixon, 2003). Analyses also included comparisons of mean changes in recidivism from the pre- to the postintervention period by group.

FINDINGS

Sample Description

The present analysis included the 162 offenders who either participated in treatment or served as the matched comparison. Chi-square

and *i*-test procedures were utilized to compare the two experimental conditions. The descriptive analysis is presented in Table 6.3. An examination of the table suggests that the research design was successful in creating comparable groups of offenders on the matched factors.

Both the treatment and control groups consisted of 81 participants, 70% male and 30% female; and 62% African American and 38% White. Although the average age of the treatment group (mean = 36) was higher than that of the control group (mean = 34), this difference was not statistically significant according to conventional standards. Similarly, there were no significant differences in supervision level between the treatment and control group, with the majority of both groups on regular supervision or intensive supervision. Most of the offenders in the sample were supervised in the central region, and 30% of each group represented both the eastern and western regions.

The type of primary offense for which each offender was convicted also did not differ significantly between groups. For both the treatment and control groups, a drug conviction constituted the majority of cases, followed by a property and a violent offense. There were slightly more property offenders in the control group, whereas more drug and violent offenders comprised the treatment group *(ns)*.

In addition to the matching factors, a number of other characteristics of the probationers are presented in Table 6.3 by experimental condition. According to information provided by probation officers, a smaller proportion of offenders in the treatment group graduated from high school or received a GED compared to the control group. The vast majority of participants in both groups were single and treatment participants had a higher prevalence of divorce/separation and lower proportion of marriage/cohabitation than their counterparts. There were also some substantial differences in employment for the two groups: those in the control group were more likely to be either employed full-time or unemployed than those in treatment, whereas treatment clients were more likely to have either a part-time job or irregular work compared to controls.

Table 6.3   Sample Characteristics by Experimental Condition ($N = 162$)

Variable	Group	
	Treatment (%)	Control (%)
Sex		
Male	70	70
Female	30	30
Race		
African American	62	62
White	38	38
Mean age (*SD*)	36.0 (8.6)	33.7 (8.3)
Supervision level		
Relaxed	4	1
Regular	62	67
Intensive	35	32
Region		
Central	41	41
Eastern	30	30
Western	30	30
Primary offense at conviction		
Drug	49	46
Property	33	40
Violent	14	11
Other	4	4
Education		
Less than high school	54	48
HS graduate/GED/more	46	52
Marital status		
Single	60	64
Married/cohabitate	9	16
Divorced/separated	31	20

(Continued)

Table 6.3 (Continued)

	Group	
Variable	Treatment (%)	Control (%)
Employment status		
Full-time	38	46
Part-time/irregular	30	15
Unemployed	33	40
History drug treatment*	58	40
History drug arrest	68	57
Prior arrest(s)	98	96
Mean number prior arrests (SD)	8.9 (7.4)	7.5 (7.1)
Prior violent arrest(s)	64	52
Mean number prior convictions (SD)	7.9 (8.0)	5.9 (6.5)
Prior incarceration(s)**	88	68

*$p < .05$. **$p < .01$.

With respect to drug treatment history, not surprisingly, probation officers reported that the treatment group had a significantly higher percentage of offenders with a history of participation in drug treatment in comparison to the control group ($\chi^2 = 5.21$, $p < .05$). Official criminal records indicated that offenders in the treatment group were more likely to have a prior drug arrest than controls but this difference was not significant.

Table 6.3 also indicates that both groups had fairly extensive criminal histories. Nearly all study participants had at least one prior official arrest (98% of the treatment group and 96% of the control group). The two groups were relatively similar on prevalence of conviction but they differed significantly on history of at least one prior incarceration. A significantly greater proportion of those in the treatment group having experienced a period of incarceration either in jail or prison relative to the control group (88% vs. 68%, respectively; $\chi^2 = 9.14$, $p < .01$). There were three criminal history measures for which the differences between groups approached significance: the treatment group had an average of 8.9 prior arrests, 7.9 prior convictions, and 64% had a violent arrest on their record. For these three measures, the criminal history of the control group was less serious; controls had an average of 7.5 prior arrests and 5.9 prior convictions, and 52% were previously arrested for at least one violent offense. These findings suggest the treatment group presents a more serious risk than the control group. The evidence that our participants displayed a history of substantial criminal involvement adheres to the principles set forth by Cullen and Gendreau (2000) recommending that treatment be directed at moderate to high-risk offenders to obtain the largest benefit.

Comparison of Residential Treatment Versus Matched Control Group

Chi-square tests were performed to investigate the hypotheses that the treatment group would perform better than the control group on a number of recidivism measures. The analyses of postprogram recidivism for the full sample are presented in the top half of Table 6.4. In all, 55% *(N=89)* of the sample was arrested during the 18-month follow-up period. There were slightly more recidivists in the treatment group with approximately 58% of treatment participants versus 52% of the control group evidencing an official arrest. Also, 48% of offenders in treatment were incarcerated during the follow-up period compared to 36% of those in the control group. Conversely, roughly 36% of controls had a new conviction in comparison to 30% of those in treatment.

To determine whether residential treatment had an effect on the type of criminal behavior, those arrested were compared on offense type. The bottom half of Table 6.4 presents chi-square test results of differences between the arrested treatment and control group. There was a statistically significant difference between the two groups for "other" offense, with those in treatment displaying a greater proportion of other arrests (60%) than those in the control group (33%; $\chi^2 = 6.13$, $p < .05$). Probation violation made up the majority of the cases in the other offense category and, in most instances, the charge was for a violation of supervision requirements rather than a new crime.

It is noteworthy to mention that the differences between groups, while not significant, were substantial for property, violent, and drug arrests. Given the small number of cases that were arrested in the follow-up period (i.e., 47 from treatment and 42 from the control group), differences would have to be quite large to obtain a statistically significant effect. Nevertheless, the findings indicate that the treatment group fared better than controls when compared on offense type. Among the arrested subsample, 15% of treatment participants

Table 6.4 Recidivism Outcomes by Experimental Condition

Recidivism Measure	Group	
	Treatment (%)	Control (%)
Full sample ($N = 162$)		
% Arrest	58	52
% Conviction	30	36
% Incarcerated	48	36
Arrest subsample ($N = 89$)		
% Property arrest	15	24
% Violent arrest	13	21
% Drug arrest	13	21
% Other arrest*	60	33

*$p < .05$.

compared to 24% of controls were arrested for a property offense. Similarly, controls who were arrested displayed a greater proportion of arrests for violent offenses than offenders in treatment who were arrested (21% vs. 13%, respectively). Finally, 21% of arrested control participants compared to 13% of treatment participants were arrested for a new drug offense.

In all, the findings show that the treatment group was more likely to be charged with a probation violation, whereas controls were substantially more likely to be arrested for a criminal offense. The literature has consistently indicated that intensive supervision significantly increases rates of technical violations (Petersilia & Turner, 1993). That was also the case in this sample of offenders. For example, among the offenders on intensive probation supervision, treatment participants were drug tested an average of 18 times compared to a mean of 11.5 for the control group ($t = 1.54$, ns). Among those on regular probation, urinalyses were administered to those in treatment an average of 16 times, double that of controls with a mean of 8 ($t = 3.04$, $p < .01$).

Mean Change in Recidivism, Pre- Versus Postintervention Period, by Group

Thus far, the analysis has focused on absolute differences in recidivism, or the observed difference in proportion between the treatment and control groups. Given that the measures of social bonds and criminal history indicated the treatment group was more high risk than the control group, a comparison at one point in time fails to account for these differences. Therefore, analyses were conducted to examine relative differences, or mean changes, in offending behavior. Table 6.5 illustrates the change in average number of rearrests and incarcerations (to jail and/or prison) within the treatment and control groups and the difference in mean change in arrests and incarcerations between the treatment and control groups from the pre- to the postintervention (T1 to T2) period.

At the preintervention period, the average number of arrests in the 18 months prior to program entry was 1.37 for the treatment group and 1.47 for the control group. At T2, the average number of official arrests decreased to 1.24 for the treatment group but increased to 1.64 for controls. This amounts to a mean reduction in number of arrests from T1 to T2 of .13 for the treatment group, whereas the control group showed a mean increase of .17. The change score between these two values equals .308. These findings indicate that exposure to treatment reduces recidivism in the form of decreasing the average number of rearrests.

The average change in number of incarcerations from T1 to T2 decreased for both groups. For the treatment group, the mean

Table 6.5   Mean Change in Measures of Recidivism, Pre- to Postintervention

	Arrest			Incarceration		
Group	Pre	Post	Change[a]	Pre	Post	Change[a]
Treatment	1.370	1.235	−0.135	2.321	1.049	−1.272
Control	1.469	1.642	+0.173	1.519	0.667	−0.852
Difference			.308			.420

a. Plus sign indicates an increase and minus sign indicates a decrease in the difference between mean averages from T1 to T2.

reduction in number of incarcerations was 1.27 compared to .85 for the control group. The change score equals .420. The treatment group experienced a larger reduction in mean incarcerations in comparison to the control group, again suggesting a positive effect of residential drug treatment.

Conclusions

The current study used a quasi-experimental research design to evaluate the effectiveness of residential drug treatment in reducing recidivism for high-risk offenders under community corrections supervision. Specifically, 82 probationers who attended one of seven drug treatment programs were matched to 82 probationers who did not attend treatment on sex, race, age, probation district, primary offense, and supervision level. The findings revealed mixed support for the efficacy of drug treatment.

Based on statistical convention, the groups did not differ on absolute measures of arrest, conviction, and incarceration during the postintervention period. For both official arrests and convictions, there was a 6% point difference *(ns)* between groups; arrests were more prevalent among treatment participants whereas control participants had a greater percentage of convictions. Furthermore, the results also showed that a substantially greater proportion of offenders who participated in treatment were incarcerated postintervention in comparison to offenders in the control group (48% vs. 36%, respectively; *ns)*. Although this outcome may call into question the efficacy of treatment, it was not unexpected.

Residential drug treatment is considered the "end of the line" in community corrections sanction options. In other words, placement in a drug treatment facility is one of the final options afforded to an offender before the probationer is sent to jail/ prison. Therefore, the offenders who made up the treatment group had generally exhausted the less-intensive sanctions, such that any subsequent violations or crimes would lead to incarceration. This may also partially explain why the treatment group was more high-risk than the control group.

In examining the subsample of offenders arrested, the findings showed that those in treatment had a significantly larger proportion of "other" offenses compared to controls. The other offenses were predominantly charges for a violation of supervision requirements rather than a new crime. These results are consistent with findings from the intensive supervision probation (ISP) literature that has shown that ISP participants have higher revocation rates, primarily for technical violations, but similar rates of new crimes than other offenders (Petersilia & Turner, 1993; Turner, Petersilia, & Deschenes, 1992). Although participants in this sample were matched according to supervision level, results indicated that probationers who received residential drug treatment were supervised more intensively than controls. It is possible, then, not that treatment and control participants were in violation of supervision at differing rates, but that offenders in treatment were more likely to be detected because of stricter monitoring levels placed on them by their supervising officer.

Conversely, the study found that treatment participants arrested at follow-up had a substantially lower prevalence of property, violent, and drug arrests than controls who were arrested. Given the strong relationship between substance use and crime (Exum, 2002; Goldstein, Bellucci, Spunt, & Miller, 1991; Klein, Maxson, & Cunningham, 1991; Lennings, Copeland, & Howard, 2003; Lurigio & Swartz, 1999; Spiess & Fallow, 2000), one possible explanation is that these types of criminal behavior were lower for those in treatment as a result of decreased drug use. Unfortunately, this conjecture is not testable with the existing data as there is no reliable information on drug test outcomes. Nevertheless, the reduction in arrests translates into increased public safety and potential correctional cost benefits. Decreases mean fewer victims (Klaus, 2002) as well as savings in costs related to detaining a defendant pending trial (VanNostrand, 2003).

An examination of mean changes in offending from pre- to postintervention indicated that the treatment group fared better than the control group in new arrests and incarcerations. Specifically, the average number of arrests from T1 to T2 decreased for the treatment group but increased for the controls. Furthermore, while the mean number of incarcerations decreased from T1 to T2 for both groups, the decrease for the treatment group was larger than that of the controls. Overall, the findings are promising and provide partial support for the hypothesis that high-risk offenders who participate in residential drug treatment will have lower rates of recidivism than a matched group of offenders who did not receive treatment. These study results justify continued examination into the efficacy of substance abuse treatment for high-risk offenders under community collections supervision.

The findings of this study highlight a number of important considerations in treatment assignment and delivery. First, the offenders participating in residential treatment were clearly moderate to high-risk offenders. According to the risk principle of evidence-based practices, residential treatment directed at high-risk offenders will produce the most positive treatment effects (Andrews, 2000; Lowenkamp & Latessa, 2005; Lowenkamp, Latessa, & Holsinger, 2006; Wexler, Melnick, & Cao, 2004). The research has also shown that intensive drug treatment is most cost effective among high-risk cases (Griffith, Hiller, Knight, & Simpson, 1999). The descriptive analysis showed that the treatment group was comprised of offenders with poor social bonds and a serious criminal history, including incidents of violence and prior incarceration(s). Large proportions of offenders lacked a high school diploma, were unemployed or only employed part-time or irregularly, were largely single or divorced, and evidenced substantial drug problems. Although this study was not able to compare high-risk to low-risk offenders on outcomes to test the veracity of the risk principle, the findings do indeed suggest that high-risk offenders were amenable to treatment and that treatment does work in reducing

reoffending among individuals often perceived to be impervious to change.

Second, in this study, the treatment group was more high risk than the control group based on measures of social bonds, substance abuse, and criminal history. For this reason, it was important to consider relative behavior change. The study found that the average number of arrests and incarcerations decreased for those participating in treatment from pre- to postintervention. It would be imprudent to assume all criminal behavior would be eliminated based on one treatment episode. The evidence consistently shows that relapse rates are high among substance abusers, ranging from 50% to 80% and that, given the chronic nature of the disease, addiction often requires multiple episodes of treatment to achieve abstinence (National Institute on Drug Abuse, 2000). Nevertheless, these results indicated that treatment participation substantially reduced the amount of criminal activity in which offenders participated; thus, drug treatment is an effective crime-reducing option for high-risk offenders.

To date, there are few treatment studies that utilize experimental methods to determine drug treatment effectiveness. The present study employed a quasi-experimental research design (i.e., matched treatment and control group) to address some of the methodological shortcomings in current treatment research. The findings were encouraging; nevertheless, there exist a number of limitations that should be noted. First, although rigorous in comparison to much of the existing drug treatment literature, because this study was not a randomized experiment, there may exist other important variables not accounted for that may distinguish the two groups. Although these other factors may explain the results, the significant findings detected in the present study could arguably be a conservative estimate of the true treatment effect as the treatment group, with a more extensive criminal history, was at higher risk for reoffending than the control group. Second, a larger sample size would have been preferable. Beyond decreasing the chance of a Type 2 error, a larger sample size would allow for additional types of comparisons, such as by offender characteristics or program components, to determine mediating effects.

Furthermore, although the residential treatment programs operated primarily from a cognitive-behavioral theoretical orientation and generally provided similar types of services (e.g., 12-Step attendance, drug education, relapse prevention, family therapy), there were potential differences between the programs that could account for the results or mask potential treatment effects. For example, not all of the treatment programs provided dual diagnosis treatment; however, research consistently finds that a large proportion of substance abusers, both in the general and offender population, also exhibit a co-occurring mental health disorders(s) (Bradizza, Stasiewicz, & Paas, 2006; Grella, Greenwell, Prendergast, Sacks, & Melnick, 2008; Kessler et al., 1997; McMillan et al., 2008; Swartz & Lurigio, 1999). Given that treating co-occurring disorders simultaneously is necessary to improve psychological functioning and reduce relapse (Curran, Flynn, Kirchner, & Booth, 2000; Hasin et al., 1996; Ouimette, Moos, & Finney, 2003; Sacks et al., 2008), it is possible that study participants who received mental health services in addition to substance abuse treatment would experience more positive outcomes than those not treated for mental illness. Similarly, because these were community-based residential programs contracted by the DOC to provide substance abuse treatment, the programs differed in the proportion of criminal justice clients who received services. Differences in client characteristics could influence the content of programming to the extent that treatment providers focus more or less on offender-specific needs in therapy. Consistent with EBP research on offenders, programs that primarily target criminogenic needs for change should have the greatest impact on reducing recidivism.

Nevertheless, clients in all of the treatment programs received individual counseling where criminal justice participants could address their particular needs. Unfortunately, it was not possible to examine differences across treatment programs because of the limited sample size. Finally, the study would have benefited greatly had reliable indicators of drug use, both during and postintervention, been available. As this was a retrospective design, a systematic data collection mechanism was not in place for recording of urinalysis results. Collecting data on drug use during treatment is essential as not only does it signal relapse but it is also a strong indicator that the offender will also return to criminal behavior.

Although we have amassed a wealth of evidence that shows "treatment works" to reduce recidivism among offenders, many policymakers continue to advocate for punitive responses for drug offenders (e.g., mandatory minimum sentences). These "get-tough" policies and practices, spurned on by the "war on drugs," have contributed to the dramatic increase in the incarceration rate that has characterized our Nation's correctional system for more than 30 years (Pew Center, 2008). The findings from the present study provide evidence that many drug offenders can safely be monitored and treated in the community. Many legislators and constituents either do not know this or do not believe it to be true—in either case, it is necessary to educate policymakers and the public about the efficacy of best practices in community corrections to increase support for prison alternatives. As many addicted offenders are aware and criminal justice practitioners will acknowledge, drug treatment is not a "slap on the wrist" but rather an effective correctional mechanism to hold offenders accountable for their actions. To suggest otherwise dismisses the fact that getting and staying clean and sober is arduous work.

References

Andrews, D. A. (2000). Principles of effective correctional programs. In L. L. Motiuk & R. C. Serin (Eds.), *Compendium 2000 on effective, correctional programming*. Ottawa, Ontario: Correctional Services of Canada.

Andrews, D. A., & Bonta, J. (1998). *The psychology of criminal conduct*. Cincinnati, OH: Anderson.

Andrews, D. A., Zinger, I., Hoge, R. D., Bonta, J., Gendreau, P., & Cullen, F. T. (1990). Does correctional treatment work? A clinically relevant and psychologically informed meta-analysis. *Criminology, 28,* 369-404.

Belenko, S. (1998). *Behind bars: Substance abuse and America's prison population.* New York: National Center on Addiction and Substance Abuse at Columbia University.

Bradizza, C. M., Stasiewicz, P. R., & Paas. N. D. (2006). Relapse to alcohol and drug use among individuals diagnosed with co-occurring mental health and substance use disorders: A review. *Clinical Psychology Review, 26,* 162-178.

Carey, M. (1997, Spring), Cog probation. *Perspectives, 21*(2), 27-42.

Chanhatasilpa, C, MacKenzie, D. L., & Hickman, L. J. (2000). The effectiveness of community-based programs for chemically dependent offenders: A review and assessment of the research. *Journal of Substance Abuse Treatment, 19,* 383-393.

Chung, I., Hill, K. G., Hawkins, J. D,, Gilchrist, L. D., & Nagin, D. S. (2002). Childhood predictors of offense trajectories. *Journal of Research in Crime and Delinquency, 39,* 60-90.

Cohen, J. (1988). *Statistical power analysis for the behavioral sciences* (2nd ed.). Hillsdale, NJ: Lawrence Erlbaum.

Cook, T. D., & Campbell, D. T. (1979). *Quasi-experimentation: Design & analysis issues for field settings.* Boston: Houghton Mifflin.

Cullen, F. T., & Gendreau, P. (2000). Assessing correctional rehabilitation: Policy, practice, and prospects. In J. Homey (Ed.), *Policies, processes, and decisions of the criminal justice system* (Vol. 3, pp. 109-175). Washington, DC: U.S. Department of Justice.

Curran, G. M., Flynn, H. A., Kirchner, J., & Booth, B. M. (2000). Depression after alcohol treatment as a risk factor for relapse among male veterans. *Journal of Substance Abuse Treatment, 19,* 259-265.

Dowden, C., Antonowicz, D., & Andrews, D. A. (2003). The effectiveness of relapse prevention with offenders: A meta-analysis. *International Journal of Offender Therapy and Comparative Criminology, 47,* 516-528.

Dixon, P. (2003). The p-value fallacy and how to avoid it. *Canadian Journal of Experimental Psychology, 57,* 189-202.

Exum, L. M. (2002). Application and robustness of the rational choice perspective in the study of intoxicated and angry intentions to aggress. *Criminology, 40,* 933-966.

Farrington, D. P. (1995). Development of offending and antisocial behaviour from childhood: Key findings from the Cambridge Study in Delinquent Development. *Journal of Child Psychology, 360,* 929-964.

Gendreau, P., & Goggin, C. (2000). Correctional treatment: Accomplishments and realities. In P. Van Voorhis, M. Braswell, & D. Lester (Eds.), *Correctional counseling and rehabilitation* (4th ed., pp. 289-297). Cincinnati, OH: Anderson.

Goldstein, P. J., Bellucci, P. A., Spunt, B. J., & Miller, T. (1991). Volume of cocaine use and violence: A comparison between men and women. *Journal of Drug Issues, 21,* 345-367.

Grella, C. E., Greenwell, L., Prendergast, M., Sacks, S., & Melnick, G. (2008). Diagnostic profiles of offenders in substance abuse treatment programs. *Behavioral Sciences & the Law, 26,* 369-388.

Griffith J. D., Hiller, M. L., Knight, K., & Simpson, D. D. (1999). A cost-effectiveness analysis of in-prison therapeutic community treatment and risk classification. *The Prison Journal, 79,* 352-368.

Hasin, D., Tsai, W. Y., Endicott, J., Mueller, T. L, Coryell, W., & Keller, M. (1996). The effects of major depression on alcoholism. *American Journal on Addictions, 5,* 144-155.

Hepburn, J. R., & Albonetti, C. A. (1994). Recidivism among drug offenders: A survival analysis of the effects of offender characteristics, type of offense, and two types of intervention. *Journal of Quantitative Criminology, 10,* 159-179.

Hiller, M. L., Knight, K., Broome, K. M., & Simpson, D. D. (1998). Legal pressure and treatment retention in a national sample of long-term residential programs. *Criminal Justice and Behavior, 25,* 463-481.

Hiller, M, L., Knight, K., & Simpson, D. D. (2006). Recidivism following mandated residential substance abuse treatment for felony probationers. *The Prison Journal, 86,* 230-241.

Karberg, J. C., & James, D. J. (2005). *Substance dependence, abuse, and treatment of jail inmates, 2002.* Bureau of Justice Statistics.

Kessler, R C., Crum, R. M., Warner, L. A., Nelson, C. B., Schulenberg, J., & Anthony, J. C. (1997). Lifetime co-occurrence of DSM-III-R alcohol abuse and dependence with other psychiatric disorders in the National Comorbidity Survey. *Archives of General Psychiatry, 54,* 313-321.

Klaus, P. A. (2002). *Crime and the nation's households, 2002.* Washington, DC: Bureau of Statistics, U.S. Department of Justice.

Klein, M. W., Maxson, C. L, & Cunningham, L. C. (1991). Crack, street gangs, and violence. *Criminology, 29,* 623-650.

Krebs, C. P., Strom, K. J., Koetse, W. H., & Lattimore, P. K. (2009). The impact of residential and nonresidential drug treatment on recidivism among drug-involved probationers. *Crime & Delinquency 55,* 442-471.

Latessa, E. J. (2004). The challenge of change: Correctional programs and evidence-based practices. *Criminology & Public Policy, 3,* 547-560.

Latessa, E. J., Cullen, F. T., & Gendreau, P. (2002). Beyond correctional quackery: Professionalism and the possibility of effective treatment. *Federal Probation, 66,* 43-49.

Lennings, C. J., Copeland, J., & Howard, J. (2003). Substance use patterns of young offenders and violent crime. *Aggressive Behavior, 29,* 414-422.

Lovins, L. B., Lowenkamp, C. T., Latessa, E. J., & Smith, P. (2007). Application of the risk principle to female offenders. *Journal of Contemporary Criminal Justice, 23,* 383-398.

Lowenkamp, C. T., & Latessa, E. J. (2004). Understanding the risk principle: How and why correctional interventions can harm low-risk offenders. *Topics in Community Corrections,* pp. 3-8.

Lowenkamp, C. T., & Latessa, E. J. (2005). Increasing the effectiveness of correctional programming through the risk principle: Identifying offenders for residential placement. *Criminology & Public Policy, 4,* 501-528.

Lowenkamp, C. T., Latessa, R. J., & Holsinger, A. M. (2006). The risk principle in action: What have we learned from 13,676 offender and 97 correctional programs? *Crime & Delinquency, 52,* 77-93.

Lurigio, A. J., & Swartz, J. A. (1999). The nexus between drugs and crime: Theory, research, and practice. *Federal Probation, 63,* 67-72.

Mackenzie, D. L. (1997). Criminal justice and crime prevention. In L. W. Sherman, D. Gottfredson, D. L. MacKenzie, J. Eck, P. Reuter, & S. Bushway (Eds.), *Preventing crime: What works, what doesn't, what's promising* (NIJ Report, NCJ 165366, pp. 9-1 to 9-76). Washington, DC: U.S. Department of Justice, National Institute of Justice.

MacKenzie, D. L. (2000). Evidence-based corrections: Identifying what works. *Crime and Delinquency, 46,* 457-471.

MacKenzie, D. L. (2001). Corrections and sentencing in the 21st Century: Evidence-based corrections and sentencing. *The Prison Journal, 81,* 299-312.

MacKenzie, D. L. (2005). The importance of using scientific evidence to make decisions about correctional programming. *Criminology & Public Policy, 4,* 249-258.

Maxfield, M. G., & Babbie, E. (1995). *Research methods for criminal justice and criminology.* Belmont, CA: Wadsworth.

McMillan, G. P., Timken, D. S., Lapidus, I., C'de Baca, J., Lapham, S. C, & McNeal, M. (2008). Underdiagnosis of comorbid mental illness in repeat DUI offenders mandated to treatment. *Journal of Substance Abuse Treatment, 34,* 320-325.

National Institute on Drug Abuse. (2000). *Principles of drug addiction treatment: A research-based guide* (NIH Publication No. 00-4180). Washington, DC: Author.

Ouimette, P. C, Moos, R. H., & Finney, J. W. (2003). PTSD treatment and 5-year remission among patients with substance use and posttraumatic stress disorders, *Journal of Consulting and Clinical Psychology, 71,* 410-414.

Petersilia, J., & Turner, S. (1993). Intensive probation and parole. In M. Tonry (Ed.), *Crime and justice: A review of research* (pp. 281-335). Chicago: University or Chicago Press.

Pew Center. (2008). *One in 100: Behind bars in America.* Washington, DC: Public Safety Performance Project, Pew Center on the States.

Sacks, J. Y., McKendrick, K., Hamilton, Z., Cleland, C. M., Pearson, F. S., & Banks, S. (2008). Treatment outcomes for female offenders: Relationship to number of Axis I diagnoses. *Behavioral Sciences & the Law, 26,* 413-434.

Sherman, L.W., Gottfredson, D. C., MacKenzie, D. L., Eck, J., Reuter, P., & Bushway, S. (1997). *Preventing crime: What works, what doesn't, what's promising.* Washington, DC: A Report to the U.S. Congress prepared by National Institute of Justice.

Spiess, M., & Fallow, D. (2000). *Drug-related crime.* Washington, DC: Office of National Drug Control Policy.

Sung, H. (2003). Differential impact of deterrence vs. rehabilitation as drug interventions on recidivism after 36 months. *Journal of Offender Rehabilitation, 37,* 95-108.

Swartz, J. A., & Lurigio, A. J. (1999) Psychiatric illness and comorbidity among adult male jail detainees in drug treatment *Psychiatric Services, 50,* 1628-1630.

Turner, S., Petersilia, J., & Deschenes, E. P. (1992). Evaluating intensive supervision probation/parole (ISP) for drug offenders. *Crime and Delinquency, 38,* 539-556.

VanNostrand, M. (2003). *Assessing risk among pretrial defendants in Virginia: The Virginia pretrial risk assessment instrument.* Richmond: Virginia Department of Criminal Justice Services.

Wexler, H. K., Melnick, G., & Cao, Y. (2004). Risk and prison substance abuse treatment outcomes: A replication and challenge. *The Prison Journal, 84,* 106-120.

Wilson, D. B., Bouffard, L. A., & MacKenzie, D. L. (2005). A quantitative review of structured, group-oriented, cognitive-behavioral programs for offenders. *Criminal Justice and Behavior, 32,* 172-204.

DISCUSSION QUESTIONS

1. What are evidence-based practices regarding criminal justice outcomes?

2. According to previous research, what should correctional treatment focus on?

3. Where did Pérez find the participants for this study? Further, what services did this program provide to the participants?

4. Pérez collected data from multiple sources. What were these sources, and what types of information did she collect?

5. How did this researcher measure social bonds, substance abuse, and criminal history? How many different dependent variables did the author include? In other words, how did she measure success?

6. What did Pérez find regarding the program's effectiveness at reducing recidivism?

7. Which attributes of a true experiment is this quasi-experimental design lacking? Were subjects randomly assigned to groups? What was done instead?

8. From Table 6.3, do you see any other variables (rival causal factors) that might possibly cause differences between the two groups on the outcomes studied?

9. What are the broader overall findings from this study regarding residential treatment of offenders?

7

SURVEY RESEARCH AND INTERVIEWS

SELF-REPORT SURVEY RESEARCH

Survey research is one of the most common ways to solicit information about attitudes and behaviors from subjects of interest. Surveys involve collecting information from persons via questionnaires, telephone interviews, face-to-face interviews, and more recently Internet and e-mail–based instruments. The researcher can record information solicited from individuals, or respondents themselves can complete the surveys. The US Census is a large-scale example of self-report survey research; individuals receive questionnaires via mail and are asked to fill them out and send them back. The NCVS (National Crime Victimization Survey) is another example of a large-scale survey research design where data is collected via telephone interviews. Although survey research is a common way to solicit information from a wide variety of individuals, it is not without its limitations.

One of the major problems in survey research is getting the respondents a researcher wants to study to fill out the survey. Response rate in survey research refers to the number of persons who respond to the survey (fill it out

and, in the case of a mail survey, send it back) in relation to the overall number of persons the researcher wanted to respond. Often, persons do not want to provide answers to questionnaires either because they do not have time, they do not think the survey is important, they are not sure how their answers are going to be used, or if a mail survey, they do not want to pay the postage to mail it back. If a researcher does not get back all of the surveys he or she sends out, it can have implications for the results of the research. Recall the discussion of sampling error in the previous chapter. If only half of the sample a researcher wanted to obtain information from fills out the surveys, the researcher has to be concerned about his or her ability to generalize the results of the survey. For purposive samples, this is not as much of a problem. For instance, maybe you have filled out a survey as part of one of your college courses. Most students in the class will provide responses on these surveys, especially if the professor is offering extra credit for doing so.

If a researcher has randomly selected a sample, however, and sent out the surveys to the sample via mail, it is very likely that not all of the surveys will be returned; this research, therefore, will contain some degree of sampling error. The individuals a researcher has selected to study are collectively referred to as the chosen sample. The individuals who actually agree to participate in the study are called the obtained sample. The difference between the two is called attrition (Ellis, Hartley, & Walsh, 2010). Attrition is one of the most problematic issues surrounding survey research. The amount of attrition in a survey may depend on its method of administration as well as its length. Figure 7.1 displays some of the different types of surveys and the ways in which they are administered as well as the typical structure and cost associated with their administration.

Response rates in survey research vary considerably depending on a number of factors. If a researcher obtains a response rate in the neighborhood of 60% to 70%, this is considered good (an attrition rate of 30% to 40%). If response rates are much lower, researchers need to be concerned about the representativeness of the sample. There are a number of techniques utilized by researchers to attempt to minimize the amount of attrition they experience. Some of the techniques include: having a credible sponsor (such as a university), including a personalized cover letter explaining the importance of the research, constructing clear and easy to understand questions, using short surveys, including a self-addressed stamped envelope for the respondent to return the survey, and even including compensation of some sort such as coupons or even a small amount of cash (Bachman & Schutt, 2008). Any methods used to increase response rates, no matter how small, will pay off in lowering attrition rates and will increase the researchers' abilities to generalize their results.

Telephone surveys have unique issues regarding response rates. Survey interviews via telephone have become an increasingly common way to collect data because of innovations such as random digit dialing and computer-assisted telephone interviewing (CATI). Researchers can now use a computer program to randomly dial the phone numbers of respondents in a quick and easy way. Problems, however, still persist even with CATI, such as persons not being home or persons hanging up because of a lack of interest. Similarly e-mail and web-based surveys are becoming increasingly popular because they can enable the selection of a large number of widely dispersed subjects in a cost-effective and time-efficient manner. Computer programs will also

Figure 7.1 Typical Features of the Five Survey Designs

Design	Manner of Administration	Setting	Questionnaire Structure	Cost
Mailed survey	Self	Individual	Mostly structured	Low
Group survey	Self	Group	Mostly structured	Very low
Phone survey	Professional	Individual	Structured	Moderate
In-person interview	Professional	Individual	Structured or unstructured	High
Electronic survey	Self	Individual	Mostly structured	Very low

automatically code and enter subject responses into a preconstructed database, saving the researcher valuable time and effort.

Nonetheless, limitations are also inherent in survey administration via this method. For example, not all households currently have access to the Internet or e-mail, or respondents can easily delete the e-mail containing the survey. Respondents may also be hesitant to respond to survey questions via the World Wide Web, especially if the questions are of a personal nature, due to fear that they are not sure who will see their responses. Despite these limitations, advances in both telephone- and computer-based survey administration have helped researchers solicit information from those they have had trouble reaching in the past and in an easy and time-efficient manner.

VERACITY OF SELF-REPORT SURVEYS

Another issue with self-reports has to do with their veracity; do respondents provide truthful answers? Survey research could produce unreliable or invalid information if the respondent does not understand the question, the respondent cannot remember certain information, or the respondent is dishonest (Ellis et al., 2010). Pilot testing survey instruments can help reduce problems with invalid answers due to lack of understanding of questions. Clear, straightforward, and simple questions that ask respondents about recent events are the most likely to elicit true and valid responses.

Dishonest responses, on the other hand, are more difficult to detect. There are some ways, however, for researchers to check the honesty of subjects' responses. At the very least, researchers should inform respondents that their responses will remain anonymous. Anonymously collecting information via surveys, especially if it is of a sensitive or criminal nature, is one of the best ways to ensure

honest and open responses from subjects (Hill, Dill, & Davenport, 1988).

Ellis and colleagues (2010) recommend other practices beyond affording anonymity that may also help to minimize dishonesty. They suggest avoiding asking respondents embarrassing questions that may make them uneasy. If questions of a sensitive nature have to be asked, researchers should try to ensure that these questions are asked in a nonjudgmental way. Another technique they recommend is to simply ask respondents at the end of the survey to rate their level of truthfulness. The problem then is what to do with surveys in which respondents report a high level of dishonesty. Ultimately, these surveys should not be included in the study. Finally, researchers can use one of the internal reliability checks discussed in Chapter 4, such as the split-half technique. Asking the same or similar questions in different sections of a survey can help researchers detect whether or not respondents were truthful in their responses. Again, those surveys in which answers are shown to be contradictory should be discarded.

Overall, survey research has proven to be a useful source of information on countless topics that would not otherwise be available if individuals did not agree to respond to surveys. Accuracy of responses will also depend somewhat on whether the survey is completed by the respondents themselves or if the researcher records the respondents' answers to the questions. Interviewing respondents in person or via telephone usually solicits more accurate responses, depending on the research topic. Regardless of method, survey research has provided social scientists with invaluable information about the nature of human interactions and behaviors.

INTERVIEWS

As stated above, although more costly and time-consuming, face-to-face interviewing is probably the best survey method at soliciting accurate responses. Bachman and Schutt (2008) report several advantages to in-person interviews: response rates are higher, researchers can seek more in-depth information, difficult questions can be clarified by the interviewer, researchers can ask follow-up questions, and finally, nonverbal behaviors can also be recorded. Face-to-face interviews can be structured, unstructured, or in-depth (Hagan, 2005). Structured interviews mainly consist of asking respondents questions with a minimal amount of response options. Generally, these interviews consist of the interviewer checking off the respondents' answers to the questions. Unstructured interviews, on the other hand, ask open-ended questions where the subjects can respond in any way they want. These types of interviews seek information that is more personal, such as a person's attitudes or opinions of various subjects. Finally, in-depth interviews are the most intensive, and the researcher and interviewee may even meet on several occasions. These types of interviews have been used extensively in research of little-known or difficult to obtain subjects. In-depth interviews, for instance, have been used to study prostitution, narcotics trafficking, residential burglary, and robbery, to name a few. Obviously, without in-depth interviews, we would know little about these behaviors other than that they exist.

Ethical issues can arise in survey research, especially regarding survey methods involving interviews of subjects and, more specifically, in-depth interviews of past and active criminal offenders. Researchers who conduct this type of research have to always be conscious about the ethical guidelines regarding the subjects of their research (protect confidentiality), as well as to the fact that their own safety could potentially be compromised. Researchers who conduct this type of research may find that there is a delicate balance between the quest for scientific knowledge and the moral and safety implications of these pursuits.

RESEARCH READING

Ruddell and colleagues use a survey research methodology to examine the perceptions that jail administrators in 39 states have about special needs populations in jail facilities. These problem populations include inmates who have mental illnesses, who are repeat offenders, who are serving long sentences, and especially those who are involved with gangs. The researchers solicited information regarding a number of issues with these populations, including the problems that they cause for correctional facilities. They also solicited information on what administrators in these facilities believe are the best institutional responses to these problems. Findings show that just over 10% of jails have gang problems, and that smaller jails report having less gang problems. Ruddell and colleagues also report that gang problems do not vary by region, and that gathering information about gangs in facilities (gang intelligence) is the best intervention for dealing with gang problems.

GANG INTERVENTIONS IN JAILS

A National Analysis

Rick Ruddell, Scott H. Decker, and Arlen Egley, Jr.

Abstract: This national-level study surveys the perceptions of 134 jail administrators in 39 states about the prevalence of gang members in their facilities. Consistent with previous empirical work, approximately 13% of jail populations are thought to be gang involved, and although there are no regional differences in these estimates, small jails report having fewer gang-involved inmates. When asked about the problems that these inmates cause in their facilities, respondents report that gang members are less disruptive than inmates with severe mental illnesses but are more likely to assault other inmates. The use and efficacy of 10 programmatic responses to gangs are evaluated, with respondents rating the gathering and dissemination of gang intelligence as the most effective intervention. Implications for practitioners and gang research are outlined.

INTRODUCTION

Most of our knowledge about gangs in correctional facilities is based on research conducted in state or federal prison systems (Camp & Camp, 1985; Gaes, Wallace, Gilman, Klein-Saffran, & Suppa, 2002; Ralph & Marquart, 1991; Stastny & Tymauer, 1983). Typically, these studies have found that the proliferation of gangs and the number of gang members in prison settings have increased substantially since the 1980s (Decker, 2003). Understanding the extent of the gang problem is an important issue for prison administrators because gang-involved inmates contribute to higher rates of prison violence (Camp & Camp, 1985), increase racial tensions within prisons (Anti-Defamation League of B'nai B'rith, 2002; Ross & Richards, 2002), challenge rehabilitative programming by supporting criminogenic values (Decker, 2003; Fortune, 2003), engage in criminal enterprises within prisons (Ingraham & Wellford, 1987), and contribute to failure in community reintegration if these parolees return to gang activities on release (Adams & Olson, 2002; Fleisher & Decker, 2001b; Olson, Dooley, & Kane, 2004).

Fischer's (2001) study of Arizona prisons, for instance, reported that "members of certified prison gangs (security threat groups [STGs]), uncertified prison gangs, and street gangs commit serious disciplinary violations at rates two to three times higher than do non-gang inmates housed in units of the same security level" (p. ii). Thus, by better understanding the scope of the problem and the efficacy of different types of interventions, jail professionals can work to reduce the influence that gangs have in their facilities. In addition, other stakeholders also need to better understand the extent of this social problem. Esbensen, Winfree, He, and Taylor (2001) observe that research about gangs is also important for researchers and theorists:

> For researchers, it is important to refine measurement: to assess the validity and reliability of the measures being used. For theorists, it is important to better understand factors associated with gang membership and associated behaviors, whether testing or constructing theory. (p. 122)

These scholars also acknowledge the importance of information sharing and collaboration between academics and policy makers, although we also suggest that jail practitioners ought to be involved in the research process as they have intimate knowledge of the success and failure of different interventions within their institutions.

Comparatively little is known about the extent of adult gangs in jails. Increasing our knowledge about gangs and tactics designed to respond specifically to these groups is an important issue given the size of the jail population—approximately 714,000 inmates are housed in local correctional facilities (Harrison & Beck, 2005b). Unlike prisons, jails are intended primarily for inmates awaiting court processes and incarceration for periods of less than 1 year. Operated by counties and local governments, there are more than 3,300 American jails that range in size from four or five beds to the Los Angeles County jail system, which held an average of 18,629 inmates in the third quarter of 2005 (Corrections Standards Authority, 2005). Parallel with federal and state prison systems, however, local jails have also experienced dramatic growth during the past two decades (Cunniff, 2002; Harrison & Beck, 2005b; Stephan, 2001). This growth has stretched county budgets (Davis, Applegate, Otto, Surette, & McCarthy, 2004), increased staff turnover (Kerle, 1998), and may contribute to higher rates of inmate violence (Tartaro, 2002). Altogether, these changes produce less predictable conditions within America's jails (Mays & Ruddell, 2004).

It is plausible that some of the problems in the day-to-day operations that jails confront are a result of expanding gang populations. As a result, an important first step is to examine the extent of the problem. Wells, Minor, Angel, Carter, and Cox (2002) surveyed jail administrators and found that approximately 16% of all jail inmates were members of STGs, whereas 13% of prison inmates were STG members. There are a number of reasons why jail populations have rates of gang involvement that closely correspond with prison systems. First, although jail populations tend to be more heterogeneous than prisons (a wide variety of persons from different demographic and socioeconomic backgrounds are admitted), this diversity is a function of the short-term nature of jail incarceration. Most inmates are held for a day or

two until they make bail, but serious or persistent offenders, such as gang members, may have more difficulty securing release and may wait months or even years for the conclusion of their trials. James (2004, p. 4) found that 11.3% of jail inmates were held more than 6 months and that an additional 6.5% were held more than 1 year.

A second reason why rates of gang membership in jails parallel prison rates is that jails act as an entry point for prisons. Virtually everyone who is admitted to prison will first spend time in jails, either awaiting court dates or pending their transfer to prison. Approximately 10% of all jail inmates have already been sentenced to a term within the state prison system, but overcrowding keeps these inmates in city or county facilities awaiting transfer (Harrison & Beck, 2005b). Finally, jails hold persons sentenced to periods of incarceration up to 1 year, and some may serve much longer periods of time in a local jail (James, 2004). Although early scholarly work reported that jail inmates were primarily members of the underclass held on relatively minor offenses (Goldfarb, 1975; Irwin, 1985), current research indicates that offenders in many urban jails are held on more serious crimes. In fact, Rainville and Reaves (2003, p. 33) found that nearly 75% of all persons sentenced to jail incarceration were felony offenders.

Organizational characteristics of jails might also contribute to gang membership. Jails hold a diverse mix of short- and long-term inmates, which can contribute to unpredictability. Although prison populations are fairly stable through periods of years, the population in a jail unit may change completely in a single week. Jails with high levels of population turnover are less predictable for jail officers and inmates alike (Richards, 2003). The short-term nature of jail confinement relative to prisons also makes classification and programming more challenging. Wright and Goring (1989) observed that "prisoners come in directly from the street as unknown quantities, often with alcohol, drug or psychiatric problems" (p. ii). A combination of this instability and high populations of gang-involved inmates recently led to riots involving thousands of inmates at a Southern California jail (Cable News Network, 2006).

Although the unpredictability of jail incarceration is bearable for a few days, it may contribute to gang affiliation as months stretch into a year. As Ross and Richards (2002) remark, "in some prisons you absolutely need to affiliate with a group that will protect you. The loners, the people without social skills or friends, are vulnerable to being physically attacked or preyed upon" (p. 133). Lhotsky (2000) describes the pressures to join a gang in a large urban jail: "Everything here is gang politics and you have to be involved, one way or another . . . and you better participate or you're gonna get beat bloody" (p. 213). Consequently, the characteristics of an individual jail or the types of inmates incarcerated within a facility (both the demographic and offense-related characteristics) may also contribute to gang membership (Santos, 2004).

Despite the problems that gang-affiliated inmates cause, there is some evidence to suggest that jails have been slow to adopt gang intervention programs, especially compared with state prison systems (see Wells et al., 2002). Moreover, there has been very little empirical attention devoted to the issue. This national-level study examines the prevalence of gang members in jails, based on information about the methods that jails use to classify gang involvement; perceptions about the types of problems that gang-affiliated inmates cause; and the efficacy of strategies intended to reduce the harm that gangs create in jails.

DATA AND METHOD

In June 2004, 418 surveys were sent to jails throughout the nation soliciting information from jail administrators about their experiences with "special needs" jail populations, including persons with mental illness, gang members, repeat offenders, and long-term inmates. With the exception of six states that had integrated state jail systems, all states were included in the sample. A random sample of jails was completed, choosing facilities listed in the American Jail Association's (2003) *Who's Who in Jail Management*. The exception to the random selection was an oversampling of large jails. Harrison and Beck (2005a) found that the largest 50 jails (mostly located in urban areas) held approximately 30% of all jail inmates, so all jails with a rated capacity of more than 1,500 inmates were surveyed.

To enhance the response rate, each facility was contacted by phone, and survey team members spoke with administrators and encouraged their participation. Survey instruments were either mailed or faxed to the administrators, although in some cases, the surveys were directed to mental health professionals or classification officers at the request of the official who was contacted. Responses to faxed surveys were somewhat better than those that were mailed and tended to be promptly returned. The survey instrument solicited responses from jail administrators about their experiences with gang members, including asking how gang affiliation or membership was defined, estimating the prevalence of these populations within their jail, and analyzing strategies that worked or that were not effective in responding to gangs. Although most respondents returned the survey within 2 or 3 weeks, we continued to receive responses to the survey for several months afterward. Altogether, 134 surveys from 39 states were returned, a response rate of approximately 32%.

There were several limitations with the survey results. Jails in the northeastern states, for example, were underrepresented in the surveys that were returned, as were returns from small jails. This underrepresentation rests on the sampling strategy used in this study. Integrated jail-prison systems in Alaska, Connecticut,

Delaware, Hawaii, Rhode Island, and Vermont were not sent surveys. Fewer surveys were also sent to smaller institutions, and the smallest jail that returned a survey had 28 beds. More than 10% of the sample were smaller jails, but the responses from these facilities were disappointing. Of one group of 25 facilities of 35 beds or less, for instance, only 1 was returned. It is plausible that larger jails are more likely to have classification experts, administrators, and mental health specialists who have more time to respond to such requests for information. Thus, the generalizability of the findings in this study is limited somewhat by the facilities that did not respond to the survey or were not included in the sampling strategy. Although the response rate was somewhat less than the Wells et al. (2002) study, the estimates in this research are based on a sample more than 3 times as large.

Table 7.1 reveals the organizational characteristics of the facilities that were represented in this study. With an average rated capacity of 941.8 inmates ($mdn = 512$ inmates), jails from large urban areas were overrepresented. The standard deviation of 1,279.37 inmates, however, indicates considerable skewness. Altogether, the facilities represented in the survey had a total rated capacity of 125,259 beds, or 19% of all jail inmates nationwide. The jails examined in this study were also smaller than those in the research reported by Wells et al., as the mean size of their sample was 5,638 beds.

Respondents reported that their facilities operated near capacity: The average jail operated at 94% of its rated capacity ($mdn = 91\%$, $SD = 26\%$). Based on the average daily population and admissions data, we extrapolated several statistics, including an average inmate turnover of approximately 31 inmates per year and an average stay of approximately 12 days. As most jail inmates only remain in custody for a day or two, this finding suggests that there are a large number of inmates who serve lengthy periods in county jails, either awaiting

Table 7.1 Jail Characteristics: National Jail Sample

Participating jails	134
States	39
Rated capacity (beds)	941.8 ($SD = 1,279.4$)
Average daily population	898.7 ($SD = 1,261.2$)
Percentage rated capacity	93.8 ($SD = 26.2$)
Daily cost	55.4 ($SD = 19.1$)
Turnover (annual admits/ average daily population)	30.8 ($SD = 64.4$)
Total rated capacity (beds)	125,259
Region	
Northeast	7
Midwest	36
South	45
West	4

their court dates, serving a sentence of less than 1 year, or some combination of these two factors. Consequently, one question on the survey asked respondents to estimate the percentage of inmates that had been in the jail for periods in excess of 1 year, and the mean was 12.7% *(mdn = 5.0%, SD - 16.8%)*.

RESULTS

Jail administrators were asked to select methods of classifying gang affiliation in their facilities. Table 7.2 outlines the five different options for classifying or defining gang membership that were provided. Respondents overwhelmingly reported that they defined gang membership on the basis of tattoos, clothing (gang colors), or hand signs, although designation of gang membership by another law enforcement agency was commonly used to define gang membership. Eighty-one percent of respondents reported that an individual's self-declaration as a gang member was used as a method of classification. Correspondingly, law enforcement agencies report frequent use of this technique as well (Egley & Major, 2004). It is important to report that there is considerable research that supports the validity of this measurement approach (see Esbensen et al., 2001). Furthermore, almost three quarters of respondents based definitions

Table 7.2   Jail Administrator Definitions of Gang Membership

	%	SD	*Range*
Inmate has been designated a gang member by another law enforcement agency	83.3		
Inmate has been identified as a gang member by a reliable informant	65.3		
Inmate claims to be a gang member	81.7		
Inmate displays symbols of membership: clothing, "colors," hand signs, or tattoos	86.8		
The inmate is known to associate with and/or has been arrested with known gang members	71.4		
Average reported gang membership (84 jails reporting estimates)	13.2	15.5	0 to 70
Jails reporting no gang membership (11 jails)[a]	131.1		
Jails reporting 1% to 10% gang membership (42 jails)	50.0		
Jails reporting 11% to 25% gang membership (19 jails)	21.4		
Jails reporting more the 25% gang membership (12 jails)	14.3		
Admissions of gang members have increased during past 5 years	45.0		
Gang members younger than other jail inmates	55.0		

Note: All figures are percentages.

a. Totals may not add up to 100% because of rounding.

of membership on the basis of the inmate's associates. Respondents were least likely, however, to base definitions of gang membership on claims by informants. These results indicate that self-report remains a viable and frequent method of identification among criminal justice practitioners. In addition, there is considerable overlap between police and jail methods of classification, extending the validity of the measurement approach to yet another group.

Using the methods of designating gang affiliation reported above, respondents were asked to estimate the prevalence of gang members in their jail. Fong and Buentello (1991) outline how correctional administrators have historically been reluctant to provide information to researchers about internal problems, such as gangs or gang violence. Anecdotal information from administrators suggests that gang members may not be forthcoming about their gang affiliation with classification or intake officers. As a result, the true rate of gang membership is likely to be undercounted in many places, especially if jails do not collect such data on admission or do not have gang intelligence officers that track these populations.

The mean (unweighted) estimate of gang membership among jail inmates was 13.2%, which closely approximates the national-level estimate of 16% reported by Wells et al. (2002). Estimates varied greatly, from 11 respondents who reported having no gang members in their facilities to 1 California jail administrator who reported that 70% of inmates in their facility were gang involved. In fact, by subtracting the facilities that reported having no gang members in their facility, the mean increased to 15.2%. Overall, half of the respondents estimated that the prevalence of gang members in their facilities ranged from 1% to 10%.

Table 7.3 presents the perceptions of jail administrators regarding the likelihood of problem behaviors in special needs populations. These problem behaviors included suicide, incidents of self-harm, victimization, assault (either inmates or staff), disruptive behavior within the facility, escapes (or attempts), or other criminal conduct. Gang members were compared to three other special needs populations: inmates with severe mental illness, "frequent flyers" (repeat offenders with more than 20 admissions), and long-term inmates (prisoners who had served more than 1 year of jail incarceration). A disruption index was calculated where 1 point was counted each time a respondent checked that a special needs group was likely to be involved in one of the disruptive behaviors listed above. Of a possible total value of 1,072 (if inmates were coded as being disruptive in all categories by all respondents),

Table 7.3 Perceptions of Jail Administrators on the Involvement of Special Needs Populations in Problem Behaviors

Population	Disruption[a]	Assault Inmates	Assault Staff
Gang members	367	44	65
Frequent flyers	233	78	81
Inmates with mental illness	610	78	81
Long-term inmates	201	35	21

a. Disruption Index = sum of the following categories; likelihood of suicide, self-harm, victimization, assault (other inmates of staff), disruptive behavior, escapes (or attempts), and other criminal conduct (highest possible value = 1,072).

inmates with mental illness had the highest disruption score of 610.4. Gang members followed with a value of 367, whereas the remaining groups had much lower scores. This finding reinforces the findings of previous research that found gang members represent a significant challenge to correctional operations (Fischer, 2001).

In addition to estimating the overall potential for disruption, perceptions of involvement in violent behavior were also collected. Jail administrators reported that gang members were more likely to assault other inmates than any other group of special needs inmates. Fischer's (2001) surveys of 463 Arizona prisoners found that inmates believe that inmates who are not members of a gang are safer than those who are: 69% said that inmates who are not members of a gang are very safe, safe, or somewhat safe, while only 57% said inmates who were members of *a* gang were very safe, safe, or somewhat safe (p. 172).

Furthermore, although inmates with mental illness were perceived as the most likely special needs group to assault officers and staff, gang members were also considered to pose a physical threat to jail staff.

Administrators were also asked about the efficacy of 10 different jail-based interventions to respond to gangs. Of the tactics presented in Table 7.4, the three that were considered most effective were segregation or

Table 7.4 Perceptions of Jail Administrators About the Efficacy of Gang Interventions (Percentage of Respondents)

Programs or Responses	Very Effective	Somewhat Effective	Not Effective	Not Applicable
Segregation or separation	36.2	30.8	1.5	31.5
Restrict outside visitors	10.9	15.5	5.4	68.2
Transfer (e.g., other jail)	5.5	20.5	4.7	69.3
Facility sanctions for gang behavior	27.5	36.6	6.1	29.8
Legal sanctions for gang behavior	11.6	20.9	9.3	58.1
Loss of "good time" credits	19.8	22.9	9.2	481
Information sharing (other agencies)	36.6	35.1	3.8	24.4
Intelligence gathering	33.1	39.2	3.1	24.6
Written policies or procedures	26.8	40.9	2.4	29.9
Limit program participation	15.4	26.9	11.5	46.2

Jails that report using none of these tactics = 15; jails that report using two or fewer of these tactics = 34.

separation of gang members, intelligence gathering, and sharing this information with other agencies. Thus, these results are consistent with the findings reported in the earlier national study of jail interventions (Wells et al., 2002) as well as Decker's (2003) research. It is interesting to note that for every category, the "not effective" category was the lowest for every intervention strategy. Stated differently, jail administrators were highly inclined to view any intervention strategy as effective.

The strategies perceived as least successful in reducing the influence of jail gangs were placing restrictions on outside visitors, transfers of gang members to other facilities, or legal sanctions for criminal behavior. Few administrators reported that they used these tactics, and those facilities that used these approaches did not deem them very effective. Transferring gang members is not, for example, a feasible approach in most local jails. Respondents also indicated that some approaches were ineffective, including the loss of "good time" credits and limiting program participation for gang-involved jail inmates.

The finding that 15 jail administrators reported their facilities used none of the interventions outlined above was surprising. Chi-square analyses were used to evaluate the relationships between the number of gang interventions used by a given jail (split at the median) and the following variables split at their median values: the daily cost to house an inmate, the estimated gang membership, and the rated capacity of the facility. Consistent with expectations, the only variable that had a significant association with high levels of gang interventions was the size of facility; larger facilities used a greater variety of interventions.

Discussion and Conclusion

This research examined the perceptions of jail administrators about the problems that gang members cause in their facilities, the prevalence of these populations, methods of classifying

gang membership, and approaches that may reduce the disruption or violence associated with these groups. The findings reported above suggest that the estimate of gang populations vary greatly by location, and although there were no statistically significant regional differences, smaller jails were less likely to report the presence of gangs. Although 11 facilities reported that they had no gang members in their populations, a number of jails reported that more than half of their populations were gang involved.

Estimating the true population of gang members is problematic, especially considering that there are different degrees of membership. Silverman (2001, p. 284) outlined seven different classifications of membership from hard core members to "sympathizers and wanna-be's." The United States Department of Justice (1992) estimated that hard core members represent only 15% to 20% of the total gang membership. It is important to distinguish between these different categories of gang membership, although there is little evidence to suggest this is regularly performed within prisons and jails. There is an intuitive conceptual appeal to the notion that strategies for long-term hard core members need to be fundamentally different than those who have less commitment to the gang.

Depending on the categories and methods of classifying gang members, estimates of the prevalence of gang members within jails are likely to vary greatly. The definition of gang membership used in this study was broadly inclusive in that it asked respondents to base their estimates on the five categories outlined in the survey and did not distinguish between "street-gangs," "prison-gangs" "unaffiliated gangs," and "STGs." Still, the finding that 13.2% of all jail inmates in this national sample were gang involved suggests that accurately estimating the gang populations is an important step for jail administrators. Extrapolating this estimate to the 2003 national jail population, for example, would result in 90,000 gang members held in American jails on any given day.

A second relevant research question is to evaluate the commitment to the gang of these 90,000 inmates: Are the estimates of 15% to 20% of hard core members accurate today? Is gang membership, for instance, a situational or temporary condition for most inmates? Furthermore, at what point of a person's incarceration does that person become gang affiliated? Knowing the answers to such questions may enable us to prevent gang affiliation in the first place or create more effective interventions to discourage jail inmates from joining such groups. Such questions can only be answered through further empirical work, including interviews with gang members.

Eleven jails reported having no gang members. Of these facilities, the mean rated capacity was 271 inmates *(mdn* = 119 beds), which is approximately one third the size of the average jail in this study. Yet one of the jails that reported having no gang members had a capacity of nearly 1,500 inmates, which does not seem plausible. Although rural communities are less likely than other localities to develop gang problems, a number of scholars have found that these areas are not immune to gangs (Egley & Major, 2004; Weisheit & Wells, 2004). It is likely that some administrators are not aware of the scope of the problem, are in denial, deliberately underreport the percentages of gang-involved inmates, or do not regard gangs as problematic (Fong & Buentello, 1991), concerns that apply elsewhere to law enforcement officials (Huff, 1990).

Most administrators reported that gang members challenged the operations of their facilities through illegal or disruptive behaviors and a greater involvement in violence. In response to these problems, jails have adopted a number of strategies to reduce the prevalence or harm that these special needs inmates pose. The foremost of these strategies was gathering intelligence and disseminating this information within the facility and to other law enforcement agencies. Also effective was the segregation or separation of gang-involved jail inmates, although this strategy may not be feasible in all locations or in some jails. An examination of the American Jail Association's (2003) national inventory of jails reveals that there are some 650 facilities of 25 beds or less, and these institutions are unlikely to have the ability to separate or segregate any inmate.

Despite the fact that most inmates serve short terms of temporary incarceration, there are long-term jail populations that may be vulnerable to gang recruitment. In some cases, inmates may serve years in local jails (James, 2004) and serve part (or all) of their state prison sentence there (see Ruddell, 2005). Moreover, of the estimated 13% of gang members in this sample, some may have weak ties with the gang. If jail-based interventions can prevent gang recruitment or prevent those "wannabes" from becoming full-fledged gang members, the benefits may be felt throughout justice systems. First, by reducing gang populations, jails will be safer. Safe jails are important not only from a human rights perspective, but high levels of violence might also contribute to increased membership as inmates affiliate themselves with gangs in search of safety (Lhotsky, 2000; Ross & Richards, 2002).

The second advantage of jail-based gang interventions is that jails serve as the entry point for prison populations. Reducing gang membership in local facilities and information sharing with state correctional systems may enhance the effectiveness of prison-based gang interventions. Furthermore, high-visibility interventions may deter nonaffiliated inmates from joining gangs by increasing the "costs" of membership. Some correctional systems, for instance, provide inmates with "guidelines" of the lost opportunities that occur when they affiliate with a gang (see Connecticut Department of Corrections, 1995).

One issue that requires careful consideration is whether society can provide realistic alternatives to the safety and status that gangs offer. Returning vulnerable young people from jails to the community with little hope of meaningful opportunities makes joining a gang more likely. Fleisher and Decker (2001a, pp. 69-70) outline the many barriers to successful reintegration of gang members into the community. Thus, although correctional interventions can attempt to reduce the prevalence of gangs and control their criminal behaviors within these institutions, these jail or prison-based programs need to be supplemented with a corresponding increase in community-based gang-intervention programs to support prisoner reentry.

REFERENCES

Adams, S., & Olson, D. E. (2002). *An analysis of gang members and non-gang members discharged from probation.* Springfield; Illinois Criminal Justice Information Authority.

American Jail Association. (2003). *Who's who in jail management.* Hagerstown, MD: Author.

Anti-Defamation League of B'nai B'rith. (2002). *Dangerous convictions: An introduction to extremist activities in prisons.* New York: Author.

Cable News Network. (2006). *One dead in California jail riot.* Retrieved February 8, 2006, from http://www.cnn.com/2006/US/02/04/prison.riot.ap/?section=cnn_mostpopular

California Board of Corrections. (2004). *Jail profile survey 2004, 1st quarter results.* Sacramento, CA: Author.

Camp, G. M., & Camp, C. G. (1985). *Prison gangs: Their extent, nature, and impact on prisons.* Washington, DC: U.S. Government Printing Office.

Connecticut Department of Corrections. (1995). *Gang membership.* Wethersfield, CP. Author.

Corrections Standards Authority. (2005). *Jail profile survey, 2005 3rd quarter results.* Sacramento, CA: Author.

Cunniff, M. A. (2002). *Jail crowding: Understanding jail population dynamics.* Washington, DC: National Institute of Corrections.

Davis, R. K., Applegate, B. K., Otto, C. W., Surette, R., & McCarthy, B. J. (2004). Roles and responsibilities: Analyzing local leaders' views on jail crowding from a systems perspective. *Crime & Delinquency, 50,* 458-482.

Decker, S. H. (2003). *Understanding gangs and gang processes.* Richmond: Eastern Kentucky University.

Egley, A. H., Howell, J. C., & Major, A. K. (2004). Recent patterns of gang problems in the United States: Results from the 1996-2002 National Youth Gang Survey. In F. Esbensen, L. Gaines, & S. G. Tibbetts (Eds.), *American youth gangs at the millennium* (pp. 90-108), Long Grove, IL: Waveland.

Egley, A. H., & Major, A. K. (2004). *Highlights of the 2002 youth gangs survey.* Washington, DC: Office of Juvenile Justice and Delinquency Prevention.

Esbensen, F., Winfree, L. T., He, N., & Taylor, T. J. (2001). Youth gangs and definitional issues: When is a gang a gang, and why does it matter? *Crime & Delinquency, 47,* 105-130.

Fischer, D. R. (2001). *Arizona Department of Corrections: Security threat group (STG) program evaluation, final report.* Retrieved September 25, 2004, from http://www.ncjrs.org/pdffiles1/nij/grants/197045.pdf

Fleisher, M. S., & Decker, S. H. (2001a). Going home, staying home: Integrating prison gang members into the community. *Corrections Management Quarterly, 5,* 65-77.

Fleisher, M. S., & Decker, S. H. (2001b). Overview of the challenge of prison gangs. *Corrections Management Quarterly, 5,* 1-9.

Fong, R. S., & Buentello, S. (1991). The detection of prison gang development: An empirical assessment. *Federal Probation, 55,* 66-69.

Fortune, S. H. (2003). *Inmate and prison gang leadership.* Unpublished doctoral dissertation, East Tennessee State University, Johnson City.

Gaes, G. G., Wallace, S., Gilman, E., Klein-Saffran, J., & Suppa, S. (2002). Influence of prison gang affiliation on violence and other prison misconduct. *The Prison Journal, 82,* 359-385.

Goldfarb, R. (1975). *Jails: The ultimate ghetto of the criminal justice system.* Garden City, NY: Anchor.

Harrison, P. M., & Beck, A. J. (2005a). *Prison and jail inmates at midyear 2004.* Washington, DC: Bureau of Justice Statistics.

Harrison, P. M., & Beck, A. J. (2005b). *Prisoners in 2004.* Washington, DC: Bureau of Justice Statistics.

Howell, J. C., Egley, A. H., & Gleason, D. K. (2002). *Modern day youth gangs.* Washington, DC:

Office of Juvenile Justice and Delinquency Prevention.

Huff, C. R. (1990). Denial, overreaction and misidentification: A postscript on public policy. In C. R. Huff (Ed.), *Gangs in America* (pp. 310-317). Newbury Park, CA: Sage.

Ingraham, B. L., & Wellford, C. F. (1987). The totality of conditions test in eighth-amendment litigation. In S. D. Gottfredson & S. McConville (Eds.), *America's correctional crisis: Prison populations and public policy* (pp.13-36). New York: Greenwood.

Irwin, J. (1985). *The jail: Managing the underclass in American society.* Berkeley: University of California Press.

James, D. J. (2004). *Profile of jail inmates, 2002.* Washington, DC: Bureau of Justice Statistics.

Kerle, K. E. (1998). *American jails: Looking to the future.* Boston: Butterworth-Heinemann.

Klein, M. W., & Maxson, C. L. (1996). *Gang structures, crime patterns and police responses.* Los Angeles: Social Science Research Institute.

Knox, G. W., & Tromanhauser, E. D. (1991). Gangs and their control in adult correctional institutions. *The Prison Journal, 71,* 15-22.

Lhotsky, N. (2000). The L.A. county jail. In R. Johnson & H. Toch (Eds.), *Crime and punishment: Inside views* (pp. 211-213). Los Angeles: Roxbury.

Mays, G. L., & Ruddell, R. (2004, November). *Frequent flyers, gang-bangers, and old-timers: Understanding the population characteristics of jail populations.* Paper presented at the annual meetings of the American Society of Criminology, Nashville, TN.

McLearen, A, M., & Ryba, N. L (2003), Identifying severely mentally ill inmates: Can small jails comply with detection standards? *Journal of Offender Rehabilitation, 37,* 25-40.

Nadel, B. A. (1997). Slashing gang violence, not victims: New York City Department of Corrections reduces violent jail incidents through computerized gang tracking data base. *Corrections Compendium, 22,* 20-22.

Norris, T. (2001). Importance of gang-related information sharing. *Corrections Today, 63,* 96-99.

Olson, D. E., Dooley, B., & Kane, C. M. (2004). *The relationship between gang membership and inmate recidivism.* Springfield: Illinois Criminal Justice Authority.

Rainville, G., & Reaves, B. A. (2003). *Felony defendants in large urban counties.* Washington, DC: U.S. Department of Justice.

Ralph, P. H., & Marquart, J. W. (1991). Gang violence in Texas prisons. *The Prison Journal, 71,* 38-49.

Richards, S. C. (2003). My journey through the Federal Bureau of Prisons. In S. C. Richards & J. I. Ross (Eds.), *Convict criminology* (pp. 120-149). Belmont, CA: Thompson/Wadsworth.

Rivera, B. D., Cowles, E. L., & Dorman, L. G. (2003). Exploratory study of institutional change: Personal control and environmental satisfaction in a gang-free prison. *The Prison Journal, 83,*149-170.

Ross, J. L., & Richards, S. C. (2002). *Behind bars: Surviving prison.* Indianapolis, IN: Alpha Books.

Ruddell, R. (2005). Long-term jail populations: A national assessment *American Jails, 19,* 22-27.

Santos, M. G. (2004). *About prison.* Belmont, CA: Thompson/Wadsworth.

Sherman, L. W., Gottfredson, D., MacKenzie, D., Eck, J., Reuter, P., & Bushway, S. (1997). *Preventing crime: What works, what doesn't, what's promising.* Washington, DC: U.S. Department of Justice.

Silverman, I. (2001). *Corrections: A comprehensive review.* Belmont, CA: Wadsworth.

Stastny, C., & Tymauer, G. (1983). *Who rules the joint? The changing political culture of maximum-security prisons in America.* Lanham, MD: Lexington Books.

Stephan, J. J. (2001). *Census of jails, 1999.* Washington, DC: Bureau of Justice Statistics.

Tartaro, C. (2002). The impact of density on jail violence. *Journal of Criminal Justice, 30,*499-510.

U.S. Department of Justice. (1992). *Management strategies in disturbances and with gangs/disruptive groups* Washington, DC: Author.

Weisheit R. A., & Wells, L. E. (2004). Youth gangs in rural America. *National Institute of Justice Journal, 251,* 2-7.

Wells, J. B. Minor, K. I., Angel, E., Carter, L., & Cox, M. (2002). *A study of gangs and security threat groups in America's adult prisons and jails.* Indianapolis, IN: National Major Gang Task Force.

Wright, C., & Goring, S. (1989). Litigation can stop unnecessary jail building. *National Prison Project Journal, 18,* i-vii.

DISCUSSION QUESTIONS

1. Why do Ruddell and colleagues study jails specifically?

2. How did these researchers go about studying jails throughout the country? Did they use random sampling techniques to obtain their sample?

3. What would be the units of analysis in this study?

4. What techniques did these researchers use to try to increase response rates? What was their final response rate? What are some of the limitations of their obtained sample?

5. According to the results from their survey data (Table 7.1), what are the various ways in which jail administrators define gang activity?

6. According to Table 7.3, which special needs populations are the most problematic for jails?

7. According to jail administrators (Table 7.4), what are the most effective responses to problematic gang behavior? What are the least effective responses?

8. According to these researchers' results, if they generalized their findings, how many jail inmates nationwide would be gang involved?

9. What are some of the implications from this research for administrators of jails?

RESEARCH READING

Tewksbury and Mustaine use survey research to study the perceptions of prison staff regarding appropriate programs and services for inmates. Most research on prison amenities focuses on what the public thinks prisoners should and should not be provided in a correctional setting. These researchers decided it may be more appropriate to ask those closest to the inmates, the correctional staff, about services and resources for inmates. The subjects of their research are prison staff from six institutions in Kentucky. These institutions were chosen because of the different types of inmates they house. The results are from 554 surveys returned to the researchers and generally show that correctional staff believes that prisoners should be afforded amenities; however, these views are dependent on the education, experience, and position held by the staff member.

Source: Tewksbury, R., & Mustaine, E. E. (2005). Insiders' views of prison amenities: Beliefs and perceptions of correctional staff members. *Criminal Justice Review, 30*(2), 174–188. Copyright © 2005 Sage Publications. Published by Sage Publications on behalf of Georgia State University Research Foundation.

INSIDERS' VIEWS OF PRISON AMENITIES

Beliefs and Perceptions of Correctional Staff Members

Richard Tewksbury and Elizabeth Ehrhardt Mustaine

Abstract: Existing research on views of prison amenities has largely focused on the general public. This research assesses the perceptions and views of correctional staff regarding what should be provided. Based on data from 554 Kentucky Department of Corrections staff members, results show that correctional staffers tend to have favorable views regarding the presence of prison amenities. Furthermore, analyses of patterns and trends across types of jobs, experience, and educational attainment show that prison staffers are accepting of most particular amenities. Finally, views on prison amenities are related to one's position and length of experience in the prison, as well as one's educational level. Policy and practical implications are discussed.

INTRODUCTION

As American correctional institutions continue to expand in number and population (Harrison & Beck, 2005), they increasingly become points of political and community attention (see No Frills Prison Act of 1996; Hensley, Miller, Tewksbury, & Koscheski, 2003). Much discourse in this arena focuses on issues of the consequences of incarceration (for society in general and offenders in particular) and what (if anything) should be done with, for, and to inmates. Should correctional administrators attempt to rehabilitate offenders, or should prisons simply warehouse offenders in stark and sparse conditions? Should inmates be provided with access to products, services, and opportunities that those at the bottom of society's economic structure are unable to access? Where is the line regarding what should and should not be available for prison inmates? These questions form the basis of the present study. What products, services, and programmatic opportunities do correctional staff persons believe are appropriate and inappropriate for incarcerated offenders? And how do variations in staff members' characteristics influence these beliefs?

Both the debate about and research assessing the beliefs of individuals (and categories of individuals) regarding the appropriateness of providing various amenities to inmates are fairly recent developments (e.g., No Frills Prison Act of 1996; Applegate, 2001; Hensley et al., 2003; Johnson, Bennett, & Flanagan, 1997; Lenz, 2002). Only during the past two decades has a discussion of whether inmates should have access to a variety of products, services, and programs been popularly debated. And research about attitudes and beliefs concerning inmates' access to amenities is a recently emerging and underdeveloped field (Applegate, 2001; Bryant & Morris, 1998; Hensley et al., 2003; Johnson et al., 1997; Lenz, 2002).

This study endeavors to add to this underdeveloped field by considering the views of correctional staff about a variety of prison amenities as well as assess any relationship between these views and correctional staff characteristics. In short, the present study goes beyond the limited available literature and assesses the perceptions of a wide range of correctional staff regarding the provision of a large number of potential prison amenities. Without consideration of how those charged with carrying out the day-to-day tasks and functions of corrections, even the best intended policies and directives may go unheeded or be implemented in ways contrary to what may be intended. To disregard the perceptions, values, beliefs, and attitudes of frontline correctional staff is to ignore the most important population regarding correctional practices.

REVIEW OF THE LITERATURE

The Public Debate Regarding Prison Amenities

At the core of the debate about what prison inmates should and should not be allowed to have or have access to is the concept of least eligibility. In short, the principle of least eligibility is the idea that "prisoners should not be given programs and services or live under conditions that are better than those of the lowest classes of the noncriminal population in society" (Champion, 2005, p. 200). According to this way of thinking, convicted and incarcerated offenders should not be provided with anything better than that provided or accessible to anyone in the general population. This is contrasted with those who take the position that by incarcerating an individual, the state assumes responsibility for providing for that individual's needs because the inmate is unable to do so oneself (the principle of *parens patriae)*.

Since the mid-1990s. there has been a sharp shift toward limiting prison inmates' access to amenities and to removing extras and luxuries from inside prisons. The most important stimulus in this movement was the passage of the 1996 federal legislation known as the No Frills Prison Act. This law prohibits in-cell televisions (except for inmates in segregation); coffee pots; hot plates; movies rated R, X, or NC-17; boxing, wrestling, or any martial art, bodybuilding, and weightlifting equipment; and possession of any personal electronics or musical instruments in federal prisons. This development also spurred state Departments of Corrections (DOCs) to pass similar state-level legislation or to remove many inmate amenities by

administrative action (see Corrections Compendium, 2002).

Where access to amenities has been maintained, access has been restricted (or curtailed) through the imposition of fees for services. According to a survey of state DOCs in 2002, the legal developments of the mid- to late 1990s did create a "trend for decreased privileges . . . and will likely continue in the future" (Corrections Compendium, 2002, pp. 8-9). The restrictions on luxuries has led to the prohibition of smoking in 53% of American prisons. R-rated movies are not allowed in 58% of prisons, and many institutions and systems have strict restrictions on books and magazines (e.g., no magazines more than 3 months old, only one book to be in an inmate's possession at a time; Corrections Compendium, 2002).

The movement toward no frills prisons appears to be in response to a perceived political belief that the public wants prisons to be austere environments. However, the veracity of this assumption has not been supported by the research literature (Applegate, 2001; Bryant & Morris, 1998; Hensley et al., 2003; Lenz, 2002). Correctional administrators largely believe that removing all amenities may pose safety risks and seriously restrict their abilities to manage inmate behavior through the availability of incentives and rewards (see below).

THE PRESENT STUDY

The present study seeks to fill the gap in our knowledge regarding how criminal justice staff—and prison staff specifically and most interestingly—perceive what are and are not appropriate programs, services, and resources for inmates. This represents a first step in assessing how those most closely associated with prison life perceive the value of amenities for institutional operations.

The existing public opinion data focus only on residents of Florida. Instead, we focus on a broad cross section of correctional staff in a medium-sized prison population (approximately 16,000) in the state of Kentucky. Our goal is to identify the views of prison staff regarding what programs, services, and resources should and should not be provided inmates. Additionally, to inform policies and policy makers, we examine patterns across job categories, demographics and levels of institutional experience, and educational attainment.

Method

Data for the present study were gathered via surveys administered to all staff working at 6 (of the 14) prisons in the Commonwealth of Kentucky during spring 2003. The institutions studied were chosen to provide diversity in the sample: one maximum security prison (average daily population [ADP] = 807), a special needs prison (ADP = 1,852), a reception and assessment center (ADP = 960), a medium security prison (ADP = 1,075), a minimum security institution (ADP = 552), and a women's institution (ADP = 697). All staff members, both those employed by the DOCs and those employed by other agencies, with their primary work assignment at one of the 6 selected prisons were provided an explanatory cover letter and copy of the research instrument with paychecks. Wardens of each institution also provided either written or e-mail encouragement and reminders to their institution's staff members to complete the survey.

The data collection instrument is a five-page, 68-item questionnaire. Staff members receiving the instrument were informed of the voluntary and anonymous nature of the project as well as the identity and both the university and DOC affiliation of the researcher. Instructions were provided both in the cover letter and at the end of the survey for returning the instrument. Locked survey collection boxes were provided to each institution and located either immediately inside the main entrance or in a high-traffic staff area (i.e., break room) for depositing completed surveys.

Survey collection boxes were kept in place for 2 weeks. After that time, all surveys were collected, coded, and evaluated.

Description of Sample

A total of 554 usable surveys were returned. Approximately 1,590 surveys were distributed; thus, the response rate is 34.9%. Although this is not a large response rate, it is adequate and the sample does fairly accurately reflect the sex and race characteristics of Kentucky correctional staff in general. Kentucky correctional staff members are 64.8% men and 35.2% women. Ninety-three percent of the staff members are White, with 7% all other races (L. Gillis, personal communication, October 24, 2003).

For this sample (see Table 7.5), in terms of demographics, respondents are 61.7% male and 38.3% female, and the mean age is 42.9 years. More than one quarter of individuals (28.4%) hold a 4-year college degree (with 11.6% of the sample also having a graduate degree). A near equal percentage (27.1%) reports a high school diploma or GED with no college courses completed. Of the sample, 43.7% report having attended college but not completing a 4-year bachelor's degree. It is important to note that the vast majority of respondents self-report their race as White (92.5%); therefore, it is not possible to assess differences and similarities in perspectives and views of Kentucky DOC staff by race.

Finally, one half (49.7%) of the sample reports working in security. An additional quarter (23.7%) of the sample works in programs. One in 6 respondents (16.6%) is from administration, and 1 in 10 (9.9%) is in a support services job. Respondents report a mean of 9 years and 8 months of experience working in corrections, with one half of the sample having at least 7 years and 2 months of experience.

Table 7.5 Description of Sample

	n	%
Sex		
Male	333	61.7
Female	207	38.3
Race		
White	493	92.5
Non-white	40	7.5
Education		
Less than high school/GED	4	0.7
High school graduate/GED	147	27.1
Attended college, did not graduate	175	32.3
2-year college degree	62	11.4
4-year college degree	91	16.8
Graduate degree	63	11.6
Type of job		
Administration	89	16.6
Security	266	49.7
Programs	127	23.7
Support services (clerical, food service, physical, plant, etc.)	53	9.9

Note: Age (years), M = 42.9, Mdn = 43.0; time working in corrections, M = 9 years, 8 months, Mdn = 7 years, 2 months.

Description of Variables

The dependent variables, or variables of primary interest in this study, are the set of 26 prison amenities commonly used in this developing line of research. The list, originally proposed by Applegate (2001), asks respondents to "indicate whether you believe each item/activity should be eliminated for prison inmates or should be kept for inmates (in prisons where these are provided)" The 26 amenities are shown in the tables that follow.

Independent variables, or the variables used for comparison, are the respondents' types of jobs (administration; program staff-unit management, education, medical, mental health, industries, or library; security-correctional officer or supervisors; or other), educational attainments (less than a college graduate and graduated from college or more education), and lengths of experience working in corrections (short job tenure is 0 to 4 years on the job, mid-level job tenure is 5 to 12 years on the job, and longer job tenure is 13 or more years on the job).

The analysis of the data proceeds in two stages. First, we report correctional staff members' views on keeping or eliminating correctional amenities in general (as highlighted in Table 7.6). Next, we create cross-tabulation tables for these amenities by correctional staff members' types of jobs (Table 7.7) and compute Pearson's chi-square statistic to assess any differences in the relationship between these groups and their views on particular correctional amenities.

Findings: Staff Members' Views of Prison Amenities

The focus of the present research concerns the views of correctional staff members regarding whether any of the available programs, services, and resources (commonly referred to as amenities) should be retained or eliminated in prisons. We assess this in general as well as consider whether any of three correctional staff characteristics (type of job, length of tenure, and educational attainment) are related to their views on these amenities.

Specifically, Table 7.6 reports the percentages of staff members who report that they believe each of the assessed amenities should be kept in prisons where they are available. The table also provides a rank ordering of the amenities, starting with the amenity that received the most support for retention and ending with the amenity that received the least support for retention (or the most support for elimination). This analysis of frequency can highlight the views of staff about particular amenities as well as give some information about the types of amenities that are seen as the most and least worthy.

To elaborate, as can be seen, there are 12 amenities that at least 90% of staff believe should be retained in prisons; these include items that represent such areas as basic prison conditions (psychological counseling, books, supervised visits with family, telephone calls, and air conditioning), educational programming (job training, GEO classes, and basic literacy programs), and

some forms of mild entertainment (radios and tape players, basic television, and newspapers and magazines). Additionally, there are six amenities (boxing and martial arts, conjugal visits, pornography, condoms, R-rated movies, and cable TV) that a majority of staff persons believe should be eliminated from prison.

The remaining amenities (HIV/AIDS treatment, arts and crafts, legal assistance, law books and legal libraries, weightlifting equipment, college education programs, cigarettes and tobacco, and tennis) are items believed by at least two thirds of staff members to be appropriate for prison. These items do not receive the same resounding support as the top amenities listed (all with more than 90% support for retention) but are still viewed as being valuable for a successful prison experience for inmates and/or successful maintenance of prison security and safety of those there (inmates and staff). As a whole, then, it is interesting to note that with the exception of six amenities, the majority of the Kentucky prison staff members felt that most of the amenities available in prisons should be kept. It is also interesting to note that several amenities that did not receive more than 90% support are amenities that have legal mandates for prisons to offer (HIV treatment and law libraries).

This is similar to Applegate's (2001) findings that the Florida public was more supportive of prison amenities than perhaps previously assumed. Fully 19 of the 26 amenities assessed were supported by the majority of those persons interviewed. Additionally, as a point of interest, the amenities supported for retention as well as those supported for elimination are very similar for those reported as such by Applegate's Florida citizens and the correctional staff in the present study. (Amenities marked for elimination in Applegate's study were identical to those in the present study, with the exceptions that the majority of the Florida public felt that tennis and cigarettes and other tobacco should be eliminated and conjugal visits should be kept.)

Of course, correctional staff members' views on amenities may be influenced by their personal attributes. As such, we turn to the cross-tabulation analysis to assess any differences in

Table 7.6 Percentage of Correctional Staff Members Believing Amenities Should Be Kept

Amenity	% Staff Advocating to Keep Amenity
Books	98.3
Psychological counseling	96.8
Basic literacy programs	96.4
Supervised family visits	96.2
GED classes	95.1
Basketball	94.8
Newspapers and magazines	93.9
Basic TV (no cable)	93.8
Telephone calls	92.2
Radios and tape players	92.0
Job training programs	91.4
Air conditioning	91.2
HIV/AIDS treatment	87.4
Art and crafts	86.8
Legal assistance	81.3
Law books and legal library	77.7
Weightlifting equipment	64.6
College education programs	62.8
Cigarettes and other tobacco	62.3
Tennis	56.2
Cable TV	47.1
R-rated movies	35.5
Condoms	19.9
Pornography	17.6
Conjugal visiting	12.5
Boxing and martial arts	12.3

Table 7.7   Results of Cross-Tabulations on Attitudes About Keeping Prison Amenities by Correctional Staff Position

Amenity	% Administrators	% Security Staff	% Program Staff	Pearson χ^2
Books	98.8	98.0	99.2	0.784
Psychological counseling	97.6	96.1	98.3	1.618
Basic literacy programs	98.8	95.2	98.3	3.945
Supervised family visits	97.6	95.3	98.3	2.688
GED classes	98.8	91.8	100	15.211*
Basketball	97.6	93.7	95.7	2.176
Newspapers and magazines	97.6	91.7	983	8.897*
Basic TV (no cable)	95.2	93.9	95.0	0.294
Telephone calls	88.2	92.5	95.9	4.243
Radios and tape players	92.9	90.2	95.8	3.630
Job training programs	96.4	86.6	97.5	15.773*
Air conditioning	92.9	92.0	94.2	0.556
HIV/AIDS treatment	97.6	82.0	90.0	15.772*
Arts and crafts	91.7	82.8	91.7	7.807*
Legal assistance	90.6	78.6	893	10.511*
Law books and legal library	88.7	72.1	91.7	20.797*
Weightlifting equipment	66.7	58.7	74.2	8.694*
College education programs	75.0	53.5	74.8	22.035*
Cigarettes and other tobacco	61.2	59.7	65.3	1.089
Tennis	59.8	53.5	59.8	1.788
Cable TV	49.4	44.3	52.9	2.590
R-rated movies	31.0	32.0	45.4	7.173*
Condoms	16.5	12.7	41.4	40.439*
Pornography	7.1	20.6	16.8	8.087*
Conjugal visiting	11.8	11.1	14.5	0.845
Boxing and martial arts	12.2	10.0	20.0	7.209*

* $t < .05$.

views on prison amenities by several correctional staff member characteristics (type of job, job tenure, and educational attainment). For this part of the analysis, we create cross-tabulation tables and use Pearson's chi-square statistic. We test the significance of the statistic (that assesses whether there is any relationship between the two variables in the table) with a two-tailed t test. Using cross-tabulation tables and the chi-square statistic is the appropriate mode of analysis for this type of comparison between groups because data for all variables are nominal (as such, ANOVA, paired t tests, and other such similar procedures are inappropriate, as they require at least one variable to be numeric; Hopkins, 2000).

Turning to Table 7.7, when examining differences across staff members based on type of job, some variation comes forth. As noted above, for this comparison, we use three broad categories of jobs (administration, security, and programs). Specifically, for 13 of the amenities, there is a significant relationship between the three types of correctional staff positions and their views on the particular amenity. First, for several of the amenities, it appears that it is security staff members who have a distinctive view from both administrators and program staff members. These seven amenities are GED classes, newspapers and magazines, job training programs, arts and crafts, legal assistance, law books and legal library, and college education programs. In all cases, security staff members have a lower level of support for retention of these amenities than do administrators and program staff members. For example, although 98.8% and 100% of administrators and program staff members are in support of the retention of GED classes for inmates in prisons, only 91.8% of security officers feel these classes should be retained. Certainly, it is the case that, overall, the vast majority of correctional staffers in general are supportive of this program. Nonetheless, a noticeably higher proportion of security officers do not support inmates taking classes to get their GEDs. Other examples are that fewer security staff members support job training programs, arts and crafts, college

education programs, newspapers and magazines, law library and legal books, and legal assistance (even though they are, for the most part, supportive of these programs) than administrators and program staff.

For three of the amenities, where there is a significant relationship between the type of job held and views on prison amenities, it appears that it is program staffers that have the distinct view. In all cases, they are significantly more likely to favor retaining the amenity than are administrators and security staff members. To elaborate, 45.4%, 41.4%, and 20% of program staff members are in favor of retaining R-rated movies, condoms, and boxing and martial arts programs, respectively. Fewer administrators (31%, 16.5%, and 12.2%, respectively) and security staff (32%, 12.7%, and 10%, respectively) support retaining these amenities.

Views on pornography are significantly related to type of job held, and in this case, it appears that administrators have the most distinctive view. Security and program staff members have similar amounts of support for the retention of pornography in prisons (20.6% and 16.8%, respectively), whereas very few administrators support retaining pornography (7.1%).

Finally, three amenity views that are significantly related to type of job held seem to have distinct views across all job categories. To specify, administrators are the most likely to support the retention of HIV/AIDS treatment (97.6%), fewer program staffers favor HIV/AIDS treatment (90.9%), and still fewer security staff want to keep HIV/AIDS treatment (82%). In this case, it may be that administrators are the most in favor of this amenity because they know it is legally mandated (but we did not directly test this assertion). Weightlifting equipment seems to be another amenity that has distinctive views across all types of jobs. Specifically, security staff have the least amount of support for it (58.7%), administrators are next with 66.7% being in support of retaining it, and the highest proportion of program staff members support keeping weightlifting equipment (74.2%). Obviously, staff members' types of jobs in prison have significant influences over their views on the retention or elimination of various prison amenities.

Discussion and Conclusion

The present study has endeavored to provide a first look at the views of correctional staff members regarding the retention or elimination of various prison amenities. Previous research has examined the attitudes of citizens as well as prison wardens, but we know very little about the views of other correctional staff members, especially those with frequent and intense inmate contact. Additionally, the present study has examined the relationship between these views and several correctional staff member characteristics.

The current study has illustrated that correctional staff members generally support the retention of most assessed amenities. There are only four amenities that received less than 20% support for retention (boxing and martial arts, conjugal visiting, pornography, and condoms), and only two additional amenities that received more than one third but less than one half support for retention (cable TV and R-rated movies). For the remaining amenities, at least a majority of the correctional staff members surveyed supported their retention in prison. Additionally, nearly half (12) of the amenities assessed received support for retention by at least 90% of the sample. This is an instructive finding. Those who actually work in the prison setting, as administrators, security staff members, or program staff members, are generally supportive of most of the prison services, programs, and activities that are currently offered (at least in some facilities) to inmates. Obviously, the belief is that there is at least some tangible benefit to having these amenities available to inmates.

References

Applegate, B. (2001). Penal austerity: Perceived utility, desert, and public attitudes toward prison amenities. *American Journal of Criminal Justice, 25,* 253-268.

Applegate, B., Cullen, F. T., Turner, M. G., & Sundt, J. L. (1996). Assessing public support for three-strikes-and-you're-out laws: Global versus specific attitudes. *Crime & Delinquency, 42,* 517-534.

Bryant, P., & Morris, E. (1998). What does the public really think? A survey of the general public's perceptions of corrections yields some surprising results. *Corrections Today, 59,* 26-28,79.

Bureau of Economic and Business Research. (1997). *Corrections in Florida: What the public, news media, and Department of Corrections staff think.* Available at www.dc.state.fl.us

Champion, D. J. (2005). *The American dictionary of criminal justice.* Los Angeles: Roxbury.

Corrections Compendium. (2002). Inmate privileges and fees for service. *Corrections Compendium, 27,* 8-26.

Cullen, F. T., Fisher, B. S., & Applegate, B. K. (2000). Public opinion about punishment and corrections. In M. Tonry (Ed.), *Crime and justice: A review of research. Vol. 27* (pp. 1-79). Chicago: University of Chicago Press.

Harrrison, P., & Beck, A. (2005). *Prison and jail inmates at midyear 2004.* Washington, DC: Bureau of Justice Statistics.

Hensley, C., Miller, A., Tewksbury, R., & Koscheski, M. (2003). Student attitudes toward inmate privileges. *American Journal of Criminal Justice, 27*(2), 249-262.

Hopkins, W. G. (2000). A new view of statistics. *Internet Society for Sport Science.* Retrieved January 23, 2005, from http//www.sportsci .org/resource/stats/

Johnson, W., Bennett, K., & Flanagan, T. (1997). Getting tough on prisoners: Results from the national corrections executive survey, 1995. *Crime & Delinquency, 43,* 24-41.

Keil, T. J., & Vito, G. F. (1991). Fear of crime and attitudes toward capital punishment: A structural equations model. *Justice Quarterly, 8*(4), 447-464.

Lenz, N. (2002). "Luxuries" in prison: The relationship between amenity funding and public support. *Crime & Delinquency, 48,*499-523.

Whitehead, J. T., & Blankenship, M. B. (2000). The gender gap in capital punishment attitudes: An analysis of support and opposition. *American Journal of Criminal Justice, 25,* 1-13.

DISCUSSION QUESTIONS

1. What are some of the differing views about the level of amenities that prisoners should be afforded? What are correctional staff members worried about that the general population probably does not think about?

2. Why did Tewksbury and Mustaine choose these six prisons?

3. Describe the general methods used by these researchers to administer the survey.

4. What was the response rate in this study? What do the authors say about response rate and the characteristics of their sample versus the population of correctional staff in Kentucky? According to Table 7.5, what do typical correctional officers look like? Are they well educated, in your opinion?

5. According to Table 7.6, which amenities receive the most support from correctional staff? The least?

6. How do the responses vary by the type of position a staff member has? Which position gives the most support for the least supported amenities? Do the authors discuss why the position one has might affect their views?

7. What is the reason given by these researchers for the generally high level of support for amenities for inmates?

RESEARCH READING

Decker and colleagues use interviews of two samples of juveniles housed at detention facilities in Arizona to examine the organization and structure of gangs and how the level of organization of a gang affects the amount of crime it is involved in. These researchers build off the framework of previous research, which has revealed that (1) gangs are not well organized, and (2) that a gang's organizational structure has no affect on the gang's behavior. They hypothesize that gangs that are better organized will be more involved in crime. They conduct their analysis of ADAM (Arrestee Drug Abuse Monitoring) data, which uses face-to-face interviews of arrestees to gather information about gang affiliation and criminal behavior. The findings from these interviews with juveniles suggest that gang organizational structure is related to the level of involvement in crime of its members.

Source: Decker, S., Katz, C., & Webb, V. (2008). Understanding the black box of gang organization: Implications for involvement in violent crime, drug sales, and violent victimization. *Crime & Delinquency*, *54*, 153–172. Copyright © 1992 Sage Publications.

UNDERSTANDING THE BLACK BOX OF GANG ORGANIZATION

Implications for Involvement in Violent Crime, Drug Sales, and Violent Victimization

Scott H. Decker, Charles M. Katz, and Vincent J. Webb

Abstract: This article examines the influence of gang organization on several behavioral measures. Using interview data from juvenile detention facilities in three Arizona sites, this article examines the relationship between gang organizational structure and involvement in violent crime, drug sales, victimization, and arrest. The gang literature suggests that gangs are not very well organized. However, the findings from the current research suggest that even low levels of gang organization are important for their influence on behavior. Indeed, even incremental increases in gang organization are related to increased involvement in offending and victimization.

INTRODUCTION

The role of gangs in crime has been examined in a large body of research (Esbensen & Huizinga, 1993; Thornberry, Krohn, Lizotte, & Chard-Weirschem, 1993). At the individual level, a growing body of research has documented that gang membership has a disproportionate impact on crime. Individuals commit more crimes while in a gang, and those crimes tend to be more serious than when individuals are not gang members. On the intervention side, there is ample evidence that dealing with gang members is more difficult than dealing with nongang offenders (Klein, 1995). Gang members who end up in prison also have longer and more serious involvement in crime than comparable nongang individuals (Fleisher & Decker, 2001).

Research on the aggregate impact of gangs in many large cities has been equally consistent. This research finds that cities with more gangs have more crimes of violence concentrated in those neighborhoods with high levels of gang presence (Klein, 1995). In addition, this research finds that the longer cities have gangs, the more difficult it is to eradicate those gangs (Spergel, 1995). Gangs also provide impediments to prevention, intervention, and suppression efforts.

These consistent findings about the salience of the relationship between gang membership and crime raise an important issue about the nature of the gang itself. Despite the considerable knowledge that has accumulated regarding the impact of gangs on crime, there is considerably less knowledge about the organizational and structural characteristics of gangs themselves. In a sense, gangs largely have been a "black box"; that is, little is known about the nature of the gang with regard to its structure and organization. Given the current dearth of knowledge of these characteristics, it comes as little surprise that there is a lack of knowledge of the relationship between such characteristics and the behavior of members. The current study attempts to fill these gaps, focusing on the structural and organizational features of gangs and the influence of these characteristics on the behavior of gang members. In this sense, we seek to better understand the role of structural and organizational aspects of the gang on gang member behavior.

THE PRESENT STUDY

Despite these advances in our understanding of the structural and organizational features of gangs, there is not enough information to specify how the organizational and structural characteristics of gangs affect criminal behavior and victimization. Stated differently, we know a fair amount about gang structures but very little about their relationship to behavior. This is a crucial omission from our understanding of gangs. After all, understanding gang structures and gang behavior without knowing their influence on behavior and victimization falls short of providing an explanation of the influence of such characteristics. Although this may seem obvious, gang research has provided more descriptive literature than analyses of relationships between gang characteristics and behavior, a notable omission. This article provides evidence about and examines in greater detail the relationship between gang structure and the behavior of gang members.

We hypothesize that members of gangs with stronger organizational structures will have higher levels of involvement in crime, commit more serious offenses, be arrested more often, and be victims of violent crime more often. These hypotheses are consistent with the enhancement approaches outlined by Thornberry, Krohn, Lizotte, Smith, and Tobin (2003), who suggest that group norms and group processes work together to increase involvement in offending while individuals are in a gang (p. 99). Group norms and group processes have a locus, which we suggest can be found in the organizational structure of the gang. We propose a similar link between gang membership and victimization. One of the most important findings in criminology in the past decade is the link between victimization and offending. Using multiple waves from the National Youth Survey, Lauritsen, Sampson, and Laub (1991) note a strong relationship between involvement in a delinquent lifestyle and victimization, particularly for males. We hypothesize that membership in a gang is a suitable proxy for involvement in a delinquent lifestyle, particularly as gang membership enhances involvement in offending.

It is important to point out from the start that this is not a test of gang member versus nongang member behavior, as much of the empirical work on gangs tends to be. Rather, this is a test of the influence of gang organization on several relevant behaviors as reported by individual gang members. The data used for the current study are particularly appropriate for this task in several ways. First, because the interviews were collected from arrestees, they represent more seriously involved juvenile offenders than school- or community-based samples. This may truncate the lower end of the distribution of gang involvement compared to at-large gang members, but is more likely to include more serious gang members. Second, the interviews were collected in three different sites in Arizona (Mesa, Phoenix, and Tucson), so the interview participants reflect more than just local enforcement practice. Finally, the demographic characteristics of gang members in this sample (race and ethnicity, gender, violent offending, drug sales, gang organization, victimization) are consistent with national trends reported by the National Youth Gang Center (Egley, 2002). The Arizona sites have a historic presence of gangs (Zatz, 1987; Zatz & Portillos, 2000), yet are not dominated by Los Angeles gangs. Finally, to provide the strongest test of these concepts, we examine the responses of current and former gang members separately. If there is consistency in the responses of these two groups, we can more strongly conclude that the findings accurately depict the relationship between organizational structure and behavior. Because there is some evidence that current and former gang members differ in their assessment of the gang (Curry, Decker, & Egley, 2002; Thornberry, Krohn, Lizotte, Smith, & Tobin, 2003), this is an important addition to any analysis of gang structure and gang behavior.

METHOD

The present study uses data collected as part of the Arrestee Drug Abuse Monitoring

(ADAM) program. The ADAM program, originally established in 1987 by the National Institute of Justice, was created to monitor drug use trends, treatment needs, and at-risk behavior among recently booked arrestees. The ADAM program collected data from recently booked arrestees in 35 sites across the United States. The data used here are from two sites. Maricopa and Pima County, Arizona (aka Arizona ADAM), that sample male and female juveniles. For 14 days each quarter, trained local staff at each site conducted voluntary and anonymous interviews with juveniles who had been arrested within the last 48 hrs. At both the Maricopa and Pima County sites the catchment area for the sample encompasses the entire county. However, only those juveniles who have been detained and booked by the police are available for the study. Just over 96% of approached juvenile arrestees agreed to participate in the study.

The core ADAM juvenile data collection instrument generates self-report data on a variety of sociodemographic and behavior variables. In this article, we focus on three demographic variables (gender, ethnicity, and age), exposure to gang activity and membership, gang crime (violent offending, drug sales), violent victimization, and gang organizational measures measured by the instrument. Gang membership was determined through self-nomination, a technique that has received strong support in the research literature (Curry, 2000; Curry, Decker, & Egley, 2002; Esbensen & Huizinga, 1993; Esbensen, Winfree, He, & Taylor, 2001; Klein, 1995). We further validated our definition of gang membership by asking respondents to name the gang they belonged to. This procedure helped distinguish between those who were members of informal peer groups and those who were members of actual gangs. Only respondents who provided the name of a gang were considered gang members for this study. As such, our final sample of gang members consisted of those who self-reported association with a gang and who could name the gang.

The Arizona Sample

Juvenile data in Arizona were collected between 1999 and 2003 in three different booking facilities located in Phoenix, Tucson, and Mesa. We combine data over multiple quarters of data collection and multiple catchment areas because of the need for large samples. However, there are considerable similarities across the three catchment areas, justifying the aggregation of data across multiple years and sites. The descriptive characteristics of the sample are presented in Table 7.8. Table 7.8 presents a format followed in subsequent tables in that data from current gang members are contrasted to results from individuals who report ever being a member, though not currently. With regard to gender, both current and former members are overwhelmingly male, with 87% of current members and 74% of former members being males. There is consistency between current and former gang members with regard to ethnic composition. The modal category for each group is Hispanic, with roughly 60% of each group falling into this category. Whites are the next largest group, 21% of current and 31% of former members. African Americans comprised 15% of current gang members and 8% of former members. With regard to age, roughly equal percentages of 15-(23%), 16-(27%), and 17-year-olds (24%) were found among current gang members. Former gang members were a little older with 17-year-olds (37%) and 16-year-olds (24%) being the two largest categories. Every individual who self-reported gang membership identified the name of their gang, adding additional validity to the self-nomination procedure.

For the majority of individuals in the sample, a misdemeanor was the most serious offense that led to their referral to the detention facility where they were interviewed. That said, 24% of current members and 31% of

Table 7.8   Characteristics of the Arizona ADAM Gang Samples

	Current Gang Member (N = 156; percentage)	Ever a Gang Member (N = 85; percentage)
Gender		
Male	87	74
Female	13	26
Ethnicity		
Hispanic	60	57
African American	15	8
White	21	31
American Indian	3	4
Other	1	
Age		
≤ 13	9	8
14	17	13
15	23	19
16	27	24
17	24	37
Most serious charge		
Felony	24	31
Misdemeanor	43	56
Status	7	13
Other	26	
Is there gang activity in your neighborhood? (percentage responding yes)	81	65
Are people who live on your street members of a gang? (percentage responding yes)	76	51
Are there rival gangs in your neighborhood? (percentage responding yes)	55	50
In your neighborhood, is there pressure to join a gang? (percentage responding yes)	26	14
Are there problems in your neighborhood because of gangs? (percentage responding yes)	55	37
During the past 12 months, have you been arrested and booked for breaking a law whether or not you were guilty? (percentage responding yes)		75

former gang members were referred for a felony. In addition, three quarters of each group reported that they had been arrested and booked for breaking the law at some time in the prior 12 months. Individuals in this sample were very familiar with gang activity. The majority of each group reported that there was gang activity in their neighborhood (81% of current, and 65% of former members), that people who lived on their street were members of a gang (76% and 51%, respectively), and that there were rival gangs in their neighborhood (55% and 50%). Though relatively small percentages of respondents indicated that there was pressure to join a gang in their neighborhood (26% and 14%), higher proportions reported that there were problems in their neighborhood because of gangs (55% and 37%). In sum, these two samples of youth were heavily involved in offending, and found themselves surrounded and influenced by gangs and gang activities. As such, these are appropriate samples with which to begin to understand the role of internal gang structure for gang behavior.

FINDINGS

In Table 7.9, we examine the four indices described above. The first index includes the measure of Gang Organization. Drawing from the earlier work of Decker, Bynum, and Weisel (1998) and Peterson, Miller, and Esbensen (2001), seven measures of gang organization were used to form an index of the level of gang organization. These measures include the presence of leaders, whether the gang had regular meetings, rules, punishment for breaking the rules, symbols of membership, responsibilities to the gang, and whether or not the members give money to the gang. These seven measures tap both the structure of the gang (leaders, rules, meetings, symbols) as well as behavior (punishment, responsibilities, and giving money) and represent important dimensions of how well organized a gang

is. For both current and former members, symbols drew the largest percentage of positive responses (89% and 84%), with giving money to the gang drawing the lowest percentage of positive responses (33% and 30%). Interestingly, the next smallest categories were for leaders (33% and 40%) and responsibilities to the gang (37% and 36%). A count index was constructed for these seven measures in which a "yes" response to each question about the organizational complexity of the gang was scored a "1" and summed across the seven measures. The mean for current members was 3.2 and for former members it was 4.5. This indicates a somewhat higher level of organizational complexity among gangs that former members were a part of, but in general a rather low level of organizational complexity. This is consistent with earlier work (Decker et al., 1998; Klein, 1995; Peterson et al., 2001; Zatz & Portillos, 2000), particularly because the individuals in this sample are juveniles.

The second index presented in Table 7.9 is Violent Victimization. We include seven variables: being threatened with a gun, being shot at, being shot, being threatened with another weapon, being injured with another weapon, being jumped or beaten up, and being robbed. These seven indicators tap into the major risks for violent victimization faced by gang members (Decker, 1996; Decker & Van Winkle, 1996; Sanders, 1994) and provide a measure of the extent to which gang members are at risk for being victims of violence. This is an important variable to examine in the context of the current analysis given our interest in the role of gang organization for involvement in criminal activities, and the link between violent offending and violent victimization (Lauritsen, Sampson, & Laub, 1991). Overall, these two samples were exposed to high levels of violent victimization. Seventy-five percent of current gang members and 62% of former gang members report being threatened with a gun. Being jumped or beaten up represented the modal category for each group with 82% of current members and 71% of former gang

Table 7.9 Organization, Violent Victimization, Drug Sale, and Violent Offending Index Measures

	Current Member	Ever Member
Gang organization index measures		
Does the gang have a leader?	33%	40%
Does the gang have regular meetings?	36%	46%
Does the gang have rules?	54%	46%
Is there punishment if rules are broken?	86%	79%
Does the gang have colors, symbols, signs, or clothes?	89%	84%
Do members have responsibilities to the gang?	37%	36%
Do members give money to the gang?	33%	30%
Range	0–7	0–7
Mean	3.2	4.5
Median	3.0	5.0
SD	1.9	1.9
Violent victimization index measures		
Have you ever been threatened with a gun?	75%	62%
Have you ever been shot at?	74%	57%
Have you ever been shot?	14%	11%
Have you ever been threatened with another weapon?	67%	59%
Have you ever been injured with some other weapon?	48%	31%
Have you ever been robbed?	28%	32%
Range	0–7	0–7
Mean	3.9	3.2
Median	4.0	3.0
SD	1.8	1.8
Drug sale index measures		
Does the gang sell marijuana?	80%	81%
Does the gang sell crack cocaine?	51%	50%
Does the gang sell powder cocaine?	53%	44%

	Current Member	Ever Member
Does the gang sell heroin?	17%	18%
Does the gang sell methamphetamine?	31%	30%
Does the gang sell drugs to other dealers?	56%	42%
Range	0–6	0–6
Mean	2.8	2.6
Median	3.0	3.0
SD	1.9	1.8
Violent crime index measures		
Does the gang intimidate or threaten others?	75%	80%
Does the gang rob people?	72%	57%
Does the gang jump or attack people?	80%	81%
Does the gang do drive-by shootings?	61%	50%
Does the gang kill people?	51%	37%
Range	0-5	0-5
Mean	2.8	3.0
Median	3.0	3.0
SD	1.9	1.5

members reporting that they had experienced this form of victimization. These results provide continued support for the observation that gang members are involved in a substantial amount of violence, certainly in this case as victims. The level of victimization as measured by this seven-item index is modestly higher for current gang members (3.9) than former members (3.2).

The third index provides a measure of involvement in drug sales. The involvement of gangs and gang members in drug sales has been a consistent theme in the research about gangs (Decker & Van Winkle, 1995; Fagan, 1989; Hagedorn, 1988, 1994a, 1994b, Maxson, Klein, & Cunningham, 1992; Skolnick, 1990). We employ six indicators of involvement in drug sales to measure this dimension of gang behavior. Five of them ask specifically whether or not the gang sells a specific drug, including marijuana, powder cocaine, crack cocaine, heroin, and methamphetamines. The sixth measure asks whether the gang sells drugs to other drug dealers. It is important to note that in each case the question is whether the *gang* sells a particular type of drug rather than individual gang members. Not surprisingly, marijuana was the drug most likely to be sold by gangs (80%, 81%), followed by crack cocaine (51%, 50%) and powder cocaine (53%, 44%). The mean number of drugs sold was 2.8 for current gang members and 2.6 for former gang members. It is interesting to note that a majority of current gang members, 56%, report that their gang was involved in the sale of drugs to other dealers.

The fourth and final index that was developed for this analysis was an indicator of involvement in violent offending. Again, there is strong evidence in the literature that gangs are heavily involved in the commission of acts of violence (Decker, 2000; Maxson & Klein, 1990; Thornberry, Krohn, Lizotte, Smith, & Tobin, 2003; Tita & Abrahamse, 2004). Five specific offenses were used in constructing this scale. Gang members were asked whether the gang intimidated or threatened others, robbed people, jumped or attacked people, did drive-by shootings, or killed people. The

majority of current gang members reported that their gang engaged in these activities, ranging from 80% of gang members who agreed with the statement that their gang jumped or attacked people, to a low of 51% who acknowledged that their gang killed people. For former gang members, the figures were generally lower, particularly for the fraction of former members who acknowledged that their gang killed people (37%). The mean score for current gang members on this five-point index was 2.8, and for former gang members it was 3.0.

We next examine the correlations between these four indices and one additional interval measure, the number of self-reported arrests in the past 12 months. We consider the correlations for each subgroup (current members and former members) separately in Table 7.10. We interpret these results as largely descriptive in nature, given the cross-sectional design of the data.

Table 7.10 Correlation Between Organization, Violent Victimization, Drug Sale, and Violent Offending Index Measures

	Organization	Violent Victimization	Drug Sale	Violent Offending	Arrests
Current gang member					
Organization		.32**	.27**	.26**	.11
Violent victimization			.41**	.32**	.25**
Drug sale				.41**	.20*
Violent offending					.12
Ever a gang member					
Organization		.47	.35*	.56**	−.25
Violent victimization			.44**	.66**	−.09
Drug sale				.56**	−.27*
Violent offending					−.14

*p = .05. ** p = .01.

Correlations between the gang organization index and three of the other scales are significant at the .01 level. Individuals who were members of more organized gangs report higher victimization counts, more gang sales of different kinds of drugs, and more violent offending by the gang than do members of less organized gangs. This can be seen in the significant and positive correlations between the gang organization index and each of these indices. The correlation between the gang organization index and violent victimizations is the strongest of the three, .32. But it is also important to note from the top panel of Table 7.10 that the level of gang organization is significantly and positively related to the number of different violent and drug crimes that a gang engages in. These results run contrary to the findings from earlier work that the level of gang organization is not sufficiently complex to have implications for how gangs behave particularly in offending patterns largely described as "cafeteria style" (Decker, Bynum, & Weisel, 1998; Klein, 1995; McGloin, 2004; Peterson, Miller, & Esbensen, 2001).

The violent victimization index is positively related to gang drug sales, gang violent offending, and being arrested. Each of these correlations is strong for individual level data (.41, .32, and .25, respectively) and significant at the .01 level. These results are consistent with a growing body of research (Lauritsen, Sampson, & Laub, 1991; Loeber, Kalb, & Huizinga, 2001; Peterson, Taylor, & Esbensen, 2004) that documents the role of involvement in crime as an offender for victimization among adolescents. Although these are cross-sectional interview data and the time order of this relationship can not be established, it is nonetheless important to point out the role of offending for victimization for current gang members, particularly in light of the consistent finding in gang ethnographies that gang members often join the gang for "protection" (Decker & Van Winkle, 1996; Hagedorn, 1988).

The pattern of relationships for former gang members is found in the bottom panel of Table 7.10. These relationships follow the general pattern found for current gang members, though where they deviate from this pattern, the relationships are stronger. Perhaps some of these differences are attributable to the fact that the former gang members are somewhat older than the current members. Specifically, the gang organization index is strongly and positively related to violent victimizations, gang drug sales, and violent offending committed by the gang. Most notable is the strength of the relationship between the degree of gang organization and violent offending for this group of former gang members. This relationship is quite strong (.56) and significant at the .01 level. These results clearly suggest that despite the relatively low overall levels of gang organization observed for this sample, what organization does exist is related to increased involvement in drug sales, violent offending, and violent victimization. We are not able to identify the specific mechanisms through which the nature of gang organization is related to increases in these forms of offending and victimization. We believe that more organized groups are effective in pursuing individual and group goals, most often offending in the case of the gang. Organizational complexity can also increase the efficacy of the organization. In this context, organizational efficacy is the extent to which an organization can influence the behavior of its members and successfully compel them to pursue group goals. Prior research (Esbensen & Huizinga, 1993; Thornberry, Krohn, Lizotte, & Chard-Wierschem, 1993) has documented the extent to which offending increases during periods of gang membership compared to the time prior to becoming a member and the extent to which offending declines after individuals leave the gang. Our results suggest it is the organizational structure of the gang (weak as it may be) that accounts for changes in behavior. However, as our results are based on cross-sectional data, they are suggestive, offering hypotheses for future research.

REFERENCES

Adler, P. (1985). *Wheeling and dealing.* New York: Columbia.

Curry, D. (2000). Self-reported gang involvement and officially recorded delinquency. *Criminology, 38(4),* 1253-1274.

Curry, G. D., Decker, S. H., & Egley, A. H. (2002). Gang involvement and delinquency in a middle school population. *Justice Quarterly, 19,* 301-318.

Decker, S. (2000). Legitimating drug use: A note on the impact of gang membership and drug sales on the use of illicit drugs. *Justice Quarterly, 17(2),* 393-410.

Decker, S. H. (1996). Gangs and violence: The expressive character of collective involvement. *Justice Quarterly, 11,* 231-250.

Decker, S. H., Bynum, T. S., & Weisel, D. L. (1998). A tale of two cities: Gangs as organized crime groups. *Justice Quarterly, 15,* 395-425.

Decker, S., & Van Winkle, B. (1995). Slingin' dope: The role of gangs and gang members in drug sales. *Justice Quarterly, 11,* 1001-1022.

Decker, S., & Van Winkle, B. (1996). *Life In the gang: Family, friends, and violence.* New York: Cambridge University Press.

Egley, A. H. (2002). *National youth gang survey trends from 1996 to 2000.* OJJDP Fact Sheet No. 03. Washington, DC: U.S. Department of Justice.

Esbensen, F., & Huizinga, D. (1993). Gangs, drugs, and delinquency in a survey of urban youth. *Criminology, 31,* 565-590.

Esbensen, F., Winfree, T., He, N., & Taylor, T. (2001). Youth gangs and definitional issues: When is a gang a gang, and why does it matter. *Crime and Delinquency, 47*(1), 105-130.

Fagan, J. (1989). The social organization of drug use and drug dealing among urban gangs. *Criminology, 27,* 633-669.

Fleisher, M. S., & Decker, S. H., (2001). Going home, staying home: Integrating prison gang members into the community. *Corrections Management Quarterly, 5,* 65-77.

Hagedorn, J. H. (1988). *People and folks.* Chicago: Lakeview Press.

Hagedorn, J. H. (1994a). Homeboys, dope fiends, legits, and new jacks. *Criminology, 32,* 197-219.

Hagedorn, J. H. (1994b). Neighborhoods, markets, and gang drug organization. *Journal of Research in Crime and Delinquency, 31,* 264-294.

Irwin, J. (1972). The inmate's perspective. In J. Douglas (Ed.), *Research on deviance* (pp. 117-137). New York: Random House.

Katz, C. M., Webb, V., & Schaefer, D. (2000). The validity of police gang intelligence lists: Examining differences in delinquency between documented gang members and non-documented delinquent youth. *Police Quarterly, 3(4),* 413-437.

Klein, M. W. (1971). *Street gangs and street workers.* Englewood Cliffs, NJ: Prentice-Hall.

Klein, M. W. (1995). *The American street gang.* New York: Oxford University Press.

Lauritsen, J., Sampson, R. J., & Laub, J. (1991). The link between offending and victimization among adolescents. *Criminology, 29,* 265-292.

Loeber, R., Kalb, L., & Huizinga, D. (2001). *Juvenile delinquency and serious injury victimization.* Juvenile Justice Bulletin. Washington, DC: Office of Juvenile Justice and Delinquency Prevention.

Maxson, C, & Klein, M. W. (1995). Investigating gang structures. *Journal of Gang Research, 3(1),* 33-40.

Maxson, C. L., & Klein, M. W. (1990). Street gang violence: Twice as great, or half as great. In C. R. Huff (Ed.), *Gangs in America* (pp. 71-100). Newbury Park, CA: Sage.

Maxson, C. L., Klein, M. W., & Cunningham, L. (1992). *Street gangs and drug sales.* Report to the National Institute of Justice.

McGloin, J. M. (2004). *Associations among criminal gang members as a defining factor of organization and as a predictor of criminal behavior: The gang landscape in Newark, New Jersey.* Ann Arbor, MI: UMI.

Mieczkowski, T. (1986). Geeking up and throwing down: Heroin street life in Detroit. *Criminology, 24,* 645-666.

Padilla, F. (1992). *The gang as an American enterprise.* New Brunswick, NJ: Rutgers.

Peterson, D., Miller, J., & Esbensen, F.-A. (2001). The impact of sex composition on gangs and gang member delinquency. *Criminology, 39,* 411-440.

Peterson, D., Taylor, T. J., & Esbensen, F.-A. (2004). Gang membership and violent victimization. *Justice Quarterly, 21(4),* 793-815.

Sanchez-Jankowski, M. (1991). *Islands in the street.* Berkeley, CA: University of California Press.

Sanders, W. B. (1994). *Gang bangs and drive-bys; Grounded culture and juvenile gang violence.* New York: De Gruyter.

Short, J. F., Jr. (1985). The level of explanation problem in criminology. In R. Meier (Ed.), *Theoretical methods in criminology* (pp. 51-72). Beverly Hills, CA: Sage.

Skolnick, J. H. (1990). The social structure of street drug dealing. *American Journal of Police, 9,* 1-41.

Skolnick, J., Correl, T., Navarro, E., & Rabb, R. (1988). *The social structure of street drug dealing.* BCS Forum, Office of the Attorney General, State of California.

Spergel, I. A. (1995). *The youth gang problem; A community approach.* New York: Oxford University Press.

Taylor, C. (1990). *Dangerous society.* East Lansing, MI: Michigan State University Press.

Thornberry, T., Krohn, M., Lizotte, A., & Chard-Wierschem, D. (1993). The role of juvenile gangs in facilitating delinquent behavior. *Journal of Research in Crime and Delinquency, 30,* 55-87.

Thornberry, T., Krohn, M. D., Lizotte, A. J., Smith, C. A., & Tobin, R. (2003). *Gangs and delinquency in developmental perspective.* New York: Cambridge.

Thrasher, F. (1929). *The gang.* Chicago: University of Chicago Press.

Tita, G., & Abrahamse, A. (2004, March). *Gang homicide in LA, 1981-2001: Perspectives on violence prevention* (No. 3). Sacramento, CA: California Attorney General's Office.

Wright, R., & Decker, S. H. (1994). *Burglars on the job.* Boston: Northeastern.

Wright, R., & Decker, S. H. (1997). *Armed robbers in action.* Boston: Northeastern.

Zatz, M. S. (1987). Chicano youth gangs and crime: The creation of a moral panic. *Contemporary Crises, 11,* 129-158.

Zatz, M., & Portillos, E. L. (2000). Voices from the barrio: Chicano/a gangs, families, and communities. *Criminology, 38,* 369-401.

DISCUSSION QUESTIONS

1. What is the impetus for this research study? What do researchers currently know about the organizational structure of gangs?

2. What is these researchers' main hypothesis? Did they state it as a null or a research hypothesis?

3. What is their main independent variable? What are their dependent variables?

4. How did these researchers operationalize gang membership? How do they provide a reliability check on the subjects interview responses to being involved in a gang?

5. How do Decker and colleagues operationalize gang organization? Similarly, how do they operationalize violent victimization, violent offending, and narcotics trafficking?

6. In Table 7.10, what do the asterisked relationships mean?

7. According to the correlations in Table 7.10, is the organization of a gang significantly related to violent offending and victimization, drug sales, or arrest?

8. Overall, what do these researchers conclude about gang organization in general and the effect of the degree of organization on criminal offending?

RESEARCH READING

In this article, Jacques and Wright propose a theoretical framework with which to understand and develop methods of recruiting, paying, and interviewing active criminal offenders. Jacques and Wright reveal how the relational distance between the researchers, recruiters, and interviewees may affect research with active offenders. They use data from their own interviews with drug dealers in Atlanta and St. Louis in an effort to provide advice to future researchers in strengthening the validity of interview data.

INTIMACY WITH OUTLAWS

The Role of Relational Distance in Recruiting, Paying, and Interviewing Underworld Research Participants

Scott Jacques and Richard Wright

Abstract: The past quarter century has witnessed the emergence of a substantial literature devoted to the mechanics of recruiting, paying, and interviewing currently active offenders. Absent from that literature, however, is a theoretical framework within which to understand, test, modify, and further develop efforts to locate such offenders and gain their cooperation. This note, based on the authors' research with active drug sellers in Atlanta and St. Louis, explores the ways in which *relational distance,* that is, the nature and degree of intimacy between recruiter, interviewee, and researcher, affects the behavior of active offender research. The note concludes with theoretically situated, practical advice for (1) recruiting active criminals, (2) cost containment, and (3) maximizing the quantity and validity of data produced in interviews.

INTRODUCTION

Interview-based research with active underworld participants has a long history in criminology, but it has enjoyed something of a renaissance in recent years, with a new generation of criminologists coming to see the importance of studying crime in situ (see, e.g., Cromwell, Olson, and Avary 1991; Jacobs 1999, 2000; Jacobs, Topalli, and Wright 2003; Mullins, Wright, and Jacobs 2004; Topalli 2005; Wright and Decker 1994, 1997). The process of interviewing unincarcerated lawbreakers presents serious challenges because they have strong incentives not to identify themselves to researchers or to talk about their illegal activities (see, e.g., Jacobs 1998, 2006; Wright et al. 1992). Challenges notwithstanding, the value of field-based interviews with active criminals has been demonstrated repeatedly; among other things, such interviews are not subject to the influence of the prison, probation, or parole setting, and they are much more likely to reflect respondents' current cultural commitments and pursuits (for a comprehensive review, see Jacobs and Wright 2006:9-22).

Source: Jacques, S., & Wright, R. (2008). Intimacy with outlaws: The role of relational distance in recruiting, paying, and interviewing underworld research participants. *Journal of Research in Crime and Delinquency, 45*(1), 22–38. Copyright © 2008 Sage Publications.

Obtaining information from active offenders is a multistep process (see, e.g., Dunlap and Johnson 1999; Wright et al. 1992) that can be broken down into three basic parts: recruitment, payment, and interview. In any given population there are only so many active criminals and, as already noted, they have good reasons to remain hidden from view, so the first step is to find and inform them about the research (see, e.g., Jacobs 1998, 1999:12-14). Once that has been accomplished, the voluntary cooperation of the offenders still must be obtained, something that often requires the expenditure of resources (see, e.g., Dunlap and Johnson 1999). That is followed by perhaps the most important stage, namely, the interview itself, during which the offender communicates to the researcher what he or she knows about the subject in question.

The past quarter century has witnessed the emergence of a substantial literature devoted to the mechanics of recruiting, paying, and interviewing various types of unincarcerated criminals (see, among many others, Adler 1990; Dunlap and Johnson 1999; Glassner and Carpenter 1985; Jacobs 1998, 2006; Mieczkowski 1988; Williams et al. 1992; Wright et al. 1992). Taken as a whole, this literature has identified a wide range of strategies that have successfully been used to locate active criminals and convince them to cooperate with researchers. Absent from this literature, however, is any sort of *theoretical* lens through which the process of penetrating the underworld can be viewed. Without such a lens, this literature amounts to little more than an interesting collection of anecdotes in the sense that it is not amenable to scientific testing, falsification, and refutation (Popper 2002a, 2002b). This not only precludes the development of a theoretical understanding of criminological research; it also has practical implications for planning and implementing real-world studies of active criminals, especially when it comes to matters like efficient recruitment, cost containment, and ensuring data quality. To be sure, recruiting, paying,

and interviewing offenders is first and foremost a means of knowledge production, but it is also a social behavior that can be quantified and, thus, theoretically explained.

In this research note, we use pure sociology's concept of relational distance (see Black 1976, 1998), defined as the degree of intimacy between actors, to explain variation in subject recruitment, resource expenditure, and the quantity and validity of interview data. In doing so, we draw on our experiences in studying low- and middle-class drug sellers in St. Louis and suburban Atlanta, and from those of our longtime field recruiter in St. Louis, Smoke Dog. We supplement this information with studies of street-based drug dealers in various urban locales across the United States, including Detroit (Mieczkowski 1988), Denver (Hoffer 2006), and New York (Bourgois 2003). We conclude with theoretically situated, practical advice for recruiting, compensating, and interviewing underworld participants.

PURE SOCIOLOGY

Pure sociology is a paradigm concerned with the science of social life, and the epistemology is unique in what it is *not* rather than what it is (Black 1995). Purely sociological explanations are formed without reference to three staples of contemporary mainstream sociological thinking (Black 1995): First, pure sociology is "pure" because its explanations do not rely on nonsociological concepts, such as emotions, motivations, or testosterone. Second, pure sociology is without teleology; it does not recognize a goal set of social life. Last but not least, pure sociology is not anthropocentric (i.e., focused on persons) but instead holds that "social life behaves and people are merely its carriers" (Cooney 2006:53; see also Black 2000a). The question is not, "How do people behave?" but instead, "How does social life behave?" The scientific benefit of nonsubjective, nonteleological, and nonanthropocentric approaches is that they increase the value of theory by making it more testable and falsifiable, general, simple, and original, all of which are common and important measures of scientific value across fields (Black 1995; Kuhn 1977:320-39; Popper 2002b).

Theories of behavior cannot precede classifications of behavior (see Cooney and Phillips 2002), and perhaps the most fundamental aspect of pure sociology is the idea of *social space* (Black 1976, 1995, 1998). Social space divides social life into five broad dimensions: (1) *vertical space,* defined by wealth and rank; (2) *horizontal space,* defined by the nature and frequency of interaction; (3) *corporate space,* defined by the number of actors working together; (4) *symbolic space,* defined by what is considered "good, true, and beautiful"; and (5) *normative space,* or "respectability," defined by the application of social control. In any given social interaction, or case, every actor has a relative social status and social distance in social space. Actors gain social status as they elevate their wealth *(vertical status),* community involvement *(radial status),* organization *(corporate status),* and knowledge or conventionality *(symbolic status):* and actors lose status as more social control is applied to their behavior *(normative status).* Actors reduce social distance as they become more intimate *(relational distance)* and culturally similar *(cultural distance).* The social statuses and distances of every actor involved in a case define the *social structure.* Social structure is the explanatory factor in producing various forms, styles, and quantities of social behavior (Black 1995, 1998, 2000b). In short, as any aspect of social structure changes, such as wealth, integration, organization, culture, or respectability, so too should the form, style, and/or quantity of social life.

Past work in pure sociology has mostly been concerned with social control (see Black, 1998; Horwitz, 1990), that is, behavior that "defines and responds to deviant behavior" (Black 1976:105), such as law (Black 1976, 1980, 1989), self-help (Black 1983; Cooney 1998; Phillips 2003; Phillips and Cooney 2005), avoidance (Baumgartner 1988), lynching (Senechal de la Roche 1997), therapy (Horwitz 1982; Tucker 1999), and terrorism (Black 2004). Beyond social control, the paradigm has also been applied to economic behaviors such as welfare (Michalski 2003) and predation (Cooney 2006; Cooney and Phillips 2002), and to cultural behaviors such as ideas (Black 2000b), medicine (Black 1998:164-65), and art (Black 1998:168-69). Whatever the social behavior concerned, whether related to wealth, community, organization, culture, or social control, it may in some way or another change as a consequence of social structure. The task for pure sociologists is to find the connections between social structure and social behavior and state them as testable propositions that can be falsified or supported through testing.

Active Offender Research and Relational Distance

This research note applies pure sociology to a new arena of social life-criminological research on active offenders. We provide a series of principles that together form a social theory of active offender research that explains and predicts (1) recruitment, (2) recruiter and subject payments, and (3) data quantity and validity, or "quality." Although all aspects of social structure may have an effect on research, our theory is restricted to one form of social variation: *relational distance,* defined by the nature and degree of intimacy between actors and their associates (Black 1976:40). "It is possible to measure relational distance in many ways, including the scope, frequency, and length of interaction between people, the age of their relationship, and the nature and number of links between them in a social network" (p. 41). The relational distance between actors decreases as the quantity of social interaction between (1) themselves and (2) those they are associated with increases.

All else equal, for example, two persons who have traded drugs are closer in relational distance than two people who have never traded, two persons who have produced marijuana together are closer in relational distance than two people who have never done so, two people who have formed a drug cartel together are closer in relational distance than two loners, and two persons who have talked together about drugs are closer in relational distance than two persons who have never communicated. Beyond direct interaction, the concept of relational distance also accounts for indirect relationships, such as "mutual friends" or "middlemen" in drug trades. The relational distance between "indirect ties" is a function of the relational distance between direct ties. All else equal, for instance, *strangers* who have bought drugs from the same dealer, or have manufactured drugs for the same cartel, or have spoken with each other's business associates are closer in relational distance than strangers who do not have those indirect social connections. In short, relational distance decreases as the quantity of social behavior in a social network increases.

The question to be addressed here is: How does relational distance between researchers, recruiters, and criminals affect subject recruitment, resource expenditure, and the quantity and validity of data produced during interviews?

RECRUITMENT

Recruitment is the process of locating criminals and convincing them to provide data. Most researchers rely on criteria-based sampling to locate active criminals, which involves recruiting only those individuals who possess the social, psychological, or biological characteristics relevant to their interests.

Although sometimes disparaged as sampling on the dependent variable, purposive sampling has the advantage of saving time and money while increasing the probability of successful recruitment (see Jacobs and Wright 2006).

To use purposive sampling successfully, of course, researchers must first be able to identify individuals with the relevant characteristics, which can be extremely difficult when those characteristics involve lawbreaking. To do so, many researchers have turned to snowball sampling, a subtype of purposive sampling whereby initial participants are called upon to identify others of the same ilk and close the relational gap with them. "Such a strategy begins with the recruitment of an initial subject who then is asked to recommend further participants" (Wright et al. 1992:150; also see Watters and Biernacki 1989; Wright and Stein 2005).

Atlanta and St. Louis Projects

For a study based in suburban Atlanta, Georgia, we sought to recruit and interview a sample of 25 unincarcerated middle-class drug sellers. The first 18 such sellers were recruited using a straightforward purposive sampling strategy; we approached and asked for the cooperation of drug sellers who the lead author already knew to be involved in this activity, largely as a result of interactions in social venues, such as sport and school. Then, knowing no further drug sellers who met the participation criteria, we turned to snowball sampling, using two prior interviewees to recruit 7 more middle-class drug sellers. Although we cannot precisely quantify our relational distance from each participant in this study, we can say that the first 18 participants were closer to us in relational distance than the last 7 were, because the former group had direct interaction with the lead author, whereas the latter group did not.

For a separate but related project, we sought to locate and interview currently active drug sellers residing in poor, inner-city neighborhoods in

St. Louis, Missouri. The recruitment of such individuals was made possible through the second author's long-standing relationship with Smoke Dog, a former street criminal who, for a fee, has helped criminologists at our university find and interview various sorts of active offenders during the past decade (see, e.g., Jacobs and Wright 2006). In effect, Smoke Dog served as a relational tie to the dealers.

In an in-depth, semistructured interview with Smoke Dog, we asked him a series of questions about the process of recruiting criminals. The answers given by Smoke Dog revealed that relational distance plays a pivotal role in the selection process. For instance, most of the criminals recruited by Smoke Dog are friends, a few are acquaintances or "friends of friends," but strangers are nonexistent:

Interviewer: How often do you try to recruit strangers? People you don't know at all?

Smoke Dog: I don't recruit them.

Interviewer: Why not?

Smoke Dog: I don't know them, and I don't know how to come back to them about this shit, so no. I don't get strangers.

Interviewer: Do you ever try to recruit people that you just kind of know through someone?

Smoke Dog: Yeah, I've done that a couple times.

As an experiment of sorts, we asked Smoke Dog a hypothetical question that required him to list the 25 drug sellers he would be most likely lo try to recruit for one of our future studies. After he had done so, we asked him about his relationship with each individual on the list. Twenty-three of the drug sellers were defined as friends, and 1 he considered an acquaintance; the remaining person was Smoke Dog himself. We also asked Smoke Dog how long he had known each of the persons listed; the average was 17.13 years, with a range of six months to 27 years (Smoke

Dog's entire life). Also relevant is the fact that Smoke Dog shared a gang affiliation with all of the persons listed. When asked how often he interacts with each of the individuals, he reported hanging out with one dealer about once a month, with another once every two weeks, with another once a week, and with yet another "on weekends." He interacted with 10 of the remaining dealers every other day or so and saw the rest nearly every day. In broad terms, then, it appears that the likelihood of Smoke Dog attempting to recruit any given drug seller increases as his relational distance from the dealer decreases, and thus, our likelihood of interviewing a dealer increases as Smoke Dog's relational distance from that person decreases.

Although we were unaware of the theoretical implications at the time, our experience with recruiting drug sellers followed a clear pattern: the likelihood of an active offender being recruited for one of our studies increased as our relational distance from that person decreased. Stated in the form of a proposition:

> Recruitment to a study increases as the relational distance between researchers, recruiters, and criminals decreases.

Thus, as relational distance between the researcher, recruiter, and potential research participant decreases, the probability that the cooperation of the potential research participant will be sought increases.

RESOURCE EXPENDITURE

A taken-for-granted aspect of convincing active criminals to take part in a social science research project is the ability to provide remuneration for their participation. As experienced street ethnographers Dunlap and Johnson (1999) pointed out, "A key element [in research] . . . is the availability of funds to pay respondents for interviews" (p. 130). Although the payments involved are often relatively modest, they are important to criminals, as the idea of doing something for nothing is anathema to many of them (see Wright and Decker 1994, 1997).

Atlanta and St. Louis Projects

Payment for participation may be ordinary in this type of research, but in our own studies of active drug sellers in Atlanta and St. Louis, the price per interview has ranged from zero to $125. The initial 18 recruits for our study of middle-class drug sellers in Atlanta—who had relatively close ties to the lead author—received no monetary compensation for talking to us. The seven middle-class sellers who were recruited with the help of prior interviewees—essentially friends of friends—were paid $20 each.

Compared to our relational distance from the middle-class friend-of-friend participants, the dealers recruited by Smoke Dog were relatively far from us. Although it is true that the second author has a long-standing relationship with Smoke Dog, the relationship between the lead author and the two middle-class recruiters is even closer in relational distance. Because we have closer relational distance with the middle-class recruiters than with Smoke Dog, we are closer in relational distance to the last 7 middle-class participants than we are to the 25 St. Louis participants.

The price expended per interview, including recruiter and interviewee payments, appears to be affected by relational distance. As already noted, the original 18 middle-class sellers were closest in relational distance and were not paid for participation; the seven middle-class dealers recruited through friends of the lead author were compensated $20 for cooperation; and the low-class sellers in St. Louis—who are strictly "business associates" known through another "business associate," that is, Smoke Dog—were paid $50 per interview. Similar to the pattern for subject payments, we gave the two middle-class recruiters $20 for each successful referral, whereas Smoke Dog charged us $75 for exactly the same service.

As with the probability of recruiting one seller or another, price per interview appears not to behave randomly but instead varies as a function of relational distance. Our experience suggests the following proposition:

> *The price per interview decreases as the relational distance between researchers, recruiters, and criminals decreases.*

In other words, the further the relational distance between respondents, recruiters, and researchers, the more it costs to interact and obtain information.

DATA QUANTITY AND VALIDITY

While the successful recruitment of active criminals is a necessary first step in research of this type, the effort and expense required to do so is wasted if the data obtained in the resulting interview are sparse or false. The basic purpose of an interview is to obtain information about how people behave, and this is a quantitative variable measurable in two ways: data provided varies both in quantity and in its congruence with actual events, or validity. Consider, for example, the difference between a 10-page-long narrative and a one-sentence synopsis, and how either of those descriptions can be entirely accurate, partially so, or completely false. Moreover, the quantity and validity of data provided varies both between and within interviews; some interviews produce more valid information than others, as a whole or per topic, and, within interviews, various topics (e.g., murder versus supplier selection) can be discussed in lesser or greater detail and in a more or less honest manner.

St. Louis Project

Some of the active drug sellers interviewed at the state university where we work have been involved in past projects and others have not. Smoke Dog, our field recruiter, suggests that whether or not a criminal has been involved in past projects has an effect on the quality of information produced in interviews thereafter:

Smoke Dog: Nobody is going to tell you everything they do. Or what they did. They'll let you know most of it, something to make you feel good and put in your book. Like shit though, you can't ever expect them to tell you the whole truth.... They'll tell you some shit, and some of it might be mixed up or something. They ain't gonna tell you exactly how it happened, but they'll tell you. That's how it is.

Interviewer: And do you think people do that less the more often they come up here?

Smoke Dog: I say people who would do it would be people who I don't know better, but the people who have been up here [at the university to do interviews], then the shit they tell you real shit, for real. They been there. "Cause we've been doing this 10 years man, 96 or 97—it's 2006 now man.

Smoke Dog's experiences as a recruiter of unincarcerated offenders suggest that the more a researcher and criminal have interacted, and the more third-party ties they share, the greater the validity and quantity of data provided by that criminal. Thus, we propose the following:

Data quantity and validity increase as the relational distance between researchers, recruiters, and criminals decreases.

This proposition predicts that as relational distance decreases, the data provided by an active criminal will become more plentiful and more congruent with actual events. For instance, active criminals who have been interviewed before should produce higher quality information than criminals who have never been interviewed (between-person variation), and the more times any given criminal is interviewed, the more plentiful and truthful the data will be (within-person variation).

CONCLUSION

Taken together, the propositions outlined above suggest a preliminary theory of how research with active criminals "behaves": The more a criminological researcher has interacted with a criminal and his or her associates, the more likely a criminal is to be recruited for an interview, the less it will cost to do the interview, and the more valid and plentiful will be the data obtained. Each of these propositions is testable because it states empirical, quantifiable, directional relationships (see Black 1995:831-33), and each is general because it applies to criminology in various times, places, and social classes (Black 1995:833-37).

Because the role of research is to test—and thereby falsify or support—theory, we strongly encourage researchers to take up the challenge of determining the limits of our proposed theory and add to it as appropriate. Surely, there will be instances in which our propositions are not accurate, but it should be remembered that relational distance is but one part of social life. Other aspects of social structure may prove to have an effect on the behavior of research and serve to offset the effects of relational distance. For instance, the quantity and validity of data likely behave as a function of the quantity of law applied to the behavior in question; all else constant, an admittance and discussion of murder would seem less likely to occur during an interview than an admittance and discussion of assault.

The likelihood of studying a ~~...~~ of criminals may also ~~...~~ status (Black 20~~...~~ difficult an~~...~~ ~~...~~ce, to recruit ~~...~~ who are wealthy than ~~...~~poor, and this could explain the a~~...~~ complete absence of studies on "elite," or high-status, criminals (but see, e.g., Adler 1993). Culture may play a role in the "behavior of method" as well; as noted by Wright and Bennett (1990; also see Douglas 1972), a "key" element in active offender research "involves 'fitting in' by dressing appropriately and, more important, learning the distinctive terminology, phrasing, and so on used by the offenders. Several commentators have stressed that researchers should modify their dress and language to accommodate those they are studying" (p. 146). In short, all aspects of social structure must be examined to fully understand the effect of each aspect of social life on recruiting, paying, and interviewing active offenders (see Black 1995:851-52).

Beyond pure sociology, we fully support the use of other theories in explaining the behavior of recruiting, paying, and interviewing active criminals. For instance, Granovetter's (1973) notions of "weak" and "strong" ties likely have important implications for obtaining data; a researcher with a few strong ties—persons very close in relational distance—to criminals may enjoy a great amount of access to cheap and valid data, but without any weak ties, the "information trail" is relatively likely to end or become more expensive to travel. Other scientists could explore the role of motivation in interview-related behavior. What role, for example, does rational choice (Clarke and Cornish 1985) play in recruitment, subject payments, and data quality? Does self-control (Gottfredson and Hirschi 1990) affect the knowledge production process? How do subcultural beliefs and norms, such as the "code of the street" (Anderson 1999), influence cooperation?

These are but a few of many conceivable theoretical questions and directions; we leave to other criminologists the task of exploring the potential of those and other theories for explaining and improving the process that produces much of the data used in criminological research.

Of course, the most valuable asset to the development of theory is data that can be used to test and reformulate explanations and predictions. For every study of active criminals attempted, the behavior "behind" the study could facilitate unique insights into the behavior of criminals and criminologists. But without a more conscious documentation of *our own* behavior and characteristics, these insights will remain hidden. In future research, we will make a more cognizant and systematic effort to record theoretically relevant factors surrounding the process (e.g., our own social status), and we urge that other criminologists do the same (also see Brenner and Roberts 2007). If this research note stimulates a series of studies that verifiably disprove our theory and demonstrate others to be more valuable to science, or vice versa, then criminology will benefit.

The theory we have proposed should be of more than theoretical interest to criminologists; it constitutes a beginning point for the development of a practical framework within which to plan and interpret research involving active criminals. Let us conclude, then, by noting that, at this early stage, the theory suggests at least three pieces of practical advice for criminologists who want to interview active underworld participants:

1. Success in recruitment will increase in tandem with the quantity of social interaction between researchers, recruiters, and criminals;

2. The price of interviews does not need to be held constant as criminals who are closer in relational distance to the researcher will do interviews for a smaller payment; and

3. The criminals who are closest in relational distance to the researcher, especially those who have done previous interviews, are the ones most likely to produce the greatest amount of valid data and thus are the most appropriate persons with whom to discuss the most serious crimes.

REFERENCES

Adler, P. 1990. "Ethnographic Research on Hidden Populations: Penetrating the Drug World." *NIDA Monograph* 98:96-111.

———. 1993. *Wheeling and Dealing. An Ethnography of an Upper-Level Drug Dealing and Smuggling Community.* 2d ed. New York: Columbia University Press.

Anderson. E. 1999. *Code of the Street: Decency, Violence, and the Moral Life of the Inner City.* New York: Norton.

Baumgartner. M. P. 1988 *The Moral Order of a Suburb.* New York: Oxford University Press.

Black, D. 1976. *The Behavior of Law.* New York: Academic Press.

———. 1980. *The Manners and Customs of the Mice.* New York: Academic Press.

———. 1983. "Crime as Social Control." *American Sociological Review* 48:34-45.

———. 1989. *Sociological Justice.* New York: Oxford University Press.

———. 1995. "The Epistemology of Pure Sociology." *Law and Social Inquiry* 20: 829-70.

———. 1998. *The Social Structure of Right and Wrong.* Rev. ed. San Diego, CA: Academic Press.

——— 2000a. "On the Origin of Morality." Pp. 107-19 in *Evolutionary Origins of Morality: Cross-Disciplinary Perspectives,* edited by L. D. Katz. Exeter, UK: Imprint Academic.

———. 2000b. "Dreams of Pure Sociology." *Sociological Theory* 18:343-67.

———. 2004. "The Geometry of Terrorism." *Sociological Theory* 22 (1): 14-25.

Bourgois, P. 2003. *In Search of Respect: Selling Crack in El Barrio.* 2d ed. New York: Cambridge University Press.

Brenner, S. and R. J. Roberts. 2007. "Save Your Notes, Drafts and Printouts: Today's Work Is Tomorrow's History." *Nature* 446 (April 12): 725.

Clarke, R. and D. Cornish. 1985. "Modeling Offenders' Decisions: A Framework for Research and Policy." Pp. 147-85 in *Crime and Justice: An Annual Review of Research,* Vol. 6, edited by M. Tonry and N. Morris. Chicago, IL: University of Chicago Press.

Cooney, M. 1998. *Warriors and Peacemakers: How Third Parties Shape Violence.* New York: New York University Press.

———. 2006. "The Criminological Potential of Pure Sociology." *Crime, Law, and Social Change* 46:51-63.

Cooney, M. and S. Phillips 2002. "Typologizing Violence: A Blackian Perspective." *International Journal of Sociology and Social Policy* 22:75-108.

Cromwell, P., J. Olson, and D. Avary. 1991. *Breaking and Entering: An Ethnographic Analysis of Burglary.* Newbury Park, CA: Sage.

Douglas, J. D., ed. 1972. *Research on Deviance.* New York: Random House.

Dunlap, E. and B. D. Johnson. 1999. "Gaining Access to Hidden Populations: Strategies for Gaining Cooperation of Drug Sellers/Dealers and Their Families in Ethnographic Research." *Drugs and Society* 14:127-49.

Entwisle, B., K. Faust, R. R. Rindfuss, and T. Kaneda. 2007. "Variation in the Structure of Social Ties." *American Journal of Sociology* 112:1495-1533.

Glassner, B. and C. Carpenter. 1985. *The Feasibility of an Ethnographic Study of Property Crime: A Report Prepared for the National Institute of Justice.* Washington, DC: National Institute of Justice. Mimeo.

Gottfredson, M. R. and T. Hirschi. 1990. *A General Theory of Crime.* Palo Alto, CA: Stanford University Press.

Granovetter, M. 1973. "The Strength of Weak Ties." *American Journal of Sociology* 78: 1360-80.

Hirsch, T. and M. R. Gottfredson. 1993. "Commentary: Testing the General Theory of Crime." *Journal of Research in Crime and Delinquency* 30:47-54.

Hoffer, L. D. 2006. *Junkie Business: The Evolution and Operation of a Heroin Dealing Network.* Belmont, CA: Thomson Wadsworth.

Horwitz, A. V. 1982. *The Social Control of Mental illness*. Orlando, FL: Academic Press.

———. 1990. *The Logic of Social Control*. New York: Plenum.

Jacobs, B. A. 1998. "Researching Crack Dealers: Dilemmas and Contradictions." Pp. 160-177 in *Ethnography at the Edge: Crime, Deviance, and Field Research*, edited by J. Pencil and M. S. Hamm. Boston, MA: Northeastern University Press.

———. 1999. *Dealing Crack*. Boston, MA: Northeastern University Press.

———. 2000. *Robbing Drug Dealers*. New York: Aldine de Gruyter.

———. 2006. "The Case for Dangerous Fieldwork." Pp. 157-68 in *The Sage Handbook of Fieldwork*, edited by D. Hobbs and R. Wright. Thousand Oaks, CA: Sage.

Jacobs, B. A. and R. Wright. 2006. *Street Justice: Retaliation in the Criminal Underworld*. New York: Cambridge University Press.

Jacobs. B., V. Topalli, and R. Wright. 2003. "Carjacking, Streetlife, and Offender Motivation." *British Journal of Criminology* 46:1-15.

Kuhn, T. S. 1977. *The Essential Tension*. Chicago, IL: University of Chicago Press.

Maruna, S. 2001. *Making Good: How Ex-Convicts Reform and Rebuild Their Lives*. Washington, DC: American Psychological Association.

Michalski, J. H. 2003. "Financial Altruism or Unilateral Resource Exchanges? Toward a Pure Sociology of Welfare," *Sociological Theory* 21 (4): 341-58.

Mieczkowski, T. 1988. "Studying heroin retailers: A research note." *Criminal Justice Review* 13:39-44.

Mullins, C., R. Wright, and B. Jacobs. 2004. "Gender, Streetlife, and Criminal Retaliation." *Criminology* 42:911-40.

Phillips, S. 2003. "The Social Structure of Vengeance: A Test of Black's Model." *Criminology* 41 (3): 673-708.

Phillips, S. and M. Cooney. 2005. "Aiding Peace. Abetting Violence: Third Parties and the Management of Conflict." *American Sociological Review* 70:334-54.

Piquero, A. R., R. Macintosh, and M. Hickman. 2000. "Does Self-Control Affect Survey Response? Applying Explanatory, Confirmatory, and Item Response Theory Analysis to Grasmick et al.'s Self-Control Scale." *Criminology* 38:897-929.

Popper, K. 2002a. *Conjectures and Refutations*. New York: Routledge.

———. 2002b. *The Logic of Scientific Discovery*. New York: Routledge.

Senechal de la Roche. R. 1997. "The Sociogenesis of Lynching." Pp. 48-76 in *Under Sentence of Death: Lynching in the South*, edited by W. F. Brundage. Chapel Hill: University of North Carolina Press.

Topalli, V. 2005. "When Being Good Is Bad: An Expansion of Neutralization Theory." *Criminology* 43:797-835.

Tucker, J. 1999. *The Therapeutic Corporation*. New York: Oxford University Press.

Watkins, A. M. and C. Melde. 2007. 'The Effect of Self-Control on Unit and Item Nonresponse in an Adolescent Sample." *Journal of Research in Crime and Delinquency* 44:267.

Watters, J. and P. Biernacki, 1989. 'Targeted Sampling: Options for the Study of Hidden Populations." *Social Problems* 36:416-30.

Weinreb, A. 2006. "Limitations of Stranger-Interviewers in Rural Kenya." *American Sociological Review* 71:1014-39.

Williams, T., E. Dunlap, B. D. Johnson, and A. Hamid. 1992. "Personal Safety in Dangerous Places." *Journal of Contemporary Ethnography* 21 (3): 343-74.

Wright, R. and T. Bennett. 1990. "Exploring the Offender's Perspective: Observing and Interviewing Criminals" Pp. 138-51 in *Measurement Issues in Criminology*, edited by K. Kempf. New York: Springer-Verlag.

Wright, R. and S. Decker. 1994. *Burglars on the Job: Streetlife and Residential Burglary*. Boston, MA: Northeastern University Press.

———. 1997. *Armed Robbers in Action*. Boston, MA: Northeastern University Press.

Wright, R., S. Decker, A. Redfern, and D. Smith. 1992. "A Snowball's Chance in Hell: Doing Fieldwork with Active Residential Burglars." *Journal of Research in Crime and Delinquency* 29:148-61.

Wright, R. and M. Stein. 2005. "Snowball sampling," Pp. 495-500 in *The Encyclopedia of Social Measurement*, edited by K. Kempf-Leonard. San Diego, CA: Elsevier.

DISCUSSION QUESTIONS

1. What do these authors cite as valuable about interviews with active criminals? What do they cite as problematic about interviewing active criminals? What are the main steps in soliciting information from active criminals?

2. Why do these authors state that without a theoretical framework the active criminal interview data is not scientific?

3. What is pure sociology, and what is included in the idea of social space? Further, what do these authors mean by relational distance?

4. What type of sampling technique did these researchers employ in Atlanta and St. Louis? What was a common theme surrounding the active criminals that the researchers were referred to by Smoke Dog? How does relational distance affect selection or recruitment of subjects for interview? How does relational distance affect payment of interview subjects?

5. How do these researchers argue that data quantity and validity are affected by relational distance? Who is most likely to give quality information, that which is truthful and complete?

6. Did these researchers discuss any ethical issues with interviewing active criminals?

7. What do these authors encourage future researchers to do with their theory?

8. How did the interview data these authors collected provide support for their theory?

9. List some specific things that Smoke Dog said that provided a clearer picture of the effect of relational distance on recruitment, payment, and interviewing of active criminals.

8

QUALITATIVE RESEARCH

Participant Observation, Focus Groups, and Case Studies

Qualitative research involves the researcher collecting data with his or her senses, often through interactions with the subjects themselves (field research). This type of research gives us more in-depth and sensitizing descriptions of reality. Berg (2004) states that qualitative research "refers to the meanings, concepts, definitions, characteristics, metaphors, symbols, and description of things" (p. 3). Although Berg lists numerous techniques under the umbrella of qualitative research methods, for the purposes of this reader, three of the most commonly used techniques in criminology and criminal justice will be discussed: ethnography and participant observation, focus groups, and case studies. The in-depth interviews discussed in the previous chapter are considered qualitative and can be used in conjunction with the three qualitative research strategies mentioned here.

Qualitative research has its roots in anthropology. Ethnographic work came from anthropologists who lived with and participated in the customs and rituals of preindustrial groups. Ethnography refers to the study of people's ways of life (Ellis, Hartley, & Walsh, 2010). In criminology specifically, ethnography and participant observation owe their beginnings to Robert Park and the sociology department at the University of Chicago in the 1920s, where Park's students and others spent their days observing life in the city. Rather than sit in a classroom and listen to a professor lecture, these students were out observing first-hand accounts of the inner workings of life in urban Chicago. The city essentially was the students' social science lab (Bachman & Schutt, 2008).

Although some would probably argue that it never waned, qualitative research in criminology and criminal justice has seen a recent resurgence as more and more researchers are realizing the importance of contextualizing criminal behaviors and events. Ethnographic research can take many forms and is most often defined by the role the researcher plays within the group setting. The researcher, for instance, could simply observe a group in its natural setting or, at the other extreme, become a member of that group and participate in its activities without the members knowing; this is known as covert participation. Most researchers who do qualitative research in the field take a role somewhere in between the above mentioned methods, making it known that they are researchers but are partaking in some of the group's activities (Bachman & Schutt, 2008). Berg (2004) refers to ethnography as research "that places researchers in the midst of whatever it is they study" (p. 148).

Specifically regarding ethnography and crime, even undercover agents from local police departments, as well as other federal agencies like the FBI and the DEA, have covertly participated in the activities of gangs, narcotics traffickers, and other organized and unorganized criminal groups, mostly with the intent to gather evidence against the individuals in the group but also in attempt to better understand the organizational structure and activities of these groups. Using this inside information, these agencies can develop better strategies to prevent these criminal enterprises from forming and engaging in criminal activities in the future.

Variations on Participant Observation

Complete observation involves researchers simply observing groups without disturbing their activities. Obviously, this can sometimes be difficult to do; subjects may get nervous if they believe they are being watched and, therefore, alter their behavior. This is called a reactive effect and refers to "the response of subjects to the presence of an intruding investigator" (Berg, 2004, p. 209). Researchers obviously want to observe natural behaviors; therefore, complete observation can be a problem, depending on the circumstances under which the observation is being conducted (Bachman & Schutt, 2008). For instance, if observations are being made in a very public place where there are many people, those being observed may not even be aware of the researcher's presence, and there would be no worries about a reactive effect. In a more intimate setting, conducting complete observation will be more problematic. In most participant observation studies, at least some of the persons being observed are aware of the researcher's presence and that the group's activities are being studied. The degree of participation may depend on the level of rapport with the group; some researchers may have to participate in group activities in order to build trust with group members and make them more comfortable in their presence.

Moral and ethical issues often arise in participant observation research depending on the behaviors the researchers are observing and the degree of participation the researchers are required to undertake. Gaining access to certain groups may also prove to be difficult. Researchers often have to find someone who can vouch for their presence in the group and who understands the goals and objectives of the research. This person is often referred to as a gatekeeper. Gatekeepers are important in participant observation research, especially in criminology, where access to groups researchers are interested in studying may be very limited. Recall the discussion of snowball sampling in Chapter 7: the gate-keeper is often the beginning of, and the momentum that forms, a study's snowball sample.

Focus Groups

Focus groups as a qualitative research method involve group discussions. They are similar to interviews but instead of soliciting information from one individual, the researcher is interested in gathering opinions and responses in a group setting. The researcher poses questions and facilitates group discussion with probing follow-up questions. The purpose of these group discussions is to explore the opinions and attitudes of persons regarding certain topics (Ellis et al., 2010). Researchers record information from these group discussions and attempt to code the data in such a way as to construct categories or thematic typologies to describe the information gleaned from the group.

These focus groups are not likely to be a representative sample, and researchers have to be cautious in generalizing the information obtained. Researchers sometimes conduct several focus groups on a particular topic in order to provide some degree of reliability to their findings (Bachman & Schutt, 2008). Although the majority of focus group research is done by marketing researchers to assess consumer preferences, focus groups have also been used to gauge opinions of new policies or laws implemented to deter crime. They have also been conducted with groups of offenders to assess whether motivations for offending are similar across individuals. In this capacity, focus groups can provide valuable insight regarding the various motivations for crime, as well as differences in offending patterns across individuals or groups.

Case Studies

Similar to focus groups, case studies involve in-depth research on one or two individuals, who are called cases. For example, serial murder is a rare phenomenon. As such, researchers may only be able to study a few cases. Criminology researchers have used case studies to analyze specific events such as school shootings or other high profile crimes. Case studies of individuals or events have also sometimes been referred to as life histories (Ellis et al., 2010; Hagan, 2005) or historiographies (Berg, 2004), especially where the researcher seeks accounts of individuals or events from multiple sources. Shaw's (1930) *The Jack-Roller*, Sutherland's (1937) *The Professional Thief*, Klockars' (1974) *The Professional Fence*, and Denzin's (1987) *The Alcoholic Self* are a few of the classical examples of case study research in criminology.

Qualitative Data Analysis

Collecting and analyzing data of a qualitative nature can be a very time consuming endeavor; qualitative researchers often spend years collecting data and organizing it into logical and meaningful results. Qualitative researchers use inductive reasoning in attempts to ground empirical and theoretical explanations in the social lives of the persons they study. In conducting qualitative research, "the observer wishes to make claims that are grounded in the claims of those who make them" (Feagin, Orum, & Sjoberg, 1991, p. 8). Qualitative research methods usually involve, but are not limited to, the following analytic procedures: collecting and recording data, conceptualizing and organizing data, examining relationships and correlations among data, validating or authenticating findings and conclusions, and reporting of results (Bachman & Schutt, 2008).

RESEARCH READING

In this article, Miller argues that covert participation is the least used of all qualitative methods, yet it may be the most fruitful for research in criminology and criminal justice because of the behaviors of interest to researchers in these disciplines. Miller demonstrates that the goals of covert participation are similar to the goals of other observational methods, yet researchers rarely consider the covert method. Pay special attention to the issues of validity and reliability of data that Miller discusses, especially as they relate to using confederates or cooperatives (gatekeepers), and how covert participation can avoid these problems. There are, however, some moral and ethical issues that may arise in covert participatory research that have to do with deception of those the researcher is observing, as well as the possibility of law enforcement scrutiny.

COVERT PARTICIPANT OBSERVATION

Reconsidering the Least Used Method

Mitch Miller

The goal of any science is not willful harm to subjects, but the advancement of knowledge and explanation. Any method that moves us toward that goal is justifiable.

—Norman Denzin (1968)

Social scientists have virtually ignored the qualitative technique covert participant observation. This variation of participant observation is either not mentioned or described in less than a page's length in social science research methods texts. The majority of qualitative methods books provide a few illustrative examples, but scarcely more in terms of detailed instruction. Manifested in the selection of alternative field strategies, this disregard has made covert observation the truly least used of all the qualitative research methods.

It is unfortunate that covert research is so rarely conducted because a veiled identity can enable the examination of certain remote and closed spheres of social life, particularly criminal and deviant ones, that simply cannot be inspected in an overt fashion. Consequently, covert research is well-suited for much subject material of concern to criminology and the criminal justice sciences. Also applicable in some situations where overt designs appear the appropriate or only option, covert schemes are infrequently considered. Clearly, complicated ethical issues inherent to secret investigations have created a methodological training bias that has suppressed their application. New generations of researchers therefore remain unfamiliar with a potentially valuable research option.

This brief commentary reintroduces covert participant observation and presents the principal advantages of using the technique. Theoretical, methodological, and pragmatic grounds are offered for exercising covert research. Ethical matters long associated with the stifling of its use are also reconsidered in the context of criminal justice research. The ethicality of secret research, relative to other qualitative methods,

Source: Miller, M. (1995). Covert participant observation: Reconsidering the least used method. *Journal of Contemporary Criminal Justice, 11*(2), 97–105. Copyright © 1995 Sage Publications.

is upheld for some research problems with certain stipulations.

DEFINING COVERT
PARTICIPANT OBSERVATION

Covert participant observation is a term that has been used rather interchangeably with other labels: "secret observation" (Roth 1962). "investigative social research" (Douglas 1976). "sociological snooping"' (Von Hoffman 1970), and most frequently "disguised observation" (Erickson 1967, 1968; Denzin 1968). Disguised observation has recently been defined as "research in which the researcher hides his or her presence or purpose for interacting with a group" (Hagan 1993:234). The distinguishing feature is that the research occurrence is not made known to subjects within the field setting.

Disguised observation is too inclusive a term often used in reference to those who simply hide in disguise or secret to observe, such as Stein's (1974) observation via a hidden two-way mirror of prostitutes servicing customers. Covert participant observation likewise involves disguise, however, the researcher is always immersed in the field setting. Additional elements – intentional misrepresentation, interpersonal deception, and maintenance of a false identity over usually prolonged periods of time are entailed. "Covert participant observation" is therefore a more technically correct term than "disguised observation" because it better indicates the active nature of the fieldwork essential to the technique (Jorgensen 1989).

Covert participant observation is essentially "opportunistic research" (Ronai and Ellis 1989) conducted by "complete-member researchers" (Adler and Adler 1987) who study phenomena in settings where they participate as full members. Admission to otherwise inaccessible settings is gained by undertaking a natural position and then secretly conducting observational research. Examples of the method include Steffensmeier and Terry's (1973) study of the relationship between personal appearance and

suspicion of shoplifting involving students dressed either conventionally or as hippies, Stewart and Cannon's (1977) masquerade as thieves. Tewksbury's (1990) description of adult bookstore patrons, and most recently Miller and Selva's (1994) assumption of the police informant role to infiltrate drug enforcement operations.

The most pronounced example of covert research, however, is Laud Humphreys' infamous Tea Room Trade (1970). Shrouding his academic interest in sexual deviance, Humphreys pretended to be a "watchqueen" (i.e., a lookout) for others so that he might observe homosexual acts in public bathrooms. He also used this role to record his subjects' license plate numbers to obtain their names and addresses in order to interview them by means of another disguise—survey researcher interested in sexual behaviors and lifestyles.

There are other versions of disguised or covert participant observation wherein certain confederates are made aware of the researcher's true identity, purpose and objectives (Formby and Smykla 1981; Asch 1951). The reasons for working with cooperatives are plain: to facilitate entry and interaction in the research site, to become familiar with nomenclature and standards of conduct, to expedite the happening of that which the researcher hopes to observe, and to avoid or at least minimize potential danger. Such reliance may be counter productive, though, in that observations and consequent analysis of the social setting may be tainted by confederates values, perceptions, and positions within the research environment.

If only a few individuals within a research site are aware of the researcher's true identity, it is possible, indeed likely, that interaction will be affected and spread to others within the setting. Hence, data distortion can become a potential validity and reliability problem with the use of confederates. The researcher must be completely undercover to avoid this problem and utilize the covert role so as to optimally exploit a social setting.

The goals of covert participant observation are no different than the standard objectives of overt participant observation: exploration, description, and, occasionally, evaluation (Berg 1989). Epistomological justification is similarly derived from an interpretive, naturalistic inquiry paradigm (Patton 1990). Most aspects of the methodological process, such as defining a problem, observing and gathering information, analyzing notes and records, and communicating results, are nearly identical to conventional participant observation as well. The covert approach may thus be considered a type of participant observation rather than a distinctive method.

There are aspects of the covert participant observation research cycle, however, that are unconventional. One controversial point is gaining entry to a setting through misrepresentation. It is the closed nature of backstage settings and the politics of deviant groups that negates announcement of the researcher's objectives and requires deception via role assumption if certain topics are to be examined.

The character of the participation is also much different and more demanding on the researcher. Covert role assumption means full participation in various group and individual activities, many of which contain risks. The direct study of crime by means of an undercover role can be doubly enigmatic to both the researcher's well-being and the inquiry. Assuming a role either as a criminal or in close proximity to crime for the purpose of research does not absolve the researcher from real or perceived culpability; thus moral decisions and the possibility of arrest and legal sanction must be considered prior to the onset of fieldwork.

The recording of notes from a clandestine position would divulge the researcher's cover and is obviously inadvisable. Extended periods of time in the field often yield rich and rare insight but, without a chance to withdraw and log events, recollection of temporal/causal sequence can become muddled due to information overload and understandable fatigue.

Resolves to this concern have been the use of mnemonics—a process of memorizing through abbreviation and association (Hagan 1993:195), taking photographs when possible, and the use of hidden mini-tape recorders and even body wires (Miller and Selva 1994).

THE ETHICS OF COVERT OBSERVATION

The ethicality of disguised or covert observational techniques has long been controversial, as evidenced by the "deception debate" (Bulmer 1980; Humphreys 1970; Roth 1962; Galliher 1973). Participants in this debate have tended to assume one of two polarized positions; moralistic condemnation or responsive justification. Deception is explicitly equated with immorality and is so unconscionable for some they would have covert observation banned from social science research altogether (Erikson 1967). The major objection is that deceptive techniques often violate basic ethical principles including informed consent, invasion of privacy, and the obligation to avoid bringing harm to subjects.

Critics further contend that misrepresentation not only causes irreparable damage to subjects, but also to the researcher, and to science by evoking negative public scrutiny and making subject populations wary of future researchers (Polsky 1967). Risk to the researcher, however, is a matter of individual decision. To set restrictions on academic investigations in an a priori fashion on the basis of potential harm is at odds with both the ideals of an open, democratic society (individual freedom and autonomy) and traditional social science precepts (free inquiry and, ironically, informed consent).

The argument of isolating future research populations is seemingly unsound as well. Many settings of interest to criminal justice researchers are essentially restricted and typically occupied with subjects already suspicious of strangers due to the threat of legal penalty associated with disclosure. Because researchers as outsiders will usually be distrusted and excluded from such settings, it is logical to assume that its occupants are already ostracized from researchers. The more substantial points that remain and must be confronted are interrelated: the use of deceit and the harm subjects may encounter as a result of the research process.

The topic of dishonesty in covert research is not as clear as opponents of the method suggest and nebulous in comparison to the frequent disregard for ethical standards demonstrated in other qualitative deviance research. Klockars' award winning *The Professional Fence,* for example, describes research conduct far more offensive than the duplicity intrinsic to covert participant observation. This case history of a thirty year career of dealing in stolen goods was enabled by an intentionally misrepresentative letter in which the researcher admittedly lied about: (1) his academic credentials, (2) his familiarity and experience with the subject of fencing, (3) the number of other thieves he had interviewed, and most seriously, (4) the possible legal risks associated with participating in the project (Klockars 1974:215). Klockars deception is reasoned in near blind pursuit of his research objective: "I thought the claim would strengthen the impression of my seriousness" and "the description of what I wanted to write about as well as the whole tone of the letter is slanted . . . and did not warn Vincet [the research subject] of his rights" (Ibid).

Surprisingly, Klockars' book and similar projects have not produced controversy on par with covert strategies. The terms "case history" and "personal interview" simply do not provoke the interest and suspicion generated by the labels "covert" and "disguise." Covert methods can be considered, relative to the exercise of some techniques, forthright in that the level of deception is predetermined and calculated into the research design (Strieker 1967). The decision of whether or not to use deception to gain entry and thus enable a study can be made based

on the ends versus the means formula described below.

A BASIS FOR COVERT RESEARCH?

Justifications for the use of covert techniques have been presented on various levels. The most common practical argument is that those engaged in illegal or unconventional behavior, such as drug dealers and users, simply will not submit to or participate in a study by overt methods. Likewise, those in powerful and authoritative positions have been considered secretive and difficult to openly observe (Shils 1975). Police chiefs, white-collar criminals, prison wardens, and drug enforcement agents benefit from the existing power structure which inhibits study of their behavior in these official roles. A covert design is often the only way to conduct qualitative evaluation research of certain enforcement and intervention programs closed to principal participants.

Beyond a "last-resort" rationale, there are other reasons, methodological and theoretical, for employing the covert technique. An evident reason is that of qualitative methodology in general—the desirability of capturing social reality. By concealing identity and objective, researchers can avoid inducing a qualitative Hawthorne effect (i.e., a covert approach can minimize data distortion). Covert participant observation is justified theoretically by dramatulurgical and conflict perspectives. If Goffman (1959) is to be taken seriously, then all researchers should be viewed as wearing masks and the appropriateness of any inquiry viewed in its context. Following Goffman, Denzin has also argued that ethical propriety depends upon the situation:

> The sociologist has the right to make observations on anyone in any setting to the extent that he does so with scientific intents and purposes in mind. (1965:50)

Dramatulurgy also provides a theoretical framework from which to assess topics of concern to the covert observer. The duplicity of roles already present in criminal settings under analysis (e.g., undercover police, fence, snitch, racketeer) are only multiplied when such a role is assumed with the additional post of social scientist.

Consideration of the well known consensus-conflict dialectic also provides logic supportive of covert research. Conventional field methods, such as in-depth interviewing and overt observation, are based on a consensus view of society wherein most people are considered cooperative and willing to share their points of view and experiences with others (Patton 1990). This assumption is highly suspect, however, in stratified and culturally diverse societies. To the extent that acute conflicts of interests, values and actions saturate social life to the advantage of some and not others, covert methods should be regarded proper options in the pursuit of truth.

This rationale should resonate with critical criminologists as it is in sync with the accepted view of much crime and delinquency as definitions and labels unjustly assigned to persons and events by operatives of an oppressive criminal justice system. John Galliher, well-known for commentaries on research ethics, supported a critical approach to covert research at a recent meeting of the Society for the Study of Social Problems by qualifying "upward snooping that might expose institutionalized corruption."

Perhaps the most compelling basis for the use of disguise in some research, however, is "the end and the means" position first stated by Roth (1962), then Douglas (1976) and Homan (1980), and most recently Miller and Selva (1994). Employing this reasoning in defense of covert observation, Douglas (1976:8-9) notes:

> Exceptions to important social rules, such as those concerning privacy and intimacy, must be made only when the research need is clear and the potential contributions of the findings to

general human welfare are believed to be great enough to counterbalance the risks.

That the purpose may absolve the process has also been acknowledged by the British Sociological Association, which condones the covert approach "where it is not possible to use other methods to obtain essential data" (1973:3): such is the case in many criminal justice research situations. The benefits of investigating and reporting on expensive, suspicious, and dysfunctional facets of the criminal justice system, then, may outweigh its potential costs. Failure to study how various initiatives and strategies are actually implemented on the street could condemn other citizens to misfortune and abuse should the behavior of the system be inconsistent with stated legitimate objectives.

To rule out study of covert behavior, whether engaged in by the powerful or the powerless, simply because it cannot be studied openly places artificial boundaries on science and prevents study of what potentially may be very important and consequential activities in society. The propriety and importance of research activities must always be judged on a case by case basis. Drug enforcement's use of asset forfeiture, for example, has been questioned by the press and media with such frequency and intensity that scholarly evaluation is warranted. The very nature of the allegations, however, have prompted the police fraternity to close ranks, thus compelling covert analysis. Abandoning such a study because it can not be carried out overtly would mean that potential misconduct and betrayal of public trust by government officials would remain unexposed.

The means and end rule, of course, requires the subjective interpretation of plausible harm to subjects, what exactly constitutes benefit, and who will be beneficiaries. To assess the balance between these elements it is necessary that they be highly specified, a requirement that is not easily met. The means and end formula is thus ambiguous and the choice to use a covert technique must be carefully deliberated. Certainly, deceptive observation carries ethical baggage less common to other qualitative methods, yet its ethicality is negotiable through detailed purpose and design.

CONCLUSION

The study of crime invites and sometimes requires the covert method as does examination of the clandestine nature of many facets of the formal social control apparatus. How other than through covert participant observation can topics such as undercover policing and inmate-correctional officer interaction be fully understood and evaluated? Those in the criminal justice system, as well as criminals, have vested interests in maintaining high levels of autonomy which require degrees of secrecy. This is evident in various labels such as "police fraternity," "gang," and "confidential informant."

The very things that make a criminal justice or criminological topic worthy of investigation and suitable for publication in a social science forum can preclude overtly exploring it. Methodologically sustained by the theoretical foundations of qualitative inquiry, covert designs tender opportunities to reach relatively unstudied topics.

The solidification of criminology and criminal justice as independent academic disciplines have resulted in a greater number, breadth, and specification level of refereed journals—all of which may indicate a general research surplus (Vaughn and del Carmen 1992). This is a debatable point for new technologies and the ever evolving nature of the criminal law present still developing and unstudied forms of deviance: but it is also true that the last thirty years have witnessed the near-exhaustion of most obvious crime oriented research foci. It is not uncommon to hear the sagely professor remark how much more difficult it is to now market one's intellectual work in choice outlets (e.g., *Justice Quarterly, Criminology*) than in years past

Covert research is simply one particularly inviting means by which to meet the expectations and competitive realities of today's social science arena.

This comment has briefly surveyed the methodological, theoretical, and practical reasons to utilize covert participant observation in criminal justice research. The most difficult facet of using this method will undoubtedly remain ethical factors that must be dealt with on a case by case basis. But these too can be overcome with caution, conviction, and adherence to established scientific guidelines for qualitative research (Glaser and Strauss 1967). The spirit of selecting methods on technical merit and relevance to research objectives rather than ethical pretense is an outlook consistent with the goals of social science. To the extent that this perspective thrives, covert participant observation may well become more commonplace: perhaps to the point of no longer being the least used method.

REFERENCES

Adler, P. A. and P. Adler. (1987) "The Past and Future of Ethnography." *Contemporary Ethnography* 16:4-24.

Asch, Solomon E. (1951) "Effects of Group Pressure upon the Modification and Distortion of Judgement." In H. Guetzkow (Ed.) *Groups, Leadership and Men*. Pittsburgh: Carnegie Press.

Berg, Bruce L. (1989) *Qualitative Research Methods for the Social Sciences*. Boston: Allyn and Bacon.

British Sociological Association. (1973) Statement of Ethical Principles and their Application to Sociological Practice.

Bulmer, Martin. (1980) "Comment on the Ethics of Covert Methods." *British Journal of Sociology* 31:59-65.

Denzin, Norman. (1968) "On the Ethics of Disguised Observation." *Social Problems* 115:502-504.

Douglas, Jack D. (1976) *Investigative and Social Research: Individual and Team Field Research*. Beverly Hills, CA: Sage.

Erikson, Kai T. (1967) "Disguised Observation in Sociology". *Social Problems* 14:366-372.

Formby, William A. and John Smykla. (1981) "Citizen awareness in Crime Prevention: Do They Really Get Involved?" *Journal of Police Science and Administration* 9: 398-403.

Galliher, John F. (1973) "The Protection of Human Subjects: A Reexamination of the Professional Code of Ethics". *The American Sociologist* 8:93-100.

Glaser, Barney G. and Anselm Strauss. (1967) *The Discovery of Grounded Theory*. Chicago: Aldine.

Goffman, Erving. (1959) *The Presentation of Self in Everyday Life*. New York: Doubleday.

Hagan, Frank E. (1993) Research Methods in *Criminal Justice and Criminology* 3rd ed. New York: Macmillian Publishing Co.

Homan, Roger. (1980) "The ethics of covert methods" British Journal of Sociology 31:46-59.

Humphreys, Laud. (1970) *Tearoom Trade: Impersonal Sex in Public Places*. New York: Aldine Publishing Co.

Jorgensen, Danny L. (1989) *Participant Observation: A Methodology for Human Studies*. Newburry Park. CA: Sage.

Klockars, Carl B. (1974) *The Professional Fence*. New York: The Free Press.

Miller, J. Mitchell and Lance Selva. (1994) "Drug Enforcement's Double-Edged Sword: An Assessment of Asset Forfeiture Programs." *Justice Quarterly* 11:313-335.

Patton, M.Q. (1990) *Qualitative Evaluation and Research Methods*. 2nd ed. Newbury Park. CA: Sage.

Polsky, Ned (1967) *Hustlers, Beats, and Others*. New York: Anchor Books.

Ronai, C.R. and C. Ellis. (1989) "Turn-ons for money: Interactional strategies of the table dancer". *Journal of Contemporary Ethnography* 18:271-298.

Roth, Julius A. (1962) "Comments on Secret Observation". *Social Problems* 9: 283-284.

Shils, Edward A. (1975) "Privacy and Power" in *Center and Periphery Essays in Macrosociology*. Chicago: University of Chicago Press.

Stein, Martha L. (1974) *Lovers, Friends, Slaves: The Nine Male Sexual Types*. Berkeley: Berkeley Publishing Corp.

Stewart, John E. and Daniel Cannon. (1977) "Effects of Perpetrator Status and Bystander Commitment on Response to a Simulated Crime." *Journal of Police Science and Administration* 5:318-323.

Strieker, LJ. (1967) "The True Deceiver." *Psychological Bulletin* 68:13-20.

Tewksbury, Richard. (1990) "Patrons of Porn: Research Notes on the Clientele of Adult Bookstores." *Deviant Behavior* 11: 259-271.

Vaughn, Michael and Rolando del Carmen. (1992) "An Annotated List of Journals in Criminal Justice and Criminology: A Guide Foe Authors." *Journal of Criminal Justice Education* 3:93-142.

Von Hoffman. N. (1970) "Sociological Snoopers." *Washington Post* (Jan. 30).

DISCUSSION QUESTIONS

1. Why does Miller argue that covert research is well-suited for criminology and criminal justice?

2. What is covert participant observation, and what does the method entail?

3. In what ways are the goals of covert participant observation the same as those of other participant observation strategies? What are the unconventional aspects of covert participation?

4. Describe the ethical issues involved in this type of research? How does Miller argue that researchers can justify deception?

5. How can covert participation contribute to the theoretical and methodological goals of research?

RESEARCH READING

This researcher used focus groups to examine four theoretical perspectives of the fear of crime, namely gang crime. Lane argues that recent crime-control-oriented responses to crime have not helped to quell public fears of crime. She discusses four theoretical perspectives that are based on social disorganization theory, which explain fear of crime in terms of environmental factors other than crime itself. She tests these four perspectives through focus group research conducted in California. Through these focus groups, Lane is able to gather information from residents about why they are afraid of crime. Her results show support for these theoretical perspectives. Lane further demonstrates how the observed data explicates the connections between these theoretical perspectives that cite different causal mechanisms for fear of crime.

——— FEAR OF GANG CRIME ———

A Qualitative Examination of the Four Perspectives

Jodi Lane

Abstract: Crime has gone down, but fear remains high. This high fear level indicates that the recent hard-hitting policy focus on crime and gang suppression is not sufficient to calm public fears. Fear-of-crime researchers have developed four theoretical perspectives grounded in social disorganization theory to explain fear on the basis of environmental factors other than crime. These perspectives are similar in their focuses on urban community factors as key elements, but they differ in how they construct the thought processes of individuals who are afraid. This study uses qualitative data from focus groups conducted in 1997 in Santa Ana, California, to describe in residents' own words how they think about gang crime and their reasons for being afraid. It confirms that each theoretical perspective on fear of crime is important and shows how each of them is connected to the others in the thoughts of these residents.

FEAR OF CRIME AFFECTS INDIVIDUALS AND POLICY

Gang crime became one of the most important social problems at the end of the twentieth century, as citizens and policymakers struggled with escalating violence and the possibility that more teens might mean even more crime and gangs. The predictions of more "teen killers" (e.g.. Fox 1996:3) did not come true during the late 1990s (Snyder and Sickmund 1999). States markedly enhanced their efforts to fight crime and gangs (e.g., passing laws to improve gang suppression and incarceration, increase juvenile transfers to adult court, and ensure only "three strikes" before "you're out"), but fear of crime remained high (Smith et al. 1999; Torbet et al. 1996). Focusing solely on eradicating crime and gangs, then, is not sufficient to calm public fears. Through analysis of focus groups in which people talked about their fears of gangs "in their own words," this article illustrates some of the reasons why.

Researchers have long known that crime rates and victimization risk are not the primary predictors of fear. For years, studies consistently showed that women and the elderly were the most fearful, even though men and the

Source: Lane, J. (2002). Fear of gang crime: A qualitative examination of the four perspectives. *Journal of Research in Crime and Delinquency*, *39*, 437–471. Copyright © 2002 Sage Publications.

young were more likely to experience crime (see Warr 1994 for a review). These findings led researchers to examine other predictive factors. Paralleling recent crime research (see Sampson 1993a), most contemporary fear-of-crime research has been driven by social disorganization theory and has examined contextual characteristics in the physical and social environment. Research has shown that important environmental cues include both physical (e.g., graffiti, litter) and social (e.g., youths hanging out, prostitutes) incivilities; as well as racial and ethnic diversity (e.g., living around people who look and act differently) (e.g., Covington and Taylor 1991; Merry 1981; Skogan 1990). Other recent fear research has focused on the impact of information that people receive about crime through the media or acquaintances (e.g., Chiricos, Eschholz, and Gertz 1997; Chiricos, Padgett, and Gertz 2000).

There are four perspectives about the primary causes of fear of crime. These perspectives are *indirect victimization, disorder/incivilities, community concern,* and *subcultural diversity* (Covington and Taylor 1991). Although all four perspectives focus on contextual factors other than crime to explain fear, each hypothesizes a different causal thought process: that is, whether residents are more worried about community disorder itself as an indicator of crime (disorder/ incivilities), their belief that the community is different than it used to be (community concern), the behaviors of those who look different (subcultural diversity), or what they hear about local crime and gangs (indirect victimization) (Covington and Taylor 1991).

This study uses qualitative data to examine these four competing perspectives and to gain a more in-depth understanding of these thought processes with regard to fear of gangs in Santa Ana, California, a primarily White and Latino city just south of Los Angeles that has struggled with social disorganization and gang crime for decades. Few studies have

specifically examined fear of gangs, even though gangs have been blamed for much recent violence. None have studied how these four perspectives apply to fear of gang crime specifically. Through analysis of focus group discussions conducted during the summer of 1997 with a diverse sample of residents from neighborhoods of various socioeconomic levels, this study examines fear of gangs and their crimes, as the residents themselves defined it. First, the analysis shows how the fear-of-crime models, which have been used primarily to describe aggregate fear levels, apply at the individual, personal level for a group of people living in Santa Ana. Second, it illustrates how people can connect in their daily lives the theoretically important environmental factors into one general thought process leading to fear of gang crime.

Knowing how perceptions of these environmental factors influence people's thoughts and fear of gang crime is important for theoretical and policy reasons. To date, fear-of-crime researchers generally have seen the four perspectives as unique and separate, although they are similar in their focuses on environmental indicators. Some have argued that there are causal connections linking these perspectives (e.g., Garofalo and Laub 1978; Skogan 1990; Skogan and Maxfield 1981; Taylor 1999b; Wilson and Kelling 1982), but the thrust of many studies has been to examine them as independent predictors of fear. I was guided by two primary questions. First, how do the fear-of-crime perspectives apply to fear of gang crime specifically? Second, when worrying about gang crime, do different people focus primarily on different problems (e.g., some diversity or some disorder), or do the same people think about all of these factors?

Understanding resident concerns about gangs is useful for policymakers and practitioners, especially police, who now often focus on improving neighborhood quality of life rather than simply on suppression (see Friedman and Clark 1999; Taylor 1999b). Legislators and other elected officials also continue to use public fear as a primary reason for supporting harsh policies. Because of the exorbitant cost of increasing prison populations, they are now forced to look for other answers to America's crime and fear problems (Little Hoover Commission 1998). More information about why some people fear gang crime may help them choose among the available crime prevention and suppression options.

RESEARCH DESIGN

The Context: Santa Ana, California

Santa Ana is an ideal location for neighborhood research on fear of gangs. Santa Ana has structured neighborhoods with geographically defined boundaries and organizations through which to recruit participants, which are not constructed to deal specifically with crime issues (as neighborhood watches are). Santa Ana has a reputation in the county as "gang infested" and reports high levels of gang crime (see Meeker et al. 1998). It has one of the highest crime rates in the county (U.S. Census Bureau 1994). However, the city's neighborhoods vary considerably in social disorganization characteristics, socioeconomic status, and levels of crime and gang-related crime.

Santa Ana is located in Orange County, just south of Los Angeles. Orange County has experienced rapid increases in population, ethnic heterogeneity, and urbanization. Between 1996 and 1997 alone, the county's population increase (54,733 people) was the fourth largest net gain in the nation (Fiore 1998). During the 1980s, the number of county residents increased 25 percent and gained another 13 percent during the 1990s, resulting in a total of about 2.7 million people by 1997. By the late 1990s, the primary minority groups were Latinos (28.5 percent) and Asians/Pacific Islanders (13.3

percent), primarily Vietnamese. African Americans were only about 2 percent of the population (Gaquin and DeBrandt 2000). In addition to a large number of documented Latino immigrants, there are many undocumented ones, especially in Santa Ana, the city with the highest concentration of Latino residents (about half of the counted population). In the mid-1990s, Santa Ana was the largest city in the county, with a counted population of about 300,000 people and a median household income of $35,000. About 18 percent of the residents were living below the poverty level.

Like many other areas of Southern California, Santa Ana has many long-term, established resident gangs and at the time of this research had the largest identified gang population in the county (Capizzi 1996). There were some indications that the number of gang members was continuing to increase during the late 1990s, but statistics showed that violent gang crime was decreasing (Capizzi 1998; Grad 1998). Although Santa Ana had the most gang-related homicides (16) in the county during 1997, the year these focus groups were conducted, homicides had been declining for four years in a row. Between 1995 and 1997, gang-related homicides dropped by 71 percent (Boucher 1998: Capizzi 1998), a trend that was occurring statewide (Carney 1998). The number of gang-related shootings in the city also dropped significantly from about 30 a month in 1996 to about 7 a month in 1997 (Capizzi 1998).

The drop in crime was not simply a local phenomenon, but the decreases in Santa Ana's gang-related violent crime may have been due in part to a hard-hitting Orange County policing approach to decrease gang crime. Since 1992, the county's law enforcement agencies have worked together on the Gang Strategy Steering Committee (GSSC). Tri-Agency Resource Gang Enforcement Teams (TARGETs) are part of their gang suppression tactics. Santa Ana has four of these teams, which are called STOP

(Street Terrorist Offender Project) teams. STOP teams, composed of police and probation officers and district attorney staff members, "target" the most serious gang members and sometimes gangs as a whole for intensive enforcement and suppression strategies. These strategies include increased surveillance by police and probation officers working together on the streets, vertical prosecution, refusal to plea bargain, and enhanced penalties under California's Street Terrorism and Enforcement and Prevention (STEP) Act. The STEP Act, passed in 1988, provides for longer prison terms for people who commit certain crimes and are members of criminal street gangs with a "pattern of criminal activity" (see California Penal Code, Section 186.22).

The Six Neighborhoods

To ensure a diverse sample, participants were recruited during the summer of 1997 from six neighborhoods in Santa Ana: two upper-income, two middle-income, and two lower-income areas. This sampling strategy allowed for variation in the socioeconomic status and "objective" social disorganization factors across neighborhoods. The community development resource coordinator in the city's housing department provided me with a list of neighborhood organizations and contacts as well as a map of the city's neighborhoods. He indicated the upper-, middle-, and lower-income areas on the basis of the city's designations, and this map served as the source for choosing study sites.

The two upper-income areas were Floral Park and Morrison Park, which were established neighborhoods. Most residents there were homeowners and were White. According to officers in the Santa Ana Police Department, at the time of this study, neither neighborhood had resident gangs, and neither had much serious crime relative to other neighborhoods (see Figure 8.1). Both areas were at

Figure 8.1 Number of Homicides, Robberies, and Assaults in Santa Ana Neighborhoods, 1994 to 1996

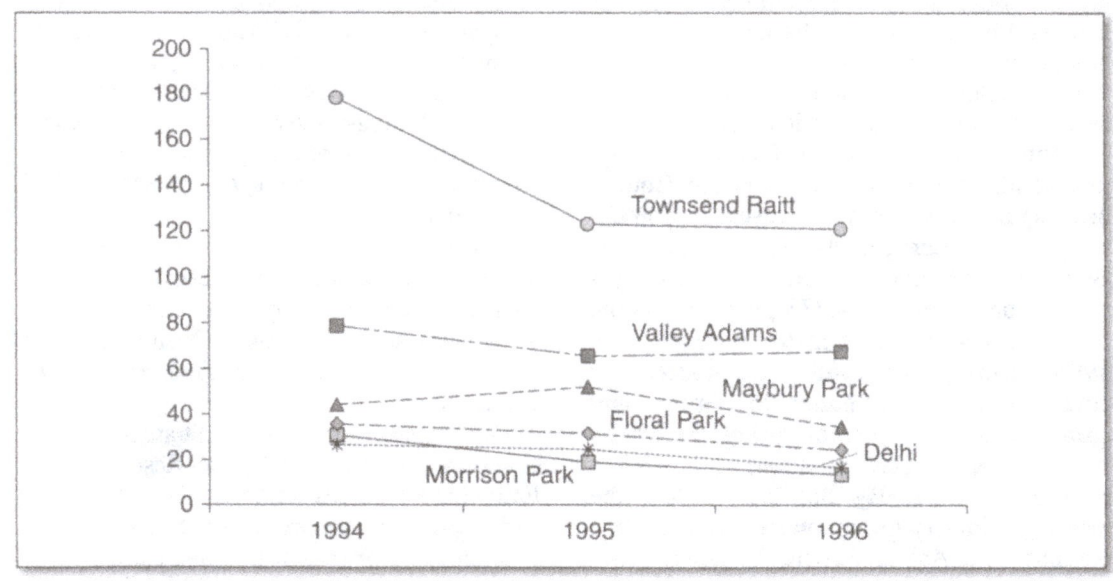

the north end of the city and were close to major freeways. Floral Park had many refurbished Victorian homes and a mix of young professionals and long-term family residents. The neighborhood association was well-organized and produced a newsletter, concerts, and a home and garden tour. Within its boundaries was the county's largest art museum. Morrison Park consisted primarily of middle-aged, long-term residents whose children had reached adulthood, although according to residents, younger professional families were beginning to move into the area. The community organization here was also organized, for example, throwing a neighborhood picnic and cleanup every year. Both neighborhoods were "well kept," with very little evidence of disorder. Both also had neighborhood parks where residents had family picnics and activities, but residents reported that these parks were much more the focus of family activities 10 to 20 years before, when the long-term families had "little" children.

Maybury Park and Valley Adams were the two middle-income neighborhoods. Both were also older neighborhoods and had many homeowners. Maybury Park had very few visible signs of disorder (except some minor graffiti), was primarily White, and did not have any resident gangs, although the police reported that a few gang members lived in the neighborhood. It was located on the northeast side of the city, also close to a freeway. Valley Adams was closer to the central city, was more ethnically diverse, and was facing more environmental and residential changes in recent years. It also had many long-term residents who owned their homes, but according to police, residents moving in recently were more likely to be poor apartment dwellers. Three or four established gangs claimed territory within Valley Adams boundaries, and the neighborhood was the focus of one of the STOP teams during the mid-1990s. There were 32 targeted gang members there by the end of 1995, and by 1996, police indicated that their efforts had eliminated a "large core group" of the targeted gang (through imprisonment), causing violent crimes to decrease (see Walters 1995, 1996). This neighborhood had more immediate visible signs of disorder (e.g., abandoned buildings, bars on store windows, graffiti in some areas).

The lower-income neighborhoods were Delhi and Townsend Raitt. Delhi was an established traditional Latino barrio very near the central city, with some residents having lived there 50 years or more. Some long-term residents owned their own homes, and others were renting, although the houses in this area were not as "nice" as in the upper- and middle-income areas. There were also more signs of disorder (e.g., graffiti, bars on windows). For years, Delhi had a strong resident gang with rival gangs in close proximity. Beginning in the mid-1990s, the police began targeting the Delhi gang with their enforcement and suppression efforts in hopes of stopping the bloody rivalries (see Orange County Chiefs' and Sheriff's Association County-Wide Gang Strategy Steering Committee 1998; Walters 1996). Partly as a result of these law enforcement efforts and partly because this gang generally did not commit crimes within their own turf, the violent gang crime in Delhi was relatively low (see Figure 8.1; Walters 1996). Between 1995 and 1996, police reported that felony assault in this area had decreased 48 percent, auto theft had decreased 18 percent, and auto burglaries had decreased 30 percent (Walters 1996). Just before the focus groups were conducted, the police reported that "this gang has been relatively inactive due to the number of gang members in custody" (Walters, 1996:5). The Delhi residents in this study, though, reported a strong fear and distrust of the police and complained about harassment, brutality, and what they saw as the police department's dismissal of their complaints (see Moore 1991; Vigil 1988).

Delhi did have a community center designed to help residents access social services and to provide them with help (e.g., health and skills workshops, food distribution, homework help, referrals to social service programs).

The Townsend Raitt neighborhood was the poorest of the neighborhoods. The residents were primarily recent, undocumented Latino immigrants from Mexico and other Central and South American countries living in high-density apartment complexes. Because of poverty, many apartments housed multiple immigrant families. This area had the most signs of disorder of the neighborhoods: bars on windows, gang graffiti, trash, rundown and abandoned buildings, and people hanging out on the street. The crime in Townsend Raitt was relatively high compared to other areas of the city, and there were many gangs who claimed territory there, including some rivals (see Figure 1). Although the STOP teams were focusing on gangs in some adjacent grids, the gang enforcement efforts were not primarily focused on this specific area during the time preceding this research. Rather, this area was the focus of the U.S. Department of Justice-funded Weed and Seed Program, designed to "weed out" criminals and "seed" the neighborhood with programs, which claimed success at decreasing crime (Kass 1997). This neighborhood also had a community center adjacent to a neighborhood park, where residents gained access to social and recreational services (e.g., welfare, food, exercise and parenting classes).

Using Focus Groups to Gain More In-Depth Responses

Focus groups are one way to examine the magnitude and intensity of residents' feelings in their own words and to gain more in-depth responses than randomized surveys allow (Goldman and McDonald 1987; Stewart and Shamdasani 1990). They permit researchers to probe respondents about their feelings (Krueger 1994), in this case to see if factors related to fear of gangs are similar to those that are related to general fear of crime. This study used a variation of the traditional focus group, called a "peer group" (Gamson 1992:192), in which residents already know one another, here because they were neighbors or because they participated in their neighborhood organizations. These peer groups were smaller than traditional focus groups, were on the "participants' turf," and did not rely heavily on the facilitator to maintain the conversation (Gamson 1992:193).

Recruiting Participants

I used a variation of "snowball sampling," a common approach to recruiting focus group participants (Krueger 1994:84; Stewart and Shamdasani 1990). I initially contacted people within the neighborhood organizations or community centers. The research was introduced as a group designed to discuss "community issues and concerns" to avoid biasing the composition of the groups toward those already sensitized to crime issues. The exact recruitment process varied depending on the neighborhood and the preference of the contact person (the leader of the neighborhood organization or community center; see Table 8.1).

The number of respondents in the focus groups ranged from 6 to 11. Because this was an exploratory study to look at how residents in different types of neighborhoods might think about factors that cause them to fear gangs, there was no attempt to regulate the demographic characteristics of the participants, although available information is noted here (see Table 8.1). This study was not designed to gather a "representative" sample of Santa Ana residents. Rather, I tried to gather a diverse group of people living in different types of neighborhoods and to gain access to people who might not have been easily contacted otherwise (e.g., poor Latinos). The method of recruiting then (neighborhood organizations and community centers) may make these respondents different from other neighborhood members; for example, they may be more attuned to or active in neighborhood life. By choosing to participate, residents also self-selected into the groups. Consequently, the findings here may not apply to other people who live in Santa Ana, its neighborhoods, or elsewhere (see Stewart and Shamdasani 1990). There were also more women than men. Prior research has shown that women are more likely than men to be afraid (see Warr 1994 for a review). In these discussions, I did not perceive major differences between men's and women's thoughts about the causes of their gang-related fears.

Conducting the Focus Groups

Because of the sensitivity of the research topic and to ensure maximum participation, the research setting was comfortable and convenient. The groups were held at times and neighborhood locations chosen by the participants (see Table 8.1). It is best to hold two focus groups with regard to each factor on which the groups were selected-here, neighborhood income levels and social disorganization characteristics (Morgan 1988)—and six groups can adequately address most research questions (Goldman and McDonald 1987). I conducted seven focus groups: one in each neighborhood (or two in each type of neighborhood), with the exception of Townsend Raitt, where the community center invited me to conduct two.

When focus group members arrived, they completed a short list of demographic questions. I brought approximately 15 open-ended questions to serve as a guide for the discussions, but the conversations were free flowing. The first question was always "What are your biggest concerns about your community?" I attempted to downplay the role of the facilitator while ensuring that the questions of interest were discussed (see Gamson

1992). According to Morgan (1988:22), the goal is to "conduct a group discussion that resembles a lively conversation among friends or neighbors." which was how these groups proceeded. However, there were multiple questions designed to ask specifically about gangs and fear of them after asking more generally about residents' communities and crime concerns. Some questions included the following: "Are you concerned about gangs? Why?" "What about gangs, in particular, scares you?" "Do you think gangs are a problem in your own community? Why?" "Do you currently take precautions to protect yourself from gangs?"

The groups generally lasted about two hours. The discussions were audiotaped and later transcribed verbatim, then coded by hand on the basis of themes that emerged. The framework guiding the search for themes was driven by the four perspectives on fear of crime discussed earlier. Quotations were then grouped and evaluated within these themes (rather than solely by question). People in all focus groups, except those in Townsend Raitt, discussed the causes of their fears in similar ways. Consequently, the findings from these five groups will be the primary focus of this article. The differences in the Townsend Raitt groups' responses will be discussed near the end of the article, in part because they echo these results but from a different perspective: that of recent Latino immigrants.

Each Perspective Is Critical to the Thought Process

Increasing (Sub)Cultural Diversity Is at the Root of Fear

The connection between Latino immigrants and gang crime has a strong history in Southern California (see Moore 1978, 1991; Vigil 1988) and especially in Santa Ana, where there are

Table 8.1 Neighborhood and Focus Group Characteristics

Focus Group by Neighborhood	SES Designation of Neighborhood	General Neighborhood Designation	Recruitment Process	Location of Focus Group	Number in Group	Age Range (years)	Ethnic Makeup[a]	Sex Breakdown	
								Female	Male
Floral Park	Upper	Professionals, remodeled Victorian homes, mostly White, no resident gangs, low crime	Attended neighborhood meeting and then called individuals who agreed to participate	Neighborhood park building (cabin), evening	7	35 to 75	White	6	1
Morrsion Park	Upper	Mostly older residents with homes and grown children, mostly White, no resident gangs, low crime	Primary contact recruited and set up group	Primary contact's backyard, evening	11	37 to 71	White	6	5
Maybury Park	Middle	Mostly middle-aged and older residents with homes, some diversity, crime in middle range	Called individual members from list provided by primary contact	Neighborhood park (picnic tables), afternoon	9	42 to 72	White 1 Latina	4	5
Valley Adams	Middle	Diverse ages and ethnic groups, crime in middle range, some gangs claim territory in neighborhood	Attended neighborhood meeting and called individual members who agreed to participate	Neighborhood restaurant, evening	6	44 to 70	Mixed (Whites, Latino/ Latina, Dutch Arabic)	5	1

Focus Group by Neighborhood	SES Designation of Neighborhood	General Neighborhood Designation	Recruitment Process	Location of Focus Group	Number in Group	Age Range (years)	Ethnic Makeup[a]	Sex Breakdown	
								Female	Male
Delhi	Lower	Long-term Latino barrio, established families, established resident gang, high crime before intense police gang suppression efforts, crime lower in late 1990s	Community center staff contacted and recruited neighborhood residents	Neighborhood community center, morning	9	19 to 63	Latino/ Latina	3	6
Townsend Raitt 1	Lower	Transitional, primarily (undocumented) Latino immigrants, Spanish speaking, established resident gangs, high-density apartments, high crime	Community center staff contacted and recruited neighborhood residents	Neighborhood community center, morning	10	21 to 41	Latina	10	0
Townsend Raitt 2	Lower	Transitional, primarily (undocumented) Latino immigrants, Spanish speaking, established resident gangs, high-density apartments, high crime	Community center staff contacted and recruited neighborhood residents	Neighborhood community centre, evening	8	28 to 49	Latino/ Latina	6	2

a. Determining the racial and ethnic makeup was difficult because I asked the residents to designate their race or ethnicity on a prequestionnaire, and many refused to indicate it. Consequently, this category is based on both self-designation and my perception and therefore may not be the best possible descriptor of the group.

many established Latino gangs that commit most of the gang crimes. Consequently, in Santa Ana, "race is part of the image of gangs" (Moore 1991:137), and the respondents were primed by "history" to believe that Latinos are more likely than others to be in gangs and commit gang crime (see Capizzi 1998).

Around the 1970s, Southern California began experiencing a surge in Latino immigration (Moore 1991). Although there is a long history of immigration in Santa Ana, the residents in these focus groups believed that more recent immigrants were different and more threatening to their communities and personal safety, primarily for two reasons. First, the long-term residents of the middle- and upper-income neighborhoods and the barrio believed that the recent (perceived to be mostly undocumented) Latinos were a *"different breed"* from those who immigrated many years ago. In their opinions, this new breed of "illegal" Latino immigrants was culturally very different not only from Whites but also from the long-term Mexican and Mexican American residents (see Madriz 1997). The residents believed that these "illegals" were more likely than not to be gang members. The immigrants' presence therefore had immediate negative impacts on the general quality of life and the level of gang crime in their areas as they moved into neighborhoods previously "untouched" by poor Latinos and gangs.

Second, these respondents believed that Latino immigration and immigrants brought with them *long-term, negative community change,* which eventually had resulted in or would result in even more gang crime. This increasing and changing ethnic and cultural mix (more Latinos, but of a different "breed") brought disorder and decline to their communities over a period of years because of major cultural differences in lifestyle (see Taub, Taylor, and Dunham 1984). This new cultural base and decline eventually meant that more gangs moved into previously "immune" but declining areas to claim territory, and gang crime increased, sometimes spiraling out of control. For the people in the upper- and middle-income areas, it was concern about what they saw as the beginning of this downward spiral that led them to be afraid in their own neighborhoods (see Madriz 1997; Taylor 1999b; Wilson and Kelling 1982). As one woman of color in Valley Adams who refused to identify her ethnicity said, with this wave of immigration, neighborhoods changed and "gangs got more violent."

The following exchange between two long-term, White female residents of Floral Park illustrates the crux of residents' worries about the differences between the primarily White and Mexican American long-term residents and the "new" Latinos:

> I think that part of the problem is that there are too many immigrants that come to this country and don't melt in. They want to bring their customs and everything and they don't want to be American.

> What it boils to for me is very simple. It's our illegal problem. It has nothing to do with, well it does have something to do with Mexicans definitely. But, the ones that are family people and that have lived here for generations and have come legally, I don't see any problems. But it's the mess, the garbage, and I mean garbage. We've got it . . . here in Santa Ana, we lived with the educated Mexican culture for generation. . . . This that we got now has nothing to do with that. . . . [Illegal immigrants] are a whole different breed. They're a whole different ball of wax.

The respondents' concerns about cultural diversity were heightened by language barriers that they believed kept them from adequately communicating neighborhood living and behavioral norms. They reported that trying to talk to their immigrant neighbors about concerns led to a response of "no habla English" (I do not speak English). Some thought that the new "illegals" were from such rural areas of Mexico that they did not "speak English or Spanish." For some of them, this was especially troubling because their parents or they themselves had been immigrants and had assimilated by learning English.

Even those in the long-established barrio, who themselves were all Latino, believed that the more recent Latino immigrants were different. Specifically, they made a clear distinction between Mexican Americans who had "American" values and the new Mexican immigrants who brought with them conflicting norms and behaviors (see Vigil 1988). As a young man there said,

> The thing is, this neighborhood is one of the oldest neighborhoods. You know, there's been a lot of camaraderie, people grown up together, and basically we have an understanding of each other. . . . Now we got an implement of new immigrant coming in and they are bringing their culture in, so we're having a culture clash. . . . I'm battling with my neighbors because, you know, yeah, true, we're the same ethnic background . . . .The thing is, I'm American. I've lived here all my life, so they come in, and they want to come in and, you know, implement their beliefs and all that, so we're going to have a culture clash right there.

More Diversity and Disorder Lead to Community Decline and More Gang Crime

The Neighborhood Is Not What It Used To Be

As noted above, the residents in the middle- and upper-income neighborhoods and the barrio believed that a major outcome of the changing cultural diversity landscape and the resulting disorder was dramatic community decline, which produced more gangs and gang crime. For some, this decline was evident in types of "disorder" the residents associated with "lower-class, gang-infested" Latino neighborhoods (see Taub et al. 1984). For example, the respondents thought that the street vendors who sold Mexican food in their neighborhoods signaled decline:

> I don't like the street vendors. I think it reflects badly on the neighborhood to have their little pushcarts come through . . . that's the thing you see in lesser neighborhoods. . . . I think it sends a negative message. Well, you don't see it in the higher-class neighborhoods, that's for sure.

Some felt that the neighborhood changes caused by this diversity resulted in grocery and drug stores leaving the area because they were "stolen blind" and unable to make profits. Others saw significant changes in the products carried by local stores as evidence of decline (more Latinos). As one woman said, "We lost our Alpha Beta that used to be just a wonderful store and now it's a Hispanic market. And our Ralph's [grocery store] caters to the [Latino] population . . . you see that in the selection." Others worried about the deterioration of the shopping areas: As buildings became rundown, more trash appealed in the parking lots, and more police calls occurred there. Changing grocery stores led the residents to shop outside the city to protect themselves from probable gang members and to get the products they wanted. Others, especially those in Delhi, believed that the community was no longer the way it used to be because they saw long-term neighbors moving out, putting bars on their windows, and refusing to go outside after dark. As one older woman there said, "After it gets dark, you go inside, you know" (see Warr 1990).

Community Decline Means More Crime and Gangs

Community members in established neighborhoods believed that the disorder and decline had occurred over time (primarily the last 10 to

15 years), was specifically related to an increase in immigration, and was the cause of more gangs and gang activity in their neighborhoods. As one older man in Maybury Park said, "I [have] been concerned about gangs here for about 10 or 15 years. We could see it—we could see a little graffiti and stuff like that . . . but before that, no." Another woman there said that gangs "[came] in with the immigrants." They believed that their own neighborhoods had been safe enclaves until "illegal" immigrants (in their minds, a clear symbol and almost synonym for gangs) began moving closer and into their areas (see Taub et al. 1984). Until recently, they had been afraid only when passing through the central part of the city. In the past, they had allowed their children to play in the neighborhood parks unsupervised, had family picnics there, and left their doors unlocked (see Sasson and Nelson 1996). Now, things were different, as the following excerpts from Valley Adams and Floral Park illustrate:

> We [do] not see the neighborhood like what we found 25 years ago . . . where we could let our children go down to the park and play. Now it's dangerous to go down there.

> I never locked the house the first 40 years I lived here. Now I got locks on the locks. It's just ridiculous. [Gangs] just kind of crept in.

The people in these middle- and upper-income neighborhoods felt that they were waging a daily struggle to keep gangs from taking over their neighborhoods. They still believed that they had the power to stop gangs from gaining "control," and some still walked their neighborhoods at night; yet they saw many signs of increasing gang activity in some spots or on the immediate outskirts of their once "really safe" areas. For example, this exchange in Floral Park:

> The only thing I'm worried about is the things on the outskirts [of her neighborhood], like bullets flying, passing through. . . .

> I mean, I go to sleep to the sound of police helicopters circling. They're not circling our neighborhood, but they're somewhere around.

> At night you hear shooting. I mean it's very nerve racking.

Still, even though most residents in the middle- and upper-income neighborhoods felt that the gang problems were encroaching rather than immediate, they reported that they constantly worried about victimization by gangs. Some worried about probable gang members in the neighborhood, who might steal things out of their garages or burglarize their houses for jewelry to pawn to support their drug habits. But others worried about the randomness of gang crime and believed that at any point, gang members might "hurt you." When talking about people they thought were gang members living in their neighborhood, three women in Maybury Park said,

> When you see people who look kind of dangerous walking down the street, you don't want to be biased or prejudiced 'cause they might be wonderful people just dressed like [gangs] for style. But, it's very scary to me.

> I think they're dangerous because they have very little value for human life.

> They have to kill somebody—to be in a gang and to make them powerful. . . . They kill for nothing.

Residents were even more afraid when they went to other areas of the city that were "gang infested." As one woman in Floral Park said, she refused to go downtown because the gangs there "scare me to death." Others took the long way to major shopping malls to avoid these "gang" areas.

People in Delhi had dealt with social disorganization and gang problems for years but believed that recent immigrants were making these problems much worse. They generally did not fear the gangs who lived in their barrio: They knew them, either as friends, people they "grew up with." or children they had helped rear (see Moore 1991; Sanchez Jankowski 1991; Sullivan 1989; Venkatesh 1997). Rather, they worried about rival gangs from other neighborhoods or new immigrant gangs trying to encroach on their area (see Sanchez Jankowski 1991; Vigil 1988), For example, one young man said,

> All these other people, they're immigrants. And, they come in here and they want to get high and they want to get doped up. . . . They're going to go hit the houses, they want to rob this and that. I've busted a couple of guys and I've threatened them, and I put across to them that, hey, you come into my neighborhood, you mess around, you're going to leave in a body bag. . . . People cannot be held hostage in their own homes. And, basically the new people coming in here into this neighborhood are immigrants from other places, and they're representing other gangs.

Their primary fears were about experiencing retaliation from gang members who might mistake them for Delhi gang members and avoiding the crossfire if their own gang members got in a shootout with their rivals. They said that they avoided certain areas of the city because just being from Delhi could get them killed there.

Discussion And Conculusions

Neighborhoods Differed on the "Urgency" of Their Fears

Although most residents reported fear of gangs, the depth and urgency of this fear differed by neighborhood (see Skogan and Maxfield 1981). For people who lived in middle- and upper-income neighborhoods, the fear was only urgent when they drove through certain parts of town or saw someone whom they believed to be a gang member. For them, crime and gangs were currently an outside problem that was encroaching on their neighborhood boundaries and threatened to harm them. They believed that in working together and with city officials, they had the social capital to protect themselves and their neighborhoods (see Sasson and Nelson 1996). They avoided areas they associated with gangs and gang violence and maintained informal social control at home (e.g., monitored people who came to the park or drove through their neighborhoods, watched homes that housed immigrants or gang members, and called the city to remove graffiti) (Lewis and Salem 1986; Sampson et al. 1997). But they also "knew" that gang violence could be random and harm them anywhere (Best 1999). Still, on a day-to-day basis, they did not feel a crippling terror but, rather, had a strong "urban unease" about their future safety from gangs (Garofalo and Laub 1978:252).

In contrast, people living in the lower-income neighborhoods were confronted daily with the possibility of violent victimization by gangs in their own neighborhoods and in others (see Sanchez Jankowski 1991). Their fear was more urgent and intense. Each of them could cite personal experience with violent victimization and/or gangs or knew people who had been killed by gangs. They did sometimes have incapacitating fear: They stayed in their homes when it got dark and even during the day. Yet they did not describe their fear as a paralyzing one. Rather, taking precautions had become a normal part of their daily lives: avoiding areas, staying home or in their backyards, putting bars on their windows, restricting their children's activities, and wondering who would be hurt next. Recovering from gang violence was also normal; some in Delhi, for example, described the community coming together to have car washes to help pay for the funerals of murder victims.

REFERENCES

Best, J. 1999. *Random Violence: How We Talk about New Crimes and New Victims.* Berkeley; University of California Press.

Best, J. and M. M. Hutchinson. 1996. "The Gang Initiation Rite as a Motif in Contemporary Crime Discourse." *Justice Quarterly* 13:383-404.

Boucher, G. 1998. "Homicide Rate Down Again for 4th Straight Year." *Los Angeles Times,* January 2, pp. Bl, B3.

Bursik, R. J., Jr., and H. G. Grasmick. 1993. *Neighborhoods and Crime: The Dimensions of Effective Community Control.* New York: Lexington.

_____. 1996. "The Use or Contextual Analysis in Models of Criminal Behavior." Pp. 236-67 in *Delinquency and Crime: Current Theories* edited by J.D. Hawkins. New York: Cambridge University Press.

California Street Terrorism Enforcement and Prevention Act, California Penal Code, Compact Edition, § 186.22 (West 1997).

Capizzi, M.R.1996. *1995 Annual Report: Gang Unit & Multi-Agency Resource Gang Enforcement Teams.* Santa Ana, CA: Orange County District Attorney's Office.

_____. 1998. *1997 Annual Report: Gang Unit & Tri-Agency Resource, Gang Enforcement Teams (TARGET).* Santa Ana, CA: Orange County District Attorney's Office.

Carney, S. 1998. "Chipping Away at Gangs' Influence in Orange County." *Los Angeles Times,* February 12. p. A15.

Chambliss, W. J. 2001. *Power, Politics, and Crime.* Boulder, CO: Westview.

Chiricos, T., S. Eschholz, and M. Gertz. 1997, "Crime, News and Fear of Crime: Toward an Identification of Audience Effects." *Social Problems* 44:342-57.

Chiricos, T., M. Hogan, and M. Gertz, 1997. "Racial Composition of Neighborhood and Fear of Crime;" *Criminology* 35:107-31.

Chiricos, T., K. Padgett, and M. Gertz. 2000. "Fear, TV News, and the Reality of Crime." *Criminology* 38:755-85.

Clinton, W. J. 1997. "State of the Union Address." Retrieved March 18, 2001, from http://clinton4.nara.gov/WH/SOU97/

Cohen, S. 1980. *Folk Devils and Moral Panics: The Creation of Mods and Rockers.* 2nd ed. New York: St, Martin's.

Covington, J., and R. B. Taylor. 1991. "Fear of Crime in Residential Neighborhoods: Implications of Between- and Within-Neighborhood Sources for Current Models." *The Sociological Quarterly* 32:231-49.

Fiore, F. 1998. "4 Area Counties among Population Gain Leaders." *Los Angeles Times.* March 18, pp. Al, A13.

Fox, J. A. 1996. *Trends in Juvenile Violence: A Report to the United States Attorney General on Current and Future Rates of Juvenile Offending.* Washington, DC: Bureau of Justice Statistics.

Friedman, W. and M. Clark. 1999. "Community Policing: What Is the Community and What Can it Do?" Pp. 121-31 in *Measuring What Matters: Proceedings from the Policing Research Institute Meetings.* Washington, DC: National Institute of Justice.

Gamson, W. A. 1992. *Talking Politics.* New York: Cambridge University Press.

Gaquin, Deirdre A. and Katherine A. DeBrandt, eds. 2000. *2000 County and City Extra: Annual Metro, City, and County Data Book.* 9th ed. Lanham, MD; Bernan.

Garofalo, J. and J. Laub. 1978. "The Fear of Crime: Broadening Our Perspective." *Victimology* 3:242-53.

Goldman, A, E. and S, Schwartz McDonald. 1987. *The. Group Depth Interview: Principles and Practice.* Englewood Cliffs, NJ: Prentice Hall.

Grad, S. 1998. "More Kids and Adults in Gangs, Study Shows." *Los Angeles Times,* January 24, pp. B1, B5.

Hall, S., C. Critcher, T. Jefferson, J. Clarke, and B. Roberts. 1978. *Policing the Crisis: Mugging, the State, and Law and Order.* London: Macmillan.

Heath, L. and K, Gilbert. 1996, "Mass Media and Fear of Crime." *American Behavioral Scientist* 39:379-86.

Hua, Thao. 1997. "Westminster Police Chief Armed With Fresh Ideas." *Los Angeles Times,* Orange County Edition, March 24, pp. Bl, B4.

Kass, J. 1997. "Reaping Success: Weed and Seed Program Cuts Crime Dramatically in Santa Ana

Target Site." *Los Angeles Times,* December 14, pp. B1, B4.

Krueger, R. A. 1994. *Focus Groups: A Practical Guide for Applied Research.* 2nd ed. Thousand Oaks, CA: Sage.

LaGrange, R. L, K. F. Ferraro, and M. Supancic. 1992. "Perceived Risk and Fear of Crime: Role of Social and Physical Incivilities" *Journal of Research in Crime and Delinquency* 29: 311-34.

Lane, J. 1998. "Crime and Gangs in an Urban Sphere: Constructing the Threat and Fearing the Future." Ph.D. dissertation, University of California, Irvine.

Lane, J. and J. W. Meeker. 2000. "Subcultural Diversity and the Fear of Crime and Gangs." *Crime & Delinquency* 46:497-521.

Lewis, D. A. and G. Salem. 1986. *Fear of Crime: Incivility and the Production of a Social Problem.* New Brunswick, NJ; Transaction.

Liska, A. E., J. J. Lawrence, and A. Sanchirico. 1982. "Fear of Crime as a Social Fact." *Social Forces* 60:760-70.

Little Hoover Commission. 1998. *Beyond Bars: Correctional Reforms to Lower Prison Costs and Reduce Crime.* Sacramento, CA: Little Hoover Commission.

Madriz, B. 1997. *Nothing Bad Happens to Good Girls: Fear of Crime in Women's Lives.* Berkeley: University of California Press.

McCleary, R., B. C. Nienstedt, and J. M. Erven. 1982, "Uniform Crime Reports as Organizational Outcomes: Three Time Series Experiments." *Social Problems* 29:361-72,

McGarrell, E. F., A. L. Giacomazzi, and Q. C. Thurman. 1997. "Neighborhood Disorder, Integration, and the Fear of Crime." *Justice Quarterly* 14:479-500.

Meeker, J. W., B. J. Vila, T. E. Fossati, J. Lane, K.J.B. Parsons, and D. Wiebe, 1998. "Gang Incident Tracking System." In Orange County Consortium COPS Project, Final Report.

Merry, S. E. 1981, *Urban Danger: Life in a Neighborhood of Strangers,* Philadelphia: Temple University Press.

Moore, J. W. 1978, *Homeboys: Gangs, Drugs, and Prison in the Barrios of Los Angeles,* Philadelphia: Temple University Press.

_____.1991. *Going Down to the Barrio: Homeboys and Homegirls in Change.* Philadelphia: Temple University Press.

Morgan, D. L. 1988. *Focus Groups as Qualitative Research.* Thousand Oaks, CA: Sage.

Orange County Chiefs' and Sheriff's Association County-Wide Gang Strategy Steering Committee. 1998. *Final Report of the Orange County Consortium COPS Project.* Santa Ana, CA: Orange County Chiefs' and Sheriff's Association County-Wide Gang Strategy Steering Committee.

Orange County Gang Prevention Alliance. 1994, *Action Plan, FY '94-'95.* Santa Ana, CA: Orange County Gang Prevention Alliance.

Perkins, D. D., P. Florin, R, C. Rich, A. Wandersman, and D. M. Chavis. 1990, "Participation and the Social and Physical Environment of Residential Blocks: Crime and Community Context." *American Journal of Community Psychology* 18:83-115.

Perkins, D. D., J. W. Meeks, and R. B. Taylor. 1992, "The Physical Environment of Street Blocks and Resident Perceptions of Crime and Disorder: Implications for Theory and Measurement." *Journal of Environmental Psychology* 12:21-34.

Perkins, D. D. and R. B. Taylor. 1996. "Ecological Assessments of Community Disorder: Their Relationship to Fear of Crime and Theoretical Implications" *American Journal of Community Psychology* 24:63-107.

Project: No Gangs. 1994. *Project: No Gangs: Awareness, Enforcement and Education* (Program Plan) Santa Ana, CA: Orange County Chiefs' and Sheriff's Association.

Rackauckas, T. 1999. *1998 Annual Report Gang Unit & Tri-Agency Resource Gang Enforcement Teams (TARGET).* Santa Ana, CA: Orange County District Attorney's Office.

Sampson, R. J. 1993a. "The Community Context of Violent Crime." Pp. 259-286 in *Sociology and the Public Agenda,* edited by William Julius Wilson, Newbury Park, CA: Sage.

_____. 1993b. "Linking Time and Place: Dynamic Contextualism and the Future of Criminological Inquiry." *Journal of Research in Crime and Delinquency* 30:426-44.

Sampson, R. J., S. W. Randenbush, and F. Earls. 1997. "Neighborhoods and Violent Crime: A Multilevel Study of Collective Efficacy" *Science* 277:918-24.

Sanchez Jankowski, M. 1991, *Islands in the Street: Gangs and American Urban Society.* Berkeley: University of California Press.

Sasson, T. and M. K. Nelson. 1996. "Danger, Community, and the Meaning of Crime Watch: An Analysis of Discourses of African American and White Participants." *Journal of Contemporary Ethnography* 25:171-200.

Skogan, W. G. 1986. "Fear of Crime and Neighborhood Change" Pp. 203-229 in *Communities and Crime,* edited by A. J. Reiss, Jr., and M. Tonry. Chicago: University of Chicago Press.

_____. 1990. *Disorder and Decline: Crime and the Spiral Decay in American Neighborhoods.* Berkeley: University of California Press.

_____. 1999. "Measuring What Matters: Crime, Disorder and Fear." Pp. 27-53 in *Measuring What Matters: Proceedings from the Policing Research Institute Meetings.* Washington, DC: National Institute of Justice.

Skogan, W. G. and M. G. Maxfield. 1981. *Coping with Crime: Individual and Neighborhood Reactions.* Beverly Hills, CA; Sage.

Smith, S. K., G. W. Steadman, T. D. Menton, and M. Townsend. 1999. *Criminal Victimization and Perceptions of Community Safety in 12 Cities, 1998.* Washington, DC: Bureau of Justice Statistics and Office of Community Oriented Policing Services.

Snyder, H. N. and M. Sickmund. 1999. *Juvenile Offenders and Victims: 1999 National Report.* Washington, DC: Office of Juvenile Justice and Delinquency Prevention.

St. John, C. and. Heald-Moore. 1996. "Racial Prejudice and Fear of Criminal Victimization by Strangers in Public Settings." *Social Inquiry* 66:267-84.

Stewart, D. W. and P. N. Shamdasani. 1990. *Focus Groups: Theory and Practice.* Newbury Park, CA: Sage.

Sullivan, M. L. 1989. *"Getting Paid": Youth Crime and Work in the Inner City.* Ithaca, NY: Cornell University Press.

Sullivan, M. L. and B. Miller. 1999. "Adolescent Violence, State Processes, and the Local Context of Moral Panic." Pp. 261-283 in *States and Illegal Practices,* edited by J. M. Heyman. New York: Berg.

Taub, R. P., D. G. Taylor, and J. D. Dunham. 1984. *Paths of Neighborhood Change: Race and Crime in Urban America.* Chicago: University of Chicago Press.

Taylor, R. B. 1999a. *Crime, Grime, Fear and Decline: A Longitudinal Look.* Washington, DC: U.S. Department of Justice.

_____. 1999b. 'The Incivilities Thesis: Theory, Measurement and Policy." Pp. 65-88 in *Measuring What Matters: Proceedings from the Policing Research Institute Meetings.* Washington, DC: National Institute of Justice.

_____. 2001. *Breaking Away from Broken Windows: Baltimore Neighborhoods and the Nationwide Fight against Crime, Grime, Fear, and Decline.* Boulder, CO: Westview Press.

Taylor, R. B. and J. Covington. 1993, Community Structural Change and Fear of Crime. *Social Problems* 40:374-95.

Taylor, R. B. and M. Hale. 1986. "Testing Alternative Models of Fear of Crime" *The Journal of Criminal Law & Criminology* 77:151-89.

Taylor, R. B., S. A. Shumaker, and S. G. Gottfredson, 1985. "Neighborhood-Level Links between Physical Features and Local Sentiments: Deterioration, Fear of Crime, and Confidence." *Journal of Architectural and Planning Research* 2:261-75.

Torbet, P., R. Gable, H. Hurst IV, L. Montgomery, L. Szymanski, and D. Thomas. 1996. *State Responses to Serious and Violent Juvenile Crime.* Washington, DC: Office of Juvenile Justice and Delinquency Prevention.

Tyler, T. R. 1980. "Impact of Directly and Indirectly Experienced Events; The Origin of Crime-Related Judgments and Behaviors." *Journal of Personality and Social Psychology* 39:13-28.

_____. 1984, "Assessing the Risk of Crime Victimization: The Integration of Personal Victimization Experience and Socially Transmitted Information." *Journal of Social Issues* 40:27-38.

U.S. Census Bureau. 1994. *County and City Data Book: 1994,* Washington, DC: U.S. Government Printing Office.

U.S. House of Representatives, Committee on the Judiciary, Subcommittee on Crime. 1997a. *Administration's Anti-Gang and Youth Violence Initiative.* 105th Cong., 1st Sess., Serial No. 91. Washington, DC: U.S. Government Printing Office.

_____. 1997b. *Gang-Related Witness Intimidation and Retaliation.* 105th Cong., 1st Sess., Serial No. 31. Washington, DC: U.S. Government Printing Office.

U.S. Senate, Committee on the Judiciary, Subcommittee on Juvenile Justice. 1994a. *The Gang Problem in America: Formulating an Effective Federal Response.* 103d Cong., 2d Sess., Serial No. J-103-40. Washington, DC: U.S. Government Printing Office.

———. 1994b. *Juvenile Crime: Breaking the Cycle of Violence.* 103d Cong., 2d Sess., Serial No. J-103-76. Washington, DC: U.S. Government Printing Office.

Venkatesh, S. A. 1997. "The Social Organization of Street Gang Activity in an Urban Ghetto." *American Journal of Sociology* 103:82-111.

Vigil, J. D. 1988. *Barrio Gangs: Street Life and Identity in Southern California.* Austin: University of Texas Press.

Walters, P.M. 1995. *S.T.O.P. Street Terrorism Offender Project: Annual Report 1995.* Santa Ana, CA: Santa Ana Police Department.

———. 1996. *S.T.O.P. Street Terrorist Offender Project: Annual Report 1996.* Santa Ana. CA: Santa Ana Police Department.

Warr, M. 1990. "Dangerous Situations: Social Context and Fear of Victimization." *Social Forces* 68:891-907.

———. 1994. "Public Perceptions and Reactions to Violent Offending and Victimization." Pp. 1-66 in *Understanding and Preventing Violence: Consequences and Control,* edited by A. J. Reiss and J. A. Roth. Washington, DC: National Academy Press.

Wilson, J. Q. and G. L. Kelling. 1982. "Broken Windows: The Police and Neighborhood Safety." *The Atlantic Monthly* 249:29-38.

Zatz, M. S. 1987. "Chicano Youth Gangs and Crime: The Creation of a Moral Panic." *Contemporary Crisis* 11:129-58.

DISCUSSION QUESTIONS

1. What does the previous research say about the relationships between crime rates, victimization risk, and fear of crime?

2. Describe the four perspectives that attempt to explain the causes of fear of crime, as well as what each hypothesizes as the cause for fear of crime.

3. Why does Lane argue that Santa Ana, California is a good location for focus group research on fear of gangs?

4. From Table 8.1, how do these focus group participants differ in terms of social status and the types of neighborhoods in which they live, as well as according to demographic factors?

5. What sampling technique did Lane use to obtain focus groups from these neighborhoods? According to Table 8.1, how did the recruitment processes differ?

6. What were the methods by which data was collected from the focus groups? How long did the focus groups last? How was the data organized after the completion of the focus groups?

7. In what ways do the opinions and attitudes from these focus groups provide support for the theoretical perspectives (look specifically at the direct quotes from participants)?

8. Overall, how did fear of crime differ according to the neighborhood in which the participants lived?

Community policing has become a popular strategy used by police departments all over the country to garner community support and develop better relationships within communities in attempts to be able to more effectively solve issues of crime and disorder. Chappell's research examines the extent to which patrol officers themselves accept and practice the community policing philosophy. Because she argues that community policing is a local phenomenon, she employs a case study methodology to collect data from one police department who had adopted a department-wide community policing strategy. Specifically, she was interested in studying police officers' views of the philosophy behind community policing, as well as the extent to which they adopted practices that were consistent with community policing.

THE PHILOSOPHICAL VERSUS ACTUAL ADOPTION OF COMMUNITY POLICING

A Case Study

Allison T. Chappell

Abstract: Community policing is the operating philosophy of the majority of American police departments in the new millennium. Though most departments claim to engage in community policing, research has shown that implementation of the strategy is uneven. One way to investigate the implementation of community policing is to study patrol officer attitudes toward community policing because research has shown that attitudes are related to behavior. The present study used qualitative data to explore the extent to which patrol officers have endorsed and implemented community policing in one medium-sized agency in Florida. Furthermore, the research sought to gain insight into the organizational barriers that prevented officers from adopting community policing in their daily work. Results indicated that although most officers agreed with the philosophy of community policing, significant barriers, such as lack of resources, prevented its full implementation in this agency. Implications of the findings and directions for future research are discussed.

INTRODUCTION

Community policing is currently touted by academicians and practitioners as the answer to crime and disorder problems and police-community conflict (Cordner, 2001; Greene & Mastrofski, 1988; Rosenbaum & Lurigio, 1994; Trojanowicz & Bucqueroux, 1990;

Walker, 1999). The federal government has also been supportive, providing financial incentives to agencies that agreed to participate in community policing activities. For example, the Office of Community Oriented Policing Services (COPS), a branch of the Department of Justice, provided funding to local police agencies to hire 100,000 new

Source: Chappell, A. T. (2009). The philosophical versus actual adoption of community policing: A case study. *Criminal Justice Review, 34,* 5–28. Copyright © 2009 Georgia State University Research Foundation Inc. Published by Sage Publications on behalf of Georgia State University Research Foundation.

community policing officers in the 1990s (Bureau of Justice Statistics, 2000). The results of a recent Government Accountability Office (GAO) study suggested that the funds contributed to a decline in crime (United States Government Accountability Office, 2005).

The definition of community policing has been the subject of much debate. Agencies, practitioners, and researchers tend to define it differently, though most definitions contain similar principles, including problem solving, community involvement, and organizational decentralization (Adams, Rohe, & Arcury, 2002; Chappell & Lanza-Kaduce, 2004; Skogan, 2004). Quality of life and crime prevention are also emphasized (Community Policing Consortium, 2006; Skogan, 2004). Trojanowicz and Bucqueroux (1990) offered the following definition of community policing:

> Community policing is a new philosophy of policing, based on the concept that police officers and private citizens working together in creative ways can help solve contemporary community problems related to crime, social and physical disorder, and neighborhood decay. The philosophy is predicated on the belief that achieving these goals requires that police departments develop new relationships with law-abiding people in the community, allowing them a greater voice in selling local police priorities and involving them in efforts to improve the overall quality of life in their neighborhoods. It shifts the focus of police work from handling random calls to solving community problems. (p. 5)

Community policing has been a topic of considerable research attention since the 1980s. Evaluations of community policing programs usually focus on large police agencies with specialized community policing units and evaluate the effectiveness of community policing by looking at variables such as crime rates, fear of crime, citizens'

perceptions, and other quantitative outcomes (MacDonald, 2002). Other studies investigate the relationship between community policing and measures of police attitudes (Cordner, 1991; McElroy, Cosgrove, & Sadd, 1993; Pate & Shtull, 1994; Rosenbaum, Yen, & Wilkinson, 1994; Wycoff & Skogan, 1994). Given the well-documented subcultural resistance to police innovations, examining police officer attitudes toward community policing is an important area of research because some research has indicated that attitudes are related to behavior (see Engel & Worden, 2003). There is still a need to examine the actual implementation of community policing in local police agencies (Skogan & Frydl, 2004).

The decision to institute community policing is usually made at the command level (i.e., by the chief or command staff) of a police agency. Hierarchical centralized bureaucracies are often resistant to change (Gaines, Worrall, Southerland, & Angell, 2003; Hannan & Freeman, 1984). Implementation problems, organizational cultural barriers, and various forms of inflexibility can interfere with attempts to transform organizations (Gaines et al., 2003). In fact, Weisburd and colleagues (Weisburd, Mastrofski, McNally, Greenspan, & Willis, 2003) discovered that police organizations were most likely to change in ways that reinforced the traditional bureaucratic structure and least likely to change in ways that challenged that structure. Community policing, with its emphasis on decentralization, certainly challenges the traditional, bureaucratic structure of police organizations. Therefore, there may be a degree of discrepancy between the adoption of the community policing philosophy at the command level and the implementation of that philosophy at the street level. Indeed, the formal effects may be swamped by informal practices and culture.

The present study examined attitudes and behaviors of police officers in one police agency that claimed to fully endorse the philosophy and practice of community policing. The purpose of the study was to discern through participant observation techniques the extent to which patrol officers working the street have endorsed and implemented community policing and problem solving. Once data collection began, it became obvious that there was a lack of full implementation of such strategies in this agency. Thus, a related goal emerged—to gain insight into the barriers preventing officers from adopting community policing and problem solving techniques in their daily work.

The current study is important for several reasons. First, community policing is, by definition, a local phenomenon (Trojanowicz & Bucqueroux, 1990; Weisburd & McElroy, 1988). Therefore, it continues to be of practical importance to investigate how it is carried out in different police agencies. Second, the majority of studies of community policing implementation are based on large, big city departments (but see studies on rural agencies by Thurman & McGarrell, 2003 and Weisheit, Wells, & Falcone, 1994). Thus, there is still a need to investigate community policing implementation in medium-sized agencies. The present study aims to investigate community policing implementation in a smaller, less extraordinary police department (Willis, Mastrofski, & Weisburd, 2004). Third, most existing studies are based on quantitative data. In this study, qualitative data are used to investigate officers' attitudes and behaviors related to community policing and problem solving. Finally, there is still relatively little research on community policing implementation (Wilson, 2004; Zhao, Thurman, & Lovrich, 1995). Indeed, a report by the Committee on Law and Justice concluded that more research is needed on community policing (Maguire, Kuhns, Uchida & Cox, 1997; Skogan & Frydl, 2004).

CURRENT STUDY

This research sought to assess the extent to which community policing was accepted and practiced by a sample of patrol officers in one police agency that had ostensibly adopted the community policing model department-wide. The purpose of the data collection effort was to discern the extent to which patrol officers (a) endorsed the philosophy of community policing and problem solving and (b) utilized techniques consistent with community policing and problem solving in their daily activities. As research progressed, it became obvious that there was a lack of commitment to the community policing philosophy at the patrol level in this agency. Thus, a final goal was to assess the reasons for the lack of commitment.

The present study makes a contribution to our knowledge of community policing in several ways. First, community policing, by definition, is a local phenomenon. One of the overarching goals of community policing is to tailor policing to local residents' needs and wants (Eck & Rosenbaum, 1994; Trojanowicz & Bucqueroux, 1990). Thus, each community policing case study adds to our understanding of the way it is being implemented in different departments. The lessons learned from these studies can help police leaders implement community policing in their own agencies. Second, most existing studies of community policing have been conducted in the largest police agencies, like Los Angeles, New York City, Houston, and Chicago (see Greene, 2000; Skogan & Hartnett, 1997; Wycoff & Skogan, 1986). Such departments likely confront different challenges compared to the majority of small- and medium-sized departments (e.g., more complicated bureaucracies, more serious crime problems; see Zhao, Thurman, & Ren, 2008). Third, most existing studies have used quantitative data. Such studies are important, but they often lack the ability to increase our understanding of why officers may or may not engage in community policing and problem solving. This study relied on qualitative data to provide the "detailed, context-specific understanding of emerging levels of commitment to community policing and the factors that link beliefs with actions" (Ford et al., 2003. p. 179). Finally, most community policing implementation occurred in the 1990s. Now that the community policing philosophy has had time to settle in, it is important to reexamine its implementation and the barriers associated with it in the 21st century (Zhao et al., 2008).

Agency Setting

The agency (XPD) is a medium-sized municipal police department in Florida. It serves a town of approximately 100,000 people and is home to a major university. At the time of data collection, there were 275 sworn officers and 90 nonsworn personnel. The agency has an aviation unit, a K-9 unit, a forensics unit, a SWAT (special weapons and tactics) team, mounted patrol, and a motorcycle unit.

In 1985, community policing began as a separate unit of XPD. In the 1990s, the agency moved toward a department-wide community policing philosophy. Their mission statement reflects the importance of building partnerships with community residents and business owners to solve problems and enhance quality of life. Current practices include permanent assignments and geographic accountability (the agency is decentralized to three districts); community involvement (neighborhood crime watch groups, citizen's academy); foot, bike, and horse patrol; crime analysis; police substations in high-crime neighborhoods; and working with social service agencies and schools. The department regularly held meet-the-officer days, participated in National Night Out (and similar activities that aimed to increase trust between police and residents),

published a monthly newsletter, and had a weekly television show. Furthermore, ranking members of the department are vocal supporters of community policing and publicly reinforce the idea that patrol officers should be engaging in problem-solving and community-building activities. XPD expects officers to use the SARA problem-solving model. In fact, the police agency was the recipient of a Goldstein award for problem-solving in the early 1990s. The regional training academy is based on a community policing, problem-solving model.

The author regularly met with ranking members of the department and attended the department's version of Compstat meetings. It was clear to the author that most members of the command staff were committed to community policing. For example, officers were often formally recognized for their problem-solving efforts at Compstat meetings (e.g., officer of the month) and command staff regularly spoke about ongoing problem solving efforts (e.g., coordinating with the local community college to provide computers to low-income children) and community-building activities (e.g., neighborhood watch [meetings and picnics], meet-the-officer days, and neighborhood cleanups). In fact, it was common for Compstat presentations to include photos of officers engaging in such activities.

It is important to note that XPD lacked two important components of community policing: their performance evaluation system was outdated (i.e., it primarily reflected traditional measures of policing performance) and they lacked in-service training in community policing. Both components are seen as major impediments to community policing implementation (see Alpert & Moore, 2000; Haarr, 2001).

Data and Methods

Student in an upper-level undergraduate community policing course at a large state university were offered an extra credit opportunity to go on one 10 hour ride along with the XPD. They were required to assess the degree to which community policing and problem solving were part of the police activity they observed. They also queried officers about whether they had received training in community-policing and what their views were toward community-policing and problem-solving. Depending on responses and rapport, students were instructed to probe where appropriate. For example, if officers were not supportive of community policing or had reservations about it, observers probed the officers about their reasons for resistance.

By the time students completed their ride along, they had 2 months' education in community policing theory and practice. The community policing course covered the theories and philosophies of community policing as well as sophisticated studies of community policing implementation and effectiveness. We also discussed research design limitations and implications of the studies that we read. Furthermore, students were provided 2 hours of training on the use of participant observation in research. The preparation session consisted of an overview of bias and reactivity in research and interviewing (Mastrofski & Parks, 1990) as well as the importance and practices of notetaking, maintaining objectivity, and lessening observer effects. The students were well-versed in community policing philosophy and practice by the time they participated in their ride along. Participant observation is an appropriate methodology for determining differences and similarities between formal goals and informal implementation, and allows the officers to be observed in their natural environment. According to Babbie (1992). "field research is especially appropriate to the study of those topics for which attitudes and behaviors can best be understood within their natural setting" (p. 286).

Students studied a questionnaire developed by the author prior to participating in the ride along (to provide questions to ask the officers), but they were not allowed to take the questionnaire with them on the ride along (to minimize observer effects). Thus, they conducted unstructured interviews with the police officers that they rode with (Babbie, 1992, p. 293). The questionnaire also served as an outline upon which their narratives were based. It was made clear that students should omit answers to questions that they did not gather complete data on. Fifty-four students completed ride alongs.

Ride-along officers were chosen by the commanders of each district. The author requested that each student ride with a different officer to minimize threats to validity. Students rode with officers in all three patrol districts on all three shifts (day, evening, night). The police department was promised anonymity and students were instructed not to reveal officers' names in their narratives.

Student narratives were analyzed by the author and a graduate student. Emergent themes, patterns, similarities, and dissimilarities were recorded. Keywords and observations were noted, color coded, and substantiated by further analysis and reading of the narratives until succinct themes had been developed.

Data consisted of qualitative narratives from observations and interviews with 54 officers. The qualitative narratives ranged in length from one page to six pages. Narratives contained a summary of the ride-along activities and a judgment on the extent to which community-policing and problem-solving were a part of the policing observed. Although the police department explicitly endorsed community policing, the ride alongs offer insight into the extent to which community policing was (or was not) internally and informally supported by a sample of patrol officers. They offered a view of the departmental environment and the extent to which community policing was practiced at the patrol level in the department.

RESULTS

Tables 8.2 and 8.3 present the demographics of the police officer sample as well as statistics on the ride alongs themselves. Of the 54 officers observed, 49 (90.7%) were male, 47 (87%) were White, 4 were Black, and 2 were Hispanic (see Table 8.2). The average age of the officers was 32 and the average tenure was 5.4 years (median 3, mode 2; see Table 8.3). Twelve of the officers (22%) had military experience and 51 (94%) of them were at the rank of patrol officer. Thirty-five (64.8%) students completed their ride alongs on the evening shift (3 p.m. to 11 p.m.), 11 (20.4%) completed them during the day shift (7 a.m. to 3 p.m.), and 8 (14.8%) completed them during the night shift (11 p.m. to 7 a.m.; see Table 8.2).

Observers asked the officers what type of academy training they had. The regional police academy had recently adopted a community policing and problem-solving philosophy, thus it was interesting to know whether or not the officers completed the traditional curriculum or the newer curriculum. Many officers, however, completed their training in another jurisdiction. Seventeen (31.5%) of the officers were trained in a regional traditional-style police academy, whereas 10 (18.5%) of the officers were trained in a regional community-oriented style police academy. The remaining 27 (50%) either completed the training elsewhere (e.g., out of state) or did not provide this information (see Table 8.2).

Observers asked officers whether or not they endorsed (or believed in) community policing. They were also asked to judge whether or not their officer engaged in problem solving techniques during their ride along. Overall, 26 (48.1%) officers said they believed in the community policing philosophy

and 19 (35.2%) were observed by students using problem-solving techniques. Observers were asked to count citizen contacts, traffic stops, and arrests during their ride along. Twenty one (39%) engaged in 5 or fewer citizen contacts during the ride along, 19 (35%) engaged in 6 to 10 citizen contacts, and 14 (26%) engaged in 11 or more citizen contacts. Twenty two (40.7%) conducted no traffic stops and 32 (59%) conducted one or more traffic stops during the ride along. Thirty-five officers (64.8%) made no arrests, and 19 officers (35.2%) made one or more arrests during the ride along (see Table 8.2). Finally, students were asked to estimate the percentage of time the officer spent being reactive versus proactive. On average, officers spent almost 75% of their time reacting to calls for service and about 25% of their time being proactive (see Table 8.3). Herein, the themes from the qualitative data are discussed.

Implementing Community Policing

Although about half of the officers believed that community policing was a good idea, many of the officers focused on barriers to the full implementation of community policing in this agency. Next, the author focuses on three broadly defined obstacles to community policing discussed by officers during the ride alongs: lack of resources, time, and organizational resistance.

Lack of resources. Many officers felt that the primary barrier to the implementation of community policing was lack of resources, especially as it relates to personnel. Specifically, officers told stories about how the department did not have enough "manpower" to implement community policing. The consequences of having too little manpower (i.e., being understaffed) were that there were too many calls for service to handle to focus on problem solving and meeting community residents.

Table 8.2 Descriptive Statistics of Police Office Sample ($N = 54$)

Office/Ride-Along Characteristics	N	Percentage
Gender		
Male	49	90.7
Female	5	9.3
Race/ethnicity		
White	47	87
Black	4	7.4
Hispanic	2	3.7
Other	1	1.9
Military experience		
Yes	12	22.2
No	40	74.1
Unknown	2	3.7
Rank		
Patrol officer	51	94.4
Corporal	2	3.7
Sergeant	1	1.9
Ride-along shift		
Day shift (7 a.m.-3 p.m.)	11	20.4
Evening shift (3 p.m.-11 p.m.)	35	64.8
Night shift (11 p.m.-7 a.m.)	8	14.8
Type of training curriculum		
Traditional	17	31.5
Community policing	10	18.5
Unknown	27	50.0
Endorsement of community policing		
Yes	26	48.1
No	27	50
Unknown	1	1.9

Office/Ride-Along Characteristics	N	Percentage
Participation in problem solving		
Yes	19	35.2
No	35	64.8
Citizen contacts (per officer)		
5 or less	21	38.9
6 to 10	19	35.2
11 or more	14	25.9
Traffic stops (per officer)		
None	22	40.7
1 or more	32	59.3
Arrests (per officer)		
None	35	64.8
1 or more	19	35.2

Table 8.3 Descriptive Statistics of Police Officer Sample (*N* = 54)

Officer/Ride-Along Characteristics	M	SD	Range
Age	32	5.3	24–43
Tenure	5.4	4.8	1–18
Percentage of time spent on reactive policing	73.25	29.26	1–100
Percentage of time spent on proactive policing	25.17	27.91	1–100

One officer commented, "XPD is too under-staffed to fully execute community policing. It would work if they were fully staffed so that they could have time to communicate more one on one with the people" (White male, age 26, evening shift).

Another officer said, "I love the idea of community policing in XPD but we are too understaffed" (White male, age 38, day shift).

A student wrote, "The officer told me from the get-go that we wouldn't be doing anything

proactive or practicing community policing because they were too short-staffed" (White male, no age given, day shift).

Similarly, another officer spoke about the agency's funding: "While it may look good on paper, the implementation of [community policing] is not reality. XPD does not have the funding or manpower to implement it" (White male, age 26, night shift).

Sadd and Grinc (1994) also found that resources were an impediment to community policing. They found that, in some cities, officers believed that community policing was difficult to implement due to a lack of resources. Future research should investigate the resources needed to successfully implement community policing.

According to the officers in the sample, lack of manpower meant that officers were assigned to larger beats than what is ideal in community policing, so officers were unable to get to know community residents. A few officers illustrated this to the students who rode along with them by driving the students around the periphery of their beat to show them the difficulty of building relationships with people in such a large area. One 35-year-old male officer on the day shift commented, "It is difficult to implement community policing because the size of our zones are so large."

A 38-year-old male officer on the evening shift argued, "Do you see a community? There is too much area to cover." Another officer asked, "Do you see how big this area is?" (White male, age 40, evening shift).

The literature suggests that size of beat is crucial to the successful implementation of community policing. Skogan and Hartnett (1997) argued that officers must be assigned to one area to ensure beat integrity, thus enabling officers and community members to build a relationship. In other words, "Agencies that assign fixed shifts and beats generally enjoy a higher success rate. Long-term and/or permanent shift assignment-the ultimate forms of decentralization-allow officers to learn more about people, places, issues, and problems within neighborhoods" (Sparrow, 1988, p. 5).

Relatedly, it has been argued that smaller police agencies are better at implementing community policing (Skolnick & Bayley, 1988; Weisheit et al., 1994). This is likely due to the fact that officers in smaller agencies have always been practicing a policing style that is similar to community policing, and that smaller agencies have fewer bureaucratic hurdles to overcome (Weisheit et al., 1994). Beats should be organized along natural neighborhood boundaries (Greene, 2000). That is, a beat should be defined by the common characteristics and interests of the populace, such as race or ethnicity, language, culture, and socioeconomic status (Greene, 2000). Beats should cover a whole neighborhood, rather than bisect it, and be small enough that officers can work within community networks. More research is needed on the relationship between beat size and officers' willingness and ability to perform community policing activities.

Time. Community policing scholars have discussed the importance of officers having enough time to engage in community policing and this has often been tied to lack of resources. In the present study, the issue of time emerged as a distinct theme for two reasons. First time constraints, as a result of responding to so many calls for service, were noted by officers as a reason why they do not practice community policing. Second, several students noted that the officer they rode with seemed to have an abundance of time, which, notably, was not used for community policing and problem-solving activities.

In terms of time constraints, many officers noted that time was limited. For example, one student commented, "I spoke with several officers and they quoted concerns such as time constraints of responding to service calls as a reason why community policing is difficult to implement."

Another officer wants to get involved, but lacks the time: "He told me that he would like to be more proactive and get involved but there are not enough hours in the day" (Black male, age 28, day shift).

An officer on the dayshift was too busy for community policing. Her student rider commented: "My officer didn't have time for community policing; she was too busy responding to calls and filling out reports from the calls" (White female, age 32, day shift).

Interestingly, many students also said they had a lot of down time during their ride along. One student and his officer on the evening shift watched a baseball game while they waited for calls to respond to. Another student and her officer went to play with the K-9 unit during their down time. Other students discussed how they spent time looking for illegally parked vehicles so that they could write parking tickets. "Sam said that, usually, he sits in front of the ATM at the grocery store and people will park next to him in a handicapped spot and get out to use the ATM. He gets out and writes them a ticket. All of our time was spent responding to calls or patrolling parking lots for illegally parked vehicles. We did not even venture into the realm of community policing" (White male, approximately 40, day shift).

Clearly, at least some of the officers had extra time that they could have used to work on community policing and problem solving. This may indicate that the resource problem cited by so many officers is more of a perception than a reality. It should be noted that cultural resistance to community policing invariably includes officers believing that responding to calls for service leaves them with too little time to practice community policing (Glensor & Peak, 1995). Another study found that officers did not engage in community policing or problem solving during their uncommitted time (Famega, Frank, & Mazerolle, 2005). They suggest that officers will not proactively engage in community policing and problem solving unless supervisors provide them with clear directives to do so (Engel & Worden, 2003).

There are practical implications to this finding. First, some officers may simply not be willing to engage in proactive community policing activities unless they are given clear guidelines regarding what to do and how to do it Second, they may not have had enough training to know how to do proactive problem solving and community engagement. Indeed, Sadd and Grinc (1994) found that many officers knew very little about community policing because they had not been trained. Third,

when officers are not evaluated on problem solving and community policing, there is no incentive to engage in such activities. These issues suggest that officers need more training and that the XPD should update their performance evaluation rubric to reflect problem solving and community policing. Finally, it may imply a need for separate units. Although usually not a suggested method of community policing implementation (see Skogan, 2004), it is likely that many officers joined the policing profession when crime fighting and law enforcement were the primary missions. These officers may never be willing to participate in community policing activities. Some research indicates that community policing specialists spend more time on problem-solving activities than do patrol generalists (Parks, Mastrofski, DeJong, & Gray, 1999).

On the other hand, there are ways that police departments can assess resource needs. Goldstein (1990) suggested that an agency may be able to obtain more time for officers to practice community policing by conducting analyses of calls for service and officer workload to assess how they spend their time. The data generated would provide information regarding resource needs and help to ensure that resources are allocated appropriately. Furthermore, research indicates that, overall, response time is not that important and quick response times only matter in a small percentage of cases (e.g., crimes in progress) (Percey, 1980). Therefore, if nonemergency calls can be shifted to nonsworn personnel (or handled via phone or Internet), sworn officers would have more time to engage in problem solving and community policing (Moslow, 1994).

The larger issue, of course, is that officers must focus on resolving substantive crime and disorder problems because focusing on these deep-seated issues will reduce calls for service in the long term. Therefore, making the effort to be creative with calls for service early on so that sworn personnel can focus on community problems is an investment in the future of the community. In the long run, it will reduce what initially feels like a need for more resources and personnel. The goal is to reduce calls for service so that ultimately fewer resources are needed.

Organizational resistance. Many officers commented on different aspects of the culture in XPD. Comments tended to relate to the lack of change in the organizational structure of the agency. Police scholars note that organizational change (e.g., decentralization) must occur in order for a cultural shift to take place and for community policing to come to fruition (Adams et al., 2002; Skogan & Hartnett, 1997).

Comments by officers suggested that the culture of XPD had not been redefined in terms of community policing and officers have not endorsed the philosophy. One student wrote,

> When I was at roll call, everyone laughed when the sergeant told me that I would ride along with officer X to learn about community policing. "Don't worry, we're not laughing at you, we're laughing at the community policing part!" Even the top guys were laughing.

Other observers noted the following examples of organizational resistance: "Officer X, who seemed to have trouble distinguishing community policing from 'liberal gibberish' just laughed when I brought up the subject" (White male, 30s, night shift).

Another officer provided a more concise response when asked about community policing. "When I asked [him] what he thought of community policing, he called it 'crap'" (White male, approximately 40, day shift).

The following excerpt is from a student who had the opportunity to discuss the issue with a group of officers. He concluded,

> What was even more funny was the officers' view of community policing. They had no interest

in it at all or in using problem-solving techniques, simply because they know the people they deal with don't want that. The police feel that no matter what they do, people they arrest and catch committing crimes will always hate them. (White male, age 26, evening shift)

This quote suggests that officers believe that community policing is geared toward offenders. Although that may be true in some cases (e.g., information gathering), community policing is a much broader concept that is geared toward increasing quality of life, building relationships with community residents (especially those that are law-abiding), and solving community-defined problems. It does not mean, however, that officers will not continue to enforce the law against those who break it. This finding clearly suggests that the officers (who expressed this) do not have a clear understanding of the philosophy and goals of community policing. Again, it indicates that the officers need more training, education, and perhaps mentoring in the philosophy and skills of community policing.

Cultural resistance has been cited as one of the biggest impediments to community policing (Giacomazzi & Brody, 2004; Paoline et al., 2000). Clearly, many of the officers saw community policing activities as unworthy of their time and consideration. Some officers were more open to the idea but were still less than optimistic about its potential for success. The following two officers referred to problems with more seasoned XPD officers:

> My officer told me that although he enjoys interactions with the public, many of the senior officers do not. They often sit in dark parking lots by themselves. He said that during their down time the officers are supposed to be doing community policing. (White male, age 26)

Another officer commented, "A lot of officers do not take it seriously and just wait for the next call. If everyone doesn't believe it will work, the odds of it being successful are really low" (White male, age 26, evening shift).

Finally, a night shift officer summed it up this way: "I believe community policing is a great idea and that is all it will ever be" (White male, age 29, night shift).

These observations reflect clear examples of organizational or cultural resistance within the police agency. The police subculture must be redefined to value the participation of other service providers and citizens as partners. Similarly, the successful transition to community policing requires a change in the management and organization of the agency. Midlevel management must provide administrative support and believe in the philosophy themselves, so that they can model altitudes and behaviors for patrol officers (Glensor & Peak, 1995; Wilson, 1968). Research shows that the failure of past innovations may have in part been attributed to lack of managerial support (Sherman, 1973). Although this issue is beyond the scope of the current study, future research should investigate the relationship between middle management support for community policing and patrol officer behavior (Engel & Worden, 2003).

Training in community policing and problem solving must be provided and required for all officers and administrators. Two officers mentioned the lack of training in community relations. In fact, one of them said that the police academy presented an adversarial relationship between the officer and the community. Obviously, if we expect officers to do community policing, they must be trained in such skills at the academy as well as in field- and in-service training (Trojanowicz & Bucqueroux, 1990). In Chicago, officers who felt that they were well-trained in community policing held much more positive views toward community policing compared to officers who did not feel well-trained. They were also more optimistic about its impact on crime (Skogan & Hartnett, 1997).

Importantly, only one of the officers mentioned his supervisor's endorsement of community policing. An observer wrote, "community policing is very important and he told me his sergeant thinks so too which also gives him motivation to do community policing" (White male, age 27, evening shift).

Many scholars agree that patrol officers adopt the beliefs of their immediate supervisors; thus their endorsement of community policing is critical (Engel & Worden, 2003; Ford et al., 2003; Rosenbaum et al., 1994; Wilson & Bennett, 1994; Wycoff & Skogan, 1994). Similarly, officers must be rewarded for problem-solving efforts and the activities associated with community policing as this sends the message that community policing is more than just lip service (Lewis et al., 1999). All levels of management must understand, support, and believe in the philosophy if they expect patrol officers to implement it. One observer sums up her experience this way:

> Community policing is not an integral part of the police work I observed. I believe that this might have been because of how busy they were responding to calls for service. I did not observe any proactive police initiated contacts. When I spoke about community policing, the officers brushed it off and at some points laughed at it. I definitely do not think it is part of XPD . . . I also noticed this during briefing before the shift. The head officer was reading off arrests from the night before and he was congratulating those officers who had made many arrests. He did not speak about the community. He was speaking more about traditional policing. (White female, age 25, evening shift)

The above quote brings together several challenges to community policing noted by officers in the narratives, such as time constraints, organizational resistance, and lack of reinforcement by supervisors. Next, we focus on officers who endorsed community policing.

Officers Who Embraced Community Policing

Several officers were proponents of community policing and discussed the benefits of it with the students who rode with them. For example, an observer noted the following in an interview with a 43-year-old White male officer from the day shift:

> He has gotten to know everyone who attends neighborhood meetings and it makes his job easier in the community. He enjoys knowing who lives where he patrols so that he can better serve the people and he actually knows what is going on in the community. People invite him to their get-togethers and it makes him feel more like a part of the community instead of just a law-enforcer.

A few other officers mentioned neighborhood meetings, getting to know business owners, enjoying the aspect of knowing the community, and having permanent beat assignments. Some students witnessed foot patrols in the downtown area and information-gathering techniques used by several officers. Many officers drove around their beat and waved to residents, mediated disputes, and discussed the importance of knowing how to communicate with citizens. One officer played football with the children in one of the neighborhoods in his beat. A student commented,

> The way [my officer] handled situations was kind of like a father, where he was trying to see what caused the problem and solve it, and at the same time be a type of friend to the people he came into contact with.

What does this tell us about the officers who claimed to have no time or resources to engage in community policing or problem solving? Clearly, making time for such activities is an option for some officers. This could be due to differences in beat activities or shift assignments. For example, officers on the day shift with a smaller beat may have more free time to engage in proactive activities, whereas officers on the evening/night shift may be too busy responding to calls for service to engage in community policing and problem solving. Again, this speaks to the importance of establishing appropriate beats and assessing workload.

Another observer writes:

> The officer felt that if you maintained close ties to the community that citizens wouldn't be as fearful of him when he was driving or walking around at night. He wanted a positive relationship so when problems arose, suspects wouldn't flee or run away. . . . The officer thought it was important to know most people's names and where they lived so he could start conversations with them and familiarize himself with the citizens and what they are involved in . . . the officer made significant attempts to acquaint himself with individuals walking throughout his zone that he had not previously met. (White male, age 27, evening shift)

The examples above illustrate the fact that at least a few officers are implementing community policing in this agency. Perhaps these officers will model their behavior for their colleagues, and the community policing philosophy will begin to permeate the traditional police subculture that characterized the majority of the sample.

DISCUSSION AND CONCLUSION

Community policing has existed in theory since the 1970s, but over 30 years later, its implementation still varies substantially across police agencies. Scholars have recognized many barriers to its implementation, including lack of community involvement, lack of organizational change, and a traditional police subculture that values law enforcement over problem solving. The present study looked at a small sample of officers from a police agency that had ostensibly adopted community policing department-wide to assess the extent to which patrol officers endorsed the philosophy and put it into practice. Furthermore, it sought to increase our understanding of the barriers that prevent line officers from implementing community policing. Results indicated that lack of resources, time constraints, and the organizational culture are significant barriers to community policing implementation in this agency.

This study is important for several reasons. First, community policing is a local phenomenon. By definition, strategies associated with the community policing philosophy should be tailored to the local community (Weisburd & McElroy, 1988). Thus, investigating the way it is done (or not done) in different types of agencies and communities continues to be important. Second, much of the extant research on community policing implementation was conducted in large agencies using quantitative methods. There continues to be a need to investigate community policing in medium-sized agencies using qualitative methods. Finally, there are still relatively few studies on community policing implementation, and the Committee on Law and Justice has called for more research in this area (Skogan & Frydl, 2004).

Results of the present study indicated that even in an agency that has claimed to fully adopt community policing, significant barriers to its implementation still exist. Data suggested that community policing in this agency is likely more of a departmental philosophy than a set of operational procedures. It appears to have been adopted at the command level but has not trickled down to the line level. This is an example of loose-coupling between administrative priorities and operational procedures. In other words, there is a disjuncture between the stated organizational goals of the agency and everyday police tasks (Maguire & Katz, 2002; Mastrofski, Ritti & Hoffmaster, 1987). Interestingly, past research suggests that patrol officers have more negative attitudes toward problem solving and community policing than those in the higher ranks (Lurigio & Skogan, 1994; Skogan et al., 1999).

Many of the officers viewed community policing as a good idea and have a positive attitude toward it but believe that XPD is not equipped to put it into practice. They believe that XPD does not have enough resources, and this in turn affects beat size and officers' relative time available to spend on problem-solving activities. Even officers who are enthusiastic about the philosophy will seldom practice it if they do not have the support that they require (Engel & Worden, 2003). This finding is similar to Schafer (2002) who found that many officers agreed with community policing in theory (i.e., positive global attitudes) but had concerns about the way it was operationalized in their particular department (i.e., negative specific attitudes).

The traditional police subculture is a significant barrier to the successful implementation of community policing in this agency. Some officers are cynical or simply laugh at the idea of community policing. An explanation for this could be that they have not seen the positive results of community policing and/or that the organization has not sufficiently prepared them for the change in philosophy and practice. Organizational change must take place-including training of all officers, supervisors, and ranking personnel-to ensure that officers not only understand the philosophy of community policing and problem solving but that they possess the skills needed to implement it well (Glensor & Peak, 1995).

REFERENCES

Adams, R., Rohe, W. M., & Arcury, T. A. (2002). Implementing community-oriented policing: Organizational change and street officer attitudes. *Crime & Delinquency, 48,* 399-430.

Alpert, G. P., & Dunham, R. G. (1997). *Policing urban America.* Prospect Heights, IL: Waveland Press.

Alpert, G. P., Flynn, D., & Piquero, A. R. (2001). Effective community policing performance measures. *Justice Research and Policy, 3,* 79-94.

Alpert, G. P., & Moore, M. (2000). Measuring police performance in the new paradigm of policing. In G. P. Alpert & A. R. Piquero (Eds.), *Community policing: Contemporary readings* (2nd ed., pp. 215-232). Prospect Heights, IL: Waveland Press.

Babbie, E. (1992). *The practice of social research.* Belmont, CA: Wadsworth.

Bayley, D. H. (1988). Community policing: A report from the devil's advocate. In J. R. Greene & S. D. Mastrofski (Eds.), *Community policing: Rhetoric or reality?* (pp. 225-238). New York: Praeger.

Boydstun, J. E., & Sherry, M. E. (1975). *San Diego community profile: Final report.* Washington, DC: Police Foundation.

Bureau of Justice Statistics. (2000). *Local police departments, 1997,* Washington, DC: Author.

Chappell, A. T., & Lanza-Kaduce, L. (2004). Integrating sociological research with community-oriented policing: Bridging the gap between academics and practice. *Journal of Applied Sociology/Sociological Practice, 21*(6), 80-98.

Community Policing Consortium. (2006). *About community policing.* Retrieved August 23, 2006, from http://www.communitypolicing .org/about2.html.

Cordner, G. W. (1991). A problem-oriented approach to community-oriented policing. In J. R. Greene & S. D. Mastrofksi (Eds.), *Community policing: Rhetoric or reality?* (pp. 135-152). New York: Praeger.

Cordner, G. W. (2001). Community policing elements and effects. In R. G. Dunham & G. P. Alpert (Eds.), *Critical issues in policing* (4th ed., pp. 493-510). Prospect Heights, IL: Waveland Press.

Cordner, G. W., & Biebel, E P. (2005). Problem-oriented policing in practice. *Criminology & Public Policy, 4,* 155-180.

DeJong, C., Mastrofksi, S. D., & Parks, R. B. (2001). Patrol officers and problem solving: An application of expectancy theory. *Justice Quarterly. 18,* 31-61.

Eck, J., & Rosenbaum, D. P. (1994). The new police order: Effectiveness, equity, and efficiency in community policing. In D. P. Rosenbaum (Ed.), *The challenge of community policing: Testing the promises* (pp. 3-24). Thousand Oaks, CA: Sage.

Eck, J., & Spelman, W. (1987). Who ya gonna call? The police as problem-busters. *Crime & Delinquency, 33,* 31-52.

Engel, R. S., & Worden, R. (2003). Police officers' attitudes, behavior and supervisory influences: An analysis of problem solving. *Criminology, 41,* 131-166.

Famega, C. N., Frank, J., & Mazerolle, L. (2005). Managing police patrol time: The role of supervisor directives. *Justice Quarterly, 22,* 540-559.

Ford, K. J., Weissbein, D. A., & Plamondon, K. E. (2003). Distinguishing organizational from strategy commitment: Linking officers' commitment to community policing to job behaviors and satisfaction. *Justice Quarterly, 20,* 159-185.

Fridell, L. (2004). The results of three national surveys on community policing. In L. Fridell & M. A. Wycoff (Eds), *Community policing: Past, present, and future* (pp. 39-58). Washington, DC: Police Executive Research Forum, The Annie E. Casey Foundation.

Gaines, L., Worrall, J. L., Southerland, M. D., & Angell, J. E. (2003). *Police administration* (2nd ed.). New York: McGraw Hill.

General Accounting Office. (2005). Community policing grants: COPS grants were a modest contributor to declines in crime in the 1990s. Washington, DC: Author.

Giacomazzi, A., & Brody, D. (2004). The effectiveness of external assessments in facilitating organizational change in law enforcement. *Policing, 27,* 37-55.

Glensor, R. W., & Peak, K. (1995). Implementing change: Community-oriented policing and problem solving. *FBI Law Enforcement Bulletin, 65*(7), 14-21.

Goldstein, H. (1979). Improving policing. A problem-oriented approach. *Crime & Delinquency. 25,* 236-258.

Goldstein, H. (1987). Toward community-oriented policing: Potential, basic requirements, and threshold questions. *Crime & Delinquency, 33,* 6-30.

Goldstein, H. (1990). *Problem-oriented policing.* Philadelphia: Temple University Press.

Greene, H. T. (1993). Community-oriented policing in Florida. *American Journal of Police, 12,* 141-155.

Greene, J. R. (1989). Police officer job satisfaction and community perceptions: Implications for community-oriented policing. *Journal of Research in Crime & Delinquency, 26,* 168-183.

Greene, J. R. (2000). The road to community policing in Los Angeles: A case study. In G. P. Alpert & A. R. Piquero (Eds.), *Community policing: Contemporary readings* (2nd ed., pp. 123-158). Prospect Heights, IL: Waveland Press.

Greene, J. R., & Mastrofski, S. (1988). *Community policing: Rhetoric or reality?* New York: Praeger.

Haarr, R. N. (2001). The making of a community policing officer: The impact of basic training and occupational socialization on police recruits. *Police Quarterly, 4,* 402-433.

Hannan, M. T., & Freeman, J. (1984). Structural inertia and organizational change. *American Sociological Review, 49,* 149-164.

He, N. P., Zhao, J. S., & Lovrich, N. P. (2005). Community policing: A preliminary assessment of environmental impact with panel data on program implementation in U.S. cities. *Crime & Delinquency, 51,*295-317.

Kelling, G. L. (1992). Measuring what matters: A new way of thinking about crime and public order. *City Journal, 2,* 21-34.

Kelling, G. L., Pate, A., Dieckman, D., & Brown, C. (1974). *The Kansas City preventive patrol experiment: A technical report.* Washington, DC: Police Foundation.

King, W. R., & Lab, S. P. (2000). Crime prevention, community policing, and training: Old wine in new bottles. *Police Practice and Research, 1,* 241-252.

Langworthy, R., & Travis, L. (2003), *Policing in America: A balance of forces* (3rd ed.). Upper Saddle River, NJ: Prentice Hall.

Lewis, S., Rosenberg, H., & Sigler, R. (1999). Acceptance of community policing among police officers and police administrators. *Policing, 22,* 567-588.

Lurigio, A. J., Rosenbaum, D. P. (1994). The impact of community policing on police personnel: A review of the literature. In D. P. Rosenbaum (Ed.), *The challenge of community policing: Testing the promises* (pp. 147-163). Thousand Oaks, CA: Sage.

Lurigio, A. J., & Skogan, W. G. (1994). Winning the hearts and minds of police officers: An assessment of staff perceptions of community policing in Chicago. *Crime & Delinquency, 40,* 315-330.

MacDonald, J. M. (2002). The effectiveness of community policing in reducing urban violence. *Crime & Delinquency, 48,* 592-618.

Maguire, E. R. (1997). Structural change in large municipal police organizations during the community policing era. *Justice Quarterly, 14,* 547-576.

Maguire, E. R., & Katz, C. M. (2002). Community policing, loose coupling, and sensemaking in American police agencies. *Justice Quarterly, 19,* 503-536.

Maguire, E. R., Kuhns, J. B., Uchida, C, D., & Cox, S. M. (1997). Patterns of community policing in nonurban America. *Journal of research in Crime & Delinquency, 34,* 368-394.

Mastrofski, S. D., & Parks, R. (1990). Improving observational studies of the police. *Criminology, 28,* 475-496.

Mastrofski, S. D., Ritti, R. R., & Hoffmaster, D. (1987). Organizational determinants of police discretion: The case of drinking-driving. *Journal of Criminal Justice, 15,* 387-402.

Mastrofski, S. D., Worden, R, E., & Snipes, J. B. (1995). Law enforcement in a time of community policing. *Criminology, 33,* 539-563.

McElroy, J. E., Cosgrove, C. A., & Sadd, S. (1993). *Community policing: The CPOP in New York.* Newbury Park, CA: Sage.

Moslow, J. J. (1994). False alarms: Cause for alarm. *FBI law enforcement bulletin, 63,* 1-5.

Muhlhausen, D. (2001). *Do community oriented policing services grants affect violent crime rates. A report of the heritage center for data analysis.* Washington, DC: The Heritage Foundation.

Paoline E., III, Myers, S. M., & Worden, R, E. (2000). Police culture, individualism, and community policing: Evidence from two police departments. *Justice Quarterly, 17,* 575-605.

Parks, R. B., Mastrofski, S. D., DeJong, C., & Gray, K. (1999). How officers spend their time with the community. *Justice Quarterly, 16,* 483-518.

Pate, A. M., & Shtull, P. (1994). Community policing grows in Brooklyn: An inside view of the New York City police department's model precinct. *Crime & Delinquency, 40,* 384-410.

Pelfrey, W. V. (2004). The inchoate nature of community policing: Differences between community policing and traditional police officers. *Justice Quarterly, 21,* 579-601.

Percey, S. L. (1980). Response time and citizen evaluation of the police. *Journal of Police Science and Administration, 8,* 75-86.

Reuss-Ianni, E. (1983). *Two cultures of policing: Street cops and management cops.* New Brunswick, NJ: Transaction.

Rosenbaum, D. P., & Lurigio, A. J. (1994). An inside look at community policing reform: Definitions, organizational changes, and evaluation findings. *Crime & Delinquency, 40,* 299-314.

Rosenbaum, D. P., Yen, S., & Wilkinson, D. L. (1994). Impact of community policing on police personnel: A quasi experimental test. *Crime & Delinquency, 40,* 331-353.

Sadd, S., & Grinc, R. M. (1994). *Innovative neighborhood-oriented policing: Descriptions of programs in eight cities.* New York: Vera Institute of Justice.

Schafer, J. A. (2002). "I'm not against it in theory. . . .": Global and specific community policing attitudes. *Policing, 25,* 669-686.

Schwartz, A., & Clarren, S. (1977). *The Cincinnati team policing experiment: A summary report.* Washington, DC: The Urban Institute and Police Foundation.

Sherman, L. (1973). *Team policing: Seven case studies.* Washington, DC: Police Foundation.

Skogan, W. (2004). Community policing: Common impediments to success. In L. Fridell & M. A. Wycoff (Eds.). *Community policing: Past, present, and future* (pp. 159-167). Washington, DC: Police Executive Research Forum, The Annie E. Casey Foundation.

Skogan, W., & Frydl, K. (Eds.). (2004) *Fairness and effectiveness in policing: The evidence.* Washington, DC: The National Academies Press.

Skogan, W., & Hartnett, S. M. (1997). *Community policing, Chicago style.* New York: Oxford University Press.

Skogan, W. G., Hartnett, S. M., Dubois, J., Comey, J. T., Kaiser, M., & Lovig, J. H. (1999). *On the beat: Police and community problem solving.* Boulder, CO: Westview Press.

Skolnick, J., & Bayley, D. (1988). Theme and variation in community policing. *Crime and Justice, 10,* 1-37.

Sparrow, M. K. (1988). *Implementing community policing. Research in brief.* Washington, DC: National Institute of Justice.

Thurman, Q., & McGarrell, E. (2003). *Community Policing in a rural setting* (2nd ed.). Cincinnati, OH: Anderson.

Trojanowicz, R. C, & Banas, D. W. (1985). *Job satisfaction: A comparison of foot patrol versus motor patrol officers.* East Lansing, MI: National Neighborhood Foot Patrol Center, Michigan State University, School of Criminal Justice.

Trojanowicz, R. C, & Bucqueroux, B. (1990). *Community policing: A contemporary perspective.* Cincinnati, OH: Anderson.

United States Government Accountability Office. (2005). *Community policing grants: COPS grants were a modest contributor to declines in crime in the 1990s* (GAO-06-104). Washington, DC: Author.

Walker, S. (1999). *Police in America: An introduction (3rd* ed.). Boston: McGraw-Hill.

Weisburd, D., & McElroy, J. D. (1988). Enacting the CPO role: Findings from the New York City pilot program in community policing. In J. R. Greene & S. D. Mastrofski (Eds.), *Community policing: Rhetoric or reality?* (pp. 89-102). New York: Praeger.

Weisburd, D. S., Mastrofski, S., McNally, A. M., Greenspan, R., & Willis, J. (2003). Reforming to preserve: COMPSTAT and strategic problem solving in American policing. *Criminology and Public Policy, 2,* 421-456.

Weisheit, R. A., Wells, L. E., & Falcone, D. N. (1994). Community policing in small town and rural America. *Crime & Delinquency, 40,* 549-567.

Wilkinson, D. L., & Rosenbaum, D. P. (1994). The effects of organizational structure on community policing: A comparison of two cities. In D. P. Rosenbaum (Ed.), *The challenge of community policing: Testing the promises* (pp. 53-74). Thousand Oaks, CA: Sage.

Willis, J. J., Mastrofski, S. D., & Weisburd, D. (2004). COMPSTAT and bureaucracy: A case study of challenges and opportunities for change. *Justice Quarterly, 21,* 462-496.

Wilson, U. G., & Bennett, S. F. (1994). Officers' response to community policing: Variations on a theme. *Crime & Delinquency, 40,* 354-370.

Wilson, J. M. (2004). A measurement model approach to estimating community policing implementation. *Justice Research and Policy, 6,* 1-24.

Wilson, J. Q. (1968). *Varieties of police behavior.* New York: Atheneum.

Wilson, J. Q., & Kelling, G. L. (1982). Broken windows. *Atlantic Monthly, 249(3),* 29-38.

Worrall, J. L., & Kovandzic, T. V. (2007). COPS grants and crime revisited. *Criminology, 45,* 159-190.

Wycoff, M. A., & Skogan, W.G. (1986). Storefront police offices: The Houston field test. In D. Rosenbaum (Ed.), *Community crime prevention: Does it work?* Beverly Hills, CA: Sage.

Wycoff, M. A., & Skogan, W. G. (1994). The effects of a community policing management style on officers' attitudes. *Crime & Delinquency, 40,* 371-383.

Yates, D. L., & Pillai, V. K. (1996). Attitudes toward community policing: A causal analysis. *Social Science Journal, 33,* 193-209.

Zhao, J., Lovrich, Q. C, & Thurman, N. P. (1999). The status of community policing in American cities: Facilitation and impediments revisited. *Policing: An International Journal of Police Strategies & Management,* 22(1), 74-92.

Zhao, J., Scheider, M. C., & Thurman, Q. (2002). Funding community policing to reduce crime: Have COPS giants made a difference? *Criminology and Public Policy, 2,* 7-32.

Zhao, J., Thurman, Q. C., & Lovrich, N. P. (1995). Community-oriented policing across the U.S.: Facilitators and impediments to implementation. *American Journal of Police, 1,* 11-28.

Zhao, J., Thurman, Q. C., & Ren, L. (2008). An examination of strategic planning in American law enforcement agencies: A national study. *Police Quarterly, 11,* 3-26.

DISCUSSION QUESTIONS

1. How does Chappell make the case for using a case study methodology to study community policing?

2. Describe the police department that was the subject of the case study.

3. How did Chappell collect information from police officers regarding community policing?

4. How did this researcher obtain the sample of officers to be part of the study?

5. How was the data gathered from the study analyzed?

6. What did Chappell find regarding officer endorsement of community policing? Do officers buy into the idea? What were some of the problems they had with the community-policing ideal? Was this group of officers proactive in their duties?

7. What does this research say about the reality of whether a police department is practicing community policing? If the chief adopts a department-wide strategy of community policing, does this mean the department is actually doing community policing?

8. According to this case study, what are some of the problems in implementing a community policing strategy?

9

UNOBTRUSIVE METHODS

Secondary Analysis, Content Analysis, Crime Mapping, and Meta-Analysis

Unobtrusive methods refer to research strategies in which the subjects do not know they are being studied. This is not to be confused with covert participation; what is meant by unobtrusive methods is that "the observer is removed from the actual events and the subject is not aware of being observed" (Hagan, 2005, p. 234). Researchers can study observations that have already been made or data that has already been collected by other researchers. In fact, researchers in criminology and criminal justice routinely study preexisting data.

Most social science researchers do not have to collect their own data. They do not have to expend effort in mailing out surveys and hoping for good response rates or spend time observing groups in order to obtain data. Numerous government and other agencies collect a tremendous amount of data that researchers can analyze for their own purposes. In criminology and criminal justice, for instance, police, courts, and correctional agencies all over the country keep records on those who have been arrested, charged, convicted, sentenced, and incarcerated. A researcher can

simply study data from police reports or court records, enter this information into a database, and perform some type of statistical analysis. Unobtrusive measures, although not synonymous with quantitative methods, usually involve some type of quantitative analysis.

One of the major criticisms with unobtrusive methods, such as analyzing police and court records, is that the individuals who have been arrested for criminal offenses do not represent the entire population of persons who have committed criminal offenses. When researchers study offenders who are being prosecuted or defendants who are being sentenced by the court, they have to be worried about what is known as sample selection bias. Police and court records suffer from sample selection bias because these data only reflect information on those who have been arrested and charged with criminal offenses.

Selection bias has to do with the fact that the sample the researcher is studying has been selected based upon an arrest, prosecution, or conviction. Recall the chapter on sampling and the discussion about how nonrepresentative samples affect a researcher's ability to generalize results to the larger population. Likewise, in analyzing preexisting data collected by criminal justice agencies, "it is the mechanism for selecting the sample that causes the sample to be not representative of the population as a whole" (Sirkin, 1999, p. 197). Researchers using unobtrusive methods also have to be careful in making generalizations from these samples of offenders. Four main types of unobtrusive measures utilized by researchers in criminology and criminal justice include secondary analysis, crime mapping, content analysis, and meta-analysis.

SECONDARY ANALYSIS

Secondary analysis involves analysis of archival data (Ellis, Hartley, & Walsh, 2010) or analysis of data that was collected by someone else for another purpose (Hagan, 2005). Bachman and Schutt (2008) point out that the research opportunities for secondary analysis in criminology and criminal justice are almost infinite because of the quantity of data that has been collected on crime. Many data warehouses exist through which researchers can gain access to thousands of sources of data on topics of interests to them; usually these are publicly available data and access is free because the data has been collected with federal research funds. The National Institute of Justice annually provides funding for secondary analysis of crime-related data. The funds are specifically targeted to researchers who propose to test new hypotheses by analyzing existing data. The archival data for this funding opportunity are maintained by the Interuniversity Consortium for Political and Social Research (ICPSR) at the University of Michigan and are housed at the National Archive of Criminal Justice Data (NACJD). The ICPSR and the NACJD maintain thousands of data sets for use by social science researchers.

The main advantage of secondary analysis is that the researcher does not have to spend time collecting the information; it has already been collected, coded, and entered into a database. Not personally collecting the data, however, does pose some limitations for the research. One of these limitations is that analyzing data that someone else has collected brings up conceptualization and measurement problems. Often, preexisting data have been collected for other purposes, and as such, the variables contained in the data may not have been conceptualized or operationalized according to the researcher's needs. In other words, there may be a lack of fit between the theoretical concepts a researcher wishes to test and the operationalized concepts present in the data. Data collected by official agencies may also be susceptible to political pressures regarding which variables and cases actually make it into the final data set.

Obviously, it is not possible to go back and recollect or recode this type of data. Researchers are usually stuck with the data as is. A related limitation, therefore, is that the validity and reliability of the data may also be suspect. Researchers conducting secondary analysis have to trust that the data was collected by the agency in an objective and accurate manner. Often, variables in these data sets are not measured with the precision that is necessary for researchers to take advantage of certain statistical techniques. Sometimes, researchers may be able to recode certain variables in order to increase the level at which they are operationalized, thereby making them amenable to meeting the assumptions of certain statistical tests. Despite these limitations, thousands of researchers study thousands of topics every year using data that has been collected by other individuals or agencies.

CRIME MAPPING

Advances in both computer technology and statistical analysis have enabled crime mapping to evolve from the city map in the police chief's office stuck with a bunch of red push pins signifying the places where crimes have occurred. Crime mapping today utilizes advanced statistical techniques to examine the correlation between the spatial distribution of crime and other socio-demographic factors. Researchers can examine areas of high crime (hot spots) to look for the factors that make them susceptible to crime. Using mapping software, researchers can examine the relationships between city and neighborhood factors and crime.

Professionals beyond the police chief are also interested in these kinds of spatial relationships. City mayors, for instance, could use crime mapping information to decide how to expend valuable city resources; determining the most cost-effective ways to reduce and prevent crime. Urban planning departments could also utilize this information to make decisions about business and residential zoning. For instance, does having too many bars or apartment complexes in one area have an effect on crime rates? Police departments and city officials around the country are making use of research on crime mapping to help them deploy the best methods at preventing and reducing crime.

CONTENT ANALYSIS

Content analysis can be defined as any method designed "to make valid inferences from text" (Weber, 1990, p. 9). Content analysis involves analyzing the content of some type of communication. This method is usually employed where researchers want to "examine artifacts of social communication" (Berg, 2004, p. 267). Most content analyses examine written or transcribed media in the form of text. Some argue, however, that this method can be employed to examine any type of communication (Abrahamson, 1983). For example, content analysis has been used to examine newspaper portrayals of crime and criminals, television newscasts of criminal events, and even gang graffiti.

Content analysis is considered an unobtrusive or quantitative method (Bachman & Schutt, 2008) because it usually involves counting (quantifying) aspects of communication. For example, where in the newspaper were articles about prostitution placed? What was the average word count for articles on crack cocaine versus those on powder cocaine? Content analysis can also be qualitative in the sense that it attempts to conceptualize meaning from the analyzed content. For instance, if all newspaper articles on prostitution appear on the first page and those on burglary are on the last page, researchers might conclude that the media are trying to portray that prostitution is a more serious crime than burglary. If crack cocaine articles are twice as long on average than those on powder cocaine, researchers might question if the newspaper is trying to portray one drug as more harmful than the other.

Often, researchers conducting content analysis examine both manifest and latent content. Manifest content is that which is "physically present and countable," whereas latent content is that which involves examining the themes "underlying the physical data" (Berg, 2004, p. 269). Researchers can learn a great deal about how offenders are portrayed in the media and the effect that these portrayals may have on public attitudes toward them.

Sample (2001) contends that because the media can disseminate large volumes of information about crime and criminals to a sizeable audience, they have the capacity to profoundly shape public opinion of these topics. Researchers have observed both television and newspaper mediums presenting distorted information on crime (Durham, Elrod, & Kincaid, 1995). Content analysis involves more than simply reading newspapers or watching television programs. Researchers have to make specific decisions about what type of content will be selected for analysis as well as what type of characteristics or content is to be examined. These characteristics need to be recorded and categorized, and then the content needs to be analyzed. Depending on how much content is to be included for study, content analysis can be a substantially time-consuming research method.

META-ANALYSIS

A meta-analysis is essentially a study of studies. Meta-analyses are unobtrusive methods that summarize the findings from many different studies of the same topic. Although rarely used in criminology and criminal justice, meta-analysis is becoming more common because of the rapid pace at which research is being conducted in these fields. In meta-analysis, other research studies are the unit of analysis. Researchers have to establish some criteria for selecting which studies will be included in the sample. In other words, what is going to be the condition for a research study to be included in the meta-analysis? Often, researchers will examine research studies on a specific variable such as age, gender, or race and their impact on crime. Researchers may also restrict studies based on other criteria such as the sample size of the original study or how dated the research is. Often, findings are weighted according to the sample size in the original study, producing a "statistically based literature review" (Ellis et al., 2010, p. 256).

An advantage of meta-analysis is that it allows researchers to uncover what is currently known about a specific topic by analyzing existing research studies published on the topic. A disadvantage, however, is that meta-analysis can become complex if the studies being studied used differing methodologies. Another criticism of meta-analysis is that, dependent on the inclusion criteria a researcher selects, the outcome of a meta-analysis could be widely different (Ellis et al., 2010). This may not help researchers make conclusions about the current knowledge of a topic.

RESEARCH READING

Arrests of female juveniles for assault have increased in recent years. There have been various explanations as to the reasons for this rise in girls' delinquency; the reason the current author contends these numbers have increased is due to policy changes in the juvenile justice system. Feld specifically argues that these increases in arrest and confinement rates for girls can be best understood through relabeling interpretation rather than an actual increase in these crimes by girls. Feld analyzes official data from criminal justice agencies to assess changes in arrest and confinement rates for both boys and girls to show support for his argument.

—— VIOLENT GIRLS OR RELABELED STATUS OFFENDERS? ——

An Alternative Interpretation of the Data

Barry C. Feld

Abstract: Policy makers and juvenile justice officials express alarm over the rise in arrests of girls for simple and aggravated assault. Others see this perceived increase as an artifact of decreased

Source: Feld, B. C. (2009). Violent girls or relabeled status offenders? An alternative interpretation of the data. *Crime & Delinquency, 55,* 241–265. Copyright © 2009 Sage Publications.

public tolerance for violence, changes in parental attitudes or law enforcement policies, or heightened surveillance of domestic violence, which disproportionately affects girls. The author contends that the social construction of girls' violence may reflect policy changes in the juvenile justice system itself, especially the deinstitutionalization of status offenders. The Juvenile Justice and Delinquency Prevention Act deinstitutionalization mandates encouraged "bootstrapping" or "relabeling" female status offenders as delinquents to retain access to facilities in which to confine "incorrigible" girls. The author analyzes data on changes in arrest patterns and confinement for boys and girls charged with simple and aggravated assault, arguing that differences in rates, victims, and confinement for "violent" boys and girls support a relabeling interpretation of the supposed rise in girls' violence consistent with the social construction thesis.

INTRODUCTION

Over the past decade, policy makers and juvenile justice officials have expressed alarm over a perceived increase in girls' violence. Official statistics report that police arrests of female juveniles for violent offenses such as simple and aggravated assault either have increased more or decreased less than those of their male counterparts and thereby augured a gender convergence in youth violence (Federal Bureau of Investigation, 2006; Steffensmeier, Schwartz, Zhong, & Ackerman, 2005). Reflecting the official statistics, popular media amplify public perceptions of an increase in "girl-on-girl" violence, "bad girls gone wild," "feral and savage" girls, and girl-gang violence (Scelfo, 2004; Sanders, 2005; Kluger, 2006; Williams, 2004). One possible explanation for the perceived narrowing of the gender gap in violence is that gender-specific social structural or cultural changes actually have changed girls' behaviors in ways that differ from boys.

On the other hand, the supposed increase in girls' violence may be an artifact of decreased public tolerance for violence, changes in parental attitudes or law enforcement policies, or heightened surveillance of several types of behaviors, such as domestic violence and simple assaults, which disproportionately affect girls (Garland, 2001; Kempf-Leonard & Johansson, 2007; Steffensmeier et al., 2005). Steffensmeier et al. (2005) compared boys' and girls' official arrest rates with other data sources that do not depend on criminal justice

system information (e.g., longitudinal self-report and victimization data) and concluded that "the rise in girls' violence . . . is more a social construction than an empirical reality" (p. 397). They attributed the changes in female arrests for violent crimes to three gender-specific policy changes: a greater propensity to charge less serious forms of conduct as assaults, which disproportionately affects girls; a criminalizing of violence between intimates, such as domestic disputes; and a diminished social and family tolerance of female juveniles' "acting out" behaviors.

Their data and analyses support a social constructionist argument that the recent rise in girls' arrests for violence is an artifact of changes in law enforcement policies and the emerging culture of control rather than a reflection of real changes in girls' behavior (Garland, 2001; Steffensmeier et al., 2005). Although cultural and police policy changes likely contribute to a greater tendency to arrest girls for minor violence, the social construction of girls' violence also may reflect policy changes that occurred within the juvenile justice system itself, especially the deinstitutionalization of status offenders (DSO). After federal mandates in the mid-1970s to deinstitutionalize status offenders, analysts described juvenile justice system strategies to "bootstrap" and/or "relabel" female status offenders as delinquents to retain access to secure facilities in which to confine "incorrigible" girls (Bishop & Frazier, 1992; Feld, 1999).

In this article, I focus on patterns of arrests and confinement of boys and girls for simple and aggravated assaults over the past quarter century. The analysis bolsters Steffensmeier et al.'s (2005) contention that much of the seeming increase in girls' violence is an artifact of changes in law enforcement activities. However, I attribute some of the increase in girls' arrests for violence to federal and state policies to remove status offenders from delinquency institutions. Initially, laws that prohibited confining status offenders with delinquent youth disproportionately benefited girls, whom states most often confined under that jurisdiction. But they provided an impetus to relabel status offenders as delinquents to continue to place them in secure institutions. Within the past two decades, deinstitutionalization polices have coincided with the generic "crackdown" on youth violence in general and heightened concerns about domestic violence in particular, further facilitating the relabeling of status offenders by lowering the threshold of what behavior constitutes an assault, especially in the context of domestic conflict.

I first examine the historical differences in juvenile justice system responses to male and female delinquents and status offenders. The next section focuses on the 1974 federal Juvenile Justice and Delinquency Prevention (JJDP) Act, which mandated DSO. In the following section, I analyze arrest data on boys and girls for certain violent crimes—simple and aggravated assault—to highlight differences in the seriousness of the crimes for which police arrest them. The analyses suggest that some girls' arrests for simple assault may be a relabeling of incorrigible girls as delinquents. I then focus on the offender-victim relationship of boys' and girls' assaults, which differentially affects the likelihood of girls' arrests for family conflicts in domestic disputes. Then I examine differences between patterns of incarceration for boys and girls sentenced for simple and aggravated assault. A discussion of the findings and conclusions follows.

ARRESTS OF BOYS AND GIRLS FOR VIOLENCE: SIMPLE AND AGGRAVATED ASSAULTS

Police arrest and juvenile courts handle fewer girls than their proportional makeup of the juvenile population. As Table 9.1 reports, in 2003, police arrested an estimated 2.2 million juveniles. Girls constituted fewer than one third (29%) of all juveniles arrested and fewer than one fifth (18%) of those arrested for Violent Crime Index offenses. Girls constituted about

Table 9.1   Juvenile and Female Arrest Estimates for Violence, 2003

Crime	Total Juvenile Arrest Estimates for All Offenses	Percentage Female Share of Arrests
Total	2,220,300	29
Violent Crime Index[a]	92,300	18
Aggravated assault	61,490	24
Simple assault	241,900	32

Source: Snyder and Sickmund (2006).

a. Violent Crime Index includes murder, forcible rape, robbery, and aggravated assault.

one quarter (24%) of all the juveniles arrested for aggravated assaults and about one third (32%) of juvenile arrests for simple assault. Girls' arrests for simple assault constitute the largest proportion of their arrests for any violent crime. Arrests for Violent Crime Index offenses—murder, forcible rape, robbery, and aggravated assault—account for a very small proportion (4.2%) of all juvenile arrests, and aggravated assaults constitute two thirds (66.6%) of the Violent Crime Index offenses (Snyder & Sickmund, 2006). Significantly, however, police arrested about 85% of all girls arrested for Violent Crime Index offenses for aggravated assault (Federal Bureau of Investigation, 2006). By contrast, police arrested fewer than two thirds (62%) of boys for aggravated assaults and a much larger proportion for the most serious Violent Crime Index crimes of murder, rape, and robbery.

Changes in gender patterns of juveniles' arrests may reflect real differences in rates of offending by boys and girls over time, or they may be justice system artifacts reflecting differences in the ways police and courts choose to respond to boys and girls (Girls Inc., 1996). Although girls constitute a smaller portion of juvenile arrestees than boys, the two groups' arrest patterns have diverged somewhat over the past decade. This divergence distinguishes more recent female delinquency from earlier decades, when male and female offending followed roughly similar patterns and when modest female increases were concentrated primarily in minor property crimes rather than violent crime (Steffensmeier, 1993).

As Table 9.2 indicates, arrests of female juveniles for various violent offenses have either increased more or decreased less than those of their male counterparts. From 1996 to 2005, the total number of juveniles arrested dropped by about 25%, primarily because arrests of boys decreased by 28.8%, whereas those of girls decreased only less than half as much (14.3%).

Table 9.2 Percentage Changes in Male and Female Juvenile Arrests, 1996 to 2005

Crime	Girls	Boys
Total	−14.3	−28.8
Violent Crime Index[a]	−10.2	−27.9
Aggravated assault	−5.4	−23.4
Simple assault	24.0	−4.1

Arrests of boys for Violent Crime Index offenses decreased substantially more than those of female offenders. Over the past decade, arrests of boys for Violent Crime Index offenses declined by 27.9%, whereas those of girls decreased by only 10.2%. Aggravated assaults constitute two thirds of all juvenile arrests for offenses included in the Violent Crime Index. Boys' arrests for aggravated assaults decreased by nearly one quarter (23.4%), whereas girls' arrests declined much more modestly (5.4%). By contrast, girls' arrests for simple assaults increased by one quarter (24%), whereas boys' arrests declined somewhat (4.1%). Thus, the major changes in arrest patterns for juvenile violence over the past decades are the sharp decrease in boys' arrests for aggravated assaults and the parallel increase in girls' arrests for less serious assaults.

Although the percentages reported in Table 9.2 reflect changes in the numbers of arrests, Figure 9.1 shows changes in the arrest rates per 100,000 male and female juveniles aged 10 to 17 years for Violent Crime Index offenses between 1980 and 2005. Overall, police arrested male juveniles at much higher rates than they did female juveniles. Consistent with Table 9.2, arrest rates for both groups peaked in the mid-1990s, and then the male rates exhibited a much sharper decline than the female rates. Indeed, the male juvenile arrest rate for Violent Crime Index offenses in 2005 was nearly one quarter (23.3%) lower than in

Figure 9.1   Male and Female Juvenile Arrest Rates, 1980 to 2005, Violent Crime Index Offenses

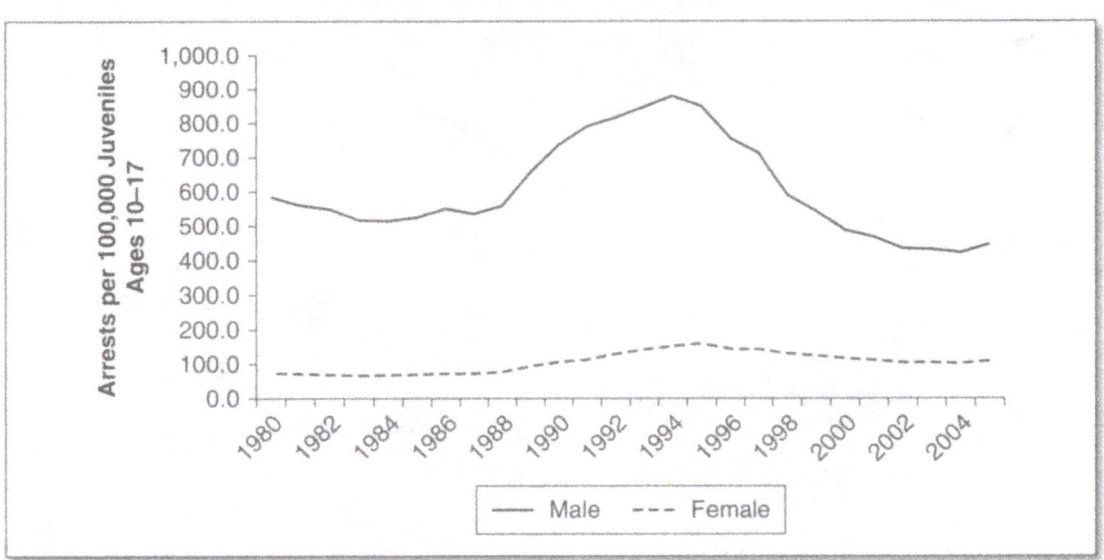

Source: National Center for Juvenile Justice (2008).

1980. By contrast, girls' arrest rate for Violent Crime Index offenses rose from 70.4 to 106.9 per 100,000 over the same period, a 51.8% increase. In 1980, Violent Crime Index arrest rates for male juveniles were about 8 times higher than those of female juveniles, whereas by 2005, they were only 4 times higher. Thus, the juvenile "crime drop" of the past decade reflects primarily a decline in boys' arrests.

Arrests for aggravated assault constituted the largest component of the Violent Crime Index, and arrests for simple assault constituted the largest component of non–Violent Crime Index arrests. Over the past quarter century, clear changes have occurred between boys' and girls' patterns of arrests for these offenses. As Figure 9.2 indicates, boys' and girls' arrests for aggravated assault diverged conspicuously. The female arrest rate in 2005 was nearly double (97%) the arrest rate in 1980 (88.8 vs. 45 arrests for girls per 100,000). Although police arrested

male juveniles for aggravated assault about 3 times more frequently than they did female juveniles, the boys' proportional increase (11.8%) was much more modest than that exhibited by the girls over the same period (267.8 vs. 239.4 arrests for boys per 100,000).

Police arrest juveniles for simple assaults much more frequently than they do for aggravated assaults. Again, changes in the arrests rates of female juveniles for simple assaults over the past quarter century greatly outstripped those of their male counterparts. The rate at which police arrested girls for simple assault in 2005 was nearly quadruple (3.9) the rate at which they arrested them in 1980 (499.8 vs. 129.7 female arrests per 100,000). Although the male arrest rate for simple assaults started from a higher base than the female rate, it only doubled (2.1) over the same period (948.9 vs. 462.7 arrests per 100,000).

Figure 9.2 Male and Female Juvenile Arrest Rates, 1980 to 2005 Simple and Aggravated Assaults

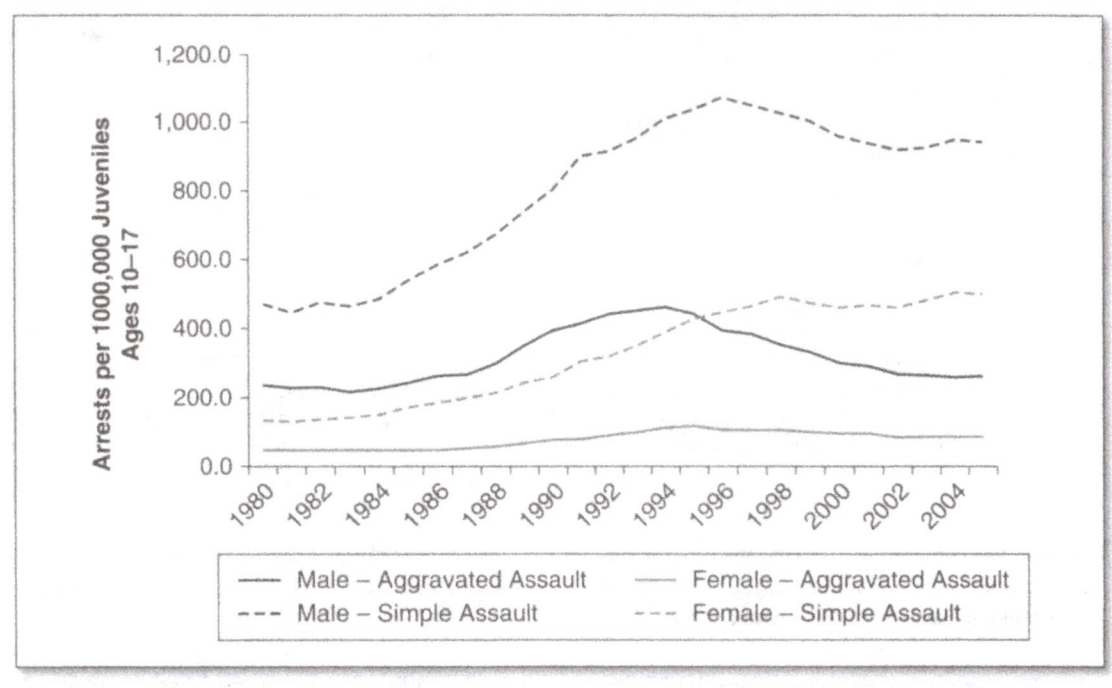

Source: National Center for Juvenile Justice (2008).

OFFENSE CHARACTERISTICS OF DELINQUENT BOYS AND GIRLS IN CONFINEMENT

Juvenile court judges possess a wide range of options to sentence delinquents: dismissal, continuance without a finding, restitution or fine, probation with or without conditions, out-of-home placement in a public or private facility or group home, confinement in a county institution or state training school, or placement in another secure public or private setting. Because male juveniles commit most of the serious crimes, evaluations of juvenile court sentencing practices typically focus on boys and examine racial rather than gender disparities (e.g., Feld, 1999; McCord, Widom, & Crowell, 2001).

Some sentencing research on gender bias focuses on "chivalrous" or lenient treatment of delinquent girls to explain why girls receive less severe sanctions than do similarly charged boys (Hoyt & Scherer 1998). Other analysts invoke "protectionist" or "paternalistic" explanations to account for why juvenile courts intervene more actively in the lives of sexually active females and status offenders than they do boys charged with minor offenses (e.g., Chesney-Lind, 1977, 1988; Johnson & Scheuble, 1991; Schlossman, 1977; Schlossman & Wallach 1978). Earlier research consistently reported a gender double standard in the sentencing of girls and boys. Juvenile courts incarcerated proportionally more girls than boys charged with status offenses and sentenced boys charged with delinquency more severely than they did girls (e.g., Bishop & Frazier 1992). More recent studies have reported fewer gender differences in sentencing status offenders once analysis control for present offense and prior record (e.g., Corley, Cernkovich, & Giordano, 1989; Hoyt & Scherer, 1998; Teilman & Landry, 1981; U.S. General Accounting Office, 1995). However, others contend that the definitions of the offenses for which the research control (e.g., status offenses) already reflect gender bias (Alder, 1984). Johnson and Scheuble (1991) summarized the inconsistent research findings on sentencing girls and reported that

> the traditional sex role model has more application to less serious types of violations, such as status offenses, for which females are given a more severe penalty than mules for violating role expectation. It also has application for the sentencing of repeat offenders. Such behavior by girls is more strongly in violation of gender role expectations than it is for boys and should result in more punitive disposition for the girls. For the more serious violations of the law, the chivalry model may have the most relevance. Girls are more likely to receive leniency and protection from the consequences of the more serious crimes. (p. 680)

Bishop and Frazier (1992) analyzed juvenile courts' use of contempt power to sanction male and female status offenders who violated valid court orders and reported differential treatment and bootstrapping of girls that covertly perpetuated gender bias.

The next analyses look at characteristics of youths in juvenile residential facilities. Police arrest and juvenile courts file petitions, detain, adjudicate, and place boys in institutions at higher rates and for more serious offenses than they do girls. However, the juvenile justice system processes girls for aggravated and simple assaults at higher rates than it does girls charged with other types of offenses, such as property, drugs, and public order crimes (Feld, in press; Snyder & Sickmund, 2006). Rather than examining the cumulative process by which judges place youths in correctional facilities, the Census of Juveniles in Residential Placement provides a 1-day count of youths in residential placements on a biennial basis.

Table 9.3 adapts the Census of Juveniles in Residential Placement data and reports on juveniles in residential placement (detention and confinement) in 1997, 1999, 2001, and 2003. In 2003, girls constituted about 14% of all delinquents in confinement and 13% of those confined for violent crimes, and both proportions have increased over the four biennia. Nearly three quarters (about 72%) of all girls confined in secure facilities for crimes against individuals were incarcerated for either simple or aggravated assault. In 2003, girls constituted about one seventh (13%) of all delinquents confined for aggravated assault and one fourth (25%) of those confined for simple assault. Confinement for simple assault represents the largest proportion for any offense for which states confine girls, and it has increased steadily over the census years.

To highlight the differences between the offenses for which states confine male and female juveniles, in 2003, girls constituted only about one in seven (14%) of all delinquents in confinement. However, suites incarcerated one quarter (25%) of all delinquent girls for either simple or aggravated assaults. By contrast, states confined boys for a more heterogeneous mix of offenses, of which simple and aggravated assaults accounted for only about one seventh (15%).

When changes in confinement for assault are examined, it is found that in each succeeding biennial census, the proportion of girls confined for aggravated and simple assaults increased. Even though boys constituted 92% of all delinquents confined for Violent Crime Index offenses (Sickmund, Sladky, & Kang,

Table 9.3 Confinement of Boys and Girls for Simple and Aggravated Assaults, 1997 to 2003

Variable	1997	1999	2001	2003
Total delinquents confined	98,222	102,958	99,297	91,831
Female proportion of all delinquents in confinement	11%	12%	13%	14%
Number of girls confined for all person offenses	3612	4365	4443	4401
Proportion of delinquent offenders confined for all person offenses who are female	10%	12%	13%	13%
Number of girls confined for simple and aggravated assault	2,535	3,147	3,211	3,198
% of total delinquents confined for aggravated assault who are female	12	14	15	16
% of total delinquents confined for simple assault who are female	22	23	24	25
% of girls confined for simple and aggravated assaults as a proportion of all girls' delinquency confinements	23	25	25	25
% of boys confined for simple and aggravated assaults as a proportion of all boys' delinquency confinements	16	16	15	16
Girls' % aggravated assaults to all assaults	45	45	40	38
Boys' % aggravated assaults to all assaults	62	60	54	51

Source: Adapted from Sickmund, Sladky, and Kang (2005).

2005), the proportion of girls confined for aggravated assaults, as a percentage of all delinquents confined for aggravated assaults, increased from 12% to 16%. In all four biennia, states confined a majority of all boys for aggravated assaults (62%, 60%, 54%, and 51%) rather than simple assaults. By contrast, the majority of girls whom states confined for assaults were incarcerated for simple assaults rather than aggravated assaults (45%, 45%, 40%, and 38%). Although violent girls may violate gender norms and thereby appear more serious (Schaffner, 1998), by contrast with the boys, larger proportions of girls are confined for less violent and injurious crimes than their male counterparts. The incarceration of larger numbers and proportions of girls for simple assaults suggests a process of relabeling other statuslike conduct, such as incorrigibility, to obtain access to secure placement facilities.

CONCLUSION AND POLICY IMPLICATIONS

Juvenile courts adapt to changes in their organizational environment, and institutional maintenance may explain juvenile courts' continued endurance at least as well as their professed ability to achieve their rehabilitative goals (Schwartz, Weiner, & Enosh, 1998; Sutton, 1988). The breadth and mutability of the juvenile court's mission enable it to redefine the boundaries of social control it administers (Sutton, 1988) and allow court personnel to maintain operational stability in the face of the delinquent male "crime drop," with an offsetting increase in female cases (Federle, 2000). DSO coincided with the emergence of a "culture of control," greater emphases on proactive policing, and aggressively addressing minor disorder and law violations (Garland, 2001). "The trend has been to lower the threshold of law enforcement, in effect to arrest or charge up and be less tolerant of low-level crime and misdemeanors, and to be more inclined to respond to them with maximum penalties" (Steffensmeier et al., 2005, p. 363).

The broad discretion available to parents, police, prosecutors, and juvenile court personnel allows them to charge many status offenders as minor delinquents and to "bring status offenders under the jurisdiction of the court at a rate almost as great as had existed prior to the [decriminalization] reform" (Schneider, 1984, p. 367). Courtroom observers report that following DSO, prosecutors charged many girls with criminal offenses for behavior that they previously charged as status offenses (Mahoney & Fenster, 1982). After Washington State temporarily decriminalized status offenders, some police and courts "redefined" them as minor criminal offenders so that juvenile courts could retain jurisdiction and authority over them (Castallano, 1986; Schneider, 1984). Analyses of the changing handling of girls' simple and aggravated assaults strongly suggest that the perceived growth in girls' "violence" may reflect a "criminalization of intra-familial conflicts and aggressive behavior" rather than an actual change in girls behavior (American Bar Association & National Bar Association, 2001, p. 14).

After three decades of DSO, the juvenile justice system remains committed to protecting and controlling girls, but without responding to their real needs. When Congress passed the JJDP Act in 1974, neither the federal nor state governments made substantial or systematic efforts to provide girls with adequate programs or services in the community (Chesney-Lind & Shelden, 1997; Maxson & Klein, 1997). Although the 1992 reauthorization of the JJDP Act included provision for "gender-specific services," the implementation of that mandate has languished. The failure to provide alternatives to institutional confinement for "troublesome girls" creates substantial pressures within the juvenile justice system to circumvent DSO restrictions by the simple expedient of relabeling them as delinquents by charging them with assault.

REFERENCES

Acoca, L. (1999). Investing in girls: A 21st century strategy. *Juvenile Justice, 6,* 3-13.

Acoca, L., & Dedel, K. (1998). *No place to hide; Understanding and meeting the needs of girls in the California juvenile justice system.* San Francisco, CA: National Council on Crime and Delinquency.

Alder, Christine. (1984). Gender bias in juvenile diversion. *Crime & Delinquency, 30,*400-414. American Bar Association & National Bar Association. (2001). *Justice by gender: The lack of appropriate prevention, diversion and treatment alternatives for girls in the justice system.* Washington, DC: American Bar Association.

Artz, S. (1998). *Sex, power, and the violent school girl.* Toronto, Canada: Trifolium.

Bishop, D. M., & Frazier, C. (1992). Gender bias in juvenile justice processing: Implications of the JJDP Act. *Journal of Criminal Law and Criminology, 82,* 1162-1186.

Bloom, B., Owen, B., Deschenes, E. P., & Rosenbaum, J. (2002). Improving juvenile justice for females: A statewide assessment in California. *Crime & Delinquency, 4,* 526-552.

Blumstein, A. (1996). Youth violence, guns, and the illicit-drug industry. *Journal of Criminal Law and Criminology, 86,* 10-36.

Blumstein, A. (2000). Disaggregating the violence trends. In A. Blumstein & J. Wallman (Eds.), *The crime drop in America* (pp. 13-44). New York: Cambridge University Press.

Bond-Maupin, L., Maupin, J. R., & Leisenring, A. (2002). Girls' delinquency and the justice implications of intake workers' perspectives. *Women & Criminal Justice, 13,* 51-77.

Bureau of Criminal Information and Analysis. (1999). Report on arrests for domestic violence in California, 1998. *Criminal Justice Statistics Center Report Series, 1*(2), 5-6.

Castallano, Thomas C. (1986). The justice model in the juvenile justice system; Washington state's experience. *Law and Policy, 8,* 397-418.

Chesney-Lind, M. (1977). Paternalism and the female status offender. *Crime & Delinquency, 23,* 121-130.

Chesney-Lind, M. (1988). Girls and status offenses: Is juvenile justice still sexist? *Criminal Justice Abstracts, 20,* 144-165.

Chesney-Lind, M. (2002). Criminalizing victimization: The unintended consequences of proarrest policies for girls and women. *Criminology & Public Policy, 1,* 81-90.

Chesney-Lind, M., & Belknap, M. (2004). Trends in delinquent girls' aggression and violent behavior: A review of the evidence. In M. Puytallaz & P. Bierman (Eds.), *Aggression, antisocial behavior and violence among girls: A developmental perspective* (pp. 203-222). New York: Guilford.

Chesney-Lind, M., & Pasko, L. (2004). *The female offender: Girls, women, and crime* (2nd ed.). Thousand Oaks, CA: Sage.

Chesney-Lind, M., & Shelden, R. (1997). *Girls, delinquency, and juvenile justice* (2nd ed.). Pacific Grove, CA: Brooks/Cole.

Chesney-Lind, M., Morash, M., & Irwin, K. (2007). Policing girlhood? Relational aggression and violence prevention. *Youth Violence and Juvenile Justice, 5,* 328-345.

Community Research Associates. (1998). *Juvenile female offenders: A status of the states report.* Washington, DC: Office of Juvenile Justice and Delinquency Prevention.

Corley, C. J., Cernkovich, S., & Giordano, P. (1989). Sex and the likelihood of sanction. *Journal of Criminal Law and Criminology, 80,* 540-556.

Costello, J. C., & Worthington, N. L. (1981). Incarcerating status offenders: Attempts to circumvent the Juvenile Justice and Delinquency Prevention Act. *Harvard Civil Rights-Civil Liberties Law Review, 16,* 41 -81.

Curran, D. J. (1984). The myth of the "new" female delinquent. *Crime & Delinquency, 30,* 386-399.

Federal Bureau of Investigation. (2006). *Uniform crime reports: Crime in the United States 2005.* Washington, DC: U.S. Department of Justice.

Federle, K. H. (2000). The institutionalization of female delinquency. *Buffalo Law Review, 48,* 881-908.

Federle, K. H., & Chesney-Lind, M. (1992). Special issues in juvenile justice: Gender, race, and ethnicity. In I. Schwartz. (Ed.), *Juvenile justice and public policy: Toward a national agenda* (pp. 165-195). New York: Lexington.

Feld, B. C. (1999). *Bad kids: Race and the transformation of the juvenile court.* New York: Oxford University Press.

Feld, B. C. (2003). Race, politics, and juvenile justice: The Warren court and the conservative "backlash." *Minnesota Law Review, 87,* 1447-1577.

Feld, B. C. (2004), *Cases and materials on juvenile justice administration* (2nd ed.). St. Paul, MN: West.

Feld, B. C. (2009). Girls in the juvenile justice system. In M. Zahn (Ed.), *The delinquent girl.* Philadelphia: Temple University Press.

Franke, T. M, Huynh-Hohnbaum, A.-L.T., & Chung, Y. (2002). Adolescent violence: With whom they fight and where. *Journal of Ethnic & Cultural Diversity in Social Work, 11* (34), 133-158.

Gaarder, E., Rodriguez, N., & Zatz, M. S. (2004). Criers, liars, and manipulators: Probation officers' views of girls. *Justice Quarterly, 21,* 547-578.

Garland, D. (2001). *The culture of control: Crime and social order in contemporary society.* Chicago: University of Chicago Press.

Girls Inc. (1996). *Prevention and parity: Girls in juvenile justice.* Indianapolis, IN: Author.

Handler, J. F., & Zatz, J. (Eds.). (1982). *Neither angels nor thieves: Studies in deinstitutionalization of status offenders.* Washington, DC; National Academy Press.

Hoyt, S., & Scherer, D. G. (1998). Female juvenile delinquency: Misunderstood by the juvenile justice system, neglected by social science. *Law and Human Behavior, 22,* 81-107.

In re Gault, 387 U.S. 1 (1967).

Johnson, D. R., & Scheuble, L. K. (1991). Gender bias in the disposition of juvenile court referrals: The effects of time and location. *Criminology, 29,* 677-699.

Kempf-Leonard, K., & Johansson, P. (2007). Gender and runaways: Risk factors, delinquency, and juvenile justice experiences. *Youth Violence and Juvenile Justice, 5,* 308-327.

Kempf-Leonard, K., & Sample. L. L. (2000). Disparity based on sex: Is gender-specific treatment warranted? *Justice Quarterly, 17,* 89-128.

Kluger, J. (2006). Taming wild girls. *Time, 167* (18), 54-55.

Krause, W., & McShane, M, D. (1994). A deinstitutionalization retrospective: Relabeling the status offender. Journal of Crime and Justice, *17,* 45-67.

Krisberg, B., Schwartz, I., Lisky, P., & Austin, J. (1986). The watershed of juvenile justice reform. *Crime & Delinquency, 32,* 5-38.

MacDonald, J. M., & Chesney-Lind, M. (2001). Gender bias and juvenile justice revisited: A multiyear analysis. *Crime & Delinquency, 47,* 173-195.

Mahoney, A. R., & Fenster, C. (1982). Female delinquents in a suburban court. In N. H. Rafter & F., A. Stanko (Eds.), *Judge, lawyer, victim, thief: Women, gender roles and criminal justice* (pp. 221-236). Boston: Northeastern University Press.

Maxson, C. L., & Klein, M. W. (1997). *Responding to troubled youth.* New York: Oxford University Press.

McCord, J., Widom, C. S., Crowell, N. A. (2001). *Juvenile crime, juvenile justice.* Washington, DC: National Academy Press.

Miller, S. L. (2005). *Victims as offenders: The paradox of women's violence in relationships.* New Brunswick, NJ: Rutgers University Press.

National Center for Juvenile Justice. (2008. October 24). Juvenile arrest rates by offense, sex, and race. Available at http://ojjdp.ncjrs .org/ojstatbb/crime/excel/jar_2007.xls.

National Council on Crime and Delinquency. (1975). Jurisdiction over status offenders should be removed from the juvenile court: A policy statement. *Crime & Delinquency, 21,* 97-99.

Platt, A. M. (1977). *The child-savers: The invention of delinquency.* Chicago: University of Chicago Press.

Poulin, A. B. (1996), Female delinquents: Defining their place in the justice system. *Wisconsin Law Review,* 1996, 541-575.

Rothman, D. (1980). *Conscience and convenience: The asylum and its alternative in progressive America.* Boston: Little, Brown.

Russ, H. (2004, February). The war on catfights. *City Limits,* pp. 19-22.

Ryerson, E. (1978). *The best-laid plans: America's juvenile court experiment.* New York: Hill & Wang.

Sanders, J. (2005, June 23). How to defuse "girl on girl" violence. *Christian Science Monitor.* Retrieved from http://www.csmonitor.com/ 2005/0623/p09s01-coop.html.

Scelfo, J. (2004). Bad girls go wild: A rise in girl-on-girl violence is making headlines nationwide and prompting scientists to ask why. *Newsweek,* Available at http://www.newsweek .com/id/50082.

Schaffner, L. (1998). Female juvenile delinquency: Sexual solutions, gender bias, and juvenile justice. *Hastings Women's Law Journal,* 9, 1-25.

Schlossman, S, L. (1977). *Love and the American delinquent: The theory and practice of "progressive" juvenile justice 1825-1920.* Chicago: University of Chicago Press.

Schlossman, S. L., & Wallach, S. (1978), The crime of precocious sexuality: Female juvenile delinquency in the progressive era. *Harvard Educational Review, 48,* 655-694.

Schneider, A. L. (1984). Divesting status offenses from juvenile court jurisdiction. *Crime & Delinquency, 30,* 347-370.

Schwartz, I. M. (1989). *(In)justice for juveniles: Rethinking the best interests of the child,* Lexington, MA: Lexington Books.

Schwartz, I. M., Steketee, M. W., & Schneider, V. W. (1990). Federal juvenile justice policy and the incarceration of girls. *Crime & Delinquency, 36,* 511-520.

Schwartz, I. M., Weiner, N. A., & Enosh, G. (1998). Nine lives and then some: Why the juvenile court does not roll over and die. *Wake Forest Law Review, 33,* 533-552.

Sickmund, M., Sladky, T. J., & Kang, W. (2005) *Census of Juveniles in Residential Placement databook.* Available at http://www.ojjdp.ncjrs .org/ojstatbb/cjrp/

Snyder, H. (2000). *Challenging the myths.* Washington, DC: U.S. Department of Justice, Office of Juvenile Justice and Delinquency Prevention.

Snyder, H. N., & Sickmund, M. (2006). *Juvenile offenders and victims: 2006 national report.* Washington, DC: U.S. Department of Justice, Office of Justice Programs, Office of Juvenile Justice and Delinquency Prevention.

Steffensmeier, D. (1993). National trends in female arrests, 1960-1990: Assessment and recommendations for research. *Journal of Quantitative Criminology, 9,* 411-441.

Steffensmeier, D., Schwartz, J., Zhong, S. H., & Ackerman, J. (2005). An assessment of recent trends in girls' violence using diverse longitudinal sources: Is the gender gap closing? *Criminology, 43,* 355-405.

Sussman, A. (1977). Sex-based discrimination and PINS jurisdiction. In L. R. Teitelbaum & A. R. Gough (Eds.), *Beyond control: Status offenders in the juvenile court* (pp. 179-199). Cambridge, MA: Ballinger.

Sutton, J. (1988). *Stubborn children: Controlling delinquency in the United States, 1640-1981.* Berkeley: University of California Press.

Tanenhaus, D. S. (2004). *Juvenile justice in the making.* New York: Oxford University Press.

Teilman, K. S., & Landry, P. H., Jr. (1981). Gender bias in juvenile justice. *Journal of Research in Crime and Delinquency, 18,* 47-80.

Tonry, M. (2004). *Thinking about crime: Sense and sensibility in American penal culture.* New York: Oxford University Press.

U.S. General Accounting Office. (1991). *Noncriminal juveniles: Detentions have been reduced but better monitoring is needed.* Washington, DC: Author.

U.S. General Accounting Office. (1995). *Minimal gender bias occurred in processing noncriminal juveniles.* Washington, DC; Author.

Williams, C. (2004, December 28). Where sugar and spice meet bricks and bats. *The Washington Post,* p. B01.

Zimring, F. E. (1998). *American youth violence.* New York: Oxford University Press.

Zimring, F. E. (2002). The common thread: Diversion in juvenile justice. *California Law Review, 88,* 2477-2495.

Zimring, F. E., & Hawkins, G. (1997). *Crime is not the problem: Lethal violence in America.* New York: Oxford University Press.

DISCUSSION QUESTIONS

1. What existing data sets did Feld analyze? Which agencies originally collected this data?

2. According to Table 9.1, what percentage of violent crime arrests were of females? What about for aggravated and simple assault?

3. According to Table 9.2, what has happened to both male and female juvenile arrests since 1996? What about these percentages between males and females? What does Figure 9.1 show about the male and female differences?

4. What does Figure 9.2 show regarding aggravated versus simple assault and for male and female juveniles? What does Feld conclude from this?

5. What does previous research say about why judges may sentence females more leniently than males?

6. What does Feld's research demonstrate about what is driving the increase in arrest and confinement rates of female juveniles?

7. What policy implications does Feld discuss that are related to the findings of his research?

RESEARCH READING

Taylor provides a good example of a content analysis of newspaper portrayals of female homicide victims. Specifically, this researcher analyzes 292 articles from a metropolitan newspaper in Florida from 1995 to 2000 to explore how the media portray female victims of homicide in domestic violence cases. Pay attention to how Taylor distinguishes between the direct and indirect tactics of the newspaper articles to portray that the femicide victim was somehow to blame for her own death.

SLAIN AND SLANDERED

A Content Analysis of the Portrayal of Femicide in Crime News

Rae Taylor

Abstract: The present study is a content analysis of crime news to determine how femicide victims are portrayed by a Florida metropolitan newspaper. The analysis consisted of 292 domestic homicide-related articles published by one newspaper from 1995 to 2000. The data were analyzed to determine effects on newsworthiness, context revealed, and patterns of victim blame. A dichotomy concerning victim blame emerged from the analysis, suggesting victims are blamed directly and indirectly for their own femicides. Direct tactics include using negative language to describe the victim, highlighting her choices not to report past incidences, and portraying her actions with other men as contributing to her murder. Indirect tactics include using sympathetic language to describe the perpetrator; emphasizing the perpetrator's mental, physical, emotional, and financial problems; highlighting the victim's mental or physical problems; and describing domestic violence in terms that assign equal blame to both partners.

INTRODUCTION

The media play a significant role in contemporary society because of the nearly exclusive power they have in deciding what issues are worthy of publicity (Chermak, 1995). In fact, the media are believed to have replaced all other social institutions as the single most influential with regard to attitudes and behavior (i.e., Chermak, 1995; Croteau & Hoynes, 1997). Consequently, the media shape public perception, influence public policy, and thus, reinforce social control and initiate necessary change (Benedict, 1992; Berkeley Media Studies Group, 2003; Berns,

2004; Bullock, 2007; Meyers, 1997; Taylor & Sorenson, 2002). With respect to crime, particularly domestic violence, this influence is very important.

Researchers have concluded that the mass media's portrayal of women reflects the overall treatment of women in society. This includes the idea that women are subjugated by men through the social structure as a whole to enforce their assigned subordinate status (Meyers, 1997; Tuchman, 1978). Croteau and Hoynes (1997) asserted "The inequality that women still face in society as a whole is clearly reflected in the unequal treatment women receive in the media" (p. 149). Men

Source: Taylor, R. (2009). Slain and slandered: A content analysis of the portrayal of femicide in crime news. *Homicide Studies*, *13*, 21–49. Copyright © 2009 Sage Publications.

may resort to violence against their female intimate partners to maintain power and control in their relationships (i.e., Daly & Wilson, 1988). In these events, the media may exonerate these men through victim blaming coverage, which also may encourage such behavior (Lowney & Best, 1995; McNeill, 1992; Meyers, 1994, 1997).

According to researchers, this treatment of women by the mass media is a fundamental problem in society, as it is the mass media that truly educate the public on social issues and transmit these messages intergenerationally (Tuchman, 1978). Thus, it is primarily the media who perpetuate harmful myths and stereotypes about victims of violence against women (Meyers, 1994, 1997).

Researchers conclude that more responsible reporting and media coverage as a whole, namely through eliminating the practice of victim blame in stories, could achieve important social change by expelling such myths and stereotypes that underlie the patriarchal foundation of our society (Carll, 2003; Meyers, 1994, 1997). According to Ryan (1971), it is the practice of victim blame that is the very barrier to social change. With regard to the media's portrayal of violence against women, the practice of blaming female victims of domestic and other forms of violence for their own plight is the primary barrier to social change relevant to this phenomenon, as it diverts attention from the true root of the social problem, which is abuse of women by men (Meyers, 1994). Berns (2004) asserted that the media have framed domestic violence in such a way that it has become a victim-centered social problem, where the focus is on the victim and what she has done, or not done, to contribute to the victimization, rather than focusing on the structural causes of the problem or on why batterers abuse.

Although media portrayal of violence against women has long been a central issue among feminists (McNeill, 1992), the ultimate act of violence against women—femicide—had received little attention by researchers with regard to the manner in which the media

portray these victims and perpetrators (Meyers, 1997), until relatively recently (i.e., Berkeley Media Studies Group, 2003; Bullock, 2007; Bullock & Cubert, 2002; Ryan, Anastario, & DaCunha, 2006; Taylor & Sorenson, 2002). This body of literature is filling an important void and beginning to effect social change in notable ways, as illustrated by Ryan et al. (2006), in their comparative analysis of coverage in Rhode Island, pre- and post collaboration between advocates and journalists. Experts emphasize that research focused on how the media cover domestic violence must continue because people rely on the media for understanding of domestic violence, and this directly affects responses by the criminal justice system, the community, and the government with regard to policy and prevention (Berns, 2004; Carll, 2003; Taylor & Sorenson, 2002). Analyzing and challenging the media's portrayal of femicide is an important step in understanding public perception and shaping intervention efforts.

Utilizing content analysis with a feminist theoretical framework, 5 years of femicide coverage by a metropolitan newspaper is examined to identify patterns of coverage. The current study seeks to respond to the call for further research to add to this growing body of work with hopes of initiating further important social change, particularly partnership among researchers, advocates, and the media community. As the analysis will reveal, media coverage of femicide is fraught with both direct, overt victim-blaming tactics as well as more indirect tactics. In addition, reporters tend to rely on convenient, biased sources for information. The methodology for the study as well as findings and implications for research and practice are discussed.

Language

The language used in a story plays a key role in both how the actors are portrayed and how they will be perceived by readers (Domingo, 1992). Content analyses of femicide coverage in newspapers reveal that stories are often completely void of blame toward the murderer for his actions (e.g., McNeill, 1992; Meyers, 1997). Even the title of an article may sufficiently illustrate the media's portrayal of the perpetrator as blameless, as can be seen from examples in a case from McNeill's (1992) work where a motorbike racer killed his wife and then himself: "Tragedy After Wife Left," "Together Again in the Grave" and "The Green Devil of Suspicion Kills Two" (pp. 180-181). Researchers have found that in cases where the perpetrator is especially respected, as with the case of an athlete or local celebrity, for example, the portrayal of the perpetrator tends to be especially sympathetic (McNeill, 1992; Meyers, 1994, 1997).

In her content analysis of media portrayal, Benedict (1992) concluded that the English language is inherently sexist and that reports of violence against women regularly include sexual, disdainful words used to describe women that are never used for men. Furthermore, she discovered that women are defined in the media in terms of their relationship to men rather than as individuals. She added that the portrayal of women in the media is not only shaped by oppressive language and the perpetuation of harmful cultural myths, but that these portrayals also reflect the overall general view the media have about women. In her study of femicide coverage in Utah newspapers, Bullock (2007) determined that "most coverage portrayed domestic violence fatalities in ways that supported patriarchal institutions such as the law enforcement and legal systems and obscured connections between violence against women and societal structures that help preserve gender-based power imbalances" (p. 36). Media coverage of femicide may reinforce patriarchal tendencies and obscure the very important context of domestic violence simultaneously.

Context

Femicide is usually preceded by chronic male-perpetrated abuse and leaving the abusive relationship heightens the victim's lethality risk (e.g., Smith, Moracco, & Butts, 1998). Despite this well-established pattern, the media seldom provide an accurate context with regard to the dynamic of domestic violence, often blaming a victim for not leaving the relationship. Websdale (1998) noted, "We learn very little of the political nature of [domestic homicide] or the gendered pattern of killings in tragedies such as domestic homicide." (p. 205), and revealing more of the structural context could be very educational for the public.

In a content analysis of three newspapers' coverage of domestic homicides, one researcher discovered that despite the fact that every female victim in every case had attempted to leave, been in the process of leaving, or actually left the abusive relationship, that fact was omitted from or buried deeply within the stories—in every story, in every newspaper (McNeill, 1992). Consalvo (1998) found *The Seattle Times* erased the context of domestic violence in their coverage of a high-profile femicide case, whereas two smaller minority newspapers offered more accurate coverage and even highlighted the omission of domestic violence from *The Seattle Times* coverage. She argued the difference in coverage was attributed to the freedom the smaller newspapers had from "the ideological and economic constraints that are present for mainstream presses such as *The Seattle Times*" (p. 199). In another study, Bullock and Cubert (2002) found that more than two thirds of the articles in their sample of 1998 newspaper coverage "elaborated little" with regard to the context of domestic violence and "seldom labeled a killing as domestic violence" (p. 483). They concluded that the media's tendency to present domestic homicide as comparable to other types "sidesteps the issues of male control, manipulation, and abuse of women" (p. 494). Furthermore, when the media frame domestic violence as a couple's problem, they are still blaming the victim, and the actions of the abused member of the couple usually takes focus over what the batterer has done and why (Berns, 2004). The value of the context provided, when provided, depends on reliable sources from which to gather this information.

Why Study the Media?

Regardless of the breadth of scholarly work on the topic or information provided by domestic violence experts, such as victim advocates, "most people learn about domestic violence from the popular media. The media are the most common and influential tour guides for exploring the landscapes of social problems" (Berns, 2004, p. 37). Berns and others who studied media portrayal of domestic violence and domestic homicide (i.e., Berkeley Media Studies Group, 2003; Bullock & Cubert, 2002; Carll, 2003; Consalvo, 1998; Meyers, 1997; Taylor & Sorenson, 2002) have been clear about this message. Not only are the media instrumental in shaping public perception of a problem, they are directly tied to changing problems. "How the media tell the story of intimate partner violence (IPV) will have a profound effect on what our society decided to do about it. News both reflects and shapes public attitudes-and these can stimulate or stymie policies that might remedy spousal and dating violence" (Berkeley Media Studies Group, 2003, p. 3). Examining the content of the media is a crucial first step in understanding the story being told about femicide, how it is told, how it is received, and ultimately, how we go about changing both the story and the problem.

Research Questions

Based on findings from the literature discussed, the following questions guide the current study:

1. How were the victim and perpetrator portrayed in the articles? Specifically, what language was used and what behaviors or conditions were disclosed that could lead to a negative or positive portrayal?

2. Was a context of domestic violence revealed? If so, how, and what were the sources for this information?

METHODOLOGY

Procedure

Research involving examinations of crime in the news media have relied on a variety of methods, including content analysis, ethnography, and interviews, with content analysis being the most common methodology utilized (Chermak, 1995). According to Berg (2004), a researcher can learn how authors of recorded material view the larger social world through content analysis. He said, "[Content analysis] is a passport to listening to the words of the text and understanding better the perspective(s) of the producer of these words" (p. 269). Berg pointed out two dimensions of text available for analysis: manifest content and latent content. Manifest content refers to "those elements that are physically present and countable," and latent content to "the deep structural meaning conveyed by the message" (p. 269). Although there is somewhat of a debate regarding which of the two should be used in content analysis, Berg proposed that the method is to use both when appropriate.

As such, the current study incorporates analysis of both the manifest and latent content in the newspaper articles. In addition, detailed examples are offered for each element of latent analysis to substantiate the author's interpretation.

Operationalization

Femicide. The definition offered by Dawson and Gartner (1998) will be used: "The killing of women by a male intimate partner" (p. 383).

Primary victims. Refers to those persons who suffer directly from a crime (Chermak, 1995). In this analysis, it will refer to those women who have been killed by their intimate partner.

Perpetrator. Refers to those persons who have committed the crime. In this analysis, it will refer to the male who has killed his female intimate partner.

Intimate partner. The definition for intimate partner offered by Dawson and Gartner (1998) will be used as well: "current or formal legal spouses, common-law partners, and boyfriends" (p. 383).

Domestic violence. The State of Florida defines domestic violence as "any assault, aggravated assault, battery, aggravated battery, sexual assault, sexual battery, stalking, aggravated stalking, kidnapping, false imprisonment, or any criminal offense resulting in physical injury or death of one family or household member by another family or household member," according to Florida state statute 741.28 to 741.31. As the sample for the study is drawn from incidences occurring in the state of Florida, this legal definition will be used in the current study.

Data Collection

Earlier content analyses of newspaper articles were based on small samples for relatively short periods of time (i.e., Chermak, 1995; Meyers, 1994). More recent work in the area of femicide news coverage includes larger samples, spanning longer periods of time (i.e., The Berkeley Media Studies Group, 2003; Bullock & Cubert, 2002; Consalvo, 1998; Taylor & Sorenson, 2002). In keeping with this approach, the current study seeks to analyze a large sample of newspaper articles, covering several years.

Rather than focus on national media, a local newspaper was chosen for the analysis. Ryan et al. (2006) noted, "National media, covering the most egregious or unusual domestic violence murders cases, would be a less reliable arena on which to evaluate coverage" (p. 217). Furthermore, they contended, "Local print news outlets serve as kingmakers directly affecting politicians, police, and other institutions" (p. 217), and that broadcast news usually follows behind print in their coverage, even using stories from print in their programs. A metropolitan newspaper published in Orlando, Florida, *The Orlando Sentinel,* was chosen for the current analysis and articles were retrieved from the NewsBank electronic archive.

The Orlando Sentinel has a daily circulation in excess of 250,000 and a Sunday circulation of more than 300,000. The readership spans several counties in Florida, extending across the state. The newspaper covers news occurring both within the area of publication and other parts of the state as well, thus widening the scope of coverage as compared to some previous studies.

Domestic homicide articles covering an incident or events subsequent to the killing (i.e., court proceedings) in the State of Florida from any section within the newspaper from 1995 to 2000 were retrieved for use in the analysis. Although the contents of the article, including the title, subtitle, and photograph captions, are precisely duplicated in the database version retrieved from the archive, an exact replica of the article is not accessible. In other words, the article retrieved from the database is not a picture of the article as it was featured in the newspaper. The archive article was provided in a standard word-processing format, so measurement of length had to be relative to that format rather than newspaper column format. In addition, the database did not include photographs that appeared with the article in the publication of the story but did note when a photograph had been included.

Certain types of incidences were omitted from the sample. Specifically, attempted murders and actual murder related to a domestic situation (i.e., a platonic roommate or extended family member) but not perpetrated against an intimate partner were not included, as to be consistent in analyzing coverage of actual femicide. An exhaustive keyword search was conducted (see Table 9.4) to maximize the goal of retrieving all articles pertaining to domestic homicide from the newspaper within the years of interest.

Table 9.4   Keyword Searches

Murder and wife

Murder and husband

Murder and girlfriend

Murder and boyfriend

Murder and spouse

Murder and intimate partner

Homicide and wife

Homicide and husband

Homicide and girlfriend

Homicide and boyfriend

Homicide and spouse

Homicide and intimate partner

Domestic homicide

Domestic murder

Intimate partner homicide

Intimate partner murder

Femicide

Wife and death

Husband and death

Girlfriend and death

Boyfriend and death

Spouse and death

Intimate partner and death

Wife and kill

Husband and kill

Girlfriend and kill

Boyfriend and kill

Spouse and kill

Intimate partner and kill

Description of Sample

This search produced a total of 292 articles representing 168 separate cases of domestic homicide. The total number of articles included in the analysis does not reflect the total number of incidents that occurred within 1995 to 2000. In some instances, articles were retrieved from coverage in the span of 1995 to 2000 that were stories pertaining to an event that occurred prior to 1995. Likewise, any incident that occurred from 1999 to 2000 would very likely have coverage of the judicial process continuing on into the years beyond the period of analysis. In addition, 124 of the articles in the overall sample were coverage of the same incident. There may have been one incident from which multiple articles were written, from the time of the incident through the judicial process. For example, the widely publicized killing of a pregnant ex-wife was featured in 29 articles during the 5 years, with most written in 1997. Thus, 39.5% $(n = 17)$ of the articles retrieved from 1997 were related to this particular incident.

Most cases in which there were multiple articles, however featured far fewer than 29. In fact, of the total sample of articles retrieved, only 7.2% $(n = 21)$ cases of femicide featured three or more articles, and only eight of those featured more than four articles on the same incident. Some notable stories featuring more than four articles include a funeral home employee who killed his wife and buried her in the same casket with an elderly woman (nine articles, 1996-1999), a woman who killed her husband, a plastic surgeon, as he was on the phone scheduling a date with his mistress (six articles, all in 2000), a man who hired a hit man to kill his ex-wife, the mother of six children, including two-year-old quadruplets who played in her blood after the slaying (nine articles, 1990-2000), and the killing of a woman by her ex-husband and his new wife after being featured on the Jerry Springer Show (four articles, all in 2000).

All articles covering a domestic homicide were collected and analyzed, including those perpetrated by men and women in both heterosexual and homosexual relationships. However, those cases involving a male-perpetrated intimate partner homicide with a female victim (i.e., femicide) were of major interest. Articles covering female-perpetrated or same-sex perpetrated intimate partner homicides were included to measure similarities and differences in the coverage of these types of incidents in comparison to femicide cases. The same criteria were used in the analysis of the femicide cases and in the comparison cases.

Analysis

A coding sheet was used for the analysis of each article. The items of interest were based on what was deemed worthy of special attention from similar studies on femicide coverage in newspapers. Articles were analyzed by first reading them to ensure again that the article met the criteria for inclusion in the study, then by going through each article carefully recording the frequencies of the items of interest. The following were included in this analysis (and others reserved for future work):

1. Title of the article

2. Negative adjectives/behaviors attributed to victim

3. Negative adjectives/behaviors attributed to perpetrator

4. Positive adjectives/behaviors attributed to victim

5. Positive adjectives/behaviors attributed to perpetrator

6. Was any domestic violence context referenced (including no known history of DV)?

7. Sources referenced for domestic violence context

8. Physical, mental, or other pathological issues concerning victim?

9. Physical, mental, or other pathological issues concerning perpetrator?

10. Tone of story

Each article was carefully analyzed for these items and were coded appropriately (listing each adjective, characteristic, etc.) by the author. Other items were also included in the

coding for future analysis but not included in the present study (examples include whether or not first names and occupations of the victim and perpetrator were revealed, location of offense, weapon used). The specific items were then divided by type (perpetrator illness, financial woes, infidelity, etc.) and counted individually.

Tone of the story was determined in conjunction with the other items of interest and involved multiple rounds of analysis. Initially, articles were given a variety of labels for tone based on the first analysis, and examples of these initial tone codes included *article focuses on perpetrator because of physical illness,* when an article was focused on the murderer or victim's history of mental or physical illness; *blames victim,* when an article was focused on the victim's suspected infidelity; and *blames perpetrator* in cases where the reporter focused on the perpetrator's proclivity for violence, for example, and still others were coded *as fact only* when they contained little detail of any sort, other than reporting that a murder had occurred with whatever information about the crime characteristics were available.

After completing the initial data collection and coding, articles were grouped together based on common patterns and themes. Articles belonging to a series about the same incident, those about female-perpetrated incidents, and articles with similar tone are examples of such groupings. Each group was reanalyzed to verify the initial coding, to identify any other elements of the story missed, and to more thoroughly investigate the relationship of the tone in conjunction with the other elements. For example, did articles focusing on a perpetrator's history of financial despair also include negative adjectives to describe the victim? Did articles with a sympathetic tone for the victim (i.e., positive adjectives, warm quotes from sources close to the victim) also include negative adjectives to describe the perpetrator? These observations were recorded on the coding sheet. All of these elements helped better define the patterns and themes identified in the initial analysis and also made the determination of whether an article was victim blaming more apparent as well as the degree to which an article was or was not victim blaming. Extensive details and examples of these elements are discussed in the findings.

FINDINGS

The 292 articles found in the search produced a wide range of stories about actual homicides and about subsequent events to a homicide, such as investigative updates and reports of judicial hearings. In addition, stories involved multiple articles about different aspects of the case, allowing for comparison within a series of articles on one case.

There was a drastic disparity in the number of cases involving male-perpetrated domestic homicides, or femicides ($n = 150$ cases; see Table 9.5), as compared to the number of female perpetrated incidences found in the sample ($n = 18$). It is widely noted that males commit most domestic homicides (e.g., Campbell, 1992; Daly & Wilson, 1988; Websdale, 1999); therefore, the breakdown of female-perpetrated versus male-perpetrated homicides in the current sample may illustrate a natural disparity of trends in domestic homicide, or that the loss of a female life is seemingly more newsworthy than the loss of a male life, as existing literature suggests (e.g., Pritchard & Hughes, 1997).

Dichotomy of Victim Blame

A great deal of time was devoted in the current study to analyzing ways in which articles portrayed victims as accountable for their own victimization, or ways in which perpetrators of femicide were exonerated for their crimes because of pathological tendencies. Beginning with victim blame, the articles in the present study presented no exception to the tendency of the media to blame victims for their own victimization. Authors of the articles in the current sample managed to discredit or altogether blame victims using several methods, some with direct and others with more indirect approaches. These direct and indirect tactics are dichotomized and illustrated in Table 9.6.

The direct approaches included the language used to describe the victim, both in adjectives and in behaviors attributed to the victim, attributing the violence to the victim's lack of reporting previous violence and/or not cooperating with the prosecution of the perpetrator in prior offenses, and highlighting when a woman had an affair, had been suspected of infidelity, when the woman had been in the company of another man during the incident, or when the woman was the mistress of her killer. Some of the more indirect approaches used to cast blame on victims and/or exonerate perpetrators included adjectives used to describe the perpetrator, behaviors attributed to the perpetrator, disclosure of mental, physical, and emotional problems of the perpetrator, disclosure of mental or physical problems of the victim, discussing the perpetrator's frustration over financial despair, and describing a history of domestic violence in neutral terms as to assign equal blame to both parties for past incidences of violence or for the troubled state of the relationship as a

Table 9.5   Sample Frequencies

292 articles were retrieved

150 = cases of male-perpetrators/female victim

18 = cases of female-perpetrated/male victim

1 = case of male-perpetrated/male victim

27.3% ($n = 41$) of male-perpetrated = murder-suicides

5% ($n = 1$) female-perpetrated = murder-suicide

57% ($n = 166$) of articles were from a multiple series on the same incident

Table 9.6 Victim Blame Tactics

Direct Victim Blame Tactics

- Negative language used to describe the victim.

- Highlighting the victim's choice not to report past incidences as contributing to her murder.

- Highlighting the victim's decision not to prosecute previous incidences as contributing to her murder.

- Highlighting her actions with other men, such as actual and suspected infidelity while married, being seen with another man, being found with another man when killed, and being the mistress of the killer.

Indirect Victim Blame Tactics

- Positive, sympathetic language used to describe the perpetrator.

- Highlighting the perpetrator's mental, physical, and emotional problems.

- Discussing the couple's financial despair.

- Highlighting the victim's mental or physical problems.

- Describing domestic violence in terms which assign equal blame to both the victim and perpetrator.

whole. Conversely, articles pertaining to female-perpetrated incidences contained very little victim blame compared to stories where females were the victims. Whereas four of the female-perpetrated stories in the sample did make mention of the fact that the perpetrator had been abused by the victim and two were clearly incidences precipitated by the victim, the remaining stories were void of any of the victim blame tactics described in reference to male-perpetrated incidences.

Language

Regarding language, the very title or subtitle of an article was the beginning of the use of language to blame victims in two articles: "Girlfriend's Cocaine Use Lead to Killing" and "Funeral Home Love Took a Deadly Turn: She Became Rebellious" (Rippel, 1999). Other uses of language to blame victims or attack the character of a victim were found in the text of 74 articles, including adjectives

used to describe the victim and/or behaviors attributed to her. A few examples of these adjectives include greedy, threatening, sexually promiscuous, flamboyant (used to describe a male killed by his boyfriend), and rebellious. Examples of certain victim behaviors that did not pertain to the fact that she or he was murdered by an intimate partner included abused drugs/alcohol, spent large amounts of money/ran up debt (usually citing the amount), hung out with gang members, was suicidal, and had recently cut the defendant out of her will. One of the most blatant uses of irrelevant adjectives and behaviors of the victim included in a story was found in the case of a man who killed his pregnant ex-wife and buried her body in his backyard. In this series of articles, reporters routinely disclosed information about the victim that had absolutely no bearing on the fact that she was brutally murdered in her last week of pregnancy and buried under a concrete slab. This included allegations that she had become pregnant with her first child at a very young age by an ex-boyfriend's friend, was known to have difficulty maintaining relationships, and that her parenting abilities had been questioned by the perpetrator and his family. The positive information included in the articles came only from the victim's immediate family members.

There were positive adjectives and behaviors attributed to victims throughout 26 articles in the sample as well. Some examples include always willing to help people, hard working, reliable, friendly, charitable, admired, and peaceful. These examples are derived from both male and female-perpetrated stories. In one case where a man had killed his ex-wife after a long history of custody disputes, the majority of the article was dedicated to portraying her as a wonderful woman who had touched the lives of her entire community. In addition to her family, members of the community gave specific examples of how she always helped those in need, was admired for being a strong single mother, and was a successful hard worker.

There were notable negative adjectives and behaviors attributed to perpetrators as well in 40 articles, such as extensive criminal record, jealous, obsessive, had admitted infidelity, has abused other women, demanding, and arrogant. There were also many positive things said about perpetrators in 35 articles. Examples of these include doting parent, hard working, affluent, gentlest person in the world, strong sense of family structure, dutiful law enforcement officer, enjoyed life, had so much potential, and always helped the neighbors.

A particular case stands out as having an abundance of coverage painting a positive picture of the perpetrator. This three story series involved a well-respected police officer who killed his wife, then himself. Every article featured several sources who commented extensively on what great character and integrity the officer was known for, how much he adored his wife, how revered he had been by the community in which he resided, and how decorated an officer he was. Coworkers were cited as saying things such as "This is the most tragic situation because it involves one of our own" (Stanfield, 1998), "he had extensive training for handling domestic violence" (Sargent, 1998b, p. C1), and "he had no reprimands in his employment record" (Sargent, 1998a, p. 1). With regard to the context of the relationship and what led to the killing, all the articles included the same interpretation, which was that "the couple had become involved in an apparent murder-suicide . . . after a quarrel" (Sargent, 1998a, p. A1). This sort of language indicates that the act of killing his wife and then himself was something that happened *to* him, and that the "quarrel" from which the incident stemmed was a mutual combat situation. In another case, a man shot and killed his wife days after learning she had cut him out of her will and planned to divorce him. The two articles on this story discuss how he had been betrayed by his wife. In the second article, reporting that the charges against him had been dismissed, the tone suggested justice had been served, pointing out that allegations of her suicidal tendencies were enough to exonerate him and that he could not be blamed for reacting violently to what *she* had done to *him*.

The Victim's Response to Violence

A history of domestic violence preceding the murder was mentioned in 99 articles. In the cases where the tone of the article was more sympathetic to the plight of the abused woman, this information would be accompanied by facts such as how the victim was too afraid of retaliation by the perpetrator either to report the violence at all or to follow through with prosecution, a common problem for battered women for a number of reasons (Belknap, Fleury, Melton, Sullivan, & Leisenring, 2001). This information came from those closest to the victim such as her family and friends as well as from prosecutors handling the murder case in 16 articles, but 15 articles contained overt blaming of the victim for prior responses. A prime example can be seen in the title of one article: "Police: Victim Protected Her Killer" with the subtitle, "A Woman Who Was Killed Had Refused to Prosecute Her Ex-Boyfriend for Stalking" (Curtis, 1996). The articles highlighting the lack of action on the part of the victim in previous incidences portrayed this as a lack of seriousness of the violence the woman had endured at the hands of her killer throughout their abusive relationship, even suggesting that she must not have really been afraid of the abuser. In seven articles on female-perpetrated incidences, however, the authors report that the perpetrator had been abused by the man she killed, even noting specific arrest records including previous domestic violence, stalking, and so on.

A story highlighting the victim's past responses to violence actually portrayed the relationship as one of complete control and domination over the victim by her husband, citing several instances of abuse she endured and the injuries she sustained at the hands of her husband. While the story emphasized the terror involved for a victim of domestic violence, the first line of the article reads "[she] knew she should leave her husband and put an end to the beating and threats that had marked their 10-month marriage" (Leithauser, 1995b, p. C1), suggesting that leaving her husband would have guaranteed an end to his controlling and physically abusive behavior. The last lines in the article describe how she had not been willing to file reports against him in prior incidences of violence and how she had not followed the advice of advocates who were trying to help her escape.

In another case where a woman had been shot and killed by her husband, the article cites several instances where the police had been called in response to domestic violence in the home, only to find the victim would not write a statement and refused to prosecute him. The incidences were portrayed by first describing the valiant efforts of the police and other criminal justice personnel to rescue her, and then followed with the actions she took to avoid criminal justice system involvement. The article systematically portrays the victim as the barrier to all the protection she was being offered without discussing how and why this behavior is common for domestic violence victims, often for the sole purpose of survival (Belknap et al., 2001). Another story claimed that the woman who had left her abusive husband and was later shot and killed "apparently stayed in the marriage longer than she should have" (Berry, 1997). One of the more unique examples of victim blame was in a case where the reporter focused the entire femicide story on another woman who had previously been involved with the perpetrator and how she could have prevented the current victim's murder by going forward and prosecuting the man when he had battered her. This was the only incident where a victim of domestic violence was indirectly blamed for another victim's murder.

Context

Literature suggests that the mention of context is an important item of analysis in articles about domestic-homicide (McNeill, 1992). Special attention was given to any discussion of a history of domestic violence because research shows that most femicides are often committed as a conclusion to a history of battering the victim (e.g., Campbell, 1992; Daly & Wilson, 1988; Websdale, 1999), and that most female-perpetrated incidences are cases of self-defense (e.g., Campbell, 1992; Daly & Wilson, 1988).

As noted previously, 99 of the articles included mention of domestic violence. This information came from a variety of sources including prior police reports, family, friends, neighbors, and from police officers and attorneys involved in the case commenting on the history of the relationship when asked. In four articles, the history of abuse was revealed in such a way as to paint a horrific picture of violence on the part of the perpetrator of the femicide and of tremendous fear on the part of the victim. However, of the 99 articles including reference to domestic violence, 42 of those did so in a way that made it impossible to determine who was responsible. A couple of examples of this trend include "some sort of domestic dispute took place and gunshots erupted" (Associated Press, 1998), "there was obviously some marital discord" (Stratton, 1996).

Family members disclosed a history of domestic violence in 14 articles. Police and police reports were also a source of this information in nearly every article including a history of domestic violence; however, this knowledge came almost exclusively from knowledge of past police reports. For example, one police officer commented, "To our knowledge, there were no domestic problems" (Quigley, 1997a). Because victims of domestic violence often choose not to report domestic violence for a variety of reasons, police may have stated there was no past domestic violence when there may have in fact been an extensive history. In any case, the articles reveal context of a history of relationship problems including domestic violence, divorce, and so on, when there was a source willing to comment on it.

In 57 of the articles noting a history of domestic violence, the history was portrayed in a neutral, equal-blame nature. The titles and subtitles of articles referenced the abuse history or the actual homicide in such a way as to completely obscure who had been battered or to present it as something that happened to the couple, as was the case in murder-suicides. A few examples include "Two Adults Die in Shooting " (1998), "Husband, Wife Shot to Death" (2000), "Eustis Husband, Wife Are Both Found Dead" (Quigley, 1997a), "Couple Die in

Nursing Home Shootings" (Lelis, 1996), and "Parents, Girl Found Shot" (2000).

In addition to titles, language throughout articles portrayed domestic violence in neutral terms, indicating that both parties were possibly to blame for the violence. For example, "some sort of domestic dispute took place and gunshots erupted" (Associated Press, 1998), "there was obviously some marital discord" (Stratton, 1996), and "they were fighting all the time, and it came to this, that someone had to pay the ultimate price" (Lelis, 1998a, 1998b). The most common was, "the couple had a history of domestic violence" (e.g., Harris, 1998; Horvitz, 1997; Lelis, 1998a, 1998b).

Discussion

On the whole, the current study serves to reinforce various findings reported in existing literature on the portrayal of femicide victims by the news media while identifying some new areas as well. One basic theme of existing literature with regard to the portrayal of victims is that the news media tend to blame victims for their own victimizations, and the present study produced key findings consistent with this theme. In addition, these findings support literature from feminist theorists who contend that the tendency of the media to cast blame on victims of femicide for their own deaths presents a significant barrier to social change concerning femicide. The exception found regarding victim blame was in cases where the incident was female perpetrated. Very little victim blame was revealed in those particular articles.

Beginning with direct tactics of victim blame, negative language used to describe the femicide victim, her behaviors, or her personal problems was pervasive throughout the sample of articles (74 articles). An additional troubling direct tactic was focusing on the victim's failure to report past incidences of violence and her failure to cooperate with the prosecution of the perpetrator in past incidences, without discussing why this behavior may have been a survival technique on the part of the victim.

CONCLUSION AND IMPLICATIONS

The present study was designed to contribute to the body of literature devoted to investigating the portrayal of femicide and its victims in the news media. Because public perception is predominantly shaped by the media, and it is perception that leads to attitudes and behaviors, it is essential to better determine how femicide is portrayed by the media to change faulty perceptions about femicide and femicide victims. This will in turn affect community, law enforcement, and justice system responses to domestic violence, and hopefully reducing the occurrence of this tragic phenomenon.

The present study is both a contribution to the growing body of literature on the topic of femicide as well additional evidence that victims of femicide are routinely blamed for their victimization through the news media, even if implicitly. This faulty portrayal is then filtered into the perceptions, and thus, attitudes and behaviors of members of society. Researchers maintain that it is important to continue analyzing the media because the media are the primary source of information and understanding, and thus, action and change (i.e., Berkeley Media Studies Group, 2003; Berns, 2004; Bullock & Cubert, 2002; Carll, 2003; Consalvo, 1998; Meyers, 1997; Taylor & Sorenson. 2002). Berns (2004) stated, "Media portrayals of social problems affect common understandings of the problem, which spill over into individual responses by police officers, judges, jurors, lawyers, clergy, friends, family, and counselors. These individual understandings are also used in making

laws, developing policy, and creating prevention programs" (p. 155).

The media play a powerful role in the construction and understanding of social problems, and the solutions for intervention and prevention begin with understanding how the media work and where changes need to be made. An important first step with regard to femicide coverage is to stop blaming the victim and to start telling an accurate story about the gendered pattern and roots in chronic domestic violence.

REFERENCES

Associated Press. (1995, May 13). Despondent man kills ex-wife, friend, self. *The Orlando Sentinel,* p. D12.

Associated Press (1998, June 30). Man kills wife, self in dispute over kids. *The Orlando Sentinel,* p. D4.

Associated Press. (2000, January 10). Suspect's life "a challenge." *The Orlando Sentinel,* p. B4.

Backhaus, E. (1999, March 7), Police: Ex-boyfriend said woman would "pay price." Reports show he called wife before 2 gunned down. *The Orlando Sentinel,* p. B1.

Belknap, J., Fleury, R. E., Melton, H, C, Sullivan, C. M., & Leisenring, A. (2001). To go or not to go? Preliminary findings on battered women's decisions regarding court cases. In H. M. Eigenberg (Ed.), *Woman battering in the United States: Till death do us part* (pp. 319-326). Prospect Heights, IL: Waveland Press.

Benedict, H. (1992). *Virgin or vamp: How the press covers sex crimes.* New York: Oxford University Press.

Berg, B. L. (2004). *Qualitative research methods for the social sciences* (5th ed.). Boston: Allyn & Bacon.

Berkeley Media Studies Group. (2003). *Distracted by drama: How California newspapers portray intimate partner violence.* Retrieved October 13, 2008, from http://www.bmsg.org/pdfs/Issue13.pdf

Berns, N. (2004). *Framing the victim: Domestic violence, media and social problems.* Hawthorne, NY: Aldine de Gruyter.

Berry, M. (1997, May 11). Man suspected of killing his wife remains at large. *The Orlando Sentinel*, p. B1.

Best, J. (1999). *Random violence: How we talk about new crimes and new victims.* Berkeley: University of California Press.

Bullock, C. F. (2007). Framing domestic violence fatalities: Coverage by Utah newspapers. *Women's Studies in Communication, 30*(1), 34-63.

Bullock, C. R, & Cubert, J. (2002). Coverage of domestic violence fatalities by newspapers in Washington state. *Journal of Interpersonal Violence, 27,* 475-499.

Byerly, C. M. (1994). An agenda for teaching news coverage of rape. *Journalism Educator, 49,* 59-69.

Campbell, J. C. (1992). "If I can't have you, no one can": Power and control in homicide of female partners. In J. Radford & D, E. H. Russell (Eds.), *Femicide: The politics of woman-killing* (pp. 99-113). New York: Twayne.

Carll, E. K. (2003). News portrayal of violence and women. *American Behavioral Scientist, 46,* 1601-1610.

Carmody, D. C. (1998). Mixed messages: Images of domestic violence on "reality" television. In M. Fishman & G. Cavender (Eds.), *Entertaining crime: Television reality programs* (pp. 159-174). New York: Aldine De Gruyter.

Chermak, S. (1995). *Victims in the news: Crime and the American news media.* Boulder, CO: Westview Press.

Consalvo, M. (1998). "3 shot dead in courthouse": Examining news coverage of domestic violence and mail-order brides. *Women's Studies in Communication, 21,* 188-202.

Croteau, D., & Hoynes, W. (1997). *Media/Society: Industries, images, and audiences.* Thousand Oaks, CA; Pine Forge Press.

Curtis, H. P. (1996, May 21). Police: Victim protected her killer. *The Orlando Sentinel*, p. D1.

Daly, M., & Wilson, M. (1988). *Homicide.* New York: Aldine de Gruyter.

Dawson, M., & Gartner, R. (1998). Differences in the characteristics of intimate femicides: The role of relationship state and status. *Homicide Studies, 2,* 378-399.

Domingo, C. (1992). What the white man won't tell us: Report from the Berkeley Clearinghouse on femicide. In J. Radford & D. E. H. Russell (Eds.), *Femicide: The politics of woman-killing* (pp. 195-202). New York: Twayne.

Duff-Hoppes, J. (1998). Altamonte Springs man held in wife's slaying. *The Orlando Sentinel,* p. C3.

Girlfriend's cocaine use lead to killing, man says. (1995, February 7). *The Orlando Sentinel,* p. C3.

Hanmer, L, Radford, J., & Stanko, E. A. (1989). Policing men's violence: An introduction. In J. Hanmer, J. Radford, & E. A. Stanko (Eds.), *Women, policing, and male violence: International perspectives* (pp. 1-12). London: Routledge.

Harris, K. A. (1998, January 12). Husband charged with killing wife. *The Orlando Sentinel*, p. C3.

Horvitz, L. (1997, October 3). Couple had history of violence. *The Orlando Sentinel,* p. D1.

Husband, wife shot to death. (2000, December 28). *The Orlando Sentinel,* p. D2.

Iovanni, L., & Miller, S. L. (2001). Criminal justice system responses to domestic violence: Law enforcement and the courts. In C. M, Renzetti, J. L. Edleson, & R. K. Bergen (Eds.), *Sourcebook on violence against women* (pp. 303-344). Thousand Oaks, CA: Sage.

Jones, A. (1994). *Next time she'll be dead: Battering & how to stop it.* Boston: Beacon Press.

Killing suspect pleads guilty. (2000, October 20). *The Orlando Sentinel,* p. D2.

Lawyer pleads for life of man who killed family. (1996, April 19). *The Orlando Sentinel,* p. D6.

Leithauser, T. (1995a, January 11). Orange family of 4 found slain in bed. *The Orlando Sentinel,* p. A1.

Leitbauser, T. (1995b, January 27). Slain wife had thought of seeking shelter. *The Orlando Sentinel,* p. C1.

Lelis, L. (1996, June 21). Couple die in nursing home shootings. *The Orlando Sentinel,* p. D1.

Lelis, L. (1998a, April 9). Husband charged in woman's slaying. *The Orlando Sentinel,* p. D1.

Lelis, L. (1998b, September 2). Man pleads guilty to wife's murder. *The Orlando Sentinel,* p. D3.

Lowney, K. S., & Best, J. (1995). Stalking strangers and lovers: Changing media typifications of a new crime problem. In J, Best (Ed.), *Images of issues: Typifying contemporary social problems* (pp. 33-57). New York: Aldine de Gruyter.

Maxwell, K. A., Huxford, J., Borum, C, & Hornik, R. (2000). Covering domestic violence; How the O.J. Simpson case shaped reporting of domestic violence in the news media. *J&MC Quarterly, 77,*258-272.

McNeill, S. (1992). Woman killer as tragic hero. In J. Radford, & D. E. H. Russell (Eds.), *Femicide: The politics of woman-killing* (pp. 178-183). New York: Twayne.

Mercer, P. (2000, June 4). Couple dead in apparent murder-suicide. *The Orlando Sentinel,* p. B3.

Meyers, M, (1994). News of battering. *Journal of Communication, 44*(2), 47-63.

Meyers, M. (1997). *News coverage of violence against women: Endangering blame.* Thousand Oaks, CA: Sage.

Millionaire who killed self, family blamed woes. (1997, March 19). *The Orlando Sentinel,* p. C3.

Murder-suicide couple in Titusville are identified. (1999, August 4). *The Orlando Sentinel,* p. D3.

Naylor, B. (2001). Reporting violence in the British print media: Gendered stories. *The Howard Journal, 40(2),* 180-194.

Parents, girl found shot. (2000, November 20). *The Orlando Sentinel,* p. B2.

Pritchard, D., & Hughes, K. D. (1997). Patterns of deviance in crime news. *Journal of Communication, 47*(3), 49-67.

Purvette, A. B. (1996, August 15). Judge sets bail for Deltona man. *The Orlando Sentinel,* p. D1.

Quigley, K. (1997a, December 27). Eustis husband, wife are both found dead. *The Orlando Sentinel,* p. A1.

Quigley, K. (1997b, December 28). Wife was strangled, autopsy shows. T*he Orlando Sentinel,* p. B3.

Rippel, A. C. (1999, October 30). Funeral-home love took a deadly turn: She became rebellious. *The Orlando Sentinel,* p. H1.

Ryan, W. (1971). *Blaming the victim,* New York: Pantheon Books.

Ryan, C., Anastario, M, & DaCunha, A. (2006). Changing coverage of domestic violence murders: A longitudinal experiment in participatory communication. *Journal of Interpersonal Communication, 21,* 209-228.

Salamone, D. (1995, January 19). Wife killer sentenced again to die. *The Orlando Sentinel,* p. C3.

Salamone, D. (1997, July 25). Killer of girlfriend still thinks he deserves to die. *The Orlando Sentinel,* p. D3.

Sanford man is indicted in deaths of woman, teen. (1994, March 24). *The Orlando Sentinel,* p. D3.

Sargent, R. (1998a, January 5). Deaths shock city: Lady Lake couple were known for civic work. *The Orlando Sentinel,* p. A1.

Sargent, R. (1998b, January 5). Deaths shock officer's friends. *The Orlando Sentinel,* p. C1.

Smith, P. H., Moracco, K. E., & Butts, J. D. (1998), Partner homicide in context: A population-based perspective. *Homicide Studies, 2,* 400-421.

Stanfield, F. (1998, January 4). Police think Lake cop killed wife and himself. *The Orlando Sentinel,* p. B1.

Stratton, J. (1996, May 10). Ocoee man kills wife, self. *The Orlando Sentinel,* p. D3.

Stutzman, R. (1998, August 19). Husband pleads no contest to shotgun slayings of wife, her lover. *The Orlando Sentinel,* p. D3.

Stutzman, R. (1999, May 30). Do notes shed new light on killings? *The Orlando Sentinel,* p. B1.

Stutzman, R. (2000, October 19). No deal for suspect in slayings. *The Orlando Sentinel,* p. D1.

Taylor, C. A., & Sorenson, S. B. (2002). The nature of newspaper coverage of homicide. *Injury Prevention, 8*(2), 121-127.

Tuchman, G. (1978). Introduction: The symbolic annihilation of women by the mass media. In G. Tuchman, A. K. Daniels, & J. Benet (Eds.), *Hearth and home: Images of women in the mass media* (pp. 3-38). New York: Oxford University Press.

2 adults die in shooting at high school. (1998, May 30). *The Orlando Sentinel,* p. D1.

Websdale, D. (1998). *Rural woman battering and the justice system: An ethnography.* Thousand Oaks, CA: Sage.

Websdale, N. (1999). *Understanding domestic homicide.* Boston: Northeastern University Press.

Zoellner, L. A., Feeny, N. C, Alzarez, J., Watlington, C., O'Neill, M. L., Zager, R., et al. (2000). Factors associated with competition of the restraining order process in female victims of partner violence. *Journal of Interpersonal Violence, 15,* 1081-1099.

DISCUSSION QUESTIONS

1. How does this researcher argue that the media has a significant role in shaping public perceptions of, and influencing policy for, crime and criminals?

2. Describe media portrayals of females in general and the social implications these characterizations have.

3. What does Taylor state is the impetus for this research study? What are her goals for the current research?

4. What is Taylor's reason for selecting the *Orlando Sentinel* as her source of data collection? How were articles from this newspaper selected to be included as part of the study? Which articles were not included?

5. How does Taylor operationalize the main variables for study? What did this researcher do regarding multiple articles of the same incident?

6. According to the findings of this study, is there a disparity in the articles on domestic violence homicides with regard to the sex of the victim? How does Taylor explain this disparity? Was victim blame as prevalent in the articles where the homicide victim was male?

7. Were there both positive and negative adjectives used in describing female victims? List some of the specific adjectives chosen when female victim behaviors were reported on.

8. Are the findings in Taylor's content analytic study consistent with previous findings that the media tend to blame victims for their own victimizations? How do these portrayals affect public perception, and ultimately solutions for prevention, of crime?

RESEARCH READING

These researchers take a geographic research approach by examining traffic stops at both microlevels and macrolevels in order to explore the causes of racial profiling. Their analyses provide for an examination of the spatial characteristics that might be influential of traffic stops. Their findings from Houston traffic stop data reveal that racial disparity existed in the frequency of traffic stops and stop outcomes. Roh and Robinson's research also reveals that neighborhood level factors also affect the likelihood of being stopped and other adverse outcomes. The authors discuss the implications of their research to problem-oriented and hot-spot policing.

Source: Roh, S., & Robinson, M. (2009). A geographic approach to racial profiling: The microanalysis and macroanalysis of racial disparity in traffic stops, *Police Quarterly*, *12*(2), 137–169. Copyright © 2009 Sage Publications.

————— A GEOGRAPHIC APPROACH TO RACIAL PROFILING —————

The Microanalysis and Macroanalysis of Racial Disparity in Traffic Stops

Sunghoon Roh and Matthew Robinson

Abstract: Despite numerous studies explaining racial disparity in traffic stops, the effects of spatial characteristics in patrolling areas have not been widely examined. In this article, the authors analyzed traffic stop data at both micro- and macrolevels. The microlevel analysis of individual stops confirmed racial disparity in the frequency of traffic stops as well as in subsequent police treatments. Blacks were overrepresented and other racial and ethnic groups were underrepresented in traffic stops, with a greater disparity in investigatory stops. The macrolevel analysis found that the likelihood of being stopped and being subjected to unfavorable police treatment (e.g., arrest, search, and felony charge) was greater in beats where more Blacks or Hispanics resided and/or more police force was deployed, consistent with the racial threat or minority threat hypothesis. These findings imply that racial disparity at the level of individual stops may be substantially explained by differential policing strategies adopted for different areas based on who resides in those areas. Policy implications for problem-oriented policing and hot spot policing are discussed.

INTRODUCTION

Racial profiling is one of the most discussed issues in policing (Weitzer & Tuch, 2006). Racial profiling occurs when "a person is treated as a suspect because of his or her race, ethnicity, nationality or religion" (American Civil Liberties Union, 2007). It can occur when police officers stop, question, search, investigate, arrest, and/ or use some degree of force against a person based on race rather than suspicious or criminal behavior (Harris, 1997; Weitzer & Tuch, 2002). A well-known form of racial profiling is referred to as "driving while Black" or "driving while Brown" (DWB).

Most American citizens believe racial profiling not only exists but is widespread. For example, a 2003 Gallup Poll showed that 59% of Americans thought police profiling was widespread, including 85% of Blacks (Ludwig, 2003). Historical analyses (Skolnick, 2007) and scholarly reviews of the literature (del Carmen, 2007) verify the realities of racial profiling by some police, at some times, in some places. Discrimination that occurs in some

places and some time periods is referred to as "contextual discrimination" (Walker, Spohn, & Delone, 2006).

The American Civil Liberties Union (ACLU) has documented evidence of racial profiling in several states, including Arizona, California, New York, Ohio, and Rhode Island. It also has led efforts to file complaints against police departments in cities in other states (ACLU, 2007). Amnesty International also has investigated racial profiling (Amnesty International, 2007). According to Amnesty, 32 million Americans "report they have already been victims of racial profiling." Furthermore, about 87 million Americans "are at a high risk of being subjected to future racial profiling during their lifetime."

When it occurs, racial profiling has dramatic negative effects on those targeted, including emotions such as fear, frustration, depression, and anger (Birzer & Smith-Mahdi, 2006; Hart, Larsen, Litton, & Sullivan, 2003). Furthermore, racial profiling hurts law enforcement efforts because it hinders trust between the police and community. Racial profiling has also been shown to be largely ineffective with regard to the wars on crime, drugs, and terrorism (Robinson, 2005).

Despite the abundant studies on racial profiling, only a few studies have paid attention to the macrolevel aspect—that is, the association between racial disparity in police practices and the spatial characteristics of patrolling areas. Such a macrolevel of analysis is important to fully understand racial profiling because police agencies do not use the same crime control strategies in different areas within their jurisdictions; deployment of police force varies geographically depending on the demand for patrol resources. In general, more patrols are allotted to communities that generate a greater number of calls for service and host higher rates of reported crime (Doerner, 1997). Differential crime control approaches, supported by problem-oriented policing strategies and "hot spot" analyses, are considered by police administrators as appropriate means to use limited police resources (Paulsen & Robinson, 2004). Crime hot spots often coincide with disadvantaged minority communities, which lead to disproportionate commission of police resources to those areas. Furthermore, police officers tend to be disproportionately assigned to minority communities, supposedly owing to a perceived threat posed by members of certain racial minority groups (Holmes, 2000; Parker, Stults, & Rice, 2005; Stolzenberg, D'Alessio, & Eitle, 2004; Stults & Baumer, 2007).

The current study examines traffic stop data at both micro- and macrolevels to assess the likelihood of racial profiling in Houston, Texas. At the microlevel, we analyze racial discrepancies in traffic stops in terms of the likelihood of being stopped and the types of police treatments after stops. At the macrolevel, we examine the spatial distribution of traffic stops and stop outcomes, especially focusing on how racial disparities in traffic stops are associated with characteristics of police beats.

The current study hypothesizes that the frequency of traffic stops and types of stop outcomes are dependent on the characteristics of areas including the police resource commitment and the proportion of minorities in the population. The macrolevel analysis examines how traffic stops and (adverse) stop outcomes are spatially distributed and how the distributions can be explained by the factors contingent on areas.

METHOD

Data

Traffic stop data were collected from January through December 2003 by the Houston Police Department, Texas. The data collection was conducted in compliance with Senate Bill 1074, which mandates every police agency to compile data about race or ethnicity whenever traffic and pedestrian stops are made. The police department uses a computer-based data compilation system whereby officers are required to select an appropriate option regarding race and gender of the person stopped, the reason for the stop, the disposition of the stop, the type of search involved, whether contraband was discovered, and the type of charge as a result of the stop.

In this study, 333,760 traffic stops in 121 beats were analyzed. Only included were the traffic stops in which the driver's race and ethnicity was White, Black or Hispanic. The baseline for comparing the frequencies of traffic stops among different racial and ethnic groups was the racial and ethnic proportion of population 15 years and above based on the American Community Survey 2003. Because no data were available for estimating the actual driving population and the racial and ethnic proportion of drivers, we chose the driving age population as a proxy of the driving population. Despite the potential risk of discrepancy between the actual driving population and the driving age population, this threshold population has been widely used in previous racial profiling studies (for review of the baseline issues, see Batton & Kadleck, 2004; Engel et al., 2002). The expected number of traffic stops for each racial and ethnic group was estimated based on the racial and ethnic proportions of driving age population.

At the macrolevel, we used the geographic files in the 2000 U.S. Census data and a beat map file to estimate populations and racial proportions in police beats. Using a GIS program (ArcGIS 9.2), TIGER/Line files downloaded from the U.S. Census Web site were overlaid with the beat map in the police department. Then, the U.S. Census demographic data layer was plotted over those maps, aggregating demographic information on the census block level into that of the beat level. Finally, patrol deployment data on the police department were used to estimate the distribution of police force over the beats. The data contain patrol assignments by beats from January through December 2003.

Measures

Table 9.7 describes the variables included in the microlevel analysis. Under the data compilation system in the department, race and ethnicity is divided into five categories: White, Black, Hispanic, Asian, and Native American. The current study included only the traffic stops in which the driver's race and ethnicity was White, Black or Hispanic.

For the police stop variables, we followed the classification in the traffic stop data. Stop reasons included nonmoving traffic violation (e.g., child restraint violation), moving-traffic violation (e.g., speeding), and investigation. Investigatory stops are justified as long as the facts and the circumstances sufficiently support that the driver is engaged in a criminal activity. Stops culminate in one of three outcomes. First, the driver is released if no law violation is found or the officer exercises discretion in favor of the driver. Second, the officer can issue a ticket for a law violation, especially traffic laws. Finally, the driver may be arrested if the driver is found to have committed more

Table 9.7 Description of Variables in Microlevel Analysis

Variables	N	%
Independent Variable		
Race		
White	91720	27.5
Black	131395	39.4
Hispanic	110645	33.2
Dependent Variable		
Stop Reasons		
Non-moving traffic	40171	12.0
Moving traffic	110854	33.2
Investigation	182735	54.8
Disposition		
Released	187255	56.1
Ticketed	86059	25.8
Arrested	60446	18.1
Search		
No search	279048	83.6
Consent search	10362	3.1
Probable cause search	44350	13.3
Contraband		
Yes	4960	1.5
No	328800	98.5
Charge		
No charge	187255	56.1
Traffic	88151	26.4
Misdemeanor	48120	14.4
Felony	10234	3.1
Total	333760	100

serious offenses such as drug possession. A police officer may conduct a search of the driver, passengers, and/or the vehicle (e.g., trunks and glove compartments) without a search warrant. However, the police officer is required either to obtain consent from the driver or to establish probable cause that the driver has committed or is about to commit a crime (e.g., observing or smelling drugs in the car). In most cases, police searches target contraband such as drugs and guns. The rate of successful searches (i.e., the ratio of contraband findings to searches) is called a *hit rate*. During the final stage of a police stop, the driver is charged with a traffic offense,

misdemeanor, or felony, depending on the type of offense accused.

Table 9.8 shows the variables included in the macrolevel analysis. We chose a variety of dependent variables that indicate racial disparity in traffic stops. The percentage of investigatory stops represents the likelihood to be stopped for the purpose of investigation, wherein the officer may exercise greater discretion than in moving or nonmoving traffic stops to decide to stop a vehicle. Adverse stop outcomes were measured by the percentages of arrests, searches, felony charges, and contraband detection.

The next group of dependent variables measures the ratio of one stop outcome variable to

Table 9.8 Description of Variables in Macrolevel Analysis

Variables	N	Minimum	Maximum	M	SD
Independent variables					
% Black population	106	.94	91.71	25.75	26.58
% Hispanic population	106	4.94	92.71	35.49	23.90
Resource commitment	106	.00	4.49	1.13	.79
Population	106	1205	57992	22172.31	11937.19
Dependent variables					
Number of stops	106	113	8682	3159.47	1650.82
% Investigatory stops	106	15.33	84.72	54.23	16.69
% Arrests	106	3.25	32.80	17.61	7.24
% Consent searches	106	.42	10.26	2.90	1.96
% Probable cause searches	106	2.21	26.85	12.82	6.28
% Felonies	106	.00	10.47	2.95	2.03
% Contraband	106	.00	7.10	1.37	1.18
Ratio of releases to investigatory stops	106	38.30	90.10	64.76	11.34
Ratio of searches to non-moving stops	106	.00	13.81	2.22	2.31
Ratio of searches to moving stops	106	.00	13.82	1.66	2.21
Ratio of contraband findings to searches	106	.00	37.55	8.13	4.75

the other. According to racial profiling claims, minority drivers are the primary target of investigatory police stops, which are often made without sufficient legal grounds. If this claim is accurate, it is predicted that many minority drivers stopped for investigation are more likely to ultimately be released because of a lack of evidence to charge them. This variable is measured by dividing the number of releases by the number of investigatory stops. Next, the pretexual stop contention posits that police use minor traffic violations as opportunities to investigate other criminal offenses (e.g., drug offenses). And the pretextual stop tactic is used disproportionately and adversely against minority drivers. Following the argument, a police officer may be more likely to conduct a search of the driver (if the driver is a minority) after moving or nonmoving traffic stops. The pretextual stop variables include the ratio of searches to nonmoving stops and the ratio of searches to moving stops. Finally, if more police searches are conducted of minority drivers—not because of legal factors, but because of extralegal factors (i.e., race and ethnicity)—the hit rate must be lower for minority drivers. The hit rate is measured by dividing the number of contraband findings by the number of searches.

The independent variables are characteristics of police beats, consisting of the percentage of Black residents, the percentage of Hispanic residents, police resource commitment, and the total population. Police resource commitment, a measure of the concentration level of patrol assignments, is calculated by dividing the number of police-initiated deployments in each beat by the total number of shifts for 1 year. Given three shifts in a day, the annual total number of shifts is the total number of days (365) times three, which equals 1,095. The outcome figure represents the average number of patrol units deployed per shift during the year of 2003 in a particular beat.

In the macrolevel analysis, 15 beats out of the total 121 are excluded for several reasons. Eleven beats are disqualified because no information is available on the amount of deployment. Three beats with population below 1,000 are excluded because the rates of stops in these beats are extraordinarily high, which is called a small area problem. Estimates based on a small population often constitute outliers, not because of characteristics on issue but because of the small population at risk. Another outlier beat is disqualified because of an extremely low number of stops (7) compared to the population size (13,556). After the clean up, the total 106 beats are left for the analysis.

FINDINGS

Racial Disparity in Traffic Stops at the Microlevel of Analysis

The descriptive statistics show that Black drivers were stopped more often than any other racial or ethnic groups (see Table 9.7). More than half of the stops were investigatory stops, followed by moving traffic offense stops. The majority of drivers were released and not subject to a search. When officers conducted warrantless searches, they justified them based on probable cause rather than consent from the driver. Only a small number of traffic stops (1.5%) ended up finding contraband. About a quarter of drivers were charged with traffic offenses and felony charges accounted for only 3% of all stops.

The first analysis compares racial disparity in the number of traffic stops among three different stop reasons. As shown in Table 9.9, the expected numbers of stops in the table were estimated by population 15 and above of each racial and ethnic group within the police department's jurisdiction. Blacks were the only racial or ethnic group that was disproportionately stopped regardless of stop reasons. Although Black drivers were stopped 13.9% more often for nonmoving traffic reasons and 7.6% more often for moving-traffic reasons than expected, both Whites and Hispanics

Table 9.9   Racial Differences in the Observed and Expected Number of Stops by Reasons for Stops

Stop Reasons			Observed	Expected	Residual
Nonmoving traffic	White		23.1% (9280)	34.8% (13979.5)	−11.7% (−4699.5)
	Black		39.6% (15891)	25.7% (10340.0)	13.9% (5551.0)
	Hispanic		37.3% (15000)	39.5% (15851.5)	−2.2% (−851.5)
	Total		40.171		
χ^2	4605.59**				
Moving traffic	White		33.6% (37275)	34.8% (38577.2)	−1.2% (−1302.2)
	Black		33.3% (36878)	25.7% (28533.8)	7.6% (8344.2)
	Hispanic		33.1% (36701)	39.5% (43743.0)	−6.4% (−7042.0)
	Total		110,854		
χ^2	3617.7**				
Investigation	White		24.7% (45165)	34.8% (63591.8)	−10.1% (−18426.8)
	Black		43.0% (78626)	25.7% (47036.0)	17.3% (31590.0)
	Hispanic		32.3% (58944)	39.5% (72107.2)	−7.2% (−13163.2)
	Total		182735		
χ^2	28958.7**				

*$p < .05$. **$p < .01$.

were less stopped than expected. Investigatory stops followed a similar distribution, with more stops for Blacks and less stops for the other groups. The greatest overrepresentation of Blacks was found in investigatory stops with 17.3% more stops than expected. Despite the statistically significant chi-square values for all the comparisons, the differences between observed and expected investigatory stops were much greater than those for the other stop reasons. These results show that racial discrepancy is greater in investigatory stops for which police officers rely on more discretionary determinants such as a probable cause, than in moving or nonmoving traffic stops, which require manifest traffic violation.

In this sense, these findings are consistent with the racial profiling claim that police officers exercise greater discretion unfavorably for Black drivers.

Table 9.10 shows racial disparity in various outcomes after traffic stops. Hispanics and Blacks were more likely than Whites to be arrested after stops, whereas White drivers

Table 9.10   Racial Differences in Stop Outcomes

Stop Outcomes	White	Black	Hispanic
Disposition			
Released	61.1% (56023)	58.3% (76663)	49.3% (54569)
Ticketed	25.8% (23677)	21.9% (28790)	30.4% (33590)
Arrested	13.1% (12020)	19.7% (25941)	20.3% (22484)
χ^2	4854.2**		
Search			
No search	89.4% (82029)	80.7% (106078)	82.2% (90939)
Consent search	2.1% (1917)	3.9% (5177)	3.0% (3268)
Probable cause search	8.5% (7774)	15.3% (20139)	14.9% (16436)
χ^2	3350.7**		
Contraband			
No	99.0% (90837)	97.8% (128541)	98.9% (109419)
Yes	1.0% (883)	2.2% (2853)	1.1% (1224)
χ^2	702.1**		
Charge			
No changes	61.1% (56023)	58.3% (76663)	49.3% (54569)
Traffic	25.5% (23365)	22.6% (29659)	31.7% (35126)
Misdemeanor	11.6% (10678)	14.5% (19000)	16.7% (18440)
Felony	1.8% (1654)		2.3% (2508)
χ^2	6009.3**		

*p < .05. **p < .01.

were more likely to be released. Police conducted searches more frequently of Black and Hispanic drivers. Although about 15% of Black or Hispanic drivers were searched based on probable cause, only 8.5% of White drivers were searched. In spite of the similar pattern, the racial difference in consent searches was not as severe as in probable cause searches: 2.1%, 3.9%, and 3.0% for Whites, Blacks, and Hispanics, respectively. The findings show that when officers stopped Black or Hispanic drivers, they were more likely not only to conduct a search but also to resort to probable cause rather than the driver's consent. The greater reliance on probable cause may be related with the finding that more Black or Hispanic drivers were stopped for an investigation purpose. When a police officer stops a vehicle to investigate a criminal offense, he or she is required to establish probable cause that the driver has engaged in a criminal activity based on the totality of circumstances. Once the police officer stops the vehicle, probable cause for a vehicle search can be developed through an observation (e.g., the driver is trembling and appears to be extremely nervous) or plain view (e.g., a bag of marijuana on the floor). Given the existence of a suspicion prior to a stop, one or more suspicious elements can easily advance the situation to a searchable one. Thus, police officers may not need to obtain consent from the driver.

The odds to discover contraband were highest when Blacks were stopped; 2.2% of traffic stops for Black drivers resulted in contraband whereas about 1% of stops led to contraband for Whites or Hispanics. This discrepancy may be a result of the greater amount of searches conducted against Black drivers. This reasoning, however, does not appear to be valid if we take into account Hispanic drivers. Although Hispanics also were subject to a disproportionate level of police searches, contraband was not found in their searches as much as in searches of Black drivers. Thus, it is likely that Black drivers actually possessed contraband

more often than their racial and ethnic counterparts. We recognize, however, that this simple conclusion may be myopic without taking into account the organizational factors in police agencies. Law enforcement activities in Black communities place more emphasis on narcotic crackdowns because of higher perceived rates of drug offenses. The police initiative to enforce drug offenses in drug hot spots, which are more likely to be located in Black communities, may lead to a higher probability of contraband for Black drivers.

Finally, although Whites were more likely to be released without being charged, the risk of being charged with a felony was highest for Blacks. Hispanics were over-represented in the categories of traffic charges and misdemeanor charges. The greater felony charges for Blacks may be a subsequent outcome of the higher likelihood to find contraband.

The primary purpose of this study was to examine the spatial association between the characteristics of patrol areas and the patterns of traffic stops. Specifically, this study assumed that more traffic stops are conducted, and more adverse outcomes are generated in the areas where minority people are concentrated and more police resource is committed. This assumption is supported by the empirical findings that these areas often spatially coincide with high crime neighborhoods in which more intensive law enforcement is performed. Although this study could not provide clear evidence that racial disparity in individual traffic stops is contingent on the disparity in traffic stops at the community level, the findings in this study suggest that these two facts may be associated. Simply put, minority drivers may be stopped, searched, arrested, and charged with a felony because they are more likely to drive in high crime areas where they reside and more vigorous law enforcement is a common practice.

The microlevel analysis of individual stops confirmed the existence of a racial disparity in the number of traffic stops and subsequent outcomes. Blacks were over-represented and the other racial or ethnic groups were under-represented in traffic stops. Furthermore, Blacks were found to be disproportionately involved with traffic stops in situations where officer discretion played a greater role in decisions to stop. The racial disparity was greater in investigatory stops than in the other two types of stop. In terms of stop outcomes, Black and Hispanic drivers, once stopped, were more likely to be arrested and searched than White counterparts. More Blacks than any other racial or ethnic group were found to possess contraband and were eventually charged with felonies.

The spatial analysis at the macrolevel found that the areas with more frequent traffic stops and more adverse stop outcomes were spatially clustered rather than dispersed, and the majority of the clusters spatially coincided with minority residential areas and/or police resource concentration areas. The multiple regression analysis, affirming the exploratory findings of the cluster map analysis, found statistically significant associations between the characteristics of patrol areas and the traffic stop patterns; a greater number of stops were made and more adverse stop outcomes were followed as more minorities live and/or more patrol is assigned in the community.

Not only are traffic stops concentrated on particular racial or ethnic groups at the microlevel but also they vary by place. That is, there are certain places (e.g., beats or streets) that traffic stops are more likely to occur and drivers are more likely to be searched or arrested. Greater police force and more intensive law enforcement are applied to hot spots where more crimes occur. The demand for police service also tends to cluster in certain areas, heightening the likelihood of traffic stops. Although selective law enforcement based on race or ethnicity is often disapproved as racially discriminatory, differentiated policing by place is supported in most police agencies as an effective crime control strategy.

Insofar as the different treatment by place is grounded on legal factors (e.g., crime rates), greater police force along with more intensive enforcement for particular areas does not bring up a discrimination issue.

A great deal of research during the last decade provided police departments with a valid justification for a geographically differentiated policing strategy. Because of the groundbreaking work by Sherman, Gartin, and Buerger (1989), a number of studies have searched for hot spots of various types of crime in different areas. In the study conducted in Minneapolis, Sherman et al. identified hot spots that produced more than 50% of calls to police but accounted for only 3% of all addresses and intersections.

Hot spots have been identified for different types of crimes, including gang violence (Block & Block, 1993), drug offenses (Block & Block, 1995), burglary (Hirschfield, Bowers, & Brown, 1995), car theft (Fleming, 1994), gun violence (Sherman & Rogan, 1995), among others. Thus, if the occurrence of crime is geographically concentrated and the hot spots are predictable, police agencies may prevent crimes or at least reduce crime rates by concentrating police force in these locations. The hot spot studies provide an empirical basis for implementing problem-oriented policing. Unlike traditional policing that attempts to deal with general crime or social disorder, the problem-oriented approach targets more specific problems or specific types of crime (Goldstein, 1977). Under the problem-oriented approach, the police are expected to analyze specific problems in a neighborhood and then respond to the problems with most appropriate strategies.

Many evaluation studies reveal that problem-solving strategies based on hot spot analysis are effective in reducing crime rates and disorder problems. For example, Sherman and Weisburd (1995), in the experimental study conducted in Minneapolis, found a substantial decrease in crime rates and disorder in hot spots when they doubled the amount of patrol. Similar crime reductions were also reported for different types of crimes, including residential burglary (Eck & Spelman, 1987), prostitution (Matthews, 1997), drug selling (Hope, 1994), as well as others.

Numerous studies also found that high crime rates, especially street crimes, are associated with neighborhoods with high rates of poverty and economic deprivation and a high proportion of non-Whites (Robinson, 2004). Macrolevel studies analyzed this as a structural problem in poor, non-White communities, which failed to develop an effective social control mechanism. As crime is spatially concentrated in particular areas, residences are also spatially segregated by different racial groups. The uneven distribution of residences may be determined either by the principle of market rules based on economic affordability (Massey, 1985), or by Whites' willingness to maintain racial homogeneity in their neighborhoods (Logan, Alba, & Leung, 1996; Logan, Alba, McNulty, & Fisher 1996; Massey & Denton, 1988; South & Crowder, 1997).

No matter what the reason is, there exist racially or ethnically minority communities where social problems are concentrated. And these communities often constitute hot spots of crime and disorder, which draw greater attention from police agencies, and consequently invite more intensive law enforcement activities. The problem-oriented policing strategy, accompanied by scientific analyses (e.g., a hot spot analysis and crime mapping with the Geographic Information System), is widely understood as a legitimate effort by police administrators to maneuver police resource more efficiently and effectively. This study found that more police resource was committed to minority communities, and in these communities, more traffic stops and more adverse outcomes occurred. If the disparity in traffic stops by geographic areas could explain a substantial amount of racial disparity at the individual level, the racial profiling argument may be seriously weakened because the police

practice that is seemingly race based (i.e., more minority drivers stopped and arrested) may be a mere consequence of legitimate policing strategies at the department level. However, it will be premature to conclude as such because of the following issues.

This study showed a likelihood of such an interaction between racial disparity at the macrolevel and at the microlevel. However, the findings in this study must be regarded as suggestive rather than conclusive. Despite the significant effects of beat characteristics on the number of traffic stops and the types of subsequent outcomes, we do not know yet how much of the racial difference on the individual level can be accounted for by the beat characteristics. Future research is recommended to conduct a multilevel analysis, which includes both macrolevel and microlevel factors in the model to examine the role of a driver's race or ethnicity in a traffic stop situation, controlling for relevant factors at the macrolevel.

Furthermore, it is still questionable if the area-specific policing strategies at the department level could neutralize completely the racial profiling claim. When police officers exercise discretion in traffic stops, decision making is often influenced by subjective perception or knowledge of the patrol area, which is developed through previous experiences or information from fellow officers (Smith et al., 2004). Thus, police officers' reactions to similar situations may vary depending on the characteristics of the community. For example, police officers may overreact simply because of their exaggerated perceived risk working in a certain community. If this is the case, the community may experience undue policing, not because of legitimate crime control efforts at the agency level, but because of abuse of discretion at the individual level.

Finally, targeting specific geographic locations (e.g., addresses, blocks) rather than neighborhoods as a whole, hot spot policing can alleviate even further the negative implications of singling out particular, mostly disadvantaged minority, neighborhoods. Indeed, most hot spot literatures also focus on clustering of crimes at the place level rather than at the neighborhood level. However, hot spot policing is not still free from the issue of adverse impact on a few selected neighborhoods because innocent residents living around hot spots, as well as the targeted subjects in the neighborhood, can be unduly influenced by disparate law enforcement.

The findings of the current study suggest important policy implications for police agencies. Granted that racial disparity in traffic stops at the individual level is substantially attributed to the disproportionate commitment of police resources at the community level, police agencies still need to consider if such policing strategies, often named *problem-oriented policing* or *hot spot policing,* resonate well with the ideal of democratic policing, the longstanding imperative for the American police. Democratic policing is often understood as the antonym of inequality, seeking an equal distribution of police service or police control over the public. Thus, unequal amount or different types of police recourses that are devoted to different communities may appear undemocratic. People living in disadvantaged minority communities may perceive that policing unduly targets their communities, if not minority individuals.

Responding to such a complaint, the police may justify that their policing strategies are race neutral and legitimate, targeting crime hot spots that are singled out through sophisticated analyses of crime data. This argument could be challenged for two reasons. First, the validity of official crime data, on which most police agencies rely to develop policing strategies, has long been questioned. It has been argued that official crime data may be a measure of "official reactions to crime" rather than an actual measure of crime (Warner & Pierce, 1993, p. 494). In this sense, a high concentration of crime in particular areas may simply represent a strong willingness for social control by the police. Thus, crime control policies

based on such data may be criticized as tautological in nature.

Second and more important, it is also questionable if police agencies are entitled to impose policing practices that communities do not want. Another important ethos of democratic policing, especially under participatory or deliberative democracy, is community control of the police through community empowerment and community participation (Sklansky, 2008). According to this aspect of democracy, a community's status should not be limited as a consumer of police service but should be a coproducer of police service, therefore playing key roles in the producing process. The pubic must participate in the decision-making process and determine the amount and the types of police service and police protection. In this sense, disproportionate commitment of police resources, no matter how it seems race-neutral, may be perceived as antidemocratic insofar as the community does not grant it.

The current study found that disparities in policing practices at the community level may lead to racial disparities at the individual level. In other words, more effective police practices at the community level (e.g., a higher hit rate to detect contraband) may generate a greater likelihood of becoming subject to more frequent and more intensive police practices at the individual level (e.g., more stops and more searches). Here is the dilemma that the police may confront: Although achieving the institutional goals as a law enforcement agency, the police also should pursue the ideal of democratic policing. The recent popularity of problem-oriented policing and hot spot policing, which champions the disproportionate allocation of police recourses by geographic locations, can be understood as an endeavor to achieve the institutional goals in a more effective and efficient way. However, it is also true that potential negative impact of such a policing approach on the ideal of democratic policing has been relatively ignored. To minimize a conflict between these two different (but relevant) imperatives, the police, when developing a policing strategy, must take into consideration the community's needs and demands, as well as crime data. The police also should strive for community support before implementing the strategy, especially if there is a chance that the strategy may arouse a sentiment among the community members that they (or their communities) are treated in an unequal way.

REFERENCES

Alpert, G. P., Dunham, R., G., & Smith, M., R. (2007). Investigating racial profiling by the Miami-Dade Police Department: A multimethod approach. *Criminology & Public Policy, 6,* 25-55.

American Civil Liberties Union. (2007). *Racial profiling: Old and new.* Retrieved January 5, 2007, from http//www.aclu.org/racialjustice/racialprofiling/index.html.

Amnesty International. (2007). *Threat and humiliation: Racial profiling, national security, and human rights in the United States.* Retrieved January 6, 2007 from http://www.amnestyusa.org/racial_profiling/report/index.html

Anselin, L. (2003). *An introduction to spatial autocorrelation analysis with GeoDa.* Urbana: Spatial Analysis Laboratory, Department of Agricultural and Consumer Economics, University of Illinois, Urbana-Champaign and Center for Spatially Integrated Social Science.

Anselin, L. (2006). *Spatial regression.* Urbana: Spatial Analysis Laboratory, Department of Agricultural and Consumer Economics, University of Illinois, Urbana-Champaign and Center for Spatially Integrated Social Science.

Baller, R. D., Anselin, L., Messner, S. F, Deane, G., & Hawkins, D. R (2001). Structural covariates of U.S. county homicide rates: Incorporating spatial effects. *Criminology, 39,* 561-588.

Barlow, D. E., & Barlow, M. H. (2002). Racial profiling: A survey of African American police officers. *Police Quarterly, 5,* 334-358.

Batton, C, & Kadleck, C. (2004). Theoretical and methodological issues in racial profiling research. *Justice Quarterly, 7,* 30-64.

Beckett, K., Nyrop, K., & Pfingst, L. (2006). Race, drugs, and policing: Understanding disparities in drug delivery arrests. *Criminology, 44,* 105-137.

Birzer, M., & Smith-Mahdi, J. (2006). Does race matter? The phenomenology of discrimination experienced among African Americans. *Journal of African American Studies, 10,* 22-37.

Block, C. R., & Block, R. L. (1993). *Street gang crime in Chicago: Research in brief.* Washington, DC: U.S. Department of Justice.

Block, R. L., & Block, C. R. (1995). Space, place and crime: Hot spot areas and hot places of liquor-related crime. In J. E. Eck & D. L. Weisburd (Eds.), *Crime prevention studies: Crime and place* (pp. 145-184). Monsey, NY: Willow Tree Press.

Bostaph, L. (2007). Race and repeats: The impact of officer performance on racially biased policing. *Journal of Criminal Justice, 35,* 405-417.

Buerger, M., & Farrell, A. (2002). The evidence of racial profiling: Interpreting documented and unofficial sources. *Police Quarterly, 5,* 272-305.

Bureau of Justice Statistics. (2005). *Contacts between police and the public.* Washington, DC: U.S. Department of Justice, Office of Justice Programs.

Chainey, S., & Ratcliffe, J. (2005). *GIS and crime mapping.* West Sussex, UK: John Wiley & Sons.

del Carmen, A. (2007). *Racial profiling in America,* Upper Saddle River, NJ: Prentice Hall.

Doerner, W. (1997). *An introduction to law enforcement: An insider's view.* New York: Butterworth-Heinemann.

Eck, J. E., & Spelman, W. (1987). *Problem-solving: Problem-oriented policing in Newport News.* Washington, DC: National Institute of Justice.

Engel, R. S., & Calnon, J. M. (2004). Examining the influence of drivers' characteristics during traffic stops with police: Results from a national survey. *Justice Quarterly, 27,* 49-90.

Engel, R. S., Calnon, J. M., & Bernard, T J. (2002). Theory and racial profiling: Shortcomings and future directions in research. *Justice Quarterly, 19,* 249-273.

Farrell, A., & McDevitt, J. (2006). *Rhode Island traffic stop statistics 2004-2005 final report.* Retrieved January 6, 2007, from http://www.rijustice.ri.gov/sac/Executive%20Summary%202004-2005.pdf

Farrell, A., McDevitt, J., Bailey, L., Andresen, C, & Pierce, E. (2004). *Massachusetts racial and gender profiling study*. Retrieved January 7, 2007, from http://www.racialprofilinganalysis.neu.edu/IRJsite_docs/finalreport.pdf.

Fleming, M. (1994). Exploring auto theft in British Columbia. In R.V. Clarke (Ed.), *Crime prevention studies* (Vol. 3, pp. 47-90). Monsey, NY: Criminal Justice Press.

Fridell, L. (2004). *By the numbers: A guide for analyzing race data from vehicle stops*. Washington, DC: Police Executive Research Forum.

Gaines, L. (2006). An analysis of traffic stop data in Riverside, California. *Police Quarterly, 9,* 210-233.

Gold, A. (2003). Media hype, racial profiling, and good science. *Canadian Journal of Criminology & Criminal Justice, 45,* 391-399.

Goldstein, H. (1977). *Policing in a free society*. Cambridge, MA: Ballinger.

Golub, A., Johnson, B., & Dunlap, E. (2007). The race/ethnicity disparity in misdemeanor marijuana arrests in New York City. *Criminology & Public Policy, 6,* 131-164.

Gross, S., & Barnes, K. (2002). Road word: Racial profiling and drug interdiction on the highways. *Michigan Law Review, 101,* 651-754.

Harris, D. A. (1997). "Driving while Black" and all other traffic offenses: The Supreme Court and pretextual traffic stops. *The Journal of Criminal Law and Criminology, 87,* 544-582.

Harris, D. A. (1999). The stories, the statistics, and the law: Why "driving while black" matters. *Minnesota Law Review, 84,* 265-326.

Harris, D. A. (2003). The reality of racial disparity in criminal justice: The significance of data collections. *Law & Contemporary Problems, 66,* 71-98.

Hart, J., Larsen, A., Litton, K., & Sullivan, L. (2003). Racial profiling: At what price? *Journal of Forensic Psychology Practice, 3,* 79-88.

Hirschfield, A. F. G, Bowers, K. J., & Brown, P. J. B. (1995). Exploring relations between crime and disadvantage on Merseyside. *European Journal on Criminal Policy and Research, 3,* 93-112.

Holmes, M. (2000), Minority threat and police brutality: Determinants of civil rights complaints in US municipalities. *Criminology, 38,* 343-368.

Hope, T. (1994). Problem-oriented policing and drug market locations: Three case studies. In R.V. Clarke (Ed.), *Crime prevention studies* (Vol. 2, pp. 5-31). Monsey, NY: Criminal Justice Press.

Institute on Race and Justice at Northeastern University. (2007). *Racial profiling data collection research center*. Retrieved January 7, 2007, from http://www.racialprofilinganalysis.neu.edu.

Lamberth, J. D. (1997). *Report of John Lamberth, Ph.D*. American Civil Liberties Union. Retrieved May 5, 2006 from http://www.aclu.org/court/lamberth.html.

Langan, P. A., Greenfeld, L. A., Smith, S. K., Durose, M.R., & Levin, D. J. (2001). *Contacts between the police and the public: Findings from the 1999 National Survey* (No. NCJ184957). Washington, DC: Bureau of Justice Statistics, U.S. Department of Justice.

Lange, J., Johnson, M., & Voas, R. (2005). Testing the racial profiling hypothesis for seemingly disparate traffic stops on the New Jersey Turnpike. *Justice Quarterly, 22,* 193-223.

Leadership Conference on Civil Rights. (2005). Leadership conference on civil rights' letter to Attorney General Gonzales expressing concern about the suppression of a Bureau of Justice Statistics report on racial profiling. Retrieved January 6, 2007, from http://www.aclu.org/racialjustice/racialprofiling/200911leg20050830.html

Lichtblau, E. (2005, August 24). Profiling report leads to a demotion. *The New York Times,* p. A1.

Lichtenberg, I. (2006). Driving while Black (DWB): Examining race as a tool in the war on drugs. *Police Practice & Research, 7,* 49-60.

Logan, J. R., Alba, R. D., & Leung, S. (1996). Minority access to White suburbs: A multi-region comparison. *Social Forces, 74,* 851-881.

Logan, J. R., Alba, R. D., McNulty, T., & Fisher, B. (1996). Making a place in the metropolis: Locational attainment in cities and suburbs. *Demography, 33,* 443-453.

Ludwig, J. (2003). Americans see racial profiling as widespread. Gallup Poll. May 13, 2003. Retrieved January 4, 2007 from http://www.gallup.org

Lundman, R. J. (2004). Driver race, ethnicity, and gender and citizen reports of vehicle searches by police and vehicle search hits: Towards a triangulated scholarly understanding. *The*

Journal of Criminal Law & Criminology, 94, 309-349.

Martin, D. (2002). Spatial patterns in residential burglary. *Journal of Contemporary Criminal Justice, 18,*132-146.

Massey, D. S. (1985). Ethnic residential segregation: A theoretical synthesis and empirical review. *Sociology and Social Science Research, 69,* 315-350.

Massey, D., & Denton, N. (1988). Suburbanization and segregation in U.S. metropolitan areas. *American Journal of Sociology, 94,* 592-626.

Matthews, R. (1997). Developing more effective strategies for curbing prostitutions. In R. Clarke (Ed.), *Situational crime prevention: Successful case studies* (2nd ed.). Guilderland, NY: Harrow and Heston.

Meehan, A. J., & Ponder, M. C. (2002). Race and place: The ecology of racial profiling African American motorists. *Justice Quarterly, 19,* 399-430.

Novak, K. J. (2004). Disparity and racial profiling in traffic enforcement. *Police Quarterly, 7,* 65-96.

Office of the New York State Attorney General (1999). *The New York City Police Department's "stop and frisk" practices: A report to the people of the state of New York.* Retrieved January 6, 2007, from http://www.oag.state .ny.us/press/reports/stop_frisk/stop_frisk.html

Parker, K., MacDonald, J., Alpert, G., Smith, M., & Piquero, A. (2004). A contextual study of racial profiling: Assessing the theoretical rationale for the study of racial profiling at the local level. *American Behavioral Scientist, 47,* 943-962.

Parker, K., Stults, B., & Rice, S. (2005). Racial threat, concentrated disadvantage and social control: Considering the macro-level sources of variation in arrests. *Criminology, 43,* 1111-1134.

Paulsen, D., & Robinson, M. (2004). *Spatial aspects of crime: Theory and practice.* Boston, MA: Allyn & Bacon.

Peruche, B. M., & Plant, E. A. (2006). The correlates of law enforcement officers' automatic and controlled race-based responses to criminal suspects. *Basic & Applied Social Psychology, 28,* 193-199.

Petrocelli, M., Piquero, A., & Smith, M. (2003). Conflict theory and racial profiling: An empirical analysis of police traffic stop data. *Journal of Criminal Justice, 31,* 1-11.

Ridgeway, G. (2006). Assessing the effect of race bias in post-traffic stop outcomes using propensity scores. *Journal of Quantitative Criminology, 27,* 1-29.

Robinson, M. (2004). *Why crime? An integrated systems theory of antisocial behavior.* Upper Saddle River, NJ: Prentice Hall.

Robinson, M. (2005). *Justice blind? Ideals and realities of American criminal justice* (2nd ed.). Upper Saddle River, NJ: Prentice Hall.

Robinson, M., & Scherlen, R. (2007). *Lies, damned lies and drug war statistics: A critical analysis of claims made by the Office of National Drug Control Policy.* Albany: State University of New York Press.

Romero, M. (2006). Racial profiling and immigration law enforcement: Rounding up of usual suspects in the Latino community. *Critical Sociology, 32,* 447-473.

Schafer, J., Carter, D., Katz-Bannister, A., & Wells, W. (2006). Decision making in traffic stop encounters: A multivariate analysis of police behavior. *Police Quarterly, 9,* 184-209.

Sherman, L. W. (1986). Policing communities: What works? In A. Reiss & M. Tonry (Eds.), *Communities and crime* (pp. 342-386). Chicago, IL: University of Chicago Press.

Sherman, L. W., Gartin, P. R., & Buerger, M. E. (1989). Hot spots of predatory crime: Routine activities and criminology of place. *Criminology, 27,* 27-55.

Sherman, L. W., & Rogan, D. P. (1995). Effects of gun seizures on gun violence: Hot spots patrol in Kansas City. *Justice Quarterly, 12,* 27-56.

Sherman, L.W., & Weisburd, D. (1995). General deterrent effects of police patrol in crime "hot spots": A randomized, controlled trial. *Justice Quarterly, 12,* 625-648.

Skolnick, J. (2007). Racial profiling: Then and now. *Criminology & Public Policy, 6,* 65-70.

Sklansky, D. A. (2008). *Democracy and the police.* Stanford, CA: Stanford University Press.

Smith, D. (1986). The neighborhood context of police behavior. In A. Reiss & M. Tonry (Eds.), *Communities and crime* (pp. 313-341). Chicago, IL: University of Chicago Press.

Smith, M. R., & Petrocelli, M. (2001). Racial profiling? A multivariate analysis of police traffic stop data. *Justice Quarterly, 4,* 4-27.

Smith, W., Tomaskovic-Devey, D., Zingraff, M., Mason, M., Warren, P., Wright, C., et al. (2004). *The North Carolina highway traffic study, final report to the National Institute of Justice.* Retrieved January 7, 2007, from http://www.ncjrs.gov/pdffiles1/nij/grants/204021.pdf

South, S. J., & Crowder, K. D. (1997). Escaping distressed neighborhoods: Individual, community, and metropolitan influences. *American Journal of Sociology, 102,* 1040-1084.

Stolzenberg, L., D'Alessio, S. J., & Eitle, D. (2004). A multilevel test of racial threat theory. *Criminology, 42,* 673-698.

Stults, B., & Baumer, E. (2007). Racial context and police force size: Evaluating the empirical validity of the minority threat population. *American Journal of Sociology, 113,* 507-546.

Tomaskovic-Devey, D., Wright, C, Czaja, R., & Miller, K. (2006). Self-reports of police speeding stops by race: Results from the North Carolina reverse record check survey. *Journal of Quantitative Criminology, 22,* 279-297.

Walker, S. (2001). Searching for the denominator: Problems with police traffic stop data and an early warning system solution. *Justice Research and Policy, 3,* 63-95.

Walker, S., Spohn, C., & Delone, M. (2006). *The color of justice: Race, ethnicity and crime in America.* Belmont, CA: Wadsworth.

Warren, P., Tomaskovic-Devey, D., Smith, W., Zingraff, M., & Mason, M. (2006). Driving while Black: Bias processes and racial disparity in police stops. *Criminology, 44,* 709-738.

Warner, B. D., & Pierce, G. L. (1993). Reexamining social disorganization theory using calls to the police as a measure of crime. *Criminology, 31,* 493-516.

Weiss, A., & Grumet-Morris, V. (2006). *Illinois traffic stops statistics study, 2005 annual report.* Retrieved January 6, 2007, from http://www.dot.state.il.us/trafficstop/2005annualreport.pdf

Weitzer, R., & Tuch, S. (2002). Perceptions of racial profiling: race, class, and personal experience. *Criminology, 40,* 435-456.

Weitzer, R., & Tuch, S. (2006). *Race and policing in America: Conflict and reform.* New York: Cambridge University Press.

West, A. (2003). Chicken little, three blind men and an elephant, and "racial profiling": A commentary on the collection, analysis, and interpretation of traffic stop data. *Journal of Forensic Psychology Practice, 3,* 63-77.

DISCUSSION QUESTIONS

1. Why has racial profiling garnered so much attention?

2. What are these authors' main hypotheses?

3. How did these researchers collect their traffic stop data? How many traffic stops did they analyze?

4. How did these researchers estimate the expected traffic stops for different racial and ethnic groups? What data source did they utilize for the mapping portion of the research?

5. According to Table 9.7, what is the reason most persons are stopped by the police? What is the most likely outcome of a police stop? Are most persons who are stopped, also searched? How do these differ by race (Table 9.9)?

6. What are the implications of this research for police departments?

RESEARCH READING

There is a long history of research examining the effect of age on sentencing outcomes. The findings from this body of research, however, present mixed results of the effects of age on sentencing. Wu and Spohn employ a meta-analytic methodology in an attempt to assess the empirical findings of age on the length of sentence from previous literature. Their results reveal that, overall, the age of the offender does not affect the length of sentence received. Further, the strength of the correlation between the variables is weak, and contradictory findings of previous studies may be due to the samples studied and the analytic techniques employed.

DOES AN OFFENDER'S AGE HAVE AN EFFECT ON SENTENCE LENGTH?

A Meta-Analytic Review

Jawjeong Wu and Cassia Spohn

Abstract: Research exploring the effects of an offender's age on unwarranted sentencing disparity has produced conflicting and inconclusive results. Some studies concluded that age was inversely correlated with sentencing severity, whereas others found a positive association. Still others found no significant impact of age on sentencing differentials or that age had a curvilinear effect. Given these inconsistencies, the present research uses meta-analytic methodology to assess empirical findings from a body of sentencing studies. In particular, this research focuses on the imposition of sentence length. Findings from this meta-analysis reveal that the age of the offender has no effect on the length of the prison term and that the strength of the association between the two variables is extremely weak. The homogeneity analysis indicates that variability in effect sizes across contrasts is not due simply to sampling error. A number of moderators related to sample and analytic characteristics account for the differences in effect sizes.

INTRODUCTION

Sentencing research has paid considerable attention to unwarranted disparity stemming from reliance on offender characteristics in judicial decision making. Theoretical perspectives on punishment assume that judges will impose sentences on offenders based on legally relevant factors, such as an offender's prior criminal record and the severity of the offense, legally irrelevant factors, particularly offender characteristics and many case processing characteristics, are viewed as inappropriate sentencing considerations, and use of these factors raises questions about fairness and equity in the sentencing process. Thus, sentencing statutes enacted by the U.S. Congress and some state legislatures (e.g., Florida, Maryland, Minnesota, North Carolina, Pennsylvania, and Washington) require judges to base their decisions regarding incarceration and sentence length on sentencing guidelines, which delineate as legally irrelevant (or as not ordinarily relevant) factors, such as the

Source: Wu, J., & Spohn, C. (2009). Does an offender's age have an effect on sentence length? A meta-analytic review. *Criminal Justice Policy Review, 20*(4), 379–413. Copyright © 2009 Sage Publications.

offender's age, education and vocational skills, employment record, race/ethnicity, gender, national origin, religion, and socioeconomic status (United States Sentencing Commission [USSC] §5H1.1, §5H1.2, §5HL5, & §5H1.10,2007). The sentencing guidelines, explicitly or implicitly, proscribe the use of legally irrelevant factors.

Among legally irrelevant factors, the age of the offender has received little attention in the sentencing literature despite its extensive use as a control variable (but see Feinberg & McGriff, 1989; Steffensmeier, Kramer, & Ulmer, 1995; Steffensmeier & Motivans, 2000; Turner & Champion, 1989; Wilbanks, 1988). Moreover, extant research on the effect of the offender's age on sentence severity has yielded inconsistent results. Using age as a control, varying effects emerge, depending on how this measure is operationalized. With age measured as a continuous variable, some studies found that older offenders were sentenced more harshly than those who were younger (Curry, Lee, & Rodriguez, 2004; Helms & Jacobs, 2002; Mustard, 2001) or that age was inversely correlated with prison terms (Kempf-Leonard & Sample, 2001; Spohn, 1990; Ulmer, 2000), whereas others found that age did not have a significant effect (Bushway & Piehl, 2001; Chiricos & Bales, 1991; Engen & Gainey, 2000; Hebert, 1997; Johnson, 2006; Kautt & Spohn, 2002; Nobiling, Spohn, & DeLone, 1998; Pasko, 2002; Ulmer & Kramer, 1996; Wooldredge, 2007). Still others concluded that the effect of age was curvilinear, with offenders who were about age 30 receiving slightly longer sentences than their younger counterparts and substantially longer sentences than their older counterparts (Steffensmeier & Demuth, 2000). The age effect, in other words, is not necessarily linear.

The second line of inquiry into the age effect uses age categories to capture the potential curvilinear relationship. Several studies found that offenders aged 30 and older, as well as those under 20, received significantly shorter sentences than did those aged 20 to 29 (Steffensmeier et al.,

1995; see also Steffensmeier, Ulmer, & Kramer, 1998). Everett and Wojtkiewicz (2002), however, found that offenders younger than 30 were treated more leniently than those aged 40 to 49 and that there was no difference between offenders aged 30 to 39 and those aged 40 to 49. These conflicting findings, then, suggest that the question of whether and how age affects the length of the sentence is far from settled.

In light of this empirical controversy, we conduct a meta-analysis using an appropriate quantitative technique that synthesizes findings to shed light on the relationship between age and sentence length. Although researchers have used meta-analysis to examine the impact of race (Mitchell, 2005; Pratt, 1998; Sweeney & Haney, 1992) and gender (Daly & Bordt, 1995) on sentencing, this methodology has not yet been used to explore the age-sentence length relationship. The main purpose of this meta-analytic study is to synthesize existing studies to determine whether age has a significant effect on the length of the prison sentence. The purpose, in other words, is to assess the magnitude of the effect of age on sentence length. A secondary purpose is to test whether variability in effect sizes across contrasts is due to sampling error, namely, the meta-analysis examines whether moderators exist that account for the differences in effect sizes and, if so, how the moderators affect the variability in effect sizes.

DATA AND METHOD

Literature Search

The current research established several criteria for a sentencing-related study to be included in the meta-analysis. These criteria are as follows:

1. The study examined the U.S. federal or state sentencing guidelines and other forms of sentencing structure (e.g., indeterminate

sentencing in Wheeler, Weisburd, & Bode. 1982). Although some meta-analytic research distinguished federal data from state data (e.g., Mitchell, 2005), this analysis made no distinction between the two sources. There is no compelling evidence to view variations between federal and state data sets as greater than those among states and thus to make a federal-and-state distinction rather than a state-and-state contrast. However, we included this factor later in the moderator analysis to conduct a close investigation.

2. The study investigated sentencing disparity in adult criminal courts, allowing for appropriate observations based on the independent variable of interest-age and because of the current research's focus on the length of the prison sentence, capital punishment cases were excluded from the analysis (Mitchell, 2005). Studies with a focus on prosecutorial discretion rather than judicial discretion were not part of the meta-analysis as well.

3. The dependent variable was not constrained solely to the actual prison term imposed. That is, a study using the expected minimum sentence (EMS) as the dependent variable was eligible for this meta-analysis. The EMS takes into consideration the maximum likelihood of good-time credit "to avoid problems posed by indeterminate sentencing, suspended sentences, good-time discounts, life sentences, and the like" (Loftin, Neumann, & McDowall, 1983. p. 290; see also Spohn, 1990). Loftin et al. (1983) indicated that the HMS "roughly corresponds to the expected length of sentence, but more precisely it is the length of time to first possible release" (p. 291). This meta-analysis also included the length of the sentence coded as a scale (e.g., Croyle, 1983) or in a discrete form (e.g., Everett & Wojtkiewicz, 2002; Farnworth & Horan, 1980), indicative of the severity of sentences from low to high.

4. The study tested the main, direct effect of age on sentence length or included age as a control. Interactions between age and other offender characteristics were not the focus of the current study and, therefore, were not employed as the source of effect size coding.

5. The scholarly work was published or produced during the years from 1970 through 2007. Advances in data collection and statistical techniques began in the 1970s. Using the data during this period ensures reliability.

6. The study provided necessary statistical information that would allow the computation of the effect size and the possibility for conversion between indexes (Gendreau, Little, & Goggin, 1996). Therefore, studies with only descriptive statistics or qualitative research methods were not eligible for the current analysis.

7. The data set had to come from different sources or the same source without thoroughly overlapping years or sites (either weighted or unweighted) effect size (Mitchell, 2005). The reason is that it is inappropriate to overestimate variation in effect size. When the statistical analyses of several studies based on the same data set use large sample sizes or produce large effect sizes, inclusion of all these studies in the meta-analysis may alter the sign direction of the average effect size and may make it unusually large or small. Consequently, the determination of significance of the relationship between the independent and dependent variables can be influenced largely by the analyses from the studies using the same data set.

This meta-analysis included published studies through the peer-reviewed process, as well as dissertations and book chapters that were unpublished or not peer reviewed. The controversy of excluding unpublished manuscripts often concerns selection bias in which journals tend to publish studies with statistically significant results (Lipsey & Wilson, 1993; Pratt, 1998). By contrast, given that unpublished manuscripts are more likely than those published to lack methodological rigor and unless the missing studies are material such as doctoral dissertations (Baier & Wright, 2001; Mitchell, 2005), the absence of unpublished products indeed reduces potential flaws that would mask the independent variable's real effect on, and relationship with, the dependent variable. In this meta-analysis, indeed, the disadvantage of missing some unpublished studies may be mitigated by the fact that age in sentencing research often plays a role of the control variable or the variable interacting with race/ethnicity and gender. Under the circumstances, research findings have reported not only significant but also nonsignificant age effects, as long as researchers have controlled for this variable in the model. The issue of availability bias, therefore, poses a relatively low threat to sentencing. More to the point, the metaanalysis covered doctoral dissertations that would further reduce biased findings to the minimum, though a number of dissertations were excluded because the authors later published their works on peer-reviewed journals using the same data set.

The meta-analysis located sources of published studies and unpublished dissertations through several tactics. First, a bibliographic database search was conducted via computer access to Criminal Justice Abstracts, Sociological Abstracts, Social Sciences Citation Index, Academic Universe, Westlaw Campus, National Criminal Justice Reference Service, PsycInfo, and PsycArticles. Cooper (1998) and Mitchell (2005) suggested combining diverse key words (e.g., sentencing, discretion, sentencing disparity, unwarranted disparity, etc.) to locate articles. Second, a library journal search was employed to locate newly published articles that have not yet been uploaded to the online databases. This approach focused merely on major criminological and sociological journals, which frequently published most sentencing studies (e.g., *Criminology, Justice Quarterly, Journal of Research in Crime and Delinquency, Crime & Delinquency, Journal of Quantitative Criminology, Criminal Justice Policy Review, Journal of Criminal Justice, Law & Society Review, American Journal of Sociology, American Sociological Review,* and *Social Forces).* Third, identified studies offered a practical alternative for the search via their references. Special attention was paid to published meta-analyses addressing the relationship between race and sentencing because the theme has triggered the most extensive discussion

about unwarranted disparity and has been associated with the role of age. Finally, the service of Dissertations and Theses Abstracts was the main source for discovering dissertation topics on sentencing.

Several additional points regarding whether to include a study in this meta-analysis are worth noting. First, the search for eligible studies could discover a study that investigated more than one jurisdiction. Aggregation bias occurs when researchers pool jurisdictions together within a state or across states (Mitchell, 2005). Aggregating data may also mask the differences between subgroups, as one of them may reveal a positive association whereas the other presents an inverse relationship (see Kautt & Spohn, 2002). To avoid aggregation bias, the coding of a single jurisdiction was preferred over the coding of multiple jurisdictions pooled together, and partitioned data for the characteristics of variables took precedence over aggregated data. For example, in case that a study partitioned multiple jurisdictions and analyzed them separately without overlapping data sets or years, each jurisdiction was treated as an independent case in this meta-analysis. Second, when an analysis had several models including different numbers of variables used to examine sentence length, we selected the model with more variables (e.g., Helms & Jacobs, 2002). Third, when the use of the same data set was at issue, the order of consideration of which study should be included in the meta-analysis is as follows: information thoroughness (more thorough over less thorough), the number of variables used (the greater number over the smaller number), sample sizes (larger sizes over small sizes), and published years (later publication over earlier publication; see Mitchell, 2005). Finally, studies reporting no information necessary for calculating effect sizes and failing to provide this information after contacts with primary authors were excluded.

As Table 9.11 indicates, the search identified 293 studies. Of the studies identified, 224 studies were excluded because they failed to

Table 9.11 Summary of Sample of Studies

Status of Study	n
Number of sentencing studies retrieved[a]	293
Number of studies excluded	224
No control for age and/or no investigation of sentence length	136
No empirical analysis	31
Inappropriate or incompatible statistics for effect size coding	27
Use of the same data set	21
No U.S. data	7
Unavailable studies	2
Number of studies without sufficient statistical information	9
Number of studies included in the analysis	60
Number of contrasts included in the analysis	110

a. Studies retrieved do not include cases that focus on prosecutorial discretion and capital punishment.

control for age, did not investigate the length of the sentence, lacked empirical analysis or appropriate statistics to yield effect sizes, were not based on U.S. data, and/or overlapped with studies selected. Two studies were not available to the authors. In addition, 9 studies met all criteria of eligibility except for the absence of sufficient information to compute effect sizes after efforts to contact primary authors. The search brought about 60 eligible studies, contributing 110 contrasts and covering 1,087,377 cases (see Appendix).

Statistical Analysis

The current meta-analysis attempted to examine (a) whether age was a significant sentencing factor in judicial decision making as to sentence length, (b) the magnitude of the age effect, (c) whether moderators existed to account for the variability in effect sizes across contrasts, and (d) how moderators impacted the variability. To answer the four research questions, this study employed two statistical techniques. First, we used z statistics to determine the extent to which age affected the length of the sentence. Second, we used Q statistics to conduct an overall homogeneity analysis. This step was to examine whether variability in effect sizes among studies was due to sampling error alone (Cooper, 1998). When the Q index appears significant, it indicates that effect sizes for different studies spread over a broad range beyond the likelihood of being explained merely by sampling error. Accordingly, explaining the variability has to rely on moderators that often involve contextual characteristics of studies or research methodology. With a significant finding from the Q statistical analysis suggesting the influence of moderator variables beyond the impact of sampling error alone, we further explored which factors contributed to explaining variations across studies. Wilson (2001) suggested that the analog to the ANOVA and meta-analytic regression analysis are two equivalently appealing methods in the moderator analysis. Following the work of Cooper (1998), Q statistics underlying the analog to the ANOVA can appropriately tackle the issue of intercorrelations between study characteristics. Likewise, Q statistics are robust when none of the moderator variables is a continuous variable (Hedges & Olkin, 1985; Wilson, 2001), as in the moderator analysis below. As a result, we used Q statistics rather than meta-analytic regression to analyze the influence of moderator variables.

FINDINGS

To further explore the distribution of the effect sizes, we used a simple vote-counting strategy to depict their significance and sign directions, as shown in Table 9.12. Each contrast represents one of five direction-significance groups: positive and significant, positive but nonsignificant, negative and significant, negative but nonsignificant, and zero effect. Approximately 41% of the contrasts found that the offender's age was a significant factor in predicting disparity in the length of incarceration, whereas 56% of the effect sizes suggested a nonsignificant effect. Moreover, roughly 40% of the contrasts found a positive association between age and sentence length, and age had a negative relationship with sentence length in 57% of the cases. Three contrasts (or 3%) presented the zero effect. Regardless of significance, the vote-counting method alone cannot precisely determine the direction of the relationship because the age effect on sentence length may vary greatly across contrasts in terms of sample sizes and the magnitude of the effect. Findings from the vote count, however, do suggest the complexity of the relationship between age and sentence length, and an advanced statistical analysis to understand the age impact is needed.

Table 9.12 Vote-Counting by Direction and Significance of Effect Sizes

Directions and Significance	F	%
Positive and significant	21	19.1
Positive but nonsignificant	23	20.9
Zero effect	3	2.7
Negative and significant	24	21.8
Negative but nonsignificant	39	35.5
Total	110	

Results of the moderator variable analysis are reported in Table 9.13. Regarding sample characteristics, as can be seen in Table 9.13, the offender's age had a stronger effect on sentence length in federal courts than in state courts. Age had a negative relationship with sentence length in federal court but a positive relationship in state courts. Southern jurisdictions had a more pronounced disparity than did nonsouthern jurisdictions. In the South, older offenders received longer sentences than did younger offenders, but this relationship was reversed in states outside of this region. Consistent with the finding of meta-analysis research on race and sentencing (see Mitchell, 2005), contrasts based on the single city or county sample resulted in greater effects, compared to those based on the single state or multiple cities and counties. The sample size also influenced unwarranted age disparity. Contrasts with a middle-sized sample (e.g., 1,000 to 9,999 cases) produced an inverse relationship between age and sentence length, but contrasts with a small sample size (e.g., 999 or smaller) and a large sample (e.g., 10,000 or greater) suggested a positive relationship. The middle-sized sample tended to produce larger disparities in sentence length than the others did.

Furthermore, moderators in terms of analytic characteristics primarily addressed

Table 9.13 Effect Size Analysis by Moderators

Moderator Variable	Mean Effect Size (r)[a]		95% Confidence Interval		n[b]
			Lower Bound	Upper Bound	
Sample characteristics					
*Source***					
Federal	−0.018	(−0.006)	−0.010	−0.002	28
State	0.002	(0.001)	−0.001	0.003	82
*Region****					
South	0.023	(0.037)	0.033	0.041	36
Non-South	−0.016	(−0.010)	−0.012	−0.008	74
*Type of jurisdiction**					
Single city or county	−0.001	(−0.012)	−0.022	−0.002	36
Single state or multiple cities, counties, or states	−0.004	(−0.001)	−0.003	0.001	74
Year of data					
1990 or later	−0.015	(−0.001)	−0.003	0.001	52
Prior to 1990	0.007	(−0.005	−0.013	0.003	58
Source of research					
Peer-reviewed/published research	−0.003	(−0.001)	−0.003	0.001	104
Not peer-reviewed/unpublished research	−0.006	(0.002)	−0.008	0.012	6
*Sample size****					
0 to 999	0.002	(0.009)	−0.004	0.022	63
1,000 to 9,999	−0.014	(−0.013)	−0.019	−0.007	27
10,000 or greater	−0.005	(0.000)	−0.002	0.002	20
Analytic characteristics					
*Source of effect size****					
Beta weight ($\beta \rightarrow r$)	−0.007	(−0.017)	−0.020	−0.014	82
t value ($t \rightarrow r$)	0.004	(0.008)	0.005	0.011	27
Pearson's correlation coefficient ($r \rightarrow r$)	0.062	(0.062)	−0.052	0.072	1

Moderator Variable	Mean Effect Size (r)[a]		95% Confidence Interval		n[b]
			Lower Bound	Upper Bound	
Statistical method***					
OLS regression without hazard rates	0.008	(0.018)	0.013	0.023	66
OLS regression with hazard rates	−0.027	(−0.008)	−0.011	−0.005	31
HLM	0.019	(−0.000)	−0.004	0.004	6
Tobit	−0.022	(−0.028)	−0.040	−0.016	3
Others	−0.021	(0.014)	0.008	0.020	4
Type of variable of sentence length**					
Continuous variable in years	−0.002	(0.000)	−0.002	0.002	78
Categorical or logged variable	−0.007	(−0.007)	−0.011	−0.003	32
Controls for prior criminal record***					
Yes	0.004	(−0.003)	−0.005	−0.001	97
No	−0.057	(0.048)	0.038	0.058	13
Controls for offense severity***					
Yes	−0.001	(−0.003)	−0.005	−0.001	80
No	−0.008	(0.040)	0.032	0.048	30
Controls for mode of conviction***					
Yes	−0.016	(−0.015)	−0.017	−0.013	58
No	0.012	(0.034)	0.030	0.038	52
Controls for pretrial status***					
Yes	−0.014	(−0.021)	−0.033	−0.009	27
No	0.000	(−0.000)	−0.002	0.002	83
Individual characteristics*					
Offender only	−0.007	(−0.002)	−0.004	0.000	96
Offender plus judge and/or victim	0.025	(0.006)	0.000	0.012	14
Interactionist perspective					
Age interactions with race and/or gender***					
Yes	−0.054	(−0.035)	−0.039	−0.031	23
No	0.010	(0.010)	0.008	0.012	87

Note: OLS = Ordinary least squares; HLM = hierarchical linear modeling.

a. Weighted *z* score in parentheses.

b. *n* = Number of contrasts.

* *p* < .05. ** *p* < .01. *** *p* < .001.

methodological differences across contrasts. Disparity in sentence length was greatest in the contrasts using the Pearson correlation coefficient to compute the effect size, followed by the use of the beta weight and then the t value. This finding is generally consistent with expectations because the use of the Pearson correlation coefficient is considered an index less precise than the beta weight and the t value. As distinguished from the use of Pearson's r and the t value, the transformation from the beta weight to the r index produced a negative relationship of age with incarceration length. Regarding statistical methods used to analyze incarceration length, disparity was greatest when Tobit was employed, and contrasts using ordinary least squares (OLS) regression with hazard rates as a control produced relatively small sentencing differentials. This was somewhat contrary to our expectation. Although researchers argue that Tobit is a procedure better than Heckman's (1974) hazard rates to correct sample selection bias resulting from in/out decisions (Bushway & Piehl, 2007; Helms & Jacobs, 2002), the two procedures function in a similar way and should generate findings that are more consistent than different. Because only 3 studies in this meta-analysis used Tobit estimation, a large effect size, coupled with a moderate-to-large sample size, might have led the weighted mean effect size in this category to be greater than expected. By contrast, there were 31 studies employing OLS regression with hazard rates as a control variable, and therefore the weighted mean effect size for this statistical procedure became less sensitive to outliers.

The findings in Table 9.13 also suggest that the length of incarceration coded as the conventional continuous variable resulted in smaller sentencing disparities than that coded as the categorical or logged variable. Contrasts without controls for criminal history, offense severity, and the mode of conviction generated greater sentencing gaps than those with appropriate controls for legally relevant and case processing factors. Relative to the former that used less precise measures and observed a positive relationship, the latter displayed that older offenders are more likely than younger offenders to get short sentences, a finding that partially reflects the theoretical prediction. As opposed to the expectation, however, failure to control for pretrial status and judge and/or victim characteristics in the model produced smaller effect sizes. In sum, findings from the moderator analyses based on analytic characteristics tend to correspond to the argument in which large effects of age on sentence length often stemmed from conventional methodology and from the absence of controls for legal and case processing factors (Mitchell, 2005).

DISCUSSION AND CONCLUSION

Using a meta-analytic methodology, the primary purpose of the present study was to examine the effect of age on disparity in the length of the sentence. Prior research has used the same methodology to explore the impact of race and gender on sentencing outcomes but has not focused on age. The line of inquiries of race and gender in sentencing disparity generally concludes that minority offenders are more likely than their White counterparts to receive longer sentences and that female offenders are treated more leniently than are male offenders. However, the literature has produced inconsistent findings on how age affects a judge's decisions on sentence length, thereby resulting in researchers' failure to reach a consensus about its effect. Therefore, it is important to have a comprehensive evaluation of whether age, as an extralegal, unwarranted characteristic, is a sentencing consideration. The result of this meta-analysis indicates that age did not have a significant effect on judicial decision making as to sentence length. Not only was the average weighted or unweighted effect size from studies examining the direct effect of age very small but the effect size also failed to reach statistical significance. Overall, older offenders received roughly the same sentences as similarly situated young offenders did.

The above finding indicates that the relationship between an offender's age and the length of the sentence is neither linear nor curvilinear. Although, as suggested by the focal concerns perspective, judges take into account multiple factors and consequences of sentencing decisions for different ages of offenders, overall, the offender's age has no direct effect on sentence length. Recent inquiries of sentencing disparity have focused on intersections of race, gender, and age (e.g., Spohn & Holleran, 2000; Steffensmeier et al., 1998) and have found that young minority men received the harshest penalties among all race-gender-age groups. It is likely that in examining the direct effect, race and gender, which are the most salient individual characteristics, suppressed the age effect. For example, Spohn and Holleran (2000) did not find the age effects in the 30-39 group and the group consisting of offenders aged over 40, but their analyses of interactions displayed that age and gender, along with age and race, jointly affected the odds of imprisonment in some jurisdictions. Therefore, explaining the age effect based on the considerations of offenders' guilty, dangerousness, and practical constraints without reference to the racial threats hypothesis or gender-centered social control thesis may present an incomplete picture (Spohn & Beichner, 2000). The interactionist argument is supported by an additional effect size analysis, which exhibited significantly larger sentencing disparity for contrasts that examined the age-race, age-gender, or age-race-gender intersection than for contrasts without this assessment.

Research suggests that the analysis of sentencing disparity with age as a continuous variable often finds a fairly small effect because the relationship between age and sentencing outcomes is likely a curvilinear one rather than a linear one (Steffensmeier et al., 1995; Steffensmeier et al., 1998). In a separate analysis (not shown), the finding revealed that contrasts that treated age as a continuous variable produced a relatively small weighted effect size of 0.011, an index that was only approximately one third of the weighted effect size (0.028) for contrasts with age as other types of variables (e.g., categorical variables). Because age as a continuous variable accounted for the majority of the contrasts (82%) and the sample size (70%), we cannot exclude the possibility that the null relationship between an offender's age and sentence length found in this metaanalysis may change when the number of studies using the noncontinuous age variable increases. Thus, the finding that age, with a considerably small effect size, had no relationship with sentence length appeared to accord with the assertion that research on the age effect should shift its focus from a linear relationship to a curvilinear one.

Our findings suggest that the focal concerns and interactionist frameworks are not incompatible. The focal concerns perspective is based on a relatively complex decision making process that involves a variety of factors and considerations. These considerations may or may not conflict with one another. For example, some judges may view age as a protective factor for younger offenders (i.e., downplaying culpability because of a lack of social experiences or serious harm caused), and they may believe that these offenders deserve lenient sentences as a result of their potential for reform (Steffensmeier et al., 1995). Other judges may not view age as a protective factor but rather may focus on the practical issue of whether older offenders are able to do time in prison without health concerns and family disruption (Steffensmeier et al., 1998). On the other hand, judges, in an attempt to identify risk factors and promote organizational efficiency, may link age to other factors to develop stereotypes of dangerousness and threat. As a result, offenders who are young, Black, and male will be singled out as the most dangerous offenders and will be viewed as the group that warrants a longer prison sentence. Therefore, age alone is not necessarily a salient factor sufficient to explain unwarranted sentencing disparities. Although the complex sentencing process with multiple factors considered shapes inconsistent research findings with respect to the age effect, our findings from this meta-analysis are consistent with the expectations of both focal concerns and interactionist perspectives.

In general, the findings are consistent with previous meta-analytic research on race, which reflected that small effect sizes stemmed primarily from studies with relatively rigorous methodology (e.g., Mitchell, 2005). Coupled with this study's finding that age did not have a significant effect on sentence length across studies, this suggests that research methodology largely accounts for whether legally irrelevant factors (e.g., race, gender, and age) will produce disparities in sentence length across studies (see also Pratt, 1998). Stated differently, the age effect found in some studies is merely an artifact of varying research methods used by researchers, and evidence is not solid enough to support the existence of age discrimination within the judicial system. Other evidence from the impact of legally relevant factors in the analyses also supports this argument. The absolute value of the weighted mean effect size for studies without controlling for the offender's criminal history (0.048) is 16 times larger than the value for studies with a control for the same legal factor (0.003). Likewise, compared to studies with a control for offense severity that produced an absolute value of the weighted mean effect size of 0.003, those without controlling for this factor resulted in a relatively large value of 0.040. Still the case is reflected in case processing factors, such as the mode of conviction. Research that did not control for the mode of conviction led to greater disparity in sentence length than did research that used the factor as a control.

The current study found a significantly greater disparity for contrasts based on federal data than for state-based contrasts. This finding may seem counterintuitive because guidelines-based federal data are highly structured, leaving judges little room to exercise discretion in determining the length of the sentence. However, unlike other legally irrelevant factors (e.g., race, gender, national origin, creed, religion, and socioeconomic status) categorically proscribed by federal sentencing guidelines (USSC §5H1.10, 2007), age operates in somewhat a different way. According to the federal guidelines, an offender's physical condition associated with age can be used as a reason for a downward departure (USSC §5H1.1, 2007), suggesting that judges do have a freer hand as faced with different ages of offenders. The guidelines grant judges the power to depart from the guidelines range for "the defendant who is elderly and infirm" (USSC §5H1.1, 2007), which is consistent with our findings regarding the inverse association between age and sentence length in federal courts. In addition, judges may also use the loose statutory restriction on age as a way to mitigate the harshness of the federal guidelines, as a substantial number of federal offenders are involved in drug, fraud, and immigration offenses that pose relatively low threat to the community. This is particularly evident in that age has been one of the top seven reasons for imposing below-range sentences on offenders (Hofer, 2007). In short, although state judges generally have greater discretionary power at the sentencing stage, the likelihood of even greater disparity resulting from an offender's age in federal courts than in state courts does exist.

The results of the current research, along with prior meta-analytic research on sentencing, suggest that policy makers should not base policy changes on the findings of any single study. Judicial decision making is a complex process, and these complexities will not necessarily be reflected in the results of quantitative research as those contained in this meta-analysis. Although critics of the sentencing process contend that evidence of sentencing disparity/discrimination based on race, ethnicity, sex, or age provides a strong justification for reforms designed to restrict judicial discretion, it is not clear that their calls for reform reflect an understanding of the dynamics and complexities of judicial decision making (Wellford, 2007). Researchers can address this issue by developing qualitative methodology to understand the complex interplay of sentencing factors, and policy makers' need to scrutinize what we call the evidence-based approach for public policy to avoid the recurrent discourse of the nothing-works notion.

REFERENCES

*Indicates studies included in the meta-analysis.

Albonetti, C. A. (1991). An integration of theories to explain judicial discretion. *Social Problems, 38*, 247-266.

*Albonetti, C. A. (1998). The role of gender and departures in the sentencing of defendants convicted of a white-collar offense under the federal sentencing guidelines. *Sociology of Crime, Law, and Deviance, 1*, 3-48.

*Auerhahn, K. (2007). Just another crime? Examining disparity in homicide sentencing. *Sociological Quarterly, 48*, 277-313.

Baier, C. J., & Wright, B. R. E. (2001). "If you love me, keep my commandments": A meta-analysis of the effect of religion on crime. *Journal of Research in Crime & Delinquency, 38*, 3-21.

*Benson, M. L., & Walker, E. (1988). Sentencing the white-collar offender. *American Sociological Review, 53*, 294-302.

Box, C., & Hale, S. (1985). Unemployment, imprisonment and prison overcrowding. *Contemporary Crises, 9*, 209-228.

Bridges, G., S., & Steen, S. (1998). Racial disparities in official assessments of juvenile offenders: Attributional stereotypes as mediating mechanisms. *American Sociological Review, 64*, 554-570.

*Britt, C. L. (2000). Social context and racial disparities in punishment decisions. *Justice Quarterly, 17*, 707-732.

*Bushway, S. D., & Piehl, A. M. (2001). Judging judicial discretion: Legal factors and racial discrimination in sentencing. *Law & Society Review, 35*, 733-764.

*Bushway, S. D., & Piehl, A. M. (2007). Social science research and the legal threat to presumptive sentencing guidelines. *Criminology Justice Public Policy, 6*, 461-482.

Champion, D. J. (1987). Elderly felons and sentencing severity: Interregional variations in leniency and sentencing trends. *Criminal Justice Review, 12*, 7-14.

*Chiricos, T. G., & Bales, W. D. (1991). Unemployment and punishment: An empirical assessment. *Criminology, 29*, 701-724.

*Chiricos, T. G., & Waldo, G. P. (1975). Socioeconomic status and criminal sentencing: An empirical assessment of a conflict proposition. *American Sociological Review, 40*, 753-772.

Cohen J. (1992). A power primer. *Psychological Bulletin, 112*, 155-159.

Cooper, H. M. (1998). *Synthesizing research: A guide for literature reviews.* Thousand Oaks, CA: Sage.

*Crow, M. S., & Bales, W. (2006). Sentencing guidelines and focus concerns: The effect of sentencing policy as a practical constraint on sentencing decisions. *American Journal of Criminal Justice, 30*, 285-304.

*Croyle, J. L. (1983). Measuring and explaining disparities in felony sentences: Courtroom work group factors and race, sex, and socioeconomic influences on sentence severity. *Political Behavior, 5*, 135-153.

*Curran, D. A. (1983). Judicial discretion and defendant's sex. *Criminology, 21*, 41-58.

*Curry, T. R., Lee, G., & Rodriguez, S. K. (2004). Does victim gender increase sentence severity? Further examinations of gender dynamics and sentencing outcomes. *Crime & Delinquency. 50*, 319-343.

Daly, K., & Bordt, R. I. (1995). Sex effects and sentencing: An analysis of the statistical literature. *Justice Quarterly, 12*, 141-175.

Demuth, S., & Steffensmeier, D. (2004). Ethnicity effects on sentence outcomes in felony cases: Comparisons among White, Black, and Hispanic defendants. *Social Science Quarterly, 85*, 994-1011,

*Engen, R. L., & Gainey, R. R. (2000). Modeling the effects of legally relevant and extralegal factors under sentencing guidelines: The rules have changed. *Criminology, 38*, 1207-1229.

*Everett, R. S., & Wojtkiewicz, R. A. (2002). Difference, disparity, and race/ethnic bias in federal sentencing. *Journal of Quantitative Criminology, 18*, 189-211.

*Farnworth, M., & Horan, P. M. (1980). Separate justice: An analysis of race differences in court processes. *Social Science Research, 9,* 381-399.

Feinberg, G., & McGriff, M. D. (1989). Defendant's advanced age as a prepotent status in criminal case disposition and sanction. In S. Chaneles & C. Burnett (Eds.), *Older offenders: Current trends* (pp. 87-124). New York: Haworth.

Frost, N. A. (2006). *The punitive state: Crime, punishment, and imprisonment across the United States.* New York: LFB.

Gendreau, P., Little, T., & Goggin, C. E. (1996). A meta-analysis of the predictors of adult offender recidivism: What works! *Criminology, 34,* 575-607.

*Hanke, P. J. (1995). Sentencing disparities by race of offender and victim: Women homicide offenders in Alabama, 1929-1985. *Sociological Spectrum, 15,* 277-297.

*Hartley, R. D., Maddan, S., & Walker, J. T. (2006). Sentencing practices under the Arkansas sentencing guideline structure. *Journal of Criminal Justice, 34,* 493-506.

Hawkins, D. (1981). Causal attribution and punishment for crime. *Deviant Behavior, 1,* 207-230.

Hebert, C. G. (1997). Sentencing outcomes of Black, Hispanic, and White males convicted under federal sentencing guides. *Criminal Justice Review, 22,* 133-156.

Heckman, J. J. (1974). Shadow prices, market wages, and labor supply. *Econometrics, 42,* 679-694.

Hedges, L. V., & Olkin, I. (1985). *Statistical methods for meta-analysis,* Orlando. FL: Academic Press.

*Helms, R., & Jacobs, D. (2002). The political context of sentencing: An analysis of community and individual determinants. *Social Forces, 81,* 577-604.

Hofer, P. J. (2007). United States v. Booker as a natural experiment: Using empirical research to inform the federal sentencing policy debate. *Criminology & Public Policy, 6,* 433-460.

*Holmes, M. D., Hoseh, H. M, Daudistel, H. C., Perez., D. A, & Graves, J. B. (1996). Ethnicity, legal resources, and felony dispositions in two southwestern jurisdictions. *Justice Quarterly, 13,* 11-30.

*Huang, W. S. W., Finn, M. A., Ruback, B. R., & Friedmann, R. R. (1996). Individual and contextual influences on sentence lengths: Examining political conservatism. *The Prison Journal, 76,* 398-419.

*Iles, G. D. (2006). America's forgotten paradise: An assessment of sentencing decisions and outcomes in the United States Virgin islands (Doctoral dissertation, University of Nebraska, Omaha, 2006). *Dissertation Abstracts International, 67,* 2329.

*Johnson, B. D. (2006). The multilevel context of criminal sentencing: Integrating judge- and county-level influences. *Criminology, 44,* 259-298.

Kant, I. (1965). *The metaphysical elements of justice.* Indianapolis, IN: Bobbs-Merrill.

*Kautt, P. M. (2000), Separating and estimating the effects of the federal sentencing guidelines and the federal mandatory "minimums": isolating the sources of racial disparity (Doctoral dissertation, University of Nebraska, Omaha, 2000). *Dissertation Abstracts International, 61,* 2048.

*Kautt, P. M., & Spohn, C. (2002). Crack-ing down on Black drug offenders? Testing for interactions among offenders' race, drug type, and sentencing strategy in federal drug sentences. *Justice Quarterly, 19,* 1-35.

*Kempf-Leonard, K., & Sample, L. L. (2001). Have federal sentencing guidelines reduced severity? An examination of one circuit. *Journal of Quantitative Criminology, 17,* 111-144.

*Klein, S., Petersilia, J., & Turner, S. (1990). Race and imprisonment decisions in California. *Science, 247,* 812-816.

Kramer, J. H., & Steffensmeier, D. (1993). Race and imprisonment decisions. *Sociological Quarterly, 34,* 357-376.

Kramer, J. H., & Ulmer, J. T. (1996). Sentencing disparity and departures from guidelines. *Justice Quarterly, 13,* 81-106.

*Kruttschnitt, C. (1980-81). Social status and sentences of female offenders. *Law & Society Review, 15,* 247-265.

*Landes, W. (1974). Legality and reality: Some evidence on criminal procedure. *Journal of Legal Studies, 3,* 287-337.

Lipsey, M. W., & Wilson, D. B. (1993). The efficacy of psychological, education, and behavioral treatment: Confirmation from meta-analysis. *American Psychologist, 48,* 1181-1209.

Loftin, C., Neumann, M., & McDowall, D. (1983), Mandatory sentencing and firearms violence; Evaluating an alternative to gun control. *Law & Society Review, 17,* 287-318.

*Miethe, T. D., & Moore, C. A. (1985). Socioeconomic disparities under determinate sentencing systems: A comparison of pre-guideline and post-guideline practices in Minnesota. *Criminology, 23,* 337-363.

Mitchell, O. (2005). A meta-analysis of race and sentencing research: Explaining the inconsistencies. *Journal of Quantitative Research, 21,*439-466.

Morris, H. (1968). Persons and punishment *Monist, 52,* 475-501.

Murphy, J. G, & Coleman, J. L. (1990). *Philosophy of law: An introduction to jurisprudence.* Boulder, CO: Westview.

*Mustard, D. B. (2001). Racial, ethnic, and gender disparities in sentencing: Evidence from the U.S. federal courts. *Journal of Law and Economics, 44,* 285-314.

*Myers, M. A. (1988). Social background and the sentencing behavior of judges. *Criminology, 26,* 649-675.

*Myers, M. A. (1989). Symbolic policy and the sentencing of drug offenders. *Law & Society Review, 23,* 295-316.

*Myers, M. A., & Talarico, S. M. (1986). The social contexts of racial discrimination in sentencing. *Social Problems, 33,* 236-251.

Myers, M. A., & Talarico, S. M. (1987). *The social contexts of criminal sentencing.* New York: Springer.

*Nagel, I. H., & Hagan, J. (1982). The sentencing of white-collar criminals in federal courts: A socio-legal exploration of disparity. *Michigan Law Review, 80,* 1427-1465.

Nobiling, T., Spohn, C., & DeLone, M. (1998). A tale of two counties: Unemployment and sentence severity. *Justice Quarterly, 15,* 459-485.

*Pasko, L. (2002). Villain or victim: Regional variation and ethnic disparity in federal drug offense sentencing. *Criminal Justice Policy Review, 13,* 307-328,

*Peterson, R. D., & Hagan, J. (1984). Changing perceptions of race: Towards an account of anomalous findings of sentencing research. *American Sociological Review, 49,* 56-70.

Pratt, T. C. (1998). Race and sentencing: A meta-analysis of conflicting empirical research results. *Journal of Criminal Justice, 26,* 513-523.

Rosenthal, R. (1984). *Meta-analytic procedures for social research.* Beverly Hills, CA: Sage.

*Simon, L. M. J. (1996). The effect of the victim-offender relationship on the sentence length of violent offenders. *Journal of Crime and Justice, 19,* 129-148.

*Sloan, J. J., & Miller, J. L. (1990). Just deserts: the severity of punishment and judicial sentencing decisions. *Criminal Justice Policy Review, 4,* 19-38.

*Smith, B. L., & Damphousse, K. R. (1996). Punishing political offenders: The effect of political motive on federal sentencing decisions. *Criminology, 34,* 289-322.

Spitzer, S. (1975). Toward a Marxist theory of deviance. *Social Problems, 22,* 638-651.

*Spohn, C. (1990). The sentencing decisions of Black and White judges: Expected and unexpected similarities. *Law & Society Review, 24,* 1197-1216.

Spohn, C, (2000). Thirty years of sentencing reform: The quest for a racially neutral sentencing process. In J. Horney (Vol. Ed.), *Criminal justice 2000: Vol. 3. Policies, processes, and decisions of the criminal justice system* (pp. 427-501). Washington, DC: U.S. Department of Justice, Office of Justice Program, National Institution of Justice.

Spohn, C., & Beichner, D. (2000). Is preferential treatment of female offenders a thing of the past? A multisite study of gender, race, and imprisonment. *Criminal Justice Policy Review, 11,* 149-184.

*Spohn, C., & DeLone, M. (2000). When does race matter? An examination of the conditions under which race affects sentence severity. *Sociology of Crime, Law, and Deviance, 2,* 3-37.

Spohn, C., & Holleran, D. (2000). The imprisonment penalty paid by young, unemployed Black and Hispanic male offenders. *Criminology, 38,* 281-306.

Spohn, C., & Sample, L. L. (in press). The dangerous drug offender in federal court: Intersections of race, ethnicity, and culpability. *Crime and Delinquency.*

*Spohn, C., & Spears, J. W. (1996). The effect of offender and victim characteristics on sexual

assault case processing decisions. *Justice Quarterly, 13,* 649-679.

*Spohn, C., & Spears, J. W. (2003). Sentencing of drug offenders in three cities: Does race/ethnicity make a difference? In D. F. Hawkins, S. L. Myers. Jr., & R. N. Stone (Eds.), *Crime control and social justice: The delicate balance* (pp. 197-231). Westport, CT: Greenwood.

*Steen, S., Engen, R. L., & Gamey, R, R. (2005). Images of danger and culpability: Racial stereotyping, case processing, and criminal sentencing. *Criminology, 43,* 435-468,

Steffensmeier, D., & Britt, C. L. (2001). Judges' race and judicial decision making: Do Black judges sentence differently? *Social Science Quarterly, 82,* 749-764.

*Steffensmeier, D., & Demuth, S. (2000). Ethnicity and sentencing outcomes in U.S. federal courts: Who is punished more harshly? *American Sociological Review, 65,* 705-729.

*Steffensmeier, D., & Demuth, S. (2001). Ethnicity and judges' sentencing decisions: Hispanic-Black-White comparisons. *Criminology, 39,* 145-178.

*Steffensmeier, D., & Demuth, S. (2006). Does gender modify the effects of race-ethnicity on criminal sentencing: Sentences for male and female While, Black, and Hispanic defendants. *Journal of Quantitative Criminology 22,* 241-261.

Steffensmeier, D., & Hebert, C. G. (1999). Women and men policymakers: Does the judge's gender affect the sentencing of criminal defendants? *Social Forces, 77,* 1163-1196.

Steffensmeier, D., Kramer, J. H., & Strelfel, C. (1993). Gender and imprisonment decisions. *Criminology, 37,* 411-446.

*Steffensmeier, D., Kramer, J. H., & Ulmer, J. T. (1995). Age differences in sentencing. *Justice Quarterly, 12,* 583-602.

*Steffensmeier, D., & Motivans, M. (2000). Older men and older women in the arms of criminal law: Offending patterns and sentencing outcomes. *Journal of Gerontology, 55B,* S141-S151.

Steffensmeier, D., Ulmer, J. T., & Kramer, J. H. (1998). The interaction of race, gender, and age in criminal sentencing: The punishment cost of being young, Black, and male. *Criminology, 36,* 763-798.

Sweeney, L. T., & Haney, C. (1992). The influence of race on sentencing; A meta-analytic review of experimental studies. *Behavioral Sciences & the Law, 10,* 179-195.

Turner, G. S., & Champion, D. J. (1989). The elderly offender and sentencing leniency. In S. Chaneles & C. Burnett (Eds.), *Older offenders: Current trends* (pp. 125-140). New York: Haworth.

Ulmer, J. T. (2000). The rules have changed-so proceed with caution: A comment on Engen and Gaincy's method for modeling sentencing outcomes under guidelines. *Criminology, 38,* 1231-1243.

*Ulmer, J. T., & Bradley, M. S. (2006). Variation in trial penalties among serious violent offenses. *Criminology, 44,* 631-670.

*Ulmer, J. T., & Johnson, B. D. (2004). Sentencing in context: A multilevel analysis. *Criminology, 42,* 137-177.

*Ulmer, J. T., & Kramer, J. H. (1996). Court communities under sentencing guidelines: Dilemmas of formal rationality and sentencing disparity. *Criminology, 34,* 383-408.

United States Sentencing Commission. (2007). *Guidelines manual* Washington, DC: Author.

Wellford, C. F. (2007). Sentencing research for sentencing reform. *Criminology & Public Policy, 6,* 399-402.

*Wheeler, S., Weisburd, D., & Bode, N, (1982). Sentencing the white-collar offender: Rhetoric and reality. *American Sociological Review, 47,* 641-659.

Wilbanks, W. (1988). Are elderly felons treated more leniently by the criminal justice system? *International Journal of Aging and Human Development, 26,* 275-288.

*Williams, M. R. (1999). Gender and sentencing: An analysis of indicators. *Criminal Justice Policy Review, 70,* 471-490.

*Wilmot, K. A., & Spohn, C. (2001). Prosecutorial discretion and real-offense sentencing: An analysis of relevant conduct under the federal sentencing guidelines. *Criminal Justice Policy Review, 75,* 324-343.

Wilson, D. B. (2001). Meta-analytic methods for criminology. *Annals of the American Academy of Political and Social Science, 578,* 71-89.

*Wooldredge, J. D. (1998). Analytic rigor in studies of disparities in criminal case processing. *Journal of Quantitative Criminology, 14,* 155-179.

*Wooldredge, J. D. (2007), Neighborhood effects on felony sentencing. *Journal of Research in Crime & Delinquency, 44,* 238-263.

*Wooldredge, J. D., & Thistlethwaite, A. (2004). Bilevel disparities in court dispositions for intimate assault. *Criminology, 42,* 417-456.

*Wu, J., & Spohn, C. (in press). Inter-district disparity in sentencing in three U.S. district courts. *Crime and Delinquency.*

*Zatz, M. S. (1984). Race, ethnicity, and determinate sentencing: A new dimension to an old controversy. *Criminology, 22,* 147-171.

DISCUSSION QUESTIONS

1. What has previous research shown about the relationship of age of offenders and the sentences they receive?

2. What criteria did these researchers use to make decisions about which previous sentencing studies would be included in their research? Do they use date of publication of the study as an inclusion criteria? What is the rationale for this?

3. How did these researchers find these studies? In other words, how did they obtain their sample?

4. How many studies do Wu and Spohn study? Why did they exclude so many of the studies that were identified through their search?

5. What were the authors' research questions? Would you consider these null hypotheses?

6. According to Table 9.12, how many of the studies found significant and positive age effects? How did this compare to those that found significant and negative effects of age?

7. In Table 9.13, how did age affect sentence lengths according to the type of court the researchers studied (state versus federal), the region of the country the study was done in, the type of jurisdiction, the sample size, and the years of data that the study covered?

8. What do the results from this meta-analytic study mean for theoretical explanations of judicial sentencing decisions?

9. What do these authors say is the reason previous studies have found a significant effect of age on sentencing? What does this say about the results of single research studies for advancing knowledge or determining policy? Do these authors' results provide support for knowledge acquisition based on the cumulative nature of science?

10

MIXED METHODS RESEARCH

The quantitative-qualitative methodological debate is nothing new (Tashakkori & Teddlie, 1998), with advocates on both sides, quants and quals (Creswell, 1995), arguing that their methods are superior. Berg (2004), in a discussion of the qual-quant debate, cites that the quants believe that everything must be counted to be examined, and the quals believe that all numbers are grounded in observation. Berg argues that "this sort of back-and-forth arguing would seem rather unproductive, and it seems more useful to consider the merits of both quantitative and qualitative research strategies" (p. 3). Indeed, some researchers have demonstrated that, in fact, the two previously thought polar-opposite methods are actually compatible. Researchers today often use multiple methodological approaches (both quantitative and qualitative) to study the same event or phenomenon. Tashakkori and Teddlie (1998), for instance, contend that the social and behavioral sciences have evolved from using single methods (what they refer to as monomethods) to employing more advanced "mixed model studies" (p. 14). Mixed methodologies have recently gained more respect as a research approach, and today, more than ever,

qualitative and quantitative methods are being integrated (Creswell, 2009).

The advantages of using mixed model strategies are that researchers are more likely to be able to overcome the limitations of single methods approaches. As discussed earlier, validity is a potential problem in all types of research methods, and no method alone is a perfect way to ensure getting accurate results. Different methods have their own unique strengths and weaknesses, and researchers are now mixing methodological strategies with the purpose of taking advantage of the strengths and overcoming the weaknesses. Researchers also believe that these mixed strategies will help uncover multiple aspects of social events or behaviors. These strategies have also been referred to as triangulation, and if the overall goal of research is to add pieces to the puzzle of knowledge, then triangulating methodological approaches makes sense. As Bachman and Schutt (2008) note, "a researcher can get a clearer picture of the social reality being studied by viewing it from several different perspectives" (p. 237).

An old African proverb states that until the lions have their historians, tales of the hunt shall always glorify the hunter. What this proverb exemplifies is that the true reality of hunting cannot be observed until it can also be examined from the lions' perspective. Indeed, a very different view of hunting might be observed if the lions could be interviewed. In much the same way, approaching the study of crime from multiple and different views may enable researchers to obtain a more complete picture of the reality of criminal offending.

TRIANGULATION

Triangulation, which comes from surveying and navigation, involves describing an unknown location based upon other known locations. Similarly, in social science research, triangulation refers to employing more than one method to study the reality of a phenomenon. Berg (2004) states that "by combining

several lines of sight, researchers obtain a better, more substantive picture of reality; a richer, more complete array of symbols and theoretical concepts" (p. 5). Finally, triangulation of approaches may also help researchers rule out rival causal factors, better enabling them to assess causal relationships by meeting the assumption of nonspuriousness.

Triangulation strategies are not limited to methodologies alone. A researcher can also triangulate data collection strategies, theoretical perspectives, observers, methodological approaches, or a combination of these (Hagan, 2005). In other words, when researchers collect data at multiple times, in different locations, using multiple observers, and test observations through different theoretical perspectives, they are in essence, using triangulation strategies in their research.

RESEARCH READING

Corsaro and colleagues employ a mixed methods strategy to examine the effect of an intervention aimed at high crime neighborhoods and drug markets. Specifically, they study the pulling levers project in Rockford, Illinois and its effectiveness at crime prevention and drug dealing in specific neighborhoods. The researchers used observational data, secondary Rockford Police Department data, and in-depth interview data to conduct both process and impact evaluations. The results from triangulation of these data sources reveal that the pulling levers strategy in Rockford had a statistically significant effect on the reduction of crime, both drug and otherwise.

PROBLEM-ORIENTED POLICING AND OPEN-AIR DRUG MARKETS

Examining the Rockford Pulling Levers Deterrence Strategy

Nicholas Corsaro, Rod K. Brunson, and Edmund F. McGarrell

Abstract: Problem-oriented policing strategies have been regarded as promising approaches for disrupting open-air drug markets in vulnerable communities. Pulling levers deterrence interventions, which are

Source: Corsaro, N., Brunson, R., & McGarrell, E. (in press). Problem-oriented policing and open-air drug markets: Examining the Rockford pulling levers deterrence strategy. *Crime & Delinquency.* Copyright © 2009 Sage Publications.

consistent with the problem-oriented framework, have shown potential as an effective mechanism for reducing and preventing youth, gun, and gang violence. This study examines the effect of a strategic, pulling levers intervention that was implemented by law enforcement officials in Rockford, Illinois, to address drug markets in a high crime neighborhood. The initiative builds on a similar effort developed in High Point, North Carolina, and represents an extension of pulling levers that was originally developed in Boston. The impact evaluation uses a mixed method of quantitative hierarchical growth curve models and qualitative interviews with residents. Study findings suggest that the Rockford strategy was associated with a statistically significant and substantive reduction in crime, drug, and nuisance offenses in the target neighborhood. Results from this examination have implications for both research and public policy.

INTRODUCTION

Since the mid-1980s, a number of criminal justice interventions have been introduced in response to a surge in drug-related offenses (Mazerolle, Soole, & Rombouts, 2006, 2007). There is considerable variation in law enforcement approaches (Weisburd & Eck, 2004), however, and this extends to strategies that target drug markets and related offending. Problem-oriented policing initiatives are directed at specific issues and rely on a host of proactive tactics in an effort to address the underlying causes of crime in varying community contexts (see Goldstein, 1990). This study evaluates a problem-oriented policing strategy used by the Rockford Police Department (RPD) to combat open-air drug markets and related offending in a high-crime neighborhood.

Drug Law Enforcement Strategies

An abundant body of research exists with regard to policing strategies designed to disrupt the flow of illegal drugs in open-air markets. Mazerolle et al. (2007) found that interventions aimed at reducing narcotic activity offer promise in terms of effect. Often-used aggressive policing tactics that rely extensively on crackdowns (e.g., arrests, sweeps, and saturation) in high crime neighborhoods have produced mixed results, however (Bynum & Worden, 1996; Wood et al., 2004). Prior investigations consistently indicate that, at best, crackdowns have a short-term effect (Best, Strang, Beswick, & Gossip,

2001; Smith, Davis, Hillenbrand, & Goresky, 1992; Smith, 2001). Thus, successful interventions directed at drug offenders in high crime communities require more than identification and arrests.

The literature indicates that the most successful drug market interventions have relied on problem-oriented policing approaches, which involve a variety of tactics designed to tackle problems in specific contexts (e.g., supply-side reductions, improving police-community relations, and nuisance abatement efforts). The use of these strategies has yielded reductions in crime and problem behaviors associated with drug markets in Chicago, Illinois (Coldren & Higgins, 2003), Jersey City, New Jersey (Mazerolle, Ready, Terrill, & Waring, 2000; Weisburd & Green, 1995), Oakland, California (Green, 1995; Mazerolle, Price, & Roehl, 2000; Mazerolle & Ransley, 2006), and San Diego, California (Clarke & Bichler-Robertson, 1998; Eck &Wartell, 1998).

A meta-analysis of drug law enforcement evaluations conducted by Mazerolle et al. (2006) concluded that problem-oriented policing tactics appear to be the most effective approach when dealing with drug crime, incivilities, and overall offenses than were community-wide policing, hot spots policing, and standard (i.e., unfocused or reactive) policing.[1] Similarly, recent research relying on simulation techniques comparing the experimental conditions of random patrol, hot spots policing, and problem-oriented policing found that the latter approach was the optimal strategy for disrupting street-level drug markets, reducing crime, and minimizing harm, regardless of the drug being trafficked (Dray, Mazerolle, Perez, & Ritter, 2008).

Although problem-oriented policing tactics seem to hold promise for minimizing criminal offenses associated with drug markets, few studies have specifically examined the utility of the "pulling levers" problem-oriented approach (see Kennedy, 1997) in an open-air drug market setting. To date, a majority of pulling levers strategies has focused on reducing violence and gang-related crime. The pulling levers intervention appears adaptable in terms of affecting youth, gang, and gun crime in a number of large U.S. cities; thus, it is reasonable to hypothesize that pulling levers can also be used as an approach to reduce nongang-related drug crime.

Pulling Levers: Combining Focused Deterrence and Social Support

Problem-oriented policing strategies have also been suggested as effective tools for preventing violence, in particular when targeted at gang-involved offenders (Decker, 2003). In response to the huge increase in firearms violence in the late 1980s and early 1990s (Blumstein & Rosenfeld, 1998), a large number of criminal justice agencies began experimenting with focused deterrence strategies often referred to as "pulling levers" (Braga, Kennedy, & Tita, 2002; Braga, Kennedy, Waring, & Piehl, 2001; McGarrell, Chermak, Wilson, & Corsaro, 2006; Weisburd & Braga, 2006). The multistage approach consists of diagnosing a specific crime problem, convening an interagency working group of criminal justice personnel, conducting research to identify patterns of chronic offenders and criminal networks, framing a specific response to law violators that uses a variety of sanctions as a coercive approach to stop continuing illegal behavior, providing social services and community resources to targeted offenders, and directly and repeatedly communicating with offenders so that they understand why they are receiving special attention

(Braga, Pierce, McDevitt, Bond, & Cronin, 2008; Kennedy, 1997, 2006).

The first pulling levers intervention was implemented in Boston and has since been recognized as an effective strategy for reducing violence, firearm offenses, and youth homicide (Braga et al., 2001). For example, pulling levers has been replicated, with promising results, in other U.S. cities including Baltimore, Maryland (Braga et al., 2002), Cincinnati, Ohio (Engel, Baker, Tillyer, Eck, & Dunham, 2008), Chicago, Illinois (Papachristos, Meares, & Fagan, 2007), High Point, North Carolina (Coleman, Holton, Olson, Robinson, & Stewart, 1999), Indianapolis, Indiana (McGarrell et al., 2006), Los Angeles, California (Tita, Riley, Ridgeway, Grammich, Abrahamse, & Greenwood, 2003), Lowell, Massachusetts (Braga et al., 2008), Minneapolis, Minnesota (Kennedy & Braga, 1998), and Stockton, California (Braga, 2008; Wakeling, 2003). At the national level, Dalton (2002) described how the pulling levers framework has been applied in a large number of U.S. cities and federal districts through the Strategic Alternatives to Community Safety Initiative and Project Safe Neighborhoods.

Summary and Research Implications

Although the promise of problem-oriented policing strategies has been well-documented as a successful law enforcement approach to combat illegal-drug markets (Mazerolle et al., 2006, 2007), and pulling levers deterrence initiatives have been regarded as promising problem-oriented policing strategies to reduce gang violence (Braga et al., 2008; Decker, 2003), very little research exists examining the capacity of pulling levers to combat open-air drug markets that are not directly driven by violent gang members. The first law enforcement agency to use pulling levers in response to persistent street-level drug markets, beyond those driven by gang members, was the High Point Police Department in North Carolina (Frabutt, Gathings, Hunt, & Loggins, 2006). Information about the High Point campaign gained the attention of RPD administrators. Further, officers from Rockford traveled to High Point to get a better understanding of the specific processes that were necessary for replication.

The purpose of this article is to assess the utility of pulling levers as an effective response to open-air drug markets in a distressed Rockford, Illinois, neighborhood. This study contributes to the drug law enforcement literature and pulling levers research by examining the utility of pulling levers as a specific response to drug sellers in drug hot spots. Although pulling levers has largely been implemented and evaluated on its ability to reduce firearms and violence, its usefulness beyond these contexts is unknown. Our results provide insight into whether the pulling levers campaign holds promise as a viable strategy for combating open-air drug markets.

METHOD AND STUDY SETTING

We employed multiple data collection and analysis methods in this study. Specifically, we used narratives and observational data with criminal justice officials to measure program implementation, RPD crime statistics to measure programmatic impact, and in-depth interviews with residents from Delancey Heights (the target neighborhood) to triangulate both process and impact data.

Activity (i.e., process) data were collected through narratives, interviews, and observations with law enforcement officials, prosecutors, and social service providers in an effort to capture detailed information on program implementation.

Specifically, we examined the extent to which the Rockford initiative adhered to the tenets of the pulling levers theoretical framework (see Braga et al, 2001; Kennedy, 1997).

Offense (i.e., impact) data include all crimes reported over a 2-year period, which were aggregated into a monthly format from June 2006 through June 2008. Crime data in Rockford are submitted and conform to the National Incident-Based Reporting System maintained by the Federal Bureau of Investigation and offer distinct advantages for both policy analysis and criminal justice research, at least compared with data submitted to the traditional Uniform Crime Report system (Maxfield, 1999). Crime data were operationalized as composite measures of violent and nonviolent offenses that occurred from the first through the last day of each month. Offense data from RPD are more reliable than conventional calls for service data because immediately following their investigations, officers enter detailed information concerning incidents into a computer system mounted in their patrol cars, allowing for improved cross-validation. In addition to employing pre- and postintervention analyses in Delancey Heights using growth curve models, we also modeled changes in citywide offense trends once the target area was subtracted from the city total for general trend and comparison purposes.

We used qualitative, in-depth interviews with 34 adults in Delancey Heights to complement the narrative, observational, and quantitative data. The interviews lasted approximately 40 minutes to 1 hour. Participation in the study was voluntary and participants were paid $25 and promised strict confidentiality. The in-depth interviews were semistructured and consisted of open-ended questions intended to elicit detailed information about participants' perceptions of and experiences with crime and disorder in Delancey Heights (prior to and following the initiative).[3] The interviews were not audiotaped. Members of the research team, however, meticulously recorded responses by hand. Furthermore, painstaking attention was paid to accurately capture study participants' statements verbatim. We analyzed the data through numerous readings of participants' accounts and were careful that the concepts developed and themes that emerged illustrated the most common (and salient) patterns of residents' descriptions in the target neighborhood,

This was accomplished using grounded theory methods involving searches for and highlighting of deviant cases (Strauss, 1987). Finally, we attempted to strengthen the reliability of the data by asking participants about their perceptions and encounters multiple times during the interview.

To place the present pulling levers intervention strategy into context, we provide descriptive information for both Delancey Heights and the city of Rockford. Table 10.1 displays key demographic characteristics of residents and households in the target community as well as the overall city. Descriptive indicators of neighborhood context include the total population, percent male, percent White, median home income, average educational attainment of inhabitants, and measures of residential stability. These data, taken from the 2000 U.S. Census, were aggregated from block groups in the target neighborhood and the overall city. Delancey Heights accounts for roughly 1.7% of the Rockford population and is generally one of the more distressed neighborhoods within the city.

Variables

Table 10.2 displays the offense data that were aggregated to create measures of violent and nonviolent outcome variables. In terms of the violent crime variable, nine offenses were selected to create an overall index measure. Violent offenses were aggregated from homicides (<1%), rapes (1.5%), kidnappings (<1%), robberies (11%), and simple and aggravated assaults (86.6%), which made up the majority of violent crimes. Similarly, nine crimes comprised the nonviolent offenses measure, which was a composite of drug-related incidents, nuisance crimes (including prostitution and vagrancy), and property offenses. Nonviolent offenses included 63.1% property damage, 15.9% drug and drug equipment violations, and 21% of nuisance crimes (including prostitution, curfew violations, vagrancy, and disorderly conduct). Identical selection criteria were employed for both the target neighborhood and citywide offense variables.

The *intervention* variable, seen in Table 10.3, captures the pulling levers intervention. In Delancey Heights, treatment was measured as a dichotomous variable (0 = pre-May 2007, 1 = May 2007 and beyond). Specifically, May 2007 was treated as the postintervention date because it was during this month that RPD (a) arrested a number of violent offenders who were involved in open-air drug trafficking, (b) conducted the pulling levers notification

Table 10.1   Demographic Characteristics of Residents: Comparison Between Target Neighborhood and Overall City of Rockford

Census Measure	Target Neighborhood	Overall City of Rockford
Percent male	47.0%	48.2%
Percent White	46.0%	72.8%
High school graduates (25 years and older)	33.3%	77.8%
Renter occupied units	84.4%	38.9%
Median income	$13,284	$37,667
Population (2000)	2,681 inhabitants	150,115 inhabitants

Table 10.2 Description of Violent and Nonviolent Offenses in Rockford

Violent Offenses (offenses against persons)	Nonviolent Offenses (nuisance, drug, and property offenses)
Murder	Stolen property
Nonnegligent manslaughter	Destruction of property
Rape	Vandalism
Kidnapping	Drug/narcotic violations
Abduction	Drug equipment violations
Unlawful restraint	Prostitution
Robbery	Violation of curfew
Aggravated assault	Vagrancy and loitering
Simple assault	Disorderly conduct

Table 10.3 Descriptive Statistics

Variable	N	M	SD	Minimum	Maximum
Violent offenses	50	299.5	298.5	10	700
Nonviolent offenses	50	482.4	475.2	9	1225
Intervention measure	50	0.28	0.453	0	1
Target neighborhood	50	0.50	0.707	0	1

meeting bringing together community leaders and key criminal justice officials to speak with nonviolent drug sellers, and (c) worked with community development officers to improve neighborhood conditions by issuing citations for a wide range of code violations. In all, these efforts resulted in 11 months of preintervention and 14 months of postintervention data for the target neighborhood. In the next section, we describe process and impact results of the pulling levers intervention employed by Rockford officials in Delancey Heights.

RESULTS

Impact and Outcome Assessment

The ultimate goal of the Rockford pulling levers strategy implemented in Delancey Heights was to reduce criminal offending, interrupt open-air drug markets, and make the once high crime community more inhabitable. The purpose of the following analyses is to assess the impact of the initiative by examining whether changes in crime patterns occurred after implementation.

As an initial step, percentage differences were examined with regard to the changes in violent and nonviolent offenses for the target neighborhood, the remainder of Rockford, and the overall city both before and after the intervention. Because the number of pre- and postintervention periods is not equivalent, the average percentage change in the number of offenses per month across the city is displayed below. Table 10.4 shows that the target neighborhood experienced an average decline of 24.10% in nonviolent and a 14.29% reduction in violent incidents between the pre- and postintervention periods. Comparatively, from a general trend perspective, the remainder of the city also experienced a decline in both nonviolent (–9%) and violent crime (–2.3%). Ultimately, a decline in both violent and nonviolent offenses occurred in the city of Rockford before and after May 2007. It is also apparent that the decline throughout the remainder of the city was not as extensive (in terms of magnitude for either offense type) and that the decline in both violent and nonviolent

crime for the entire city was influenced by specific declines in the target neighborhood.

To visually display the results seen in the HGLM estimates, nonviolent crime trends were standardized (per 1,000 residents) for the target neighborhood and the remaining city (see Figure 10.1). The target area experienced a decline from 10.8 nonviolent offenses per 1,000 residents before to 8.3 nonviolent offenses after pulling levers was implemented in May 2007. Comparatively, the remainder of Rockford experienced a reduction from 6.8 nonviolent offenses to 5.9 nonviolent offenses per 1,000 residents over this same period. Figure 10.1 also indicates that the decreases in the nonviolent offenses within the target area occurred a few months after the intervention and have since remained relatively proximate to nonviolent offense rates seen in the remainder of the city. Thus, an observed lag in the reduction of nonviolent offenses and the observed statistical effect occurred after the early summer months following program implementation. Although this lag was included in the parameter estimates in the growth curve models, it was not specifically

Table 10.4 Changes in Nonviolent and Violent Offenses in Rockford Before and After May 2007 Call-In

Location	*Number of Offenses per Month (preintervention)*	*Number of Offenses per Month (postintervention)*	*Percentage Δ*
Target neighborhood			
Nonviolent	29	22	–24.10
Violent	21	18	–14.29
Remainder of city			
Nonviolent	944	859	–9.00
Violent	567	554	–2.29
Overall city			
Nonviolent	1013	881	–13.03
Violent	588	573	–2.55

Figure 10.1 Nonviolent Crime Trends in Rockford

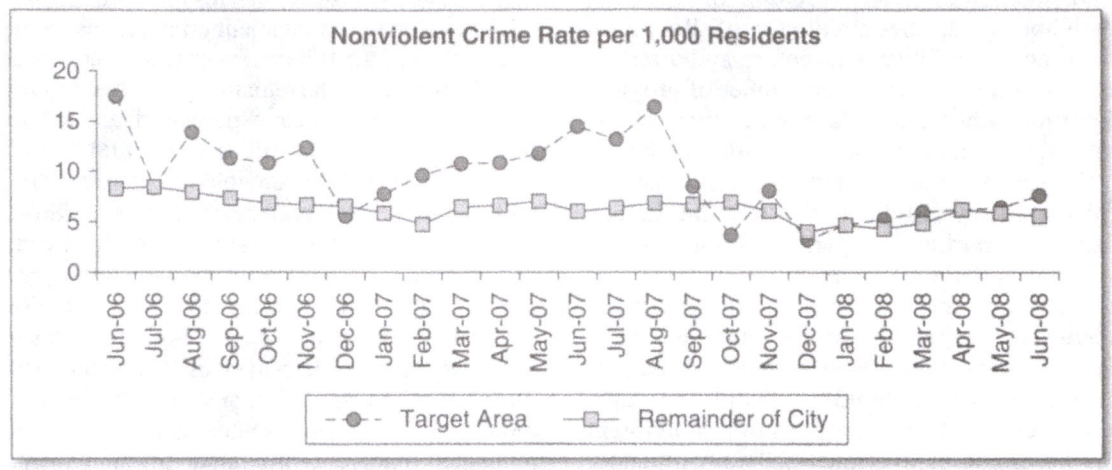

isolated using this approach. Although not displayed here, we also used the Autoregressive Integrated Moving Average (ARIMA) identification procedure to identify and isolate the lag effect, which was statistically significant $(p < .01)$. Data obtained from interviews with residents cross-validated the lag-effect finding, which we note in the next section.

Resident Interviews

The majority of study participants report being very pleased with the RPD intervention and tout it as an innovative crime-reduction strategy. For example, several participants noted that they have seen reductions in crime and incivilities in Delancey Heights following the intervention. For instance, Ted remarked, "Now the people who walk down the street aren't outsiders trafficking drugs. Now [when you see people outside] it's residents from this community. Outsiders don't come in and cause problems anymore, at least not as much as they did before." Similarly, James stated, "We used to have 'trash pickup' days every couple of months to make the neighborhood look good. We've had to cancel several of those because we just don't have the amount of trash in this

neighborhood as we used to. And that's a good thing." And finally, Mary explained,

I wouldn't say it's one hundred percent better, but it's a heck of a lot better. There are a lot less dealers, hookers, and noise around here than there used to be. It's been a long time since we have seen something bad happen, like a shooting. The big difference around here is at night; it's just a lot more peaceful at night now.

These statements highlight that residents in Delancey Heights have noticed a tangible change with regard to drug dealing, crime, nuisance offenses, litter, and incivilities in the neighborhood.

In terms of specifying when the positive changes occurred, a majority of Delancey Heights residents identified the period when RPD publicly announced its intervention efforts. Furthermore, study participants consistently attributed the observed crime reduction in their neighborhood to increased police presence and shorter response times. This perception was consistent among both heavily involved and disengaged neighborhood residents. For example, William, who attended the pulling levers community notification, noted,

It took several months after the call-in before we saw real impact. There were some remaining drug dealers in the neighborhood that refused to leave because this was their turf and they were going to stay. Police were able to eventually drive them out, but it took a few months.

Similarly, Carla, a resident who was uninvolved in the pulling levers call-in, remarked,

Things changed for the better when police got the dealers out of here. Really, when police boarded up [an abandoned building], locked the gates to it, and put up a camera, things got a lot better around then; maybe a little after that. After the dealers couldn't find anywhere else to go, this place has just been a lot better.

It is also important to note that as time has elapsed since the intervention, a number of participants expressed dissatisfaction with what they considered poor police response times. They were especially troubled because according to them, they enjoyed appreciably quicker response times during the earliest period of the intervention. And in their view, the police department no longer showed the same level of commitment to Delancey Heights. Jason's comment illustrates this point. He reported, "There's a perception among residents in this neighborhood that police [no longer] make us a priority when we call. We'd like to know why this is, especially since problems in this neighborhood used to be a priority." Likewise, Jan said, "Police response takes longer now than it used to. For a long time, police were always here and were so quick to respond to our calls. Now they seem to care less about what goes on here than they used to and that is something they should address." There were other underlying issues and concerns that the interviews seemed to uncover.

Although participants remarked that the most blatant forms of open-air drug dealing had dissipated, they noted that many remaining dealers had simply adapted to enforcement efforts and now sold drugs more covertly (i.e., inside cars and residences rather than on the street). Sheila commented, "We have less dealers than we *used* to, but the ones we still have are also different. They don't sell out on the street anymore but rather in their cars. Now they have to be sneaky about it." In agreement, Kendall noted,

I think the dealers that have been able to avoid getting caught try hard not to bring too much attention to themselves. People who used to sell drugs here sold to outsiders who were coming in, bringing attention to themselves. We don't have those types of dealers anymore, out in the street.

And finally, Kim advised, "I know there are still people here who deal. But it's not 'in and out' anymore. People who are selling drugs now are doing it out of their homes or in their cars. It's not gone, but it's much more out of sight."

Although study participants were consistent in the belief that drug crime and related offenses in Delancey Heights had indeed subsided, they desired a continued commitment from RPD to the area.

DISCUSSION

Results from the HGLM growth curve models indicate that Delancey Heights experienced a statistically significant, substantive, and noticeable reduction in property, drug, and nuisance offenses after pulling levers was implemented. This is important given the relationship between these specific types of behaviors and open-air drug markets documented in prior research (Pettiway, 1995; Rengert & Wasilchick, 1989). Comparative statistical analyses reveal that the greater city did not experience a similar effect with regard to changes in crime rates over the same period. Interviews with residents demonstrated that they observed an appreciable transformation in the neighborhood shortly after RPD introduced proactive, strategic, and focused approaches to interrupt the open-air markets that had once flourished in the community. Regardless of their level of involvement with and knowledge of the intervention strategy, the majority of study participants agreed that crime and disorder in Delancey Heights had dropped precipitously as a result of the multiagency crime-control effort.

In sum, our findings consistent with previous studies, which indicate that strategies relying on both proactive and reactive policing tactics appear to be extremely promising for reducing drug and related crime (Mazerolle et al., 2006, 2007; Weisburd & Green, 1995). It is important that RPD and other public officials sought to strengthen informal social control in Delancey Heights throughout the initiative by involving residents in various stages of the intervention process (Bursik & Grasmick, 1993; Sampson, Raudenbush, & Earls, 1997). Interviews with residents, and in particular with those who were engaged in the pulling levers notification meeting, indicated a heightened sense of awareness and responsibility in terms of cooperating with police to regulate neighborhood behaviors.

In terms of sustainability, once drug, nuisance, and property offense rates declined in the target neighborhood, they remained consistent with those experienced by the remainder of the city. It is not surprising that RPD officials have since implemented additional proactive law enforcement and pulling levers strategies in other high crime, Rockford communities in an effort to replicate the effect seen in Delancey Heights. Resident interviews indicated that many citizens in the target area believed that RPD was not prioritizing Delancey Heights as it did when intervention dosage was highest (i.e., during the implementation of strategies), despite the apparent and sustained effect. In fact, residents feared that RPD had shifted its attention and resources to other problem neighborhoods. As Tyler and Folger (1980) observed, citizens' perceptions of procedural fairness from a criminal justice perspective are directly related to issues such as police response time, regardless of whether quicker responses by law enforcement would actually solve their specific problems. Given that prior research indicates that crime victims want compassion, concern, and sensitivity from law enforcement personnel (see Mawby & Walklate, 1994), it should come as no surprise that residents who greatly appreciate the benefits of enhanced policing strategies (i.e., quicker response times, greater police presence, etc.) struggle with a perceived withdrawal or reduction of those resources once crime rates subside. Further research should be invested in effective "weaning" strategies focused on neighborhood residents' perceptual vantage points as well as on crime rates.

It is interesting that although violent crime in the target area declined following the intervention, it did not reduce at a statistically significant level. A likely explanation is the lack of statistical power given that violent offenses were relatively infrequent in Delancey Heights. As mentioned previously, more than 86% of the violent offenses were classified as assaults. A more detailed analysis should attempt to delineate those physical attacks that were drug market related, such as retaliatory violence as a means of debt collection (see Anderson, 1999) or assaults that occurred in public, in an effort to better understand this phenomenon. It is unfortunate that our data do not allow for a more in-depth investigation of these events. The fact that only nonviolent offenders were included in the pulling levers program also has implications for the lack of a significant violent crime reduction. It is difficult to assess the generalizability concerning the lack of an observed violent crime reduction that has been seen in other pulling levers strategies because the Delancey Heights neighborhood had such a small number of robberies and homicides, which have been the major focus of pulling levers research to this point (Piquero, 2005).

On a related note, the observed gradual or lagged effect on nonviolent crime rates in the Rockford strategy also differs from those seen in prior research. Specifically, some of the initial pulling levers initiatives had an immediate effect, which was seen in Boston, Massachusetts (Piehl, Cooper, Braga, & Kennedy, 2004), Indianapolis, Indiana (Corsaro & McGarrell, 2009), Minneapolis, Minnesota (Kennedy & Braga, 1998), and other sites. Whereas the immediate or "light-switch" effect (see Kennedy, 2006, p. 158) of pulling levers is consistently observed where reducing youth, gang, and gun crime is the target of the strategy, much less is known about how much time should be expected until an effect is observed in an open-air drug market setting. Rather than having an immediate and abrupt effect when dealing with gang offenders, the pulling levers intervention strategy may serve more as a catalyst for change (requiring more lag time before an effect is observed) when directed at open-air drug market offenders. Further research that examines pulling levers in different contexts is vital to our obtaining a better understanding of its utility.

There are a number of limitations to this study that we mention with the hope of informing further research on this topic. First, the pulling levers intervention assessment here is not isolated from the combination of reactive, directed, and proactive/partnership strategies that have been established as successful interventions, which are outlined in Mazerolle et al.'s (2007) systematic review of drug enforcement strategies. In essence, the Rockford intervention could be referred to as "pulling-levers plus" because there were supplemental strategies associated with the antidrug, law enforcement tactics. The effect of a pulling levers intervention strategy without the nuisance abatement and civil remedy approaches that were also included in the Rockford initiative would be extremely beneficial to this line of inquiry. It is certainly plausible that the correlation between the reduction in nonviolent crime in the target neighborhood and the implementation of the pulling levers strategy could be heavily influenced and confounded by the nuisance abatement programs

implemented in Rockford. Future studies that examine pulling levers would benefit from a more singularly focused strategy to address this issue.

The use of more rigorous, time consuming and expensive drug offender identification methods would also strengthen research in this area. For example, Beckett, Nyrop, and Pfingst (2006) used needle exchange survey data and extensive ethnographic research methods to uncover discrepancies between official arrest data and the dark figure of crime associated with drug use in open-air drug markets. Future drug market intervention research would benefit greatly from approaches such as those used by Beckett and colleagues, especially if collected throughout the duration of program implementation. In addition, although the use of a baseline comparison of the remainder of Rockford helps reduce the concern that crime in Delancey Heights simply went through a natural reduction (i.e., regression to the mean), a more appropriate methodology would be to use comparisons between multiple neighborhoods that were consistent in terms of size, social structure, and crime rates. Officials in RPD maintained that the target area was unique from all other communities within the city and, thus, a quasi-experimental analysis of within-city neighborhoods would be somewhat unreliable. Future studies should draw from the use of more powerful analytical methodologies including the application of a quasi-experimental or experimental design to assess the effect of the localized intervention (Cook & Campbell, 1979).

Summary

The statistically significant reduction in nonviolent offenses that occurred after pulling levers was implemented in Delancey Heights suggests that the extension of the initiative to drug markets holds promise. On the other hand, the lack of a statistically significant reduction in violent offenses requires further exploration. To this point, most of the research on pulling levers has focused on reducing youth, gun, and gang violence. These prior studies have consistently indicated a reduction in violent offenses driven by changes in gang-related activity. This study builds on prior problem-oriented policing research and suggests that the use of pulling levers, at least in combination with other drug law enforcement strategies, is not limited to affecting youth violence and gang-related offenses but also can be adapted to nuisance, drug, and property crimes. Future studies are needed to assess the capacity of pulling levers both independent of and in addition to other drug law enforcement strategies for eliminating drug markets in crime-ridden communities. The results of the Rockford initiative highlight the utility of such an approach.

Appendix A   Summary of the Process Indicators of the Pulling Levers Strategy

Strategy	Description
Identification (February 2007)	Research analysts at RPD mapped index offenses, drug arrests, and drug complaints for the entire city.
Mobilization (March 2007)	Law enforcement officials determined that the Delancey Heights target neighborhood, consisting of two sub-beats, would be the ideal locale for the pulling levers intervention.
Intelligence gathering (March 2007)	A narcotics unit officer at RPD supervised intelligence gathering on individuals who engaged in chronic drug dealing in the target neighborhood.
Incident review (March 2007)	Narcotics detectives conducted a complete incident review of all known offending in the target area. All reports and contacts with police, including intelligence gathered from cooperating witnesses, were examined. Twelve persistent offenders were identified.
Undercover investigation (March-April 2007)	Narcotics detectives made controlled buys from the twelve identified drug dealers over the course of eight weeks. Surveillance equipment was used to record the purchases. And, cooperating witnesses were recruited.
DMI eligibility meeting (April 2007)	A multi-agency committee reviewed the cases made against the twelve individuals and relied upon the suspects' criminal histories (e.g., the number of violent offenses and the total number of offenses) to identify five dealers who would be eligible for the pulling levers meeting.
Notice to residents (May 2007)	RPD notified residents at a local community meeting that an undercover investigation had been conducted over the past couple of months and that an immediate response was about to take place.
Sweep of violent offenders (May 2007)	Within 48 hours of the initial notification meeting, the seven violent offenders who were ineligible for the pulling levers strategy were subsequently arrested and received $500,000 bonds.
Contact with eligible offenders' families (May 2007)	RPD made phone calls, and relied upon a pastor at a local church, to notify offenders of the call-in by contacting their families. The police chief also wrote a letter to each offender guaranteeing they would not be arrested at the meeting. RPD provided assistance for those out of town to ensure their attendance.

Strategy	Description
The call-in (May 2007)	The offenders, their families, key criminal justice personnel, and community members attended the pulling levers meeting. First, residents spoke of the harm that drug dealing caused in their community. Next, offenders and their families received the deterrent message from multi-agency members that continued offending would not be tolerated. Finally, an immediate needs assessment was made by social support services, followed by a more detailed assessment in the following weeks.
Community follow-up (May 2007)	RPD and housing inspectors seized five housing complexes where prior drug offending had been prominent. Social service officials assisted in moving residents who did not previously engage in illegal drug distribution into new homes. Maintenance code citations (e.g., lawn, trash, and poor fencing) were written for violations throughout the neighborhood. A street-sweeper cleaned the streets to symbolize the change that was occurring.
Long-term follow-up	RPD continues routine and saturated patrols in the neighborhood. Community source officers and community leaders maintain communication for up-to-date information on neighborhood issues.

REFERENCES

Anderson, E. (1999). *Code of the Street: Decency, violence, and the moral life of the inner city.* New York: Norton.

Beckett, K., Nyrop, K., & Pfingst, L. (2006). Race, drugs, and policing: Understanding disparities in drug delivery arrests. *Criminology, 44,* 105-137.

Best, D., Strang, J., Beswick, T., & Gossip, M. (2001). Assessment of concentrated, high-profile police operations. *British Journal of Criminology, 41,* 738–745.

Blumstein, A., & Rosenfeld, R. (1998). Explaining recent trends in U.S. homicide rates. *Journal of Criminal Law and Criminology, 88,* 1175-1216.

Box, G. R, & Jenkins, G. M. (1976). *Time series analysis: Forecasting and control.* San Francisco: Holden Day.

Braga, A. A. (2008). Pulling levers focused deterrence strategies and the prevention of gun homicide. *Journal of Criminal Justice, 36,* 332-343.

Braga, A. A., Kennedy, D., & Tita, G. (2002). New approaches to the strategic prevention of gang and group-involved violence. In C. R. Huff (Ed.), *Gangs in America* (3rd ed., pp. 271-286). Thousand Oaks, CA: Sage.

Braga, A. A., Kennedy, D. M., Waring, E. J., & Piehl, A. M. (2001). Problem-oriented policing, deterrence, and youth violence: An evaluation of Boston's Operation Ceasefire. *Journal of Research in Crime and Delinquency, 38,* 195-226.

Braga, A. A., Pierce, G. L., McDevitt, J., Bond, B. J., & Cronin, S. (2008). The strategic prevention of gun violence among gang-involved offenders. *Justice Quarterly, 25,* 132-162.

Bursik, R. J., & Grasmick, H. G. (1993). *Neighborhoods and crime: The dimensions of effective community control.* Lexington, NY: Lexington.

Bushway, S. D., & McDowall, D. (2006). Here we go again-can we learn anything from aggregate-level studies of policy interventions? *Criminology and Public Policy, 5,* 461-470.

Bynum, T., & Worden, R. (1996). *Police drug crackdowns: An evaluation of implementation and effects.* Washington, DC: National institute of Justice.

Clarke, R. V, & Bichler-Robertson, G. (1998). Place managers, slumlords and crime in low rent apartment buildings. *Security Journal, 11,* 11-19.

Coldren, J. C, & Higgins, D. F. (2003). Evaluating nuisance abatement at gang and drug houses in Chicago. In S. H. Decker (Ed.), *Policing gangs and youth violence* (pp. 131-166). Belmont, CA: Thomson and Wadsworth.

Coleman, V., Holton, W., Olson, K., Robinson, S., & Stewart, J. (1999, October). Using knowledge and teamwork to reduce crime. *National Institute of Justice Journal,* pp. 16-23.

Cook, T. D., & Campbell, D. T, (1979). *Quasi-experimentation: Design and analysis for field settings.* Chicago: Rand McNally.

Corsaro, N., & McGarrell, E. F. (2009). Testing a promising homicide reduction strategy: Re-assessing the impact of the Indianapolis "pulling levers" intervention. *Journal of Experimental Criminology, 5,* 63-82.

Cullen, F. T. (1994). Social support as an ongoing concept for criminology: Presidential address to the Academy of Criminal Justice Sciences. *Justice Quarterly, 11,* 527-559.

Dalton, E. (2002). Targeted crime reduction efforts in ten communities: Lessons for the Project Safe Neighborhoods initiative. *U.S. Attorney's Bulletin, 50,* 16-25.

Decker, S. H. (2003). *Policing gangs and youth violence.* Belmont, CA: Wadsworth.

Dray, A., Mazerolle, L., Perez, P., & Ritter, A. (2008). Policing Australia's "heroin drought": Using an agent-based model to simulate alternative outcomes. *Journal of Experimental Criminology, 4,* 267-287.

Eck, J., & Wartell, J. (1998). *Reducing crime and drug dealing by improving place management: A randomized experiment,* Washington, DC: National Institute of Justice.

Engel, R. S., Baker, S. G., Tillyer, M. S., Eck, J., & Dunham, J. (2008). *Implementation of the Cincinnati Initiative to Reduce Violence (CIRV): Year 1 report.* Cincinnati, OH: University of Cincinnati Policing Institute.

Frabutt, J. M, Gathings, M. J., Hunt, E. D., & Loggias, T. J. (2006). *High Point West End Initiative: Project description, log and preliminary impact analysis.* Greensboro: University of North Carolina at Greensboro, Center for Youth, Family and Community Partnerships.

Goldstein, H. (1990). *Problem-oriented policing.* New York: McGraw-Hill.

Green, L. (1995). Cleaning up drug hot spots in Oakland, California: The displacement and diffusion effect. *Justice Quarterly, 12,* 737-754.

Kennedy, D. (1997). Pulling levers: Chronic offenders, high-crime settings, and a theory of prevention. *Valparaiso University Law Review, 31,*449-484.

Kennedy, D. (2006). Old wine in new bottles: Policing and the lessons of pulling levels. In D. Weisburd & A. A. Braga (Eds.), *Police innovation: Contrasting, perspective* (pp. 155-170). New York: Cambridge University Press.

Kennedy, D., & Braga, A. A. (1998). Homicide in Minneapolis: Research for problem solving. *Homicide Studies, 2,* 263-290.

Klofas, J., Hippie, N. K., McDevitt, J., Bynum, T., McGarrell, E. F., & Decker, S. H. (2006). *Crime incident reviews: A Project Safe Neighborhoods strategic intervention.* Washington, DC: U.S. Department of Justice, Office of Justice Programs.

Mawby, R., & Walklate, S. (1994). *Critical victimology: International perspectives.* London: Sage.

Maxfield, M. G. (1999). The National Incident-Based Reporting System: Research and policy applications. *Journal of Quantitative Criminology, 15,* 119-149.

Mazerolle, L., Price, J., & Roehl, J. (2000). Civil remedies and drug control: A randomized field trial in Oakland, California. *Evaluation Review, 24,* 212-241.

Mazerolle, L., & Ransley, J. (2006). *Third party policing.* Cambridge, UK: Cambridge University Press.

Mazerolle, L. G., Ready, J., Terrill, W., & Waring, E. (2000). Problem-oriented policing in public housing: The Jersey City evaluation. *Justice Quarterly, 17,* 129-158.

Mazerolle, L., Soole, D. W., & Rombouts, S. (2006). Street-level drug law enforcement: A meta-analytical review. *Journal of Experimental Criminology, 2,* 409-435.

Mazerolle, L., Soole, D., & Rombouts, S. (2007). Drug law enforcement: A review of the evaluation literature. *Police Quarterly, 10,* 115-153.

McGarrell, E. F, Chermak, S., Wilson, J. M., & Corsaro, N. (2006). Reducing homicide through a "lever-pulling" strategy. *Justice Quarterly, 23,* 214-231.

Papachristos, A., Meares, T., & Fagan, J. (2007). Attention felons: Evaluating Project Safe Neighborhoods in Chicago. *Journal of Empirical Legal Studies, 4,* 223-272.

Pettiway, L. (1995). Copping crack; The travel behavior of crack users. *Justice Quarterly, 12,* 499-524.

Piehl, A., Cooper, S., Braga, A., & Kennedy, D. (2004). Testing for structural breaks in the evaluation programs. *The Review of Econometrics and Statistics, 85,* 550-558.

Piquero, A. R. (2005). Reliable information and rational policy decisions: Does gun research fit the bill? *Criminology and Public Policy, 4,* 479-498.

Raudenbush, S. W., & Bryk, A. (2002). *Hierarchical linear models: Applications and data analysis methods* (2nd ed.). Thousand Oaks, CA: Sage.

Rengert, G., & Wasilchick, J. (1989). *Space, time, and crime: Ethnographic insights into residential burglary.* Washington, DC: National Institute of Justice.

Sampson, R. J., Raudenbush, S., & Earls, F. (1997). Neighborhoods and violent crime: A multi-level study of collective efficacy. *Science, 277,* 918-924.

Smith, B., Davis, R., Hillenbrand, S., & Goresky, S. (1992). *Riding neighborhoods of drug houses in the private sector.* Washington, DC: American Bar Association.

Smith, M. (2001). Police-led crackdowns and cleanups: An evaluation of a crime control initiative in Richmond, VA. *Crime & Delinquency, 47,* 60-83.

Strauss, A. L. (1987). *Qualitative analysis for social scientists.* Cambridge, UK: Cambridge University Press.

Tita, G., Riley, K. J., Ridgeway, G., Grammich, C., Abrahamse, A., & Greenwood, P. (2003). *Reducing gun violence: Results from an intervention in East Los Angeles.* Santa Monica, CA: RAND Corporation.

Tyler, T. R. (1990). *Why people obey the law.* New Haven. CT: Yale University Press.

Tyler, T. R., & Folger, R. (1980). Distributional and procedural aspects of satisfaction with citizen-police encounters. *Basic and Applied Social Psychology, 1,* 281-292.

Wakeling, S. (2003). *Ending gang homicide: Deterrence can work.* Sacramento, CA: California Attorney General's Office.

Weisburd, D., & Braga, A. A. (2006). *Police innovation: Contrasting perspectives.* New York: Cambridge University Press.

Weisburd, D., & Eck, J. E. (2004). What can police do to reduce crime, disorder, and fear? *The ANNALS of the American Academy of Political and Social Science, 593,* 43-65.

Weisburd, D., & Green, L. (1995). Policing hot spots: The Jersey City drug market analysis experiment. *Justice Quarterly, 12,* 711-735.

Wood, E., Spittal, P., Small, W., Kerr; T., Li, K., Hogg, R., et al. (2004). Displacement of Canada's largest public illicit drug market in response to a police crackdown. *Canadian Medical Association Journal, 170,* 1551-1556.

Xie, M., & McDowall, D. (2008). The effects of residential turnover on household victimization. *Criminology, 46*(3), 539-575.

DISCUSSION QUESTIONS

1. What has past research on police strategies to thwart open drug dealing revealed in terms of effectiveness?

2. What did these researchers triangulate in this study of the effectiveness of pulling levers? What reasons do they give for this triangulation?

3. In Table 10.1, what do you notice about the differences between the target neighborhood and the larger city of Rockford?

4. What did this particular pulling levers intervention consist of?

5. What did the quantitative results reveal about the success of the program? What about the qualitative results? What were some specific statements from residents about the program's success?

6. How do both the quantitative and qualitative results come together to provide a more accurate picture of the effectiveness of this intervention program? What aspects of the program's effectiveness would we not know without the qualitative data? Similarly, what would we not know without the quantitative analysis?

7. Were the residents of this neighborhood happy that the Rockford police targeted their neighborhood? List some ways in which this mixed methods approach led to a greater understanding of pulling levers as a drug crime reduction strategy.

RESEARCH READING

These researchers use a mixed methods approach to studying the drinking behavior of US Navy sailors—specifically, drinking that occurs during shore leave while these sailors are deployed. The authors discuss each of the components of their research, as well as the purposes of each, which include both qualitative and quantitative data collection; they refer to the points where these two approaches intersect as nodes of integration. These researchers gathered data via qualitative interviews, longitudinal surveys, and naturalistic field observations to examine how the culture of the US Navy, its drinking policies, and its work environment influence beliefs about drinking behavior. These researchers triangulate methods, data, and investigators to explore this phenomenon.

THE IMPACT OF OCCUPATIONAL CULTURE ON DRINKING BEHAVIOR OF YOUNG ADULTS IN THE U.S. NAVY

Genevieve M. Ames, Michael R. Duke, Roland S. Moore, and Carol B. Cunradi

Abstract: A mixed method study assessed how work culture and drinking norms affect heavy drinking patterns of young adults during their first 3 years in the U.S. Navy. Multivariate logistic regression analysis of the longitudinal survey data showed that normative beliefs were significantly associated with changes in drinking. Findings from thematic analyses of qualitative interviews and naturalistic observations on bases and aboard ships explained those elements of U.S. Navy culture and work environments that affect normative beliefs about drinking behavior.

INTRODUCTION

Worldwide, few workplaces are as linked in the popular imagination to alcohol consumption as the Navy, from the rationing of rum in the British Royal Navy (Pack, 1983; Standage, 2005) to the alcohol-fueled revelry of leave time ashore where drinking rates are high (Federman, Bray, & Kroutil, 2000). Although heavy drinking is widely perceived to be an integral part of a sailor's life, little is known about specific elements of the U.S. Navy workplace that may influence alcohol consumption (Bray, Bae, Federman, & Wheeless, 2005; Federman et al., 2000; Saltz, 1987; Schuckit & Gunderson, 1974).

Over the past 20 years, surveys that focus on occupational drinking (e.g., Delaney & Ames, 1995; Frone, 2006; Gleason, Veum, & Pergamit, 1991; Hingson, Mangione, & Barrett, 1981; Hollinger, 1988; Leigh, 1995) consistently show higher rates of drinking among employed young adults than among their older employed counterparts. When compared with civilian youth in the same age group (Office of Applied Studies, 2000), rates of heavy drinking are consistently higher for young adults in the military. Civilian-military differences in past 30-day heavy drinking rates are greatest for young men aged between 18 and 25 years (19.7% vs. 28.7%, respectively; Bray et al., 2006). Although heavy drinking rates generally decline after the age of 25, overall rates among military populations remain elevated in comparison with their civilian counterparts of all ages (12.9%) (Bray et al., 2006).

Author's Note: This research was supported by NIAAA Grant AA-06282.

Source: Ames, G. M., Duke, M. R., Moore, R. S., & Cunradi, C. B. (2009). The impact of occupational culture on drinking behavior of young adults in the US Navy. *Journal of Mixed Methods Research, 3*(2), 129–150. Copyright © 2009 Sage Publications.

There are several important features of the Navy as an occupational setting that contribute to problem drinking. Recruits are teenagers or in their early 20s, a demographic segment already more susceptible to problem drinking than the general population. In addition, their basic training and initial assignment is typically the first time that they have lived away from home (Ames & Cunradi, 2004-2005). Furthermore, Navy life is characterized by alternating periods of exertion and boredom, in contexts where work and leisure are highly regulated and ritualized, including those times when it is deemed appropriate to "blow off steam" through drinking (Russ & Ames, 2006). Last, and perhaps most important, Navy culture has emphasized, through ritual and habitus, drinking as a mechanism for male bonding, recreation, and stress relief (Ames, Cunradi, Moore, & Stern, 2007).

Research that is attentive both to changes in drinking patterns resulting from entrance into this occupational setting and the multiple contextual factors that influence these patterns poses multiple challenges. For example, an important mechanism for elucidating the role of the workplace on drinking behavior is to survey workers on their alcohol use at two or more time points. However, our research (see Ames, Cunradi, & Moore, 2002) is one of the few studies to date (e.g., Gleason et al., 1991; Newcomb, 1988; Richman, Flaherty, & Rospenda, 1996) that have conducted more than one wave of surveys to assess changes in work-related alcohol and drug use by young adults in the workplace. Longitudinal survey data alone, however, are limited in their ability to illuminate those occupationally specific factors that contribute to increases in problematic drinking behaviors, despite the fact that a clear understanding of these factors is critical to designing effective interventions. Therefore, to shed light on the underlying cultural, structural, and other contextual factors that may affect drinking behavior among this population, we also carried out extensive ethnographic research on U.S. Navy bases, as well as aboard ships and submarines. The complexity of the resulting research design, consisting of both longitudinal survey data collection with a highly mobile population coupled with qualitative interviewing in diverse settings, required the formation of a methodologically diverse research team and a clear delineation of the temporal sequence by which qualitative and quantitative findings would be used to inform and enrich one another.

The purposes of this article, therefore, are twofold. One is descriptive, presenting the results of a mixed method study on the impact of work culture and drinking norms on heavy drinking patterns of young adults during their first 3 years in the Navy. A second purpose of the article is methodological in scope: to use the study findings as a springboard for discussing the challenges and opportunities in carrying out collaborative mixed method research among this population. We argue that the success of the collaboration was enhanced by the fact that the study's Principal Investigator had significant prior experience in leading mixed method research teams, and that three members of the team had worked together previously.

Conceptual Framework of the Study

In this study, we sought to identify and explain the changes in young adults' drinking patterns after entering the U.S. Navy by focusing on the relationships between elements of the work environment and drinking norms and drinking patterns. A key component of our conceptual framework is the role of occupational culture in shaping behavioral norms around alcohol use. By occupational culture, we mean an organized set of understandings shared by workers and acquired through socialization into the workplace with its concepts of ideal conduct of work, and values associated with particular types of work. An occupational culture has its own formal and informal structure, vocabulary, social organization, rules, history, rituals, and collective beliefs (Ames & Janes, 1992, p. 112). As we have found in studies of other occupations, these characteristics of an occupational culture are generated in response to working conditions, shape the way work is done, and affect the behavior of workers both on and off the job, including drinking behavior (Ames, Grube & Moore, 2000). However, workplaces vary considerably in the degree to which they are able to shape occupation-related beliefs, attitudes, and behaviors. The Navy, for example, is particularly influential in this regard, because that occupational culture is highly ritualized and behaviorally regimented. Furthermore, unlike most civilian occupations, the Navy exercises considerable control over behavior during non-work hours (Duke & Ames, 2008; Hutchins, 1995).

The conceptual approach that we employ grows out of observations from former studies that workplace cultures, from whole organizations to small work teams, develop a set of shared beliefs and practices that have the potential to promote or inhibit undesirable behaviors, such as problematic drinking behavior (see Ames & Janes, 1992; Trice & Sonnenstuhl, 1990). Although demographic characteristics and prior exposure to alcohol have some influence over the workers' drinking, we postulate that the work environment itself shapes drinking norms and behaviors through the organizational and regulatory structure of particular worksites, the broader occupational norms, values, and behaviors in which these worksites are embedded, and the self-selection process whereby workers predisposed to problem drinking are attracted to work environments that reinforce those behaviors (Ames et al., 2000). Observed elements of work culture that reflect these elements include drinking rituals and traditions (Janes & Ames, 1989), expectancies around positive or negative consequences of work-related drinking or coming to work with a hangover (Grube, Ames, & Delaney, 1994), alcohol availability in and around the workplace (Ames & Grube, 1999), and alcohol policy and enforcement (Ames et al., 2000).

Our focus on normative beliefs, drawn from social learning theory, posits that people will practice behaviors that they learn from observing others' verbal expressions and behaviors, if they are rewarded and if these behaviors are reinforced (Bandura, 1977; Neumark-Sztainer, 1999). In the present study, we hypothesized that elements of the Navy—work environment influence normative beliefs, which in turn influence drinking behavior. Furthermore, because both work and leisure are structured and ideologically shaped by the military environment, we hypothesized that normative beliefs about drinking would have substantial influence on behavior. We assessed normative beliefs with questions about perceived approval or disapproval by others of one's own drinking behavior and perceived involvement in drinking by one's supervisors, coworkers, and other peers.

A key feature of Navy life that is intimately connected with heavy drinking is the recreational time that accompanies the work period known as deployment. Deployment, defined as those periods when Navy personnel are at sea and away from their home base, can last from 3 to 9 months, or longer during a time of war. Navy policy disallows any drinking of alcohol aboard ship while at sea (except under rare, officially sanctioned, and tightly regulated circumstances), and anyone caught doing so faces severe disciplinary action, including possible dismissal from the service. Periodically, however, Navy vessels dock at foreign ports for periods of relaxation and recreational activities (referred to by enlisted personnel as liberty and by officers as shore leave), during which heavy drinking frequently occurs. Based on knowledge that frequent deployment and its attendant drinking activities during liberty are fundamental aspects of contemporary Navy culture (Ames et al., 2007), and because heavier and binge drinking are known to ensue during deployment liberty (Federman et al., 2000), we further hypothesized that deployment experiences would have a significant impact on normative beliefs about drinking during deployment, and thereafter, drinking behavior generally. Specifically, we expected that changes in heavy drinking (i.e., males who reported drinking at least five drinks per typical drinking occasion at least once a week, and females at least four drinks per typical drinking occasion at least once a week) between preenlistment and follow-up 2 years later would be associated with anticipated approval for drinking during deployment liberty and perceived involvement in these behaviors by significant others.

METHOD: OVERVIEW OF STUDY FRAMEWORK

The Research Team

This study integrated survey and qualitative data to describe the changes of rates of drinking patterns and problems in our study population, as well as the cultural and environmental elements of Navy life that may predict these changes, including those that constitute actual and potential risk factors. Accordingly, the research required a transdisciplinary approach to explicate the complex linkages between drinking behavior and Navy life. In contrast to multi-disciplinary (in which researcher team members work separately from discipline-specific bases) and interdisciplinary approaches (in which researchers work together, but still from discipline-specific bases), in transdisciplinary research investigators work together using a common conceptual framework informed by theories, concepts, and methodologies drawn from multiple disciplines (Rosenfield, 1992; see also Nichter, Quintero, Nichter, Mock, & Shakib, 2004). Some scholars have recently begun using the term *interprofessional research* to refer to collaborative efforts between researchers from different disciplinary and professional backgrounds (Aagaard-Hansen & Ouma, 2002; Hart, Lymbery, & Gladman, 2005). However, we prefer the term *transdisciplinary research,* because of its emphasis both on multidisciplinary collaboration and the potential of such collaborations to transcend narrow disciplinary or methodological boundaries. Methodologically, the study design drew from approaches associated with social psychology (e.g., survey measures on normative beliefs), public health (e.g., survey measures on drinking quantity, frequency, and outcomes over time), and anthropology (e.g., semistructured interviewing to explicate beliefs, policies, and group interactions that inform drinking behavior), reflecting the disciplines of research team members.

Implementation Design and Mixed Method Integration

In keeping with our transdisciplinary orientation, we designed the study to create what we refer to as nodes of integration (Delaney & Ames, 1993a) between these two methodological approaches, thereby increasing the "yield" (O'Cathain, Murphy, & Nicholl, 2007) of unique, contextually rich insights produced by the research. Because this approach had been used successfully by the research team in previous workplace studies (Ames et al., 2000; Ames & Grube, 1999; Delaney & Ames, 1993b), coupled with the fact that the team was already accustomed to working together, the researchers maintained a high degree of collegiality, recognizing that the disciplinary and methodological training of each member would contribute to the success of the project. Furthermore, because the Principal Investigator was herself a qualitative researcher, power imbalances that often privilege quantitative over qualitative research (Hart et al., 2005) were largely mitigated, and both forms of data collection received equal weight throughout.

During the initial phase of the study, pilot qualitative interviews were carried out with key participants who had unique insights into Navy policy, labor practices, and rituals that may influence drinking behavior (i.e., medical personnel, officers, master chiefs, and counselors who interact regularly with enlisted personnel). The purpose of these initial interviews was threefold: to elucidate for the research team the dimensions and characteristics of alcohol use in the Navy, to uncover pertinent themes and workplace vocabulary pertaining to Navy life, and to provide data for developing a heuristic model of military work-related alcohol use that would guide the remainder of the study. Material from these interviews was subsequently incorporated into the qualitative interview guide, the survey design, and the model, thus constituting the initial node of integration for the study. For example, key participants noted that ports of call were sites where sailors' problematic drinking was particularly acute. As a result, we incorporated questions pertaining to these sites into the survey instrument and interview guide. Moreover, these interviews revealed a rich, specialized vocabulary pertaining both to time spent away from home port and the consequences of problem drinking (e.g., deployment, under way, liberty, shore leave, captain's mast), which were likewise incorporated into the survey as well as subsequent qualitative interview guides. Finally, the key informant interviews were used to develop a heuristic model of the study. The study's initial conceptualization was derived from a generic model developed by the research team in previous studies (Ames & Janes, 1992) on the influence of the workplace setting, psychosocial factors, and occupational cultural norms on workers' drinking patterns. Given the uniqueness of the Navy as an institution and as a site of labor, however, the research team felt it important to modify the model to better accommodate this occupational setting. Data from the key informant interviews were used to tease out some of these particularities. For example, these interviews revealed that, whereas drinking on the job is rare and subject to severe disciplinary action, heavy drinking occurs in the context of leisure activities associated with Navy life (e.g., deployment liberty, drinking at establishments within or in proximity to bases). Because the Navy, unlike most occupational settings, regulates both work and leisure time, we altered our model to reflect the unique relationship between work and leisure.

Although the qualitative and survey data collection were carried out in tandem, Time 2 survey data collection was completed approximately 1 year before the conclusion of qualitative data collection. As a result, a node of integration was introduced during this phase of the research, whereby survey findings from both time points guided the final phase of the ethnography. Specifically, we used the results from preliminary survey data runs to redirect the ethnography toward contextualizing those findings, and establishing new lines of inquiry based on those results. For example, as discussed below, despite the severity of drinking among some survey respondents, the majority reported no preenlistment or postenlistment heavy drinking. Moreover, approximately 11% had actually reduced their heavy drinking between enlistment and their follow-up interview. This caused the qualitative researchers to be more attentive to protective factors that reduced the likelihood of problem drinking, both in respondents' preenlistment histories (e.g., religiosity) and in Navy culture itself (e.g., stigma against women sailors who drink to excess) during the remainder of the study.

For the final node of integration in the study design, quantitative and qualitative analyses were carried out in tandem during Years 4 and 5 to gain both generalizable and finegrained analyses of the characteristics and consequences of Navy occupational culture as it applies to drinking, as will be described in greater detail below.

In summary, the goal of the survey was to determine the extent to which drinking patterns of sailors changed from preenlistment through their first 3 years in the Navy, and to inform the latter stages of ethnographic data collection regarding findings that may require greater qualitative explication. The purpose of the qualitative component was to gather empirical data that would (a) provide a background for the study and address first hand the complexity of the cultural underpinnings of young adults' drinking behaviors, (b) inform the content and language of the survey instrument, and (c) after completion of the survey, provide social, cultural, and occupational contexts for findings on risk factors for heavy drinking. Although current Navy regulations do not allow military personnel less than the age of 21 years to drink alcohol at any port of call, at the time of the research, drinking ages were determined by the legal drinking age of the country in which that port was located.

We obtained full authorization and cooperation from the U.S. Navy to carry out the mail survey and to conduct the ethnographic field work on Navy bases and worksites, including submarines, carriers, and other military vessels within or outside of the continental United States. Additionally, we obtained human subjects' approval for the ethnography and survey from the Institutional Review Boards of the Pacific Institute for Research and Evaluation and the U.S. Navy through the Naval Health Research Center, San Diego, California, and a Certificate of Confidentiality from the National Institutes of Health. Informed consent was obtained from all research subjects prior to study participation. During the consent procedures for both the survey and qualitative components, we informed participants that we were not under contract with the U.S. Navy; that Navy personnel would not have access to individual survey and qualitative interview data; that participants would not be penalized for refusing to participate; and that research findings, including those presented to the U.S. Navy, would only be presented in aggregate form.

Baseline Survey
Sample and Data Collection

The study population for our longitudinal study on changes in drinking patterns of young adults in their first 3 years in the military was initially enrolled at the Recruit Training Command in Great Lakes, Illinois (see Ames et al., 2002). A total of 2,160 Navy enlisted recruits were identified as eligible to participate while undergoing basic training at the Recruit Training Command during August 1998 (Year 2 of the study design). Of these, 2,002 voluntarily completed confidential self-administered Time 1 questionnaires (SAQ) on their preenlistment alcohol use and other baseline characteristics, yielding a 93% response rate. Military personnel (other than survey respondents) were present during survey administration. The enlisted component consisted of 1,507 men and

495 women with an average age of 19 years. Approximately 81% had a high school degree, and 18% had completed some postsecondary education. The officer component of the survey cohort ($n = 836$) was recruited among those entering Officer Candidate School in Pensacola, Florida between August 1998 and May 1999. A total of 856 were eligible to participate; 20 refused participation, and 836 (97.7%) voluntarily provided confidential baseline data using an SAQ. (Results of the analysis of survey data obtained from officers enrolled in the study while at Officer Candidate School will be reported elsewhere.)

Time 2 Survey Data Collection

Between February and August 2000 (Year 4), self-administered follow-up questionnaires (Time 2) were mailed to participants at their duty stations within and outside of the continental United States. The purpose of the study and voluntary nature of their participation in the follow-up were reiterated in a cover letter that accompanied the SAQ. All potential responders were free to refuse participation. For a detailed description of follow-up data collection procedures, see Cunradi, Moore, Killoran, and Ames (2005). Approximately 40% of the 2,838 baseline participants ($n= 1,132$) responded to follow-up in 2000. Our response rate, although low, is similar to those seen in other military survey studies (Bray et al., 1999; Woodruff, Edwards, & Conway, 1998). Among responders, 713 were enlisted Navy personnel. Among nonresponders, 447 (15.8%) had separated from the Navy by the time Wave 2 follow-up was undertaken. An additional 266 (9.4%) were unreachable because of undeliverable addresses (e.g., base transfer, mail not forwarded), 14 (.5%) conveyed explicit refusal to participate, and 979 (34.5%) did not respond despite multiple attempts at follow-up.

Survey Nonresponse Analysis

Nonresponse analysis among the cohort is discussed in detail elsewhere (Cunradi,

Moore et al., 2005). Briefly, chi-square tests of independence were used to analyze differences in rates of panel attrition by baseline sample characteristics, including substance use. Multivariate logistic regression models were developed to estimate the odds of panel attrition in relation to baseline frequent heavy drinking, tobacco, and drug use. The models were adjusted for sociodemographic factors (i.e., age and marital status at baseline, gender, ethnicity, religion, education). Because education and rank were highly correlated ($r = .91$, $p < .001$), rank was not included in the logistic regression analysis. Given that both substance use and lower levels of education have been found to predict attrition, we sought to test whether these factors would interact when predicting attrition. The results indicated that preenlistment frequent heavy drinking was not a predictor of nonresponse at follow-up. Multivariate logistic regression analysis, however, indicated that men, participants who were aged 29 or younger at baseline and tobacco users at baseline were significantly more likely than females, those aged 30 or older at baseline, and nontobacco users to be nonresponders at follow-up. In addition, a significant interaction between level of education and baseline drug use indicated that respondents with less than a college education who were drug users were more likely to be nonresponders.

Qualitative Data Collection

Qualitative data collection procedures included naturalistic observations and face-to-face interviews carried out on five large military bases: two on the East Coast, one on the Gulf Coast, one on the West Coast, and one in the South Pacific. Pilot interviews were carried out at the beginning of the study, to elucidate the issues of concern and to inform the survey design and qualitative interview guide. The remaining interviews were carried out after the Time 1 (T1) survey, and through the end of Time 2 (T2) survey data collection in Year 4. As a result of the high mobility of this population, coupled with the importance of carrying out qualitative interviews face-to-face, we conducted a single interview with each participant in the qualitative sample. However, during those interviews, we asked respondents to discuss changes in their drinking behaviors over the course of their Navy careers.

In all, we collected 50 tape-recorded, semistructured, open-ended interviews with a quota sample of 24 young male and female sailors, 7 junior officers, and 19 key experts to include medical personnel, alcohol counselors, master chiefs, and line officers. Recruitment was stratified by gender, job category, and geographical location and these demographic variables proved to be salient in terms of alcohol exposure and use. Our interviews and observations (Bernard, 1994) were conducted in selected work, recreational, dining, and sleeping areas on board ships and submarines in port with 1 week on board a carrier at sea. At each base, with permission, flyers were posted in various locations (including on ships in port) explaining the project and seeking participants who had been active duty Navy for 3 years or less, and older key experts. The purpose of these hour-long interviews was to ask questions that allowed open-ended answers in order to gather first-hand perspectives on alcohol-related traditions, rituals, peer pressure, and role modeling while working at home base and during deployment. We also inquired about job stress, social and physical availability of alcohol, and alcohol policies and disciplinary action.

Survey Measures

Frequent heavy drinking. Both in first and second survey waves, participants were asked questions about their usual quantity and frequency of beer, wine, and liquor consumption in the previous 12 months. In accord with previous research on gender-based heavy episodic drinking measures (e.g., Wechsler & Austin, 1998; Wechsler, Dowdall, Davenport, & Rimm, 1995), we classified males who reported drinking at least five drinks per typical drinking occasion at least once a week, and females who reported drinking at least four drinks per typical drinking occasion at least once a week, as frequent heavy drinkers. Respondents who reported frequent heavy drinking at T1 and in T2 were coded as *recurrent* frequent heavy drinkers at follow-up. Respondents who did not report frequent heavy drinking at T1, but reported frequent heavy drinking at T2 were coded as *incident* frequent heavy drinkers at follow-up. Respondents who reported frequent heavy drinking at T1, but not at T2, were coded as *remission* frequent heavy drinkers at follow-up. Respondents who did not report frequent heavy drinking at either T1 or T2 were coded as the *reference* group. Prevalence of frequent heavy drinking at follow-up was calculated as the percentage of all respondents reporting frequent heavy drinking at T2 (see Table 10.5).

Sociodemographic factors. Data were collected on gender, ethnicity (Black, Hispanic, White, Other), age at follow-up (measured as a continuous variable), and marital status (single/separated/divorced vs. married/cohabiting) at follow-up.

Normative beliefs. Respondents were asked a series of questions measuring normative beliefs for drinking during deployment liberty. The first set of questions measured perceived approval for binge drinking:

> Think about drinking on liberty during sea duty. How much do you think the following people (your immediate supervisor, closest friend at work, other friends at work, other co-workers) would disapprove or approve if you were to have four or five whole drinks within a 2-hour period?

This definition of binge drinking is in accord with the criteria adopted by the National Institute of Alcohol Abuse and Alcoholism (2004); namely a drinking pattern characterized by consuming five or more drinks (for males), or four or more drinks (for females), in about 2 hours. Responses were measured on a 5-point Likert-type scale *(disapprove strongly*

Table 10.5 Frequent Heavy Drinking Classification

	Frequent Heavy Drinking	
Group Type	*Time 1*	*Time 2*
Recurrent	+	+
Incident	–	+
Remission	+	–
Reference	–	–

to *approve strongly).* The second set of questions measured perceived drinking among work referents:

> Think about drinking on liberty during sea duty (or for officers, shore leave). How many whole drinks of an alcoholic beverage would you guess the following people (your immediate supervisor, closest friend at work, other friends at work, other co-workers) usually had when they drank?

Response categories for each referent ranged from *none* to *more than ten*. Reliability for both measures was excellent (Cronbach's $\alpha = .94$ & .90, respectively). Principal axis factoring produced one-factor scores that explained 85% and 76% of the variance for each set of measures, respectively.

Deployment factor. Based on a 7-point scale *(none* to *more than 9 months),* respondents were asked about how much time they spent deployed at sea in the previous 12 months.

RESULTS

Survey Sample Characteristics

Sample characteristics of the cohort at follow-up ($n = 713$) are shown in Table 10.6. There were significant gender differences in the race/ethnicity of the respondents; most males were White, and most females were non-White. Similarly, approximately a quarter

Table 10.6   Sample Characteristics at Follow-Up, Enlisted Respondents, Young Adults in the Workplace (n = 713)

	Males (n=493)	Females (n=220)	χ^2 or t
Heavy drinking			
Pre- and postenlistment (recurrent)	13.6	7.4	18.2***
Postenlistment only (incident)	13.2	5.1	
Preenlistment only (remission)	11.0	12.5	
None	62.2	75.0	
Ethnicity (%)			
Black	17.0	25.9	13.4**
Hispanic	14.1	15.7	
White	56.6	42.6	
Other	12.3	15.7	
Marital status (%)			
Single/separated/divorced	73.2	63.4	6.8**
Married/cohabiting	26.8	36.6	
Mean age (standard deviation)	21.3 (1.9)	21.5 (2.5)	ns

** $p < .01$; *** $p < .001$; ns = not significant.

of the males and a third of the females were married or cohabiting. On average, respondents were 21 years old; there was no significant gender difference in the age of the respondents at follow-up.

Drinking Status at Follow-up

There were significant gender differences in drinking status at follow-up ($\chi^2 = 18.2$, 3df, $p < .001$; Table 10.5). In terms of overall prevalence, more than twice as many men than women reported engaging in frequent heavy drinking at follow-up (26.8% vs. 12.5%; Cunradi, Ames, & Moore, 2005). About twice as many men than women (13.6% vs. 7.4%) reported recurrent heavy drinking, and more than twice as many men than women (13.2% vs. 5.1%) reported incident heavy drinking. Similar percentages of men (11.0%) and women (12.5%) reported remission of their preenlistment heavy drinking. The majority of men (62.2%) and women (75%) reported no preenlistment or postenlistment heavy drinking.

Normative Beliefs and Heavy Drinking

For young sailors, most of whom are under the legal drinking age, Navy life is characterized by alternating periods of tedium and intense activity, gruelingly long work hours and periods of unsupervised leisure, lengthy periods on board ship (known in Navy parlance as "away from home port") and periods of recreation in U.S. or foreign ports. Navy workplace culture both reflects and responds to these antinomies, particularly with regard to the use of alcohol.

The results in Table 10.7 show that for enlisted men, cultural norms (normative beliefs) were important predictors of frequent heavy drinking recurrence, and to a less extent,

incidence. For example, perceived heavy drinking of work referents during liberty was significantly associated with recurrent frequent heavy drinking (odds ratio [OR] = 2.86, 95% confidence interval [CI] = 1.62-5.03; $p < .001$) and incident heavy drinking (OR = 3.34; 95% CI = 1.89-5.93; $p < .001$). Perceived approval for binge (heavy episodic) drinking during liberty was significantly associated with heavy drinking recurrence (OR = 1.82; 95% CI = 1.19-2.77;

Table 10.7   Predictors of Frequent Heavy Drinking Recurrence and Incidence at Follow-Up Among Enlisted Men, Young Adults in the Workplace Study

	Recurrence		Incidence	
	Odds Ratio	95% Confidence Interval	Odds Ratio	95% Confidence Interval
Normative beliefs				
Perceived approval for binge drinking during liberty	1.82**	1.19-2.77	1.25	0.84-1.87
Perceived heavy drinking of work referents during liberty	2.86**	1.62-5.03	3.34***	1.89-5.93
Deployment	1.16	0.96-1.40	1.14	0.94-1.39
Age	1.06	0.88-1.29	1.04	0.86-1.26
Ethnicity				
Black	0.35	0.01-1.28	0.75	0.25-2.24
Hispanic	0.51	0.18-1.43	0.97	0.37-2.53
Other	1.18	0.39-3.57	2.70	0.99-7.34
White (reference)	1.00	—	1.00	—
Marital status				
Single/separated/ divorced	1.05	0.49-2.25	1.03	0.48-2.20
Married/cohabiting (reference)	1.00	—	1.00	—

** $p < .01$. *** $p < .001$.

$p < .01$), but not incidence. Length of deployment was associated with elevated odds of frequent heavy drinking recurrence and incidence, but the associations were not significant. Last, the results in Table 10.8 show that perceiving that their work referents were heavy drinkers during liberty decreased the odds of postenlistment heavy drinking remission at follow-up ($OR = 0.52$; 95% CI = 0.31–0.88; $p < .05$).

Ethnicity and Heavy Drinking

Of note, respondent race/ethnicity was not associated with frequent heavy drinking recurrence, incidence, or remission in the survey data. This finding is in contrast to the results of our baseline analysis of factors associated with preenlistment frequent heavy drinking (Ames et al., 2002). In that study, African American recruits were about half as likely to report that they had engaged in frequent heavy drinking in the year prior to enlistment compared with White recruits ($OR = 0.50$; 95% CI = 0.33–0.77; $p < .01$). Similarly, in our study of Navy careerists, we found that African Americans were significantly less likely than Whites to endorse positive social norms for heaving drinking during liberty deployment (Ames et al., 2007). We did not sample for ethnicity in the qualitative component of the study, but rather for gender and rank (i.e., sailors, chief petty officers, officers).

Overall, survey findings support the view that normative beliefs and behaviors in Navy occupational settings are associated with

Table 10.8 Predictors of Frequent Heavy Drinking Remission at Follow-Up Among Enlisted Men, Young Adults in the Workplace Study

	Odds Ratio	95% Confidence Interval
Normative beliefs		
Perceived approval for binge drinking during liberty	0.82	0.51–1.31
Perceived heavy drinking of work referents during liberty	0.52*	0.31–0.88
Deployment	0.91	0.74–1.12
Age	0.94	0.73–1.22
Ethnicity		
Black	0.92	0.24–3.45
Hispanic	0.85	0.29–2.50
Other	0.52	0.16–1.76
White (reference)	1.00	—
Marital status		
Single/separated/divorced	0.65	0.28–1.51
Married/cohabiting (reference)	1.00	—

* $p < .05$.

changes in pre- and postenlistment frequent heavy drinking among enlisted males, and with the continuation (recurrence) of heavy drinking. In particular, perceived heavy drinking of one's work associates appears to be an important influence on frequent heavy drinking recurrence, incidence, and remission among male cohort respondents. Perceived approval for binge drinking on deployment liberty was a significant factor among recurrent frequent heavy drinkers only. Although these findings are provocative in and of themselves, they offer little clarity into the ways in which normative beliefs regarding alcohol use are formed, reinforced, and contribute to drinking behavior in the context of the occupational setting of the U.S. Navy. For that, we next turn to the findings from the qualitative component of the study.

Contextualizing Normative Beliefs and Workplace Culture: Qualitative Findings

Given the study's triangulation design convergence model (Creswell & Piano Clark, 2007) and the study's heuristic model on occupational culture and alcohol use, qualitative data were collected more or less simultaneously with, and continued after, the T1 and T2 surveys to further explicate the relationship between normative beliefs and behaviors in Navy occupational settings and heavy drinking. These models required establishing a deeply contextual understanding of the complex relationships between policy, alcohol availability, cultural norms, role modeling, and drinking behavior, with the ultimate goal of explicating the causal factors that affect drinking behavior over time. Qualitative inquiry is uniquely suited to this purpose, because it is fundamentally concerned with the explanatory importance of context in uncovering causal processes (Maxwell, 2004). These relationships, and the underlying relationships that shape them, are discussed below.

Alcohol policies and policy enforcement
Starting in 1980, the U.S. Military adopted strict policies with the aim of reducing problems with alcohol, tobacco, and illicit drug use. However, in general, the Navy still exercises flexibility in alcohol policy enforcement, and disciplinary action is not equivalent across commands, locations, and job categories. Many older officers and enlistees are still perplexed by the changes in rules that clash with embedded traditions around alcohol use and handling of alcohol-related problems, leading to ambivalence in policy enforcement. Many of the young sailors and officers voiced an opinion that there was no standardized alcohol policy, and that disciplinary action depended on the commanding officer. Almost all the sailors believe that sailors are more likely to get "caught" and are more severely punished than officers if they get a DUI ("driving under influence"), arrive for work at their base job with a severe hangover, or return to ship after deployment so drunk that they are unable to work.

In general, officers believe it is important to assess the value of the rule breaker before handing out disciplinary action that may curtail or abolish advancement in a career. For serious offenses, sailors are sent to "Captain's Mast" where the captain makes the final judgment, and decides on the severity of disciplinary action. One captain and commanding officer of a ship, like others, has his own set of guidelines for enforcing policy. He gave an example where a sailor was caught drinking onboard ship, an offense that, according to policy, is grounds for dismissal:

> Just had a kid last week on marital problems, divorce, stress, and drunk on duty and all that, you name it. And you have to make a decision on guys and usually I do the same thing. Haul in everybody who knows him and talk to them and everyone involved in the incident and make an assessment of the guy's future and capability and desire, which is important to me. . . . Now somebody who is a two or three time guy, it's a little different. Then I usually find him guilty and I suspend him for 6 months.

In sum, we found a great deal of confusion regarding the alcohol policy, and resentment of that policy among older officers. The latter in particular resulted in a high degree of ambivalence in policy enforcement. Moreover, among enlisted personnel, there was a widespread belief that in terms of policy enforcement, they were held to a more stringent standard than officers.

Physical and social availability of alcohol. Alcohol availability, a well-known risk factor for higher drinking rates in the general population (Abbey, Scott, Oliansky, Quinn, & Andreski, 1990; Gruenewald et al., 1996; Holder, 1993), has been found to be equally important in occupational settings (Ames & Grube, 1999; Sonnenstuhl & Trice, 1987). Deeply embedded cultural traditions that support physical and social availability of alcohol in our study population emerged as risk factors for the heavy and binge drinking reported in the survey findings (see Tables 3 and 4), especially given the largely underage drinking population of the sample, and the relative lack of drinking experiences for many of the younger men and women. In short, the high physical, and particularly social, availability of alcohol in the Navy shapes workplace norms regarding its consumption, as well as the cultural meanings ascribed to alcohol (Moore, Ames, & Cunradi, 2007).

References to the ease with which a newly conscripted sailor could find inexpensive alcohol and the planning of drinking groups were recurring themes throughout the qualitative interviews. On stateside bases, regardless of age, alcohol could be obtained with relative ease. Although underage purchase laws are adhered to by most bars located near U.S. bases, underage recruits reported that it was not difficult to obtain alcohol in bars, in the Naval Exchange (i.e., on-base commissary), barracks, or hotel rooms near the base. When asked how underage sailors get alcohol, a 20-year-old male offered,

> Last week . . . a couple of my Marine friends went and they got a hotel room and a couple of them were 22 I think . . . And I think I drank maybe like nine beers that night. I mean, it's probably a lot. But, I really don't consider it a lot because I look at the whole week.

For sailors on liberty in a foreign port, alcohol is even more readily available, given the lower drinking ages and lax enforcement at many ports of call. In most ports, a beer costs less than one U.S. dollar, there are no restrictions on drinking age, and enforcement of underage rules are lax. Furthermore, as reflected in the survey results, cultural norms regarding excessive alcohol use on liberty are especially robust. In sum, there are few barriers to obtaining alcohol, finding peer-group networks to drink with over a typical 72-hour liberty period, drinking to excess, or getting drunk.

Drinking and workplace cultural norms. Consistent with the survey findings, qualitative interview respondents' normative beliefs and expectancies concerning alcohol use were informed by a Navy culture that places high social value on drinking during leisure hours. This suggests that many recruits are attracted to the Navy because it corresponds to preexisting cultural norms, that is, normative beliefs and expectancies concerning alcohol use (as represented by the recurrent group in the analysis above) or that participation in this occupational setting resulted in increased problem drinking behaviors (i.e., the incident group) for many young sailors.

For the most part, interview respondents described these cultural norms regarding drinking behavior in terms of normative routines that reflect preestablished traditions for socializing, reducing boredom, and alleviating stress in Navy culture. As we have found in other studies with factory workers, established routines of drinking with groups of coworkers play a role in the development of drinking networks, and thereby drinking patterns (Delaney & Ames, 1993b). For Navy recruits, the desirability to participate in drinking networks is naturally encouraged because of isolation from their recently abandoned civilian networks, and reinforced with the understanding that group drinking is a culturally prescribed way of addressing boredom and loneliness. When asked if they thought they and their peers drink more in the Navy than before they joined, the following comment by a 22-year-old female recruit typifies perspectives on group drinking:

> Yes. I didn't drink before I joined. You're away from home, around people you don't even know, people from different states. We're all so different— what else do we have in common? But after a couple of drinks, we're all the same, you know?

Likewise, a young man, responding to the question of whether people increase their drinking when they join the Navy, responded, "Definitely. Definitely. I think it is stress, actually, I think (that becoming accustomed to Navy life is) definitely something you don't acquire overnight, you know, it takes a lot of getting used to." Despite elaborate policies designed to curtail drinking, deep-seated behavioral norms regarding alcohol use in the Navy, coupled with recruits' separation from their preenlistment social networks, resulted in periodic heavy drinking among sailors, including those under the legal drinking limit.

Peer pressure and role modeling. Because drinking group membership tends to be organized around rank, cultural norms for drinking behavior are largely learned through peer pressure and role modeling. For recruits, the first foreign liberty builds excitement and anticipation of new adventures along with some anxiety, as demonstrated in the words of an 18-year-old leaving for his first deployment:

> The other day I was told if you got $28 and, I can't remember which country it was, [but] you've got everything. You can get yourself a girl, and you can get yourself drunk and a hotel room all in one shot of 28 bucks.

Peer pressure for behavioral conformity on liberty is prevalent with almost all job categories and within the contained cultural boundaries of a ship. In response to a question regarding the events that take place during a typical first night in port, a 21-year-old enlisted woman stated,

> Usually, you pull in early, but they have you clean the ship before you leave, they have you taking out the trash before you leave, they have you making sure everything is done before, so by this time, it's 6:00 in the afternoon. What are you going to do at 6:00, at somewhere you have no idea where you are? You're going to go to the bar. Plus, you've been underway [at sea], and that's the thing to say, "I'm going to go get f-ed up" is the thing that everybody says.

The hierarchical nature of Navy life and the restrictions around socializing with lower ranked personnel tend to produce drinking groups that are largely horizontal, with minimal fraternization between lower ranked sailors (E-1 to E-5), and petty and warrant officers and chiefs (E-6 to E-9). However, deployment liberty provides one of the few culturally prescribed work domains that allow for the possibility of young sailors and officers to participate in the same drinking networks. The risk here is that when officers join underage recruits in the heavy drinking networks on deployment, they serve as role models, and thereby reinforce the belief that heavy and binge drinking is acceptable, if not expected, behavior. Older sailors, enlisted officers (chiefs), and line officers who have firsthand knowledge about drinking locales around Navy bases and in foreign ports, particularly those that facilitate casual sexual encounters, are afforded an elevated status by young recruits. One high ranking commanding officer with more than 20 years in the Navy had positive views when he talked about role modeling for drinking and carousing on liberty as an important part of training for young sailors:

> It starts out at sea. That's part of the brotherhood—the fraternal order of the Navy. The fraternal order deck guys, the fraternal order of aviation guys—the handlers on the flight decks. There's all kinds of traditions and one of them is, when we go to port liberty, I'm going to show you this bar, I'm going to show you this and that—it's self-fulfilling. Let's put it this way, you educate a lot of young men.

In contrast, one experienced senior chief was concerned about the power of role modeling as an added risk factor for young sailors' drinking behavior. "If you're pulling into Thailand, and some guy who's been there before says 'Oh, when I was there, I did this and this' and then the youngsters will listen to him and say, 'Wow! You're cool!'"

A 19-year-old recruit talked about round drinking with officers:

> We do rounds, we buy for each other, or sometime there will be a senior person there, and he'll say "round!" because he has money. On shore duty, back where we belong, we don't hang out with senior people. On liberty it's a kind of different world, and we don't talk about it when we get back. Everything that happens there stays there. So, it's like the rules get bent.

For the most part, cultural norms regarding drinking are highly gendered. In particular, the association of liberty with alcohol-related sexual adventures and elevated male status, and the concomitant pressures on women sailors to drink in order to fit in (and to perhaps become more sexually vulnerable) points to the importance of gender in understanding beliefs and expectations about alcohol use in the Navy (see Russ & Ames, 2006). The prestige that men derive from excessive drinking in this context undoubtedly contributes to males' significantly higher rates of heavy drinking than those of women once they join the Navy, as reflected in the survey data cited above.

Rationales for heavy drinking behaviors. Given cultural norms that emphasize alcohol's multiple roles as a relief from boredom, rite of passage, and marker of social status, it is perhaps not surprising that many young sailors indulge in heavy drinking. A 20-year-old male expressed those aspects of Navy social life that encouraged his drinking:

> You get this mass boredom type thing to where there's not a whole lot to do. You are stuck with the same rut. And you just want to go out and do something. That's why I feel like military people drink so much.

A recruit who had just returned from his first deployment expressed his belief that excessive drinking was the expected way to relax after days at sea. His statement typifies others who hold similar beliefs:

> When you go to the port, you're pretty much looking for a good time. It might be your first time being there, you're on the ship maybe for 8 weeks straight and the only thing that you see is the sea and you've worked your butt off. I think that it's impressed on people's minds that alcohol is a good way to relax and kick back.

Descriptions of the amount of alcohol consumed at one setting on brief deployment liberties varied from 5 to 20 drinks, and the young recruits usually described the number of drinks at bars in terms of someone else's drinking, as in the following:

> It's just drink after drink after drink, for hours, as long as you're at that place. You know, I remember a buddy of mine, he was drinking hard liquor, and each one they give you a straw, and he was there from like noon in the day, drinking . . . and his straws were like piled up, and we didn't leave the club 'til about 10, and he was still drinking.

Another incentive for engaging in heavy drinking is the desire to follow the traditional pattern of getting drunk before returning to the ship and facing weeks or months without alcohol. One sailor describes his experience in drinking to get drunk after spending half his 36-hour liberty doing other things:

> We had to be back, because the ship was leaving at 12:00 a.m. and we know we had to be on board by 12:00. So we'd drink fast. I don't know why we do it, but what the concept of it is, to be drunk by the time we show up for ship. The officers would only say anything if you show up unable to walk or throwing up, because that poses a medical issue.

Participants' rationales for engaging in excessive drinking are shaped by cultural norms that equate the use of alcohol with stress relief, and perceive drinking as a mechanism for social bonding and (at least for men) social status inflation, particularly when used to excess. Moreover, in the context of these norms, Navy regulations that preclude drinking aboard ship produce a scarcity mentality among Navy personnel when they are on leave, which greatly facilitates heavy drinking.

Protective factors. Despite participating in an occupational culture that places high value on alcohol consumption, some respondents reported protective factors that reduced or diminished such hazardous drinking. Some, for example, noted that their religious beliefs precluded them from drinking to excess. Others, particularly women, noted that the cultural currency accorded to those who can "hold their liquor" applied to men only. Women who drank heavily, in contrast, were viewed as sexually promiscuous, a label that is not only stigmatizing, but potentially dangerous given the high rates of sexual assault in the U.S. military (Duke & Ames, 2008). Many of those who reported that their drinking behaviors had diminished during their tenure in the Navy attributed these changes to life events, particularly promotions, marriage, or parenthood. However, these individualized circumstances nonetheless operate within a context in which, despite policies designed to curb problem drinking, alcohol is deeply embedded in Navy culture.

CONCLUSION

One of the major strengths of this study is its mixed method approach, which resulted from the distinctly transdisciplinary orientation of the investigators regarding the study's conceptual and analytic design, which entailed incorporating nodes of data integration into the project timeline. For example, as mentioned above, both the qualitative and quantitative data mutually informed one another in terms of instrument design, model building, the triangulation and contextualization of findings, and the ability to focus simultaneously on emic conceptualizations and expressions of cultural norms as they pertain to alcohol on the one hand, and on generalizable, longitudinal data regarding drinking quantity and frequency, and normative beliefs and expectancies concerning alcohol on the other. In particular, the survey described the changes in drinking rates over the first 3 years in the Navy (between baseline and follow-up), and identified risk factors associated with problematic drinking, as well as the role of cultural norms in predicting heavy drinking. The qualitative component of the study focused on elucidating the specific, occupationally based, behavioral norms that shape problematic drinking behaviors among this population. Specifically, the qualitative data provided a clearer understanding of the cultural and social contexts of risk factors, which include the easy availability of alcohol, widespread ambivalence in rule enforcement, role modeling by higher ranked personnel, use of alcohol for stress relief, and pressure from older peers to join drinking groups. These risk factors were supported by the fact that minimum legal drinking age laws did not apply in most foreign ports at the time of the study and could be easily evaded in and around most Navy bases. The qualitative data, guided by survey results regarding abstainers, moderate drinkers, and drinkers who were in remission (i.e., who reported frequent heavy drinking at baseline, but not at Time 2), also uncovered important individual and cultural protective factors among some respondents.

Study Limitations and Strengths

Limitations of the study include the low response rate at survey follow-up, as discussed above and in detail elsewhere (Cunradi, Moore, et al., 2005). The inability to model predictors of heavy drinking among female enlisted personnel was due to unstable estimates. The lower rates of frequent heavy drinking recurrence and incidence among females, however, suggests that understanding the factors associated with heavy drinking behavior among enlisted males is the more urgent public health issue.

A strength of our study is that the conceptual approach to describing links between workplace culture and drinking that we examined in this study can be generalized to occupations other than the military. Our findings may heighten awareness of both military and civilian employers worldwide to the fact that elements of organizational culture can put young adults entering the workplace at risk for unhealthy drinking patterns. In order for workplace-based prevention to be successful in either military or civilian occupations, it will be necessary for management and young adult workers alike to come to an understanding of how their workplace supports problematic drinking, and to take a unified approach toward instituting changes.

References

Aagaard-Hansen, J., & Ouma, J. H. (2002). Managing interdisciplinary health research: Theoretical and practical aspects. *International Journal of Health Planning and Management, 17,* 195-212.

Abbey, A., Scott, R. O., Oliansky, D. M., Quinn, B., & Andreski, P. M. (1990). Subjective, social and physical availability: II. Their simultaneous effects on alcohol consumption. *International Journal of Addictions, 25,* 1011-1023.

Ames. G., & Cunradi, C. (2004-2005). Alcohol use and preventing alcohol-related problems among young adults in the military. *Alcohol Research & Health, 28,* 252-257.

Ames, G. M., Cunradi, C. B., & Moore, R. S. (2002). Alcohol, tobacco, and drug use among young adults prior to entering the military. *Prevention Science, 3,* 135-144.

Ames, G. M., Cunradi, C. B., Moore, R. S., & Stem, P. (2007). Military culture and drinking behavior among U.S. Navy careerists. *Journal of Studies on Alcohol and Drugs, 68,* 336-344.

Ames, G., & Grube, J. (1999). Alcohol availability and workplace drinking: Mixed method analyses. *Journal of Studies on Alcohol, 60,* 383-393.

Ames, G. M., Grube, J., & Moore, R. (2000). Social control and workplace drinking norms: A comparison of two organizational cultures. *Journal of Studies on Alcohol, 61,* 203-219.

Ames, G. M., & Janes, C. (1992). A cultural approach to conceptualizing alcohol and the workplace. *Alcohol Health & Research World, 16,* 112-119.

Bandura, A. (1977). *Social learning theory.* Orrville, OH: Prentice-Hall.

Bernard, H. R. (1994). *Research methods in anthropology: Qualitative and quantitative approaches.* Newbury Park, CA: Sage.

Bray, R. M., Bae, K. E, Federman, E. B., & Wheeless, S. C. (2005). Regional differences in alcohol use among U.S. military personnel. *Journal of Studies on Alcohol, 66,* 229-238.

Bray, R. M., Hourani, L. L., Rae Olmstead, K. L., Witt, M-, Brown, J. M., Pemberton, M. R., et al. (2006). *2005 Department of Defense Survey of Health Related Behaviors among Active Duty Military Personnel* (Tech. Rep. No. RTI/7841/106-FR). Research Triangle Park, NC: Research Triangle Institute.

Bray, R. M., Sanchez, R. P., Omstein, M. L., Lentine, D., Vincus, A. A., Baird, T. U, et al. (1999). *1998 Department of Defense Survey of Health Related Behaviors among Military Personnel* (Tech. Rep. No. RT1/7034/006-FR). Research Triangle Park, NC: Research Triangle Institute.

Creswell, J. W., & Piano Clark, V. L. (2007), *Designing and conducting mixed methods research.* Thousand Oaks, CA: Sage.

Cunradi, C. B., Ames G., & Moore, R. (2005). Prevalence and correlates of interpersonal violence victimization in a junior enlisted Navy cohort. *Violence and Victims, 20,* 679-694.

Cunradi, C. B., Moore, R. S., Killoran, M., & Ames, G. (2005). Survey nonresponse among young adults: The role of alcohol, tobacco, and drugs. *Substance Use & Misuse, 40,* 171-185.

Delaney, W., & Ames, G. M. (1993a). Integration and exchange in multidisciplinary alcohol research. *Social Science & Medicine, 37,* 5-13.

Delaney, W., & Ames, G. M. (1993b). Shop steward handling of alcohol-related problems. *Addiction, 88,* 1205-1214.

Delaney, W. P., & Ames, G. M. (1995). Work team attitudes, drinking norms, and workplace drinking. *Journal of Drug Issues, 25,* 275-290.

Duke, M. R., & Ames, G. M. (2008). Challenges of contraceptive use and pregnancy prevention among women in the U.S. Navy. *Qualitative Health Research, 18,* 244-253.

Federman, E. B., Bray, R. M., & Kroutil, L. A. (2000). Relationships between substance use and recent deployments among women and men in the military. *Military Psychology, 12,* 205-220.

Frone, M. R. (2006). Prevalence and distribution of alcohol use and impairment in the workplace: A U.S. national survey. *Journal of Studies on Alcohol, 67,* 147.

Gleason, P. M., Veum, J. R., & Pergamit, M. R. (1991). Drug and alcohol use at work: A survey of young workers. *Monthly Labor Review, 114,* 3-7.

Grube, J. W., Ames, G. M., & Delaney, W. (1994). Alcohol expectancies and workplace drinking. *Journal of Applied Social Psychology, 24,* 646-660.

Gruenewald, P. J., Millar, A. B., Treno, A. J., Yang, Z., Ponicki, W. R., & Roeper, P. (1996). The geography of availability and drinking and driving. *Addiction, 91,* 967-983.

Hart, E., Lymbery, M., & Gladman, J. R. F. (2005). Methodological understandings and misunderstandings in interprofessional research: Experiences of researching transitional rehabilitation for older people. *Journal of Interprofessional Care, 19,* 614-623.

Hingson, R., Mangione, T., & Barrett, J. (1981). Job characteristics and drinking practices in the Boston metropolitan area. *Journal of Studies on Alcohol, 42,* 725-738.

Holder, H. (1993). Changes in access to and availability of alcohol in the United States: Research and policy implications. *Addiction,* 88(Suppl.), 67S-74S.

Hollinger, R. C, (1988). Working under the influence (WUI): Correlates of employees' use of alcohol and other drugs. *Journal of Applied Behavior Science, 24,* 439-454.

Hutchins, E. (1995). *Cognition in the wild.* Cambridge: MIT Press.

Janes, G., & Ames, G. M. (1989). Men, blue collar work and drinking: Alcohol use in an industrial subculture. *Culture, Medicine and Psychiatry, 13,* 245-274.

Leigh, J. P. (1995). Dangerous jobs and heavy alcohol use in two national probability samples. *Alcohol and Alcoholism, 50,* 71-86.

Maxwell, J. (2004). Using qualitative methods for causal explanation. *Field Methods, 16,* 243-264.

Miles, M. B., & Huberman, A. M. (1994). *Qualitative data analysis: An expanded sourcebook* (2nd ed.). Thousand Oaks, CA: Sage.

Moore, R. S., Ames, G. M., & Cunradi, C. B. (2007). Physical and social availability of alcohol for young enlisted naval personnel in and around home port. *Substance Abuse Treatment, Prevention, and Policy,* 2(17). Retrieved November 5, 2008, from http://www.substance abusepolicy.com/content/2/1/17

Muhr, T. (2004). ATLAS,ti: The Knowledge Workbench (Version 5) [Computer software]. Berlin, Germany: Scientific Software Development.

National Institute on Alcohol Abuse and Alcoholism (NIAAA). (2004, Winter). NIAAA Council approves definition of binge drinking. *NIAAA Newsletter, 3,* 3.

Neumark-Sztainer, D. (1999). The social environments of adolescents: associations between socio-environmental factors and health behaviors during adolescence. *Adolescent Medicine, 10,* 41-56.

Newcomb, M. D. (1988). *Drug use in the workplace: Risk factors for disruptive substance use among young adults.* Dover, MA: Auburn House.

Nichter, M., Quintero, G., Nichter, M., Mock, J., & Shakib, S. (2004). Qualitative research: Contributions to the study of drug abuse, and drug use(r)-related interventions. *Substance Use & Misuse, 59*(10-12), 1907-1969.

O'Cathain, A., Murphy, E., & Nicholl, J. (2007). Integration and publications as indicators of "yield" from mixed methods studies. *Journal of Mixed Methods Research, 1*(2), 147-163.

Office of Applied Studies. (2000). *National Household Survey on Drug Abuse: Main findings 1999.* Rockville, MD: Substance Abuse and Mental Health Services Administration.

Pack, A. J. (1983). *Nelson's blood: The story of naval rum.* Annapolis, MD: Naval Institute Press.

Richman, J. A., Flaherty, J. A., & Rospenda, K. M. (1996). Perceived workplace harassment experience and problem drinking among physicians: Broadening the stress/alienation paradigm. *Addiction, 91,* 391-403.

Rosenfield, P. L. (1992). The potential for transdisciplinary research for sustaining and extending linkages between the health and social sciences. *Social Science & Medicine, 53,* 1343-1357.

Russ, A. J., & Ames, G. M. (2006). Policy and prevention as competing imperatives in U.S. Navy life and medicine. *Culture, Health and Sexuality, 8,* 1-15.

Saltz, R. (1987). The roles of bars and restaurants in preventing alcohol-impaired driving: An evaluation of server education. *Evaluation in Health Professions, 10,* 5-27.

Schuckit, M. A., & Gunderson, E. K. E. (1974). Alcoholism among Navy and Marine Corps officers. *Military Medicine, 139,* 809-811.

Selvin, S. (1991). *Statistical analysis of epidemiologic data.* New York: Oxford University Press.

Sonnenstuhl, W. R., & Trice, H. M. (1987). The social construction of alcohol problems in a union's peer counseling program. *Journal of Drug Issues, 17,* 223-254.

Standage, T. (2005). *A history of the world in 6 glasses.* New York: Walker & Company.

Strauss, A. (1987). *Qualitative analysis for social scientists.* Cambridge, UK: Cambridge University Press.

Trice, H. M., & Sonnenstuhl, W. J. (1990). On the construction of drinking norms in work organizations. *Journal of Studies on Alcohol, 51,* 201-220.

Wechsler, H., & Austin, S. B. (1998). Binge drinking: The five/four measure. *Journal of Studies on Alcohol, 59,* 122-124.

Wechsler, H., Dowdall, G. W., Davenport, A., & Rimm, E, B. (1995). A gender-specific measure of binge drinking among college students. *American Journal of Public Health, 85,* 982-985.

Woodruff, S. L., Edwards, C. C, & Conway, T. L. (1998). Enhancing response rates to a smoking survey for enlisted U.S. Navy women. *Evaluation Review, 22,* 780-791.

DISCUSSION QUESTIONS

1. What are some of the attributes of the Navy as a workplace that may contribute to problem drinking behaviors?

2. Which theory are these authors' hypotheses drawn from? What are their hypotheses?

3. What is deployment and liberty, and why does heavy drinking often occur during these?

4. Did these researchers have to obtain Navy approval to conduct this study? What entities approved this research project?

5. How did they obtain their survey sample? Why was their response rate so high at Time 1 data collection? Why was their response rate at Time 2 so low compared with Time 1?

6. What methods did these authors use to collect their qualitative data?

7. How did these researchers conceptualize or define whether sailors were frequent, heavy drinkers? Did these vary by gender? According to the results in Table 10.6, do men engage in frequent heavy drinking more than women?

8. According to the results in Table 10.7, what influences heavy drinking behavior? Did any of the demographic factors influence drinking behavior? What does this say about how Navy life influences heavy drinking behavior?

9. How do the findings from the qualitative analysis support findings from the quantitative analysis? In what ways do these authors believe that their mixed methods approach strengthened this study of drinking behavior?

11

EVALUATION RESEARCH AND POLICY ANALYSIS

THE PURPOSES OF EVALUATION RESEARCH

The main purpose of evaluation research is to examine the effectiveness of social policies and programs. Evaluation research is sometimes called applied research because it seeks to solve more immediate social problems. Rather than specifically acquiring knowledge for the discipline or testing of theoretical concepts, evaluation research looks to assess the success of policies and programs in achieving their goals. Many criminology and criminal justice researchers seek grant funding to evaluate various government-sponsored programs each year. The United States Department of Justice spends billions annually on programs to reduce and prevent crime, but very little of these monies are actually spent on evaluating the effectiveness of them (Bachman & Schutt, 2008). Recently, there has been a call for more evaluation of government-run, crime prevention programs, and the US government has recently vowed to make policy decisions based upon sound scientific research.

Researchers who conduct evaluation research are interested in examining programs with the goal that their research results will be used to guide policy decisions. Evaluation research can be undertaken using any of the research methods discussed in this reader. Many of those who evaluate programs utilize experimental research designs because of their ability to better assess causality. Evaluators want to be sure that the outcomes they observe are an accurate description of the effectiveness of the program or policy being examined. Many alternatives to conventional criminal justice system processing of offenders, such as boot camps or drug courts, have been evaluated to assess if they are more effective at reducing recidivism than the more traditional criminal justice processes. Many of these alternative programs have been adopted by jurisdictions around the country in attempt to try different approaches to crime prevention. Often, these programs are also more cost-effective than the traditional criminal justice system processing.

Evaluation researchers often study program success. Researchers doing evaluation, therefore, must carefully conceptualize what success means. For example, for drug courts, does success mean not being rearrested for a drug offense, or does success include not being rearrested for any offense? Further, does success also include beating drug addiction?

Often, researchers can define success based on the mission or goals of the program; however, sometimes they may want to define success beyond narrower program goals and make broader judgments regarding success related to crime prevention. In the case of drug courts, for example, evaluators could examine the percentage of persons who cease using narcotics. Researchers could alternatively examine arrest rates of the drug court attendees for a period of time after they have completed drug court (one year, for example). Researchers might also want to compare the drug court attendees to another group of drug arrestees who received jail or probation and examine drug relapse and recidivism rates for the two groups. In this way, they can determine the effectiveness of drug courts compared to traditional sanctions.

Evidence-Based Evaluations

A recent buzzword in the criminal justice world is evidence-based research or evaluation. Many jurisdictions, the federal criminal justice system included, are placing emphasis on implementing programs that show evidence of success. Evidence-based practices are those that are established or implemented based upon scientific research (Welsh & Farrington, 2001). Recall in Chapter 1 that the scientific method, because of its sound and principled procedures, is the best approach for arriving at accurate and reliable results. Because of these features, policies and programs designed based on scientific research are likely to be the most effective. Traditional criminal justice system responses to crime are not having the success that citizens and the powers that be would like to see by way of crime prevention. Recidivism rates around the country are a little over 60%. What this means is that two-thirds of those who are released from jail and prison end up being rearrested and sent back to jail or prison. Because of this so-called revolving

door effect, legislators, scholars, and concerned citizens alike are demanding that more effective responses to crime be implemented.

With the recent economic downturn and most state budgets in the red, evidence-based practices are going to continue to become popular. As such, researchers who conduct evidence-based research evaluations are also going to be in need. MacKenzie (2000) cites that "As prison populations grow nationally and corrections makes up an increasing proportion of state and local budgets, many jurisdictions are seeking to determine if their funds are being spent effectively. In particular, they ask whether the programs have an impact on criminal behavior" (p. 457). Indeed, programs can be evaluated in many different ways: Researchers could evaluate programs according to their implementation (are they being implemented in the correct way?), their impact (are they achieving their stated goals?), or their efficiency (are they cost-effective, given their success or benefits?) (Bachman and Schutt, 2008).

Types of Evaluation Research

Process evaluations are important because in order for a program to be effective, it has to be implemented as planned (Hagan, 2005). Maybe the reason for a program's failure is not that it does not work in reducing recidivism or in treating addiction but rather because the program staff is not implementing it correctly. It may very well be that a program is not effective because the persons in charge of implementing it are running it how they want to and not how they are supposed to.

Impact or outcome evaluation is assessing the extent to which a program or treatment is effective (Hagan, 2005). Most programs or treatments are established because of a belief that they will effect change of some sort. Crime and justice programs usually have stated goals of correcting individual's behavior and reducing crime. If programs or treatments are not realizing their intended outcomes, funding may be better spent elsewhere. The evidence-based evaluations discussed above are the heart and soul of implementing successful programs. Most evaluation research in the fields of criminology and criminal justice are centered on assessing the impact that current programs and policies have on crime.

Efficiency evaluations are those that evaluate the costs of the program against its outcomes or impact (Hagan, 2005). The goal of these evaluations is to assess whether the benefits of the program are worth the costs to implement it. Obviously, this involves some subjective determination about what success is worth. If a program, for example, is only successful for some of those who take part in it but the costs are low, or another program shows success for almost all those enrolled but is extremely expensive, then the decision of an efficiency analysis might be to continue to fund the former but to abandon the latter. Despite that, in the second case, the program is very successful, and in the first, success is only moderate; the purpose of an efficiency evaluation is to compare success to cost. A particular jurisdiction simply may not be able to continue to afford to implement a program despite its success and may, therefore, have to replace it with a less successful but more cost-efficient one.

ETHICAL ISSUES IN EVALUATION RESEARCH

Ethical issues in evaluation research arise because programs designed for the prevention, or reduction, of crime involve human beings. Thus, usually the subjects of evaluation research are those who are in need of some type of assistance. In other words, the success of programs often has a direct impact on those who are participating in them (Ellis, Hartley, & Walsh, 2010). These concerns will vary dependent on the type of program being evaluated; those who conduct evaluation research should keep ethical concerns in the forefront of their minds (Bachman & Schutt, 2008). Finally, evaluation researchers may feel pressure from stakeholders (those who have a vested interest in program success) to report only positive outcomes or to minimize results that reveal areas of ineffectiveness. The employment of those who manage or implement these programs may depend on the results of both outcome and efficiency evaluations. Researchers, therefore, need to uphold the objectivity of their research evaluations and, if possible, avoid contact with those who oversee program management (Ellis et al., 2010).

RESEARCH READING

Listwan and colleagues examine whether methamphetamine users can be treated effectively in a community-based setting, namely a drug court, without compromise to community safety. Their sample includes drug court participants who were convicted for a felony drug offense. Their quasi-experimental research design aims to assess whether drug of choice has an effect on treatment outcomes. In other words, are community-based drug courts less successful for methamphetamine users? Their sample is made up of those who are still enrolled in the drug court, those who have successfully completed drug court, and those who were unsuccessful and were terminated from drug court. According to their results, type of drug has no effect on treatment outcome; meth users can be safely and successfully treated through community-based drug courts.

—— COMBATING METHAMPHETAMINE USE IN THE COMMUNITY ——

The Efficacy of the Drug Court Model

Shelley Johnson Listwan, Deborah Koetzle Shaffer, and Jennifer L. Hartman

Abstract: Methamphetamine use was historically a problem facing Western states; however, in recent years it has methodically spread throughout the nation. Methamphetamine use impacts communities, families, and the criminal justice system in a variety of ways. As such, many Jurisdictions are developing policies to reduce the sale and consumption of this drug as well as increase penalties for its use. The question of whether methamphetamine users can be safely and effectively treated in the community is unresolved. This study explores whether community-based drug courts are a reasonable option for treating this population. Results of the study indicate that drug of choice does not influence outcome in a drug court setting. Policy implications are discussed.

INTRODUCTION

Methamphetamine (meth) use is perceived to be one of the fastest growing drug problems in America. Historically, meth was considered a problem only for Western states and rural areas, however, evidence of its spread can be found throughout the country. For example, admissions to substance abuse treatment for meth users nationwide increased from 10 per 100,000 in 1992 to 52 per 100,000 in 2002. In the Midwest, 7 of the 12 states experienced an increase in admission rates in 2002 (Substance Abuse and Mental Health Services Administration [SAMSHA], 2004). The Drug Abuse Warning Network also found a 67% increase in the number of meth-related emergency room episodes between 1994 and 2001 (SAMSHA, 2002). Given that more than 8 million people have at least tried meth (Wright & Sathe, 2006), there is a growing fear that we are becoming entrenched in a nationwide "meth epidemic."

Although it is not clear whether meth is more addictive than other drugs, there is evidence to suggest that meth users may progress along a continuum of addiction more quickly (Castro,

Barrington, Walton, & Rawson, 2000). In contrast to drugs such as marijuana and alcohol that may be initially distasteful, meth users are more likely to find the drug "instantly pleasurable" (Weisheit & Fuller, 2004, p. 8). Immediate effects include feelings of euphoria, a decreased need for sleep, and an increased energy (Herz, 2000). The instant desire for meth, along with its longer lasting effects, may help explain why meth use is pervasive among a variety of individuals (Rawson, Anglin, & Ling, 2002).

Meth use is a serious concern for law enforcement agencies and correctional officials. A recent telephone survey conducted by the National Association of Counties (NACo) of 500 law enforcement officials in 44 states found that nearly half of the counties surveyed reported meth as their primary drug problem. Furthermore, approximately 50% of the sample reported that "1 in 5 inmates are incarcerated because of meth related crimes and seventeen percent report that 1 in 2 inmates are incarcerated because of meth related crimes" (Hansell, 2006, p. 3).

To combat the use and production of meth, many states and the federal government have begun to enact specific legislation. Most of the counties surveyed by the NACo indicated they had existing legislation or were in the process of developing laws to make it more difficult to obtain the ingredients necessary to produce meth (Hansell, 2006). At the same time, the federal government, via the Combat Methamphetamine Epidemic Act of 2005, placed restrictions on the sale of ingredients used to manufacture meth and increased penalties for smuggling and trafficking the drug (Yeh & Doyle, 2005).

Parallels can be seen between the current response to meth and the response to the rise in crack cocaine use during the 1980s. As communities became increasingly concerned about the crack cocaine epidemic, legislation was enacted establishing tougher penalties for drug users convicted of abusing or trafficking drugs (see Currie, 1998; Fagan, 1994; Walker, 1994). The subsequent war on drugs resulted in a tremendous burden placed on the criminal justice system, including the correctional system (see Belenko, Peugh, Califano, Usdansky, & Foster, 1998).

As the concern surrounding meth use escalates, it is important to consider viable options for treating this population rather than simply revisiting the failed drug policies of the 1980s (see, e.g., Belenko, Mara-Drita, & McElroy, 1992; Fagan, 1994). An alternative strategy may be community-based drug courts, which merge the treatment and supervision of drug offenders. Although drug courts have been the subject of many empirical studies, few, if any, evaluations have explored the impact of drug court programming on meth users.

Literature Review

Drug courts first emerged in the late 1980s partially in response to the war on drugs. One of the consequences of the war on drugs was an overburdened court system and, consequentially, a taxed correctional system. During this time, drug offenders cycled between the community and prison but were rarely provided with any type of substance abuse treatment. As prison populations rapidly increased, so did the call for alternative strategies for dealing with drug offenders. Together, these forces were the catalyst for the development of community-based drug courts (Listwan, Sundt, Holsinger, & Latessa, 2003). A strong body of evidence suggesting that intensive drug treatment can successfully reduce drug use and criminality (Anglin & Hser, 1990; French, Zarkin, Hubbard, & Valley, 1993; Prendergast, Anglin, & Wellisch, 1995; Van Stelle, Mauser, & Moberg, 1994), combined with immense political support for the drug court model, led to a rapid expansion in drug courts nationwide. Today, there are more than 1,000 drug courts operating in 48 states (Office of Justice Programs Drug Court Clearinghouse and Technical Assistance Project, 2004) having served an estimated 229,000 offenders (Belenko, 2002).

Although drug courts often differ by agency and jurisdiction, there are several key components central to this model. The National Association of Drug Court Professionals (NADCP, 1997) identified several key components, including the integration of judicial case processing with drug treatment services via a nonadversarial approach. Drug court programs are not required to adhere to these components per se; however, these components are intended to provide a framework for the specialized courts. Essentially, the drug court model can be viewed as integrating treatment and supervision through a collaborative relationship among the court, probation, and treatment providers.

The current study seeks to add to the existing literature by examining the recidivism rates of meth users as compared to nonmeth users being served by a community-based drug treatment court. It builds on previous research in two ways. First, it uses drug of choice to distinguish between meth users and nonmeth users. This distinction is an improvement over previous research because the meth group is limited to those who prefer meth rather than including those who may have tried meth a single time. By using drug of choice as a grouping variable, it is likely that the meth group is more homogenous than if groups had been divided between ever used or never used. Second, the current study explores differences in outcomes between the two groups. By comparing these two groups on measures of arrest and program completion, this study is able to better assess whether drug of choice, namely meth, mediates the efficacy of the drug court model.

METHOD

Sample

Participants included individuals who entered the drug court between March 1999 and June 2002. The adult felony drug court served those convicted of a felony drug or drug related offense(s). The drug court program under study was a court-supervised, comprehensive outpatient treatment program for selected chemically dependent defendants. The program combined accelerated case management, ongoing court involvement, and community-based drug treatment. Before acceptance, defendants completed an intake and screening process with the treatment provider. Defendants accepted into the program were required to plead guilty but still received representation throughout their participation in the court. Successful completion and "graduation" from the program resulted in having the guilty plea set aside and the charges dismissed. Failure or dismissal from the program resulted in the case proceeding to sentencing on the basis of the guilty plea.

Once admitted to the drug court program, participants received a combination of services and interventions designed to increase offender accountability, decrease the likelihood of recidivism, and reduce drug dependence. These services and interventions included regular drug testing, periodic one-on-one contact with the drug court judge in the form of status review hearings, and placement in community-based drug treatment programming. In addition, offenders placed in the drug court program received a sentence to probation or intensive supervision probation.

The drug court program was designed to provide community-based substance abuse treatment coupled with close supervision and frequent urinalyses. The treatment protocol included a four-phase, highly structured, outpatient treatment program lasting a minimum of 1 year, which could be extended depending on individual progress. Each phase lasted approximately 3 months and consisted of specified treatment objectives, therapeutic and rehabilitative activities, and specific requirements for movement into the next phase. Phase 1 included urinalysis at least two times per week and participation in cognitive self-change, substance abuse education, and process groups. Phase 2 required urinalysis at least once a week and participation in individual sessions and cognitive and substance abuse relapse packets. Phase 3 included urinalysis at least once a week and individualized treatment focusing on living in recovery. Finally, Phase 4 required the completion of a treatment plan, which focused on using all of the program tools to establish a long-term recovery plan. During this phase, participants were subjected to urinalysis at least once a week. Throughout each phase, counselors assisted participants in obtaining education and skills assessments and provided referrals for vocational training, education, and/or job placement services.

The sample consisted of individuals who were admitted to the program and received drug court services, including, but not limited to, drug treatment and court supervision $(N = 250)$. The group is a consecutive sample of all persons accepted into the drug court between March 1999 and June 2002. Within this group of drug court participants, individuals were those identified as meth users $(n = 129)$ and nonmeth users $(n = 101)$. Drug of choice was determined through self-disclosure during an intake process with the caseworker.

Table 11.1 describes the overall sample of individuals processed through the court. The two groups are similar on several key demographic variables such as race, employment, education, marital status, and prior record. Specifically, clients in both groups were more likely to be Caucasian, unemployed, high school graduates, and not married. The vast majority, more than 90% in both groups, were likely to have a criminal history that included drugs or drug-related criminal behavior. However, one important difference emerged with regard to gender. Women were significantly more likely to report meth use as their drug of choice as compared to other types of drugs.

Measures

Independent variables. To explore the predictors of outcome, the study examined the effects of several independent variables. Of primary interest was whether the impact of drug court programming was mitigated by drug of choice. To assess this issue, the study explored whether being identified as a meth user versus a nonmeth user affected various outcomes (meth is the reference category). Also of interest was whether social demographic variables influenced the probability of future offending or predicted the likelihood of success. As such, four demographic classifications were used in these analyses: gender, employment status, education level, and marital status. The variables were dichotomized for the multivariate analysis (0 = women, 0 = unemployed, 0 = less than high school, 0 = not married). Similarly, given that each participant was at risk for differing periods, the analysis included a measure of time at risk as a control.

Dependent variables. The impact of the drug court was assessed by examining criminal behavior through arrest for any charge and whether the arrest was drug related. We also explored factors related to program

completion given its relationship to recidivism. Information regarding arrest was collected in October and November 2002, allowing for an average follow-up time of 886 days (2.4 years). Arrest for any charge and arrest for a drug-related offense were measured as dichotomous variables, as was program completion.

Results

Drug Use History

During the intake process, treatment personnel conducted an interview with individuals to determine their eligibility for drug court. During this process they inquired about the client's drug use. Both the meth and nonmeth groups reported daily use of their primary drug of choice. Similarities between the groups are also found in terms of their reported first use. Approximately 45% of both groups reported that their use of drugs (although not necessarily their current drug of choice) began when they were between the ages of 14 and 18. Many of the participants started using drugs before age 14, with more than 30% of both groups reporting that their use began between the ages of 7 and 13.

Outcome Information

At the time of this study, the drug court had been in operation for 4 years. As such, the sample includes individuals who were still receiving drug court services (23%), had graduated successfully (approximately 40% to 43%), and were unsuccessfully terminated (approximately 30% to 33%) from the program.

Of primary interest was whether clients identified as meth users differed significantly on various indicators of criminality. The results of these analyses are summarized in Table 11.2. The two groups were similar when an arrest for any new offense was examined.

Table 11.1 Frequency and Percentage Distribution of Drug Court Participants' Intake Information

Characteristic	Methamphetamine		Nonmethamphetamine	
	N	*%*	*N*	*%*
Primary drug of choice				
Marijuana	0	0.0	56	55.4
Alcohol	0	0.0	17	16.8
Cocaine	0	0.0	8	7.9
Methamphetamine	129	100.0	0	0.0
Heroin	0	0.0	13	12.9
Other	0	0.0	7	7.0
Gender				
Male	67	52.3	66	66.7
Female	61	47.7	33	33.3
($\chi^2 = 4.720; p = .03$)				
Race				
Caucasian	128	100.0	98	99.0
African American	0	0.0	1	1.0
Employment				
35 hr or more	43	33.6	36	36.0
15-34 hr	15	11.7	17	17.0
14 hr or less	5	1.0	1	1.0
Unemployed	65	50.8	46	46.0
Education				
Less than high school	35	27.6	20	19.8
High school	58	45.7	51	50.5
Some college	34	26.8	30	29.7

	Methamphetamine		Nonmethamphetamine	
Characteristic	*N*	*%*	*N*	*%*
Marital status				
Not married	93	72.7	74	73.3
Married	35	27.3	27	26.7
Prior record				
Yes	128	100.0	96	97.0
Prior record with drugs				
Yes	120	93.8	94	94.9
Frequency of drug use				
Daily	39	72.2	34	85.0
1 time per week	7	13.0	2	5.0
<1 time per week	8	14.8	4	10.0
Age of first use				
7-13 years old	20	36.4	14	35.0
14-18 years old	24	43.6	18	45.0
19-23 years old	7	12.7	6	15.0
24 and older	4	7.3	2	5.0

These data revealed that 34% of the meth users and 41% of the nonmeth users were rearrested.

While immediate measures of drug use were not available, we examined whether either group experienced arrests for drug-related offenses to assess possible differences in drug-using behavior between the groups. There were no significant differences between the two groups. Of those who were arrested, 41% of the meth group and 49% of the nonmeth group were arrested for a drug-related charge.

In addition to examining whether the meth group was more or less likely to be arrested than the nonmeth group, we explored whether the mean number of arrests differed between the two groups. This analysis allowed us to determine whether drug of choice was a predictor in the number of arrests the client experienced during the follow-up period. The results were not statistically significant, as both groups experienced an average of 1.9 arrests during the 2.5-year follow-up period.

Table 11.2 Frequency and Percentage Distribution of Participants' Outcome Information

Characteristic	Methamphetamine		Nonmethamphetamine	
	N	%	N	%
Current Status				
Currently enrolled	27	23.5	21	23.6
Graduated	50	43.5	41	46.1
Discharged	38	33.0	27	30.0
Rearrested for a new offense				
Yes	43	33.9	41	41.1
No	84	66.1	58	58.6
Rearrest charge (of those rearrested)				
Drug related	18	40.9	20	48.8
Trafficking	1	2.3	1	2.4
Theft	9	20.5	7	17.1
Violent	2	4.5	2	4.9
Probation violation	5	11.4	8	19.5
Other	9	20.5	3	7.3
Level of initial rearrest				
Felony	34	77.3	29	70.7
Misdemeanor	10	22.7	12	29.3
Arrested multiple times				
Yes	22	20.8	18	23.7
M	1.9		1.9	
Follow-up period (days)				
M	878.8		895.1	
SD	380.8		378.3	

Multivariate Analyses

Several multivariate models were calculated to determine the significant predictors of recidivism and the odds of failure for both groups under consideration. Regression analyses help pinpoint the effects of each measure relative to other measures included in the model. Three models were created exploring the predictors of arrest, arrest for a drug-related charge, and program completion.

For the model predicting arrest, the value of the model chi-square was 59.57, which was statistically significant. As noted in Table 11.3, the analysis revealed that gender and employment status were significantly related to arrest. In particular, men and those who were unemployed were more likely to be arrested. Noteworthy is the finding that drug of choice was not significantly related to arrest. Consistent with the bivariate analyses, this model suggested that drug of choice among this sample does not substantially influence the odds of being arrested.

The results of the model predicting an arrest for a drug-related offense revealed different findings. The model chi square of 11.1 was not statistically significant at less than the .05 level. As illustrated in Table 11.4, only gender was significantly related to the dependent variable of an arrest for a drug-related charge. Specifically, women were more likely to be arrested for a drug-related charge.

Finally, for the model predicting program completion, the model chi-square of 65.8 was statistically significant. As noted in Table 11.5, the analysis revealed that education, employment status, and time at risk were significantly related to program completion. In particular, those with less than a high school education and those who were unemployed were less likely to complete the drug court program. The variable time at risk was significantly associated with program completion, indicating that those who failed to complete the program were discharged more quickly. This model suggested that drug of choice among this sample does not substantially influence the odds of successful completion.

Discussion

The current study builds on existing research by exploring whether drug of choice predicts

Table 11.3 Logistical Regression Predicting Arrest

Variable	B	SE	Wald	df	Significance
Gender	.759	.340	4.972	1	.026*
Marital status	−.585	.378	2.401	1	.121
Education	−.295	.366	.647	1	.421
Employment	−1.987	.347	32.890	1	.000*
Drug of choice	−.354	.328	1.158	1	.282
Time at risk	.001	.000	3.267	1	.071

*$p < .05$.

Table 11.4 Logistical Regression Predicting Arrest for a Drug-Related Offense

Variable	B	SE	Wald	df	Significance
Gender	−1.127	.520	4.700	1	.030*
Marital status	−1.102	.647	2.903	1	.088
Education	−.187	.541	.119	1	.730
Employment	−.861	.599	2.067	1	.151
Drug of choice	−.522	.490	1.135	1	.287
Time at risk	−.001	.001	2.075	1	.150

*$p < .05$.

Table 11.5 Logistical Regression Predicting Program Completion

Variable	B	SE	Wald	df	Significance
Gender	.520	.436	1.426	1	.232
Marital status	.256	.467	.300	1	.584
Education	−1.119	.501	4.996	1	.025*
Employment	−3.554	.619	32.940	1	.000*
Drug of choice	−.044	.428	.011	1	.918
Time at risk	−.003	.001	9.688	1	.022*

*$p < .05$.

successful outcomes in a community-based drug court. The drug court model is based on the premise that a flexible approach to the treatment of drug-addicted offenders, in combination with increased court involvement and oversight of the offender's behavior, will reduce the likelihood of recidivism. Less clear, however, is whether this approach is reasonable for clients who use particular types of drugs, in this case, meth. To assess this question, two indicators of criminal behavior were assessed: arrest and arrest for a drug-related charge. The recidivism rates between meth users and non-meth users were similar to one another for both arrests (34% vs. 41%) and drug-related arrests (41% vs. 49%).

The study further explored the role of drug of choice in predicting recidivism (e.g., arrest, arrest for a drug-related charge, and program completion) through the multivariate analysis. Consistent with the bivariate findings, in each of the models, drug of choice failed to be a significant predictor of outcome. The findings suggest that the drug court had a similar impact on both meth and nonmeth users. Arguably, the lack of differences between the two groups is an important finding, namely, that meth users did no worse than nonmeth users.

Several other findings warrant consideration. Gender was significant in the bivariate analysis and in two of the three models predicting outcome. Specifically, whereas men were more likely to be arrested overall, we found women were more likely to be meth users and they were more likely to be arrested for a drug-related charge. These findings suggest the need for further inquiry into the impact of drug courts among women generally and among women meth users more specifically (see Hartman, Listwan, and Shaffer, 2007). Finally, previous research has also suggested that women from all social backgrounds may be attracted to meth given the desirable effects of increased energy and weight loss (Rawson et al., 2002). As such, future research should explore whether gender combined with social class and drug of choice influences outcomes in drug courts.

Education and employment were significant predictors of recidivism and program completion. Those who were unemployed were more likely to be arrested and less likely to graduate. Individuals with less than a high school education were more likely to experience difficulty when measured by program completion. The previously mentioned findings indicate that drug courts should pay close attention to the way individuals of different statuses and backgrounds respond to treatment. The implication is that drug courts are not a one-size-fits-all solution to the drug problem. Drug courts need to recognize that drug offenders have varying needs and difficulties, which must be managed to reduce their criminal behavior.

There are several methodological issues that should be considered. First, determination of the drug of choice was self-reported through semistructured interviews with the client. The self-classification of client's drug of choice does not preclude the fact that those who are categorized as nonmeth users may have used meth before. However, the use of self-reported drug of choice as a grouping variable helps ensure that our point of comparison is between those who regularly use meth and those who prefer other substances such as alcohol, marijuana, or heroin.

A second limitation concerns the lack of assessment data. Although the use of drug of choice allows for a distinction to be made between those who regularly use meth and those who do not, we do not have explicit data on the severity of substance use. It is important to note, however, that the groups are similar in terms of the frequency of their drug use and their age of first drug use. Both of these measures provide support for the idea that the groups are likely similar in terms of their level of addiction. However, future research should consider this issue further.

Third, it is also important to acknowledge that our bivariate models have limited statistical power. The low level of statistical power may explain our failure to find a significant difference in recidivism between the two groups despite a 7-point difference in arrest rates and an 8-point difference in drug-related arrest rates. This limitation, however, is tempered in two ways. First, the multivariate analyses, which had sufficient statistical power, failed to detect a significant relationship between drug of choice and recidivism. Second, despite the failure to find a significant relationship, our findings suggest that drug courts should be considered an option for meth users.

A fourth limitation is that, although the drug court provides similar types of treatment as drug courts across the nation, we do not have detailed treatment data. As such, we are unable to report the impact of treatment dosage on outcome. Finally, it is important to note that the drug court described in this study is located in a Northwestern state that is relatively rural in nature. The clients served by this drug court are potentially different from clients served in other drug courts.

Despite these limitations, the current study has several implications. First, although the growing concern surrounding meth use could lead to the development of punitive-based strategies, our findings suggest such a response may not be necessary. Instead, they lend further support to previous research suggesting meth users are responsive to treatment (Hser, Huang, Chou, Teruya, & Anglin, 2003; Rawson et al., 2004). Second, rather than viewing meth offenders as a unique group, our findings concur with previous research (see Bouffard and Richardson, 2007) that finds they may be similar to other types of drug-addicted offenders. As such, they should be treated similarly, with an emphasis on supervision and treatment rather than incarceration. Together, these implications suggest that officials should be treated similarly, with an emphasis on supervision and treatment rather than incarceration. Together, these implications suggest that officials should consider drug courts as an option when discussing policies for how to effectively deal with the "growing meth epidemic."

REFERENCES

Anglin, M. D., & Hser, Y. (1990). Treatment of drug abuse. In M. Tonry & J. Q. Wilson (Eds.), *Drugs and crime* (pp. 393-460). Chicago: University of Chicago Press.

Aos, S., Phipps, P., Bamoski, R., & Lieb, R. (2001). *The comparative costs and benefits of programs to reduce crime.* Olympia: Washington State Institute for Public Policy.

Belenko, S. (2002). The challenges of conducting research in drug treatment court settings. *Substance Use and Misuse, 37,* 1633-1664.

Belenko, S., Mara-Drita, I., & McElroy, J. (1992). Drug tests and the prediction of pretrial misconduct: Findings and policy issues. *Crime & Delinquency, 38,* 557-382.

Belenko, S., Peugh, J., Califano, J. A., Usdansky, M., & Foster, S. B. (1998). Substance abuse and the prison population: A three-year study by Columbia University reveals widespread substance abuse among offender population. *Corrections Today, 60,* 82-89, 154.

Bouffard, J. A., & Richardson, K. A. (2007). The effectiveness of drug court programming for specific kinds of offenders: Methamphetamine and DWI offenders versus other drug-involved offenders. *Criminal Justice Policy Review, 18*(3), 274-293.

Brewster, M. P. (2001). An evaluation of the Chester County (PA) drug court program. *Journal of Drug Issues, 31,* 177-206.

Castro, F. G., Barrington, B. H., Walton, M. A., & Rawson, R. A. (2000). Cocaine and methamphetamine: Differential addiction rates. *Psychology of Addictive Behaviors, 14.* 390-396.

Currie, E. (1998). *Crime and punishment in America.* New York: Owl Books.

Deschenes, B. P., & Greenwood, P. W. (1994). Maricopa County's drug court: An innovative program for first-time drug offenders on probation. *The Justice System Journal, 17,* 99-115.

Dynia, P., & Sung, H. (2000). The safety and effectiveness of diverting felony drug offenders to residential treatment as measured by recidivism. *Criminal Justice Policy Review, 11,* 299-311.

Fagan, J. A. (1994). Do criminal sanctions deter drug crimes? In D. L. MacKenzie & C. D. Uchida (Eds.), *Drugs and crime: Evaluating public policy initiatives* (pp. 89-131). Thousand Oaks, CA: Sage.

Faul, F., & Erdfelder, E. (1992). *GPOWER: A priori, post-hoc, and compromise power analyses for MS-DOS* [computer program]. Bonn University, Department of Psychology.

French, M. T., Zarkin, G. A., Hubbard, R. L. & Valley, R. J. (1993). The effects of time in drug abuse treatment and employment on post-treatment drug use and criminal activity. *American Journal of Drug and Alcohol Abuse, 19,* 19-25.

Goldkamp, J. S. (1999). Challenges for research and innovation: When is a drug court not a drug court? In W. C. Terry (Ed.), *The early drug courts: Case studies in judicial innovation* (pp. 166-177). Thousand Oaks, CA: Sage.

Gottfredson, D. C., Najaka, S. S., & Kearley, B. (2003). Effectiveness of drug treatment courts: Evidence from a randomized trial. *Criminology & Public Policy, 2,* 171-196.

Granfield, R., Eby, C., & Brewster, T. (1998). An examination of the Denver drug court: The impact of a treatment-oriented drug-offender system. *Law & Policy, 20,* 183-202.

Hansell, B. (2006). *The meth epidemic in America; The criminal effects of meth on communities: A 2006 survey on US counties.* Washington, DC: National Association of Counties.

Harrell, A., Roman, J., & Sack, E. (2001). *Drug court services for female offenders, 1996-1999: Evaluation of the Brooklyn Treatment Court* Washington, DC: Urban Institute, Justice Policy Center. Retrieved February 12, 2004, from http://www.urban.org/url.cfm?ID-410356

Hartley, R. E. & Phillips, R. C. (2001). Who graduates from drug courts? Correlates of client success. *American Journal of Criminal Justice, 26,* 107-119.

Hartman, J. L., Listwan, S. J., and Shaffer, D. K. (2007). Methamphetamine users in a community based drug court: Does gender matter? *Journal of Offender Rehabilitation, 45*(3/4), 109-130.

Herz, D. C. (2000), *Drugs in the heartland: Methamphetamine use in rural Nebraska.* Washington, DC: National Institute of Justice.

Hser, Y., Huang, D., Chou, C., Teruya, C., & Anglin, M. D. (2003). Longitudinal patterns of treatment utilization and outcomes among methamphetamine abusers: A growth curve modeling approach. *Journal of Drug Issues, 33,* 921 -938.

Huddleston, C. W. (2005). *Drug courts: An effective strategy for communities facing methamphetamine.* Alexandria, VA: National Drug Court Institute.

Jensen, E., & Mosher, C. (2006). Adult drug courts: Emergence, growth, outcome evaluations, and the need for a continuum of care. *Idaho Law Review. 42,* 443-470.

Listwan, S. J., Sundt, J., Holsinger, A. M., & Latessa, E. J. (2003). The effect of drug court programming on recidivism: The Cincinnati experience. *Crime & Delinquency, 49,* 389-411.

Loman, L. A. (2004). *A cost-benefit analysis of the St. Louis City Adult Felony Drug Court.* St. Louis, MO: Institute of Applied Research. Retrieved August 2, 2005, from http://www.iarstl.org/papers/SLFDCcostbenefit.pdf

Longshore, D., Turner, S., Wenzel, S., Morral, A., Harrell, A., McBride, D., et al. (2001). Drug courts: A conceptual framework. *Journal of Drug Issues, 31,* 7-26.

Lowenkamp, C. T., Holsinger, A. M.. & Latessa, E. J. (2005, Fall). Are drug courts effective: A meta-analytic review. *Journal of Community Corrections,* 5-10, 28.

Martinez, A. I., & Eisenberg, M. (2003). *Initial process and outcome evaluation of drug courts in Texas.* Austin, TX: Criminal Justice Policy Council.

Miethe, T. D., Lu, H., & Reese, E. (2000). Reintegrative shaming and recidivism risks in drug court: Explanations for some unexpected findings. *Crime & Delinquency, 46,* 522-541.

Miller, J. M., & Shutt, J. E. (2001). Considering the need for empirically grounded drug court screening mechanisms. *Journal of Drug Issues, 31,* 91-106.

National Association of Drug Court Professionals, Drug Court Standards Committee. (1997). *Defining drug courts: The key components.* Washington. DC: U.S. Department of Justice, Office of Justice Programs, Drug Courts Program Office.

Office of Justice Programs Drug Court Clearinghouse and Technical Assistance Project. (2004). *Summary of drug court activity by state and country.* Retrieved August 22, 2006, from http://spa.american.edu/justice/publications/drgchart2k.pdf#search=%22ojp%20drug%20court%20clearing%20house%22.

Peter, R. R. Haas, A. L., & Murrin, M. R. (1999). Predictors of retention and arrest in drug courts. *National Drug Court Institute Review, 2*, 33-60.

Peters, R., & Murrin, M. R. (2000). Effectiveness of treatment-based drug courts in reducing criminal recidivism. *Criminal Justice and Behavior, 27*, 72-96.

Prendergast, M., Anglin, M. D., & Wellisch, J. (1995). Up to speed: Treatment for drug-abusing offenders under community supervision. *Federal Probation, 59*, 66-75.

Rawson, R. A., Anglin, M. D., & Ling, W. (2002). Will the methamphetamine problem go away? *Journal of Addictive Diseases, 21*, 5-19.

Rawson, R. A., Marinelli-Casey, P., Anglin, M. D., Dickow, A., Frazier, V., Gallagher, C. et al. (2004). A multi-site comparison of psychosocial approaches for the treatment of methamphetamine dependence. *Addiction, 99*, 708-717.

Rempel, M., Fox-Kralstein, D., Cissner, A., Cohen, R.. Labriola, M., Farole, D., et al. (2003). *The New York State Adult Drug Court evaluation: Policies, participants and impacts.* Technical Report, Center for Court Innovation.

Schiff, M., & Terry, W. C, III. (1997). Predicting graduation from Broward County's dedicated drug treatment county. *Justice Systems Journal, 19*, 291-310.

Shaffer, D. K. (2006). Reconsidering drug court effectiveness: A meta-analytic review (Doctoral dissertation, University of Cincinnati, 2006). *Dissertation Abstracts International, 67*, 09A (AAT No. 3231113).

Shaffer, D. K., Listwan, S. J., Latessa, E. J., & Lowenkamp, C. T. (2007). The drug court phenomenon: Findings from Ohio. *Drug Court Review, 6*, 33-66.

Stoops, W. W, Tinchill, M. S., Maleyoke-Scrivner, A., & Leukefold, C. (2005). Methamphetamine use in non-urban and urban drug court clients. *International Journal of Offender Therapy and Comparative Criminology. 49*, 260-276.

Substance Abuse and Mental Health Services Administration, Office of Applied Statistics. (2002). *Emergency department trends from the Drug Abuse Warning Network, final estimates 1994-2001* (DHHS Publication No. SMA 02-3635). Rockville, MD: Author.

Substance Abuse and Mental Health Services Administration, Office of Applied Statistics. (2004). *Treatment Episode Data Set (TEDS): 1992-2002. National admissions to substance abuse treatment services* (DHHS Publication No. SMA 04-3965). Rockville, MD: Author.

Truitt, L., Rhodes, W. M., Hoffmann, N. G., Seeherman, A. M., Jalbert, S. K., Kane, M., et al. (2002). *Evaluating treatment drug courts in Kansas City, Missouri and Pensacola, Florida: Executive summary.* Technical Report, Abt Associates. Retrieved September 7, 2005, from http://www.abtassociates com/reports/es-eval_treatment.pdf.

Van Stelle, K. R., Mauser, E., & Moberg, P. D. (1994). Recidivism to the criminal justice system of substance abusing offenders diverted into treatment. *Crime and Delinquency, 40*, 175-196.

Vito, G., & Tewksbury, R. A. (1998). The impact of treatment; The Jefferson County (Kentucky) drug court program. *Federal Probation, 62*, 46-52.

Walker, S. (1994). *Sense and nonsense about crime and drugs: A policy guide* (3rd ed.). Belmont, CA: Wadsworth.

Weisheit, R. A., & Fuller, J. (2004). Methamphetamines in the heartland: A review and initial exploration. *Journal of Crime and Justice, 27*, 131-151.

Wilson, D. B., Mitchell, O., & MacKenzie, D. L. (2002, November). *A systematic review of drug court effects on recidivism.* Paper presented at the annual meeting of the American Society of Criminology, Chicago.

Wolfe, E., Guydish, J., & Termondi, J. (2002). A drug court outcome evaluation comparing arrests in a two year follow-up period. *Journal of Drug Issues, 32*, 1155-1172.

Wright, D., & Sathe, N. (2006). *State estimates of substance use from the 2003-2004 National Surveys on Drug Use and Health* (DHHS Publication No. SMA 06-4142, NSDUH Series H-29). Rockville. MD: Substance Abuse and Mental Health Services Administration, Office of Applied Statistics.

Yeh. B. T., & Doyle, C. (2005). *USA Patriot Improvement and Reauthorization Act of 2005: A brief look.* Library of Congress. Congressional Research Service (RS22348).

DISCUSSION QUESTIONS

1. Why do these authors believe meth users may be a concern if being treated in a community setting? How did meth and meth users become such a great concern?

2. Who are the participants in this experiment? How were they selected? How did this drug court naturally produce an environment for conducting an experiment?

3. What does this drug court program consist of? What services does the drug court provide in attempt to reduce drug dependence and the likelihood of rearrest?

4. Do the authors list any limitations of this research? Do they have data on whether the program was being implemented correctly?

5. Were these subjects randomly assigned to treatment and control groups? Why or why not? What do these authors cite as evidence that the treatment and control groups (meth and nonmeth) are similar?

6. What was the main independent variable of interest to these researchers?

7. How was success, or rather failure, conceptualized in this study? Was drug court completion included in the authors' conceptualization? What about rearrest?

8. Which variables were significant (< 0.05) in predicting any arrest? A drug arrest? Program completion? What does it mean that drug of choice was not significant for an arrest, a drug arrest, or program completion?

9. How do the authors explain the gender, education, and employment effects?

10. What are some of the listed limitations, and what do the authors' findings mean for treating drug users with different drugs of choice?

RESEARCH READING

Braga and colleagues conducted an evaluation of a problem-oriented policing program in Boston called Operation Ceasefire. This program aimed to reduce youth gun violence and homicide through a deterrence strategy, which focused on a particular group of youth responsible for a great deal of the youth homicide in Boston. Their evaluation reveals that this program was effective at reducing youth homicide as well as other crime involving guns. The authors discuss the specifics of this program, which they believe made it successful, and offer advice for other communities in implementing successful problem-oriented policing programs that fit their needs.

Source: Braga, A., Kennedy, D., Waring, E., & Morrison Piehl, A. (2001). Problem-oriented policing, deterrence, and youth violence: An evaluation of Boston's Operation Ceasefire. *Journal of Research in Crime and Delinquency, 38,* 195–225. Copyright © 2001 Sage Publications.

PROBLEM-ORIENTED POLICING, DETERRENCE, AND YOUTH VIOLENCE

An Evaluation of Boston's Operation Ceasefire

Anthony A. Braga, David M. Kennedy, Elin J. Waring, and Anne Morrison Piehl

Abstract: Operation Ceasefire is a problem-oriented policing intervention aimed at reducing youth homicide and youth firearms violence in Boston. It represented an innovative partnership between researchers and practitioners to assess the city's youth homicide problem and implement an intervention designed to have a substantial near-term impact on the problem. Operation Ceasefire was based on the "pulling levers" deterrence strategy that focused criminal justice attention on a small number of chronically offending gang-involved youth responsible for much of Boston's youth homicide problem. Our impact evaluation suggests that the Ceasefire intervention was associated with significant reductions in youth homicide victimization, shots-fired calls for service, and gun assault incidents in Boston. A comparative analysis of youth homicide trends in Boston relative to youth homicide trends in other major U. S. and New England cities also supports a unique program effect associated with the Ceasefire intervention.

INTRODUCTION

Although overall homicide rates in the United States declined between the 1980s and 1990s, youth homicide rates, particularly incidents involving firearms, increased dramatically. Between 1984 and 1994, juvenile (younger than 18) homicide victimizations committed with handguns increased by 418 percent, and juvenile homicide victimizations committed with other guns increased 125 percent (Fox 1996). During this time period, adolescents (ages 14 to 17) as a group had the largest proportional increase in homicide commission and victimization, but young adults (ages 18 to 24) had the largest absolute increase in numbers, and there was a good deal of crossfire between the two age groups (Cook and Laub 1998). All of the increase in youth homicide was in gun homicides (Cook and Laub 1998). For many cities, the bulk of this dramatic increase in youth homicide occurred in the late 1980s and early 1990s. In Boston, youth homicide (ages 24 and younger) increased more than three-fold—from 22 victims in 1987 to 73 victims in 1990 (see Figure 11.1). Youth homicide remained high even after the peak of the epidemic; Boston averaged about 44 youth homicides per year between 1991 and 1995.

At the same time that the United States was experiencing this sudden increase in youth violence, the capacity of police departments to design and implement creative new operational strategies also increased through the advent of "community" and "problem-oriented" policing (Goldstein 1990; Sparrow, Moore, and Kennedy 1990). In Boston, an interagency problem-solving intervention, based in part on a tight link between research, the design of interventions, and operations, has shown much promise in reducing youth homicide (Kennedy, Braga, and Piehl 1997; Kennedy, Piehl, and Braga 1996). Nationally, without the support of a formal evaluation, the Boston program has been hailed as an unprecedented success (see, e.g., Butterfield 1996; Witkin 1997). This article describes the results of a National Institute of Justice–funded evaluation of Boston's youth homicide reduction initiative. Our analyses of Boston's youth homicide prevention program suggests that it was a very effective intervention; not only was the intervention associated with a significant reduction in youth homicide victimization, it also was associated with significant reductions in shots-fired calls for service and gun assault incidents.

Figure 11.1 Boston Homicide Victims Ages 24 and Younger

THE BOSTON GUN PROJECT AND THE OPERATION CEASEFIRE INTERVENTION

Problem-oriented policing holds great promise for creating a strong local response to youth homicide problems. Problem-oriented policing works to identify why things are going wrong and to frame responses using a wide variety of often untraditional approaches (Goldstein 1979). Using a basic iterative approach of problem identification, analysis, response, evaluation, and adjustment of the response, problem-oriented policing has been effective against a wide variety of crime, fear, and other concerns (Braga, Weisburd et al. 1999; Eck and Spelman 1987; Goldstein 1990). This adaptable and dynamic analytic approach provides an appropriate framework to uncover the complex mechanisms at play in youth homicide and develop tailor-made interventions to reduce youth homicide victimization.

The Boston Gun Project is a problem-oriented policing initiative aimed at reducing homicide victimization among young people in Boston. *Youth* was initially defined as "age 21 and under" and, as the project developed, "age 24 and under." Sponsored by the National Institute of Justice, the project was designed to proceed by (1) assembling an interagency working group of largely line-level criminal justice and other practitioners; (2) applying quantitative and qualitative research techniques to create an assessment of the nature of, and dynamics driving, youth violence in Boston; (3) developing an intervention designed to have a substantial, near-term impact on youth homicide; (4) implementing and adapting the intervention; and (5) evaluating the intervention's impact. The project began in early 1995 and implemented what is now known as the Operation Ceasefire intervention beginning in the late spring of 1996.

Core participating agencies, as defined by regular participation in the Boston Gun Project Working Group over the duration of the project, included the Boston Police Department; the Massachusetts departments of probation and parole; the office of the Suffolk County District Attorney; the office of the U.S. Attorney; the Bureau of Alcohol, Tobacco, and Firearms; the Massachusetts Department of Youth Services (juvenile corrections); Boston School Police; and gang outreach and prevention "streetworkers" attached to the Boston Community Centers program. Other important participants, either as regular partners later in the process or episodically, have included the Ten Point Coalition of activist Black clergy, the Drug Enforcement Administration, the Massachusetts State Police, and the office of the Massachusetts Attorney General.

Project research showed that firearms associated with youth, especially with gang youth, tended to be semiautomatic pistols, often ones that were quite new and apparently recently diverted from retail (Kennedy et al. 1996; Kennedy et al. 1997). Many of these guns were first sold at retail in Massachusetts, and others were smuggled in from out of state. Project research also showed that the problem of youth homicide was concentrated among a small number of chronically offending gang-involved youth. Only about 1,300 gang members—less that 1 percent of their age group citywide—in about 61 gangs were responsible for at least 60 percent of all youth homicides in the city. These gangs were well known to the authorities and streetworkers; gang members were also often well known and tended to have extensive criminal records (Kennedy et al. 1996). Chronic disputes, or "beefs," among gangs appeared to be the most significant driver of gang violence (Braga, Piehl, and Kennedy 1999).

The research findings were discussed and analyzed within the working-group problem-solving process and were instrumental in the development of an operational strategy. The research findings and the working-group process thus led to the Operation Ceasefire intervention (for a complete discussion of the program development and implementation process, see Kennedy, Braga, and Piehl 1999). Operation Ceasefire included two main elements: (1) a direct law-enforcement attack on illicit firearms traffickers supplying youth with guns and (2) an attempt to generate a strong deterrent to gang violence. The working group framed a set of activities intended to systematically address the patterns of firearms trafficking identified by the research. These included the following:

- Expanding the focus of local, state, and federal authorities to include *intrastate* trafficking in Massachusetts-sourced guns, in addition to interstate trafficking.
- Focusing enforcement attention on traffickers of those makes and calibers of guns most used by gang members.
- Focusing enforcement attention on traffickers of those guns showing short time to crime and thus most likely to have been trafficked. The Boston Field Division of ATF set up an in-house tracking system that flagged guns whose traces showed an 18-month or shorter time to crime.
- Focusing enforcement attention on traffickers of guns used by the city's most violent gangs.
- Attempting restoration of obliterated serial numbers and subsequent trafficking investigations based on those restorations.
- Supporting these enforcement priorities through analysis of crime gun traces generated by the Boston Police Department's comprehensive tracing of crime guns and by developing leads through systematic debriefing of, especially, arrestees involved with gangs and/or involved in violent crime.

The "pulling levers" strategy, as the second element came to be known by working-group members, involved deterring violent behavior by chronic gang offenders by reaching out directly to gangs, saying explicitly that violence would no longer be tolerated, and backing that message by "pulling every lever" legally available when violence occurred (Kennedy 1997, 1998). Simultaneously, streetworkers, probation and parole officers, and later churches and other community groups offered gang members services and other kinds of help. The Ceasefire working group delivered this message in formal meetings with gang members, through individual police and probation contacts with gang members, through meetings with inmates of secure juvenile facilities in the city, and through gang outreach workers. The deterrence message was not a deal with gang members to stop violence. Rather, it was a promise to gang members that violent behavior would evoke an immediate and intense response. If gangs committed other crimes but refrained from violence, the normal workings of police, prosecutors, and the rest of the criminal justice system dealt with these matters. But if gang members hurt people, the working group focused its enforcement actions on them.

When gang violence occurred, the Ceasefire agencies addressed the violent group or groups involved, drawing from a menu of all possible legal levers. The chronic involvement of gang members in a wide variety of offenses made them, and the gangs they formed, vulnerable to a coordinated criminal justice response. The authorities could disrupt street drug activity, focus police attention on low-level street crimes such as trespassing and public drinking, serve outstanding warrants, cultivate confidential informants for medium- and long-term investigations of gang activities, deliver strict probation and parole enforcement, seize drug proceeds and other assets, ensure stiffer plea bargains and sterner prosecutorial attention, request stronger bail terms (and enforce them), and focus potentially severe federal investigative and prosecutorial attention on, for example, gang-related drug activity. The multitude of agencies involved in the working group assessed each gang that behaved violently and subjected them to such crackdowns. These operations were customized to the particular individuals and characteristics of the gang in question and could range from probation curfew checks to DEA investigations.

The Ceasefire crackdowns were not designed to eliminate gangs or stop every

aspect of gang activity but to control and deter serious violence. To do this, the working group explained its actions against targeted gangs to other gangs, as in "this gang did violence, we responded with the following actions, and here is how to prevent anything similar from happening to you." The ongoing working-group process regularly watched the city for outbreaks of gang violence and framed any necessary responses in accord with the Ceasefire strategy. As the strategy unfolded, the working group continued communication with gangs and gang members to convey its determination to stop violence, explain its actions to the target population, and maximize both voluntary compliance and the strategy's deterrent power.

A central hypothesis within the working group was the idea that a meaningful period of substantially reduced youth violence might serve as a "firebreak" and result in a relatively long-lasting reduction in future youth violence (Kennedy et al. 1996). The idea was that youth violence in Boston had become a self-sustaining cycle among a relatively small number of youth, with objectively high levels of risk leading to nominally self-protective behavior such as gun acquisition and use, gang formation, tough street behavior, and the like; behavior that then became an additional input into the cycle of violence (Kennedy et al. 1996). If this cycle could be interrupted, a new equilibrium at a lower level of risk and violence might be established, perhaps without the need for continued high levels of either deterrent or facilitative intervention.

IMPACT EVALUATION

Like most evaluations of crime prevention programs (Ekblom and Pease 1995), our evaluation design departs from the desirable randomized controlled experimental approach. The Operation Ceasefire strategy was aimed at all areas of the city with a serious youth violence problem. There were no control areas (or control gangs) set aside within the city because of the following: (1) The aim was to do something about serious youth violence wherever it presented itself in the city, (2) the target of the intervention was defined as the self-sustaining cycle of violence in which all gangs were caught up and to which all gangs contributed, and (3) the communications strategy was explicitly intended to affect the behavior of gangs and individuals not directly subjected to enforcement attention (Kennedy et al., 1996). Therefore, it was not possible to compare areas and groups affected by the strategy to similar areas and groups not affected. Our analysis of impacts within Boston associated with the Ceasefire intervention follows a basic one-group time-series design (Campbell and Stanley 1966; Cook and Campbell 1979); we also use a nonrandomized quasi-experiment to compare youth homicide trends in Boston to youth homicide trends in other large U.S. cities (Cook and Campbell 1979; Rossi and Freeman 1993).

Within-Boston Outcome Measures: Homicide and Gun Violence

The key outcome variable in our assessment of the impact of the Ceasefire intervention was the monthly number of homicide victims ages 24 and younger. The Ceasefire intervention mostly targets violence arising from gang dynamics; our earlier research suggests that most gang members in Boston are ages 24 and younger (Kennedy et al., 1996; Kennedy et al., 1997). Therefore, our impact evaluation focuses on the number of youthful homicide victims in this age group. The homicide data used in these analyses were provided by the Boston Police Department's Office of Research and Analysis. The youth homicide impact evaluation examined the monthly counts of youth homicides in Boston between January 1, 1991, and May 31, 1998; the preintervention period included the relatively stable but still historically high postepidemic years of 1991 to 1995 (see Figure 11.1).

Beyond preventing youth homicides, the Ceasefire intervention was also designed to reduce other forms of nonfatal serious violence.

As such, our evaluation also examines monthly counts of city wide shots-fired citizen calls for service data and citywide official gun assault incident report data. These data are available for a slightly shorter time period than our homicide data set due to lags in the Boston Police Department's data collection and preparation procedures. These data are examined for the January 1, 1991, through December 31, 1997, time period. The computerized Boston Police Department incident data have what is, for our purposes, an important shortcoming—the records do not capture the age of the victim (this is, of course, also true for shots-fired calls for service). To assess the effects of the intervention on gun assaults in specific age groups, we collected information on the age of the victim from hard copies of gun assault incident reports for the study time period. Because the collection and coding of this information was a time-consuming task, we chose to collect these data for one high-activity police district. District B-2 covers most of Boston's Roxbury neighborhood and has a very dense concentration of gangs; 29 of 61 identified gangs (47.5 percent) had turf in B-2 (Kennedy et al. 1997). Furthermore, there were 217 homicide victims ages 24 and younger in Boston between 1991 and 1995; a third of these victims were killed in B-2 (71 of 217, 32.7 percent).

Simple Pre/Post Comparisons

In these analyses, we selected May 15, 1996, the date of the first direct communications with Boston gangs, as the date Ceasefire was implemented because all elements of the strategy-the focus on gun trafficking, a special interagency response to gang violence, and the communications campaign with gangs were in place as of that date. No other rival programs were implemented in Boston even roughly close to this time period (Piehl, Kennedy, and Braga 2000). The well-known large reduction in yearly Boston youth homicide numbers certainly suggests that something noteworthy happened after Operation Ceasefire was implemented in mid-1996. As discussed earlier, Boston averaged 44 youth homicides per year between 1991 and 1995. In 1996, the number of Boston youth homicides decreased to 26 and then further decreased to 15 youth homicides in 1997. It is noteworthy that the yearly total of youth homicides in 1997—the first full calendar year of data after the implementation of Operation Ceasefire—represents the smallest number of youth homicides in Boston since 1976. This suggests that it was unlikely that the youth homicide reduction was due to a regression to the mean number of yearly youth homicides of the pre-youth homicide epidemic years. Figure 11.2 presents the monthly counts of youth homicides in Boston during the study time period. The time series shows a 63 percent reduction in the mean monthly number of youth homicide victims

from a pretest mean of 3.5 youth homicides per month to a posttest mean of 1.3 youth homicides per month. This simple analysis suggests that Operation Ceasefire was associated with a large reduction in youth homicides in Boston (see also Piehl et al. 2000).

Youth Homicide Trends
in Boston Relative to Youth
Homicide Trends in Other Cities

Although the within-Boston analyses support that a large reduction in youth homicide and gun violence was associated with the Ceasefire intervention, it is necessary to distinguish youth homicide trends in Boston from national trends in youth homicide. Many major cities in the United States have enjoyed noteworthy reductions in homicide

Figure 11.2   Monthly Counts of Youth Homicides in Boston

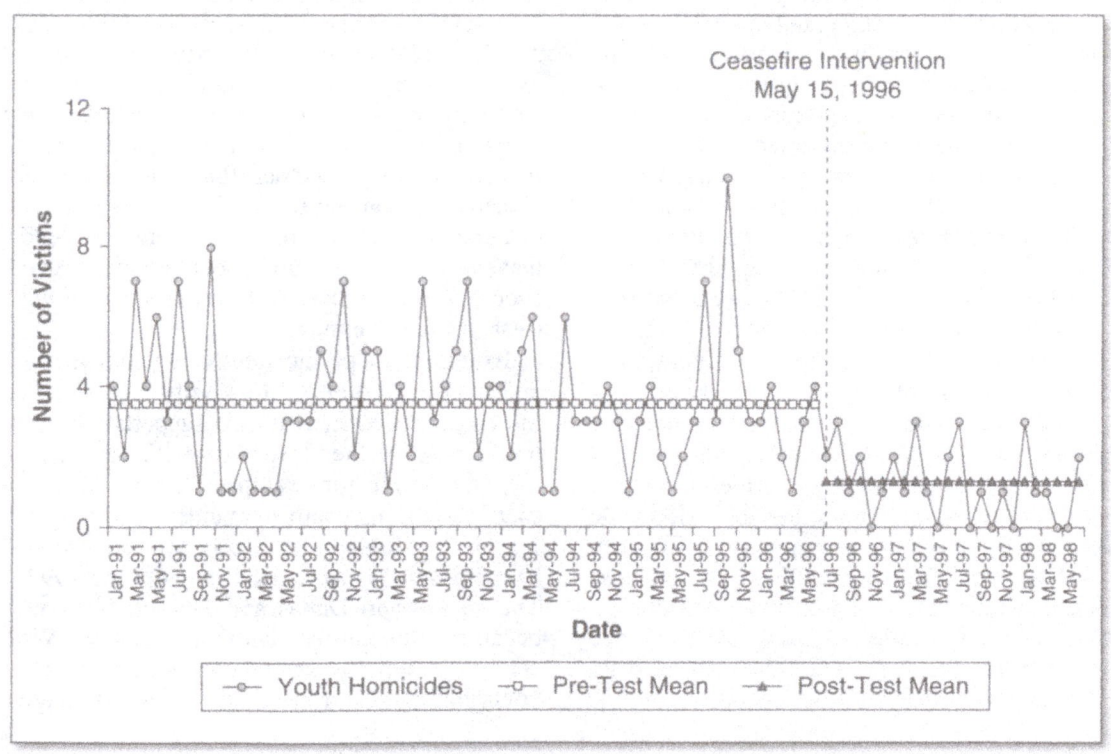

and nonfatal serious violence (see, e.g., Blumstein and Rosenfeld 1998); the reductions in other cities could be associated with a number of complex and tightly interwoven endogenous or exogenous factors such as positive changes in the national economy, shifts in the age distribution of offending populations, or the stabilization of urban drug markets. Moreover, many cities, most notably New York (Kelling and Bratton 1998), have implemented crime prevention interventions that have been credited with substantial reductions in violence. The following analyses provide insight on whether Boston's reduction in youth homicide was part of national youth homicide trends and whether the program impact associated with the Ceasefire intervention was distinct in magnitude from other youth homicide reductions occurring at the same time as the Ceasefire intervention. Furthermore, because other cities were also taking intervention action to reduce youth homicide, these analyses will suggest whether any program impact in Boston was larger than, or distinct from, any other deliberate interventions implemented during the same time period. A priori, we predicted that Boston would experience a significant reduction in monthly youth homicide counts associated with the timing of the Ceasefire intervention.

To compare youth homicide trends in Boston to national youth homicide trends, we analyzed youth homicide data for the largest cities in the United States. By rank ordering U.S. Census population data in 1990 and 1996, we selected 41 of the most populous cities in the US. Boston was ranked 20th in population size among these cities in both 1990 and 1996 with an average population of about 565,000. We then obtained monthly counts of the number of homicide victims ages 24 and younger for the 41 comparison cities from Supplementary Homicide Report (SHR) data for the time period of January 1991 through December 1997. After a close examination of these data, 2 cities (Washington, D.C. and New Orleans) were excluded due to extensive missing data. This left us with 39 major U.S. cities in the comparison group.

Recognizing that youth homicide trends can vary greatly across 39 major U.S. cities, we built a model that would maximize our ability to control for the various sources of error in the time series of each city.

Table 11.6 presents the results of the Poisson regressions for the 39 comparison cities plus Boston. Four cities—Boston, Jacksonville, Dallas, and Virginia Beach—had differences in youth homicides at the time of the intervention that were statistically significant at the .05 level; Boston had the largest estimated effect. Because our cross-city analysis involved 40 statistical tests, the expected number of effects significant at the .05 level is two. Thus, we need to be especially sensitive to the possibility of Type II error in our results. We would expect that 14 percent of the time we would find four or more statistically significant effects by chance alone. However, these cities would be a randomly selected set; we made an a priori prediction that Boston would have a significant reduction. The probability of finding four or more successes one of which is Boston (or any specific city) by chance alone is .0155. The inter-city results, therefore, fit what would be expected if Boston had a change that was not due to chance alone. However, the statistical analysis cannot provide a basis for determining whether this was the case. Nonetheless, on the basis of these results, we can conclude that there was no national trend that explains the change in youth homicide that occurred in Boston at the time of the Operation Ceasefire intervention.

Examination of the trends in youth homicides in the other cities with significant intervention coefficients also supports the distinctiveness of the Boston case (Figure 11.3). Virginia Beach, for example, shows a significant increase in youth homicides occurring in June 1996, although the yearly counts of youth homicides were stable between 1995 and 1997. The declines in Dallas and Jacksonville both began months earlier than that in Boston. We are unaware of any known connection between youth homicides in these four cities. Although based on exploratory analysis, the presence of these differences undermines the argument that the changes in Boston reflect trends in other major U.S. cities.

Of course, other cities may have experienced a sudden significant decrease in youth homicide either before or after Boston experienced its significant decrease in youth homicide, and these might be missed by the single-time-period analysis presented in Table 11.6. Therefore, we conducted an exploratory analysis to identify abrupt significant youth homicide reductions in the comparison cities occurring in other months during the time series. We performed our main analysis of youth homicides in 39 major U.S. cities with a varying intervention point from month 12 to month 72 in the time series. Five out of 39 cities experienced a sudden significant youth homicide reduction at some point in the time series. These cities were Philadelphia; Tucson, Arizona; Dallas, Texas; Los Angeles; and New York City. A sharp and sustained break will lead to significant before and after differences for several time periods around the intervention. This is because the analyses are, in essence, comparisons of two means adjusted for other factors (Piehl et al. 1999). For this reason, significant breakpoints in Boston are found in months 65 through 67 rather than just in month 66 (the June 1996 start date). Results in the 5 cities with significant breaks indicate that each had a series of successive significant breaks.

Although five cities experienced large reductions in youth homicide at some point within the time series, it is difficult to make a direct link between youth homicide trends in the five cities and Boston, as the yearly trends across cities look different. Philadelphia experienced significant reductions in monthly counts of youth homicides in months 36 (December 1993) through 38 (February 1994), 30 months before the implementation of Operation Ceasefire (Figure 11.4). This was followed by a steady increase in youth homicide between 1994 and 1997 (Figure 11.4). Tucson experienced significant decreases in monthly youth homicide counts between

month 59 (November 1995) and month 60 (December 1995). This sudden decrease was followed by an increase in Tucson youth homicides in 1997 (Figure 11.4). Dallas experienced a significant decrease in the monthly count of youth homicides between month 63 (March 1996) and month 65 (May 1996). Although this significant reduction coincides with the implementation of Operation Ceasefire, youth homicide in Dallas declined almost linearly between 1991 and 1997 (Figure 11.4).

Los Angeles experienced a significant reduction in monthly counts of youth homicides during months 30 and 31 (June and July 1993). New York City experienced sudden significant reductions in monthly counts of youth homicides during months 39 and 40 (March and April 1994) and also during months 44 and 45 (August and September 1994). As in Dallas, youth homicide trends in Los Angeles and New York show steep declines during the mid 1990s (see Figure 11.5). Superficially, the steady declines in New York, Los Angeles, and Dallas seem different from the trajectory of youth homicide in Boston. Overall, the results from this analysis do not support the idea that changes in Boston either followed or trailed national changes or changes in other major cities.

We also used this technique to examine whether Boston's youth homicide reduction could have been influenced by decreases in regional youth homicide trends. We obtained monthly counts of the number of homicide victims ages 24 and younger for 29 large New England cities from SHR data for the time period of January 1991 through December 1997. The majority of the New England cities experienced very small numbers of youth homicides and did not exhibit any discernable trends. The youth homicide time series of 11 (37.9 percent of 29) New England cities were analyzed statistically. When the main analyses were run with the varying intervention point, none experienced a significant reduction in the monthly count of youth homicides.

Careful within-city studies are necessary to unravel youth homicide trends in these cities.

Table 11.6 Results of the Poisson Regressions for 39 Comparison Cities Plus Boston

City	Estimate	Standard Error	df	t	Prob (t)	AR(1)
Albuquerque, New Mexico	−0.1195	0.5783	24.18	−0.21	0.8380	0.1751
Atlanta, Georgia	−0.336	0.3635	22.42	−0.09	0.9273	0.1973
Austin, Texas	−0.5207	0.4801	28.89	−1.08	0.2870	−0.0780
Baltimore, Maryland	0.2505	0.1974	26.03	1.27	0.2155	0.0134
Boston, Massachusetts	−1.1351	0.3771	25.98	−3.01	0.00057*	−0.0009
Charlotte, North Carolina	0.2948	0.4321	27.30	0.68	0.5009	0.0197
Chicago, Illinois	0.1764	0.1421	24.03	1.24	0.2264	0.2671
Cleveland, Ohio	0.2811	0.3947	21.94	0.71	0.4839	0.0877
Columbus, Ohio	0.3246	0.3478	21.83	0.93	0.3610	0.0470
Dallas, Texas	−0.5254	0.1786	28.79	−2.94	0.0064*	−0.1270
Denver, Colorado	−0.6698	0.4514	24.55	−1.48	0.1505	0.0576
Detroit, Michigan	0.2675	0.1873	21.57	1.43	0.1677	0.2207
El Paso, Texas	−0.1672	0.6274	28.03	−0.27	0.7918	−0.0866
Fort Worth, Texas	0.1385	0.4273	24.45	0.32	0.7485	0.1756
Fresno, California	0.0347	0.4260	25.14	0.08	0.9357	0.1952
Honolulu, Hawaii	−0.0443	0.6515	27.94	−0.07	0.9463	−0.0447
Houston, Texas	−0.3069	0.1972	24.97	−1.56	0.1322	−0.0108
Indianapolis, Indiana	−0.0577	0.3267	27.65	−0.18	0.8611	−0.0313
Jacksonville, Florida	−0.5670	0.2693	29.28	−2.11	0.0439*	−0.1637
Kansas City, Missouri	−0.5239	0.3483	24.75	−1.50	0.1452	0.0106
Los Angeles, California	−0.2324	0.1421	26.09	−1.64	0.1140	−0.0156
Long Beach, California	−0.3046	0.4892	24.59	−0.62	0.5393	0.1625
Memphis, Tennessee	−0.0328	0.3147	23.78	−0.10	0.9178	0.1029
Milwaukee, Wisconsin	−0.3408	0.2659	28.52	−1.28	0.2102	−0.1194
Nashville, Tennessee	0.1387	0.2936	31.11	0.47	0.6400	−0.1854
New York, New York	0.1583	0.1442	23.63	1.10	0.2833	0.1144
Oakland, California	−0.1766	0.3877	23.11	−0.46	0.6530	0.1336
Oklahoma City, Oklahoma	0.2657	0.6092	28.94	0.44	0.6659	−0.0299
Philadelphia, Pennsylvania	0.3227	0.1659	25.19	1.95	0.0629	0.0177

City	Estimate	Standard Error	df	t	Prob (t)	AR(1)
Phoenix, Arizona	−0.4195	0.2500	26.31	−1.68	0.1053	0.0207
Portland, Oregon	−0.3787	0.5133	30.06	−0.74	0.4663	0.0107
San Antonio, Texas	−0.2199	0.2907	30.09	−0.76	0.4553	−0.1754
San Diego, California	0.2118	0.5302	22.54	0.40	0.6933	0.1404
San Francisco, California	0.1256	0.4518	27.36	0.28	0.7831	0.0357
San Jose, California	−0.2445	0.6483	24.19	−0.38	0.7094	0.2625
Seattle, Washington	0.4182	0.6829	22.71	0.61	0.5463	0.1630
St. Louis, Missouri	−0.5068	0.2925	24.22	−1.73	0.0959	0.0772
Tucson, Arizona	−0.1741	0.4770	25.63	−0.37	0.7180	0.0143
Tulsa, Oklahoma	0.0213	0.6573	28.78	0.03	0.9744	0.1115
Virginia Beach, Virginia	1.2287	0.5968	29.43	2.06	0.0485*	−0.1935

Note: Deviance = 3613.23; dispersion parameter = 0.8616.

*p < .05.

Figure 11.3   Youth Homicide in Boston, Dallas, Jacksonville, and Virginia Beach, 1991 to 1997 (annual)

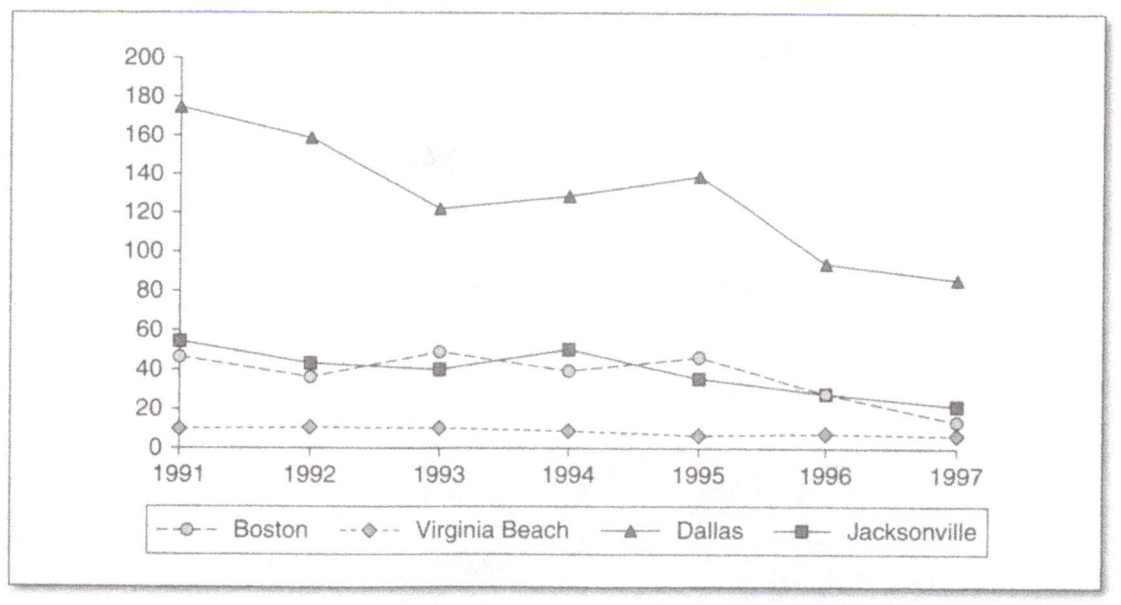

Figure 11.4 Youth Homicide in Boston, Dallas, Tucson, and Philadelphia, 1991 to 1997 (annual)

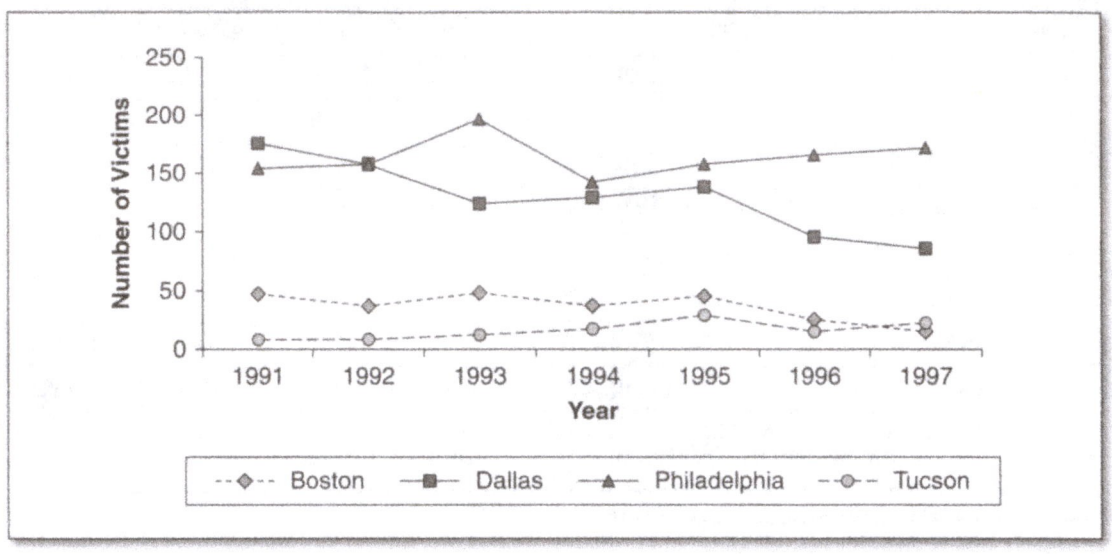

Figure 11.5 Youth Homicide in Boston, Los Angeles, and New York City, 1991 to 1997 (annual)

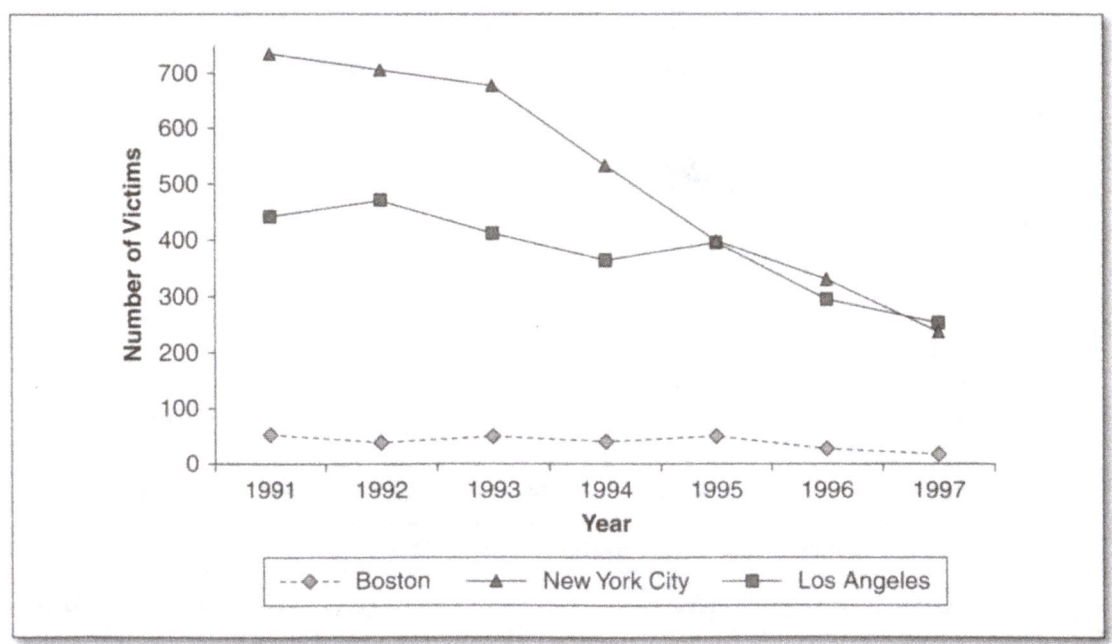

Without the benefit of a detailed analysis, it is difficult to know whether there is some broad link between the youth homicide trajectories in such diverse cities. Although some cities may have experienced a similar decrease, these analyses suggest that Boston's significant youth homicide reduction associated with Operation Ceasefire was distinct when compared to youth homicide trends in most major U.S. and New England cities.

The Role of Preventing Illegal Firearms Trafficking

Finally, there is the question of what degree, if any, of violence reduction in Boston should be attributed to the prevention of illegal firearms trafficking. Trafficking was, of course, one of the principal original foci of the Gun Project and attention to trafficking one of Operation Ceasefire's two fundamental planks. Evaluating the particular contribution of supply-side interventions in Boston is, we believe, essentially impossible. Antitrafficking efforts were implemented at the same time as violence deterrence efforts, and both might be expected to influence, for example, gun carrying, gun use, and the mix of illegal guns found on the street. A stand-alone trafficking prevention intervention would not face these difficulties and could lead to definitive answers on the impact of supply-side interventions. Operation Ceasefire, however, was not a stand-alone trafficking prevention intervention.

Here, as well, the distinctive characteristics of the decline in homicide and shootings in Boston offer the best insight into what might have happened. Two things are certain. First, supply-side efforts cannot be responsible for the abrupt reductions in gun-related violence over the summer of 1996. Boston trafficking cases follow that reduction rather than anticipate it. Second, antitrafficking efforts in Boston did nothing to reduce the existing stockpile of illegally acquired and possessed firearms in Boston. Those guns held by gang members in Boston in May of 1996 were, for the most part, still held by them several months later when the violence reached its new, lower equilibrium. The change that had occurred was not in the extent of gun *ownership* but in gun *use*. The principal impact therefore was nearly certainly a demand-side, deterrence-based effect rather than a supply-side effect. It may well be that antitrafficking efforts strengthened and prolonged that impact. Whether any such effects were large or small cannot be independently established in this case.

CONCLUSION

The Boston Gun Project was an attempt to bring problem-oriented policing to bear on one important problem, youth violence, in one city, Boston. The project assembled a working group with members from a wide variety of agencies and representing a wide variety of law enforcement, social service, and other operational capacities (Kennedy et al. 1996). It went through a variety of shifts typical of problem-solving operations: shifts in the problem definition, in the shape of the intervention, and in the management and membership of the core operational partnership. Its core operational intervention, Operation Ceasefire, was designed to operate anywhere in the city where youth violence was a serious problem and was intended to interrupt the self-sustaining cycle the Gun Project hypothesized to be driving youth violence in the city (Kennedy et al. 1996). The pulling-levers deterrence strategy at the heart of Operation Ceasefire was designed to influence the behavior, and the environment, of the core population of chronic-offender gang-involved youth Gun Project research found to be at the heart of the city's youth violence problem (Kennedy 1997).

As we have noted, these interests and diagnoses—the desire to operate wherever youth violence presented itself and the belief that there was essentially one dynamic, which had to be addressed, driving violent behavior by various groups in various places within the city—made a classic experimental evaluation design impossible. It was appropriate neither from the viewpoint of participating agencies nor from the perspective of the forces believed to be driving youth violence to set aside particular areas, groups, or individuals as controls. There are thus irreducible limits to attributing any violence reduction in Boston to any particular operational intervention.

This article makes a weaker but still meaningful case: that there was an innovative intervention implemented, there were subsequent substantial reductions in youth violence in Boston, the timing of those reductions is consistent with the intervention having impact, those reductions were robust relative to proxy measures of rival causal factors in the city, the reductions in Boston were significantly larger than those in most other American cities at the time, and the large and abrupt changes that characterized the reduction in Boston differed from those of other American cities. There seems, then, to be reason to believe that something distinct happened in Boston and that its impact was both larger and of a different character than either secular trends or deliberate interventions then operating in other cities.

The results of the impact evaluation support the growing body of research that asserts that problem-oriented policing can be used to good effect in controlling crime and disorder problems (Braga, Piehl, et al. 1999; Clarke 1992; Eck and Spelman 1987; Goldstein 1990). In particular, the Ceasefire intervention suggests a new approach to controlling violent offenders from a more focused application of deterrence principles. In contrast to broad-based "zero tolerance" policing initiatives that attempt to prevent serious offending by indiscriminately cracking down on minor crimes committed by all offenders, the pulling-levers deterrence strategy controlled violence by focusing on particular groups that were behaving violently, subjecting them to a range of discretionary criminal justice system action, and directly communicating cause and effect to a very specific audience. Unfortunately, we were not able to collect the necessary pretest and posttest data to shed light on any shifts in street-level dynamics that could be associated

with the pulling-levers deterrence strategy. Our research efforts during the pretest phase were focused on problem analysis and program development. A priori, we did not know what form the intervention would take and who our target audience would be. In this regard, our assessment is very much a "black box" evaluation. Additional research on the deterrence mechanisms of the pulling-levers approach to controlling offenders is necessary.

We believe that the research presented here shows that the Boston Gun Project was a meaningful problem-oriented policing effort, bringing practitioners and researchers together in new ways, leading to a fresh assessment of the youth violence problem in Boston, and leading to operational activities that were a substantial departure from previous practice. The principal intervention, Operation Ceasefire, was likely responsible for a substantial reduction in youth homicide and youth run violence in the city. At first blush, the effectiveness of the Operation Ceasefire intervention in preventing violence may seem unique to Boston. Operation Ceasefire was constructed largely from the assets and capacities available in Boston at the time and deliberately tailored to the city's particular violence problem. Operational capacities of criminal justice agencies in other cities will be different, and youth violence problems in other cities will have important distinguishing characteristics. However, we believe that the working-group problem-solving process and the pulling-levers approach to deterring chronic offenders are transferable to other jurisdictions. A number of cities have begun to experiment with these frameworks and have experienced some encouraging preliminary results (see, e.g., Coleman et al. 1999; Kennedy and Braga 1998). These cities include Minneapolis, Minnesota; Baltimore; Indianapolis, Indiana; Stockton, California; Lowell, Massachusetts; Los Angeles; Bronx, New York; High Point, North Carolina; Winston-Salem, North Carolina; Memphis, Tennessee; New Haven, Connecticut; and Portland, Oregon.

The Boston Gun Project applied the basic principles of problem-oriented policing to a substantial public safety problem. Addressing this problem required the involvement of multiple agencies and the community as well as substantial investments in analysis, coordination, and implementation. The experience of the Gun Project suggests that deploying criminal justice capacities to prevent crime can yield substantial benefits. The problem-solving orientation of the project means that the problem definition, the core participants, and the particulars of the intervention evolved over the course of the collaboration. Operation Ceasefire itself was highly customized to the goals of the collaboration, the particular nature of the youth violence problem in Boston, and the particular capacities available in Boston for incorporation into a strategic intervention. Therefore, Operation Ceasefire as such is unlikely to be a highly specifiable, transportable "technology," However, certain process elements of the Boston Gun Project, such as the central role of the line-level working group and the use of both qualitative and quantitative research to "unpack" chosen problems, should be generally applicable to other problem-solving efforts. Using the working-group problem-solving approach, criminal justice practitioners in other jurisdictions will develop a set of intervention strategies that fits both the nuances of their youth violence problem and their operational capacities. Although the resulting package of interventions may not closely resemble the tactics used in Operation Ceasefire, the frameworks will be similar.

REFERENCES

Aldrich, John and Forrest Nelson. 1984. *Linear Probability, Logit, and Probit Models*. Paper Series on Quantitative Applications in the Social Sciences. Beverly Hills, CA: Sage.

Ball, Richard and G. David Curry. 1995. "The Logic of Definition in Criminology: Purposes and Method for Defining 'Gangs,'" *Criminology* 33:225-46.

Beha, James A. 1977. "'And Nobody Can Get You Out': The Impact of a Mandatory Prison Sentence for the Illegal Carrying of a Firearm on the Use of Firearms and on the Administration of Criminal Justice in Boston-Part I." *Boston University Law Review* 57:96-146.

Blumstein, Alfred, Jacqueline Cohen, and Daniel Nagin. eds. 1978. *Deterrence and Incapacitation: Estimating the Effects of Criminal Sanctions on Crime Rates*. Washington. DC: National Academy of Sciences.

Blumstein, Alfred and Richard Rosenfeld. 1998. "Explaining Recent Trends in U.S. Homicide Rates." *Journal of Criminal Law and Criminology* 88:1175-216.

Braga, Anthony A., Anne M. Piehl, and David M. Kennedy. 1999. "Youth Homicide in Boston: An Assessment of Supplementary Homicide Report Data." *Homicide Studies* 3:277-99.

Braga, Anthony A., David L Weisburd, Elin J. Waring, Lorraine Green Mazerolle, William Spelman, and Francis Gajewski. 1999. "Problem-Oriented Policing in Violent Crime Places: A Randomized Controlled Experiment." *Criminology* 37:541-80.

Butterfield, Fox. 1996. "In Boston, Nothing Is Something." *New York Times,* November 21, p. A20.

Cameron, Samuel. 1988. "The Economics of Crime Deterrence: A Survey of Theory and Evidence." *Kyklos* 41:301-23.

Campbell, Donald T. and Julian Stanley. 1966. *Experimental and Quasi-Experimental Designs for Research*. Chicago: Rand McNally.

Clarke. Ronald V., ed. 1992. *Situational Crime Prevention: Successful Case Studies*. New York: Harrow and Heston.

Coleman, Veronica, Walter C. Holton, Kristine Olson, Stephen Robinson, and Judith Stewart. 1999. "Using Knowledge and Teamwork to Reduce Crime." *National Institute of Justice Journal,* October, 16-23.

Cook, Philip J. 1977. "Punishment and Crime: A Critique of Current Findings Concerning the Preventive Effects of Punishment." *Law and Contemporary Problems* 41:164-204.

_____. 1980. "Research in Criminal Deterrence: Laying the Groundwork for the Second Decade." Pp. 211-68 in *Crime and Justice: An Annual Review of Research,* Vol. 2, edited by Norval Morris and Michael Tonry. Chicago: University of Chicago Press.

Cook, Philip J. and John H. Laub. 1998. "The Unprecedented Epidemic in Youth Violence." Pp. 27-64 in *Youth Violence,* edited by Michael Tonry and Mark H. Moore, Chicago: University of Chicago Press.

Cook, Thomas and Donald Campbell. 1979. *Quasi-Experimentation: Design and Analysis Issues for Field Settings.* Boston: Houghton Mifflin.

Curry, G. David, Richard Ball, and Richard Fox. 1994. *Gang Crime and Law Enforcement Record Keeping* (NCJ 148345). Washington, DC: National Institute of Justice.

Dobson, Annette. 1990. *An Introduction to Generalized Linear Models.* New York: Chapman and Hall.

Eck, John E. and William Spelman. 1987. *Problem-Solving; Problem-Oriented Policing in Newport News,* Washington, DC: National Institute of Justice.

Ekblom, Paul and Ken Pease. 1995, "Evaluating Crime Prevention." Pp. 585-662 in *Building a Safer Society: Crime and Justice,* Vol. 19, edited by Michael Tonry and David Farrington. Chicago: University of Chicago Press.

Fox, James Alan. 1996. *Trends in Juvenile Violence.* Washington, DC: U.S. Department of Justice, Bureau of Justice Statistics.

Gibbs, Jack P. 1975. *Crime, Punishment, and Deterrence.* New York: Elsevier.

Goldstein, Herman. 1979. "Improving Policing: A Problem-Oriented Approach" *Crime & Delinquency* 25:236-58.

_____. 1990. *Problem-Oriented Policing.* Philadelphia: Temple University Press.

Kelling, George L. and William J. Bratton, 1998. "Declining Crime Rates: Insiders' Views of the New York City Story." *Journal of Criminal Law and Criminology* 88:1217-32.

Kennedy, David M. 1997. "Pulling Levers: Chronic Offenders, High-Crime Settings, and a Theory of Prevention." *Valparaiso University Law Review* 31:449-84.

_____. 1998. "Pulling Levers: Getting Deterrence Right." *National Institute of Justice Journal,* July:2-8.

Kennedy, David M. and Anthony A. Braga. 1998. "Homicide in Minneapolis: Research for Problem Solving." *Homicide Studies* 2 (3): 263-90.

Kennedy, David M., Anthony A. Braga, and Anne M. Piehl. 1997. "The (Un)Known Universe: Mapping Gangs and Gang Violence in Boston." Pp. 219-62 in *Crime Mapping and Crime Prevention,* edited by David Weisburd and J. Thomas McEwen. New York: Criminal Justice Press.

_____. 1999. "Operation Ceasefire: Problem Solving and Youth Violence in Boston." Unpublished report submitted to the National Institute of Justice. Available on request from authors.

Kennedy, David M., Anne M. Piehl, and Anthony A. Braga. 1996. "Youth Violence in Boston: Gun Markets, Serious Youth Offenders, and a Use-Reduction Strategy" *Law and Contemporary Problems* 59:147-96.

Kleck, Gary. 1995. *Targeting Guns: Firearms and Their Control.* New York: Aldine de Gruyter.

Klein, Malcolm. 1993. "Attempting Gang Control by Suppression: The Misuse of Deterrence Principles." *Studies on Crime and Crime Prevention* 2:88-111.

Littell, Ramon C., George A. Milliken, Walter W. Stroup, and Russell D. Wolfinger. 1996. *SAS System for Mixed Models.* Cary, NC: SAS Institute, Inc.

McCullagh, Peter and John Nelder. 1989. *Generalized Linear Models.* 2nd ed. New York: Chapman and Hall.

McDowall, David, Richard McCleary, Errol Meidinger, and Richard Hay. 1980. *Interrupted Time Series Analysis.* Sage University Series on Quantitative Applications in the Social Sciences. Newbury Park, CA: Sage.

Paternoster, Raymond. 1987. "The Deterrent Effect of the Perceived Certainty and Severity of Punishment: A Review of the Evidence and Issues." *Justice Quarterly* 4:173-217.

Piehl, Anne M., Suzanne J. Cooper, Anthony A. Braga, and David M. Kennedy. 1999. "Testing for Structural Breaks in the Evaluation of Programs." NBER working paper no. 7226, National Bureau of Economic Research, Cambridge, MA.

Piehl, Anne M., David M, Kennedy, and Anthony A. Braga. 2000. "Problem Solving and Youth Violence: An Evaluation of the Boston Gun Project." *American Law and Economics Review* 2:58-106.

Rossi, Peter H. and Howard E. Freeman. 1993. *Evaluation: A Systematic Approach.* 5th ed. Newbury Park, CA: Sage.

SAS Institute. 1993. *SAS/STAT Software: The GENMOD Procedure.* Release 6.09, technical report P-243. Cary, NC: SAS Institute, Inc.

———. 1997. *SAS/STAT Software: Changes and Enhancements through Release 6.12.* Cary, NC; SAS Institute, Inc.

———. 1998. "V6 SAS Note: PROCMIXED Can Return Incorrect DF with DDFM=SATTERTH and REPEATED." February 18 (http://www .sas.com/service/techsup/unotes/ V6/E/E660 .html).

Sherman, Lawrence. 1990. "Police Crackdowns: Initial and Residual Deterrence" Pp. 1-48 in *Crime and Justice: A Review of Research,* Vol. 12, edited by Michael Tonry and Norval Morris. Chicago: University of Chicago Press.

Sherman, Lawrence and Richard Berk. 1984. "The Specific Deterrent Effects of Arrest for Domestic Assault." *American Sociological Review* 49:261-72.

Sparrow, Malcolm, Marie H. Moore, and David M. Kennedy. 1990. *Beyond 911: A New Era for Policing.* New York: Basic Books.

Weisburd, David, Elin J. Waring, and Ellen F. Chayet. 1995. "Specific Deterrence in a Sample of Offenders Convicted of White Collar Crimes." *Criminology* 33:587-607.

Witkin, Gordon. 1997. "Sixteen Silver Bullets: Smart Ideas to Fix the World." *U.S. News and World Report,* December 29, p. 67.

Zimring, Franklin and Gordon Hawkins. 1973. *Deterrence: The Legal Threat in Crime Control* Chicago: University of Chicago Press.

DISCUSSION QUESTIONS

1. Why do these authors believe that problem oriented policing can provide a promising response to youth violence?

2. What happened to the homicide rate for those under 24 in the late 1980s in Boston?

3. What does the Boston gun project involve? What were the main components of Operation Ceasefire? What is the pulling levers component of this program?

4. What kind of research methodology did these authors employ to evaluate the effectiveness of this program? What was their main outcome (dependent) variable?

5. What does Figure 11.2 show regarding monthly homicide counts in Boston after implementation of Operation Ceasefire?

6. How many of the 39 cities they compared also experienced reductions in youth homicide?

7. Do these authors believe that decrease in gun ownership can explain the decrease in youth homicide? Why or why not?

8. What rival causal factors did these authors control for to attempt to isolate whether Operation Ceasefire was responsible for the youth homicide reduction?

9. What are the conclusions of this evaluation research study? What do these authors say about not having pretest measures?

REFERENCES

Abrahamson, M. (1983). *Social research methods*. Englewood Cliffs, NJ: Prentice Hall.

Akers, R. L. (2000). *Criminological theories: Introduction, evaluation and application*. Los Angeles: Roxbury.

Ames, G. M., Duke, M. R., Moore, R. S., & Cunradi, C. B. (2009). The impact of occupational culture on drinking behavior of young adults in the US Navy. *Journal of Mixed Methods Research, 3*(2), 129–150.

Anderson, A. L., & Sample, L. L. (2008). Public awareness and action resulting from sex offender community notification laws. *Criminal Justice Policy Review, 19*(4), 371–396.

Armstrong, T. A., Lee, D. R., & Armstrong, G. S. (2009). An assessment of scales measuring constructs in tests of criminological theory based on national youth survey data. *Journal of Research in Crime and Delinquency, 46*(1), 73–105.

Babbie, E. R. (2010). *The practice of social research*. Belmont, CA: Wadsworth.

Bachman, R., & Schutt, R. (2008). *Fundamental of research in criminology and criminal justice*. Thousand Oaks, CA: Sage.

Batton, C., & Kadleck, C. (2004). Theoretical and methodological issues in racial profiling research. *Police Quarterly, 7*(1), 30–64.

Berg, B. L. (2004). *Qualitative research methods for the social sciences*. Boston: Allyn & Bacon.

Berk, R. (2004). *Regression analysis: A constructive critique*. Thousand Oaks, CA: Sage.

Blalock, H. M. (1982). *Conceptualization and measurement in the social sciences*. Thousand Oaks, CA: Sage.

Chamlin, M. B., & Cochran, J. K. (2007). An evaluation of the assumptions that underlie institutional anomie theory. *Theoretical Criminology, 11*(1), 39–61.

Champion, D. J., & Hartley, R. D. (2010). *Statistics for criminal justice and criminology* (3rd ed.). Upper Saddle River, NJ: Prentice Hall.

Chappell, A. (2009). The philosophical versus actual adoption of community policing: A case study. *Criminal Justice Review, 34*, 5–28.

Corsaro, N., Brunson, R., & McGarrell, E. (in press). Problem-oriented policing and open-air drug markets: Examining the Rockford pulling levers deterrence strategy. *Crime & Delinquency*.

Creswell, J. W. (1995). *Research design: Qualitative and quantitative approaches*. Thousand Oaks, CA: Sage.

Creswell, J. W. (2009). *Research design: Qualitative and quantitative and mixed methods approaches*. Thousand Oaks, CA: Sage.

Daly, K. (1989). Rethinking judicial paternalism: Gender, work-family relations, and sentencing. *Gender & Society, 3*(1), 9–36.

Daly, K. (1994). *Gender, crime, and punishment*. New Haven, CT: Yale University Press.

Decker, S., Katz, C., & Webb, V. (2008). Understanding the black box of gang organization: Implications for involvement in violent crime, drug sales, and violent victimization. *Crime & Delinquency, 54*, 153–172.

Denzin, N. K. (1987). *The alcoholic self*. Thousand Oaks, CA: Sage.

Department of Health and Human Services. (2003). *Guidance on certificates of confidentiality*. Office for Human Research Protections, Department of Health and Human Services. Retrieved July 1, 2010, from http://www.hhs.gov/ohrp/humansubjects/guidance/certconf.htm

Dixon, J. (1995). The organization context of criminal sentencing. *American Journal of Sociology, 100*, 1157–1198.

Durham, A. A., Elrod, H. P., & Kincade, P. T. (1995). Images of crime and justice. *Journal of Criminal Justice, 23*, 143–152.

Ellis, L., Hartley, R., & Walsh, A. (2010). *Research methods in criminal justice and criminology: An interdisciplinary approach*. Lanham, MD: Rowman & Littlefield.

Feagin, J. R., Orum, A. M., & Sjoberg, G. (Eds). (1991). *A case for the case study.* Chapel Hill: University of North Carolina Press.

Feld, B. (2009). Violent girls or relabeled status offenders? An alternative interpretation of the data. *Crime & Delinquency, 55,* 241–265.

Frankfort-Nachmias, C., & Nachmias, D. (1992). *Research methods in the social sciences* (4th ed.). New York: St. Martin's Press.

Gibbs, J. P. (1989). Conceptualization of terrorism. *American Sociological Review, 54*(3), 329–340.

Hagan, F. E. (2005). *Essentials of research methods in criminal justice and criminology.* Boston: Allyn & Bacon.

Hagan, F. E. (2010). *Research methods in criminal justice and criminology* (8th ed.). Upper Saddle River, NJ: Prentice Hall.

Heilbron, J. (1990). Auguste Compte and modern epistemology. *Sociological Theory, 8*(2), 153–162.

Hill, P. C., Dill, C. A., & Davenport, E. C. (1988). A reexamination of the bogus pipeline. *Educational and Psychological Measurement, 48,* 587–601.

Jacques, S., & Wright, R. (2008). Intimacy with outlaws: The role of relational distance in recruiting, paying, and interviewing underworld research participants. *Journal of Research in Crime and Delinquency, 45*(1), 22–38.

Johnson, B. D., Ulmer, J., & Kramer, J. (2008). The social context of guidelines circumvention: The case of the U.S. District Courts. *Criminology, 46*(3), 737–783.

Klockars, C. B. (1974). *The professional fence.* New York: Free Press.

Lane, J. (2002). Fear of gang crime: A qualitative examination of the four perspectives. *Journal of Research in Crime and Delinquency, 39,* 437–471.

Logan, T. K., Walker, R., Shannon, L., & Cole, J. (2008). Combining ethical considerations with recruitment and follow-up strategies for partner violence victimization research. *Violence Against Women, 14*(11), 1226–1251.

Lowenkamp, C. T., Hubbard, D., Makarios, M. D., & Latessa, E. J. (2009). A quasi-experimental evaluation of thinking for a change: A "real-world" application. *Criminal Justice and Behavior, 36,* 137–146.

Lowman, J., & Palys, T. (2001). The ethics and law of confidentiality in criminal justice research: A comparison of Canada and the United States. *International Criminal Justice Review, 11*(1), 1–33.

MacKenzie, D. L. (2000). Evidence-based corrections: Identifying what works. *Crime & Delinquency, 46*(4), 457–471.

Meldrum, R. C., Young, J. T. N., & Weerman, F. M. (2009). Reconsidering the effect of self-control and delinquent peers: Implications of measurement for theoretical significance. *Journal of Research in Crime and Delinquency, 46*(3), 353–376.

Merton, R. K. (1957). *Social theory and social structure.* New York: Free Press.

Miller, M. (1995). Covert participant observation: Reconsidering the least used method. *Journal of Contemporary Criminal Justice, 11*(2), 97–105.

Moffitt, T. E. (1993). "Adolescence-limited" and "Life-course-persistent" antisocial behavior: A developmental taxonomy. *Psychological Review, 100,* 674–701.

Monaghan, P. (1993, April). Facing jail, a sociologist raises questions about a scholar's right to protect sources. *Chronicle of Higher Education,* p. A10.

Morgan, S. E., Reichert, T., & Harrison, T. R. (2002). *From numbers to words: Reporting statistical results for the social sciences.* Boston: Allyn & Bacon.

Pearson, G. (2009). The researcher as hooligan: Where 'participant observation' means breaking the law. *International Journal of Social Research Methodology, 12*(3), 243–255.

Perez, D. M. (2009). Applying evidence-based practices to community corrections supervision: An evaluation of residential substance abuse treatment for high-risk probationers. *Journal of Contemporary Criminal Justice, 25*(4), 442–458.

Rand, M. (2008). *Criminal victimization, 2007.* Washington, DC: United States Department of Justice, Bureau of Justice Statistics.

Rand, M. (2009). *Criminal victimization, 2008.* Washington, DC: United States Department of Justice, Bureau of Justice Statistics.

Roh, S., & Robinson, M. (2009). A geographic approach to racial profiling: The microanalysis and macroanalysis of racial disparity in traffic stops, *Police Quarterly, 12*(2), 137–169.

Ruddell, R., Decker, S. H., & Egley, A., Jr. (2006). Gang intervention in jails: A national analysis. *Criminal Justice Review, 31*(1), 33–46.

Sample, L. L. (2001). *The social construction of the sex offender*. Unpublished dissertation, University of Missouri, St. Louis.

Shaw, C. R. (1930). *The jack-roller: A delinquent boy's own story*. Chicago: The University of Chicago Press.

Sirkin, R. M. (1999). *Statistics for the social sciences* (2nd ed.). Thousand Oaks, CA: Sage.

Steffensmeier, D. (1980). Assessing the impact of the women's movement on sex-based differences in the handling of adult criminal defendants. *Crime & Delinquency, 26*, 344–357.

Steffensmeier, D., Kramer, J., & Streifel, C. (1993). Gender and imprisonment decisions. *Criminology, 31*, 411–446.

Steffensmeier, D., Kramer, J., & Ulmer, J. (1998). The interaction of race, gender, and age in criminal sentencing: The punishment cost of being young, black, and male. *Criminology, 36*, 763–797.

Stevens, S. S. (1946). On the theory of scales of measurement. *Science, 103*, 677–680.

Sutherland, E. H. (1937). *The professional thief*. Chicago: The University of Chicago Press.

Sutherland, E. H. (1939). *Principles of criminology* (3rd ed.). Philadelphia: J. B. Lippincott.

Sutherland, E. H. (1947). *Principles of criminology*. (4th ed.). Philadelphia: J. B. Lippincott.

Tashakkori, A., & Teddlie, C. (1998). *Mixed methodology: Combining qualitative and qualitative approaches*. Thousand Oaks, CA: Sage.

Taylor, R. (2009). Slain and slandered: A content analysis of the portrayal of femicide in crime news. *Homicide Studies, 13*, 21–49.

Tewksbury, R., & Mustaine, E. E. (2005). Insiders' views of prison amenities: Beliefs and perceptions of correctional staff members. *Criminal Justice Review, 30*(2), 174–188.

Ulmer, J., & Kramer, J. (1996). Court communities under sentencing guidelines: Dilemmas of formal rationality and sentencing disparity. *Criminology, 34*, 383–408.

United States Department of Justice (2009a). Crime in the United States by metropolitan statistical area, 2008. *Uniform Crime Reports*. Clarksburg, WV: Criminal Justice Information Services Division, Federal Bureau of Investigation.

United States Department of Justice (2009b). Offenses cleared (Table 26). *Uniform Crime Reports*. Clarksburg, WV: Criminal Justice Information Services Division, Federal Bureau of Investigation.

Unnever, J. D., Benson, M. L., & Cullen, F. T. (2008). Public support for getting tough on corporate crime: Racial and political divides. *Journal of Research in Crime and Delinquency, 45*(2), 163–190.

Vold, G. B., Bernard, T. J., & Snipes, J. B. (2002). *Theoretical Criminology*. New York: Oxford University Press.

Wallace, W. L. (1971). *The logic of science in sociology*. New York: Aldine de Gruyter.

Wallace, W. L. (1983). *Principles of scientific sociology*. New York: Aldine de Gruyter.

Weber, R. P. (1990). *Basic content analysis*. Newbury Park, CA: Sage.

Weinberg, R. A. (1989). Intelligence and IQ: Landmark issues and great debates. *American Psychologist, 44*(2), 98–104.

Weisburd, D. (2000). Randomized experiments in criminal justice policy: Prospects and problems. *Crime & Delinquency, 46*(2), 181–193.

Welsh, B. C., & Farrington, D. P. (2001). Toward an evidence-based approach to preventing crime. *The ANNALS of the American Academy of Political and Social Science, 578*, 158–173.

Wilcox, P., Skubak Tillyer, M., & Fisher, B. (2009). Gendered opportunity? School-based adolescent victimization. *Journal of Research in Crime and Delinquency, 46*, 245–269.

Williams, T., Dunlap, E., Johnson, B. D., & Hamid, A. (1992). Personal safety in dangerous places. *Journal of Contemporary Ethnography, 21*(3), 343–374.

Wolff, H., Jing, S., & Bachman, R. (2008). Measuring victimization inside prisons: Questioning the questions. *Journal of Interpersonal Violence, 23*(10), 1343–1362.

Wright, R., Decker, S., Redfern, A. K., & Smith, D. L. (1992). A snowball's chance in hell: Doing fieldwork with active residential burglars. *Journal of Research in Crime and Delinquency, 29*(2), 148–161.

Wu, J., & Spohn, C. (2009). Does an offender's age have an effect on sentence length? A meta-analytic review. *Criminal Justice Policy Review, 20*(4), 379–413.

ABOUT THE AUTHOR

Richard D. Hartley is an assistant professor in the Department of Criminal Justice at the University of Texas at San Antonio. He holds a PhD from the School of Criminology and Criminal Justice at the University of Nebraska at Omaha. He teaches courses relating to criminal courts and the administration of justice as well as research methods and statistics. Dr. Hartley's research interests include prosecutorial and judicial discretion, race/ ethnicity and crime, and quantitative methods. He has been involved with a number of research projects for which he analyzed sentencing outcomes, especially those for federal narcotics and immigration offenders. Some of his recent and forthcoming publications appear in *Aggression and Violent Behavior, Crime & Delinquency, Criminal Justice Review, Journal of Criminal Justice,* and *Journal of Pediatrics.*

SAGE Research Methods Online
The essential tool for researchers

**Sign up now at
www.sagepub.com/srmo
for more information.**

An expert research tool

- An **expertly designed taxonomy** with more than 1,400 unique terms for social and behavioral science research methods

- **Visual and hierarchical search tools** to help you discover material and link to related methods

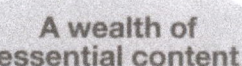

- Easy-to-use navigation tools
- Content organized by complexity
- Tools for citing, printing, and downloading content with ease
- Regularly updated content and features

A wealth of essential content

- The most comprehensive picture of quantitative, qualitative, and mixed methods available today

- More than **100,000 pages of SAGE book and reference material** on research methods as well as editorially selected material from SAGE journals

- More than **600 books** available in their entirety online

Launching 2011!

⑤SAGE research methods online

9 781412 989190